PSYCHOLOGY
IN THE WORLD TODAY

AN INTERDISCIPLINARY APPROACH

SECOND EDITION

PSYCHOLOGY IN THE WORLD TODAY

AN INTERDISCIPLINARY APPROACH

SECOND EDITION

Edited by

ROBERT V. GUTHRIE

University of Pittsburgh

ADDISON-WESLEY PUBLISHING COMPANY

Reading, Massachusetts · Menlo Park, California · London · Don Mills, Ontario

This book is in the
ADDISON-WESLEY SERIES IN PSYCHOLOGY

Cited below by page numbers are sources for photographs which were not credited in the text: p. 120, Columbia Spectator/EPA University Newsphoto Alliance; p. 247, Ellen Levine/Editorial Photocolor Archives; pp. 278, 332, 348, 429, 436, Tower News Service/EPA University Newsphoto Alliance.

PREFACE
TO THE SECOND EDITION

This edition, like the earlier one, is intended to meet the needs of the college student for a well-integrated and modern book of readings. The success of the first edition was gratifying, for it illustrated an agreement of this need. While the direction and scope of the present edition remain unchanged, about three-quarters of the materials are new. It is felt that neither the professor nor the student deserves to be bored; consequently, in making the new selections, I have tried to update and to bring together pertinent, challenging, and interesting articles. In other words, this is not just a routine scissors-and-paste collection of readings. Instead here is a freshly conceived textbook that has been planned and tested with precaution to ensure that it should contribute importantly to an understanding of the behavioral sciences.

Two features distinguish this book from other collections of readings available in the field: (1) a wider coverage of areas; and (2) a sense of audience that makes the writing in the book genuinely appealing to college students. These two features work together to promote interested learning that is not only meaningful but also *relevant*. In addition, these features help to fulfill two objectives:

a) This book is committed to a *realistic approach to the teaching of psychology*. The fourteen units are designed to complement most lecture materials and basic texts. The versatility of these units allows for an interdisciplinary approach to the field. The materials are meaningful and useful whether the professor's approach is behavioral, experimental, clinical, humanistic, or general.

b) The emphases of these materials are not on formal definitions of the various aspects of psychological knowledge but on presenting *meaningful explanations of concepts*. As a result, conventional classical studies and experimental reports are not stressed since it is felt that they are most appropriately discussed in lectures and basic texts. The rules and expectations that govern basic texts do not apply to collections of readings. The reasoning is obvious. Such collections complete a third-line of offense, i.e., basic texts, lecture-discussions, and outside readings. It therefore becomes imperative that outside readings are not only informative, but also challenging and provocative. It is the appeal nature of these materials that will aid in stimulating the student to seek a deeper understanding and application of scientific knowledge. *Psychology in the World Today* is an attempt to achieve these goals.

My especial thanks go to the several anonymous reviewers whose candid advice aided me in the final selections of materials. However, I assume full responsibility of any shortcomings of this volume. I acknowledge my indebtedness and appreciation to the authors, editors, and publishers who granted permission to use copyrighted materials.

Pittsburgh, Pennsylvania
November, 1970

R. V. G.

PREFACE
TO THE FIRST EDITION

Psychology In The World Today: An Interdisciplinary Approach has been compiled to meet the need of the college student for a well-integrated and modern book of readings which will contribute to his understanding of the behavioral sciences. This volume contains readings and discussions of how the behavioral sciences are in use today. Each of the fourteen units is introduced by a discussion designed to establish the relevancy of the unit and to aid the student in understanding the significance of the selections.

The absence of so-called classical studies and experimental reports is intentional. Though they give a scholarly appearance, they are likely to be confusing to students who, for the most part, will never become professional psychologists. Therefore, this is not just another traditional book of readings; rather, the emphasis is on the student.

These readings have been carefully selected from sources which, although scientifically accurate, are of primary interest to the layman rather than to psychologists or advanced psychology students. The selections, written by either behavioral scientists or outstanding science writers, are not ends in themselves. I have attempted to present different and opposing viewpoints within many of the units in order to provoke thought and discussion. In this way, the student becomes intellectually involved in his study of psychology.

The book is flexible in that it can be used as a text, when supplemented by classroom lectures and/or discussions, or it can be used as a helpful adjunct to a basic text.

To the many authors, editors, and publishers who directly or indirectly contributed suggestions and permission to use copyrighted materials I gratefully acknowledge my indebtedness and appreciation.

San Diego, California   R. V. G.
March 1968

CONTENTS

UNIT ONE
INTRODUCTION

Psychology, a relatively new science, has grown from a varied foundation. Not until 1879 was the first laboratory established with behavior as its principal subject. When Wilhelm Wundt established his laboratory in Leipzig, Germany, he ushered in a new era in the study of behavior. Prior to this point, man's attempt to understand himself, his fellow man, and his environment was based primarily on speculations. Earlier views of behavior can be found in the writings of ancient civilizations and outstanding religious figures. Philosophers of other centuries introduced many ideas that today serve as a foundation for modern psychology. For example, the Greek philosophers Plato and Aristotle wrote concerning the "psyche" or "soul" as the basis of behavior. Between 1600 and 1800, Descartes, Hobbes, Locke, Hume, Leibnitz, and others contributed much to the understanding of human behavior.

Today's psychology is the scientific study of behavior; it attempts to understand life as it is lived. The student of psychology finds himself involved in a most interesting, interwoven kind of investigation. He finds himself concerned with struggles, pleasures, interests, desires, habits, aims, drives, motivations, feelings, actions, wants —all those bits of behavior that mold man into a complex, unique living being. Psychology not only attempts to understand behavior, it strives to predict and control behavior.

Psychology finds itself akin to various fields: psychiatry, sociology, linguistics, biology, anthropology, and political science. In emphasizing the fusion of our discipline with others, one psychologist recently stated that psychology thrives on polygamy with her kindred disciplines and that the marriage between psychology, anthropology, sociology, and the biological sciences has produced significant knowledge. This interdisciplinary involvement creates psychology as a behavioral science.

The behavioral sciences are those areas of academic inquiry which study the behavior of man. *Sociology* is the study of group life and social organization. *Anthropology* is the comparative study of man and his works, including physical characteristics, social habits, and customs. *Biology* is the study of living things. *Psychiatry* is the branch of medicine which studies and treats behavioral disorders. *Linguistics* is the study of languages which are expressive of man. *Political Science* is the study of human relationships that involve, to a significant extent, power and authority.

At the present time there are more than 30,000 American psychologists involved in a myriad of activities. The fact that the American Psychological Association is subdivided into 29 divisions testifies to the diversity of the field.

Divisions of the American Psychological Association

1. Division of General Psychology
2. Division of the Teaching of Psychology
3. Division of Experimental Psychology

*5. Division of Evaluation and Measurement
6. Division of Physiological and Comparative Psychology
7. Division on Developmental Psychology
8. Division of Personality and Social Psychology
9. The Society for the Psychological Study of Social Issues
10. Division of Esthetics
12. Division of Clinical Psychology
13. Division of Consulting Psychology
14. Division of Industrial and Business Psychology
15. Division of Educational Psychology
16. Division of School Psychologists
17. Division of Counseling Psychology
18. Division of Psychologists in Public Service
19. Division of Military Psychologists
20. Division on Maturity and Old Age
21. The Society of Engineering Psychologists
22. National Council on Psychological Aspects of Disability
23. Division on Consumer Psychology
24. Division of Philosophical Psychology
25. Division for the Experimental Analysis of Behavior
26. Division of the History of Psychology
27. Division on Community Psychology
28. Division of Behavioral Pharmacology
29. Division of Psychotherapy
30. Division of Psychological Hypnosis
31. Division of State Psychological Association Affairs

The purpose of the APA is to advance psychology as a science, as a profession, and as a means of promoting human welfare. It attempts to further these objectives by holding annual meetings, publishing psychological journals, and working toward improved standards for psychological training and service.

The first selection by Erasmus Hoch, *Psychology Today: Conceptions and Misconceptions,* answers some of the questions which are posed more frequently about psychology as a profession. His insight into the notion of "common sense" is particularly noteworthy. Finally, the American Psychological Association's *Psychology as a Profession* presents important statistical analyses of the major work activities of psychologists; employers of psychologists; and responsibilities of the profession.

---

* Note: Owing to reorganizations and other changes made since the introduction of a divisional structure in the APA, there are currently no divisions numbered 4 or 11.

1 | PSYCHOLOGY TODAY:
CONCEPTIONS AND MISCONCEPTIONS

Erasmus Hoch

Small wonder that psychology and psychologists are often misunderstood. The field is old, yet new; it seems too mysterious to grasp, yet excites everyone's curiosity; its doctrines (or supposed doctrines) sound at once uncanny and self-evident; and the profession itself looks one day like society's Good Samaritan, the next like its Machiavelli.

There are good reasons for the perplexity. Although respecting his ability, most people seem to have relatively little personal investment in how the chemist fills his beakers or what the oceanographer dredges up from the ocean bottom. The psychologist, by contrast, is seen as doing things pretty directly *for* us, or even *to* us. He designs teaching machines; he is expected to give counsel; he samples public opinion. And there is more than a little feeling, it seems, about needing to pass a test to get a job, or hearing that advertisements are made "psychological," presumably to get us to buy products we may not really want.

It is precisely because psychology is seen as touching us so intimately that the public has developed ideas of its own about the profession, its members, and their objectives. If the ideas are sometimes faulty or actually untrue, it is partly because the field has not stood still long enough to let anyone get a good look at it. The psychology of 1960 is not the psychology of 1920; it is not even the psychology of 1940. Many things have happened to give the field a "new look" within the past two decades, and when change takes place so rapidly, it may well breed some confusion.

True, one can watch a monkey in a laboratory cage; one can even "take" a test. It is not quite as easy to "see" how the psychologist gets at the basis of prejudice, studies problems of morale among refugees, or helps a person feel less uncomfortable in the presence of the opposite sex. The gadgets are few; the relationships often subtle (at least not easily represented); the jargon of the profession sometimes esoteric. Add to this the fact that the psychologist has not been around very long, as far as most people are concerned, and the discipline and its disciples begin to look like scientific Martians of a sort.

At least three circumstances have contributed to making psychology something of an enigma for the average person:

Popular misconceptions about the profession

The semantic problem of sharing terms and settings with other professions

The nature of the field

In this chapter, we shall examine some of the sources of misunderstanding and look at the difficulties inherent in getting across a clearer, truer picture of the field.

POPULAR MISCONCEPTIONS ABOUT THE PROFESSION

Let us back into our problem, correcting a number of common and somewhat fundamental misconceptions by running through a series of things psychology is *not*, the better to understand what it really is. We shall be concerned in turn with the focus of the field, the attributes of its members, and the scope of its problems.

PSYCHOLOGY IS NOT ILLNESS-ORIENTED

In the minds of most people, psychology is associated with correcting something that has gone wrong. Psychologists help people solve problems, find out why a child is doing poorly in school, attempt to patch up a marriage, and perform other psychological first aid. True, they do—not as directly or as simply as people hope they can, and not always successfully—but they do. The story, however, hardly ends there.

The Psychological Continuum

Psychologists deal not only with "sick" people. Theirs is the whole spectrum of behavior, from the very maladjusted to the very well adjusted, from earthworm to human being, from infancy to old age. They are concerned as much with potentialities as with limitations; their interest lies not only in traits that make life miserable but especially in the thoughts, feelings, aspiration, and actions that can ennoble and enrich and inspire.

This has not always been the case. Psychology, along with other disciplines, has needed time to realize that we know much more about sickness than about health. We realize many things about what makes people break down, fewer about what keeps them going. The slow learner has drawn our attention, his gifted classmate has been left, until recently, to shift largely for himself. A good deal is known about marital disharmony, far less about the happier side. We can keep the space voyager from going "stir-crazy," find it much harder to help him keep his thoughts on the lofty plane at which he is cruising.

The situation holds not only for the "clinical" areas of knowledge. The social psychologist knows more about the foundations of prejudice than about the bases of international accord. Although able to shed considerable light on the problems of Suburbia, he would probably admit to knowing less about the impact of a Schweitzer on our culture. In any case, his interest too is coming increasingly to include the potentially creative forces at work in today's society.

The Notion of "Treatment"

Probably no psychologist has escaped the experience of being edged into a corner at a party as soon as someone has found him out. Public information efforts notwithstanding, the field continues to be associated in the public mind with couch, distress, and advice to parents of problem children.

In point of fact, even the psychologist who works primarily in such treatment centers as mental hospitals does not only "treat" people. The term itself smacks of the practice of medicine, of which he desires no part. Technicalities aside, however, even the clinical psychologist does much more than provide such direct services as testing and psychotherapy. He conducts research, he provides in-service training, he serves as consultant to other professions, he studies the "therapeutic community," among others.

His colleague at the university may seldom if ever "treat" anyone except perhaps the monkeys being studied to determine which problems cause them ulcers and which situations help them get "cured." Psychologists working in other settings and performing other functions may have even less occasion to engage in treatment, unless it be statistical "treatment" of the data their research studies have netted.

The Problem of Professional Hierarchies

As a younger profession joins the council of scientific elders, problems invariably arise. Integration tends to involve some questions of status, mayhap a mite of ill will. At the very least, outsiders have some difficulty discerning in what relationship the newer profession stands to the older ones, to which of these it is beholden, and whether there is a hierarchy in terms of either scientific respectability or actual power of one over the other.

Psychology has proved no exception in the process of finding its place among fellow professions. On the one hand, it has needed to mesh gears with such allied fields as sociology, which had already spoken of some of its members as "social psychologists" at the turn of the century. On the other hand, the psychologist entering such settings as hospitals found that the psychiatrist had been there long before him. Consequently, not only had the latter gained a reputation as leader of the "hospital team"; what was more, he was psychologically unprepared to accept a newcomer as peer, let alone as leader of a sort.

The problem has become at once more complicated and more simple as psychologists in other than the "applied" areas have found their way into clinical situations. Recently social psychologists have appeared in order to study the hospital as a therapeutic community. They are joined by the physiological psychologist, who feels quite at home in speaking about functions of the central nervous system, the effects of tranquilizers, and the concomitants of organic brain damage. When the experimental psychologist comes upon the scene, he likewise brings with him the feeling of being peer of or consultant to such other professions as happen already to be in the picture. A recent book—*Role Relations in the Mental Health Professions* (Zander *et al.*, 1957)—assures us that, if the problem is a complicated one, it is at least receiving serious and constructive consideration.

PSYCHOLOGISTS ARE NOT TECHNICIANS

However incorrect it may be, the conception of the psychologist as technician is understandable. Psychologists do work in some very dissimilar and seemingly specialized settings—the university, the secondary school, the industrial plant, the hospital. Furthermore, people seek out a psychologist because they have, as they see it, an identifiable problem—their son is flunking, their product won't sell, their avia-tion cadets "wash out" too frequently in flight training. The presenting problem, it turns out, is usually part of a much larger situation, frequently not the real problem at all. But too often there is the hope that a psychologist can take a problem of a specific sort and come up with a solution of an immediate type.

The Matter of Specialization

Judging from typical inquiries, prospective psychologists are some of the prime of-fenders. Among enterprising high school and even college students, wishful thinking has it that a set of rather specialized psychology courses qualifies one to become a "marriage counselor," a "child expert," a "psychological warfare specialist," or a "test designer." Unfortunately, or fortunately, the thought is not father to the deed. The consummation, in terms of career, involves a less direct route to the goal and a delayed reward.

The psychologist is neither technician nor narrow specialist. His training empha-sizes general, over-all knowledge as the necessary condition for later specialization. He is expected to be conversant with the several areas of knowledge which feed into his field; he must be a scientist first, a practitioner second (if at all); his training stresses the acquisition of basic information and underlying concepts rather than *expertise* in techniques. Where such *expertise* exists, as in the case of the psychologist with special competence in the area of projective methods, the skills gain meaning only as parts of larger wholes. If one needed to speak of a basic skill, one common to all psychologists, it would be none other than a thoroughgoing conversance with scientific method. Any other is subsidiary.

At major conferences on education and training, there is still room for debate about the place of the nondoctoral person in psychology, the nature of the "core curriculum," and related considerations. The fact remains, however, that psycho-logical training, at least in the early years, involves much that is broad and general rather than narrow and circumscribed, and that specialization takes place later rather than sooner. The doctoral degree, the saying goes, is a license to practice psychology, not an end in itself. If anything, it marks the beginning of the real kind of learning that takes place postdoctorally. All the while, psychologists remain psychologists first, "specialists" second.

The Roles of Tomorrow

Not only are psychologists not technicians; they do not even necessarily deal directly with their clients. On the basis of manpower shortage alone (and this is not the sole reason!), there is some justification. At the present time it is estimated that there are three vacancies for every psychologist. If the needs of the community are to be met at all, the profession must rethink the role it plays, could play, and should play.

The situation is akin to that in which the educator finds himself. Faced with a teacher shortage exacerbated by increased enrollments, he begins to wonder about and experiment with new ways of teaching. Are small classes really more effective than large ones? If so, does the advantage hold in all subjects and for all teaching purposes? How can the teacher extend his effectiveness with the techniques which television puts at his disposal? Although the answers to such questions are not easy to come by, the questions themselves prompt a re-examination of one's role; the consequent soul searching may well bring to light new and more effective ways of using oneself.

Psychologists have been especially prone to such self-examination in the past two decades. With a phenomenal rise in demand for their services, a demand with which neither recruitment nor training has been able to contend, they have been faced with the choice of letting many needs go unfilled or else finding more productive roles to play. The profession leans toward the latter alternative, unsure as it may be about what the new roles really are.

One thing seems clear. It is not necessary that the psychologist have a direct one-to-one relationship with every client. The clinician in the hospital need not, in fact probably should not, expend his talents intensively on five patients while another fifty remain unaffected. Neither must the school psychologist restrict his activities to direct work with a handful of students when, by dint of some imagination, he might have an effect on several grades or even the total school. The practice is becoming less that of dealing directly with a few clients, more that of "treating the treaters," as it were. Because the nurse, the teacher, and the foreman are in close contact with their charges, they represent mediating influences of the most significant kind. By serving as consultants to them—that is, by operating at a level once removed, so to speak—the psychologist exerts his influence less directly but, by the same token, perhaps more effectively in terms of the social realities.

PSYCHOLOGICAL PROBLEMS ARE NOT FINITE

Indebted as it is to its forebears, psychology is more than two parts biology, one part physics, three parts philosophy, and the like. Psychology is more than anything else simply psychology. It has a language of its own (sometimes strange, to be sure), has developed tools and methods, and, most important, makes distinctive contributions to problems of its own choosing. This is not to say that it divorces itself from allied sciences and operates unilaterally. Psychologists find themselves working ever more closely alongside colleagues in other fields. In so doing, however, they retain their identity as psychologists, members of a distinct species of the genus scientist. Above all, they do not wait for problems to come to them; they search them out— and the latter are everywhere.

The Notion of "Common Sense"

One thing seems clear: Everyone fancies himself a psychologist after a fashion. It is in the nature of man to have ideas on and feelings about how children are best reared, what makes for a successful marriage, how the student should study, and what motivates the Communist.

Whereas most people have relatively little inclination to tell the physician how he should practice or what he should prescribe (aside from suggestions that his fees may be too high or that he seems "too ready to operate"), the set toward the psychologist (and the psychiatrist, for that matter) is a different one. Terms such as "inferiority complex" and "repression" are common currency, and whole psychological philosophies seem to hinge on how the particular layman feels about a thing called "will power."

The result is an interesting, albeit somewhat perplexing situation. Many of us may practice some favorite home remedies; few would fancy themselves physicians of sorts. Where problems of human behavior are involved, however, there is noticeably less reluctance on the part of the average person to diagnose a situation, prescribe a solution, or even treat what seems like the problem. Ironically, when the trained psychologist proceeds less boldly, his wisdom is often questioned, his motives impugned.

Small wonder, then, that some research findings strike the layman as something he "knew all along," whereas others impress him as much scientific ado about nothing, and still others as outlandishly irrelevant to the business of living. The concept of "basic" research, as compared with the "applied" variety, is not the easiest to grasp. Nor are the problems psychologists choose to study always those which make most sense to the person concerned with the earthier problems of sleeping well at night and seeing the dawn of peace come upon the world.

The Field and Its Boundaries

The following chapters will show that psychology hardly stops at the IQ, counseling, or rats running mazes. It consists of many areas rather than few, some of them of recent origin, many of them hardly known to the public and, if known, scarcely associated with psychology.

As it happens, the field need not look far for its problems. Some of them have been with us for a long time, with their psychological aspects coming only now to be appreciated. The educational world waited long for systematic investigation of whether the architecture of a school building and its classrooms has significant effects on the learning that takes place within it. Only recently has research suggested that the recovery of mental patients may depend as much on how the hospital staff gets along as on the severity of the illness itself. Physicists and engineers have worried for some time about how to get a manned vehicle into space and back; only recently have they emphasized that unless the astronaut can stand confinement, weightlessness, and the upsetting of his cycle of eating and sleeping, the whole project may literally go up in smoke.

His subject matter being the kind it is, the psychologist finds himself being pulled in many directions at once. The stuff of human problems is everywhere. To define the boundaries of the science today is to have to shift them tomorrow. Where behavior or thought or attitude or motivation is, there psychology is.

The Staking Out of Claims

Time was when the situation in psychology was fairly simple and clear-cut. Psychologists taught at universities, did their research in the college laboratory, and, by and large, pretty much resembled one another despite the several "schools" to which they might subscribe. Things are hardly pat now. The American Psychological Association has twenty Divisions, each of them pertaining to a fairly distinct area of concern, while the "applied" wing of psychology has fanned out in all directions. The titles of the psychological journals themselves demonstrate a rather vivid panorama of interests.

This is not to say that psychologists have mapped out several dozen pockets of activity and, as a result, are walled off from one another. If anything characterizes psychology at the present time, it is its fluidity, its reluctance to sanction any greater degree of specialization than is necessary, its effort to promote concourse among all breeds of psychologists, its abhorrence of a separate professional school.

Whereas a decade ago it was the clinical psychologist who seemed to be going his own way, forsaking his university background for the unacademic life elsewhere, today finds almost any kind of psychologist in almost any kind of setting. Thus, an experimental psychologist may be working in a mental hospital, a clinical psychologist in a university laboratory, a social psychologist in an industrial plant. What is more, the problems are everybody's business. The experimental psychologist may be devoting his attention to the "clinical" problem of recovery potential of patients, the social psychologist working on the "experimental" problem of perception, and the clinical psychologist concerned with the "social" problem of getting the businessmen of the community to hire discharged patients. Psychologists feel more alike than different, and this is how they would have it.

The Forward Movement

If the public does not yet know what to make of psychology, neither do psychologists quite. Conference after conference finds the profession asking itself broad yet pointed questions. Where is the field moving? What can be done to steer its course? If, indeed, this is possible, in which direction ought the psychology of tomorrow be channeled? Should further special-interest groups (as represented by Divisions of the American Psychological Association, for example) be allowed, even encouraged, to develop? Or should the profession hold the line until the complexion of the field clears up?

Apparently some of the same questions are asked when physicists suddenly find themselves in such new roles as rocket launchers, consultants on problems of fall-out, and designers of "cleaner" bombs. And no doubt the physicist faces then some of the same difficult, if not agonizing, decisions about the why and how and whither of his science.

Yet the prospective physicist has at least a relatively clear notion of the outlines of his field. The prospective psychologist, by contrast, sees his career in fainter, fuzzier form. The science of psychology is still a protean affair. Although moving forward steadily and with determination, it does so neither like the tortoise nor like the hare but perhaps like the ameba, feeling its way as it goes.

2 | PSYCHOLOGY AS A PROFESSION

American Psychological Association

In 1954 the American Psychological Association, with the consent of the Council of Representatives, published a policy statement entitled Psychology and Its Relations with Other Professions. *Fourteen years have passed since the adoption and publication of this statement, and many changes have taken place in the interim. The present article represents a revision, updating, and retitling of the former statement in order to reflect the development and the growth of the profession. The Board of Professional Affairs was given the responsibility for preparing this statement subject to the review and approval of the Board of Directors and other governing bodies of the Association. This new document was approved by the Council of Representatives on September 5, 1967, as an official policy statement of the Association and replaces the previous booklet.*

Arthur H. Brayfield
Executive Officer
American Psychological Association

Like other professions, American psychology is a social entity operating in a supporting society. As a relative newcomer among the sciences and professions, psychology is not widely known or fully understood by the public at large. This article, prepared by the American Psychological Association, provides information about this emerging science and profession and describes some of the values that guide its members as they seek to move psychology toward greater maturity, responsibility, and public usefulness.

Psychology has three major purposes: to increase the body of knowledge in its content area, to communicate this knowledge, and to apply it in a socially useful and responsible manner. Within this threefold mission, however, one encounters marked diversity in the work of people who are called psychologists.

Psychologists engage in research, teaching, psychological services to individuals and groups, consultation, and administration. Individual psychologists generally devote themselves to more than one of these activities. For example, most research psychologists also teach, many teachers also engage in some applied or service functions, some practitioners also do research. Psychologists also differ from one another in their type and amount of training, in their areas of subsequent professional specialization, and in their work settings. The settings for their work vary from labora-

From *American Psychologist*, **23** (1968), pp. 195–200. Copyright © 1968 by the American Psychological Association, and reproduced by permission.

TABLE 1

Division Membership for 1967*

Division	Fellows	Members	Associates	Total members
1. General psychology	165	748	337	1,250
2. Teaching of psychology	319	1,424	509	2,252
3. Experimental psychology	405	656	—	1,061
5. Evaluation and measurement	216	598	—	814
6. Physiological and comparative psychology	82	413	—	495
7. Developmental psychology	244	583	26	853
8. Personality and social psychology	353	2,661	885	3,899
9. The society for the psychological study of social issues—A division of the APA	285	1,076	188	1,549
10. Psychology and the arts	44	161	47	252
12. Clinical psychology	771	2,467	—	3,238
13. Consulting psychology	278	332	—	610
14. Industrial psychology	248	660	111	1,019
15. Educational psychology	366	1,632	593	2,691
16. School psychologists	134	700	276	1,110
17. Counseling psychology	228	1,226	210	1,664
18. Psychologists in public service	55	459	135	649
19. Military psychology	156	213	20	389
20. Maturity and old age	107	180	11	298
21. The society of engineering psychologists— A division of the APA	66	293	43	402
22. Psychological aspects of disability	70	814	171	1,055
23. Consumer psychology	26	220	—	246
24. Philosophical psychology	97	370	61	528
25. Experimental analysis of behavior	54	435	—	489
26. History of psychology	93	200	—	293
27. Community psychology	86	550	—	636
28. Psychopharmacology	74	254	—	328
29. Psychotherapy	—	—	—	—

* Note: There are no figures available for Division 29. Since 1967 there are 2 additional divisions. See listing on page 2 [Ed.].

tory to factory, from classroom to hospital ward, from nursery school to university, from school of education to school of medicine, from outpatient clinic to private consulting room, and [from] large governmental or military agency to local community project.

The great majority of American psychologists are members of the American Psychological Association; in 1967 the APA had 25,800 members.[1] Basic information about the membership of this national organization should indicate the complex nature of psychology and the heterogeneity among those who constitute the profession. Many of the Association's activities are organized around divisions, presently twenty-seven in number, which represent different areas of specialized interest in psychology; however, some members join more than one division. Divisional titles and membership totals are presented in Table 1.

State psychological associations represent American psychologists in their geographical areas. Psychological associations in all but one of the fifty states (Alaska), in the District of Columbia, in Puerto Rico, and in the province of Ontario in Canada are affiliates of APA. In recent years there has also been a rapid expansion of local professional groups—estimates based on a recent survey indicate approximately 125 local groups—which represent further geographical subunits.

The diverse activities of American psychologists are graphically portrayed in their responses to a recent questionnaire. The questionnaire covered (*a*) their stated area of specialization (or subfield), (*b*) their major employment, and (*c*) their primary work activities.[2] (Data for Figures 1, 2, and 3 are based on information obtained from the National Science Foundation's National Register of Scientific and Technical Personnel in the Field of Psychological Science Questionnaire, 1966.)

PSYCHOLOGY AND ITS RELATIONS WITH OTHER PROFESSIONS

Psychology today finds itself involved in intricate relations with many other fields. Historically rooted in both philosophy and the natural sciences, some of the content of psychology overlaps that of other academic and professional disciplines. Many applications of psychology occur in settings where other professions are also involved. Thus, psychologists apply their techniques and insights to problems of concern to clergymen, lawyers, social workers, educators, administrators, politicians, physicians, engineers, and other professionals. This state of affairs is not unusual. Almost every emerging profession brings new viewpoints and methods to old problems. By joining with other professions having related concerns for human welfare, psychology has contributed new techniques and distinctive theoretical approaches for understanding and modifying behavior.

To a marked extent, professions supplement one another in their interrelations, each bringing some unique and desirable contribution. They also overlap; many problems can be appropriately and effectively met by two or more professions. When a psychologist's contribution is supplementary and distinctive, he is usually welcomed; when it overlaps with the contributions of other professions, misunderstandings may arise. The effectiveness of a psychologist's contribution, and occasionally even his opportunity to make it, are determined in part by the relations he establishes with the other disciplines and professions that share his interests and concerns.

Professional persons have an obligation to know and take into account the traditions and practices of other professional groups with whom they work and to cooperate fully with members of such groups with whom research, service, and other functions are shared.

PRINCIPLES UNDERLYING THE ROLES OF PSYCHOLOGISTS

The American Psychological Association, as the official national organization of psychologists functioning in all their specialties, accepts responsibility for coordinating the development and functioning of psychology as a profession. In this role the Association is guided primarily by general criteria of human welfare. For psychologists

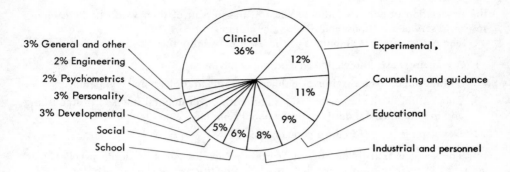

FIG. 1. Subfields of psychology ($N = 18,026$).

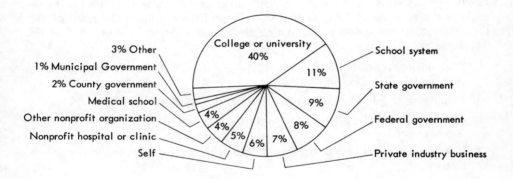

FIG. 2. Employers of psychologists ($N = 19,027$).

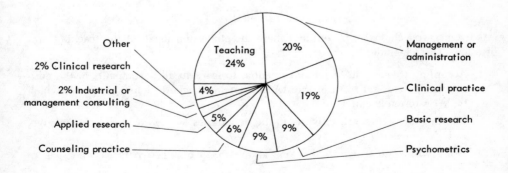

FIG. 3. Primary work activities of psychologists.

the Association provides a national voice in the pursuit of their work, be it teaching, research, service functions, consultation, or administration.

The Association has among its purposes responsibility for:

1. Advancing basic knowledge concerning behavior
2. Setting standards for training qualified aspirants to professional competence
3. Cooperating with state associations and with governmental bodies in establishing and maintaining standards of professional competence
4. Developing and enforcing a code of ethics.

The sections that follow identify certain principles which underlie psychologists' activities in their roles as researcher, teacher, practitioner, and administrator.

RESEARCH

Psychologists are concerned with the application of the methods of science to the study of the behavior of living organisms. The profession assumes the responsibility for encouraging research and facilitating the communication of research findings. This includes:

1. Encouraging research by emphasizing its importance during the preparation of students for careers in psychology
2. Identifying and developing sources of support for behavioral research
3. Sponsoring journals, professional meetings, and other means for the dissemination of research findings
4. Protecting freedom of investigation and fostering a climate favorable to scientific inquiry
5. Fostering high ethical standards in the conduct of research
6. Encouraging cooperation with other scholarly disciplines in the development of new knowledge about behavior.

TEACHING

As teachers, psychologists accept and share the ethics and ideals of the teaching profession. These include:

1. According freedom to teach and freedom to learn to all participants in the educational process set forth in the AAUP Statement on Academic Freedom, which the APA formally endorses
2. Limiting one's teaching activities to the boundaries of one's own skill, knowledge, and competence
3. Being willing to teach all that one knows to all qualified persons who seek to learn
4. Contributing to the maximum attainment of potential of students in their area of instruction.

SERVICE

As appliers of their knowledge, skills, and techniques, psychologists accept and share the values and guiding principles of those professions which deal with human welfare. Psychologists accept the responsibilities for:

1. Demanding for themselves and their colleagues the highest quality account of their abilities in utilizing psychological knowledge consonant with the state of the art and science
2. Engendering in aspirant members of the profession and displaying in their own practice a keen sense of social responsibility
3. Employing available psychological knowledge for the enhancement of human effectiveness and the betterment of human welfare
4. Making the services of psychologists available to all persons who seek and may benefit from such services
5. Sharing with related professions knowledge of research methods and findings, training techniques, and skills in the application of psychological knowledge.

ADMINISTRATION

As administrators of the professional activities of psychologists and other persons, psychologists share the responsibilities and accept the values of persons serving in such capacities. These include:

1. Accepting a primary loyalty to the overall purposes of the organization in which he has administrative responsibilities rather than to special interests within the organization
2. Willingness to utilize to the maximum the professional competence of all staff members in achieving the goals of the organization
3. Protecting the maximal freedom of behavior of staff members consonant with the effective functioning of the organization.

STANDARDS OF PRACTICE

The national Association accepts responsibility for (a) encouraging the establishment of meaningful standards of professional competence through statutory enactment and administrative policy particularly at the state level and by other means, (b) effectively informing the public concerning the meaning of the established standards of competence, and (c) designating to the public those members of the profession who have met these standards. In performing their applied functions, either alone or in association with other professions, psychologists accept the responsibility for taking appropriate steps to protect the public from the incompetent or unwise application of psychological knowledge and techniques and to establish and maintain high standards of professional competence and practice in all settings.

The public interest is advanced by the competent performance of socially useful services by a number of professions. The American Psychological Association believes it is undesirable to attempt to control the practice of all psychological functions by restricting them to members of any single profession except insofar as it can be clearly demonstrated that such restriction is necessary for the protection of the public. The Association's policy, therefore, is to oppose narrowly restrictive legislation or administrative policies which provide that only psychologists (or teachers, or physicians, or any other designated professional group) may engage in applications of certain knowledge and techniques of their field.

For example, the psychologist may engage in psychotherapy, other forms of behavior modification, and psychodiagnosis when his training and experience qualify him for such pursuits. In his practice he is responsible for assisting his client in obtaining professional help for problems that fall outside the boundaries of good psychological practice. The psychologist makes referrals to or seeks consultation with other specialists as needed. It is recognized that other professions are by virtue of their training and experience also qualified to render such services.

In the interest of both the public and the client and in accordance with the requirements of good professional practice, the profession of psychology seeks recognition of the privileged nature of confidential communications with clients preferably through statutory enactment or by administrative policy where more appropriate.

The APA has formulated a code of ethics to protect the public and has accepted responsibility for enforcing this code among its members (APA, 1967).

INDEPENDENT PRACTICE

Independent practice is one form of activity for qualified members of the profession. Good professional practice is usually facilitated by the maintenance of ongoing and meaningful working relationships with one's professional colleagues, and this principle applies with equal relevance to all forms of activity including independent or private practice.

Psychologists regarded as qualified for independent practice are those who (a) have been awarded a diploma by the American Board of Examiners in Professional Psychology, or (b) have been licensed or certified by state examining boards, or (c) have been certified by voluntary boards established by state psychological associations.

Psychologists who do not yet meet the qualifications recognized for independent practice should gain experience under qualified supervision. The Association strongly supports efforts in state legislation regulating the practice of psychology for a fee, which move toward a requirement of a doctoral degree and two years of acceptable experience.

RIGHTS AND RESPONSIBILITIES OF A PROFESSION

As a profession, psychology in America is sensitive to its rights and responsibilities. In this concluding section, some principles and statements are presented which describe the Association's policies and points of view.

THE QUESTION OF RIGHTS

As a member of an autonomous profession, a psychologist rejects limitations upon his freedom of thought and action other than those imposed by his moral, legal, and social responsibilities. The Association is always prepared to provide appropriate assistance to any responsible member who becomes subjected to unreasonable limitations upon his opportunity to function as a practitioner, teacher, researcher, administrator, or consultant. The Association is always prepared to cooperate with any responsible professional organization in opposing any unreasonable limitations on the professional functions of the members of that organization.

This insistence upon professional autonomy has been upheld over the years by the affirmative actions of the courts and other public and private bodies in support of the right of the psychologist—and other professionals—to pursue those functions for which he is trained and qualified to perform.

SOME CRITERIA FOR PSYCHOLOGY AS A PROFESSION

Psychologists share enough common values which yield a description of what they regard as criteria for a good profession. A combination of values which psychologists share and strive to protect is a respect for evidence combined with a recognition of the dignity of the human being. These give rise to the following characteristics of a good profession to which psychologists subscribe and aspire. As members of a good profession, psychologists:

1. Guide their practice and policies by a sense of social responsibility

2. Devote more of their energies to serving the public interest than to "guild" functions and to building ingroup strength

3. Represent accurately to the public their demonstrable competence

4. Develop and enforce a code of ethics primarily to protect the client and only secondarily to protect themselves

5. Identify their unique pattern of competencies and focus their efforts to carrying out those functions for which they are best equipped

6. Engage in cooperative relations with other professions having related or overlapping competencies and common purposes

7. Seek an adaptive balance among efforts devoted to research, teaching, and application

8. Maintain open channels of communication among "discoverers," teachers, and appliers of knowledge

9. Avoid nonfunctional entrance requirements into the profession, such as those based on race, nationality, creed, or arbitrary personality considerations

10. Insure that their training is meaningfully related to the subsequent functions of the members of the profession

11. Guard against premature espousal of any technique or theory as a final solution to substantive problems

12. Strive to make their services accessible to all persons seeking such services, regardless of social and financial considerations.

NOTES

1. The Association presently recognizes three major types of membership—Member, Associate, and Fellow. Qualifications for *Member* include a doctoral degree based in part upon a psychological dissertation and conferred by a graduate school of recognized standing. *Associate* (nonvoting) membership requires a master's degree in psychology from a recognized school plus a year of acceptable experience, or two years of graduate work in psychology in a recognized graduate school. *Fellow* status may be conferred upon members for whom sponsoring divisions present evidence of unusual and outstanding contribution or performance in psychology.

2. Primary work activity is defined in terms of working time devoted to that activity. ($N = 17,707$)

REFERENCE

American Psychological Association. *Casebook on ethical standards of psychologists.* Washington, D.C.: APA, 1967.

UNIT ONE | DISCUSSION QUESTIONS

1 | PSYCHOLOGY TODAY: CONCEPTIONS AND MISCONCEPTIONS

List and discuss some of the popular misconceptions of psychology as a science.

In what ways does the notion of "common sense" impair "scientific" thinking? Give examples to support your discussion.

2 | PSYCHOLOGY AS A PROFESSION

Which subfield of psychology do you think will experience the most rapid growth during the 1970's? Why?

Discuss which specific area of psychology interests you the most. Support your selection.

UNIT TWO
THE SCIENCE OF BEHAVIOR

By defining a science as "any body of organized knowledge which has been gathered through the use of systematic methods of investigation" (English and English)*, we establish a context in which to consider psychological study. The goals of science are description, prediction, and control. Present scientific knowledge is the result of the many investigations conducted by scientists all over the world. The conclusions they have reached have grown out of their objective and critical observations. Objectivity is a basic requirement for scientific observation. Inquiries are made under carefully controlled conditions in which the results are obtained and recorded by a predetermined method. Two well-defined methods are: (1) *introspection,* and (2) *observation.*

Introspection involves the contemplation of one's own experiences and behavior. Since introspection, by its very nature, is subjective, clinical objectivity is lost. However, not all behavior can be empirically verified by the scientist; some is implicit and requires the use of introspection.

Objectivity, on the other hand, may be gained by observation which is either (a) scientific or critical, or (b) uncritical. Scientific observation involves the employment of accurate laboratory methods using instruments suitably precise. It is performed by way of experimentation. Uncritical observation is the casual notice given to that which catches the eye or, for some reason or another, stimulates interest. Noticing the behavior of others while you are walking on the campus, riding in an automobile. or waiting for the bus is an example of uncritical observation. This kind of observation, like introspection, is generally unreliable. Rather it is critical observation which is mainly responsible for the accumulation of professionally recognized knowledge now available concerning human behavior. Such knowledge is accurate whenever the observations are accurate. Obviously the preferred method of learning about behavior is through critical observation.

In the first reading, *Methodology in Behavioral Research,* Bernard Berelson and Gary Steiner discuss three designs frequently used by the behavioral sciences: (1) the experiment, (2) the sample survey, and (3) the case study.

Occasionally the collection of research data has led to discussions concerning the propriety of certain procedures in gathering data. Research into the social behavior of man has often been done without the knowledge of the individuals involved. As a result, it is frequently questioned whether this constitutes an invasion of privacy. Thus the behavioral scientist, in his attempt to understand behavior without sacrificing validity, finds himself faced with a moral issue. *Privacy and Behavioral Research* is a condensation of a report on this pressing subject.

---

*   Horace B. English and Ava Champney English, *A Comprehensive Dictionary of Psychological and Psychoanalytic Terms.* David McKay, Inc., New York, 1958.

Psychological Assessment and Public Policy is a position statement of the American Psychological Association (APA) regarding quantification of individual characteristics. This document serves as a guideline for psychologists in offering services to public as well as private agencies.

---

3 | METHODOLOGY IN BEHAVIORAL RESEARCH

Bernard Berelson and Gary A. Steiner

DESIGN

In the broadest terms, there are three designs used in the behavioral sciences: the experiment, the sample survey, and the case study.

THE EXPERIMENT

By *experiment* is meant any investigation that includes two elements: manipulation or control of some variable by the investigator and systematic observation or measurement[1] of the result. In short, it means active intervention on the phenomena of interest to see what, if any, effects are produced by the intervention.

The experiment has had a central place in the history of science. The importance of experimentation depends not so much on its precision, its objectivity, or its instruments as on the inherent efficiency of intervention in disentangling cause-and-effect relationships. Whenever its use is feasible, intentional intervention is the method that most readily exposes cause and effect; and if the behavioral sciences were able to experiment more widely on their materials they would be better equipped today with important findings. For example, we would know much more about the effects on personality of different ways of rearing children if experimentation were not precluded on moral and humanitarian grounds. And the field is currently making some progress on such basic problems as mental disease and emotional disturbance by means of physiological intervention in the nervous system accompanied by controlled observation of the behavioral results. The implantation

---

From *Human Behavior: An Inventory of Scientific Findings* by Bernard Berelson and Gary A. Steiner, © 1964, by Harcourt Jovanovich, Inc., and reprinted with their permission.

of tiny electrodes in the brain has been used to induce fear, rage, joy, even "pleasure"; and ultimately such mapping of the brain centers that mediate emotions may have far-reaching clinical implications. Similarly, in human beings, chemical intervention has produced behavior that closely resembles certain manifestations of schizophrenia; and, in animals, certain parts of the brain have been systematically removed to see what effect that has on learned problem-solving.

THE CLASSICAL EXPERIMENT

The prototype of scientific experimentation, and in many ways its most foolproof form, is the classical experiment. The general question it answers is whether, and to what extent, one variable (called the experimental or independent variable) affects another variable (the dependent variable).

The logic is simple. Two groups are matched at the outset; one is given the experimental intervention (a piece of propaganda, a new drug that affects behavior, a French lesson taught in a new way, a special procedure that can introduce changes in working procedures in a factory); the result of the intervention is subsequently measured (i.e., its effect on attitudes, on personality, on the amount of French learned, on morale and productivity). The essentials of the classical experiment can be schematized as follows:

Experimental group, but not control group, exposed to intervention
(the experimental or independent variable)

	Before	After
Experimental group or subject	B_e	A_e
Control group or subject	B_c	A_{cc}

The figures represent measurements of the dependent variable, and the effect of the experimental variable is $(A_e - A_c) - (B_e - B_c)$.

Here is an illustration of a classical experiment concerned with the effects of a new tranquilizer pill on psychotic behavior:

1. Define the population of subjects and draw a sample—e.g., a random sample of all the patients with a given diagnosis at a certain institution.

2. Divide the sample at random into two groups. By definition the two groups will now be similar, within limits of sampling error, on *any* measurement. Thus there is no reason to expect one group to behave any differently in the future than the other. Flip a coin to decide which will be "experimental" and which "control."

3. Define the dependent variable ("psychotic behavior"): How will it be measured or rated? Take a "before" measurement on each group.

4. Define the experimental variable precisely—What doses of the tranquilizer over what period of time?—and administer it to the experimental group only. The control group will probably get a placebo—a pill that looks the same but has no active ingredients—to control for the effects of autosuggestion, and even for the effect of participating in the experiment at all (since that will involve some special attention, at the least. In some cases of this kind, for extra precaution, the experiment is

"double blind": not only does the subject not know which pill he gets but, in order to control the expression of his own (conscious or unconscious) wishes in the matter, the experimenter does not know at the time either.

5.   Take "after" measurements of the dependent variable on each group.

6.   The difference between the two groups after the experiment, beyond any difference that may have existed before, is the effect of the experimental variable. In this case, it is the effect of the tranquilizer upon psychotic behavior.

The glory of the classical experiment is that its logic has no loophole. When all the conditions of the classical experiment have been met, and all four cells have been filled in, the final difference between control and experimental group *must* be due to the effect of the experimental or independent variable: both groups reflect the effects of any other variables not directly manipulated by the experimenter (such as time itself, atmospheric conditions, or the effects of having been selected to participate in the study). Thus the control group protects the experimenter against many of the common fallacies that plague less rigorous studies. Before-and-after observation of an experimental group alone is particularly vulnerable to the fallacy of *post hoc, ergo propter hoc*. Without a control group there is a temptation to attribute any subsequent change in the observed subjects to the experimental variable, whereas the change may have occurred without the experimenter's intervention.

Although there is a logical model for the classical experiment, in actual experiments the design is frequently modified for various reasons: costs, practical difficulties, and so on. In some cases, statistical approximations will do. For example, if the experimental and control groups are truly divided at random, the before-measurement may be omitted in the knowledge that the two groups will vary only within known limits of sampling error. The experiment simply consists of the administration of the experimental condition to one group and the subsequent after-measurements of both. If this after-measurement records a difference between the two groups that cannot be attributed to chance variation, it is taken to be the result of the experimental variable.[2]

Similarly, many experiments add onto the basic four-fold model. Some measure the effect of the experimental variable over time: propaganda may be effective right after its administration, but how long does it last? Others assess the effects of several experimental variables within a single investigation. The simplest form of this involves two or more experimental groups, each of which is measured against a single control group. For example, the patients can be divided into three or more groups: one is the control, one gets tranquilizer A, one gets tranquilizer B, etc.

Moreover, modern statistical designs make it possible to evaluate the relative effects of a number of independent variables acting simultaneously and in combination. An investigation of classroom learning might vary the method of instruction, the sex of the teacher, the room lighting, and student motivation, all at one stage of observations; and then conclude which of these factors is the most important influence on learning, and how they act in combination.

So much for the general logic of experimental design: the principal point, worth repeating, is that the fundamental advantage of experimentation is not its precision or its instrumentation but its inherent logical rigor. Now let us apply the method to the settings and subjects of behavioral science experimentation. In our field, we can distinguish experiments in the laboratory and in natural settings.

THE LABORATORY EXPERIMENT—ANIMAL. Behavioral scientists, notably psychologists, conduct intensive studies on animals in the laboratory: historically, the animals have usually been rats, pigeons, or apes. Why study lower animals when the objective is to understand people? The reasons are both practical and theoretical.

On the practical side, many experiments cannot be conducted on human subjects for legal and moral reasons—e.g., the behavioral effect of systematic destruction of various parts of the nervous system. In general, any experimental variable that involves bodily harm or undue pain, discomfort, embarrassment, or psychological or social damage is naturally excluded from experimental intervention with human subjects. In addition, animals are cheap, they cannot resist captivity, they are almost always available, and they do not have to be paid for their services.

On the theoretical side, the environment of animals, unlike that of human beings, can be completely and systematically controlled twenty-four hours a day. The lower animals reproduce more quickly and in greater numbers than human beings, and their mating can be controlled, thus making possible longitudinal studies of hereditary effects. With animals, far greater homogeneity of subjects can be attained by inbreeding, thus reducing sources of behavioral variation that are irrelevant and bothersome for some purposes. Animals are presumably simpler and thus more easily understood than people, hence some scientists argue that the study of human behavior must begin with the simpler forms (in the sense that arithmetic has to be mastered before the calculus). Finally, the acceptance of evolution as a biological fact leads to the assumption that, in principle, the processes underlying human behavior are an outgrowth of those represented in lower forms, and therefore the study of animals cannot be irrelevant. Findings from animal studies are not expected to be directly replicated in human behavior, but they may well provide the foundations on which the elaborations introduced at the human level must be built.

THE LABORATORY EXPERIMENT—HUMAN. Human beings are also studied intensively in laboratory situations, both individually and in groups. Given the practicalities of the matter, the human beings involved are usually college students, and many of the practical advantages of using lower animals apply as well with students as subjects: they do not have to be paid, they are readily accessible, and they often cannot effectively resist the experimentation.[3]

We have reviewed the theoretical justification for studying rats and pigeons. What is the justification for using college sophomores or, more generally, representatives of any selected type of human subject for laboratory investigation?

The answer depends largely upon the expected variation of the phenomenon under study. There is little reason to suspect for example, that the visual or auditory processes of college students vary considerably from those of other types of people; or that their eye movements, which signal dreams, are unique. Accordingly, the tendency to generalize to people at large on such issues is frequently supported by further studies, and college students turn out to be a reasonably good sample of human beings on such limited topics as those closely tied to physiological processes.

However, when the question deals with political attitudes, feelings toward the family, reactions to stress, life values, or such complicated or culturally determined matters, it is safest to assume, until proved otherwise, that there *are* important differences between college students and other categories of citizens. Hence, a priori generalizations of findings of this character must be avoided.

Another general problem of much experimental work done in the laboratory is that of "translation." Some laboratory experiments deal with phenomena that can be reproduced directly in the laboratory, such as depth perception, small-group problems, or the learning of certain skills. In these cases, the experimenter simply brings the behavior of interest into the laboratory for more careful scrutiny under experimental conditions. Many phenomena, however, cannot be transplanted to a laboratory either in principle or for such practical considerations as time, money, cooperation of subjects, and so on; or the phenomenon that interests the experimenter is a general one (motivation, love, hostility) that must be delineated to one specific instance for a given investigation. Such conditions require acts of "translation": before the experiment, translation of the phenomena of interest to the experimenter into the specific laboratory operations that will "tap" them; after the experiment, translation of the results of the specific operations performed back into the original concepts and phenomena.

An illustration will, we hope, make the point. The psychoanalytic notion of "repression" states that under certain circumstances individuals will force out of their awareness the memories of certain traumatic or psychologically damaging events. In addition, some impulses or desires that are unacceptable (e.g., killing or having sexual relations with one's father) may be repressed, that is, not be consciously acknowledged although they are actively present in the personality. When experimentally inclined psychologists wanted to test some of these notions in the laboratory, one design used was to show subjects a series of pictures—some pleasant, some unpleasant or gruesome—and at a later sitting ask them to describe the pictures seen. So the hypothesis that traumatic events get repressed is translated into the test: "Gruesome pictures will be accurately recalled less frequently than nongruesome pictures."

Evaluation of such experimental results demands critical consideration of the translation involved and its validity. Students of repression might reject the experiment (as many of them did) not because it was poorly designed or failed to produce conclusive results but simply because they considered it irrelevant to their views of the concept of repression.

Note how this example illustrates the scientific requirement that results be reported operationally (what was done) as well as conceptually or theoretically (what they mean). When the experimenter reports that gruesome pictures were not described accurately with the same frequency as non-gruesome pictures, behavioral scientists can decide for themselves what relevance, if any, the finding has for issues in which they are interested.

The Natural Experiment

Frequently the major elements of an experiment occur or are produced in the natural habitat of the behavior under study. Such experimentation avoids many of the problems of the laboratory situation discussed above, e.g., oversimplification and artificiality. In the natural experiment the subjects ordinarily do not know they are under investigation and hence do not modify their behavior as a result of being watched. On the other hand, natural experimentation is usually less precise, because the pertinent events are less fully under the experimenter's control.

THE PLANNED NATURAL EXPERIMENT. In this type, as in the laboratory, the investigator intentionally manipulates the independent variable and then makes systematic measurements of the result. The tranquilizer study is an example; so is the illustrative study mentioned above dealing with classroom learning. A planned natural experiment often used in advertising research is the "split-run" technique: metropolitan newspapers frequently offer advertisers the opportunity to run two versions of an advertisement in the same issue, with coupons or other coded devices enabling "returns" from the two versions to be compared.

THE SPONTANEOUS NATURAL EXPERIMENT. Sometimes behavioral scientists are fortunate enough to come on a situation that happened by itself yet has most or all of the elements of a successful experiment. In such cases, an approximation of experimental results may be obtained.

For example, when television was being introduced, there was a period during which technical considerations were the principal determinants of which towns and cities would have stations. Thus it was possible to find a number of cities without TV and to know about when the medium would be introduced in them. This provided an opportunity to study "what television does" on a before-and-after basis, as compared with matched towns without TV (the controls.) Similarly, studying the culture of a primitive community during and after the advent of technological developments provides an attenuated natural experiment under spontaneous conditions. Since, as noted above, the absence of a proper control is the technical failing of such studies, the investigator must often decide between naturalness and control, or compromise on some of each.

THE SAMPLE SURVEY

The sample survey, as a type of research design, does not refer simply to a public opinion poll, though a properly designed poll is certainly one example of a sample survey, and probably the most familiar one. In our sense, a sample survey is properly named in that it contains the indicated two elements:

1. A sample. The investigator first decides what group or "population" he is interested in (American adults, voters, women of childbearing age, college students, etc.) and then selects a sample in the statistical sense. It may be "random," "representative," "quota," "weighted," or any of a number of technical types. The main point is that the sample is so chosen as to enable the experimenter to draw conclusions regarding the entire "population" and not simply those members of the population who happen to turn up in the sample.

2. A survey. The investigator then collects some measures on the appropriate characteristics of the population being studied (number of television sets or children in the household; how the members feel about Russia or religion; what they know about India or space; and so on).

Obviously there are certain questions that can be answered only by a sample survey. The question, "To what extent do American psychologists today believe that extrasensory perception exists?" can be answered by specifying a population and then asking a selected sample. No experiment will answer the question once and for all and neither will a case study. In general, whenever the investigator is interested in assessing or estimating the present state of affairs with regard to some variable that changes over time for a large group of subjects, a sample survey is the only practical way to get the answer. If the variable did not change over time, we could probably learn the answer once and for all by experiment; or if there were interest in only one or a few instances, case studies could provide the answer. These are certainly not the only conditions under which the sample survey is useful, but these are the conditions under which it is the imperative form of design.

In addition to simple measures of magnitude (How many people will vote?), sample surveys provide clues to relations between variables (and thus ultimately to cause and effect) by correlation of the various measures obtained. For example, a survey of number of children per family can provide a series of tables showing how fertility varies by families of differing class, race, rural-urban residence, religion, etc. This example, incidentally, illustrates another advantage of the sample survey in the study of relationships: many times the variables of interest are difficult or impossible to manipulate by experiment (years of schooling, race), so the only approach is to compare people who already differ on the characteristic in question and see how their behavior differs.

Such correlations are difficult to disentangle causally, because the direction of the influence is uncertain (and it is often reciprocal, which makes the matter more difficult still). To take a simple example, a correlation between reading an advertisement for a given make of car and buying the car could go either way—reading influenced purchase, purchase influenced reading. Even when the direction is clear, when one characteristic (e.g., race) antedates and is not affected by another (e.g., fertility), the nature of the causal relationship is quite complex, with several other factors usually involved (e.g., income, social position, religion, place of residence, age at marriage).

To handle change over time in certain investigations, a variant of the sample survey has been developed that is called the panel. This requires repeated measures of the appropriate characteristics on the same people, so that the investigation can study how changes were brought about over time. This method is particularly useful in campaigns that bring a variety of stimuli to the subjects' attention, and it is no accident that the method is used mainly in studies of marketing and voting. A major limitation of the panel technique is that, as the same people are queried repeatedly, they may change their behavior simply as a result of panel membership. As a control, panel responses are often checked against samples of "fresh" respondents.

THE CASE STUDY

The case study is complementary to the sample survey. The sample survey measures many people on few characteristics, usually at one point in time. The case study intensively examines many characteristics of one "unit" (person, work group, company, community, culture), usually over a long period of time. The goal of such investigations is to learn "all" about the area of interest for the one case involved. Typical case studies in the behavioral sciences might include: the life history of a psychotic; an intensive analysis of a patient's psychological disturbance;[4] an anthropological monograph describing in detail the technology and customs of a primitive culture; a detailed description and analysis of the socioeconomic classes existing in a small Southern town.

As the examples suggest, the detail and the depth of information over time that the case study provides makes this design particularly relevant for questions involving etiology and development: How does a particular neurotic manifestation emerge and change over time? What are the critical incidents that lead up to an industrial strike? How does the industrialization of a traditional society affect the family?

The chief limitation of this method is that the results are based on a sample of one, so that the degree of their generality is not known. Would another individual, another company, another community, another culture respond in the same way? In addition, the case study is often subject to the *post hoc, ergo propter hoc* fallacy, since neither a "control group" nor intervention by the investigator is provided as a safeguard.

Hence, case studies rarely *prove* anything, although they are frequently rich in clues and insights for further investigation. In many areas the case study is the idea-getting investigation par excellence. But since in this book we limit ourselves to what is more or less proved about human behavior, we shall bring in the results of case studies only when they have been verified in some way.

NOTES

1. By *measurement* the behavioral scientist typically means something broader than what the term means to the layman. The behavioral scientist considers that an attitude has been measured if it can simply be distinguished as "for" or "against," "more" or "less." Finer quantitative distinctions, of course, are also measurements, but so are dichotomies or classificatory categories in general.

2. It is sometimes hard to believe, but it is still true, that when a group has been divided at random into two groups, the groups will differ by no more than chance on *any* characteristic whatsoever. The proportion of blue-eyed people in the two groups, of redheads, of people over and under 5'7", of Catholics, of those who skipped breakfast this morning, of those opposed to capital punishment or in favor of a stronger United Nations—all will be roughly equivalent. There are statistical procedures that determine the probability of a given difference having arisen simply by such random division. Therefore, when a difference is greater than that which could reasonably be expected on the basis of random division, and the groups have in fact been randomly divided, the conclusion is that the difference is not due to their division but to something that happened to them afterward.

3. In this connection, it is worth recalling an observation of the late Edward Tolman, a distinguished psychologist. He once noted how much of American psychology was based on two sets of subjects, rats and college sophomores, and enjoined his colleagues to remember that the former certainly are not people and the latter may not be!

4. In fact, case studies are one of the principal sources of data on many questions in clinical psychology, since the practicing clinician is interested in specific individuals and collects intensive data on his patients. The most important questions in this area revolve around such time-bound issues as how and when the various syndromes arise, develop, and change. Thus, clinical histories have practical significance for the therapist and stimulate many hypotheses in personality theory.

RECOMMENDED READINGS

R. G. Barker and H. F. Wright, *One Boy's Day: A Specimen Record of Behavior*. Harper, 1951.

W. G. Cochran and Gertrude M. Cox, *Experimental Designs*, 2nd Ed. Wiley, 1950.

John Dollard, *Criteria for the Life History*. Yale University Press, 1935.

A. L. Edwards, *Experimental Design in Psychological Research*, Rev. Ed. Holt, Rinehart & Winston, 1960.

R. A. Fisher, *The Design of Experiments*. 4th Ed. Oliver & Boyd, 1947.

Herbert Hyman, *Survey Design and Analysis*. Free Press, 1955.

Herbert Hyman *et al.*, *Interviewing in Social Research*. University of Chicago Press, 1954.

Henry Murray, ed., *Explorations in Personality: A Clinical and Experimental Study of Fifty Men of College Age*. Oxford University Press, 1938.

Samuel A. Stouffer *et al.*, *Measurement and Prediction*. Princeton University Press, 1950.

---

4 | PRIVACY AND BEHAVIORAL RESEARCH

Preliminary Summary of the Report of the Panel on Privacy and Behavioral Research

In recent years there have been growing threats to the privacy of individuals. Wiretapping, electronic eavesdropping, the use of personality tests in employment, the use of the lie detector in security or criminal investigations, and the detailed scrutiny of the private lives of people receiving public welfare funds all involve invasions of privacy. Although the social purpose is usually clear, the impact on the persons involved may be damaging. Our society has become more and more sensitive to the need to avoid such damage.

This concern has led to extensive discussion about the propriety of certain procedures in behavioral research, by the Congress, by officials in the various agencies of the Government, by university officials, by the scientific community generally, and by leaders in professional societies in the behavioral sciences. The Office of Science and Technology appointed a panel, in January 1966, to examine these issues and to propose guidelines for those who are engaged in behavioral research or associated with its support and management.

From *Science*, **155**, pp. 535–538, 3 February 1967. Copyright © 1967 by the American Association for the Advancement of Science. Reprinted by permission.

The panel has restricted its attention to issues of privacy arising in connection with programs of data collection and study which are intimately associated with behavioral research. For example, it has not reviewed a number of the programs for data collection which are sponsored by the Federal Government, such as the various censuses, health and welfare statistics, and financial information secured from business and industry. These programs may also encroach upon the privacy of individuals, either through the burden of disclosure which they impose on respondents or through their availability for unintended purposes.

It is our opinion that the principles described in this report for protection of privacy in behavioral research should apply equally to such inquiries. When response is mandatory, as in the case of information that must be furnished to the Government, there is an even greater burden on the sponsoring agency to protect the individual against disclosure unless disclosure is specifically sanctioned by statute.

The panel has not reviewed in detail the wide variety of mechanical or electronic devices which make it possible to intrude into private lives. We have become acquainted with a few of the problems in that field, however, and are dismayed to observe the disregard for human values indicated by the advocacy or actual practice of eavesdropping, the use of lie detection without clear justification, and the frequent willingness to institute surveillance procedures to handle the problems of a small proportion of our population at the risk of eroding the rights and the quality of life for the majority.

Likewise, the panel has not reviewed in detail the propriety of procedures involved in employment or social welfare activities. Enough examples have been brought to our attention, however, to make us feel that examination of procedures in these spheres is needed also.

The attitudes of various segments of our society about proper procedures for the protection of privacy and the right to self-determination have been explored by the panel. It has reviewed relevant research in the behavioral sciences and the administrative practices of universities and Government agencies. It has also consulted with the scientific community through its professional organizations.

THREATS TO PRIVACY

The right to privacy is the right of the individual to decide for himself how much he will share with others his thoughts, his feelings, and the facts of his personal life. It is a right that is essential to insure dignity and freedom of self-determination. In recent years there has been a severe erosion of this right by the widespread and often callous use of various devices for eavesdropping, lie detection, and secret observation in politics, in business, and in law enforcement. Indeed, modern electronic instruments for wiretapping and bugging have opened any human activity to the threat of illicit invasion of privacy. This unwholesome state of affairs has led to wide public concern over the methods of inquiry used by agencies of public employment, social welfare, and law enforcement.

Behavioral research, devoted as it is to the discovery of facts and principles underlying human activity of all types, comes naturally under scrutiny in any examination of possible threats to privacy. All of the social sciences, including economics, political science, anthropology, sociology, and psychology, take as a major object of study the behavior of individuals, communities, or other groups. In one context or another, investigators in all of these disciplines frequently need to seek information that is private to the men, women, and children who are the subjects of their study. In most instances this information is freely given by those who consent to cooperate in the scientific process. But the very nature of behavioral research is such that there is a risk of invasion of privacy if unusual care is not taken to secure the consent of research subjects, or if the data obtained are not given full confidentiality.

While the privacy problem in scientific research is small in comparison to that which exists in employment interviewing, social welfare screening, and law enforcement investigations, the opportunity for improper invasion is not negligible. About 35,000 behavioral scientists are engaged in research in the United States, 2,100 new PhDs are graduated each year, and the total number of students enrolled for advanced degrees in the behavioral sciences exceeds 40,000 at the present time.

It is probable that relatively few of the studies undertaken by these scientists raise serious questions of propriety in relation to privacy and human dignity. From a survey of articles published in professional journals and of research grant applications submitted to Government agencies, we have concluded that most scientists who conduct research in privacy-sensitive areas are aware of the ethical implications of their experimental designs and arrange to secure the consent of subjects and to protect the confidentiality of the data obtained from them.

It cannot be denied, however, that, in a limited number of instances, behavioral scientists have not followed appropriate procedures to protect the rights of their subjects, and that in other cases recognition of the importance of privacy-invading considerations has not been as sophisticated, or the considerations as affirmatively implemented, as good practice demands. Because of this failure there has been pressure from some quarters, both within the Government and outside of it, to place arbitrary limits on the research methods which may be used. Behavioral scientists as a group do not question the importance of the right to privacy and are understandably concerned when suggestions are made that the detailed processes of science should be subjected to control by legislation or arbitrary administrative ruling. All scientists are opposed to restrictions which may curtail important research. At the same time they have an obligation to insure that all possible steps are taken to assure respect for the privacy and dignity of their subjects.

CONFLICTING RIGHTS

It is clear that there exists an important conflict between two values, both of which are strongly held in American society.

The individual has an inalienable right to dignity, self-respect, and freedom to determine his own thoughts and actions within the broad limits set by the requirements of society. The essential element in privacy and self-determination is the privilege of making one's own decision as to the extent to which one will reveal thoughts, feelings, and actions. When a person consents freely and fully to share himself with others—with a scientist, an employer, or a credit investigator—there is no invasion of privacy, regardless of the quality or nature of the information revealed.

Behavioral science is representative of another value vigorously championed by most American citizens, the right to know anything that may be known or discovered about any part of the universe. Man is part of this universe, and the extent of the Federal Government's financial support of human behavioral research (on the order of $300 million in 1966) testifies to the importance placed on the study of human behavior by the American people. In the past there have been conflicts between theological beliefs and the theoretical analyses of the physical sciences. These conflicts have largely subsided, but the behavioral sciences seem to have inherited the basic conflict that arises when strongly held beliefs or moral attitudes—whether theologically, economically, or politically based—are subjected to the free ranging process of scientific inquiry. If society is to exercise its right to know, it must free its behavioral scientists as much as possible from unnecessary restraints. Behavioral scientists in turn must accept the constructive restraints that society imposes in order to establish that level of dignity, freedom, and personal fulfillment that men treasure virtually above all else in life.

The root of the conflict between the individual's right to privacy and society's right of discovery is the research process. Behavioral science seeks to assess and to measure many qualities of men's minds, feelings, and actions. In the absence of informed consent on the part of the subject, these measurements represent invasion of privacy. The scientist must therefore obtain the consent of his subject.

To obtain truly informed consent is often difficult. In the first place, the nature of the inquiry sometimes cannot be explained adequately because it involves complex variables that the nonscientist does not understand. Examples are the personality variables measured by questionnaires, and the qualities of cognitive process measured by creativity tests. Second, the validity of an experiment is sometimes destroyed if the subject knows all the details of its conduct. Examples include drug testing, in which the effect of suggestion (placebo effect) must be avoided, and studies of persuasibility, in which the subjects remain ignorant of the influences that are being presented experimentally. Clearly, then, if behavioral research is to be effective, some modification of the traditional concept of informed consent is needed.

Such a change in no sense voids the more general proposition that the performance of human behavioral research is the product of a partnership between the scientist and his subject. Consent to participate in a study must be the norm before any subject embarks on the enterprise. Since consent must sometimes be given despite an admittedly inadequate understanding of the scientific purposes of the research procedures, the right to discontinue participation at any point must be stipulated in clear terms. In the meantime, when full information is not available to the subject and when no alternative procedures to minimize the privacy problem are available, the relationship between the subject and the scientist (and between the subject and the institution sponsoring the scientist) must be based upon trust. This places the scientist and the sponsoring institution under a fiduciary obligation to protect the privacy and dignity of the subject who entrusts himself to them. The scientist must agree to treat the subject fairly and with dignity, to cause him no inconvenience or discomfort unless the extent of the inconvenience and discomfort has been accepted by the subject in advance, to inform the subject as fully as possible of the purposes of the inquiry or experiment, and to put into effect all procedures which will assure the confidentiality of whatever information is obtained.

Occasionally, even this degree of consent cannot be obtained. Naturalistic observations of group behavior must sometimes be made unbeknownst to the subjects.

In such cases, as well as in all others, the scientist has the obligation to insure full confidentiality of the research records. Only by doing so, and by making certain that published reports contain no identifying reference to a given subject, can the invasion of privacy be minimized.

Basically, then, the protection of privacy in research is assured first by securing the informed consent of the subject. When the subject cannot be completely informed, the consent must be based on trust in the scientist and in the institution sponsoring him. In any case the scientist and his sponsoring institution must insure privacy by the maintenance of confidentiality.

In the end, the fact must be accepted that human behavioral research will at times produce discomfort to some subjects, and will entail a partial invasion of their privacy. Neither the principle of privacy nor the need to discover new knowledge can supervene universally. As with other conflicting values in our society, there must be constant adjustment and compromise, with the decision as to which value is to govern in a given instance to be determined by a weighing of the costs and the gains —the cost in privacy, the gain in knowledge. The decision cannot be made by the investigator alone, because he has a vested interest in his own research program, but must be a positive concern of his scientific peers and the institution which sponsors his work. Our society has grown strong on the principle of minimizing costs and maximizing gains, and, when warmly held values are in conflict, there must be a thoughtful evaluation of the specific case. In particular we do not believe that detailed Governmental controls of research methods or instruments can substitute for the more effective procedures which are available and carry less risk of damage to the scientific enterprise.

ETHICAL ASPECTS OF HUMAN RESEARCH

Greater attention must be given to the ethical aspects of human research. The increase in scientists and in volume of research provides more chance for carelessness or recklessness and, in the hurried search for useful findings, can lead to abuses. Furthermore, if standards are not carefully maintained, there could develop an atmosphere of disregard for privacy that would be altogether alien to the spirit of American society. The increased potentials for damage and for fruitful outcomes from new knowledge are in no small part results of increased Federal support of behavioral science. While no one would suggest that ethical standards should be different for scientists supported by public funds and for those supported by private funds, the Government has an especially strong obligation to support research only under conditions that give fullest protection to individual human dignity. Government must avow and maintain the highest standards for the guidance of all.

To summarize, three parties—the investigator, his institution, and the sponsoring agency—have the responsibility for maintaining proper ethical standards with respect to Government-sponsored research. The investigator designs the research and is in the best position to evaluate the propriety of his procedures. He has, therefore, the ultimate responsibility for insuring that his research is both effective and ethical. The formalization of our ethics concerning privacy in connection with research is too recent, and perhaps too incomplete, to permit the assumption that all investigators have a full understanding of the proper methods for protecting the rights of subjects.

Furthermore, the investigator is first and foremost a scientist in search of new knowledge, and it would not be in accord with our understanding of human motivation to expect him always to be as vigilant for his subject's welfare as he is for the productiveness of his own research.

We conclude, therefore, that responsibility must also be borne by the institution which employs the investigator. The employing institution is often a university or a Government laboratory in which there are other scientists capable of reviewing the research plan. Such persons, drawn in part from disciplines other than the behavioral sciences, can present views that are colored neither by self-interest nor by the blind spots that may characterize the specific discipline of the investigator.

Finally, the sponsoring agency is obligated to make certain that both the investigator and his institution are fully aware of the importance of the ethical aspects of the research and that they have taken the necessary steps to discharge their responsibility to the human subjects involved. We believe that, in the majority of instances, it is neither necessary nor desirable for an agency to exceed this level of responsibility.

CONCLUSIONS

From our examination of the relation of behavioral science research to the right to privacy, we have been led to the following conclusions.

1.   While most current practices in the field pose no significant threat to the privacy of research subjects, a sufficient number of exceptions have been noted to warrant a sharp increase in attention to procedures that will assure protection of this right. The increasing scale of behavioral research is itself an additional reason for focusing attention in this area.

2.   Participation by subjects must be voluntary and based on informed consent to the extent that this is consistent with the objectives of the research. It is fully consistent with the protection of privacy that, in the absence of full information, consent be based on trust in the qualified investigator and the integrity of his institution.

3.   The scientist has an obligation to insure that no permanent physical or psychological harm will ensue from the research procedures, and that temporary discomfort or loss of privacy will be remedied in an appropriate way during the course of the research or at its completion. To merit trust, the scientist must design his research with a view to protecting, to the fullest extent possible, the privacy of his subjects. If intrusion on privacy proves essential to the research, he should not proceed with his proposed experiment until he and his colleagues have considered all of the relevant facts and he has determined, with support from them, that the benefits outweigh the costs.

4.   The scientist has the same responsibility to protect the privacy of the individual in published reports and in research records that he has in the conduct of the research itself.

5.   The primary responsibility for the use of ethical procedures must rest with the individual investigator, but Government agencies that support behavioral research should satisfy themselves that the institution which employs the investigator has effectively accepted its responsibility to require that he meet proper ethical standards.

6.   Legislation to assure appropriate recognition of the rights of human subjects is neither necessary nor desirable if the scientists and sponsoring institutions fully discharge their responsibilities in accommodating to the claim of privacy. Because of its relative inflexibility, legislation cannot meet the challenge of the subtle and sensitive conflict of values under consideration, nor can it aid in the wise decision making by individuals which is required to assure optimum protection of subjects, together with the fullest effectiveness of research.

RECOMMENDATIONS

These conclusions lead us to make the following recommendations.

1.   That Government agencies supporting research in their own laboratories or in outside institutions require those institutions to agree to accept responsibility for the ethical propriety of human research performed with the aid of Government funds.

2.   That the methods used for institutional review be determined by the institutions themselves. The greatest possible flexibility of methods should be encouraged in order to build effective support for the principle of institutional responsibility within universities or other organizations. Institutions differ in their internal structures and operating procedures, and no single, rigid formula will work for all.

3.   That investigators and institutions be notified of the importance of consent and confidentiality as ethical requirements in research design, and that when either condition cannot be met, an explanation of the reasons be made in the application for funds.

4.   That when research is undertaken directly by, or purchased on specification by, a Government agency, responsibility for protection of privacy lies with the agency. When independent research is funded by the Government, however, responsibility lies primarily with the scientist and his institution, and research instruments or design should not be subject to detailed review by Government agencies with respect to protection of privacy.

5.   That universities and professional associations be encouraged to emphasize the ethical aspects of behavioral research. When a training grant is made, a university should be requested to indicate its understanding that support of education on the ethics of research is one of the purposes of the grant.

5 | PSYCHOLOGICAL ASSESSMENT AND PUBLIC POLICY

American Psychological Association

The nature of man and of society makes it necessary that we attempt to assess psychological characteristics. Individual human beings differ from one another in a variety of ways; society requires a variety of diverse contributions from its members. The more accurately we can judge each person's suitability for potential roles consistent with his interests, the more successfully a society will function. Accurate assessment brings benefits to the individual as well by enabling him to locate the particular kinds of situations in which he can function most effectively as he seeks education, employment, medical and psychological services, and fuller personal development.

In attempting to understand others and to predict how they will function under various circumstances, all of us utilize a great variety of assessment methods—observations, careful or casual, interviews, formal or informal, and comments and recommendations based on varying degrees of acquaintance with the person being judged. Specialized psychological assessment techniques have been developed as refinements on these general methods or as supplements to them. What such specialized techniques add is some indication of the validity and usefulness of the information. They also provide some degree of *standardization of conditions* under which observations are made or samples of behavior obtained and, where possible, some *quantification* of the findings. This makes possible systematic comparisons of the individual's characteristics with those of reference or norm groups. But the psychological procedures are similar in many ways to the more informal appraisals of people that constantly go on.

SPECIAL FEATURES OF PSYCHOLOGICAL ASSESSMENT

Because techniques of psychological assessment are *instruments* designed and built for specific tasks, they require specialized knowledge if they are to be used correctly. One cannot choose the most appropriate instrument for a particular purpose or make valid interpretations of the scores or protocols that respondents produce

"Psychological Assessment and Public Policy," *American Psychologist*, **25**, March 1970, No. 5, pp. 264–266. Copyright © 1970 by the American Psychological Association, and reproduced by permission. Adopted as a position statement of the American Psychological Association by its Board of Directors on January 17, 1970. The initial draft was written by Dr. Leona Tyler of the University of Oregon. The BPA Assessment Committee (Samuel J. Messick, *Chairman,* Abraham Carp, Chester W. Harris, A. G. Bayroff, and Warren T. Norman) and the Board of Professional Affairs were responsible for the development of the statement in its final form.

unless he possesses such knowledge. It is much more a matter of proper administration and scoring procedures. Indeed, for conventional objective tests, little more is needed than adheres to the instructions for administering and scoring. It is the body of research information associated with an instrument that furnishes the basis for decisions about what it does and does not measure or reveal, how accurate or reliable it is under various circumstances, and what special cautions must be observed in its use.

The accumulation of this essential information requires the cooperation of large numbers of persons, persons who are not themselves being assessed for any particular purpose. Millions of men, women, and children, for example, have taken intelligence and achievement tests as participants in research projects designed to establish test validity and develop norms. Persons in all walks of life have filled out interest inventories, attitude scales, and personality questionnaires in order to furnish the data psychologists needed to develop scoring systems and scaling procedures. A test or other standardized assessment instrument represents this total effort, not simply the intentions of its author. It cannot lead to sound inferences about an individual's characteristics unless this research has been done, and the person interpreting the test is familiar with it.

Often a test is used solely as a predictor of probable successful performance, as in selecting candidates for a job or school. In this case the score is treated as if it provides no information on the person's characteristics other than likelihood of success. No interpretations of test performance of inferences about personal characteristics are required for this kind of use. Although a practitioner employing a test for such purposes need not be familiar with the supporting research, the person responsible for prescribing its use should be.

Information derived from instruments used in psychological assessment as well as the instruments themselves become *dated,* and their significance may change markedly over time. A person's score or protocol indicates only his present status, and while it may constitute a basis for predicting future status, such predictions have not turned out to be very accurate except over short periods of time. Although dated or obsolete information should not be used for decision-making purposes, it may be valuable for research and should be retained using adequate coding procedures to protect the identity of the individual. The instruments themselves also require frequent updating to replace obsolete items and stimuli and to insure that norms are representative of the appropriate segments of the population.

A special difficulty in psychological assessment, particularly when used in employment or placement rather than treatment situations, is the problem of faking and response sets. It has been obvious from the beginning to anyone who examines a typical personality inventory or questionnaire that it is quite possible for respondents to falsify their answers. In circumstances where one wishes to make a good impression, this *social desirability* response set may have a considerable effect on the scores from which inferences are to be made. This and other effects of various response sets have been exhaustively studied, and ways of at least partially controlling them have been developed. The appropriate use of techniques for psychological assessment requires a thorough familiarity with this body of research knowledge.

Several policy implications follow from these essential features of psychological assessment. First, the individual assessed should be protected against unwarranted *inferences* by persons not equipped with the requisite background of knowledge. It cannot be expected that psychiatrists, classroom teachers, personnel managers, or heads of government agencies will have this kind of expertise, although some of them may possess it. Normally, therefore, arrangements will need to be worked out for collaboration with psychologists who have specialized in the kinds of assessments being conducted.

Second, the individual assessed should be protected against unfavorable evaluation based on obsolete information. This is a problem not peculiar to psychological assessment methods. An old letter of recommendation may be fully as damaging as a low IQ recorded on one's record, although the quantitative appearance of the latter makes it less apparent, perhaps, that it is no longer relevant. All proposals for data banks and permanent record systems must grapple with this problem and provide appropriate safeguards for verifying the accuracy of the records and for discarding periodically the obsolete information.

Third, the individual must be protected against unnecessary intrusions into his privacy. The assessment procedures used should be intelligently selected for particular purposes. Unnecessary tests should not be administered, and unnecessary questions should not be asked.

Fourth, whatever policies are set up to insure these kinds of protection should be of such a nature as to maintain conditions that will facilitate the research on which new and improved assessment procedures can be based. Flat prohibitions of certain kinds of tests or questions would retard research on the ways in which such tests and questions might be validly used. To require the destruction of all records of test scores and protocols along with the interpretations derived from them would make impossible some very significant kinds of longitudinal research on personality. The objective of whatever policies are adopted should be to protect the right of each individual to be soundly evaluated, realizing that to do this requires a constant effort to improve the techniques by means of which evaluations are made. The proper control is to vest responsibility in the person carrying out the assessment rather than to place arbitrary restrictions on the methods he is permitted to use.

ADDITIONAL PROBLEMS IN PERSONALITY ASSESSMENT

While not differing in principle from the assessment of abilities, the assessment of personality (sometimes called noncognitive) characteristics involves extra complications related to policy issues. In instruments for personality assessment the relationship of the respondent's test behavior to his behavior in life situations is more indirect than it is in the typical ability testing situation, where the items to which he is responding are often samples of the problems he must solve in the world outside the testing room. Whether the instrument for assessing personality requires the individual to answer questions about his attitudes, symptoms, and feelings, or whether it asks him to read meaning into inkblots or tell stories about ambiguous pictures, the psychologist's task of *validating* the instrument is a complex and difficult one. The fact that there is as yet no general agreement about what the most important personality traits are adds to the difficulty.

A special problem that may arise in personality assessment is that some of the item content is drawn from areas of human experience most likely to be regarded as private, so that such assessment techniques are especially likely to raise questions about whether a respondent's right to privacy has been infringed. For a variety of reasons it has seemed necessary or important to include some inquiry into the individual's sexual and religious ideas in instruments designed for personality assessment. Interpretations of these measures are dependent on the context in which they were standardized. If there is too much deviation from the standardized contexts by eliminating items, some distortion might be introduced into interpretations.

In formulating policies to deal with these problems, the basic requirement is the one emphasized in the previous section—that decisions about what assessment procedures are to be used and how they are to be handled should be based on recommendations from persons competent to make them—ordinarily a psychologist with specialized training in assessment. It is the responsibility of organizations and agencies in which assessment is carried on to place such persons in charge of the operations. It is the responsibility of universities and colleges to educate them in such a way that they can carry out this complex task. It is the responsibility of professional societies, such as the American Psychological Association, to formulate standards and ethical codes controlling their activity. Many states have statutory procedures for qualifying psychologists who meet legally established standards of competence and ethical conduct controlling their activity. Legal proscriptions of certain kinds of tests, items, or procedures can only handicap them in their efforts to make sound, relevant judgments about individuals.

The central concept governing what information is to be obtained from a person whose characteristics are to be assessed for a particular purpose is *relevance*. In employment situations, for example, inquiry about family, sexual, or religious matters should be carried on only if its relevance to the employee's fitness for the position in question has been established; in such instances its use may be justifiable. Always, however, relevance must be weighed and justified in terms of socially accepted values and principles.

The right of an individual to decline to be assessed or to refuse to answer questions he considers improper or impertinent has never been and should not be questioned. This right should be pointed out to the examinee in the context of information about the confidentiality of the results. Whenever possible, he should be told who will have access to the information and for what purposes. The burden of proof that assessment techniques are relevant to the situation falls on the professional person responsible for the undertaking. His competence is the foundation on which the whole structure must rest.

UNIT TWO | DISCUSSION QUESTIONS

3 | METHODOLOGY IN BEHAVIORAL RESEARCH

Why do behavioral scientists study lower animals when the objective of behavioral science is to understand people?

List and discuss three designs used in the behavioral sciences.

4 | PRIVACY AND BEHAVIORAL RESEARCH

Do you agree with the recommendations presented by the panel? Why?

Discuss how the protection of privacy can be assured during research.

5 | PSYCHOLOGICAL ASSESSMENT AND PUBLIC POLICY

Discuss what aspect of the APA policy statement is most meaningful to you.

Assuming records are maintained on an individual's test scores, would there be a time limit placed on the validity of the scores? Support your answers.

UNIT THREE
THE PSYCHOBIOLOGICAL DETERMINANTS
OF BEHAVIOR

Survival is a matter of adaptation. If human beings are to survive, they must be capable of adapting to their environment. The ability of a species to reproduce, to develop, and to pass on to its progeny the qualities which favor individual survival is the object of the study of psychobiology. The uniqueness and complexity of human behavior result from the interaction of certain inherited factors with the environment via maturation. If we wish to understand this particular combination of factors, we obviously need to study both the physiological and psychological bases of behavior.

The human being, developing from a single-cell zygote, grows into an adult with about twenty-five billion cells. Many of these cells are capable of reproducing themselves in a like manner. What is the key to this phenomenon? What are the biological determinants that distinguish the difference between you and another? To answer these questions, we must first acknowledge the contributions of the Austrian monk Gregor Mendel who, in 1866, formed the basis for our understanding of psychobiology. His inquiry into the physical differences of garden peas led to the establishment of the science of *genetics,* the branch of biology concerned with heredity and the transmission of hereditary characteristics. Mendel's discovery was of major importance because it showed that genetic data come to the individual as *units* rather than as a blending of qualities from one's ancestors. He called these units of life *genes.* In recent years, this construct was further spelled out to be a polynucleotide called deoxyribonucleic acid, DNA. Although DNA itself has been known for quite some time the discovery of its function was made by the Englishman, Francis H. C. Crick, and the American, James D. Watson, who were awarded the Nobel Prize in medicine in 1962 for their efforts.

In mid-1970, scientists announced they had created a man-made gene. With this first artificial gene, the team of scientists headed by H. Gobind Khorana, a Nobel Prize winner, took a profound step toward correction of inherited diseases, which could perhaps be extended to the genetic "engineering" of improved humans and animals and perhaps, ultimately to the artificial creation of life itself. In the first reading, Alicia Hills and Albert Rosenfeld cite advances made in molecular biology to provide necessary background for understanding of gene construction. *DNA's Code: Key to All Life* relates the importance of RNA, ribonucleic acid, which serves as a kind of chemical messenger for DNA. In addition, the authors question what man's knowledge of the code will ultimately reveal concerning the behavior of man.

Behavioral processes are affected by the organism's responses to stimulation; behavioral activity is experienced through the functioning of the central nervous system as it is affected internally and/or externally by a stimulus that brings about a response. The nervous system serves as a connecting branch between the receptor and the brain. In the second reading, D. O. Hebb is concerned with the rationale

41

of the neurological model in psychological theory. In his *Role of Neurological Ideas in Psychology* a lucid argument is presented in favor of "physiologizing" the science of psychology.

In the last selection, *The Interpretive Cartex,* Wilder Penfield discusses the structure and functions of the human brain. This article tells how "the stream of consciousness" in the brain can be electrically activated.

---

6 | DNA'S CODE: KEY TO ALL LIFE

Alicia Hills and Albert Rosenfeld

The unveiling of the DNA molecule, the delineation of its architecture, and the growing comprehension of how it performs its genetic wonders, together constitute the most exciting frontier in all of science today. The frontier is expanding rapidly and the pioneers are pushing their explorations into the new country with impatient vigor.

This new country is called "molecular biology," and it promises to yield unprecedented power for man—power to manipulate nature in ways that he cannot now even imagine. The pioneers are a new breed called "molecular biologists." Many began as mathematicians, physicists and chemists, then turned their attention, their ingenious techniques and their precision instruments to the study of living organisms. Their forays into the new country have resulted in a series of seven-league-boot advances in man's knowledge that have already won them a hatful of Nobel Prizes. In fact, their collective research will certainly go down as one of the grandest intellectual adventures in human history.

What really distinguishes molecular biology from all biology before it is that it penetrates down to individual molecules—molecules like DNA and RNA. Biologists were once limited to studying gross organisms, or pieces of them. Later they refined their techniques so that they could deal with individual cells. But getting down to the manipulation of individual molecules represents a revolutionary advance.

To appreciate what this means, imagine a Martian scientist who has been studying life on earth. He has done the best he can do from way out there, observing us through the best instruments at his command—just as the biologist has done the best

---

Life Magazine, August 15, 1963. Reprinted by permission of *Time-Life.*

he can do, looking through his microscopes. All the Martian could observe were the mass activities of entire populations. He had no idea that a Napoleon or an Einstein might exist or how his deeds might affect the destinies of millions. What he knows about human behavior is understandably limited.

But suddenly, through some remarkable new techniques and instruments, he finds out about individual people. He learns that they communicate and order their lives with the help of a language. More than that, he figures out all the letters of their alphabet. Now, if he can only learn to spell with the letters. . . . You can imagine his excitement. You can see how rapidly his knowledge of life on earth will begin to proliferate.

Biologists have arrived at exactly this stage. Heretofore they could only observe cells. A cell is not an individual, but a community—a highly organized community in which a vast and diverse population of molecules go about their business. When Dr. James Watson of Harvard and Dr. Francis Crick of Cambridge worked out the spiral-ladder structure of DNA, biologists found out what individual molecules look like. Since then they have learned the four-letter alphabet of the molecular language —the genetic code. They are much more excited than the imaginary Martian scientist, for what they are studying is not life on another planet but the life pulsing in their own bodies. "We must now learn to spell with the genetic code," says Dr. Marshall Nirenberg of the National Institutes of Health. "Only then can we hope to write genetic messages of our own."

Nirenberg is the brilliant young biochemist who took the first great stride toward cracking the genetic code. His experiment has already become historic though it was performed only two years ago. Before 1961 the genetic code was as indecipherable as Egyptian hieroglyphics before the discovery of the Rosetta Stone. Nirenberg provided the biological Rosetta Stone, the crucial key to translating the hieroglyphics of life's code.

When they began their work, Nirenberg and his associates were of course familiar with the knowledge about DNA and RNA. In all this complexity, the most promising place to look for clues to the code seemed to be in the making of proteins. They knew that RNA, using a code of only four letters, makes proteins out of 20 amino acids. They also knew that each of the 20 amino acids has a specific RNA code word for it; otherwise, how would the RNA know which amino acid to select? The amino-acid words had to contain more than two letters because there would not be enough two-letter words to go around for all 20 amino acids. Three-letter words however, ought to work just fine. But which three-letter words, out of 64 possible combinations, would select which amino acids?

It was as if there were a pack of 20 dogs whose names you had to learn. Though you don't know their names, you do know that all the names are different, and that each dog will answer to his own name and to no other. All you can do, then, is start thinking of possible dogs' names and calling them out. If you holler "Rover" and nothing happens, you try again. If you holler "Fido" and one comes running, then there are only 19 names left to learn.

This is the same sort of technique Nirenberg used. First, he mixed up a batch of chemicals prepared from living cells, including all the amino acids. He made sure that his precise recipe contained no messenger-RNA of its own to foul up the experiment. Then he manufactured an artificial messenger-RNA, made up entirely of only one of its four code chemicals—uracil, which can be thought of as the letter U. The only three-letter word that can possibly be made out of U's is UUU, and the order doesn't matter since, whichever way you scramble it, it still comes out UUU.

Adding his artificial RNA, made of nothing but U's, to the amino-acid soup, Nirenberg got a protein made entirely of a single amino acid, phenylalanine. There could be no mistake—he had talked to the amino acid in its own language. Instead of "Fido," he had hollered "UUU," and phenylalanine had come running. It was clear that UUU meant phenylalanine. In the new molecular dictionary, phenylalanine was the first word to be translated from the genetic.

Other scientists quickly joined Nirenberg, hollering "Rover" and "Sport" and all the other names they could think of. Their hollering, of course, consisted of delicate and painstaking chemical operations, often using radioactive tracers to signal the whereabouts of specific substances. In their work they had to deal with complications which did not concern Nirenberg in his pioneer undertaking. For one thing, they had to make their artificial RNA out of more letters than merely U. For another, in words with more than one letter, the order begins to matter—cta does *not* spell cat.

Despite these disadvantages, scientists have gradually come to know the code words—or, at least, the letters in the code words—for all 20 amino acids. They have also learned that sometimes there is more than one word for the same amino acid—just as "car" and "auto" can convey the same message in English. This gives the organism a better chance to survive. If one of the key code chemicals were knocked out, or in short supply for any reason, the amino acid would have an alternate choice, and protein manufacture would not necessarily come to a stop.

Still another recent discovery is genetic punctuation. It turns out that the DNA molecule is not a single, uninterrupted chain full of nothing but the code chemicals. Every so often the genetic messages are interrupted by punctuation marks. Instructions for how to make a specific protein may take up, say, a thousand rungs in the DNA ladder. At the end of this set of instructions there is a bit of protein which acts as the period at the end of the sentence.

To an earlier generation of biologists, the word "gene" was a vague abstraction to specify whatever-it-was in the cell that governed a specific hereditary trait. Molecular biologists now believe they can pinpoint the gene physically as that uninterrupted stretch of DNA code rungs—the sentence of instructions between the two punctuation marks.

Apart from their all-out assault on the problem of deciphering the code, scientists have been working intensively at solving other DNA mysteries. One of the most perplexing of these was posed by the discovery of DNA—or, rather, by the discovery of DNA's function (DNA itself was actually discovered way back in 1870). DNA is present in every cell of the body, and the DNA in every cell contains all the same information as the original fertilized egg contained. How then does DNA manage to employ only the information it wants—and only when it wants it? How does the DNA in a liver cell suppress all its voluminous instructions except those that the liver cell needs to keep going?

Fascinating partial answers have already been found in a series of substances which cover up those portions of the DNA molecule not in use, thus stopping the flow of information. Providing this protection for itself is one more job for DNA to do—since it, after all, is the source of all the cell's instructions. Added to the burden of information which DNA must carry, then, are the directions for making these cover-up substances, informing them which parts of itself to cover up and when—and then arranging to have the covered-up parts uncovered at the right times.

It has been speculated that the breaking down of this cover-up mechanism might be a cause of cancer. If the entire molecule—or even substantial parts of it—suddenly became exposed, the DNA would go haywire. It might begin multiplying again, cells would begin to divide, and the result would be an abnormal growth, perhaps a malignant one.

Every new advance in molecular biology opens up new territories to be explored. Today there is hardly an area of research in biology or medicine that is not eagerly investigating DNA and RNA—and hardly an area of human life that will not be touched by these investigations.

One of the most puzzling facets of the human mind, for example, is memory. This phenomenon may soon be a little less puzzling, thanks to a startling series of recent experiments in animals. The surprising results make it appear that RNA plays a key role in memory. It might be the very stuff that memory is made of.

Memory is really stored learning. When an animal is trained to do something, the training represents stored memories. Scientists do not know precisely how the storage is achieved, but, suspecting that the nucleic acids had something to do with it, they set out to pursue their hunch.

They have been using a variety of animals to carry out their experiments. One is a lowly flatworm called the planarian. The planarian can be taught, by means of electrical shocks, to cringe whenever a light is turned on or to avoid parts of a maze. When well-trained planarians are cut up and fed to untrained planarians, the cannibalistic worms learn much faster than those on a less educated diet.

When scientists first observed this, they wondered if the memory of the trained worms—or at least part of it—had in some way been passed on to the untrained ones. They had reason to believe that RNA might be the transmitting substance. To test this belief, another experiment was carried out.

A planarian, when cut in half, regenerates itself into two new flatworms. Scientists had already confirmed that when a trained planarian is cut in half, each of the new flatworms gets some of the benefit of the training. Knowing this, they cut a trained planarian in half. The top half developed, as expected, into a new planarian, partly trained. But the lower half was treated with a substance that destroys RNA, and this half became a worm with no training—hence no memory—at all.

There have been intriguing experiments with rats, too. In some of these, it was ascertained that rats learn faster when their RNA production is increased, and slower if their RNA production is lowered. Rats trained to walk a tightwire have more RNA in their brain cells after training than untrained rats. Moreover, their RNA contains proportions of the four code chemicals which vary considerably from the RNA in untrained rats, indicating that the training has changed the nature of the RNA code molecules.

The changes caused in the RNA by training appear to be permanent changes. The new information is retained in the nerve cells, which somehow get copies of the new RNA. Exactly how this can help us remember a telephone number is yet to be determined, but some evidence of RNA's influence on human memory has already been offered. Old people with failing memories were dosed with RNA prepared from yeast, and their memories did seem to improve.

The aging process itself seems to be tied up in some way with the nucleic acids. Scientists now theorize that, with the passing years, the DNA and RNA in human cells are subjected to all sorts of disturbing influences, from chemical action to random radiation. Thus, in steadily increasing numbers of cells, the code message is garbled, making the organism correspondingly less efficient.

Long before senility has set in, though, the body is subject to a host of ills. Some of these are directly traceable to defects in the genes. As one example, sickle-cell anemia—a debilitating and often fatal blood disease known to be hereditary—has been traced to a single amino acid in a single protein molecule—hence probably to a single fault on the DNA chain. Aside from those ailments known to be hereditary, there are a number of others—illnesses as diverse as diabetes, muscular dystrophy, feeblemindedness and cancer—which may prove to be tied in directly with faulty information in the DNA molecule. When enough is learned about DNA and RNA, might such defects be corrected and the diseases wiped out? Can the human memory be substantially improved by biochemical means? Can the clock of aging be turned back, or even slowed down? Scientists are cautious about making predictions. But in view of what has already been achieved, they see no reason to set any limits to the possibilities.

No one is quite clear exactly how man will put DNA and RNA to practical use after he learns how to read and write messages in the genetic code. Unlike the planarian, whose primitive digestive tract can absorb and use molecules virtually in the same form they are eaten, man must break down all his food and process it in quite a complicated manner before his body can use it. So merely eating genetic materials is not the answer.

However, one possible answer which scientists are giving close scrutiny is the making of artificial viruses. A virus is simply a packet of DNA or RNA, wrapped in a protective protein overcoat. Some forms of artificial DNA, RNA and protein have already been made in the laboratory. There seems to be no technical barrier to the ultimate manufacture of viruses—beneficial viruses rather than infective ones—containing nucleic acids and proteins built according to specifications. Assuming that man can turn out made-to-order viruses, how can he use them?

We have already described—at the end of the color section of this article—how a virus's nucleic acid sneaks in, takes over a cell and begins ordering the manufacture of its own materials. This does not always happen right away. A virus's DNA or RNA can quietly integrate itself with the cell's and lie dormant for years before being triggered into subversive activity. The virus's genetic material may even be passed on for several generations before it acts up. There is no telling what strange maladies may suddenly and inexplicably turn up in this fashion—including cancer, which has been more and more linked with viruses.

Here again, no one is sure what happens. But it is speculated that one way in which a virus might cause cancer, apart from taking over the cell, is to dictate the manufacture of substances alien to the cell and perhaps damaging to it. In man's war against the virus, the virus has so far won most of the battles. But when he really cracks the virus's secret code, man will win the war. When he does, he will put the tamed virus to work for his own purposes.

If artificial viruses were available, they might be injected into the body. Their snythetic protein overcoats would keep them from acting up—just as with natural viruses—until their nucleic acids entered cells. If the DNA or RNA in the virus was a wholesome, friendly type designed to help the cell rather than destroy it, it is quite possible that memory-bearing RNA might be carried to the nerve and brain cells to improve people's memories, that efficient new supplies of DNA might hold back the ravages of old age, that the cells could be better armed against all sorts of invading enemy viruses.

There is simply no calculating at this point the amount of benefit man might gain medically through his mastery of the genetic code. This mastery will not only permit him to improve the lot of individuals. By manipulating the DNA in human eggs and sperm cells, he may be able to correct genetic defects and thus save countless future generations from illness and premature death. Most scientists regard this potential as a mixed blessing, however, for if man can manipulate the genes of all humankind in this fashion, it means he can decide what characteristics he deems desirable in future generations and simply write the genetic messages into the DNA.

Evolution up to now has apparently been carried out largely by means of chance mutations—that is, through changes in the genetic material caused by, say, random impact of cosmic radiation or by chemical action. But in the future most mutations may not be left to chance. Nobel Prizes have already been awarded to Dr. Arthur Kornberg of Stanford and Dr. Severo Ochoa of New York University for making DNA and RNA artificially in their laboratories. By tampering with DNA other scientists have been able to produce new hereditary traits in bacteria and insects. There seems to be no insurmountable obstacle to eventually doing this with human genes.

The DNA molecule has been called "the atom of life." When man succeeds in harnessing *this* atom, the problems raised by the harnessing of the uranium atom will look simple indeed. As they contemplate the golden opportunities the new powers will give man, scientists also stop to think about the opportunities for the abuse of these powers—and, when they do, their thoughts sometimes make them shudder.

RECOMMENDED READINGS

Bonner, D. and S. Mills, *Heredity* (2nd Ed.). Englewood Cliffs, N.J.: Prentice-Hall, 1964, $1.75.

Dobzhansky, T., *Evolution, Genetics, and Man.* New York: Wiley & Sons, Science Editions, 1955, $2.45.

Galton, F., *Hereditary Genius.* Cleveland, Ohio: World Publishing, Meridian Books, $1.95.

Goldstein, P., *Genetics is Easy.* New York: Viking, 1961, $1.45.

McKusick, V. A., *Human Genetics.* Englewood Cliffs, N.J.: Prentice-Hall, 1964.

Moore, J. A., *Heredity and Development.* New York: Oxford University Press, 1963, $1.95.

(All books listed above are inexpensive paperbacks.)

7 | THE ROLE OF NEUROLOGICAL IDEAS IN PSYCHOLOGY

D. O. Hebb

This is partly a public profession of faith (although, to paraphrase W. H. Fowler, the writer's opinions have already been allowed to appear with indecent plainness elsewhere). It is my conviction that we have no choice but to physiologize in psychology, overtly or covertly. Tolman[1] has said that conscious theory is better than unconscious, even if bad. As the author of a bad theory, in what I conceive to be Tolman's sense, I am in an excellent position to spell out his point. But—a warning to the reader—this is not modesty. My argument is that it is only with the rubble of bad theories that we shall be able to build better ones, and that without theory of some kind, somewhere, psychological observation and description would at best be chaotic and meaningless.

There is not space here to develop any neurologically biased treatment of personality. This task must be left for other papers, including the results of some animal experiments now going on.[2] What we shall be concerned with here is the rationale of the neurological model in psychological theory,[3] including the theory of personality.

PHYSIOLOGY NO SIN WHEN PUBLICLY RECOGNIZED

Christian thought has always held that sexual congress is inherently sinful, but man is frail. The church therefore has realistically provided for biological facts in the solemn rite of marriage while still stoutly opposing any illicit, unblessed, transient, or haphazard union that has not had formal public approval. Matrimony removes the stigma. More, it makes the family possible; so one can even argue that the openly recognized sexual union has positive virtues.

For all this there is a parallel in the dealings of psychology with physiology. Here too there are biological facts that cannot be overlooked, and there is the same superiority of a recognized liaison over furtive ones. Let me try to justify such ideas.

For twenty years or so there has been a vigorous attempt in psychology (and psychiatry) to be rid of "physiologizing" or "neurologizing." It has been said that physiological concepts are too limited, restrict theory too much. Krech[4] has argued that instead of turning away from a narrow physiology (narrow presumably because incomplete), we must expand neurological and physiological conceptions to

From *Journal of Personality*, **20**, 1951, pp. 39–55. Reprinted by permission of the publisher and the author.

meet the psychological facts. This is sound enough, although I shall try to show later that there are in practice limits to such a theoretical procedure. By using exactly the procedure that Krech advocates, psychology has repeatedly anticipated neuro-physiology, the purely behavioral evidence indicating the existence of neural pro-cesses not known at the time but discovered independently by the physiologist later.

But one must seriously doubt that it was the narrowness of physiological concep-tions that made them unpopular with psychologists. With some men, yes, but not with others, because the antiphysiological point of view shows no positive correlation with the breadth and flexibility of the theory that has resulted in each case.

Those who renounced the shackles of neurology did not, in general, go on un-shackled to develop a richer and fuller account of behavior. Some of them retreated instead into the chains of an earlier and still less enlightened neurology, dated 1890 instead of 1930 or '40. This particular group can be discussed first, leaving others like Tolman to a later section.

The idea in rejecting physiology was to use only "purely behavioral" concep-tions, but some of these were actually of physiological origin and continue to exert a physiological influence on psychology. The influence is evident in several ways, but most convincingly I think in certain omissions that can be traced back to Sherring-ton, Waldeyer, and Cajal: to the neuron theory and the irreversibility of conduction at the synapse (without the significant qualification of such ideas that has been made since 1930 or thereabouts by electrophysiology). Murphy[5] has noted (pp. 188–189) how great an effect the neuron-synapse conception had. The effect was of two kinds. Primarily, in my opinion, it was clarifying and stimulating; but it was also negative, leading to the exclusion of ideas that otherwise could have remained in psychological theory. Among them one can list (a) association between sensory processes (as dis-tinct from sensori-motor association), and (b) ideation, imagery, and related notions. In 1890, an association of one sensory event with another (or of one image with an-other) was not only an acceptable notion, it was the cement that held psychological theory together. By 1920 such association was doubtful at best, and so was the mere existence of ideas, or of anything central but one-way connections running from re-ceptor to effector. Why? Not on psychological grounds, surely—psychologically, the existence of images and sensory associations is hard to deny; even in a com-pletely objective psychology there are observations of animal or man that would be much easier to account for by postulating such things. But in that thirty-year interval between 1890 and 1920, a valuable neurological hypothesis had been developed which had plenty of room for S-R connections and motor thought, but none for S-S connections or "autonomous" central processes (i.e., ones that do not depend moment by moment on any particular sensory stimulation). It should be clear that this was not a bad development for theory. The increased precision of ideas and better formulation of problems far outweighed a temporary loss of breadth. The point here is that the exclusion of S-S connections and ideation was of physiological origin.

Any later theory that continues the exclusion is permitting the faulty neurophysi-ology of 1920 (at the latest) to determine its main outlines. If we must be influenced by ideas about how the nervous system works, those of the 1940 variety make it pos-sible to regain some of James's breadth without losing the benefits gained from Cajal and Sherrington and built into psychological theory by the litigation of Hobhouse vs. Thorndike and Lashley vs. Pavlov. I do not suggest any subordination of psychology to physiology, but only that psychology must be influenced by physiological evidence, as neurophysiology is influenced by psychological evidence. It is clear that the psychologist's first concern is the behavior of the normal, intact animal, and theory must not do violence to the facts of behavior (though it may be very difficult sometimes to show that violence has been done—that is, to refute a theory decisively by behavioral evidence). But though behavioral evidence is not inferior to anatomical and physiological evidence, neither is it superior.

Again, the conception of mental set or of attention as a causal agent in perception (instead of a by-product)—how are we to understand the absence of this from a "pure" psychology, except by the fact that it is inconsistent with the 1920 conception of the nervous system as a collection of through routes, one-way streets, from sense organs to muscle or gland? Why has there been such a profound reluctance[6] to postulate something going on within the animal that opens the door to one kind of stimulation and closes it to another? There is plenty of factual evidence that this sort of thing happens all the time in behavior, and plenty of physical models to suggest how, conceivably, it might come about. There is the modern dial telephone's selector switch, for example, or the catalyst idea from chemistry, or the joint action of dust and water vapor to form fog or rain. It is not mysterious therefore to postulate attention as something that acts as co-chairman in charge of response, jointly with the present stimulus itself. Not mysterious, that is, unless one's thinking is controlled unwittingly by the picture of a nervous system in which such things are impossible.

It thus appears that S-R theory is not merely physiological in descent or in its Pavlovian terminology, but by its persistent exclusion of psychologically justified conceptions it also shows that it is still essentially physiological. Failing to recognize this is to disregard one source of error. If we must be chained to physiological ideas, we should at least choose the modern ones that allow more freedom of movement.

In short, let us espouse our physiology openly so that we know which member of the family it is that we are sleeping with and especially so that we can avoid the one who, charming and mature as she was in 1920, is less satisfying now, not to say less fertile.

TOLMAN, PHENOMENOLOGY, AND THE NEED OF THEORY

So much for the influence of neurology and physiology as exerted through the stimulus-response idea. Does the psychologist who rejects S-R theory thereby avoid the influence?

No one I believe has been as successful as Tolman in giving a systematic but nonphysiological account of behavior (assuming that Hull's is physiological). At the same time, I think it is clear (a) that his starting point was Holt's or Watson's scheme of the nervous system together with the destructive effect on it of Lashley's extirpation experiments, and (b) that the subsequent course of his work shows how short the tether is on which explanation can stray from its physiological origins.

What Tolman did essentially was to have responses initiated by stimulus patterns instead of stimuli, and to replace the ideation that Thorndike had thrown out. He also included a postulate of attention, in his "means-end-readiness," which psychology clearly needed but which no one else had the stomach for. But this effort, while it represents both imagination and courage, is by no means a holus-bolus rejection of

Watson and the earlier Thorndike or of the products of their physiologizing. By not making a neural hypothesis explicit, Tolman *may* have been freer to postulate things that are not immediately reduceable to neural terms, but this is doubtful. The same kind of thing is done in another way: "There is a neural process X with such-and-such behavioral manifestations, whose exact mechanism and locus cannot be specified for the moment, but which the behavioral evidence requires." This is what Krech has said the psychologist must do to broaden neurological theory for his own purposes, and it has been historically an important part of the psychological method. Tolman might have neurologized and still been free to recognize the facts of behavior.

The absence of neurological terms in Tolman's writing does not per se mean any real discontinuity with the physiological thinking of Holt and Watson, nor for that matter with the equally physiological thought of the Gestalt group. What Tolman offered was a modification and synthesis of these two superficially incompatible approaches, both of which were affected in their main outlines by ideas of neural function. He did not start with a clean slate, and to suppose that he did, that he could really have freed himself from the influence of earlier physiologizing, is to forget how short the steps are in the growth of theory.

Furthermore, the extent to which Tolman and his students have been negative and defensive in their later work in the latent-learning argument, looking for phenomena that their opponents could not explain more than developing their own theoretical structure, demonstrates the trouble that theory has had in getting far from the physiologically intelligible. Tolman's group have apparently felt a continuous pressure to show that ideation is still a necessary conception. The reason seems to be that the charge of mysticism and an unscientific vagueness has always hung over their heads. It could not have done so if they had turned to a modern neurophysiology and shown that it makes ideation, in a crude way at least, necessary as well as intelligible. The question of ideation at bottom is the question of whether central neural processes go on in the absence of an adequate sensory arousal, and all modern electrophysiology indicates that the activity of the brain is continuous and that the effect of a sensory event is not to arouse inactive tissue but to modify the activity already going on. Denny-Brown[7] made a similar point about set or attention: the effect of a sensory event upon motor behavior must always be subject to modification by the pre-existent activity of the brain. In other words, the work of Berger, Adrian, Lorento de Nó, and Morison and Dempsey could have been a safe-conduct to free Tolman from the necessity of continual defense—even defense in the form of attack—and to allow him to develop his own ideas further.

It has been suggested that physiology "cannot cast any vote" in the choice of psychological principles. Whether it should or not, it always has. It is now clear that Wertheimer and Köhler were on the right track about 1920 in their account of the afferent visual process, well in advance of the neurologist. Essentially, they were postulating an interaction among cells at the same level in transmission from the retina. If one will read for example Marshall and Talbot[8], one will find a very Gestalt-like account of activity in area seventeen of the cortex, based on physiological knowledge derived mostly after 1930. But despite the actual soundness of the Gestalt position, both psychologically and neurologically, it was vehemently rejected as mystical because it was "known" in 1920 that the nervous system does not act in that way.

Was such a vote (in this case, a wrong one) possible only in the neurologically deluded twenties? Not at all. Spence's brilliant treatment of insight and the sudden solution in discrimination learning[9,10] had a profound effect on those "tough-minded" psychologists who were (and are) opposed to physiologizing. For them, to judge from the literature, the evidence of insight reported by Köhler[11] and Krech[12] was not so until Spence showed how it might be dealt with. But Spence's solution could be tough-minded (i.e., provide an intelligible mechanism of response) because the conception of physiological gradients was already familiar from embryological studies; familiarized in biology by Kappers and Child (it is credited to them by Lashley[13], who also used the idea theoretically), it was used as well in a frankly physiological sense by Pavlov and the Gestalt group. Spence had a physiological passport even while he denied physiologizing.

A final and extreme example of the present day: why do we not accept ESP as a psychological fact? Rhine has offered enough evidence to have convinced us on almost any other issue where one could make some guess as to the mechanics of the disputed process. Some of his evidence has been explained away, but as far as I can find out, not all of it. Until a complete rebuttal is provided or until we accept ESP, let us not talk about enlarging our notions of neurology to meet the psychological "facts" with no external criterion of what those facts are. We are still trying to find our way out of the magic wood of animism, where psychology began historically, and we cannot give up the talisman of a knowledge of material processes. Personally, I do not accept ESP for a moment, because it does not make sense. My external criteria, both of physics and of physiology, say that ESP is not a fact despite the behavioral evidence that has been reported. I cannot see what other basis my colleagues have for rejecting it; and if they are using my basis, they and I are allowing psychological evidence to be passed on by physical and physiological censors. Rhine may still turn out to be right, improbable as I think that is, and my own rejection of his views is—in the literal sense—prejudice.

The theory of behavior must ultimately be consistent with both behavioral and physiological evidence. Either discipline can blackball the idea that strays too far from existing knowledge, even conceivably the sound idea that it should not. If some ultra-genius, with divine revelation, suddenly turned up one day with a "true" and complete theory of behavior as it may ultimately be known some millennia from now, he might find it impossible even to get a hearing from psychologists for what would seem preposterously unreal notions. The situation would be like one in which Einstein on being admitted to the houseboat on the Styx tried to explain quantum mechanics to Archimedes and Euclid, these persons not having yet heard of the electron, of the way in which electromagnetic waves can exist in a nonexistent ether, or even of the theory of gravitation. We commonly think of a theory as right or wrong, true or untrue: but is there any possibility at all of having a true theory of behavior today? Newton was a genius because his theories could be accepted for 250 years or so, but they are not thought to be correct or adequate today. The best we can ask therefore is that a theory should be good, not correct.

And in psychology, we must expect to have to work our way progressively through a series of ideas, of better and better theories. It is not by any means a condemnation of S-R theory to say that it is narrow or that there are facts which (we are now pretty sure) it cannot comprehend. The significant question is not whether Thorndike's account of animal learning was right, but whether it helped us to see better the problems involved and led to new analyses. In Hull's systematizing, in Tolman's ability to define purpose without philosophic teleology, in Lashley's analysis of animal perception, or Köhler's and Krech's experimental demonstrations of insight, the evidence is clear concerning the stimulating and clarifying value of stimulus-response theory and its erroneous (because incomplete) physiological foundation.

This point of view shows how to clear up a possible ambiguity in the discussion by MacLeod[14] and Smith[15] concerning the way in which a phenomenologist goes about his business. The suggestion is that the phenomenologist is one who puts aside bias (either of theory or of common sense) and simply observes what is before him. But MacLeod then adds that this is never entirely possible and speaks of observing with a "disciplined naïveté." The ambiguity comes in the possible interpretation that getting rid of theory completely would make for the clearest observation (or in the apparent contradiction of discipline and naïveté). From the point of view we have now arrived at, an answer is possible for this difficulty. It is not getting rid of theory entirely that is needed (otherwise the thing to do would be to get a backwoodsman, or someone else who had never heard of psychology, to observe in one's experiments), but to put theory in the background instead of the foreground where it blocks one's vision. The "discipline" is in a thorough knowledge of theory; the "naïveté" consists of trying to find other ways of looking at the world besides the one dictated by existing theory. Essentially, phenomenology means looking for new biases, not getting rid of bias.

I have spoken of the common observation that theory moves by short steps. This observation may be thought of as implying only a negative influence from earlier theory, as providing evidence simply of the inertia of human thought. But there must be more to the process than that. Einstein's formulation would not have been possible without the observations gathered under the influence of Newton's ideas. Earlier theories, then, are limiting for a very good reason. They are what one climbs on to get to the next stage—it is also a common observation that a stepladder is *very* narrow and limiting, when one is using it.

In other words, we must recognize the positive value even of "wrong" theories as guides to observation. If the phenomenologist could really divest himself of all his theoretical knowledge and tried then to record the facts of his own perception or of an animal's behavior, what would he choose to put down on paper? There are an infinite number of relationships and aspects of behavior, an infinitude of possible subdivisions of animal activity or of human thought. *Some* theoretical guide is necessary as a principle of selection.

What the phenomenologically minded individual has always recorded is what he sees that is related to, but inconsistent with, existing theory. It is in such a sense only that he avoids bias, and this of course is not really avoiding it. A better way of defining a phenomenologist might be to say that he is one of those who, at the extreme, do not like existing theories (and perhaps never will) but are interested in attacking them and finding evidence that is hard for theory to handle: an "agin-the-established-order" attitude, anti-theoretical but not a-theoretical, which historically has been an important source of new ideas and experiments.

A figure of speech used elsewhere may help to clear this up. There appears to be a left wing and a right wing in psychology, paralleling Left and Right in politics, and the activity of the Left cannot be understood if one does not see that the only continuity in its behavior is in being against the Right. In psychology the Right favors parsimony of explanatory ideas, a simple or mechanical account of behavior, and definiteness even at the cost of being narrow. The Left is prepared to postulate more freely and can better tolerate vagueness and a lack of system in its account of behavior. Thus Gestalt psychology, especially in its early years, could develop a theory of perception and a theory of thought that were not brought into any clear relationship with one another, and a theory of memory ("traces") that seemed downright inconsistent with the Gestalt account of perception. But the primary motivation was not to develop a theory; it was to demonstrate the shortcomings of stimulus-response theory, and the scientific benefits that accrued from this effort are obvious—just as obvious as the fact that such an attitude (which includes the phenomenologist's) is not possible without a theory to attack.

THE BACONIAN FALLACY

The idea that one could observe more clearly if one could divest himself of all preceding theory, or that psychology would be better off without theory, is related to a widespread epistemological misconception concerning the scientific method. This notion goes back through J. S. Mill to Francis Bacon and can, for convenience here, be called the Baconian fallacy. It is in the first place the idea that scientific generalizations are arrived at by "induction," by counting noses, and from this derives the idea that scientific laws are empirical. It implies that there are a limited number of "facts," "events," or properties of any object or situation, so that the scientist can proceed by simply describing, even, if it is desirable, by recording *everything* that happens in conjunction with whatever phenomenon he is interested in. There is no useful purpose for creative imagination. Causes can be discovered simply by assiduity: list everything that preceded the to-be-explained event, on a thousand or ten thousand occasions if necessary, and if your lists are complete, the cause will be the one thing that is on every list. (In practice there are short cuts, and the lists may be remembered instead of written out.)

But anyone can see that there is something wrong here when the crude implications of the induction idea are followed up in this way. The next step is to abandon an interest in causes (especially hypothetical causes that can hardly get into one's lists) and at a high level of sophistication regard scientific law as a statement of probability only, and science as description. Theory is tautology and self-delusion.

To such views the following propositions may be opposed.

A. Induction and counting cases are only methods of demonstration or of testing a generalization already arrived at (often on the basis of a single case).

B. The typical scientific law is not a summary of observations and has nothing to do with probability but is a working postulate or mode of thought. If apparent contradictions of a useful law are observed, one promptly postulates something else to account for them instead of discarding the law.

C. Of such modes of thought, the cause-and-effect one is still generally used though not a necessary way of thinking nor valuable in all situations.

D. The scientist is characteristically concerned with his postulated entities more than with the phenomena they were inferred from (the chemist interested in atomic weights rather than in weights of actual materials, the physicist interested in neutrons and mesons rather than photographs of cloud chambers or even bombs.) Science itself is characteristically an elaborate structure of imagined entities and events.

E. Since there is an infinity of things that can be recorded in any situation, a complete description is a meaningless conception along with a purely descriptive science. Constructs may be formally tautological and yet have the practical function of guiding observation.

These propositions may be clearer with a few examples. Newton's first law of motion has been a profoundly valuable theoretical tool, but it certainly was not an induction or summary description, for no such event as an object's continuing to move indefinitely with uniform speed in a straight line has ever been observed—not even once, nor an approximation thereto. To make the law a statement of probability is nonsense. One can assume that it is true, or that it is not true; and one can then go on to see what other assumptions must also be made and what deductions can be made from them. Experimental verification amounts to showing that the whole set is consistent with facts or leads to the discovery of new facts, also consistent.

The law of gravitation *is* a vast and impressive tautology: forces are mythical, and postulating a force of gravitation that is known only through the phenomena it is supposed to explain really adds nothing to the facts—not in this sense. But if we think of the construct of gravity as a statement of a new way of thinking, which made the tide, the orbit of the earth, and falling downstairs all examples of a single class of phenomena, one can see better the practical role of even a tautological construct. Reclassifying a group of facts does not add to the number of facts classified, but the reclassification is a significant fact itself. Logically, perhaps explanation reduces to ordering and classifying phenomena only, but it is impossible for man to think consistently in such terms.

The atom and the electron are just as much constructs as gravity, for no one has ever seen or handled either though it is now hard to realize that they are not facts (i.e., directly known phenomena). Their function too must be heuristic, as long as one is being utterly logical. It is perhaps a weakness of the human intellect that it must resort to such devices, but I think it is clear that thought is incorrigible in this respect. Thinking does not proceed according to formal logic, even in natural science or mathematics (Courant and Robbins[16], Conant[17] Hadamard[18] and attempting to act as if it did must be sterile.

If, as it seems, the scientist inveterately resorts to imagined things and properties of things to fill in the gaps as if it were in natural phenomena, his problem is to imagine the right things, to choose the constructs that do increase order in perceived events (or make possible an orderly universe that is more imagined than perceived). Sometimes the clarifying effect of a newly postulated entity is so immediate and extensive that its value is obvious. It is a "discovery," at once accepted as "true." But often, because one is dealing with a number of postulates at once, so that the same effect might perhaps be achieved by changing some other postulate, the fruitfulness of the new conception is not clear at once, and often it is only an approximation to the fruitful one. At this stage in investigation the philosophically naïve scientist merely asks of his hunch, "Is it so?" and tries to test its reality in every way he can. He does not stay at the level of his original observations but applies any test he can think of. Such an idea of reality may be an innocent one, but it makes for scientific results.

Perhaps we should describe the process of testing the value of a construct in other terms; but we cannot afford to omit it. In psychology the intervening variables, we know, are actually neural and physiological; the refusal to neurologize amounts to discarding a guide to the selection of one's constructs. It is refusing to look at data that might show that one's theory is wrong.

If only because of the frailty of man's intellect, we must theorize. In theorizing, we cannot afford to neglect any available information, so that theory must be consonant with knowledge of the nervous system although, if one wishes, one can choose terms that conceal the fact. Skinner[19] is the one, of course, whose effective experimental work may make the strongest argument against such conclusions. But I believe that it is only Skinner's high personal level of ability, in despite of an erroneous epistemology, that has made these successes possible. Even he slips into the use of constructs occasionally (e.g., in the "reflex reserve"), and he may be much more dependent on earlier neurologizing than he thinks, as I have argued above of Spence and Tolman. If all theoretical systems of behavior were really forgotten, not even Skinner could continue with simple description.

THE NERVOUS SYSTEM AND PERSONALITY

And now finally for the specific relevance of neurology to the theory of personality. In such a discussion as this the proof of the pudding is in the eating, and my argument may ultimately stand or fall with the usefulness of my own neurologically related theory[20] or the better theory it helps to engender.

The S-R model did not really offer a very good framework for the theory of personality, and even Mowrer[21], ingenious and stimulating as he is, shows signs of strain in trying to make it serve such a purpose. In earlier days, before the elaborate structure of "secondary reinforcement" had been developed to allow one to have the law of effect without its consequences, it is probable that not even a beginning at a rapprochement between S-R neurological theory and personality would have been possible. Freud and Lewin very likely were wise to choose other models.

My argument has not been that a neurologically based model is essential to psychological thought (all the literary insights based on the common-sense, animistic model of "mind" bear witness to the contrary). The argument is (a) that some scheme or model is necessary in practice, if not logically; (b) that the S-R model has served well and (with alterations) is the base of further theorizing; and (c) that psychology eventually will be using a "real" neurological model. Freud's schematizing would have been severely cramped, at the very least, by any effort to stick to the then available neurological conceptions. On the other hand, the models of both Freud and Lewin have serious defects as well as advantages; and when neurologically based theory can be enlarged to fit in the Freudian and Lewinian ideas, modified as necessary, our understanding both of personality and of apparently less complex phenomena should be greatly increased.

It is important however to say that there is no question of attempting to translate complex human processes directly into terms of neuron and synapse. At the very least there must intervene hypothetical "central motive states," "dynamic systems," "symbolic processes," or "phase cycles." The number of functional relations between the single cells in Mr. Doe's brain, determining his behavior, is for practical purposes infinite. Even if we put aside the things men have in common and try only to record the connections that are different from those in Mr. Roe's brain, the number must still be impossibly large. We need grosser units of analysis. What shall they be?

For the present they must be at the level of such familiar working conceptions as irritability, self-confidence, attitudes toward society, and so on and so forth: the rough sort of psychological analysis of personality that we now make. Further, the analysis in my judgment will always be in psychological terms. They will not be our present terms, and they may have explicit physiological reference (as "stimulus" and "reflex" have) but nonetheless will be ones which have been developed by psychologists to deal with a psychological problem.

The study of behavior requires co-operative analysis at a number of levels at once. This process implies a series of reductions, from the level of personality study to phenomena of isolated nerve fibers. Since "reductionism" seems well on its way to becoming a new term of abuse (like "molecular") I should like to be more explicit here.

The student of social psychology for example tries to understand crowd behavior by analyzing it, or reducing it, to the behavior of a number of individuals, which indeed it is. However, he finds at once the interesting thing about crowds, that they do not act as one would predict from what we know about the individual members of the crowd, at the present state of knowledge. The whole seems quite different from the sum of its parts; that is, it shows that the parts have properties that were not detected in isolation. The analysis is unsuccessful in a sense, but making it, and finding it unsatisfactory, tells one more about the crowd and the individuals therein. Similarly, the student of spinal-cord function tries to reduce it to a collection of independent reflexes, and the failure to make this work means a better understanding of the individual reflex and of reflex integration.

First, analysis, real or hypothetical; then synthesis, putting the parts back together again to see what was lost or distorted in the analysis—which is one's guide to a better analysis next time. Understanding a complex process means nothing else than that one can make the hypothetical analysis without loss or distortion. We do not yet fully understand behavior, which is to say that our present analytical conceptions are unsatisfactory and that we must look for better ones. It is not the attempt to analyze that is bad, but the being content with a poor analysis.

Thus the social psychologist is continually pressing for better conceptions from the student of emotion, of perception, of learning, and so forth. But the student of emotion (is it necessary to say that this may actually be the same person working at another level because no one else is interested in making the experiments he wants done?)—the student of emotion has in turn a similar relation to the student of conditioning, or of sensory mechanisms, or of the anatomy of the hypothalamus. The thinker in each area is guided by those around him, provided he can use their language. It is not necessary that the student of personality talk in neurological terms, but his terms should be translatable when necessary into neurology. Physiologizing is not a substitute for psychology but an aid to it.

The theory that I have proposed[20] is primarily a psychological one, not neurological. Its main outlines are determined by an effort to comprehend certain behavioral facts. If it were really a neurological (rather than neurologically oriented) one, it would be concerned mainly with anatomical and electrophysiological data and only extended into the behavioral realm as far as solid neurological warrant is available (which is not very far). If my presentation is examined, however, one will find that the solid neurological warrant is frequently missing—as the critics have noted, my explanations are vague or incomplete in places, and there is a considerable use of neurological assumption. The theory really operates at a number of levels at once, the neurologizing consisting of a search for liaison of (a) psychological construct with (b) anatomical and physiological fact, to the extent that the facts are available.

But it is also significant, I believe, that this search for liaison, the attempt to stick as far as possible to the physiologically intelligible, produced a broadening of the psychological horizon. The conceptions developed to deal with a very restricted set of problems (retention of ability after brain operation) opened my eyes to the significance of von Senden's[22] data on vision after congenital cataract, for example; provided for the first time a conceptual frame into which the variable causes and forms of emotion would fit; and led from there to a more inclusive account of human motivation. The apparent necessity of assuming two stages of learning, on purely neurological grounds, at once drew attention to a number of commonly known facts of child development that have not been comprehended by theory. And so on. Though the theory must be wrong in detail throughout, the way in which it repeatedly drew attention to behavioral relationships not noted before, or rearranged the evidence more meaningfully, gives some basis for feeling that the general line it follows may be the direction that future theory will take. Physiologizing need not be limiting and narrow in its psychological effects but may actually broaden.

To return to an earlier figure of speech, the moral is that an interest in neural anatomy and physiology may make more work for the midwife of psychological ideas than for the undertaker.

REFERENCES AND NOTES

1. Tolman, E. C. Discussion. *J. Personal.*, 1949, **18**, 48–50.
2. Clarke, R. S., Heron, W., Fetherstonhaugh, M. L., Forgays, D. G., and Hebb, D. O. Individual differences in dogs: preliminary report on the effects of early experience. *Canad. J. Psychol.*, 1951, **5**, No. 4.
3. On attempting to review the literature, I find that I cannot begin to acknowledge aid from all the various sources that have influenced this discussion, but I do wish to cite English,[23] Geldard,[24] Pratt,[25] Köhler,[26] and Loucks,[27] in addition to those referred to in the text.
4. Krech, D. Dynamic systems, psychological fields, and hypothetical constructs. *Psychol. Rev.*, 1950, **57**, 283–290.
5. Murphy, G. *Historical introduction to modern psychology* (2nd Ed.). New York: Harcourt, Brace, 1949.
6. Gibson, J. J. A critical review of the concept of set in contemporary experimental psychology. *Psychol. Bull.*, 1941, **38**, 781–817.
7. Denny-Brown, D. Theoretical deductions from the physiology of the cerebral cortex. *J. Neurol. Psychopath.*, 1932, **13**, 52–67.
8. Marshall, W. H., and Talbot, S. A. Recent evidence for neural mechanisms in vision leading to a general theory of sensory acuity. *Biol. Symp.*, 1942, **7**, 117–164.
9. Spence, K. W. Gradual versus sudden solution of discrimination problems by chimpanzees. *J. comp. Psychol.*, 1938, **25**, 213–224.

10. Spence, K. W. Continuous versus noncontinuous interpretations of discrimination learning. *Psychol. Rev.*, 1940, **47**, 271–288.
11. Köhler, W. *The mentality of apes.* New York: Harcourt, Brace, 1925.
12. Krech, D. "Hypotheses" versus "chance" in the pre-solution period in sensory discrimination-learning. *Univ. Calif. Publ. Psychol.*, 1932, **6**, 27–44.
13. Lashley, K. S. *Brain mechanism and intelligence.* Chicago: Univ. of Chicago Press, 1929.
14. MacLeod, R. B. The phenomenological approach to social psychology. *Psychol. Rev.*, 1947, **54**, 193–210.
15. Smith, M. B. The phenomenological approach in personality theory: some critical remarks. *J. abnorm. soc. Psychol.*, 1950, **45**, 516–522.
16. Courant, R., and Robbins, H. *What is mathematics?* London: Oxford Univ. Press, 1941.
17. Conant, J. B. *On understanding science.* New Haven: Yale Univ. Press, 1947.
18. Hadamard. J. *The psychology of invention in the mathematical field.* Princeton: Princeton Univ. Press, 1945.
19. Skinner, B. F. *The behavior of organisms.* New York: Appleton Century, 1938.
20. Hebb, D. O. *The organization of behavior: a neuropsychological theory.* New York: Wiley, 1949.
21. Mowrer, O. H. *Learning theory and personality dynamics: selected papers.* New York: Ronald, 1950.
22. Senden, M. v. *Raum- und Gestaltauffassung bei Operierten Blindgeborenen vor und nach der Operation.* Leipzig: Barth, 1932.
23. English, H. B. The ghostly tradition and the descriptive categories of psychology. *Psychol. Rev.*, 1933, **40**, 498–513.
24. Geldard, F. A. "Explanatory principles" in psychology. *Psychol. Rev.*, 1939, **46**, 411–424.
25. Pratt, C. C. *The logic of modern psychology.* New York: Macmillan, 1939.
26. Köhler, W. *Dynamics in psychology.* New York: Liveright, 1940.
27. Loucks, R. B. The contribution of physiological psychology. *Psychol. Rev.*, 1941, **48**, 105–126.

8 | THE INTERPRETIVE CORTEX

Wilder Penfield

There is an area of the surface of the human brain where local electrical stimulation can call back a sequence of past experience. An epileptic irritation in this area may do the same. It is as though a wire recorder, or a strip of cinematographic film with sound track, had been set in motion within the brain. The sights and sounds, and the thoughts, of a former day pass through the man's mind again.

The purpose of this article is to describe, for readers from various disciplines of science, the area of the cerebral cortex from which this neuron record of the past can be activated and to suggest what normal contribution it may make to cerebral function.

The human brain is the master organ of the human race. It differs from the brains of other mammals particularly in the greater extent of its cerebral cortex. The gray matter, or cortex, that covers the two cerebral hemispheres of the brain of man is so vast in nerve cell population that it could never have been contained within the human skull if it were not folded upon itself and refolded, so as to form a very large number of fissures and convolutions (Fig. 1). The fissures are so deep and so devious that by far the greater portion of this ganglionic carpet (about 65 percent) is hidden in them, below the surface (Fig. 2).

The portion that is labeled "interpretive" in Figs. 1 and 3 covers a part of both temporal lobes. It is from these two homologous areas, and from nowhere else, that electrical stimulation has occasionally produced physical responses which may be divided into (i) experiential responses and (ii) interpretive responses.

EXPERIENTIAL RESPONSES

Occasionally during the course of a neurosurgical operation under local anesthesia, gentle electrical stimulation in this temporal area, right or left, has caused the conscious patient to be aware of some previous experience.[1] The experience seems to be picked out at random from his own past. But it comes back to him in great detail. He is suddenly aware again of those things to which he paid attention in that distant interval of time. This recollection of an experiential sequence stops suddenly when the electrical current is switched off or when the electrode is removed from contact with the cortex. This phenomenon we have chosen to call an experiential response to stimulation.

From *Science,* **129**, pp. 1719–1725, 1959. Copyright © 1959 by the American Association for the Advancement of Science. Reprinted by permission of the author and publisher.

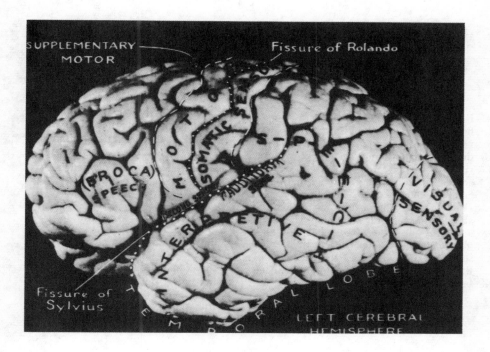

FIG. 1. Photograph of the left hemisphere of a human brain. The frontal lobe is on the left, the occipital lobe on the right. The major motor and sensory areas are indicated, as well as, the speech areas and the interpretive area. [Penfield and Roberts (*18*)]

CASE EXAMPLES[2]

The patient S.Be. observed, when the electrode touched the temporal lobe (right superior temporal convolution), "There was a piano over there and someone playing. I could hear the song you know." When the cortex was stimulated again without warning, at approximately the same point, the patient had a different experience. He said: "Someone speaking to another, and he mentioned a name but I could not understand it. . . . It was like a dream." Again the point was restimulated without his knowledge. He said quietly: "Yes, 'Oh Marie, Oh Marie'! Someone is singing it." When the point was stimulated a fourth time he heard the same song again and said it was the "theme song of a radio program."

The electrode was then applied to a point 4 centimeters farther forward on the first temporal convolution. While the electrode was still in place, S.Be. said: "Something brings back a memory. I can see Seven-Up Bottling Company—Harrison Bakery." He was evidently seeing two of Montreal's large illuminated advertisements.

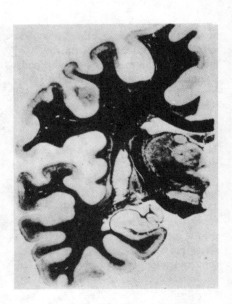

FIG. 2. (Right) Photograph of a cross section of the left cerebral hemisphere [Jelgersma (19)]. The white matter is stained black and the gray matter is unstained. The major convolutions of the cerebral cortex and the subcortical masses of gray matter can be identified by reference to the diagram below. (Bottom) Drawing of the cross section shown at right, above, with additions. The surfaces and convolutions of the temporal lobe are identified, and the relationship of one hemisphere to the other and the relationship of the hemispheres to the brain stem and cerebellum are shown.

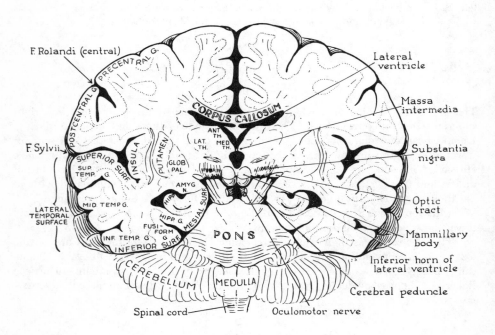

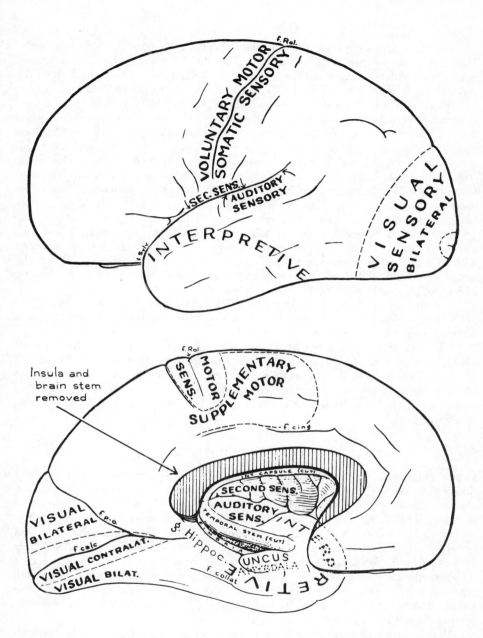

FIG. 3. The left cerebral hemisphere; the lateral surface is shown above and the mesial surface below. In the lower drawing the brain stem with the island of Reil has been removed to show the inner banks of the fissure of Sylvius and the superior surface of the temporal lobe. The interpretive cortex extends from the lateral to the superior surface of the temporal lobe. [Penfield and Roberts (18)]

The surgeon then warned him that he was about to apply the electrode again. Then, after a pause, the surgeon said "Now," but he did not stimulate. (The patient has no means of knowing when the electrode is applied, unless he is told, since the cortex itself is without sensation.) The patient replied promptly, "Nothing."

A woman (D.F.)[3] heard an orchestra playing an air while the electrode was held in place. The music stopped when the electrode was removed. It came again when the electrode was reapplied. On request, she hummed the tune, while the electrode was held in place, accompanying the orchestra. It was a popular song. Over and over again, restimulation at the same spot produced the same song. The music seemed always to begin at the same place and to progress at the normally expected tempo. All efforts to mislead her failed. She believed that a gramaphone was being turned on in the operating room on each occasion, and she asserted her belief stoutly in a conversation some days after the operation.

A boy (R.W.) heard his mother talking to someone on the telephone when an electrode was applied to his right temporal cortex. When the stimulus was repeated without warning, he heard his mother again in the same conversation. When the stimulus was repeated after a lapse of time, he said, "My mother is telling my brother he has got his coat on backwards. I can just hear them."

The surgeon then asked the boy whether he remembered this happening. "Oh yes," he said, "just before I came here." Asked again whether this seemed like a dream, he replied: "No, it is like I go into a daze."

J.T. cried out in astonishment when the electrode was applied to the temporal cortex; "Yes doctor, yes. Now I hear people laughing—my friends in South Africa!"

When asked about this, he explained the reason for his surprise. He seemed to be laughing with his cousins, Bessie and Ann Wheliow, whom he had left behind him on a farm in South Africa, although he knew he was now on the operating table in Montreal.

INTERPRETIVE RESPONSES

On the other hand, similar stimulation in this same general area may produce quite a different response. The patient discovers, on stimulation, that he has somehow changed his own interpretation of what he is seeing at the moment, or hearing or thinking. For example, he may exclaim that his present experience seems familiar, as though he had seen it or heard it or thought it before. He realizes that this must be a false interpretation. Or, on the contrary, these things may seem suddenly strange, absurd. Sights or sounds may seem distant and small, or they may come unexpectedly close and seem loud or large. He may feel suddenly afraid, as though his environment were threatening him, and he is possessed by a nameless dread or panic. Another patient may say he feels lonely or aloof, or as though he were observing himself at a distance.

Under normal circumstances anyone may make such interpretations of the present, and these interpretations serve him as guides to action or reaction. If the interpretations are accurate guides, they must be based upon previous comparable experience. It is conceivable, therefore, that the recall mechanism which is activated by the electrode during an experiential response and the mechanism activated in an interpretive response may be parts of a common inclusive mechanism of reflex recognition or interpretation.

No special function had been previously assigned by neurologists to the area in each temporal lobe that is marked "interpretive" in Figs. 1 and 3, though some clinicians have suggested it might have to do with the recall of music. The term *interpretive cortex,* therefore, is no more than slang to be employed for the purposes of discussion. The terms *motor cortex, sensory cortex,* and *speech cortex* began as slang phrases and have served such a purpose. But such phrases must not be understood to signify independence of action of separated units in the case of any of these areas. Localization of function in the cerebral cortex means no more than specialization of function as compared with other cortical regions, not separation from the integrated action of the brain.

Before considering the interpretive cortex further, we may turn briefly to the motor and sensory areas and the speech areas of the cortex. After considering the effects of electrical stimulation there, we should be better able to understand the results of stimulation in the temporal lobes.

SPECIALIZATION OF FUNCTION IN THE CORTEX

Evidence for some degree of localization within the brain was recognized early in the 19th century by Flourens. He concluded from experiment that functional subdivision of "the organ of the mind" was possible. The forebrain,[4] he said [cerebral hemispheres and higher brain stem (Fig. 4)] had to do with thought and will power, while the cerebellum was involved in the coordination of movement.

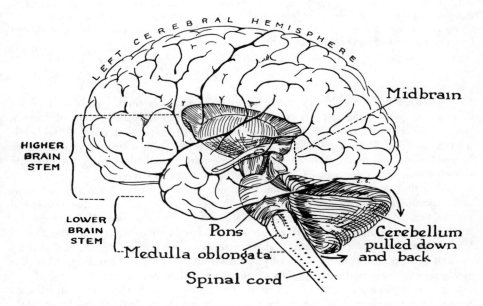

FIG. 4. Drawing of the left cerebral hemisphere, showing the higher brain stem, including the thalamus, within and the lower brain stem and spinal cord emerging below. The cerebellum is shown, attached to the lower brain stem. [Penfield and Roberts (18)]

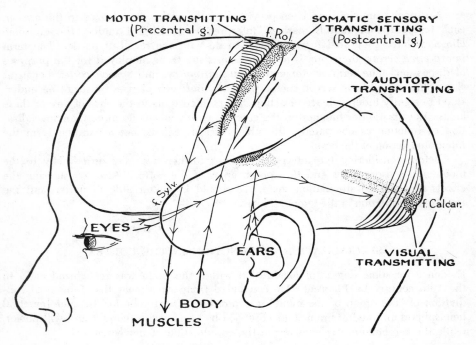

FIG. 5. Sensory and motor projection areas. The sensory areas are stippled, and the afferent pathways to them from eyes, ears, and body are indicated by entering arrows. The
motor cortex is indicated by parallel lines, and the efferent cortico-spinal tract is indicated
by emerging arrows. [Penfield and Roberts (18)]

In 1861, Paul Broca showed that a man with a relatively small area of destruction
in a certain part of the left hemisphere alone might lose only the power of speech.
It was soon realized that this was the speech area of man's dominant (left) hemisphere. In 1870, Fritsch and Hitzig applied an electric current to the exposed cortex
of one hemisphere of a lightly anesthetized dog and caused the legs of the opposite
side to move. Thus, an area of cortex called motor was discovered.

After that, localization of function became a research target for many clinicians
and experimentalists. It was soon evident that in the case of man, the precentral
gyrus (Fig. 5) in each hemisphere was related to voluntary control of the contra-
lateral limbs and that there was an analogous area of motor cortex in the frontal
lobes of animals. It appeared also that other separate areas of cortex (Figs. 1 and 5)
in each hemisphere were dedicated to sensation (one for visual sensation, others for
auditory, olfactory, and discriminative somatic sensation, respectively).

It was demonstrated, too, that from the "motor cortex" there was an efferent
bundle of nerve fibers (the pyramidal tract) that ran down through the lower brain
stem and the spinal cord to be relayed on out to the muscles. Through this efferent
pathway, voluntary control of these muscles was actually carried out. It was evident,

too, that there were separate sensory tracts carrying nerve impulses in the other direction, from the principal organs of special sense (eye, ear, nose, and skin and muscle) into separate sensory areas of the cortex.

These areas, motor and sensory, have been called "projection areas." They play a role in the projection of nerve currents to the cortex from the periphery of the body, and from the cortex to the periphery. This makes possible (sensory) awareness of environment and provides the individual with a means of outward (motor) expression. The motor cortex has a specialized use during voluntary action, and each of the several sensory areas has a specialized use, when the individual is seeing, hearing, smelling, or feeling.

TRAVELING POTENTIALS

The action of the living brain depends upon the movement, within it, of "transient electrical potentials traveling the fibers of the nervous system." This was Sherrington's phrase. Within the vast circuits of this master organ, potentials travel, here and there and yonder, like meteors that streak across the sky at night and line the firmament with trails of light. When the meteors pass, the paths of luminescence still glow a little while, then fade and are gone. The changing patterns of these paths of passing energy make possible the changing content of the mind. The patterns are never quite the same, and so it is with the content of the mind.

Specialized areas in the cortex are at times active and again relatively quiet. But, when a man is awake, there is always some central integration and coordination of the traveling potentials. There must be activity within the brain stem and some areas of the cortex. This is centrencephalic integration.[5]

SENSORY, MOTOR, AND PHYSICAL RESPONSES TO CORTICAL STIMULATION

My purpose in writing this article is to discuss in simple words (free of technical terms) the meaning of the "psychical" responses which appear only on stimulation of the so-called interpretive cortex. But before considering these responses let us consider the motor and sensory activity of the cortex for a moment.

When the streams of electrical potentials that pass normally through the various areas of sensory cortex are examined electrically, they do not seem to differ from each other except in pattern and timing. The essential difference is to be found in the fact that the visual stream passes to the visual cortex and then to one subcortical target and the auditory stream passes through the auditory cortex and then on to another subcortical target.

When the surgeon stimulates the intact sensory cortex he must be sending a current along the next "piece of road" to a subcortical destination. This electrode (delivering, for example, 60 "waves" per second of 2-milli-second duration and 1-volt intensity) produces no more than elementary sight when applied to visual cortex. The patient reports colors, lights, and shadows that move and take on crude outlines. The same electrode, applied to auditory cortex, causes him to hear a ringing or hissing or thumping sound. When applied to postcentral gyrus it produces tingling or a false sense of movement.

Thus, sensation is produced by the passage inward of electrical potentials. And when the electrode is applied to the motor cortex, movement is produced by passage of potentials outward to the muscles. In each case positive response is produced by conduction in the direction of normal physiological flow—that is, by dromic conduction.[6]

Responses to electrical stimulation that may be called "psychical," as distinguished from sensory or motor, have been elicited from certain areas of the human cortex (Fig. 6). But they have never been produced by stimulation in other areas. There are, of course, other large areas of cortex which are neither sensory nor motor in function. They seem to be employed in other neuron mechanisms that are also associated with psychical processes. But the function of these other areas cannot, it seems, be activated by so simple a stimulus as an electric current applied to the cortex.

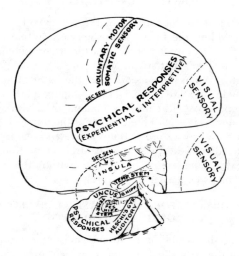

FIG. 6. The left cerebral hemisphere is shown with the temporal lobe cut across and turned down. The areas of cortex from which psychical responses have been elicited are indicated. Penfield [(1)]

DREAMY STATES OF EPILEPSY

"Epilepsy" may be defined, in Jackson's words, as "the name for occasional, sudden, excessive, rapid and local discharges of grey matter." Our aim in the operations under discussion was to remove the gray matter responsible for epileptic attacks if that gray matter could be spared. When the stimulating electrode reproduced the psychical phenomenon that initiated the fit, it provided the guidance sought.[7]

During the 19th century clinicians had recognized these phenomena as epileptic. They applied the term *intellectual aura* to such attacks. Jackson substituted the expression *dreamy states*.[8] These were, he said, "psychical states during the onset of certain epileptic seizures, states which are much more elaborate than crude sensations." And again, he wrote, "These are all voluminous mental states and yet of different kinds; no doubt they ought to be classified, but for my present purpose they may be considered together."

"The state," he said, "is often like that occasionally experienced by healthy people as a feeling of 'reminiscence.'" Or the patient has "dreamy feelings," "dreams mixing up with present thoughts," "double consciousness," a "feeling of being somewhere else," a feeling "as if I went back to all that occurred in my childhood," "silly thoughts."

Jackson never did classify these states, but he did something more important. He localized the area of cortex from which epileptic discharge would produce dreamy states. His localization was in the anterior and deep portions of the temporal lobes, the same area that is labeled "interpretative" cortex in Fig. 3.

CASE EXAMPLE

Brief reference may be made to a specific case. The patient had seizures, and stimulation produced responses which were first recognized as psychical.

In 1936, a girl of 16 (J.V.) was admitted to the Montreal Neurological Institute complaining of epileptic attacks, each of which was ushered in by the same hallucination. It was a little dream, she said, in which an experience from early childhood was reenacted, always the same train of events. She would then cry out with fear and run to her mother. Occasionally this was followed immediately by a major convulsive seizure.

At operation, under local anesthesia, we tried to set off the dream by a gentle electrical stimulus in the right temporal lobe. The attempt was successful. The dream was produced by the electrode. Stimulation at other points on the temporal cortex produced sudden fear without the dream. At still other points, stimulation caused her to say that she saw "someone coming toward me." At another point, stimulation caused her to say she heard the voices of her mother and her brothers.[9]

This suggested a new order of cortical response to electrical stimulation. When the neighboring visual sensory area of the cortex is stimulated, any patient may report seeing stars of light or moving colors or black outlines but never "someone coming toward me." Stimulation of the auditory sensory cortex may cause any patient to report that he hears ringing, buzzing, blowing, or thumping sounds, perhaps, but never voices that speak. Stimulation in the areas of sensory cortex can call forth nothing more than the elements of visual or auditory or tactile sensation, never happenings that might have been previously experienced.

During the 23 years that have followed, although practically all areas of the cerebral cortex have been stimulated and studied in more than 100 craniotomies, performed under local anesthesia, psychical responses of the experiential or interpretive variety have been produced only from the temporal cortex in the general areas that are marked "psychical responses" in Fig. 3.[10, 11]

CLASSIFICATION

It seems reasonable to subdivide psychical responses and psychical seizures (epileptic dreamy states) in the same way, classifying them as "interpretive" or "experiential." Interpretive psychical responses are those involving interpretations of the present experience, or emotions related to it; experiential psychical responses are reenactments of past experiences. Interpretive seizures are those accompanied by auras and illusions; experiential seizures are those accompanied by auras and hallucinations.

The interpretive responses and seizures may be divided into groups[11] of which the commonest are as follows: (i) recognition, the illusion that things seen and heard and thought are familiar (*déjà vu* phenomenon); (ii) visual illusion, the illusion that things seen are changing—for example, coming nearer, growing larger (macropsia); (iii) auditory illusion, the illusion that things heard are changing—for example, coming near, going away, changing tempo; (iv) illusional emotion, the emotion of fear or, less often, loneliness, sorrow, or disgust.

Experiential phenomena (hallucinations) are an awareness of experiences from the past that come into the mind without complete loss of awareness of the present.

DISCUSSION

What, then, is the function of the interpretive cortex? This is a physiological question that follows the foregoing observations naturally.

An electrode, delivering, for example, 60 electrical pulses per second to the surface of the motor cortex, causes a man to make crude movements. When applied to the various sensory areas of the cortex, it causes him to have crude sensations of sight or sound or body feeling. This indicates only that these areas have something to do with the complicated mechanism of voluntary action or conscious sensation. It does not reveal what contribution the cortex may make, or in what way it may contribute to skill in making voluntary movement or qualify the incoming sensory streams.

In the case of the interpretive cortex, the observations are similar. We may say that the interpretive cortex has something to do with a mechanism that can reactivate the vivid record of the past. It has also something to do with a mechanism that can present to consciousness a reflex interpretation of the present. To conclude that here is the mechanism of memory would be an unjustified assumption. It would be too simple.

What a man remembers when he makes a voluntary effort is apt to be a generalization. If this were not so, he might be hopelessly lost in detail. On the other hand, the experiential responses described above are detailed reenactments of a single experience. Such experiences soon slip beyond the range of voluntary recall. A man may summon to mind a song at will. He hears it then in his mind, not all at once but advancing phrase by phrase. He may sing it or play it too, and one would call this memory.

But if a patient hears music in response to the electrode, he hears it in one particular strip of time. That time runs forward again at the original tempo, and he hears the orchestration, or he sees the player at a piano "over there." There are details he would have thought forgotten.

A vast amount of work remains to be done before the mechanism of memory, and how and where the recording takes place, are understood. This record is not laid down in the interpretive cortex, but it is kept in a part of the brain that is intimately connected with it.

Removal of large areas of interpretive cortex, even when carried out on both sides, may result in mild complaints of memory defect, but it does not abolish the capacity to remember recent events. On the other hand, surgical removals that result in bilateral interference with the underlying hippocampal zone do make the recording of recent events impossible, while distant memory is still preserved.[12, 13]

The importance of the hippocampal area for memory was pointed out long ago in a forgotten publication by the Russian neurologist Bechterew.[14] The year before publication Bechterew had demonstrated the case before the St. Petersburg Clinic for Nervous and Mental Diseases. The man on whom Bechterew reported had "extraordinary weakness of memory, falsifications of memory and great apathy." These defects were shown at autopsy to be secondary to lesions of the mesial surface of the cortex of both temporal lobes. The English neurologists Glees and Griffith[15] reported similar defects, a half century later, in a patient who had symmetrical lesions of the hippocampus and of hippocampal and fusiform gyri on both sides.

The way in which the interpretive cortex seems to be used may be suggested by an example: After years of absence you meet, by chance, a man whose very existence you had forgotten. On seeing him, you may be struck by a sudden sense of familiarity, even before you have time to "think." A signal seems to flash up in consciousness to tell you that you've seen that man before. You watch him as he smiles and moves and speaks. The sense of familiarity grows stronger. Then you remember him. You may even recall that his name was Jones. The sight and the sound of the man has given you an instant access, through some reflex, to the records of the past in which this man has played some part. The opening of this forgotten file was subconscious. It was not a voluntary act. You would have known him even against your will. Although Jones was a forgotten man a moment before, now you can summon the record in such detail that you remark at once the slowness of his gait or a new line about the mouth.

If Jones had been a source of danger to you, you might have felt fear as well as familiarity before you had time to consider the man. Thus, the signal of fear as well as the signal of familiarity may come to one as the result of subconscious comparison of present with similar past experience.

One more example may be given from common experience. A sudden increase in the size of objects seen and in sounds heard may mean the rapid approach of something that calls for instant avoidance action. These are signals that, because of previous experience, we sometimes act upon with little consideration.

SUMMARY

The interpretive cortex has in it a mechanism for instant reactivation of the detailed record of the past. It has a mechanism also for the production of interpretive signals. Such signals could only be significant if past records are scanned and relevant experiences are selected for comparison with present experience. This is a subconscious process. But it may well be that this scanning of past experience and selection from it also renders the relevant past available for conscious consideration as well. Thus, the individual may refer to the record as he employs other circuits of the brain.

Access to the record of the past seems to be as readily available from the temporal cortex of one side as from that of the other. Auditory illusions (or interpretations of the distance, loudness, or tempo of sounds) have been produced by stimulation of the temporal cortex of either side. The same is true of illusional emotions, such as fear and disgust.

But, on the contrary, visual illusions (interpretations of the distance, dimension, erectness, and tempo of things seen) are only produced by stimulation of the temporal cortex on the nondominant (normally, right) side of the brain. Illusions of recognition, such as familiarity or strangeness, were also elicited only from the nondominant side, except in one case.

CONCLUSION

"Consciousness," to quote William James,[16] "is never quite the same in successive moments of time. It is a stream forever flowing, forever changing." The stream of changing states of mind that James described so well does flow through each man's waking hours until the time when he falls asleep to wake no more. But the stream, unlike a river, leaves a record in the living brain.

Transient electrical potentials move with it through the circuits of the nervous system, leaving a path that can be followed again. The pattern of this pathway, from neuron to neuron along each nerve-cell body and fiber and junction, is the recorded pattern of each man's past. That complicated record is held there in temporal sequence through the principle of durable facilitation of conduction and connection.

A steady stream of electrical pulses applied through an electrode to some point in the interpretive cortex causes a stream of excitation to flow from the cortex to the place where past experience is recorded. This stream of excitation acts as a key to the past. It can enter the pathway of recorded consciousness at any random point, from childhood on through adult life. But having entered, the experience moves forward without interference from other experiences. And when the electrode is withdrawn there is a likelihood, which lasts for seconds or minutes, that the stream of excitation will enter the pathway again at the same moment of past time, even if the electrode is reapplied at neighboring points.[17]

Finally, an electric current applied to the surface of what may be called the interpretive cortex of a conscious man (i) may cause the stream of former consciousness to flow again or (ii) may give him an interpretation of the present that is unexpected and involuntary. Therefore, it is concluded that, under normal circumstances, this area of cortex must make some functional contribution to reflex comparison of the present with related past experience. It contributes to reflex interpretation or perception of the present.

The combination and comparison of present experience with similar past experience must call for remarkable scanning of the past and classification of similarities. What contribution this area of the temporal cortex may make to the whole process is not clear. The term *interpretive cortex* will serve for identification until students of human physiology can shed more light on these fascinating findings.

REFERENCES AND NOTES

1. Penfield, W. *J. Mental Sci.* **101**, 451 (1955).
2. These patients, designated by the same initials, have been described in previous publications in much greater detail. An index of patients (designated by initials) may be found in any of my books.

3. This case is reported in detail in W. Penfield and H. Jasper, *Epilepsy and the Functional Anatomy of the Human Brain* (Little, Brown, Boston, 1954) [published in abridged form in Russian (translation by N. P. Graschenkov and G. Smirnov) by the Soviet Academy of Sciences, 1958].

4. The forebrain, or prosencephalon, properly includes the diencephalon and the telencephalon, or higher brain stem, and hemispheres. Flourens probably had cerebral hemispheres in mind as distinguished from cerebellum.

5. "Within the brain, a central transactional core has been identified between the strictly sensory or motor systems of classical neurology. This central reticular mechanism has been found capable of grading the activity of most other parts of the brain" — H. Magoun, *The Waking Brain* (Thomas, Springfield, Ill., 1958).

6. Penfield, W. *The Excitable Cortex in Conscious Man* (Thomas, Springfield, Ill., 1958).

7. It did more than this; it produced illusions or hallucinations that had never been experienced by the patient during a seizure.

8. Taylor, J., Ed., *Selected Writings of John Hughlings Jackson* (Hodder and Stoughton, London, 1931), vol. 1, *On Epilepsy and Epileptiform Convulsions*.

9. Twenty-one years later this young woman, who is the daughter of a physician, was present at a meeting of the National Academy of Sciences in New York while her case was discussed. She could still recall the operation and the nature of the "dreams" that had preceded her seizures [W. Penfield, *Proc. Natl. Acad. Sci. U.S.* **44**, 51 (1958)].

10. In a recent review of the series my associate, Dr. Phanor Perot, has found and summarized 35 out of 384 temporal lobe cases in which stimulation produced experiential responses. All such responses were elicited in the temporal cortex. In a study of 214 consecutive operations for temporal lobe epilepsy, my associate Sean Mullan found 70 cases in which interpretive illusion occurred in the minor seizures before operation, or in which an interpretive response was produced by stimulation during operation. In most cases it occurred both before and during operation.

11. Mullan, S., and Penfield, W. *A.M.A. Arch. Neurol. Psychiat,* **81**, 269 (1959).

12. This area is marked "Hipp" and "Hipp. G" in Fig. 2 (bottom) and "g. Hippoc." and "amygdala" in Fig. 3.

13. Penfield, W., and Milner, B. *A.M.A. Arch. Neurol. Psychiat.* **79**, 475 (1958).

14. Bechterew, W. V. "Demonstration eines Gehirns mit Zerstörung der vorderen und inneren Theile der Hirnrinde beider Schläfenlappen," *Neurol. Zentralbl. Leipzig* **19**, 990 (1900). My attention was called to this case recently by Dr. Peter Gloor of Montreal.

15. Glees, P., and Griffith, H. B. *Monatsschr. Psychiat. Neurol.* **123**, 193 (1952).

16. James, W. *The Principles of Psychology* (Holt, New York, 1910).

17. Thus, it is apparent that the beam of excitation that emanates from the interpretive cortex and seems to scan the record of the past is subject to the principles of transient facilitation already demonstrated for the anthropoid motor cortex [A. S. F. Grünbaum and C. Sherrington, *Proc. Roy. Soc.* (London) **72B**, 152 (1901); T. Graham Brown and C. S. Sherrington, *ibid.* **85B**, 250 (1912)]. Similarly subject to the principles of facilitation are the motor and the sensory cortex of man [W. Penfield and K. Welch, *J. Physiol* (London) **109**, 358 (1949)]. The patient D. F. heard the same orchestra playing the same music in the operating room more than 20 times when the electrode was reapplied to the superior surface of the temporal lobe. Each time the music began in the verse of a popular song. It proceeded to the chorus, if the electrode was kept in place.

18. Penfield, W., and Roberts L. *Speech and Brain Mechanisms* (Princeton Univ. Press, Princeton. N.J., 1959).

19. Jelgersma, G. *Atlas anatomicum cerebri humani* (Scheltema and Holkema, Amsterdam).

UNIT THREE | DISCUSSION QUESTIONS

6 | DNA'S CODE: KEY TO ALL LIFE

Discuss what is meant by the term "the genetic code."

Support the view that most behavioral characteristics are acquired.

7 | THE ROLE OF NEUROLOGICAL IDEAS IN PSYCHOLOGY

In what ways does the nervous system have relevance to the theory of personality?

Select one of the earlier theories in psychology and show in what ways it is lacking in accuracy.

8 | THE INTERPRETIVE CORTEX

Do we forget? Why are some people able to remember better than others?

What is the "*déjà vu*" phenomenon? Give examples.

UNIT FOUR
MATURATION, LEARNING, AND MOTIVATION

Heredity is fixed at the moment of conception; maturation begins at the time of conception. Maturation is a physiological growth process that is closely related to age, and is characterized by an orderly sequence of events. Consider the prenatal stage, identified by the *germinal, embryonic,* and *fetal* periods. This is a time of rapid growth and development during which various structures of the organism take form. Each structure is dependent upon the successful prior development of other structures. For example, the development of the spinal cord must be complete before the nervous system can reach functional maturity. If one stage is slowed or delayed, for one reason or another, the progress of the succeeding functions dependent on it is impeded. Illustrations of this may be found in the period of adolescence when the onset of sexual maturity, called *puberty,* sets the stage for other forms of maturity, such as physiological growth and emotional development. Although the sequences of development are generally the same for all, individuals may, and often do, differ in the rate of development. Recognition of the varying patterns of development offers invaluable knowledge for understanding the behavior of individuals.

Maturational readiness refers to periods of life in which it is easier for a person to learn particular tasks. For example, teaching a child to say *da-da* and *ma-ma* is appropriate during the baby's babbling stage because these words are much like the sounds he is making. Any attempt to teach other words, at this stage, generally ends with failure.

Varying skills that call for muscular coordination are most easily learned when muscular maturation is at its peak. It is apparent that learning and maturation are interwoven and related. J. P. Scott's *Critical Periods in Behavioral Development* summarizes research relating to "critical periods" of survival which are best for certain kinds of learning. Scott's article questions the frequent generalizations made from animal to human behavior.

Since Pavlov's first experiments with dogs salivating to the sound of a bell, behavioral scientists have been working to create satisfactory *laws* of learning. Many *theories* have been created with varying degrees of interpretation; for example, one psychologist, Clark Hull, attempted to explain learning through the use of mathematically stated formulas. Whether man will be able to establish *laws* of learning remains to be answered; however, there is much we are attempting to gain in the understanding of learning. David Krech in *Psychoneurobiochemeducation* discusses brain biochemistry and behavior research in terms of the physical basis for memory. Krech's document suggests that we are on the verge of great discoveries, which psychologists may soon talk about in terms of enzyme-assisted instruction, protein memory consolidators, or antibiotic memory repellers. His hypothesis regarding "species-specific enrichment experiences" and his interpretation of the importance of language development make this article an important contemporary contribution.

Among the various theories of human motivation, one of the most well-organized and sound is that formulated by A. H. Maslow. His popular *A Theory of Human Motivation* describes most people as being motivated by a hierarchy of needs and further suggests that the sequence of these needs is determined by life's circumstances.

Finally Lewis L. Robbin's *Unconscious Motivation* presents in a simplified and interesting fashion the various ways in which unconscious motives affect behavior. The concept of unconscious motives, like other Freudian terms, is debated among psychologists.

---

9 | CRITICAL PERIODS IN BEHAVIORAL DEVELOPMENT

J. P. Scott

A number of years ago I was given a female lamb taken from its mother at birth. My wife and I raised it on the bottle for the first 10 days of life and then placed it out in the pasture with a small flock of domestic sheep. As might have been expected from folklore, the lamb became attached to people and followed the persons who fed it. More surprisingly, the lamb remained independent of the rest of the flock when we restored it to the pasture. Three years later it was still following an independent grazing pattern. In addition, when it was mated and had lambs of its own it became a very indifferent mother, allowing its offspring to nurse but showing no concern when the lamb moved away with the other members of the flock.[1]

Since following the flock is such a universal characteristic of normal sheep, I was impressed by the extensive and permanent modification of this behavior that resulted from a brief early experience. The results suggested that Freud was right concerning the importance of early experience, and pointed toward the existence of critical periods in behavioral development. As I soon discovered, there is considerable evidence that a critical period for determining early social relationships is a

---

From *Science*, **138**, 30 November 1962, pp. 949–958. Copyright © 1962 by the American Association for the Advancement of Science. Reprinted by permission of the publisher and the author.

widespread phenomenon in vertebrates; such a critical period had long been known in ants.[2]

The theory of critical periods is not a new one in either biology or psychology. It was strongly stated by Stockard in 1921, in connection with his experiments on the induction of monstrosities in fish embryos, although he gave credit to Dareste for originating the basic idea 30 years earlier.[3] In experimenting with the effects of various inorganic chemicals upon the development of *Fundulus* eggs, Stockard at first thought one-eyed monsters were specifically caused by the magnesium ion. Further experiments showed him that almost any chemical would produce the same effect, provided it was applied at the proper time during development. These experiments and those of Child[4] and his students established the fact that the most rapidly growing tissues in an embryo are the most sensitive to any change in conditions, thus accounting for the specificity of effects at particular times.

Meanwhile Freud had attempted to explain the origin of neuroses in human patients as the result of early experience and had implied that certain periods in the life of an infant are times of particular sensitivity. In 1935, Lorenz[5] emphasized the importance of critical periods for the formation of primary social bonds (imprinting) in birds, remarking on their similarity to critical periods in the development of the embryo, and McGraw soon afterward[6] pointed out the existence of critical periods for optimal learning of motor skills in the human infant.

Since then, the phenomenon of critical periods has excited the imagination of a large group of experimenters interested in human and animal development. In describing this fast-moving scientific field, I shall point out some of the most significant current developments. More detailed information is available in some excellent recent reviews.[7, 8]

To begin with, three major kinds of critical-period phenomena have been discovered. These involve optimal periods for learning, for infantile stimulation, and for the formation of basic social relationships. The last of these has been established as a widespread phenomenon in the animal kingdom and consequently receives major attention in this article.

PERIODS ARE BASED ON PROCESSES

In the dog, the development of behavior may be divided into several natural periods marked off by important changes in social relationships (Table 1). Only a few other species have been studied in sufficient detail for making adequate comparisons, but enough data have been accumulated to show that similar periods can be identified in other mammals and in birds.[9, 10] I originally expected to find that the course of postnatal development, like that of embryonic development, would be essentially similar in all vertebrates, and that while the periods might be extended or shortened, the same pattern of development would be evident in all.[11] However, comparison of only two species, man and the dog, shows that the periods can actually occur in reverse order, and that there is an astonishing degree of flexibility in behavioral development.[12]

This leads to the conclusion that the important aspect of each developmental period is not time sequence but the fact that each represents a major developmental process. Thus, the neonatal period is chiefly characterized by the process of neonatal

TABLE 1

Periods of development in the puppy and song sparrow. The six periods of development described by Nice[10] for the song sparrow correspond to the first four periods in the puppy, as indicated in the table. The young of the two species are born or hatched in an immature state, require intensive parental care and feeding, and go through much the same stages before becoming independent. Development is much more rapid in the bird than in the puppy, although small mammals such as mice mature at about the same rate as birds.

Puppy			Song Sparrow		
Name of period	Length of period (weeks)	Initial event	Name of period	Length of period (days)	Initial event
I. Neonatal	0–2	Birth, nursing	Stage 1 (nestling)	0–4	Hatching, gaping
II. Transition	2–3	Eyes open	Stage 2	5–6	Eyes open
III. Socialization	3–10	Startle to sound	Stage 3	7–9	Cowering — first fear reactions
			Stage 4 (fledgling)	10–16	Leaving nest — first flight
			Stage 5	17–28	Full flight
IV. Juvenile	10–	Final weaning	Stage 6 (juvenile)	29–	Independent feeding

nutrition—nursing in mammals and parental feeding in many birds. The transition period is characterized by the process of transition to adult methods of nutrition and locomotion and the appearance of adult patterns of social behavior, at least in immature form. The period of socialization is the period in which primary social bonds are formed. If we consider processes alone, it is apparent that they are not completely dependent on each other and that they can therefore be arranged in different orders. It is also apparent that certain of these processes persist beyond the periods characterized by them. For example, a mammal usually retains throughout life the ability to suck which characterizes the neonatal period, although in most cases this ability is little used.

PROCESS OF PRIMARY SOCIALIZATION

Since one of the first acts of a young mammal is to nurse, and since food rewards are known to modify the behavior of adult animals, it once seemed logical to suppose that the process of forming a social attachment begins with food rewards and develops as an acquired drive. However, the experimental evidence does not support this extreme viewpoint. Brodbeck reared a group of puppies during the critical period of socialization, feeding half of them by hand and the other half by machine, but giving all of them the same degree of human contact.[13] He found that the two sets of puppies became equally attached to people. This result was later confirmed by Stanley and his co-workers,[14] who found that the only difference in response between the machine-fed and the hand-fed puppies was that the latter yelped more when they saw the experimenter. Elliot and King[15] fed all their puppies by hand but overfed one group and underfed another. The hungry puppies became more rapidly attached to the handlers. We can conclude that, in the dog, food rewards per se are not necessary for the process of socialization, but that hunger will speed it up.

Fisher[16] reared fox terrier puppies in isolation boxes through the entire socialization period. The puppies were fed mechanically (thus, food was entirely eliminated as a factor in the experiment), but they were removed from the boxes for regular contacts with the experimenter. One group of puppies was always rewarded by kind social treatment. A second group was sometimes rewarded and sometimes punished, but in a purely random way. Still a third group was always punished for any positive approach to the experimenter. The puppies that were both rewarded and punished showed most attraction and dependency behavior with respect to the experimenter, and the puppies that were always punished showed the least. After the treatment was discontinued, all the puppies began coming toward the experimenter, and the differences rapidly disappeared. This leads to the surprising conclusion that the process of socialization is not inhibited by punishment and may even be speeded up by it.

At approximately 3 weeks of age—that is, at the beginning of the period of socialization—young puppies begin to bark or whine when isolated or placed in strange places. Elliot and Scott[17] showed that the reaction to isolation in a strange place reaches a peak at 6 to 7 weeks of age, approximately the midpoint of the critical period, and begins to decline thereafter. Scott, Deshaies, and Morris[18] found that separating young puppies overnight from their mother and litter mates in a strange pen for 20 hours per day produced a strong emotional reaction and speeded up the process of socialization to human handlers. All this evidence indicates that any sort of strong emotion, whether hunger, fear, pain, or loneliness, will speed up the process of socialization. No experiments have been carried out to determine the effects of pleasant types of emotion, such as might be aroused by play and handling, but these were probably a factor in Brodbeck's experiment with machine-fed puppies.

The results of these experiments on dogs agree with evidence from other species. While they were going on, Harlow[19] was performing his famous experiments with rhesus monkeys isolated at birth and supplied with dummy "mothers." When given the choice between a comfortable cloth-covered mother without a nipple and an uncomfortable mother made of wire screening but equipped with a functional nursing bottle, the young rhesus monkeys definitely preferred the cloth-covered models from which they had received no food rewards. Harlow concluded that the acquired-drive theory of the origin of social attachment could be discarded.

Later, Igel and Calvin[20] performed a similar but more elaborate experiment with puppies. These animals had more opportunity to choose, being provided with four kinds of mother models: comfortable and uncomfortable, each type with and without nipples. Like rhesus monkeys, the puppies preferred the comfortable "mother" but usually chose one with a nipple. Thus, it appears that food rewards do contribute something to the social relationship, although they do not form its prime basis.

Since then Harlow[21] has raised to maturity the monkeys raised on dummy mothers, has mated them, and has observed their behavior toward their own young. They become uniformly poor mothers, neglecting their offspring and often punishing them when they cry. In spite of such rejection, the young rhesus infants desperately crawl toward their mothers and give every evidence of becoming attached to them, although perhaps not as strongly as in the normal relationship. Here again punishment does not inhibit the formation of a social bond.

The hypothesis that the primary social bond originates through food rewards had already been shown to be invalid in the precocial birds, many of which form attachments prior to the time when they begin to feed. Lorenz[5] was the first to point out the significance of this phenomenon, which he called "imprinting." He also stated that it differed from conditioning, primarily in that it was very rapid and apparently irreversible. However, rapid formation and great persistence are also characteristic of many conditioned responses and other learned behavior. Fabricius[22] pointed out that no sharp line can be drawn between imprinting and conditioning, and Collias[23] concluded that imprinting is a form of learned behavior that is self-reinforcing.

The process of imprinting in young ducklings and chicks has since been experimentally analyzed in much detail, with results that invariably confirm the conclusion that it takes place without any obvious external rewards or reinforcement. Hess[24] found that if he caused young ducklings to follow a model over varying distances or over hurdles, the ducklings which had to make the greater effort became more strongly imprinted. He also found that the drug meprobamate and its congener carisoprodol, which are muscle relaxants as well as tranquilizers, greatly reduce imprinting if given during the critical period. James[25] found that chicks would become attached to an object illuminated by a flickering light, even though they were not allowed to follow, and Gray[26] later showed that they will become attached to a motionless object illuminated by a steady light and viewed from an isolation box. It is therefore apparent that chicks can become imprinted without following, although muscular tension may still be important.

Guiton[27] found that chicks allowed to follow a model in a group become less strongly imprinted than chicks exposed singly, and he attributed the results to the greater fear shown by the isolated chicks. Recently, Pitz and Ross[28] subjected young chicks following a model to a loud sound and found that this increased the speed with which they formed a social bond. Hess[29] has given a mild electric shock to chicks following a model and finds that this also increases the strength of imprinting. Instead of avoiding the model, the distressed chick runs after it more closely.

We may conclude that these young birds become attached to any object to which they are long exposed during the critical period, even when their contact is only visual. We may also conclude that the speed of formation of a social bond is dependent upon the degree of emotional arousal, irrespective of the nature of that arousal. Whether attachment is the result of the emotion itself or of the reduction of emotion as the chick or duckling approches the model is still a matter of conjecture.[30]

TIMING MECHANISMS

The basic timing mechanisms for developmental periods are obviously the biological processes of growth and differentiation, usually called maturation. For various reasons, these are not precisely correlated with age from birth or hatching. For example, birds often retain newly formed eggs in their bodies overnight, thus incubating them for several hours before laying. By chilling duck eggs just before placing them in an incubator (thus killing all embryos except those in the earliest stages of development) Gottlieb[31] was able to time the age of ducklings from the onset of incubation rather than from hatching and found that variation in the timing for the critical period was much reduced. No such exact timing studies have been made in mammals, but I have estimated that there is at least a week's variation in development among puppies at 3 weeks of age, and the variation among human infants must be considerably greater.[32]

Another approach to the problem is to try to identify the actual mechanisms which open and close a period. Since an important part of forming a primary social relationship appears to be emotional arousal while the young animal is in contact with another, it is obvious that the critical period for socialization could be timed by the appearance of behavior mechanisms which maintain or prevent contact, and this indeed is the case. There are demonstrable positive mechanisms, varying from species to species, which bring young animals close to other members of their kind: the clinging response of young rhesus monkeys; the following response of chicks, ducklings, and lambs and other herd animals; the social investigation, tail wagging, and playful fighting of puppies; and the visual investigation and smiling of the human infant.[33] These are, of course, accompanied by interacting responses from adult and immature members of the species: holding and clasping by primate mothers, brooding of mother hens and other birds, calling by mother sheep, investigation and play on the part of other young puppies, and the various supporting and nurturing activities of human mothers.

If contact and emotional arousal result in social attachment, there must be negative mechanisms which prevent such attachment once the critical period is past. Perhaps the most widespread of these is the development of a fear response which causes the young animal to immediately leave the vicinity of a stranger and hence avoid contact. This developing fear response is found in young chicks,[7] ducklings,[22, 34] dogs,[35] rhesus monkeys,[36] and in many other birds and mammals. Even in children there is a period between the ages of 5 and 12 months in which there is a mounting fear of strangers,[37] sometimes called "8-months anxiety."[38] As already pointed out, there is a time in development when certain fear responses actually facilitate imprinting, but, as they grow stronger, the escape reaction follows so quickly that it prevents contact altogether.

Another sort of negative mechanism is the rejection of strange young by adult sheep, goats, and many other herd animals.[39] In these species the mothers become strongly attached to the young within a few hours after birth and refuse to accept strangers thereafter. This indicates that the rapid formation of emotional bonds is not limited to young animals.

These timing mechanisms all depend primarily on the development of social behavior patterns, but both sensory and motor development can also influence timing. For example, a very immature animal cannot maintain contact by following, and in slowly developing altricial birds such as jackdaws and doves,[5, 40] the period of imprinting comes much later than it does in the precocial species. In the human infant the process of socialization begins before the adult motor patterns develop, but contact is maintained by visual exploration and by the smiling response to human faces.[33] Thus, understanding the process of socialization and its timing mechanisms

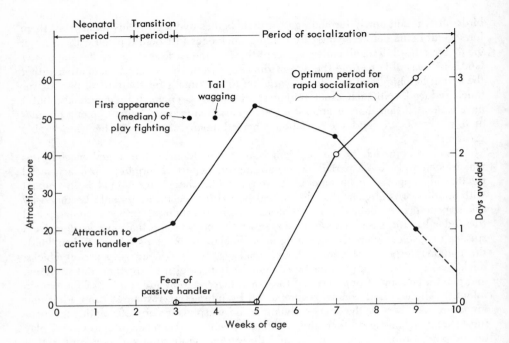

FIG. 1. Timing mechanisms for the critical period in puppies.[35] The period is initiated by positive behavior mechanisms, such as playful fighting, which result in attraction to a strange individual, and it is brought to a close by the development of a fear response which causes the attraction to decline. The optimum period for rapid and permanent socialization comes shortly after the appearance of prolonged avoidance reactions.

in any particular species requires a systematic study of the development of the various capacities which affect the time of onset and the duration of the critical period. These include sensory, motor, and learning capacities as well as the ability to perform essential patterns of social behavior.

The fact that emotional arousal is so strongly connected with the process of primary socialization suggests that the capacity to produce emotional reactions may also govern the time of onset of a critical period. Figure 1 summarizes the results of a study of emotional development in the dog during the critical period. If puppies are kept in large fields, totally isolated from people, fear and escape responses toward human beings very nearly reach a maximum by the time the puppies are 14 weeks old—a finding that fixes the upper limit of the period of socialization.[35] On the other hand, the peak of the emotional response to isolation in a strange place occurs when puppies are approximately 6 to 7 weeks old, as does the peak of the heart-rate response to handling. At this age, such emotional arousal actually contributes to the strength of the social bond. Fuller[41] was unable to condition the heart-rate response consistently until puppies were 5 weeks old. This indicates that one of the factors that brings the critical period to a close may be the developing ability of the young puppy to associate fear responses with particular stimuli.

All this suggests that if the development of the escape response to strangers could be held in check, the critical period might be extended indefinitely. Raising puppies in small isolation boxes during the critical period inhibits the development of the escape response, but they still show obvious signs of fear when they are first removed from their cages. Fuller[42] reports some success in socializing these older pups by overcoming their fear responses, either by careful handling or through the use of tranquilizing drugs.

Fear responses thus have the dual effect of facilitating the formation of the social bond during the critical period (along with other emotions) and of bringing the period to a close. This is understandable because the type of fear which terminates the critical period is a developing fear of strange animals. In the early part of the critical period the escape reaction is either lacking or is momentary and weak. At the close of the period it is strong enough to prevent contact altogether.

FORMATION OF AFFECTIONAL BONDS IN ADULT LIFE

Until recently, most investigators have concentrated their attention on the critical period for primary socialization or imprinting and few have gone on to study similar phenomena in later development. This field of investigation is just beginning to open up, though many related facts have long been known. For example, many birds form strong pair bonds which are maintained as long as both members survive. In studying the development of various types of social bonds in different species of ducks, Schutz[43] finds that, while attachments to particular individuals may be formed in the early critical period from 12 to 17 hours after hatching, the critical period for the attachment to the species may not come until sometime later, in some cases as late as 30 days after hatching, and the attachment to a particular member of the opposite sex, or the pair bond, does not come until the age of 5 months or so. Schutz also finds that female mallards cannot be sexually imprinted with respect to other species but always mate with other mallards no matter what their earliest experience has been. A similar phenomenon is reported by Warriner,[44] who finds that male pigeons prefer to mate with birds whose color is similar to that of the parents who reared them, whether of the same or another color from themselves, but females show no preference.

Certain species of mammals, such as foxes,[45] form long-lasting mating bonds. It is possible that the violence of the sexual emotions contributes to the formation of the adult bond, just as other sorts of emotional arousal are important to the primary socialization of the infant. Klopfer[46] has suggested that the rapid formation of the social bond in a mother goat toward her kid is the result of the high degree of emotional arousal which accompanies the birth of the offspring.

In short, it seems likely that the formation of a social attachment through contact and emotional arousal is a process that may take place throughout life, and that although it may take place more slowly outside of certain critical periods, the capacity for such an attachment is never completely lost.

At this point it may be remarked that, in attempting to analyze the development of affection and social bonds objectively, scientists have often tried to simplify the problem by postulating various unitary, unromantic, and sometimes unesthetic explanations. One of these was the "acquired drive" hypothesis—that children love you because you feed them. Taking a more moderate view Harlow[19] has emphasized "contact comfort" as a major variable—that the young monkey begins to love its mother because she feels warm and comfortable—but that a number of other factors are involved. As this article indicates, evidence is accumulating that there is a much less specific, although equally unromantic, general mechanism involved—that given any kind of emotional arousal a young animal will become attached to any individual or object with which it is in contact for a sufficiently long time. The necessary arousal would, of course, include various specific kinds of emotions associated with food rewards and contact comfort.

It should not be surprising that many kinds of emotional reactions contribute to a social relationship. The surprising thing is that emotions which we normally consider aversive should produce the same effect as those which appear to be rewarding. This apparent paradox is partially resolved by evidence that the positive effect of unpleasant emotions is normally limited to early infancy by the development of escape reactions.

Nevertheless, this concept leads to the somewhat alarming conclusion that an animal (and perhaps a person) of any age, exposed to certain individuals or physical surroundings for any length of time, will inevitably become attached to them, the rapidity of the process being governed by the degree of emotional arousal associated with them. I need not dwell on the consequences for human behavior, if this conclusion should apply to our species as well as to other animals, except to point out that it provides an explanation of certain well-known clinical observations such as the development by neglected children of strong affection for cruel and abusive parents, and the various peculiar affectional relationships that develop between prisoners and jailors, slaves and masters, and so on. Perhaps the general adaptive nature of this mechanism is that since the survival of any member of a highly social species depends upon the rapid development of social relationships, a mechanism has evolved which makes it almost impossible to inhibit the formation of social bonds.

CRITICAL PERIODS OF LEARNING

Unlike the process of socialization, the phenomenon of critical periods of learning was first noticed in children rather than in lower animals. McGraw's[47] famous experiment with the twins Johnny and Jimmy was a deliberate attempt to modify behavioral development by giving one of a pair of identical twins special early training. The result varied according to the activity involved. The onset of walking, for example, was not affected by previous practice or help. Other activities, however, could be greatly speeded up—notably roller skating, in which the favored twin became adept almost as soon as he could walk. In other activities performance was actually made worse by early practice, simply because of the formation of unskillful habits. McGraw[6] concluded that there are critical periods for learning which vary from activity to activity; for each kind of coordinated muscular activity there is an optimum period for rapid and skillful learning.

In an experiment with rats, Hebb[48] used the technique of providing young animals with many opportunities for spontaneous learning rather than formal training. Pet rats raised in the rich environment of a home performed much better on learning tasks than rats reared in barren laboratory cages. Since then, other experiments[49] have standardized the "rich" environment as a large cage including many objects and playthings and have gotten similar effects.

Forgays[50] finds that the age at which the maximum effect is produced is limited to the period from approximately 20 to 30 days of age, immediately after weaning. A similar experience in adult life produces no effect. In rats, at any rate, the critical period of learning seems to coincide with the critical period of primary socialization, and it may be that the two are in some way related. Candland and Campbell[51] find that fearful behavior in response to a strange situation begins to increase in rats between 20 and 30 days after birth, and Bernstein[52] showed earlier that discrimination learning could be improved by gentle handling beginning at 20 days. It may well be that the development of fear limits the capacity for future learning as well as the formation of social relationships.

In addition to these studies on motor learning and problem solving, there are many experiments demonstrating the existence of critical periods for the learning of social behavior patterns. It has long been known that many kinds of birds do not develop the characteristic songs of their species if they are reared apart from their own kind[53]. More recently, Thorpe[54] discovered a critical period for this effect in the chaffinch. If isolated at 3 or 4 days of age, a young male chaffinch produces an incomplete song, but if he hears adults singing, as a fledgling 2 or 3 weeks old or in early juvenile life before he sings himself, he will the next year produce the song characteristic of the species, even if he has been kept in isolation. In nature, the fine details of the song are added at the time of competition over territory, within a period of 2 or 3 weeks, when the bird is about a year old. At this time it learns the songs of two or three of its neighbors, and never learns any others in subsequent years. The critical period for song learning is thus a relatively long one, but it is definitely over by the time the bird is a year old. There is no obvious explanation for its ending at this particular time, but it is possible that learning a complete song pattern in some way interferes with further learning.

King and Gurney[55] found that adult mice reared in groups during youth fought more readily than animals isolated at 20 days of age. Later experiments showed that most of the effect was produced in a 10-day period just after weaning, and that similar experience as adults produced little or no effect.[56] Thus, there appears to be a critical period for learning to fight through social experience, and this experience need be no more than contact through a wire. In this case the effect is probably produced by association with other mice before the fear response has been completely developed. Similarly, Fisher[16] and Fuller[57] inhibited the development of attacking behavior in fox terriers by raising them in isolation through the critical period for socialization. The animals would fight back somewhat ineffectually if attacked, but did not initiate conflicts. Tinbergen[58] found a critical period in dogs for learning territorial boundaries, coinciding with sexual maturity.

The results of corresponding experiments on sexual behavior vary from species to species. In mice, rearing in isolation produced no effects[59]. Beach[60] found that male rats reared with either females or males were actually slower to respond to sexual behavior than isolated males, and he suggested that habits of playful fighting established by the group-reared animals interfered with sexual behavior later on. In guinea pigs, contact with other young animals improves sexual performance.[61]

On the other hand, young chimpanzees[62] reared apart from their kind can only be mated with experienced animals. Harlow[21] discovered that his rhesus infants reared on dummy mothers did not develop normal patterns of sexual behavior, and he was able to obtain matings only by exposing females to experienced males. Normal behavior can be developed by allowing 20-minute daily play periods with other young monkeys, but if rhesus infants are reared apart from all other monkeys beyond the period when they spontaneously play with their fellows, patterns of both sexual and maternal behavior fail to develop normally. These results suggest that play has an important role in developing adult patterns of social behavior in these primates, and that the decline of play behavior sets the upper limit of the critical period during which normal adult behavior may be developed.

Such great changes in the social environment rarely occur in humans even by accident, but Money, Hampson, and Hampson[63] have studied the development of hermaphroditic children who have been reared as one sex and then changed to the other. They find that if this occurs before 2½ years of age, very little emotional disturbance results. Thus, there is a critical period for learning the sex role, this capacity persisting unchanged up to a point in development which roughly corresponds to the age when children begin to use and understand language. Perhaps more important, this is the age when children first begin to take an interest in, and play with, members of their own age group.

It is difficult to find a common factor in these critical periods for learning. In some species, such as rats, mice, dogs, and sheep, certain critical periods for learning coincide with the period for primary socialization and seem to be similarly brought to a close by the development of fear reactions. Other critical periods, in chaffinches and dogs, coincide with the formation of adult mating bonds. However, the critical period for sexual learning in the rhesus monkey comes later than that for primary socialization[64], as do critical periods for various kinds of learning in human beings.

Part of this apparent inconsistency arises from our ignorance regarding timing mechanisms. One such mechanism must be the development of learning capacities, and we have evidence in dogs[65], rhesus monkeys[66], and human infants[12] that learning capacities change during development, sometimes in a stepwise fashion. One element in these capacities is the ability to learn things which facilitate subsequent learning.

It is equally possible, however, to "learn not to learn," and such a negative learning set may act to bring the critical period to a close. At this point, we can only state a provisional general hypothesis: that the critical period for any specific sort of learning is that time when maximum capacities—sensory, motor, and motivational, as well as psychological ones—are first present.

CRITICAL PERIODS FOR EARLY STIMULATION

Experiments to determine the effects of early stimulation have been mainly performed on infant mice and rats, which are usually weaned at about 21 days at the earliest, and have been concerned with the effect of stimulation during this preweaning period. All investigators beginning with Levine[67] and Schaefer[68], agree that rats handled during the first week or 10 days of life have a lessened tendency to urinate and defecate in a strange "open field" situation, learn avoidance behavior more readily, and survive longer when deprived of food and water. In short, early stimulation produces an animal that is less timorous, learns more quickly, and is more vigorous. Levine found that the effect could be obtained by a variety of stimuli, including electric shock and mechanical shaking as well as handling. This ruled out learned behavior as an explanation of the effect, and Levine, Alpert, and Lewis[69] discovered that animals handled in the early period showed a much earlier maturation of the adrenocortical response to stress. Levine interpreted these results as indicating that the laboratory environment did not provide sufficient stimulation for the proper development of the hormonal systems of the animals. This interpretation is an agreement with Richter's finding[70] that laboratory rats are quite deficient in adrenocortical response as compared with the wild variety. Schaefer, Weingarten, and Towne[71] have duplicated Levine's results by the use of cold alone, and have suggested temperature as a possible unitary mechanism. However, their findings are not necessarily in disagreement with those of Levine, as the hormonal stress response can be elicited by a variety of stimuli, and temperature may simply be another of the many kinds of stimuli which produce the effect.

According to Thompson and Schaefer[72] the earlier the stimulation the greater the effect. If the hormonal mechanism is the chief phenomenon involved, we can say that there is a critical period during the first week or 10 days of life, since the adrenal response in any case matures and becomes fixed by 16 days of age.

Denenberg[73] takes a somewhat different approach, pointing out that there should be optimal levels of stimulation, so that either very weak or very strong stimulation would produce poor results. He suggests that there are different critical periods for the effect of early stimulation, depending on the intensity of stimulation and the kind of later behavior measured. Working within the critical first 10 days, Denenberg found that the best avoidance learning was produced by stimulation in the second half of the period whereas the best survival rates were produced by stimulation in the first half. Weight was approximately equally affected, except that there was little effect in the first 3 days[74].

Analyzing the effect on avoidance learning, Denenberg[75] and his associates found that both unhandled controls and rats handled for the first 20 days performed poorly, the former because they were too emotional and the latter because they were too calm to react quickly. An intermediate amount of emotional response produces the best learning, and this can be produced by handling only in the first 10 days of life; handling during the second 10 days has a lesser effect. No handling produces too much emotionality, and handling for 20 days results in too little. Irrespective of the effect on learning, the data lead to the important conclusion that emotional stimulation during a critical period early in life can lead to the reduction of emotional responses in later life.

More precisely, there appear to be two critical periods revealed by research on early stimulation of rats, one based on a physiological process (the development of the adrenal cortical stress mechanism) and extending to 16 days of age at the latest, the other based on a psychological process (the reduction of fear through familiarity[51], beginning about 17 days when the eyes first open and extending to 30 days. The effects of handling during these two periods are additive, and many experiments based on arbitrary time rather than developmental periods undoubtedly include both.

The deleterious effects of excessive stimulation in the life of the infant may also be interpreted as a traumatic emotional experience. Bowlby[76], in studying a group of juvenile thieves, found that a large proportion of them had been separated from their mothers in early infancy, and he postulated that this traumatic emotional experience had affected their later behavior. Since this conclusion was based on retrospective information, he and his co-workers have since studied the primary symptoms of separation and have described in detail the emotional reactions of infants sent to hospitals, and thus separated from their mothers[77]. Schaffer[78] found a difference in reaction to separation before 7 months and separation afterward. Both sets of infants were disturbed, but they were disturbed in different ways. Infants show increasingly severe emotional reactions to adoption from 3 through 12 months of age[33]. It seems logical to place the beginning of the critical period for maximum emotional disturbance at approximately 7 months—at the end of the critical period for primary socialization, which Gray[79] places at approximately 6 weeks to 6 months. Infants whose social relationships have been thoroughly established and whose fear responses toward strangers have been fully developed are much more likely to be upset by changes than infants in which these relationships and responses have not yet been developed.

However, not all apparently "traumatic" early experiences have such a lasting effect. Experimental work shows that young animals have a considerable capacity to recover from unpleasant emotions experienced in a limited period in early life[80], and that what is traumatic in one species may not be in another. While young rats become calmer after infantile stimulation, young mice subjected to excessive auditory stimulation later become more emotional.[81] At this point it is appropriate to point out that critical periods are not necessarily involved in every kind of early experience. Raising young chimpanzees in the dark produces degeneration of the retina, but this is a long and gradual process.[82]

Another approach to the problem is to stimulate emotional responses in mothers and observe the effect on the offspring. Thompson[83] and other authors[84] have shown that the offspring of rats made fearful while pregnant are more likely to be over-emotional in the open-field situation than the offspring of animals not so stimulated. Since any direct influence of material behavior was ruled out by cross-fostering experiments, it seems likely that the result is produced by modification of the adreno-cortical stress mechanism—in this case, by secretion of maternal hormones acting on the embryo rather than by stimulation after birth of the young animal itself. No precise critical period for the effect has been established, but it is probably confined to the latter part of pregnancy. Similar effects have been obtained in mice,[85] and if such effects can be demonstrated in other mammals, the implications for prenatal care in human beings are obvious.

It is interesting to note that, whereas shocking the mother both before and after parturition has the effect of increasing emotional responses in the young, the emotional responses of young rats are *decreased* when the treatment is applied directly to them. The explanation of this contradiction must await direct experiments on the endocrine system.

GENERAL THEORY OF CRITICAL PERIODS

There are at least two ways in which experience during critical periods may act on behavioral development. The critical period for primary socialization constitutes a turning point. Experience during a short period early in life determines which shall be the close relatives of the young animal, and this, in turn, leads the animal to develop in one of two directions—the normal one, in which it becomes attached to and mates with a member of its own species, or an abnormal one, in which it becomes attached to a different species, with consequent disrupting effects upon sexual and other social relationships with members of its own kind.

The concept of a turning point applies equally well to most examples of critical periods for learning. Up to a certain point in development a chaffinch can learn several varieties of song, but once it has learned one of them it no longer has a choice. Similarly, the human infant can learn either sex role up to a certain age, but once it has learned one or the other, changing over becomes increasingly difficult. What is learned at particular points limits and interferes with subsequent learning, and Schneirla and Rosenblatt[86] have suggested that there are critical stages of learning— that what has been learned at a particular time in development may be critical for whatever follows.

A second sort of action during a critical period consists of a nonspecific stimulus producing an irrevocable result, not modifiable in subsequent development. Thus, almost any sort of stimulus has the effect of modifying the development of the endocrine stress mechanism of young rats in early infancy.

Is there any underlying common principle? Each of these effects has its counterpart in embryonic development. Up to a certain point a cell taken from an amphibian embryo and transplanted to a new location will develop in accordance with its new environment. Beyond this turning point it develops in accordance with its previous location. Some cells retain a degree of lability, but none retain the breadth of choice they had before. Similarly, specific injuries produced by nonspecific causes are also found in embryonic development: damage to an embryonic optic vesicle results in a defective eye, no matter what sort of chemical produces the injury. It is obvious that the similarity between this case and the critical period for early stimulation can be accounted for by the single common process of growth, occurring relatively late in development in the case of the endocrine stress mechanism and much earlier in the development of the eye. The effects are nonspecific because of the fact that growth can be modified in only very limited ways, by being either slowed down or speeded up.

Both growth and behavioral differentiation are based on organizing processes. This suggests a general principle of organization: that once a system becomes organized, whether it is the cells of the embryo that are multiplying and differentiating or the behavior patterns of a young animal that are becoming organized through learning, it becomes progressively more difficult to reorganize the system. That is, organization inhibits reorganization. Further, organization can be strongly modified only when active processes of organization are going on, and this accounts for critical periods of development.

CONCLUSION

The concept of critical periods is a highly important one for human and animal welfare. Once the dangers and potential benefits for each period of life are known, it should be possible to avoid the former and take advantage of the latter.

The discovery of critical periods immediately focuses attention on the developmental processes which cause them. As these processes become understood, it is increasingly possible to deliberately modify critical periods and their results. For example, since the development of fear responses limits the period of primary social-ization, we can deliberately extend the period by reducing fear reactions, either by psychological methods or by the use of tranquilizing drugs. Or, if it seems desirable, we can increase the degree of dependency of a child or pet animal by purposely in-creasing his emotional reactions during the critical period. Again, if infantile stimu-lation is desirable, parents can be taught to provide it in appropriate amounts at the proper time.

Some data suggest that for each behavioral and physiological phenomenon there is a different critical period in development. If this were literally true, the process of development, complicated by individual variability, would be so complex that the concept of critical periods would serve little useful purpose. Some sort of order can be obtained by dealing with different classes of behavioral phenomena. For example, it can be stated that the period in life in which each new social relationship is initiated is a critical one for the determination of that relationship. Furthermore, there is evidence that critical-period effects are more common early in life than they are later on, and that the critical period for primary socialization is also critical for other effects, such as the attachment to particular places,[87] and may overlap with a critical period for the formation of basic food habits.[88]

We may expect to find that the periods in which actual physiological damage through environmental stimulation is possible will turn out to be similarly specific and concentrated in early life.

A great deal of needed information regarding the optimum periods for acquiring motor and intellectual skills is still lacking. These skills are based not merely on age but on the relative rate of maturation of various organs. Any attempt to teach a child or animal at too early a period of development may result in his learning bad habits, or simply in his learning "not to learn," either of which results may greatly handicap him in later life. In the long run, this line of experimental work should lead to greater realization of the capacities possessed by human beings, both through avoid-ance of damaging experiences and through correction of damage from unavoidable accidents.[89]

REFERENCES AND NOTES

1. Scott, J. P. Comp. Psychol. Monogr. 18, 1 (1945).
2. Fielde, A. M. Biol. Bull. 7, 227 (1904).
3. Stockard, C. R. Am. J. Anat. 28, 115 (1921).
4. Child, C. M. Patterns and Problems of Development (Univ. of Chicago Press, Chicago, 1941).
5. Lorenz, K. J. Ornithol. 83, 137, 289 (1935).
6. McGraw, M. B. in Manual of Child Psychology, L. C. Carmichael, Ed. (Wiley, New York, 1946), pp. 332–369.
7. Hess, E. H. in Nebraska Symposium on Motivation (Univ. of Nebraska Press, Lincoln, 1959), pp. 44–77.
8. Moltz, H. Psychol. Bull. 57, 291 (1960); J. L. Gewirtz, in Determinants of Infant Behaviour, B. M. Foss, Ed. (Methuen, London, 1961), pp. 213–299.
9. Scott, J. P. in Social Behavior and Organization in Vertebrates, W. Etkin, Ed. (Univ. of Chicago Press, Chicago, in press).
10. Nice, M. M. Trans. Linnaean Soc. N.Y. 6, 1 (1943).
11. Scott, J. P., and M. V. Marston, J. Genet. Psychol. 77, 25 (1950).

12. Scott, J. P. *Child Develop. Monogr.*, in press.
13. Brodbeck, A. J. *Bull. Ecol. Soc. Am.* **35**, 73 (1954).
14. Stanley, W. C., private communication (1962).
15. Elliot, O., and King, J. A. *Psychol, Repts.* **6**, 391 (1960).
16. Fisher, A. E., thesis, Pennsylvania State Univ. (1955).
17. Elliot O., and Scott, J. P. *J. Genet. Psychol.* **99**, 3 (1961).
18. Scott, J. P., Deshaies, D., Morris, D. D. "Effect of emotional arousal on primary socialization in the dog," address to the New York State Branch of the American Psychiatric Association, 11 Nov. 1961.
19. Harlow, H. *Am. Psychologist* **13**, 673 (1958).
20. Igel, G. J., and Calvin, A. D. *J. Comp. Physiol. Psychol.* **53**, 302 (1960).
21. Harlow, H. F., and Harlow, M. K., personal communication (1962).
22. Fabricius, E. *Acta Zool. Fennica* **68**, 1 (1951).
23. Collias, N. in *Roots of Behavior,* E. L. Bliss, Ed. (Harper, New York, 1962), pp. 264–273.
24. Hess, E. H. *Ann. N.Y. Acad. Sci* **67**, 724 (1957); in *Drugs and Behavior,* L. Uhr and J. G. Miller, Eds. (Wiley, New York, 1960), pp. 268–271.
25. James, H. *Can. J. Psychol.* **13**, 59 (1959).
26. Gray, P. H. *Science* **132**, 1834 (1960).
27. Guiton, P. *Animal Behavior* **9**, 167 (1961).
28. Pitz, G. F., and Ross, R. B. *J. Comp. Physiol. Psychol.* **54**, 602 (1961).
29. Hess, E. H. "Influence of early experience on behavior," paper presented before the American Psychiatric Association, New York State Divisional Meeting, 1961
30. Moltz, H., Rosenblum, L., Halikas, N. *J. Comp. Physiol. Psychol.* **52**, 240 (1959).
31. Gottlieb, G., *ibid.* **54**, 422 (1961).
32. Scott, J. P. *Psychosomat. Med.* **20**, 42 (1958).
33. Caldwell, B. M. *Am. Psychol.* **16**, 377 (1961).
34. Hinde, R. A., Thorpe, W. H., Vince, M. A. *Behaviour* **9**, 214 (1956).
35. Freedman, D. G., King, J. A., Elliot, O. *Science* **133**, 1016 (1961).
36. Harlow, H. F., and Zimmermann, R. R., *ibid.* **130**, 421 (1959).
37. Freedman, D. G. *J. Child Psychol. Psychiat.* **1961**, 242 (1961).
38. Spitz, R. A. *Intern. J. Psychoanalysis* **31**, 138 (1950).
39. Collias, N. E. *Ecology* **37**, 228 (1956).
40. Craig, W. *J. Animal Behavior* **4**, 121 (1914).
41. Fuller, J. L., and Christake, A. *Federation Proc.* **18**, 49 (1959).
42. Fuller, J. L., private communication.
43. Schutz, F., private communication.
44. Warriner, C. C., thesis, Univ. of Oklahoma (1960).
45. Enders, R. K. *Sociometry* **8**, 53–55 (1945).
46. Klopfer, P. H. *Behavioral Aspects of Ecology* (Prentice-Hall, New York, in press).
47. McGraw, M. B. *Growth: a Study of Johnny and Jimmy* (Appleton-Century, New York, 1935).
48. Hebb, D. O. *Am. Psychologist* **2**, 306 (1947).
49. Forgays, D. G., and Forgays, J. W. *J. Comp. Physiol. Psychol.* **45**, 322 (1952).
50. Forgays, D. G. "The importance of experience at specific times in the development of an organism," address before the Eastern Psychological Association (1962).
51. Candland, D. K., and Campbell, B. A., private communication (1962).
52. Bernstein, L. *J. Comp. Physiol. Psychol.* **50**, 162 (1957).
53. Scott, W. E. D. *Science* **14**, 522 (1901).
54. Thorpe, W. H., in *Current Problems in Animal Behaviour.* W. H. Thorpe and O. L. Zangwill, Eds. (Cambridge Univ. Press, Cambridge, 1961).
55. King, J. A., and Gurney, N. L. *J. Comp. Physiol. Psychol.* **47**, 326 (1954).

56. King, J. A. *J. Genet. Psychol.* **90,** 151 (1957).
57. Fuller, J. L. "Proceedings, International Psychiatric Congress, Montreal," in press.
58. Tinbergen, N. *The Study of Instinct* (Oxford Univ. Press, Oxford, 1951).
59. King, J. A. *J. Genet, Psychol.* **88,** 223 (1956).
60. Beach, F. A., *ibid.* **60,** 121 (1942).
61. Valenstein, E. S., Riss, W., Young, W. C. *J. Comp. Physiol. Psychol.* **47,** 162 (1954) .
62. Nissen, H. *Symposium on Sexual Behavior in Mammals, Amherst, Mass.* (1954), pp. 204–227.
63. Money, J., Hampson, J. G., Hampson, J. L. *Arch. Neurol. Psychiat.* **77,** 333 (1957).
64. Harlow, H., in *Determinants of Infant Behaviour,* B. M. Foss, Ed. (Wiley, New York, 1961), pp. 75–97.
65. Fuller, J. L., Easler, C. A., Banks, E. M. *Am. J. Physiol.* **160,** 462 (1950); A. C. Cornwell and J. L. Fuller, *J. Comp. Physiol. Psychol.* **54,** 13 (1961).
66. Harlow, H. F., Harlow, M. K., Rueping, R. R., Mason, W. A. *J. Comp. Physiol. Psychol.* **53,** 113 (1960).
67. Levine, S., Chevalier, J. A., Korchin, S. J. *J. Personality* **24,** 475 (1956).
68. Schaefer, T., thesis, Univ. of Chicago (1957).
69. Levine, S., Alpert, M., Lewis, G. W. *Science* **126,** 1347 (1957).
70. Richter, C. P. *Am. J. Human Genet.* **4,** 273. (1952).
71. Schaefer, T., Jr., Weingarten, F. S., Towne, J. C. *Science* **135,** 41 (1962).
72. Thompson, W. R., and Schaefer, T., in *Functions of Varied Experience,* D. W. Fiske and S. R. Maddi, Eds. (Dorsey, Homewood, Ill., 1961), pp. 81–105.
73. Denenberg, V. H., in *The Behaviour of Domestic Animals,* E. S. E. Hafez, Ed. (Bailliere, Tindall and Cox, London), 109–138.
74. ————, *J. Comp. Physiol. Psychol.,* in press.
75. ———— and Karas, G. G. *Psychol. Repts.* **7,** 313 (1960).
76. Bowlby, J. *Intern. J. Psychoanalysis* **25,** 19, 107 (1944).
77. Heinicke, C. M. *Human Relations* **9,** 105 (1956).
78. Schaffer, H. R. *Brit. J. Med. Psychol.* **31,** 174 (1950).
79. Gray, P. H. *J. Psychol.* **46,** 155 (1958).
80. Kahn, M. W. *J. Genet. Psychol.* **79,** 117 (1951). A. Baron, K. H. Brookshire, R. A. Littman, *J. Comp. Physiol. Psychol.* **50,** 530 (1957)
81. Lindzey, G., Lykken, D. T., Winston, H. D. *J. Abnormal Soc. Psychol.* **61,** 7 (1960).
82. Riesen, A. H., in *Functions of Varied Experience,* D. W. Fiske and S. R. Maddi, Eds. (Dorsey, Homewood, Ill., 1961), pp. 57–80.
83. Thompson, W. R. *Science* **125,** 698 (1957).
84. Hockman, C. H. *J. Comp. Physiol. Psychol.* **54,** 679 (1961); R. Ader and M. L. Belfer, *Psychol. Repts.* **10,** 711 (1962).
85. Keeley, K. *Science* **135,** 44 (1962).
86. Schneirla, T. C., and Rosenblatt, J. S. *Am. J. Orthopsychiat.* **31,** 223 (1960).
87. Thorpe, W. H. *Learning and Instinct in Animals* (Methuen, London, 1956).
88. Hess, E. H., in *Roots of Behavior,* E. L. Bliss, Ed. (Harper, New York, 1962), pp. 254–263.
89. Part of the research described in this article was supported by a Public Health Service research grant (No. M-4481) from the National Institute of Mental Health.

10 | PSYCHONEUROBIOCHEMEDUCATION

David Krech

I am a rat-brain psychologist with a weakness for speculation. Now time was when rat research was a fairly harmless activity, pursued by underpaid, dedicated, well-meaning characters. The world took little note and cared even less about our researches on how rats learned to thread their way through mazes. Oh, occasionally a misguided educator would take us seriously and try to fashion an educational psychology out of our rats-in-a-maze studies. But the classroom teachers—once removed from the school of education—would quickly see through such nonsense, and, forsaking all rats, would turn to the serious and difficult task of teaching children—unencumbered and unaided by our research and theory.

But time no longer is. Our psychology—especially when combined with educational practice and theory—must now be listed among the Powerful and, even perhaps, the Dangerous sciences. I refer specifically to the recent research developments in brain biochemistry and behavior—to some of which research I now turn.

The research I will discuss really concerns itself with the venerable mind-body problem beloved of philosophers and theologians. For brain biochemistry and behavior research seeks to find the *physical* basis for memory. In essence it asks the following question: In what corporal forms do we retain the remembrance of things past? What are the chemical or neurological or anatomical substrates of the evocative ghosts we call "memories"? Over the centuries of thought and decades of scientific research we have gained but very little on this question. Today, however, there is a feeling abroad that we are on the verge of great discoveries. Indeed, some researchers believe that we already know, in the rough, the form the final answer will take to the question I have raised. And it is this: The physical basis of any memory, whatever else it may be, involves either the production of new proteins, the release of differentiated molecules of ribonucleic acids (RNA's) or the induction of higher enzymatic activity levels in the brain. In a word, for every separate memory in the mind we will eventually find a differentiated chemical in the brain—"chemical memory pellets," as it were.

What warrant do we have for such a prophecy? To begin with, we have reason to believe that the storage of memory in the brain is a many-splendored, multi-phased, actively changing affair. That is, any single memory is not merely "deposited" in a completed form in the brain. Rather, it goes through a complex developmental history in the brain in which it changes from a short-term into a long-term memory. And each stage in this consolidation process seems to be dependent upon different although interrelated chemical mechanisms. Let me indicate to you one set

From *California Monthly*, LXXIX, No. 7, June–July 1969, California Alumni Association, Berkeley, California. Reprinted by permission.

(of quite a number which are now available) of speculative hypotheses concerning this developmental transformation of memories.

First we can assume that immediately after every experience, a relatively short-lived reverberatory process is set up within the brain. This process continues for a time after the stimulus disappears and permits us to remember events which occurred moments or minutes ago. But this reverberatory process fairly quickly decays and disappears—and as it does, so does the related memory. However, under certain conditions, the short-term reverberatory process, before it disappears completely from the scene, triggers off a second and quite different series of events in the brain. This second series of events involves the release of new RNA's or the production of new proteins and other macromolecules. And these chemical changes are relatively long-lasting and serve as the physical bases of our long-term memories.

Now it can be supposed that if we increased the robustness or the survival time of the initial reverberatory process we might increase the probability of converting the short-term memory into a long-term memory. There are several ways one could do that. Through the repetition of the same stimulus one could presumably prolong or continually reinstate the reverberatory process and thus, perhaps, make it more effective in inducing permanent chemical changes in the brain. The old-fashioned term for this procedure is "drill" or "practice," and drill and practice are indeed effective techniques for helping the conversion of short-term memories into long-term ones.

But James McGaugh, at the University of California at Irvine, got the bright idea that he could achieve much the same results chemically. His argument—very much simplified—went something like this: A drug which would increase neural and chemical activity within the brain might either increase the vigor of the reverberatory process, or the ease with which the long-term chemical processes would "take-off," and thus facilitate the conversion of short-term memories into long-term ones. Apparently his idea was a sound one, for with the use of chemical compounds like strychnine and metrazol, which are central nervous system stimulants, McGaugh has been eminently successful in raising the intellectual level of hundreds of southern California mice.

In one of his experiments which is most pregnant with social implications and promises and forebodings for the future, McGaugh tested the maze-learning ability of two quite different strains of mice. One of the strains was, by heredity, particularly adept at maze learning; the other, particularly stupid at that task. Some animals from each strain were injected with different doses of metrazol after each daily learning trial to see whether there would be an improvement in their ability to retain what they had learned on that trial—and some were not. The findings pleased everyone—presumably even the mice. With the optimal dosage of metrazol, the chemically treated mice were 40 percent better in remembering their daily lessons than were their untreated brothers. Indeed, under metrazol treatment the hereditarily stupid mice were able to turn in better performances than their hereditarily superior but untreated colleagues. Here we have a "chemical memory pill" which not only improves memory and learning but can serve to make all mice equal whom God—or genetics—hath created unequal. May I suggest that some place in the back of your mind, you might begin to speculate on what it can mean—socially, educationally, politically—if and when we find drugs which will be similarly effective for human beings.

But let me continue with my story. What chemistry can give, it can also take away—as Agranoff and his now notorious goldfish at the University of Michigan have shown. Agranoff argued that if we could prevent the brain from manufacturing the chemicals involved in the long-term memory process, then we would create an animal which might have normal short-term memories, but would be incapable of establishing enduring memories. Agranoff trained his fish to swim from one side of an aquarium to another, whenever a signal light was turned on, in order to avoid an electric shock. Goldfish can learn this task within a 40-minute period, and once it is learned, they remember it over many days. Now Agranoff varied his experiments. Immediately before, and in some experiments immediately after, training, Agranoff injected puromycin or actinomycin-D (two antibiotics which prevent the formation of new proteins or nuclear RNA) into the brains of a new group of goldfish. His findings were most encouraging (to Agranoff, that is, not necessarily to the goldfish). The injected goldfish were not impaired in their *learning* of the shock-avoidance task since, presumably, the short-term reverberatory process which enables a fish to remember its lesson from one trial to another—a matter of a few seconds—does not involve the synthesis of new proteins or nuclear RNA. But when tested a day or two later the fish showed almost no retention for the task they had known so well the day before—indicating that the long-term process *is* dependent upon the synthesis of these compounds in the brain. Here, then, we find not only support for our general theory but we have a suggestion that there exist in antimetabolites whole families of chemical memory preventatives which seem not to interfere with the individual's immediate capacity to obey immediate orders, but which do prevent him from building up a permanent body of experiences, expectations, and skills. Conjure up, if you are of that mind, what evils such weapons can wreak in the hands of the Orwellian authorities of 1984—but I must hurry on to our next set of experiments.

A number of years ago, James McConnell at the University of Michigan threw all the brain researchers into a tizzy by reporting that he had succeeded in teaching planaria—a fairly primitive type of flatworm—to make a simple response to a light signal, that he then ground up his educated flatforms, fed the pieces to untrained fellow worms—and lo and behold, the uneducated flatworms wound up with the *memories* of the worms which they had just eaten, and, without any training, could perform the response of the late-lamented and digested "donor" worms!

But then all hell broke loose when other workers in other laboratories and in other countries reported that they could train a *rat,* make an extract from its brain, inject this extract into an untrained rat, and by so doing cause the recipient rat to acquire the memories of the now-dead donor rat. It is one thing to claim this for the primitive planaria, which, after all, do not have very much in the way of a structurally differentiated and organized brain. It is a very different thing to claim it for the rat, which *is* a serious mammal, with a highly developed brain, not too different in complexity, in differentiation, and in organization from our own.

The dust raised by these reports has not yet settled. Indeed, most scientists are definitely on the side of the nonbelievers—but the work goes on, and we cannot predict the final outcome of these experiments, many of which have given negative results. However, as a result of this work, a number of brain researchers have been moved, over the last two or three years, from the position of stiff-necked disbelief to the position of "well, maybe—I don't believe it, but well, maybe." And this is where *I* stand at the moment—fearless and foursquare proclaiming "well, maybe. . . ." Now, if it should come to pass that McConnell and his fellow believers are right, then we will indeed have made a huge jump forward. For we would then have a most effective behavioral assay method which should enable us to zero in on this marvelous brain-goulash which can transfer information from one brain to another, and isolate and identify in detail all the "memory" proteins, enzymes, RNA's, or other macromolecules. After that—the world of the mind is ours! But that day is not here yet. Let me leave these brave new world experimenters and go on with another question and another set of experiments.

Does the research I have reviewed mean that if and when we will have developed get-smart pills (*a la* McGaugh), or chemical erasures of wrong mental habits (*a la* Agranoff), or specific knowledge pills (*a la* McConnell), we will be able to do without Head Start programs, educational enrichment programs, school supervisors, educational research, and, indeed, without most of our educational paraphernalia? The answer to this question, gentlemen, is a most reassuring "NO." I might even say, "*Au contraire.*" Precisely because of the advances in brain biochemistry, the significance of the educator will be greatly increased—*and just as greatly changed.* Let me tell you why I think so by describing to you the results of some of your own work in the Berkeley laboratories.

Some time ago we set ourselves the following problem: If the laying down of memories involves the synthesis of chemical products in the brain, then one should find that an animal which has lived a life replete with opportunities for learning and memorizing would end with a brain chemically and morphologically different from an animal which has lived out an intellectually impoverished life. For almost two decades, now, E. L. Bennett, Marian Diamond, M. R. Rosenzweig, and I, together with technical assistants, graduate students, and thousands of rats, have labored— and some of us have even sacrificed our lives—to find such evidence. Let me tell you some of what we found.

At weaning time we divide our experimental rats into two groups, half of the rats being placed in an "intellectually enriched" environment, the other half—their brothers—in the deprived environment. While both groups receive identical food and water, their psychological environments differ greatly. The animals in the first group live together in one large cage, are provided with many rat toys (tunnels to explore, ladders to climb, levers to press), and they are assigned to graduate students who are admonished to give these rats loving care and kindness, teach them to run mazes, and in general to provide them with the best and most expensive supervised higher education available to any young rat at the University of California. While these rats are thus being encouraged to store up many and varied memories, their brother rats, in the deprived group, live in isolated, barren cages, devoid of stimulation by either their environmental appurtenances, fellow rats, or graduate students. After about 80 days of this differential treatment, all the animals are sacrificed, their brains dissected out and various chemical and histological analyses performed. The results are convincing. The brain from a rat from the enriched environment—and presumably, therefore, with many more stored memories—has a heavier and thicker cortex, a better blood supply, larger brain cells, more glia cells, and increased activity of two brain enzymes, acetylcholinesterase and cholinesterase, than does the brain from an animal whose life has been less memorable.

We can draw several morals from these experiments. First, the growing animal's psychological environment is of crucial importance for the development of its brain.

By manipulating the environment of the young, one can truly create a "lame brain" —with lighter cortex, shrunken brain cells, fewer glia cells, smaller blood vessels, and lower enzymatic activity levels—or one can create a more robust, a healthier, a more metabolically active brain. If it should turn out that what is true for the rat brain is also true for the human brain, and that by careful manipulation of this or that group's early environment we can develop among them bigger and better brains or smaller and meaner ones, the wondrous promises of a glorious future or the monstrous horrors of a Huxlian brave new world are fairly self-evident.

The second conclusion I draw from our experiments is this: Since the effect of any chemical upon an organ is, in part, a function of the beginning chemical status of that organ, and since—as we have just seen—the chemical and anatomical status of the individual's brain is determined by his educational experience, then the effectiveness of the biochemist's "get smart pill" will depend upon how the educator has prepared the brain in the first instance. Indeed, a review of all the data indicates that manipulating the educational and psychological environment is a more effective way of inducing long-lasting brain changes than direct administration of drugs. Educators probably change brain structure and chemistry to a greater degree than any biochemist in the business. Another way of saying this is: The educator *can potentiate or undo the work of the brain biochemist.*

But there is still more to report, and more lessons to draw. Consider the experimental problem we faced when we tried to create a psychologically enriched environment for our Berkeley rats. We did not really know how, so we threw everything into the environment, including almost the kitchen sink, and called it "a psychologically enriched environment." The cages were kept in brightly lighted, sound-filled rooms; the rats were given playmates to relate to, games to manipulate, maze problems to solve, new areas to explore. They were fondled and tamed and chucked under the chin at the drop of a site-visitor. In other words, we provided our happy rats with almost every kind of stimulation we could think of—or afford. And it seems to have worked. But of course it is quite possible that in our "kitchen-sink design," many of the things we did were not at all necessary—indeed, some may have had an adverse effect. And so we undertook a series of experiments to discover which elements of our environment were effective and which were not. I shall not bore you with the details of the many experiments already run and many more which are now being run in the Berkeley laboratory. Let me list, however, some of the tentative conclusions which one can already make:

First: Sheer exercise or physical activity alone is not at all effective in developing the brain. A physical training director seems not to be an adequate substitute for a teacher.

Second: Varied visual stimulation, or indeed any kind of visual stimulation, is neither necessary nor sufficient to develop the brain, as we were able to demonstrate by using rats blinded at weaning age.

Third: Handling, or taming, or petting is also without effect in developing the growing rat's brain. Love is Not Enough.

Fourth: The presence of a brother rat in our intellectually deprived rat's cage helps him not a whit. *Bruderschaft* is not enough.

Fifth: Teaching the rat to press levers for food—that and only that seems to help somewhat, but only minimally. Not every problem-set will do, either.

The only experience we have thus far found really effective is freedom to roam around in a large object-filled space. From a recent experiment in Diamond's laboratory there are some suggestions that if the young rat is given continuous and varied maze-problems to solve—that and little else—the rat will develop a number of the same brain changes (at least the morphological ones) which we had observed in our randomly "enriched" environment.

It is clear, then, that not *every* experience or variation in stimulation contributes equally to the development of the brain. But of even greater interest is the suggestion in the above data that the most effective way to develop the brain is through what I will call *species-specific enrichment experiences.* Here is what I mean: The ability of a rat to learn its way through tunnels and dark passages, to localize points in a three-dimensional space full of objects to be climbed upon, burrowed under, and crawled through is, we can assume, of particular survival value for the rat as he is now constituted. Presumably, through the selective evolutionary process, the rat has developed a brain which is peculiarly fitted to support and enhance these skills. The "effective rat brain," therefore, is one which is a good "space-brain"—not a lever-pressing brain or an arithmetic-reasoning brain. The effective stimulating environment, correspondingly, would be one which makes *spatial learning* demands on that brain—which "pushes" that particular kind of brain in that particular way. To generalize this hypothesis, I would suggest that *for each species there exists a set of species-specific experiences which are maximally enriching and which are maximally efficient in developing its brain.*

If there be any validity to my hypothesis, then the challenge to the human educator is clear. For the educator, too, you may have noticed, has been using the kitchen-sink approach when he seeks to design a psychologically or educationally enriched environment for the child. Some educators would bombard the child—practically from infancy on—with every kind of stimulus change imaginable. His crib is festooned with jumping beads and dangling colored bits and pieces of wood (all sold very expensively to his affluent parents); he is given squishy, squeaking, squawking toys to play with, to fondle, to be frightened by, to choke on. He is jounced and bounced and picked up and put down. And when he goes to school—he finds the same blooming, buzzing confusion. He is stimulated with play activities, with opportunities for social interaction, with rhythmic movements, with music, with visual displays, with contact sports, with tactual experiences, and with anything and everything which the school system can think of—or afford. But it may be that a "stimulating environment" and an "enriched environment" are not one and the same thing. It is not true that a brain is a brain is a brain. The rat is a rat and he hath a rat's brain; the child is a child and he hath a child's brain—and each, according to my hypothesis, requires its own educational nutrient. What, then, are the species-specific enrichments for the human child?

Of course I do not know the answer to this question, but let me share with you my present enthusiastic guess that in the language arts will you find part of the answer.

I can start with no better text than a quotation from my teacher, Edward Chace Tolman, who was a completely devoted rat psychologist. "Speech," he wrote, ". . . is in any really developed and characteristic sense, the sole prerogative of the human being. . . . It is speech which first and foremost distinguishes man from the great apes." (1932)[1] In my opinion, it is in the study of language, above anything else, that the psychologist will discover the psychology of man, and that the educator will discover how to educate man.

In the first place, and we must be clear about this, human language, with its complex and *abstract structure,* has *nothing* in common with animal communication. Language is probably the clearest instance of a pure species-specific behavior. This is true whether you study language as a neurologist, or as a psychologist. Let us look at some brain research first.

Recently Robinson, at the National Institute of Mental Health (1967), attempted to discover which areas of the monkey's brain controlled its vocalizations.[2] Now the monkey most certainly uses vocalization for communication, but principally for communications with emotional tone such as threat, fear, pain, and pleasure. In Robinson's study 15 unanesthetized animals, with brains exposed by surgery, were used. Some 5,880 different loci or spots in the brain were stimulated by electrodes to see whether such stimulation could bring forth vocalization. The loci explored included neocortical areas as well as areas in the limbic system, that older part of the mammalian brain which is most intimately involved with motivational and emotional responses.

Robinson's results were clear-cut: First, despite his exploration of several hundred different neocortical sites he was unable to raise a single sound from his animals by stimulating their *neocortex.* Second, stimulation of the limbic system brought forth regular, consistent, and identifiable vocalizations.

These results differ sharply from those found with the human brain. While there is some evidence that human cries and exclamations—uttered in moments of excitement—are also controlled by the limbic system, *speech and language clearly depend upon neocortical areas*—areas for which there simply are no analogues in the brain of any other animal. These areas are, of course, the well-known Broca and Wernicke areas in the left hemisphere of the human brain. It seems clear, as Robinson puts it, that "human speech did not develop 'out of' primate vocalization, but arose from *new tissue* [italics my own] which permitted it the necessary detachment from immediate, emotional situations." Man's brain, *and man's brain alone,* is a language-supporting brain.

Corresponding to the neurological picture is the psycholinguist's view of language. Almost every psycholinguist is impressed not only with the unique nature of language itself but with its unique mode of achievement by the child. Whatever value so-called reinforcement or stimulus-response theories of learning may have for describing acquisition of motor skills by people, maze-learning by rats, and bar-pressing by pigeons—these theories are assessed as completely trivial and utterly irrelevant when it comes to understanding that "stunning intellectual achievement" (McNeill, 1966)[3], the acquisition of language by the child. Indeed, in reading the psycholinguist's work one is left with the impression that we will have to develop a species-specific learning theory for this species-specific behavior of language. I must confess that I agree with them. And if we ever achieve an understanding of language development, and if we learn how to push the *human* brain with this *human* experience, then will we indeed be on our way.

I know that other people have proposed other ways with which to enrich the child's education. Some plug for what are referred to as "cognitive" experience or "productive thinking" experiences, etc. Let me hasten to record that I quite agree with them. As a matter of fact, I am not at all certain that I am saying anything other than what my cognitive friends propose. For I hold with McNeill's judgment that ". . . the study of how language is acquired may provide insight into the very basis of mental life." And, I would go on, being human *means* having an effective mental, cognitive life.

It is for these and many, many other reasons that I would urge the educator to turn to the psycholinguist—as well as to Piaget and Crutchfield and Bruner—for his major guides in designing a rational educational enrichment program.

Whether my guess merits this enthusiasm or not will perhaps eventually be determined by research. But here is the challenge and here is the promise for the educator. Drop your kitchen-sink approach, and specify and define for us the species-specific psychologically enriching experiences for the child—and we will be off and running!

Where will we run? Let me speculate out loud. It is perfectly reasonable to suppose that we will be able to find specific biochemical boosters and biochemical inhibitors for different kinds of memories and imagery, or for different kinds of abilities, or for different kinds of personality or temperament traits. With such chemical agents in hand, and with appropriate educational and training procedures, we may use them as supplementary therapy for those failing in this or that trait and thus will we be able to rectify and heal some of the mentally retarded and the senile. Of course we may use these agents for evil—to create docile, intellectually limited, but efficient human beasts of burden without memories beyond the order of the day (remember Agranoff's fish?).

But above all, there will be great changes made in the first and foremost and continuing business of society: the education and training of the young. The development of the mind of the child will come to rest in the knowledge and skills of the biochemist, and pharmacologist, and neurologist, and psychologist, and educator. And there will be a new expert abroad in the land—the psychoneurobiochemeducator. This multi-hybrid expert will have recourse—as I have suggested elsewhere—to protein memory consolidators, antimetabolite memory inhibitors, enzymatic learning stimulants, and many other potions and elixers of the mind from our new psychoneurobiochemopharmacopia.

There is a grievous problem here, however. Experts, whatever else they may be, are notorious order-takers. *Who* will direct our psychoneurobiochemeducator where to work his expertise, and *what* shall we tell him to do? Here we are talking about goals, values, and aims. Shall our expert raise or lower docility, aggressiveness, musical ability, engineering ability, artistic sensitivity, effective intellectual functioning? Shall different ethnic or racial or national or social groups receive different treatments? In past centuries, and even today, this differential group treatment is precisely what our relatively primitive but quite effective medical and educational experts have been ordered by us to carry out. And lo, they have done so! On one side of the town they have created enclaves of the sickly, the weak, the ignorant, the unskilled—in a word, the brutalized social vanquished. On the other side of the town they have created the social victors—the healthy, the strong, the knowledgeable, the skilled. Will we continue to do this in the future with our much more sophisticated and effective psychoneurobiochemeducators? Who, in other words, will control the brain controllers—and to what ends?

I have thought and worried about these questions, and I must confess to you that I cannot avoid a dread feeling of unease about the future.

At the same time I keep whistling the following tune in an attempt to cheer myself up: If there be any validity at all to my speculations this afternoon, they add up to this: The biochemist, neurologist, psychologist, and educator will eventually add to the intellectual stature of man. With this in mind, and clinging to a life-long faith in the virtues of knowledge and the intellect (for certainly, at this stage I can do no less), I find myself believing that man who by taking thought will have added cubits to his intellectual stature, will also acquire the added bit of wisdom and humaneness that will save us all. Let me stop on this note—before I scrutinize this faith and this hope too carefully.

REFERENCES

1. Tolman, Edward Chace. *Purposive Behavior in Animals and Men.* New York: The Century Company, 1932.
2. Robinson, B. W. "Vocalization Evoked from Forebrain in *Macaca Mulatta,*" *Physiology and Behavior,* 1967, No. 2, pp. 345–54.
3. McNeill, D. "The Creation of Language," *Discovery,* 1966, No. 27, pp. 34–38.

---

11 | A THEORY OF HUMAN MOTIVATION

Abraham H. Maslow

INTRODUCTION

In a previous paper[1] various propositions were presented which would have to be included in any theory of human motivation that could lay claim to being definitive. These conclusions may be briefly summarized as follows:

1. The integrated wholeness of the organism must be one of the foundation stones of motivation theory.

2. The hunger drive (or any other physiological drive) was rejected as a centering point or model for a definitive theory of motivation. Any drive that is somatically

A. H. Maslow, "A Theory of Human Motivation," *Psychological Review,* L, 1943, pp. 370–396. Copyright © 1943 by the American Psychological Association and reproduced by permission of the publisher and the author.

based and localizable was shown to be atypical rather than typical in human motivation.

3. Such a theory should stress and center itself upon ultimate or basic goals rather than partial or superficial ones, upon ends rather than means to these ends. Such a stress would imply a more central place for unconscious than for conscious motivations.

4. There are usually available various cultural paths to the same goal. Therefore conscious, specific, local-cultural desires are not as fundamental in motivation theory as the more basic, unconscious goals.

5. Any motivated behavior, either preparatory or consummatory, must be understood to be a channel through which many basic needs may be simultaneously expressed or satisfied. Typically an act has *more* than one motivation.

6. Practically all organismic states are to be understood as motivated and as motivating.

7. Human needs arrange themselves in hierarchies of prepotency. That is to say, the appearance of one need usually rests on the prior satisfaction of another, more prepotent need. Man is a perpetually wanting animal. Also no need or drive can be treated as if it were isolated or discrete; every drive is related to the state of satisfaction or dissatisfaction of other drives.

8. *Lists* of drives will get us nowhere for various theoretical and practical reasons. Furthermore, any classification of motivations must deal with the problem of levels of specificity or generalization of the motives to be classified.

9. Classifications of motivations must be based upon goals rather than upon instigating drives or motivated behavior.

10. Motivation theory should be human-centered rather than animal-centered.

11. The situation or the field in which the organism reacts must be taken into account, but the field alone can rarely serve as an exclusive explanation for behavior. Furthermore, the field itself must be interpreted in terms of the organism. Field theory cannot be a substitute for motivation theory.

12. Not only the integration of the organism must be taken into account, but also the possibility of isolated, specific, partial, or segmental reactions.

It has since become necessary to add to these another affirmation.

13. Motivation theory is not synonymous with behavior theory. The motivations are only one class of determinants of behavior. While behavior is almost always motivated, it is also almost always biologically, culturally, and situationally determined as well.

The present paper is an attempt to formulate a positive theory of motivation which will satisfy these theoretical demands and at the same time conform to the known facts, clinical and observational, as well as experimental. It derives most directly, however, from clinical experience. This theory is, I think, in the functionalist tradition of James and Dewey, and is fused with the holism of Wertheimer,[2] Goldstein,[3] and Gestalt Psychology, and with the dynamicism of Freud[4] and Adler.[5] This fusion or synthesis may arbitrarily be called a "general-dynamic" theory.

It is far easier to perceive and to criticize the aspects in motivation theory than to remedy them. Mostly this is because of the very serious lack of sound data in this area. I conceive this lack of sound facts to be due primarily to the absence of a valid theory of motivation. The present theory then must be considered to be a suggested program or framework for future research and must stand or fall, not so much on facts available or evidence presented, as upon researches yet to be done, researches suggested perhaps by the questions raised in this paper.

THE BASIC NEEDS

THE "PHYSIOLOGICAL" NEEDS

The needs that are usually taken as the starting point for motivation theory are the so-called physiological drives. Two recent lines of research make it necessary to revise our customary notions about these needs, first, the development of the concept of homeostasis, and second, the finding that appetites (preferential choices among foods) are a fairly efficient indication of actual needs or lacks in the body.

Homeostasis refers to the body's automatic efforts to maintain a constant normal state of the blood stream. Cannon[6] has described this process for (1) the water content of the blood, (2) salt content, (3) sugar content, (4) protein content, (5) fat content, (6) calcium content, (7) oxygen content, (8) constant hydrogen-ion level (acid-base balance), and (9) constant temperature of the blood. Obviously this list can be extended to include other minerals, the hormones, vitamins, etc.

Young in a recent article[7] has summarized the work on appetite in its relation to body needs. If the body lacks some chemical the individual will tend to develop a specific appetite or partial hunger for that food element.

Thus, it seems impossible as well as useless to make any list of fundamental physiological needs for they can come to almost any number one might wish, depending on the degree of specificity of description. We can not identify all physiological needs as homeostatic. That sexual desire, sleepiness, sheer activity, and maternal behavior in animals, are homeostatic, has not yet been demonstrated. Furthermore, this list would not include the various sensory pleasures (tastes, smells, tickling, stroking) which are probably physiological and which may become the goals of motivated behavior.

In a previous paper[1] it has been pointed out that these physiological drives or needs are to be considered unusual rather than typical because they are isolable, and because they are localizable somatically. That is to say, they are relatively independent of each other, of other motivations, and of the organism as a whole, and secondly, in many cases, it is possible to demonstrate a localized, underlying somatic base for the drive. This is true less generally than has been thought (exceptions are fatigue, sleepiness, maternal responses) but it is still true in the classic instances of hunger, sex, and thirst.

It should be pointed out again that any of the physiological needs and the consummatory behavior involved with them serve as channels for all sorts of other needs as well. That is to say, the person who thinks he is hungry may actually be seeking more for comfort, or dependence, than for vitamins or proteins. Conversely, it is possible to satisfy the hunger need in part by other activities such as drinking water or smoking cigarettes. In other words, relatively isolable as these physiological needs are, they are not completely so.

Undoubtedly these physiological needs are the most prepotent of all needs. What this means specifically is, that in the human being who is missing everything in life in an extreme fashion, it is most likely that the major motivation would be the physiological needs rather than any others. A person who is lacking food, safety, love, and esteem would most probably hunger for food more strongly than for anything else.

If all the needs are unsatisfied, and the organism is then dominated by the physiological needs, all other needs may become simply nonexistent or be pushed into the background. It is then fair to characterize the whole organism by saying simply that it is hungry, for consciousness is almost completely preempted by hunger. All capacities are put into the service of hunger-satisfaction, and the organization of these capacities is almost entirely determined by the one purpose of satisfying hunger. The receptors and effectors, the intelligence, memory, habits, all may now be defined simply as hunger-gratifying tools. Capacities that are not useful for this purpose lie dormant or are pushed into the background. The urge to write poetry, the desire to acquire an automobile, the interest in American history, the desire for a new pair of shoes are, in the extreme case, forgotten or become of secondary importance. For the man who is extremely and dangerously hungry, no other interests exist but food. He dreams food, he remembers food, he thinks about food, he emotes only about food, he perceives only food and he wants only food. The more subtle determinants that ordinarily fuse with the physiological drives in organizing even feeding, drinking, or sexual behavior, may now be so completely overwhelmed as to allow us to speak at this time (but *only* at this time) of pure hunger drive and behavior, with the one unqualified aim of relief.

Another peculiar characteristic of the human organism when it is dominated by a certain need is that the whole philosophy of the future tends also to change. For our chronically and extremely hungry man, Utopia can be defined very simply as a place where there is plenty of food. He tends to think that, if only he is guaranteed food for the rest of his life, he will be perfectly happy and will never want anything more. Life itself tends to be defined in terms of eating. Anything else will be defined as unimportant. Freedom, love, community feeling, respect, philosophy, may all be waved aside as fripperies which are useless since they fail to fill the stomach. Such a man may fairly be said to live by bread alone.

It cannot possibly be denied that such things are true but their *generality* can be denied. Emergency conditions are, almost by definition, rare in the normally functioning peaceful society. That this truism can be forgotten is due mainly to two reasons. First, rats have few motivations other than physiological ones, and since so much of the research upon motivation has been made with these animals, it is easy to carry the rat picture over to the human being. Secondly, it is too often not realized that culture itself is an adaptive tool, one of whose main functions is to make the physiological emergencies come less and less often. In most of the known societies, chronic extreme hunger of the emergency type is rare, rather than common. In any case, this is still true in the United States. The average American citizen is experiencing appetite rather than hunger when he says, "I am hungry." He is apt to experience sheer life-and-death hunger only by accident and then only a few times through his entire life.

Obviously a good way to obscure the "higher" motivations, and to get a lopsided view of human capacities and human nature, is to make the organism extremely and chronically hungry or thirsty. Anyone who attempts to make an emergency picture into a typical one, and who will measure all of man's goals and desires by his behavior during extreme physiological deprivation is certainly being blind to many things. It is quite true that man lives by bread alone—when there is no bread. But what happens to man's desires when there *is* plenty of bread and when his belly is chronically filled?

At once other (and "higher") needs emerge and these, rather than physiological hungers, dominate the organism. And when these in turn are satisfied, again new (and still "higher") needs emerge and so on. This is what we mean by saying that the basic human needs are organized into a hierarchy of relative prepotency.

One main implication of this phrasing is that gratification becomes as important a concept as deprivation in motivation theory, for it releases the organism from the domination of a relatively more physiological need, permitting thereby the emergence of other more social goals. The physiological needs, along with their partial goals, when chronically gratified cease to exist as active determinants or organizers of behavior. They now exist only in a potential fashion in the sense that they may emerge again to dominate the organism if they are thwarted. But a want that is satisfied is no longer a want. The organism is dominated and its behavior organized only by unsatisfied needs. If hunger is satisfied, it becomes unimportant in the current dynamics of the individual.

This statement is somewhat qualified by a hypothesis to be discussed more fully later, namely, that it is precisely those individuals in whom a certain need has always been satisfied who are best equipped to tolerate deprivation of that need in the future, and that, furthermore, those who have been deprived in the past will react differently to current satisfactions than the one who has never been deprived.

THE SAFETY NEEDS

If the physiological needs are relatively well gratified, there then emerges a new set of needs, which we may categorize roughly as the safety needs. All that has been said of the physiological needs is equally true, although in lesser degree, of these desires. The organism may equally well be wholly dominated by them. They may serve as the almost exclusive organizers of behavior, recruiting all the capacities of the organism in their service, and we may then fairly describe the whole organism as a safety-seeking mechanism. Again we may say of the receptors, the effectors, of the intellect, and the other capacities that they are primarily safety-seeking tools. Again, as in the hungry man, we find that the dominating goal is a strong determinant not only of his current world outlook and philosophy but also of his philosophy of the future. Practically everything looks less important than safety (even sometimes the physiological needs which, being satisfied, are now underestimated). A man in this state, if it is extreme enough and chronic enough, may be characterized as living almost for safety alone.

Although in this paper we are interested primarily in the needs of the adult, we can approach an understanding of his safety needs perhaps more efficiently by observation of infants and children in whom these needs are much more simple and obvious. One reason for the clearer appearance of the threat or danger reaction in infants is that they do not, inhibit this reaction at all, whereas adults in our society have been taught to inhibit it at all costs. Thus even when adults do feel their safety to be threatened, we may not be able to see this on the surface. Infants will react in a total fashion and as if they were endangered, if they are disturbed or dropped suddenly, startled by loud noises, flashing light, or other unusual sensory stimulation, by rough handling, by general loss of support in the mother's arms, or by inadequate support.[8]

In infants we can also see a much more direct reaction to bodily illnesses of various kinds. Sometimes these illnesses seem to be immediately and *per se* threatening and seem to make the child feel unsafe. For instance, vomiting, colic, or other sharp pains seem to make the child look at the whole world in a different way. At such a moment of pain, it may be postulated that for the child the appearance of the whole world suddenly changes from sunniness to darkness, so to speak, and becomes a place in which anything at all might happen and in which previously stable things have suddenly become unstable. Thus a child who because of some bad food is taken ill may, for a day or two, develop fear, nightmares, and a need for protection and reassurance never seen in him before his illness.

Another indication of the child's need for safety is his preference for some kind of undisrupted routine or rhythm. He seems to want a predictable, orderly world. For instance, injustice, unfairness, or inconsistency in the parents seems to make a child feel anxious and unsafe. This attitude may be not so much because of the injustice *per se* or any particular pains involved, but rather because this treatment threatens to make the world look unreliable, or unsafe, or unpredictable. Young children seem to thrive better under a system which has at least a skeletal outline of rigidity, in which there is a schedule of a kind, some sort of routine, something that can be counted upon, not only for the present but also far into the future. Perhaps one could express this more accurately by saying that the child needs an organized world rather than an unorganized or unstructured one.

The central role of the parents and the normal family setup are indisputable. Quarreling, physical assault, separation, divorce, or death within the family may be particularly terrifying. Also parental outbursts of rage or threats of punishment directed to the child, calling him names, speaking to him harshly, shaking him, handling him roughly, or actual physical punishment sometimes elicit such total panic and terror in the child that we must assume more is involved than the physical pain alone. While it is true that in some children this terror may represent also a fear of loss of parental love, it can also occur in completely rejected children who seem to cling to the hating parents more for sheer safety and protection than because of hope of love.

Confronting the average child with new, unfamiliar, strange, unmanageable stimuli or situations will too frequently elicit the danger or terror reaction, as, for example, getting lost or even being separated from the parents for a short time, being confronted with new faces, new situations or new tasks, the sight of strange, unfamiliar, or uncontrollable objects, illness, or death. Particularly at such times, the child's frantic clinging to his parents is eloquent testimony to their role as protectors (quite apart from their roles as food-givers and love-givers).

From these and similar observations, we may generalize and say that the average child in our society generally prefers a safe, orderly, predictable, organized world which he can count on, in which unexpected, unmanageable, or other dangerous things do not happen, and in which, in any case, he has all-powerful parents who protect and shield him from harm.

That these reactions may so easily be observed in children is in a way a proof of the fact that children in our society feel too unsafe (or, in a word, are badly brought up). Children who are reared in an unthreatening, loving family do *not* ordinarily react as we have described above.[9] In such children the danger reactions are apt to come mostly to objects or situations that adults too would consider dangerous.[10]

The healthy, normal, fortunate adult in our culture is largely satisfied in his safety needs. The peaceful, smoothly running, "good" society ordinarily makes its members feel safe enough from wild animals, extremes of temperature, criminals, assault and murder, tyranny, etc. Therefore, in a very real sense, he no longer has any safety needs as active motivators. Just as a sated man no longer feels hungry, a safe man no longer feels endangered. If we wish to see these needs directly and clearly we must turn to neurotic or near-neurotic individuals, and to the economic and social underdogs. In between these extremes, we can perceive the expressions of safety needs only in such phenomena as, for instance, the common preference for a job with tenure and protection, the desire for a savings account, and for insurance of various kinds (medical, dental, unemployment, disability, old age).

Other broader aspects of the attempt to seek safety and stability in the world are seen in the very common preference for familiar rather than unfamiliar things, or for the known rather than the unknown. The tendency to have some religion or world philosophy that organizes the universe and the men in it into some sort of satisfactorily coherent, meaningful whole is also in part motivated by safety-seeking. Here too we may list science and philosophy in general as partially motivated by the safety needs (we shall see later that there are also other motivations to scientific, philosophical, or religious endeavor).

Otherwise the need for safety is seen as an active and dominant mobilizer of the organism's resources only in emergencies, *e.g.*, war, disease, natural catastrophes, crime waves, societal disorganization, neurosis, brain injury, chronically bad situations.

Some neurotic adults in our society are, in many ways, like the unsafe child in their desire for safety, although in the former it takes on a somewhat special appearance. Their reaction is often to unknown psychological dangers in a world that is perceived to be hostile, overwhelming, and threatening. Such a person behaves as if a great catastrophe were almost always impending, *i.e.*, he is usually responding as if to an emergency. His safety needs often find specific expression in a search for a protector, or a stronger person on whom he may depend, or perhaps, a Fuehrer.

The neurotic individual may be described in a slightly different way with some usefulness as a grown-up person who retains his childish attitudes toward the world. That is to say, a neurotic adult may be said to behave "as if" he were actually afraid of a spanking, or of his mother's disapproval, or of being abandoned by his parents, or having his food taken away from him. It is as if his childish attitudes of fear and threat reaction to a dangerous world had gone underground, and untouched by the growing up and learning processes, were now ready to be called out by any stimulus that would make a child feel endangered and threatened.[11]

The neurosis in which the search for safety takes its clearest form is in the compulsive obsessive neurosis. Compulsive-obsessives try frantically to order and stabilize the world so that no unmanageable, unexpected, or unfamiliar dangers will ever appear.[12] They hedge themselves about with all sorts of ceremonials, rules, and formulas so that every possible contingency may be provided for and so that no new contingencies may appear. They are much like the brain-injured cases, described by Goldstein,[3] who manage to maintain their equilibrium by avoiding everything unfamiliar and strange and by ordering their restricted world in such a neat, disciplined, orderly fashion that everything in the world can be counted upon. They try to arrange the world so that anything unexpected (dangers) cannot possibly occur. If, through no fault of their own, something unexpected does occur, they go into a panic reaction as if this unexpected occurrence constituted a grave danger. What we can see only as a none-too-strong preference in the healthy person, e.g., preference for the familiar, becomes a life-and-death necessity in abnormal cases.

THE LOVE NEEDS

If both the physiological and the safety needs are fairly well gratified, then there will emerge the love and affection and belongingness needs, and the whole cycle already described will repeat itself with this new center. Now the person will feel keenly, as never before, the absence of friends, or a sweetheart, or a wife, or children. He will hunger for affectionate relations with people in general, namely, for a place in his group, and he will strive with great intensity to achieve this goal. He will want to attain such a place more than anything else in the world and may even forget that once, when he was hungry, he sneered at love.

In our society the thwarting of these needs is the most commonly found core in cases of maladjustment and more severe psychopathology. Love and affection, as well as their possible expression in sexuality, are generally looked upon with ambivalence and are customarily hedged about with many restrictions and inhibitions. Practically all theorists of psychopathology have stressed thwarting of the love needs as basic in the picture of maladjustment. Many clinical studies have, therefore, been made of this need, and we know more about it perhaps than any of the other needs except the physiological ones.[12]

One thing that must be stressed at this point is that love is not synonymous with sex. Sex may be studied as a purely physiological need. Ordinarily sexual behavior is multi-determined, that is to say, determined not only by sexual but also by other needs, chief among which are the love and affection needs. Also not to be overlooked is the fact that the love needs involve both giving *and* receiving love.[13]

THE ESTEEM NEEDS

All people in our society (with a few pathological exceptions) have a need or desire for a stable, firmly based, (usually) high evaluation of themselves, for self-respect, or self-esteem, and for the esteem of others. By firmly based self-esteem, we mean that which is soundly based upon real capacity, achievement, and respect from others. These needs may be classified into two subsidiary sets. These are, first, the desire for strength, for achievement, for adequacy, for confidence in the face of the world, and for independence and freedom.[14] Secondly, we have what we may call the desire for reputation or prestige (defining it as respect or esteem from other people), recognition, attention, importance, or appreciation.[15] These needs have been relatively stressed by Alfred Adler and his followers and have been relatively neglected by Freud and the psychoanalysts. More and more today, however, there is appearing widespread appreciation of their central importance.

Satisfaction of the self-esteem need leads to feelings of self-confidence, worth, strength, capability, and adequacy of being useful and necessary in the world. But thwarting of these needs produces feelings of inferiority, of weakness, and of helplessness. These feelings in turn give rise to either basic discouragement or else compensatory or neurotic trends. An appreciation of the necessity of basic self-confidence and an understanding of how helpless people are without it can be easily gained from a study of severe traumatic neurosis.[16, 17]

THE NEED FOR SELF-ACTUALIZATION

Even if all these needs are satisfied, we may still often (if not always) expect that a new discontent and restlessness will soon develop, unless the individual is doing what he is fitted for. A musician must make music, an artist must paint, a poet must write, if he is to be ultimately happy. What a man *can* be, he *must* be. This need we may call self-actualization.

This term, first coined by Kurt Goldstein, is being used in this paper in a much more specific and limited fashion. It refers to the desire for self-fulfillment, namely, to the tendency for him to become actualized in what he is potentially. This tendency might be phrased as the desire to become more and more what one is, to become everything that one is capable of becoming.

The specific form that these needs will take will, of course, vary greatly from person to person. In one individual it may take the form of the desire to be an ideal mother, in another it may be expressed athletically, and in still another it may be expressed in painting pictures or in inventions. It is not necessarily a creative urge, although in people who have any capacities for creation, it will take this form.

The clear emergence of these needs rests upon prior satisfaction of the physiological, safety, love, and esteem needs. We shall call people who are satisfied in these needs, basically satisfied people, and it is from these that we may expect the fullest (and healthiest) creativeness.[18] Since in our society basically satisfied people are the exception, we do not know much about self-actualization, either experimentally or clinically. It remains a challenging problem for research.

THE PRECONDITIONS FOR THE BASIC NEED SATISFACTIONS

There are certain conditions which are immediate prerequisites for the basic need satisfactions. Danger to these is reacted to almost as if it were a direct danger to the basic needs themselves. Such conditions as freedom to speak, freedom to do what one wishes so long as no harm is done to others, freedom to express one's self, freedom to investigate and seek for information, freedom to defend one's self, justice, fairness, honesty, orderliness in the group are examples of such preconditions for basic need satisfactions. Thwarting in these freedoms will be reacted to with a threat or emergency response. These conditions are not ends in themselves but they are *almost* so, since they are so closely related to the basic needs which are apparently the only ends in themselves. These conditions are defended, because without them the basic satisfactions are quite impossible, or at least, very severely endangered.

If we remember that the cognitive capacities (perceptual, intellectual, learning) are a set of adjustive tools which have among other functions the satisfaction of our basic needs, then it is clear that any danger to them, any deprivation or blocking of their free use, must also be indirectly threatening to the basic needs themselves. Such a statement is a partial solution of the general problems of curiosity, the search for knowledge, truth, and wisdom, and the ever-persistent urge to solve the cosmic mysteries.

We must therefore introduce another hypothesis and speak of degrees of closeness to the basic needs, for we have already pointed out that *any* conscious desires (partial goals) are more or less important as they are more or less close to the basic needs. The same statement may be made for various behavior acts. An act is psychologically important if it contributes directly to satisfaction of basic needs. The less directly it so contributes, or the weaker this contribution is, the less important this act must be conceived to be from the point of view of dynamic psychology. A similar statement may be made for the various defense or coping mechanisms. Some are very directly related to the protection or attainment of the basic needs, others are only weakly and distantly related. Indeed if we wished, we could speak of more basic and less basic defense mechanisms, and then affirm that danger to the more basic defenses is more threatening than danger to less basic defenses (always remembering that this is so only because of their relationship to the basic needs).

THE DESIRES TO KNOW AND TO UNDERSTAND

So far, we have mentioned the cognitive needs only in passing. Acquiring knowledge and systematizing the universe have been considered as, in part, techniques for the achievement of basic safety in the world, or, for the intelligent man, expressions of self-actualization. Also freedom of inquiry and expression have been discussed as preconditions of satisfactions of the basic needs. True though these formulations may be, they do not constitute definitive answers to the question as to the motivation role of curiosity, learning, philosophizing, experimenting, etc. They are, at best, no more than partial answers.

This question is especially difficult because we know so little about the facts. Curiosity, exploration, desire for the facts, desire to know may certainly be observed easily enough. The fact that they often are pursued even at great cost to the individual's safety is an earnest of the partial character of our previous discussion. In addition, the writer must admit that, though he has sufficient clinical evidence to postulate the desire to know as a very strong drive in intelligent people, no data are available for unintelligent people. It may then be largely a function of relatively high intelligence. Rather tentatively then, and largely in the hope of stimulating discussion and research, we shall postulate a basic desire to know, to be aware of reality, to get the facts, to satisfy curiosity, or as Wertheimer phrases it, to see rather than to be blind.

This postulation, however, is not enough. Even after we know, we are impelled to know more and more minutely and microscopically on the one hand, and on the other, more and more extensively in the direction of a world philosophy, religion, etc. The facts that we acquire, if they are isolated or atomistic, inevitably get theorized about, and either analyzed or organized or both. This process has been phrased by some as the search for "meaning." We shall then postulate a desire to understand, to systematize, to organize, to analyze, to look for relations and meanings.

Once these desires are accepted for discussion, we see that they too form themselves into a small hierarchy in which the desire to know is prepotent over the desire to understand. All the characteristics of a hierarchy of prepotency that we have described above, seem to hold for this one as well.

We must guard ourselves against the too easy tendency to separate these desires from the basic needs we have discussed above, *i.e.*, to make a sharp dichotomy between "cognitive" and "conative" needs. The desire to know and to understand are themselves conative, *i.e.*, have a striving character, and are as much personality needs as the "basic needs" we have already discussed.[2]

FURTHER CHARACTERISTICS OF THE BASIC NEEDS

THE DEGREE OF FIXITY OF THE HIERARCHY OF BASIC NEEDS

We have spoken so far as if this hierarchy were a fixed order, but actually it is not nearly as rigid as we may have implied. It is true that most of the people with whom we have worked have seemed to have these basic needs in about the order that has been indicated. However, there have been a number of exceptions.

1. There are some people in whom, for instance, self-esteem seems to be more important than love. This most common reversal in the hierarchy is usually due to the development of the notion that the person who is most likely to be loved is a strong or powerful person, one who inspires respect or fear, and who is self-confident or aggressive. Therefore such people who lack love and seek it, may try hard to put on a front of aggressive, confident behavior. But essentially they seek high self-esteem and its behavior expressions more as a means to an end than for its own sake; they seek self-assertion for the sake of love rather than for self-esteem itself.

2. There are other apparently innately creative people in whom the drive to creativeness seems to be more important than any other counter determinant. Their creativeness might appear not as self-actualization released by basic satisfaction, but in spite of lack of basic satisfaction.

3. In certain people the level of aspiration may be permanently deadened or lowered. That is to say, the less prepotent goals may simply be lost and may disappear forever, so that the person who has experienced life at a very low level, *i.e.*, chronic unemployment, may continue to be satisfied for the rest of his life if only he can get enough food.

4. The so-called "psychopathic personality" is another example of permanent loss of the love needs. These are people who, according to the best data available,[19] have been starved for love in the earliest months of their lives and have simply lost forever the desire and the ability to give and to receive affection (as animals lose sucking or pecking reflexes that are not exercised soon enough after birth).

5. Another cause of reversal of the hierarchy is that when a need has been satisfied for a long time, this need may be underevaluated. People who have never experienced chronic hunger are apt to underestimate its effects and to look upon food as a rather unimportant thing. If they are dominated by a higher need, this higher

need will seem to be the most important of all. It then becomes possible, and indeed does actually happen, that they may, for the sake of this higher need, put themselves into the position of being deprived in a more basic need. We may expect that after a long-time deprivation of the more basic need there will be a tendency to reevaluate both needs so that the more prepotent need will actually become consciously prepotent for the individual who may have given it up very lightly. Thus, a man who has given up his job rather than lose his self-respect, and who then starves for six months or so, may be willing to take his job back even at the price of losing his self-respect.

6. Another partial explanation of *apparent* reversals is seen in the fact that we have been talking about the hierarchy of prepotency in terms of consciously felt wants or desires rather than of behavior. Looking at behavior itself may give us the wrong impression. What we have claimed is that the person will *want* the more basic of two needs when deprived in both. There is no necessary implication here that he will act upon his desires. Let us say again that there are many determinants of behavior other than the needs and desires.

7. Perhaps more important than all these exceptions are the ones that involve ideals, high social standards, high values, and the like. With such values people become martyrs; they will give up everything for the sake of a particular ideal or value. These people may be understood, at least in part, by reference to one basic concept (or hypothesis) which may be called "increased frustration-tolerance through early gratification." People who have been satisfied in their basic needs throughout their lives, particularly in their earlier years, seem to develop exceptional power to withstand present or future thwarting of these needs simply because they have strong, healthy character structure as a result of basic satisfaction. They are the "strong" people who can easily weather disagreement or opposition, who can swim against the stream of public opinion and who can stand up for the truth at great personal cost. It is just the ones who have loved and been well loved, and who have had many deep friendships who can hold out against hatred, rejection, or persecution.

I say all this in spite of the fact that there is a certain amount of sheer habituation which is also involved in any full discussion of frustration tolerance. For instance, it is likely that those persons who have been accustomed to relative starvation for a long time are partially enabled thereby to withstand food deprivation. What sort of balance must be made between these two tendencies, of habituation on the one hand, and of past satisfaction breeding present frustration tolerance on the other hand, remains to be worked out by further research. Meanwhile we may assume that they are both operative, side by side, since they do not contradict each other. In respect to this phenomenon of increased frustration tolerance, it seems probable that the most important gratifications come in the first two years of life. That is to say, people who have been made secure and strong in the earliest years tend to remain secure and strong thereafter in the face of whatever threatens.

DEGREES OF RELATIVE SATISFACTION

So far, our theoretical discussion may have given the impression that these five sets of needs are somehow in step-wise, all-or-none relationships to each other. We have spoken in such terms as the following: "If one need is satisfied, then another emerges." This statement might give the false impression that a need must be satisfied 100 per cent before the next need emerges. In actual fact, most members of our society who are normal are partially satisfied in all their basic needs and partially unsatisfied in all their basic needs at the same time. A more realistic description of the hierarchy would be in terms of decreasing percentages of satisfaction as we go up the hierarchy of prepotency. For instance, if I may assign arbitrary figures for the sake of illustration, it is as if the average citizen is satisfied perhaps 85 per cent in his physiological needs, 70 per cent in his safety needs, 50 per cent in his love needs, 40 per cent in his self-esteem needs, and 10 per cent in his self-actualization needs.

As for the concept of emergence of a new need after satisfaction of the prepotent need, this emergence is not a sudden, saltatory phenomenon but rather a gradual emergence by slow degrees from nothingness. For instance, if prepotent need A is satisfied only 10 per cent, then need B may not be visible at all. However, as this need A becomes satisfied 25 per cent, need B may emerge 5 per cent, as need A becomes satisfied 75 per cent, need B may emerge 90 per cent, and so on.

UNCONSCIOUS CHARACTER OF NEEDS

These needs are neither necessarily conscious nor unconscious. On the whole, however, in the average person, they are more often unconscious rather than conscious. It is not necessary at this point to overhaul the tremendous mass of evidence which indicates the crucial importance of unconscious motivation. It would by now be expected, on *a priori* grounds alone, that unconscious motivations would on the whole be rather more important than the conscious motivations. What we have called the basic needs are very often largely unconscious although they may, with suitable techniques and with sophisticated people, become conscious.

CULTURAL SPECIFICITY AND GENERALITY OF NEEDS

This classification of basic needs makes some attempt to take account of the relative unity behind the superficial differences in specific desires from one culture to another. Certainly in any particular culture an individual's conscious motivational content will usually be extremely different from the conscious motivational content of an individual in another society. However, it is the common experience of anthropologists that people, even in different societies, are much more alike than we would think from our first contact with them, and that as we know them better we seem to find more and more of this commonness. We then recognize the most startling differences to be superficial rather than basic, *e.g.*, differences in style of hairdress, clothes, tastes in food, etc. Our classification of basic needs is in part an attempt to account for this unity behind the apparent diversity from culture to culture. No claim is made that it is ultimate or universal for all cultures. The claim is made only that it is relatively *more* ultimate, more universal, more basic, than the superficial conscious desires from culture to culture, and makes a somewhat closer approach to common-human characteristics. Basic needs are *more* common-human than superficial desires or behaviors.

MULTIPLE MOTIVATIONS OF BEHAVIOR

These needs must be understood *not* to be *exclusive* or single determiners of certain kinds of behavior. An example may be found in any behavior that seems to be physiologically motivated, such as eating, or sexual play, or the like. The clinical psychologists have long since found that any behavior may be a channel through which flow various determinants. Or to say it in another way, most behavior is multi-motivated. Within the sphere of motivational determinants any behavior tends to be determined by several or *all* of the basic needs simultaneously rather than by only one of them. The latter would be more an exception than the former. Eating may be partially for the sake of filling the stomach, and partially for the sake of comfort and amelioration of other needs. One may make love not only for pure sexual release, but also to convince one's self of one's masculinity, or to make a conquest, to feel powerful, or to win more basic affection. As an illustration, I may point out that it would be possible (theoretically if not practically) to analyze a single act of an individual and see in it the expression of his physiological needs, his safety needs, his love needs, his esteem needs and self-actualization. This contrasts sharply with the more naïve brand of trait psychology in which one trait or one motive accounts for a certain kind of act, *i.e.*, an aggressive act is traced solely to a trait of aggressiveness.

MULTIPLE DETERMINANTS OF BEHAVIOR

Not all behavior is determined by the basic needs. We might even say that not all behavior is motivated. There are many determinants of behavior other than motives.[20] For instance, one other important class of determinants is the so-called "field" determinants. Theoretically, at least, behavior may be determined completely by the field, or even by specific isolated external stimuli, as in association of ideas, or certain conditioned reflexes. If in response to the stimulus word "table," I immediately perceive a memory image of a table, this response certainly has nothing to do with my basic needs.

Secondly, we may call attention again to the concept of "degree of closeness to the basic needs" or "degree of motivation." Some behavior is highly motivated; other behavior is only weakly motivated. Some is not motivated at all (but all behavior is determined).

Another important point[21] is that there is a basic difference between expressive behavior and coping behavior (functional striving, purposive goal seeking). An expressive behavior does not try to do anything; it is simply a reflection of the personality. A stupid man behaves stupidly, not because he wants to, or tries to, or is motivated to, but simply because he *is* what he is. The same is true when I speak in a bass voice rather than tenor or soprano. The random movements of a healthy child, the smile on the face of a happy man even when he is alone, the springiness of the healthy man's walk, and the erectness of his carriage are other examples of expressive, non-functional behavior. Also the *style* in which a man carries out almost all his behavior, motivated as well as unmotivated, is often expressive.

We may then ask, is *all* behavior expressive or reflective of the character structure? The answer is "No." Rote, habitual, automatized, or conventional behavior may or may not be expressive. The same is true for most "stimulus-bound" behaviors.

It is finally necessary to stress that expressiveness of behavior and goal-directed-ness of behavior are not mutually exclusive categories. Average behavior is usually both.

GOALS AS CENTERING PRINCIPLE IN MOTIVATION THEORY

It will be observed that the basic principle in our classification has been neither the instigation nor the motivated behavior, but rather the functions, effects, purposes, or goals of the behavior. It has been proven sufficiently by various people that this is the most suitable point for centering in any motivation theory.[22]

ANIMAL- AND HUMAN-CENTERING

This theory starts with the human being rather than any lower and presumably "simpler" animal. Too many of the findings that have been made in animals have been proven to be true for animals but not for the human being. There is no reason whatsoever why we should start with animals in order to study human motivation. The logic or rather illogic behind this general fallacy of "pseudo-simplicity" has been exposed often enough by philosophers and logicians as well as by scientists in each of the various fields. It is no more necessary to study animals before one can study man than it is to study mathematics before one can study geology or psychology or biology.

We may also reject the old, naïve behaviorism, which assumed that it was some-how necessary, or at least more "scientific" to judge human beings by animal stan-dards. One consequence of this belief was that the whole notion of purpose and goal was excluded from motivational psychology simply because one could not ask a white rat about his purposes. Tolman[23] has long since proven in animal studies them-selves that this exclusion was not necessary.

MOTIVATION AND THE THEORY OF PSYCHOPATHOGENESIS

The conscious motivational content of everyday life has, according to the foregoing, been conceived to be relatively important or unimportant accordingly as it is more or less closely related to the basic goals. A desire for an ice cream cone might actu-ally be an indirect expression of a desire for love. If it is, then this desire for the ice cream cone becomes extremely important motivation. If however the ice cream is simply something to cool the mouth with, or a casual appetitive reaction, then the desire is relatively unimportant. Everyday conscious desires are to be regarded as symptoms, as *surface indicators of more basic needs*. If we were to take these super-ficial desires at their face value we would find ourselves in a state of complete con-fusion which could never be resolved, since we would be dealing seriously with symptoms rather than with what lay behind the symptoms.

Thwarting of unimportant desires produces no psychopathological results; thwarting of a basically important need does produce such results. Any theory of psychopathogenesis must then be based on a sound theory of motivation. A conflict or a frustration is not necessarily pathogenic. It becomes so only when it threatens or thwarts the basic needs, or partial needs that are closely related to the basic needs.[24]

THE ROLE OF GRATIFIED NEEDS

It has been pointed out above several times that our needs usually emerge only when more prepotent needs have been gratified. Thus gratification has an important role in motivation theory. Apart from this, however, needs cease to play an active determining or organizing role as soon as they are gratified.

What this means is that, *e.g.*, a basically satisfied person no longer has the needs for esteem, love, safety, etc. The only sense in which he might be said to have them is in the almost metaphysical sense that a sated man has hunger, or a filled bottle has emptiness. If we are interested in what *actually* motivates us, and not in what has, will, or might motivate us, then a satisfied need is not a motivator. It must be considered for all practical purposes simply not to exist, to have disappeared. This point should be emphasized because it has been either overlooked or contradicted in every theory of motivation I know.[25] The perfectly healthy, normal, fortunate man has no sex needs or hunger needs, or needs for safety, or for love, or for prestige, or self-esteem, except in stray moments of quickly passing threat. If we were to say otherwise, we should also have to aver that every man has all the pathological reflexes, *e.g.*, Babinski, etc., because if his nervous system were damaged, these would appear.

It is such considerations as these that suggest the bold postulation that a man who is thwarted in any of his basic needs may fairly be envisaged simply as a sick man. This is a fair parallel to our designation as "sick" of the man who lacks vitamins or minerals. Who is to say that a lack of love is less important than a lack of vitamins? Since we know the pathogenic effects of love starvation, who is to say that we are invoking value questions in an unscientific or illegitimate way, any more than the physician does who diagnoses and treats pellagra or scurvy? If I were permitted this usage, I should then say simply that a healthy man is primarily motivated by his needs to develop and actualize his fullest potentialities and capacities. If a man has any other basic needs in any active, chronic sense, then he is simply an unhealthy man. He is as surely sick as if he had suddenly developed a strong salt hunger or calcium hunger.[26]

If this statement seems unusual or paradoxical the reader may be assured that this is only one among many such paradoxes that will appear as we revise our ways of looking at man's deeper motivations. When we ask what man wants of life, we deal with his very essence.

SUMMARY

1.   There are at least five sets of goals, which we may call basic needs. These are briefly physiological, safety, love, esteem, and self-actualization. In addition, we are motivated by the desire to achieve or maintain the various conditions upon which these basic satisfactions rest and by certain more intellectual desires.

2.   These basic goals are related to each other, being arranged in a hierarchy of prepotency. This means that the most prepotent goal will monopolize consciousness and will tend of itself to organize the recruitment of the various capacities of the organism. The less prepotent needs are minimized, even forgotten or denied. But when a need is fairly well satisfied, the next prepotent ("higher") need emerges,

in turn to dominate the conscious life and to serve as the center of organization of behavior, since gratified needs are not active motivators.

Thus man is a perpetually wanting animal. Ordinarily the satisfaction of those wants is not altogether mutually exclusive, but only tends to be. The average member of our society is most often partially satisfied and partially unsatisfied in all of his wants. The hierarchy principle is usually empirically observed in terms of increasing percentages of nonsatisfaction as we go up the hierarchy. Reversals of the average order of the hierarchy are sometimes observed. Also it has been observed that an individual may permanently lose the higher wants in the hierarchy under special conditions. There are not only ordinary multiple motivations for usual behavior, but in addition many determinants other than motives.

3.   Any thwarting or possibility of thwarting of these basic human goals, or danger to the defenses which protect them, or to the conditions upon which they rest, is considered to be a psychological threat. With a few exceptions, all psychopathology may be partially traced to such threats. A basically thwarted man may actually be defined as a "sick" man, if we wish.

4.   It is such basic threats which bring about the general emergency reactions.

5.   Certain other basic problems have not been dealt with because of limitations of space. Among these are (a) the problem of values in any definitive motivation theory, (b) the relation between appetites, desires, needs, and what is "good" for the organism, (c) the etiology of the basic needs and their possible derivation in early childhood, (d) redefinition of motivational concepts, i.e., drive, desire, wish, need, goal, (e) implication of our theory for hedonistic theory, (f) the nature of the uncompleted act, of success and failure, and of aspiration level, (g) the role of association, habit, and conditioning, (h) relation to the theory of interpersonal relations, (i) implications for psychotherapy, (j) implication for theory of society, (k) the theory of selfishness, (l) the relation between needs and cultural patterns, (m) the relation between this theory and Allport's theory of functional autonomy. These as well as certain other less important questions must be considered as motivation theory attempts to become definitive.

REFERENCES AND NOTES

1. Maslow, A. H. A preface to motivation theory. *Psychosomatic Med.*, 1943, 5, 85–92.
2. Wertheimer, M. Unpublished lectures at the New School for Social Research.
3. Goldstein, K. *The organism*. New York: American Book Co., 1939.
4. Freud, S. *New introductory lectures of psychoanalysis*. New York: Norton, 1933.
5. Adler, A. *Social interest*. London: Faber & Faber, 1938.
6. Cannon, W. B. *Wisdom of the body*. New York: Norton, 1932.
7. Young, P. T. The experimental analysis of appetite. *Psychol. Bull.*, 1941, 38, 129–164.
8. As the child grows up, sheer knowledge and familiarity as well as better motor development make these "dangers" less and less dangerous and more and more manageable. Throughout life it may be said that one of the main conative functions of education is this neutralizing of apparent dangers through knowledge, e.g., "I am not afraid of thunder because I know something about it."
9. Shirley, M. Children's adjustments to a strange situation. *J. abnorm (soc.) Psychol.*, 1942, 37, 201–217.

10. A "test battery" for safety might be confronting the child with a small exploding fire-cracker, or with a bewhiskered face, having the mother leave the room, putting him upon a high ladder, a hypodermic injection, having a mouse crawl up to him, etc. Of course I cannot seriously recommend the deliberate use of such "tests" for they might very well harm the child being tested. But these and similar situations come up by the score in the child's ordinary day-to-day living and may be observed. There is no reason why these stimuli should not be used with, for example, young chimpan-zees.

11. Not all neurotic individuals feel unsafe. Neurosis may have at its core a thwarting of the affection and esteem needs in a person who is generally safe.

12. Maslow, A. H. and Mittelmann, B. *Principles of abnormal psychology.* New York: Harper & Bros., 1941.

13. For further details see (27) and (28, Chap. 5).

14. Whether or not this particular desire is universal we do not know. The crucial question, especially important today, is "Will men who are enslaved and dominated inevitably feel dissatisfied and rebellious?" We may assume on the basis of commonly known clinical data that a man who has known true freedom (not paid for by giving up safety and security but rather built on the basis of adequate safety and security) will not willingly or easily allow his freedom to be taken away from him. But we do not know that this is true for the person born into slavery. The events of the next decade should give us our answer. See discussion of this problem in (29).

15. Perhaps the desire for prestige and respect from others is subsidiary to the desire for self-esteem or confidence in oneself. Observation of children seems to indicate that this is so, but clinical data give no clear support for such a conclusion.

16. Kardiner, A. *The traumatic neuroses of war.* New York: Hoeber, 1941.

17. For more extensive discussion of normal self-esteem, as well as for reports of various researches, see (30).

18. Clearly creative behavior, like paintings, is like any other behavior in having multiple determinants. It may be seen in "innately creative" people whether they are satisfied or not, happy or unhappy, hungry or sated. Also it is clear that creative activity may be compensatory, ameliorative, or purely economic. It is my impression (as yet uncon-firmed) that it is possible to distinguish the artistic and intellectual products of basically satisfied people from those of basically unsatisfied people by inspection alone. In any case, here too we must distinguish in a dynamic fashion the overt behavior itself from its various motivations or purposes.

19. Levy, D. M. Primary affect hunger. *Amer. J. Psychiat.,* 1937, 94, 643–652.

20. I am aware that many psychologists and psychoanalysts use the term "motivated" and "determined" synonymously, e.g., Freud. But I consider this an obfuscating usage. Sharp distinctions are necessary for clarity of thought and precision in experimentation.

21. To be discussed fully in a subsequent publication.

22. The interested reader is referred to the very excellent discussion of this point in Mur-ray's *Explorations in Personality* (31).

23. Tolman, E. C. *Purposive behavior in animals and men.* New York: Century, 1932.

24. Maslow, A. H. Conflict, frustration, and the theory of threat. *J. abnorm.* (*soc.*) *Psychol.,* 1943, 38, 81–86.

25. Note that acceptance of this theory necessitates basic revision of the Freudian theory.

26. If we were to use the word "sick" in this way, we should then also have to face squarely the relations of man to his society. One clear implication of our definition would be that (1) since a man is to be called sick who is basically thwarted, and (2) since such basic thwarting is made possible ultimately only by forces outside the individual, then (3) sickness in the individual must come ultimately from a sickness in the society. The "good" or healthy society would then be defined as one that permitted man's highest purposes to emerge by satisfying all his prepotent basic needs.

27. Maslow, A. H. The dynamics of psychological security-in-security. *Character & Pers.*, 1942, 10, 331–344.
28. Plant, J. *Personality and the cultural pattern.* New York: Commonwealth Fund, 1937.
29. Fromm, E. *Escape from freedom.* New York: Farrar and Rinehart, 1941.
30. Maslow, A. H. Dominance, personality and social behavior in women. *J. soc. Psychol.*, 1939, 10, 3–39.
31. Murray, H. A., *et al. Explorations in personality.* New York: Oxford University Press, 1938.
32. Freud, A. *The ego and the mechanisms of defense.* London: Hogarth, 1937.
33. Horney, K. *The neurotic personality of our time.* New York: Norton, 1937.
34. Young, P. T. *Motivation of behavior.* New York: John Wiley & Sons, 1936.

---

12 | UNCONSCIOUS MOTIVATION

Lewis L. Robbins

One of the most important postulates of modern psychiatric thinking, which came about largely, but not exclusively, through the discoveries and the work of Sigmund Freud, is that most human behavior is determined by forces within the individual of which he is not consciously aware. People often act in ways which they themselves are unable to explain. Some may give explanations for their behavior which they believe are quite correct, which satisfy them, as it were. However, an observer —particularly a psychiatrist—may see that these are not the real motives.

Freud's pronouncements about the dynamic unconscious were about as disturbing to man as the discovery by Copernicus that the earth was not the center of the universe; they were even more devastating than Darwin's theory of evolution. Man liked to think of the earth as the center of everything in the universe. He liked to think of himself as something special and different from lower animals. Above all, he likes to think that he is completely rational. He deeply cherishes the thought that he can always control his behavior and has a great reluctance to relinquish this thought.

Today, most people are somewhat willing to believe man's behavior is unconsciously determined in most instances, but they usually believe this only about the other fellow and not about themselves. They still prefer to think that they are not subject to distant, hidden impulses and motivations.

In psychiatry and psychology, the mind is divided roughly into three areas: the *conscious, pre-conscious, and unconscious.*

Abridged from the *Menninger Quarterly*, 1956, 10, 24–28. Reprinted by permission of the author and The Menninger Foundation.

The conscious is that segment of the mind which is concerned with immediate awareness. You know you are reading right now. This is conscious.

The pre-conscious is the portion where are stored those things which we can recall more or less at will. You can probably remember the address where you lived when fifteen years old. This awareness is now conscious. A moment before, it was pre-conscious.

The unconscious is that segment containing a great deal of "forgotten" material which cannot be recalled at will. It contains ideas, wishes, and strivings which were once conscious, but now have been buried or, as psychiatrists say, repressed. The unconscious also contains many primitive, instinctual strivings and desires which have never been conscious.

This is a tremendous storehouse of forgotten memories, forgotten experiences. One might say that, like the iceberg, about one-seventh of the human mind is exposed to consciousness or to pre-conscious awareness and about six-sevenths or more is below the surface. But even though the unconscious is not apparent, its effects certainly are.

Is there evidence the unconscious exists? Yes, a great deal.

One of the simplest clinical evidences comes from hypnosis. When a person is hypnotized, it is possible to have him recall many events of his past life which he cannot remember in his normal state of consciousness. Another interesting and easily demonstrated phenomenon is post-hypnotic suggestion. An individual, while hypnotized, is told that after he is awakened he will do something at a given signal. And he does. The impulse on which he acts is determined by suggestion which has become unconscious.

We all make slips of the tongue. Many of them are funny, or embarrassing, because they tell a partial truth and expose a thought or feeling which we may not wish to express consciously. We say what we unconsciously mean or have an impulse to say, but had not consciously intended to say. An example is the mother who carefully warned her children not to stare at or remark about the unusually large, red nose of an expected guest. Then when he came, she introduced him as "Mr. Nose." These slips tell us there is mental activity which is not conscious.

Forgetting is another evidence of the unconscious. We are apt to forget some things about which we have conflict. Some people, for example, often forget important appointments. If they stop and honestly reflect, they will probably find they had been reluctant to keep these appointments in the first place. Of course we may have intense preoccupations and simply forget something which in itself doesn't carry much conflict. If someone in our family is seriously ill, for instance, we're apt to forget little things. But there is much of this other—that is, forgetting because in a sense we do not want to remember. I recall a patient who said, "I always lose my gloves, I don't know why." I knew why. Hers was a very fashionable family in which a lady always wore gloves when in public. She had some conflict about being a fashionable lady all the time. The gloves represented gentility, which was somewhat of a burden to her.

The most common example of forgetting is that practically everybody has totally "forgotten" the events of his early childhood. Can you remember when you were weaned, or when you got your first tooth? We may think we recall some early events because we have been told about them over and over again. But most of these memories are really buried in the unconscious and, without knowing it, influencing our behavior today.

In the amnesias, there is gross and pathological forgetting. Some people have particularly horrible traumatic experiences, in war for instance, and not only forget the experience but can't even remember their own names. We can see in such an example some of the function of forgetting. If one remembers who he is, he is likely to recall what he has experienced, and the painful feelings associated with it. So, for psychic self protection, there follows a total blotting out of his own identity.

Dreams also furnish us evidence of unconscious mental activity. We know by the study of dreams that many early childhood events, primitive impulses, and infantile wishes, which somehow have been stimulated by the course of a day's events, reappear in a distorted form in dreams. They are not revealed consciously because when one is conscious he exercises much control. In sleep there is a loss of control which results in mental activity which is reflected in dreams. If we set up proper conditions, it's possible to understand the meanings of dreams. However, only with a certain specific and special relationship to the individual and an understanding of him as an individual, as in the psychotherapeutic situation, could one know what the dreams really mean.

You probably have experienced the interesting phenomenon of solving problems in your sleep. Let us say you were leaving the office yesterday afternoon and could not remember where you put that letter from Bill Smith. You look everywhere, but you can't find it. The more you try to think of where that letter is, the further you are from a solution. Finally you quit searching, go home, go to sleep, wake up in the morning, and, while having your breakfast, you know where it is. You solved it in your sleep. Many problems are solved that way. Here again is a curious kind of evidence that an aspect of mental activity is going on without our being conscious of it.

We all have rituals. For instance, each morning nearly everyone puts on the same shoe first, not necessarily the one that comes to hand first. Or some of us feel we *must* straighten every picture that's crooked. These compulsive things we all do may seem illogical or ridiculous, but they all have some meaning. We are forced to do them because of unconscious impulses of which we are not remotely aware. Take the person at the party who goes from one room to the next constantly emptying ash trays. That this has something to do with how he or she was toilet trained as a child may seem very remote, but it does.

Some of us have very marked tics that we, though unaware, do over and over again. We may blink our eyes, or pick at our teeth, or scratch. All these have unconscious meaning which would become apparent to a psychiatrist working with an individual having them. They, too, are evidence of the existence of the unconscious.

There is another broader and most meaningful evidence: "automatic" reactions. For example, you meet people whom you immediately like or dislike for no reason you can explain. These spontaneous reactions are often determined by past events or attitudes within us that come from the past. The reasons we consciously ascribe for such reactions are often very invalid substitutes for the real ones.

Similarly, many of our prejudices and preferences are determined unconsciously, even though we frequently give them conscious reasons. This is true of many political convictions, though certainly not all. Without even thinking about it a great majority of the people in a certain area vote Republican and a similar proportion in another area vote Democrat. They have all kinds of wonderful reasons for political preferences, aside from the one they never thought about: this is the thing to do in this particular culture. Most of us follow the religious precepts we've been taught and are relatively intolerant of those who seem to deviate, who are different from us. We have good reasons, they have good reasons. But most of these reasons are beside the point. The tradition, the culture, the way in which we were brought up—it is these with which we have identified. We have not necessarily learned them. We have acquired them through a rather simple process in which the conscious elements are the least important.

There are other evidences of the unconscious in the change in peoples' behavior when they are under the influence of alcohol, drugs, or anesthesia. The facade of conscious control may dissolve in alcohol and the more primitive personality come through. A nice genial fellow may, under the influence of alcohol, pick a fight with somebody. A very sweet, demure, decorous lady may start to flirt. Some people drink to bring about a change in themselves. Rarely does an alcoholic drink because he likes the taste of liquor. He drinks because it does something to him psychologically, because it is a way of bringing a change in himself. We all have heard stories about people who do funny things when they come out of anesthesia—for example, people who had learned a foreign language in childhood and had forgotten it. They talked in that language when they were coming out of an anesthetic. Some drugs have similar effects and occasionally can—as can hypnosis—be useful to the psychiatrists in helping patients express thoughts ordinarily unconscious.

The unconscious is seen in more gross and more bizarre personality peculiarities in severe mental illness. Under this severe stress, some of the methods for maintaining a kind of control, logical behavior, and rationality are weakened; some of the unconscious impulses break through and become part of the conscious behavior. Many of the illusions and hallucinations that people have when severely mentally ill are reflections of this. Severely mentally ill people are just like you and me, only more so, in the sense that lots of the little things that you and I do have the same origins as the more distorted and more persistent behavior seen in certain types of mental disorder.

Basically, what we are is a reflection of this vast area of mental processes which are unconscious. They have a most dynamic effect upon our behavior. Although these unconscious drives, wishes, and conflicts can be made known under certain conditions—psychiatric treatment, hypnosis, drugs, etc.—we usually do not need to know them. Yet an awareness of their existence and their extraordinary functioning can be extremely important to all of us in dealing with other people, for whatever purpose.

UNIT FOUR | DISCUSSION QUESTIONS

9 | CRITICAL PERIODS IN BEHAVIORAL DEVELOPMENT

Briefly discuss the formation of affectional bonds in adult life.

The discovery of critical periods focuses attention on the developmental processes which cause them. List some of the critical learning periods of early adulthood.

10 | PSYCHONEUROBIOCHEMEDUCATION

Discuss Krech's hypothesis regarding "species-specific enrichment experiences."

What are your views on the following statement? "The study of how languages are acquired may provide insight into the very basis of mental life."

11 | A THEORY OF HUMAN MOTIVATION

What are some of the limitations inherent in generalizing from animal to human behavior according to Maslow?

What single aspect of Maslow's hierarchy of needs has most relevance to your life?

12 | UNCONSCIOUS MOTIVATION

What does the author mean by the statement, "We all have rituals"?

List and discuss the evidence supporting unconscious motivation.

UNIT FIVE
INDIVIDUAL DIFFERENCES

When we observe friends, neighbors, or people from distant lands speaking different languages, exhibiting different cultures, and representing varying ethnic backgrounds, we are aware that individuals are more alike than they are different. Differences in individuals are differences in degree rather than in kind of traits or attributes. Differences are based on *units,* rather than on *wholeness,* of behavior. It is these units of behavior which affect our perception of one's total behavior. Differing capacities for hate, greed, love, friendliness, and coordination are examples of interpersonal, or social, variables. Differences in skin color, hair color, eye color, height, and weight are determined by heredity and are strictly physical variables.

Variances prove to be helpful in selecting desirable traits. For example, different strains of plants yield healthier crops and are more resistant to disease. We select these traits to reproduce more plants of this kind. Likewise with human beings, society emphasizes the importance of and need for certain qualities, and we attempt to cultivate these traits in ourselves and in our children. Traits which society considers detrimental are discouraged and an attempt is made to correct or alter such behavior.

Attributes of masculinity and femininity are for the most part, acquired as a result of cultural demands. In western cultures, masculinity is related to aggressiveness, competitiveness, and strength. Femininity, on the other hand, is often related to submissiveness, weakness, and dependence. Consequently, females are often referred to as the "weaker sex." *How Different Are They?* is an exploration by Stanley F. Yolles into the differences between the sexes as related to the demands of our culture. Interestingly enough, the author illustrates that many of the so-called masculine tasks are accomplished readily and efficiently by females. The same is true for so-called feminine tasks when performed by males.

Wagner H. Bridger investigates *Individual Differences in Behavior and Autonomic Activity in Newborn Infants.* Bridger suggests that human infants are born with certain predetermined temperamental differences and he points out that while the origins and consequences of these differences are not known, it is possible to make significant implications for the future.

Can a man be born a criminal? Can his genetic endowment predispose him to bizarre sexual acts and violent attacks on other people? So far, geneticists have more questions than answers; legal courts debate the issue. Robert W. Stock in *The XYY and the Criminal* explores this highly controversial question of the XYY male and individual differences.

The "idiot savant" is a mentally deficient person possessed of a high degree of some special ability, such as the ability to calculate. This phenomenon has been subject to frequent discussion in many psychology classes. In the final reading, William A. Horwitz, et al., present a profoundly interesting case report in *Identical Twin—"Idiot Savants"—Calendar Calculators.*

13 | HOW DIFFERENT ARE THEY?

Stanley F. Yolles

Experts on behavior hesitate when Henry Higgins asks, "Why can't a woman be more like a man?" Parents who wonder why little girls don't act like boys are assured by one authority that the differences are of "no consequence." A Stanford University professor of psychology now documents what little boys and girls are made of. The details, distilled from some 900 studies, shows that boys and girls are indeed quite different. This notion is hardly a news bulletin for parents, but science has documented the obvious generalizations with facts and has also uncovered some fresh answers to the eternal question of Henry Higgins. Here they are as outlined in the book, "The Development of Sex Differences," written in part with National Institute of Mental Health support and edited by Dr. Eleanor E. Maccoby:

Little boys start more fights, make more noise, take more risks, think more independently, are harder to educate and are the more fragile of the sexes. While many more males are conceived, more miscarried fetuses are male. More males than females die in the first year of life and in each decade after that. They are much more likely to stutter, to have reading problems and to suffer emotional quirks of every sort. They lag a year or more behind girls in physical development. By the time they start school, even their hand muscles are markedly less mature.

In contrast, little girls are more robust and mature, yet much more dependent, passive, submissive, conforming, unadventurous. They are more interested in people than in things, show more concern for others and are more sensitive to their reactions and are more likely, by far, to remember names and places.

Science has found no difference in I.Q. between boys and girls in childhood, yet their styles of thinking and learning are different. Girls excel in verbal abilities— even before they know they are girls. They talk first, and later on they spell better and write more. Boys outclass them in abstract thinking including math and science. Boys are also more likely to be creative.

How do we explain the basic and early differences? Some experts believe most of these differences are taught to the child. Other experts, such as Dr. David Hamburg, chairman of the department of psychiatry at Stanford, think there may be hormonal and genetic causes. Dr. Hamburg writes that hormones may act on the brain even before birth or right after, to organize certain circuits into male or female patterns. The evidence for this comes from experiments with the hormonal systems of newborn rats. When male rats are castrated within the first 24 hours after birth, they retain a basic female-type system for regulating hormonal secretions later in

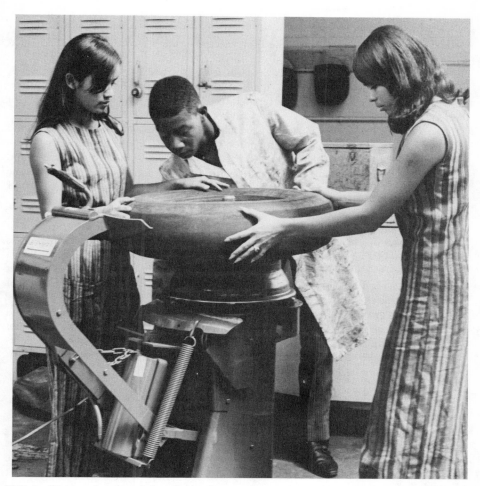

FIG. 1. "Science has found that the brightest girls are those whose interests extend into the masculine range." Above, girls repair tire in an auto mechanics class. (Photograph courtesy of San Diego City Schools)

life. If castration is delayed until the second 24 hours, only a few males retain the female patterns. By the third day, all male rats have developed a male-type pattern.

In addition, Dr. Hamburg points out that their genetic make-up is different. The female has a chromosomal composition that seems to lend her protection against disease and infection. It protects her against blood-clotting disorders, color-vision defects and one type of rickets.

Scientists at the National Institute of Mental Health who have observed infants right after birth and in the weeks that follow have seen sharp differences too early in life to have been caused by the environment. These differences have been uncovered through ingenious tests. Drs. George Weller and Richard Q. Bell hooked up recording devices to 40 newborns by placing sensors on their skins. By this method they were able to detect the faint electrical activity of the skin called "conductance," a property which turned out to be greater in the female. Since this increases as the baby gets older, it is taken as a sign of maturity. The female infant, therefore, is more mature than the male of the same age. The females also show more sensitivity to contact and the temperature changes on the skin, more proof of their greater maturity in this very early period of life.

Dr. Howard Moss, an institute psychologist who has watched three-week-old and three-month-old infants for seven and eight hours at a time is impressed with the "striking differences" between boys and girls. Boys sleep less, cry more, demand more attention. "Much more is happening with the male infants," he reports. Some boys, he found, also seem to be much more "inconsolable" than the girls, a sign of lesser maturity.

When children go to school, their differences become magnified. From first grade until well into high school, the girls usually make better grades. One ingenious researcher found that as early as the second grade, little boys think of school as a female institution and, therefore, one which is hostile to them. Our psychologists at the N.I.M.H. asked teachers in Arlington County, Va., to write their impressions of 153 seventh-graders.

According to the teachers, girls are 20 per cent better than boys at sticking to a task. They are more conscientious, compliant, methodical. They are also friendlier to the teacher, and more attentive. And boys are 35 per cent more hostile, domineering, aggressive, also more irritable, boastful, argumentative, quarrelsome. Paradoxically, boys are more introverted—depressed, sad, withdrawn.

Several years ago, educators in Fairfax County, Va., near Washington, D.C., decided to experiment with separate elementary classes for boys and girls.

One teacher said: "I learned things about boys and girls that I had never understood before. I had spent years trying to keep boys from disturbing everyone. This was just wasted effort. I found that boys can still concentrate even when they are noisy. You can learn to work in a boiler factory, if you have to, and that is just what I have done."

Another said: "I always liked girls best until I got a whole classful of them. In the beginning of the experiment, it dawned on me that the girls were not doing their own thinking. Parrot-like, they repeated everything that the teacher had ever said. What are we doing to these girls, I began to wonder, to make them so conforming?"

The results of the experiment were impressive. Both sexes did significantly better in their studies. The boys became much more interested in school. The girls grew more independent and original in their thinking.

Since it is scarcely practical to separate the boys and girls in most of our school systems today, educators might consider what they can do to achieve some of the same results. Principals and teachers can keep the differences in school performance between boys and girls in mind when they deal with problems in the classroom— either of discipline or of underachievement. Devices such as all-boy or all-girl contests, debates, or dramatic and musical clubs might give students the sense of confidence and enthusiasm found in the separate class.

If schools can capitalize on the differences between boys and girls, parents can do so, too. Parents of a boy can now see that he may be at a disadvantage in early years at school, under the twin burden of the girls' better performances and the teachers' disapproval. If parents don't expect their sons' reading or handwriting to be of the best, it may take some unnecessary pressure off the boys.

The girl's problem is even more complex. Many families feel that education is not so important for a girl as a boy. Today, only one in 10 Ph.D.'s is a woman, a drop from the one in seven of the nineteen-thirties. Teen-age marriages are on the rise, with an accompanying rise in the divorce rate. The question is, are we properly fitting girls for a woman's life as it really is?

After raising a girl to conform and to be subordinate we expect her to face problems that require education, originality, dominance and drive. A new study of young married people points out that conformity and submissiveness often lead only to boredom in marriage.

Science has found that the brightest girls are those whose interests extend into the masculine range. They like math, motors and abstract problems. The brighter boys also show a sensitivity and responsiveness we call "feminine" although these children are by no means effeminate. The most creative boys, for example, are dominant and aggressive, yet show much more sensitivity to their surroundings than other boys.

In my experience, the most successful personalities are those who have the widest range of interests and abilities. I would like to see our boys and girls brought up with as broad and varied an experience as possible, with attention to the many facets of the human mind. This includes insight into the thinking of the opposite sex.

What can parents do to offer this kind of insight to the young child? One psychologist bought his 3-year-old girl a truck when she asked for it, to the consternation of her grandmother. Another brought home an abandoned engine his pretty 12-year-old daughter had longed to tinker with. One father makes a point of answering his girls' questions about science and about his business world, although he has to fight an ingrained tendency against it. He tries to pique them into forming interesting solutions to problems, and to build self-confidence in their mental abilities.

As for the boys, one mother encourages hers to experiment with cooking. She enjoys giving them the benefit of her feminine insight into human behavior and motivation. This insight into the female skills will stand them in good stead professionally as well as in their marriages. It augments rather than reduces their manliness, she argues.

It might be in order to revise our ideas about what the proper sex role is for our boys and girls, and how best to train them for it. Society needs men who are not limited to the so-called tougher masculine characteristics of aggressiveness and dominance. It needs men who are capable of showing the more "feminine" traits of warmth and sensitivity toward the feelings of others. And we need women who are less conforming, more original and daring, women who can think hard and straight.

Henry Higgins, who yearned for more "logic" in women, and Eliza Doolittle, for "a little kindness" in men, surely would agree.

14 | INDIVIDUAL DIFFERENCES IN BEHAVIOR AND AUTONOMIC ACTIVITY IN NEWBORN INFANTS

Wagner H. Bridger

Before the turn of the century, it was rather common practice to ascribe to temperament and biological predisposition the origin of both mental and medical illnesses. In the twentieth century the emphasis has turned from these intrinsic factors to a search for extrinsic or environmental factors. In the field of mental health and personality development, both Watsonian behaviorism and Freudian psychoanalysis have put prime responsibility upon the parents for the personality, health, or ill-health of their offspring.

In recent years there has been a trend away from this unilateral approach, since specific environmental variables that would be responsible for many psychiatric and medical syndromes have not been found. The possible role of biological predispositions in interacting with environmental factors has been gaining a theoretical acceptance. This new emphasis seems particularly applicable to the psychiatric syndromes of schizophrenic and manic-depressive psychoses and the psychosomatic syndromes of hypertension and peptic ulcer.

The return of the potential significance of intrinsic factors is also true in regard to personality development. Several investigators, Bayley, Escalona, Thomas, and Schaeffer, have emphasized the probable role of intrinsic factors in the individual personality differences they found in the children of their respective studies. In particular, at least one factor—the infant's activity level—is predictive of subsequent behavior in childhood. However, all studies were started after the children were a few months old, and thus there is no conclusive evidence that these individual differences were present at birth.

It is within this framework that our laboratory at Albert Einstein College of Medicine has been intensively studying the human neonate for the past five years. Specifically, we were interested in determining whether or not there are individual differences in behavioral and autonomic functions at birth, which may influence later personality development and which may represent predisposition to later psychosomatic illnesses.

From *American Journal of Public Health,* **55,** 12, December 1965, p. 1899. Reprinted by permission of the author and publisher. This paper was presented before a Joint Session of the American Orthopsychiatric Association and the Mental Health Section of the American Public Health Association at the Ninety-Second Annual Meeting in New York, N.Y., October 7, 1964.

TYPES OF EXPERIMENTS

The following types of experiments have been performed: Our basic technic is to take two-to-five-day-old infants, Apgar above 8,* and, using a team of raters, make a series of repeated behavioral rating and heart rate measurements. When studying day-to-day constancy, we rotate observers to diminish halo bias. The ratings are on a 6-point scale, 1 = quiet, no movement to 6 = extreme agitation with severe crying. We rated the infants' responses to a loud sound, a soft sound, an air puff applied to the abdomen, a cold disc applied to the thigh, and a pacifier inserted into the baby's mouth. With this last procedure the vigor of the sucking was monitored on a polygraph.

Using correlation technics, we found that there are significant individual differences between these babies in behavioral response to these stimulations, and these differences are consistent during the first few days of life. The babies were ranked according to their median behavioral ratings to the stimuli, and the analysis revealed that a baby who gave intense responses to the soft sound also gave intense responses to the loud sound and cold disc and also sucked vigorously on the pacifier. The babies who gave gentle responses to the soft sound also gave gentle responses to the loud sound and cold disc and sucked weakly. Thus, most babies could be characterized as being either slightly, moderately, or intensely responsive to stimuli, regardless of the modality or nature of the stimulus. In addition, this characteristic behavior was present on successive days. The baby who responded vigorously on the second day of life also responded vigorously on the third, fourth, and fifth days.

In addition to these behavioral ratings, the heart rate of the babies was monitored on a polygraph. The experimental question being investigated was whether or not the neonates showed individual differences in autonomic lability, a possible predisposition to psychosomatic disorders. The infants' heart rates were compared at the same behavioral states. The babies were ranked according to their heart rates when they were asleep, active, and crying. The data revealed consistent individual differences between the babies in cardiovascular functioning. Infants who slept with relatively high heart rates (e.g., 140 beats per minute) had high heart rates when active and when crying (e.g., 220). Infants who had relatively low heart rates when asleep (e.g., 70 beats per minute) had low heart rates when active and when crying (e.g., 150). The autonomic and behavioral factors seemed to be independent in that the behavioral hyperreactor did not necessarily have a labile autonomic nervous system. The individual differences just described were in response to excitatory stimuli.

The next experiment investigated whether or not there were individual differences with respect to inhibitory stimuli. In other words, do infants differ from one another in their ability to be soothed when in a state of distress? In this study, the babies were brought to a high level of excitation by flicking the soles of their feet. Then, an inhibitory stimulus was applied for one minute each. Among these stimuli were continuous low-pitch sounds, rocking, warmth, and sucking on a pacifier. The

---

* A rating system based on a scale of ten in which a newborn infant is rated in terms of health. Factors of heart rate, reflexes, color, muscle tone, and breathing are taken into consideration. [Ed.]

results indicated that, in general, all these experimental manipulations were equally effective in soothing the infants as compared to a control period during which no stimulus was applied.

DATA EVALUATED

While the analysis of the data from this study is not complete, it appears that there are consistent individual differences in soothability. In addition, some babies have a predisposition to be more effectively soothed by one or another of the stimuli. For example, one baby was most effectively soothed by the loud sound, another by rocking, still another by sucking a pacifier. We are in the process of analyzing whether or not there is a relationship between individual differences in excitability and soothability. During these soothing studies, we also recorded the heart rate. Some babies demonstrated a labile cardiovascular reaction in that while showing behavioral inhibition, their heart rates reached the same level as when they were crying.

Summarizing the results of this research, it is evident that human infants show stable temperamental differences right after birth. These differences are present in respect to levels of behavioral activity, reactivity, soothability, and autonomic lability. The implications of these findings can only be tentative at this time, because we do not know their origin or the consequences of these differences. In view of these differences, however, it seems likely that similar maternal behavior will have a different effect upon different babies. In addition, the behavior of the neonate may determine in part the behavior of the mother. In any case, it seems obvious that advice in regard to child-rearing practice might best be adjusted in each instance to the specific qualities of the individual child.

In conclusion, it is suggested that the role of environmental variables in growth and development must be evaluated in the context of the biological endowment of the individual. There are significant implications for public health if we can find controllable pre- and perinatal factors, which may be important determinants of neonatal individual differences.

15 | THE XYY AND THE CRIMINAL

Robert W. Stock

The sketch is tacked to the door of a laboratory at the Downstate Medical School in Brooklyn. Two fish, standing on their tails, lovingly entwined. The legend: "It takes two to tango." But beyond the door, the romance is by threes—hundreds of trios of tiny killifish in individual glass tanks filled with water at a constant 27 degrees centigrade. "Normally," says Dr. James B. Hamilton, head of the anatomy department, "they would breed once a year. At that temperature, they breed once a day."

The tangoers are accorded little privacy, for they are very special fish with some very special implications for their scientific *voyeurs* and the rest of mankind. Each trio consists of a normal female, a normal male and a rare kind of killifish supermale whose cells contain a double dose of the male sex-determining chromosome called Y.

The behavior of this supermale takes on particular interest because of recent investigations of human males with a somewhat analogous sex chromosome make-up. Geneticists have found that boys born with XYY chromosomes (XY is normal) seem to have an uncommon chance of becoming tall, stupid, pimply-faced criminals. The suspicion is that the extra Y causes the problem, and Hamilton's experiments with his YY killifish[1] are one means of gaining greater understanding of the phenomenon.

The results of his study? In the competition for the female's favors, the YY fish wins 88 per cent of the time—and not because the XY isn't trying. The supermale emerges victorious from almost every physical combat with the normal male. He shows greater homosexual, as well as heterosexual, activity. He is, if not more aggressive (a term often applied to the human XYY), at least, in Hamilton's phrase, more competitive.

All of which lends some animal-kingdom credence to the theory that when a human male has an extra Y chromosome, it may have an important, and potentially antisocial, effect upon his behavior. Though by no means universally accepted, the theory is supported by impressive evidence, perhaps the most dramatic example being a report last year on a study of XYY males at a state hospital for the criminally insane in Scotland. Their I.Q.'s ranged from 60 to 80, they had been convicted at an earlier age than XY inmates (13 vs. 18 years of age), they had severe personality disorders. They often behaved violently and aggressively. And there was no sign of family environments that would predispose them to lives of crime. Since, according to the latest estimates, as many as 1 in 300 men may have an XYY chromosomal make-up, such reports have aroused widespread concern.

The lawyer: If a man has an inborn tendency toward criminal behavior, can we fairly hold him legally accountable for his acts?

The penologist: If a criminal's chromosomes are at fault, how can we possibly rehabilitate him?

The philsopher: If the human being's personality and behavior are dictated to such an important degree by his genes, what happens to free will, to morality?

These are some of the questions raised by the so-called double-Y syndrome, basic social and ethical questions of a kind that will become more and more common, more and more insistent, as the implications of the "new biology" take root in the public mind. Scientists are laying bare the arcane mechanisms in the body that in large measure determine and control what we are—the chemical sleight-of-hand whereby 46 impossibly tiny bits of matter called chromosomes order up our appearance and intelligence, our physical and emotional health, perhaps even our capacity for love. And with such knowledge, they are on the threshold of an awesome new power—the ability to alter these inborn traits, to turn a tenor into a basso profundo, to correct at the source such inherited diseases as cystic fibrosis and diabetes, to erase genetically determined personality flaws.

More than half a century ago, the sex chromosomes led a Columbia University zoologist, Thomas Hunt Morgan, to the first concrete proof that chromosomes carry genes, the factors that govern our inheritance. Today, the double-Y syndrome and other new insights into the workings of the sex chromosomes point the way toward a time, undoubtedly still some decades hence, when man will be able to consciously control his inheritance. Suddenly genetics has become a matter too important to be left to the scientists. Willy-nilly, we are being forced to pay some attention to their ravings about such abstruse items as mitosis and DNA—and to take a closer look into the inner space of ourselves.

It is a world that can be seen only through a glass, and even then darkly. Start with the run-of-the-mill cell—itself too small to be made out by the naked eye. Smaller still, the nucleus of that cell. And finally, within the nucleus, the chromosomes.

They begin as a mass of long, threadlike filaments. Just before the cell is to divide—the basic process of bodily growth and development—they double their numbers, from 46 to 92. They then take on the appearance of short, fat rods, and the membrane round the nucleus dissolves. Meanwhile, the cell has been changing shape, roughly from that of a sphere to that of a salami. Now half the rods move to one end of the salami, half to the other, the salami divides and the rods in each end revert to the filament shape; we're back where we started—but with two cells instead of one.

It is by means of this elaborate minuet, known as mitosis, that we develop from a one-cell fertilized egg to a 10-trillion-cell adult. And the dance master is the chromosome. For in the chromosome are the genes, some 40,000 units of hereditary material which determine the traits we will have—blue eyes or brown, square head or round.

That such objects as chromosomes exist was first established by a 24-year-old German bookseller named Wilhelm Hofmeister in 1848. He saw them in flower cells. Some four decades later, a fellow national, biologist Walther Flemming, treated the cell nucleus of a salamander with a synthetic red dye and found that the chromosomes absorbed the dye, making them relatively easy to observe. Which is how they earned the misnomer "chromosome" from the Greek word for color; they are actually quite colorless.

Gradually scientists came to recognize that the 46 chromosomes in the human cell (the number varies with the species but not within the species) come in pairs and that each pair has a different size and shape from the others. So the first 22 pairs were numbered for easy reference, starting with the longest as No. 1.

The 23d pair was a problem: sometimes its chromosomes matched, sometimes they didn't. Scientists called the larger of the two "X," as an unknown; the smaller, another unknown, was dubbed "Y." Since males always have an X and a Y making up their 23d pair and females always have two X's, it was not long before the suspicion arose that these particular chromosomes have something to do with sex determination.

The fact that chromosomes come in pairs led scientists to another piece of speculation. Back before Hofmeister's day, the Austrian monk Gregor Mendel had found that each new pea plant carries genetic material from both parent plants. If one parent passed along a gene for smooth seeds, and the other a gene for wrinkled seeds, the new plant would have smooth seeds; smooth was the dominant, wrinkled was the recessive. Was it not obvious that, if the chromosomes carried the genes, then one member of any given pair of chromosomes would bear the genes of the mother and the other the genes of the father?

What the scientists really needed, however, was less speculation and more proof. Where was the direct, proven link between chromosomes and heredity? It came, in the end, on the wings of *Drosophila melanogaster,* the fruit fly used by Columbia's Thomas Morgan for his epochal genetic experiments. Morgan concentrated on the sex chromosomes. He found, for example, that, when he bred a particular strain of fruit fly, only the male ever had white eyes; the female's eyes were always red. His conclusion: There had been a mutation in the genes for eye color. The mutation was recessive, and it was carried in the sex chromosome, specifically the X. By 1915 he had uncovered some 20 such X-linked traits in the fruit fly.

So now the microscopic bits of matter called chromosomes had been tied directly to hereditary traits. And the list of such linkages mounted, not only for the fruit fly but for man. Hemophilia, color-blindness, a kind of Vitamin-D-resistant rickets—these are among the more than 100 ailments which, according to the National Foundation-March of Dimes, have been pinned to the human X chromosome. Hundreds more were found that could be traced to the other 22 pairs of chromosomes. Still, the mechanism by which the genes and their chromosomes control human traits remained as mysterious as ever.

Enter the biochemists, who painstakingly analyzed the chemical structure of the chromosome. They found that it contained a large quantity of that much-discussed and little-understood item called DNA, short for deoxyribonucleic acid, a most complex molecule. And in 1953, the now-renowned J. D. Watson, Maurice Wilkins, and F. H. C. Crick suggested just how the DNA molecule might look (it is too small to be seen) and behave.

Reduced to oversimplified fundamentals, DNA is made up of four molecules that are linked in pairs, each pair forming one rung of a ladder. The sides of the ladder are composed of two other molecular groupings. Take the ladder firmly at each end, twist it and presto: DNA, the famed double helix.

The prime task of DNA in the chromosome is to order the production of protein —the substance which, in the form of an enzyme, triggers the body's biochemical reactions, from a thought to a wink. The orders are issued in this manner:

Proteins are composed of molecules arranged in a special sequence; vary the sequence, and you have a different protein. The particular sequence of molecules in any given protein is determined by the sequence of molecules on the controlling DNA ladder. Thus, the arrangement of molecules in your DNA (the sequence that existed in the cells of your parents and which you inherited) is a kind of code for making proteins, which in turn determine the traits you will have—your height, your hair color, possibly your I.Q. And the gene for any one of those traits consists of sections of the DNA ladder in one or more chromosomes.

The DNA in the 46 chromosomes of any one cell has the capacity to direct the creation of an entire human being. Which explains, of course, how we manage to develop human forms from a single, fertilized, one-cell egg. But in fact, in the vast majority of the cells of our body, only a tiny fraction of DNA's protein-ordering potential is operative. As the egg divides, new cells are formed, and eventually they become specialists: blood cells, liver cells, brain cells. In their specific roles and locations, they have no use for all the 40,000 genes carried in the chromosomes; it would be a waste of time, for example, for a brain cell to produce all the proteins needed by a blood cell, and vice versa. So most of the genes in most of the cells are turned off, just another in the miraculous series of events masterminded by DNA.[2]

Thus man develops from the fertilized egg. And the egg itself? It is the end product of a process that starts with the production of the germ cell—the egg in the woman, the sperm in the male. By means of a procedure called meiosis, a 46-chromosome cell creates germ cells that contain only 23 chromosomes each, one from each chromosome pair in the parent cell. Since the normal woman has an XX chromosome make-up, the egg cell will always carry an X; but because the normal male has both an X and a Y chromosome in each body cell, the sperm will carry either an X or a Y.

The sex of the child-to-be depends entirely upon which of the 200 million sperm in an ejaculation wins the race to fertilize the egg—an X-bearing sperm or a Y-bearer. Once the race is over, the fertilized egg, having absorbed the sperm's 23 chromosomes, returns to the normal 46-chromosome count. And the egg proceeds to divide again and again, the new cells going to make up the substance of the developing fetus—each of the cells bearing 23 chromosomes from the mother and 23 chromosomes from the father, including an X from the mother and an X or Y from the father.

Now, the two sex chromosomes are an oddly assorted pair. The X, one of the larger chromosomes in the cell, is about three times the size of the Y. It is apparently far more active in the body's working, containing many more protein-ordering genes. According to the well-accepted theories of Dr. Sasumu Ohno of California's City of Hope Medical Center, the X is the conservative partner— it has undergone little change in the course of evolution. The Y has grown progressively smaller and less influential as mammals have evolved. Its only proven role is as a determiner of sex. In that role, however, the Y is the more powerful of the two—a single Y in your cells is usually enough to make you a male, no matter how many X's you may carry.

Just how the X and Y determine sex is still a most uncertain business. Why, for example, should 80 per cent of the children born to British deep-sea divers' wives be girls rather than boys? Why has one Midwestern family had 50 boys born in six generations, and not a single girl? Scientists don't know the answers. This much, however, they do know:

The gonadal tissue of the human fetus is neuter until about the second month; it has the capacity to go either way. At about that time, genes in the X or Y chromosome trigger a mechanism that causes the primitive gonadal tissue to develop into female or male sex organs. The mechanism is little understood, but it obviously starts —though does not complete—the physical conversion of the person to a particular gender.

How "male" or "female" the mature person will look or act also depends upon the balance of male and female hormones he may secrete (both sexes produce both male and female hormones) and on a multitude of environmental influences, not excluding Oedipus. A woman with a normal XX chromosome make-up and normal sex organs may grow a beard if her ovaries, which normally secrete tiny amounts of androgen, the male hormone, start working overtime. Contrariwise, a woman may be to all appearances a normal female, even though she carries a Y chromosome, if the production of the male hormone is held down.

An apparent example of the latter case was reported last year when Ewa Klobukowska, a Polish track star, was ruled ineligible for international competition. A chromosome test had revealed that she had "one chromosome too many" to qualify as a woman for athletic competition. Details of the test results were not released, but the International Amateur Athletic Federation withdrew ratification of all the medals she had won and all the records she had broken. It was something of a prestige setback for her nation, and for the 21-year-old girl the affair was an intimate personal tragedy that she had to share with the whole world. "It's a dirty and stupid thing to do to me," she said. "I know what I am and how I feel." She is, and feels, a woman—but with the aid of modern science, she has been effectively declared a man.

Aside from its more obvious effects, the sex-determining mechanism in man has another vital consequence. It enables women to live longer and healthier lives than men. There seems to be a compensation for this male weakness—the Y-bearing sperm has a slightly better chance of fertilizing the egg than the X-bearing one; 106 boys are born for every 100 girls. (The odds are actually somewhat higher at the time of conception, but more boys die *in utero*.) Even so, in the game of life, the "second sex" comes in first. The secret lies in the sex chromosomes.

Happily for the human being, most genetic defects are recessive; that is, when the gene in one of the 23 pairs of chromosomes in his cell is abnormal, its influence will be negated by the normal gene in the other chromosome in the pair. And that mechanism works very well for most defects carried on the X chromosome—if you're a woman. You may carry the X-linked defect known as hemophilia in one of your X's; but you will not actually suffer the symptoms unless the other X also bears the defect—that is, unless both your parents have passed along the bad gene. And since so many male hemophiliacs do not live long enough to sire children, the chances of that are slight. Like zoologist Morgan's female fruit flies, who were always red-eyed because red eyes were dominant over white, you will express the dominant gene—in this case, good health.

The male, however, like the white-eyed male fruit fly, has no second X to counter the effects of a recessive, X-linked gene. The Y doesn't carry a matching gene. If his lone X is programmed for hemophilia, he will suffer.

Over the years, scientists have made a number of intriguing discoveries about the female's double-X. The Barr body, for example. It was found that, early in the cell's life, one of a woman's two X's coils itself into a tight spiral and becomes genetically inactive. In some of her cells, this condensed chromosome, known as a Barr body, is the X from the woman's mother; in others, the inactive X is from her father.

Recently, however, Dr. Harold P. Klinger of New York's Albert Einstein College of Medicine has provided some experimental evidence indicating that not all the genes on the Barr body are permanently inactivated. He put into a cell an antibiotic that inhibits the cell's protein-making process and found that the number of Barr bodies increased. This suggests, he says, that when the cell's protein-making activity is in high gear both X's may be operating. When the antibiotic is washed out of the cell, the number of Barr bodies decreases again.

Because the Barr body is large and can be seen under the microscope where the chromosome cannot, it has also come in handy as a means of determining the sex of a cell. The more exacting way of dividing the ewes from the rams, is known as karyotyping. It involves a complicated procedure for sorting out and matching all the cell's 46 chromosomes, using sample blood, bone or skin cells, and may cost $100 or more. The Barr-body search is faster and cheaper; it is routinely used in such far-out experiments of the new biology as sex selection.

This feat was recently achieved with rabbits by two scientists from Cambridge University. Physiologists Robert Edwards and Richard Gardner take early-stage embryos from pregnant rabbits, examine a sampling of the cells for Barr bodies and separate the embryos into male and female groups. They then re-implant the embryos, deciding which mother rabbit will have a boy, which a girl. If the technique is perfected for other mammals, it will be a boon to dairy farmers (who have a preference for cows) and meat ranchers (the best meat comes from steers).

There is, incidentally, a method for determining the sex of a human fetus while it is still in the mother's womb. A hypodermic needle is inserted through the mother's abdomen and a small sample of amniotic fluid, containing cells sloughed off from the fetus, is removed. The cells of the sample can then be analyzed for Barr bodies and the sex of the unborn fetus thus determined. The cells can also be studied for signs of chromosomal aberrations. One such aberration involving the No. 21 chromosome pair produces Mongoloid children; some United States physicians are aborting fetuses that manifest this defect.

The process by which the body sorts out and distributes X's and Y's to the next generation is a model of efficiency—a tribute to the stability of sex, at least in its chemical manifestations. Yet it sometimes happens, back in the sperm-forming or egg-forming stage, that meiosis misfires—one or more chromosomes go into the wrong cell. Thus, for example, instead of a sperm's ending up with a single X or Y sex chromosome, it may have two or three or none. The result of such a mix-up is trouble.

The majority of women with three or more X's show some form of mental retardation. Two X's in combination with a Y cause Klinefelter's syndrome; boys so afflicted are frequently of low intelligence, sterile and possessed of an assortment of physical abnormalities which physicians like to call "anomalies." And when the fertilized egg bears an X and two Y's—well, then the boy may be a victim of the double-Y "criminal" syndrome.

The evidence for the existence of a double-Y syndrome has surfaced only within the last six years. It came first from Sweden, where chromosome studies showed an unusually large number of XYY men among "hard-to-manage" patients in mental hospitals. These observations received impressive confirmation in studies of maximum-security prisons and hospitals for the criminally insane in Scotland. Then the double-Y excitement crossed the Atlantic. American doctors began reporting case after case, and a composite picture of the XYY emerged. He was invariably tall and usually of below-average intelligence with a tendency toward acne; he was likely to have unusual sexual tastes, often including homosexuality, and a record of criminal or antisocial behavior.

By no means, however, have all reported XYY's manifested this full range of traits. Some come very close—Richard Speck, for example, who was convicted last year in the slaying of eight nurses in Chicago. He is tall, dull, acned—and, according to his attorney, an XYY. But two cases recently reported by Dr. D. S. Borgaonkar of the Johns Hopkins School of Medicine in Baltimore are more typical of the variations among XYY's:

1. A 31-year-old, 6 feet 8 inches tall, a patient in a psychiatric hospital. Though the son of eminently respectable upper-middle-class parents, he was a troublemaker at school, later got into the habit of buying cars on time and selling them for cash. He attended four colleges in three years, served two and a half years in the Air Force —and earned bad marks for behavior in both endeavors. He was sentenced to a year in jail on a charge of sodomy. But he has no acne nor any record of violent antisocial behavior, and he has an I.Q. of 125.

2. A 15-year-old, 6 feet 5½ inches tall, a member of a special class for retarded children (his I.Q. is 75). He is a bully, talks loudly, enjoys breaking things. He has some acne. But he has shown no inclination toward abnormal sexual acts nor has he demonstrated any criminal tendencies.

In the light of such evidence, most biologists are wary of proclaiming the double-Y theory a fact. Dr. Hamilton warns that killifish and humans are worlds apart in their genetic complexity and that the results of his fish-tank experiments may be quite inapplicable to man. (He also points out that an XYY chromosome make-up can hardly be the whole story of human aggressiveness: "The classic mother-in-law is as good an example of aggression as any you can find, but she's assuredly not YY.") Dr. Kurt Hirschhorn, chief of the Division of Medical Genetics at New York's Mount Sinai School of Medicine, is somewhat willing to accept tallness as a part of a double-Y syndrome, but he has his doubts about aggressiveness. Most of the studies of XYY males to date have been based on prison and mental-institution populations; he is awaiting control studies of normal, noninstitutionalized examples. (He may not have too long to wait. The search for XYY's in the general population is on. It was a chromosome examination of some 3,700 infants in the United States, Canada and Scotland that yielded the latest projection of one XYY for every 300 males.)

Yet it is in the nature of the scientist to be speculative as well as cautious. Thus Hirschhorn suggests: "What if the genes for aggression and tallness do exist in the Y? They would have had survival value for the caveman, and there might have been an evolutionary selection for them. But civilized man has been breeding against aggressive genes—aggressive people have been killed in wars, put away in jail, and they don't pass on these genes. The average male has just the single Y. Now, today, we find a man who gets a double dose of Y's; it's understandable that they might well be too much for him to handle."

There are also those outside the biology laboratory who have their doubts about the validity of the double-Y syndrome. The psychologist, for example. Personality and behavior, he insists, are functions, in the main, of environment—the family, the peer group, the society as a whole; there are no genes for love, for empathy, for aggression. And in the sophisticated reaches of our nation, among educators and sociologists and urbanologists, his view has triumphed.

Yet the psychologist's explanations are not universally accepted. Man has long spoken of the "bad seed," the evil or merely unpleasant traits of his children, assumed to come from his mate's side of the family. We have always felt that there were "born criminals," and the fact that men are many times more prone to criminal behavior than women lent support to that feeling. As long ago as the nineteen-thirties, studies of one-egg twins indicated that if one twin is a criminal the other will follow suit—the chances of this being five times greater than among two-egg twins, who are not genetically identical. But not until the double-Y syndrome came along was there anything approaching a direct link between the criminal and the chromosome.

The evidence to date may neither clinch the validity of the syndrome nor convict all of the world's estimated five million XYY's of innate aggressive or criminal tendencies. There does, however, seem good reason to keep an eye on it—and them.

And if, as now seems quite possible, the syndrome is proven—if it can be conclusively demonstrated, for example, that most babies born with an XYY chromosomal complement have a strong tendency toward criminal behavior—what then?

The first step, of course, will be to find the XYY infants in the general population, and some leading geneticists have suggested the need for a nationwide program of automatic chromosome analysis of all newborns. It might be possible to counter the defect through special educational and psychological treatment.

If not, the techniques envisioned by the practitioners of the "new biology" may provide an answer. Theoretically, the genes in the extra Y chromosome of the XYY that cause the behavioral defect might be identified and their influence suppressed. The theory of such genetic engineering is already well understood: the practice is another matter.

Scientists have succeeded in altering the genetic code of a fruit fly by soaking its eggs in a solution containing DNA from other flies. Viruses have been used to transfer genetic information from one bacterial cell to another: a virus grown with a cell resistant to a particular drug is introduced into a cell that is susceptible to the drug and the second cell becomes resistant. By infecting an XYY infant with a harmless but well-trained virus, it might be possible to alter his DNA to avoid the effects of the double-Y syndrome.

The day may even come when a collection of cells from a newborn XYY—or any child with a gross chromosome defect—will be corrected in the laboratory and returned to the child to flourish and reproduce, overwhelming the defective cells.

But before such a day arrives, there is much to be learned. The specific locations of genes on the DNA in specific chromosomes must be charted, a process still barely begun. And the procedures for inducing precise genetic alterations must be developed; the tiniest miscalculation that might change genes other than those intended could have disastrous consequences for the patient.

That all this and more will in the end be accomplished is an article of faith for many scientists. "We are the heirs of Icarus," says Dr. Robert Sinsheimer, chairman of the division of biology at California Institute of Technology. "We have become the latter-day Prometheus. In the ancient myths . . . man could not rise above his nature to chart his destiny. But we can now begin to confront that chance and choice, and soon we shall have the power consciously to alter our inheritance, our very nature."

It may be hubris; but it begins more and more to look like fact.

NOTES

1. The YY killifish is produced by the unlikely expedient of mating two males. One of the males, however, has been given so much female hormone that he has become a functional "she" with female organs and the capacity to bear young. (This trick is possible only with the simplest of organisms, not including man—at least, not yet including man.) The four offspring of the match between the two killifish are: an XX (normal female), two XY's and a YY.

2. If an entire human being can develop from a single cell, scientists have suggested, it should theoretically be possible to bypass sexual reproduction. The technique would work this way: The nucleus of an unfertilized egg removed from a woman's body would be destroyed and replaced with the nucleus from any 46-chromosome cell in another person's body. The egg would then be replaced in the woman's uterus; the DNA in the egg nucleus would be reactivated, and from the egg there would develop a new human being with a genetic complement identical to that of the nucleus donor. This feat has been accomplished with frogs. The nucleus in a frog's egg is killed and replaced with the nucleus from a tadpole's intestinal cell—and the egg produces a tadpole in many ways identical to the donor of the intestinal cell. Of course, frogs' eggs are 100 times as large as human eggs and develop naturally outside the mother's body—two reasons why a Brave New World version of the frog experiment for man will be many years in coming, if it comes at all.

16 | IDENTICAL TWIN—"IDIOT SAVANTS" CALENDAR CALCULATORS

William A. Horwitz, Clarice Kestenbaum, Ethel Person, and Lissy Jarvik

The phenomenon of the "idiot savant" has long been known in psychological literature. Classically, the term describes those individuals with sub-normal intelligence, frequently in imbecile range, who have a special highly developed intellectual skill incongruous with other areas of mental functioning. Theories attempting to explain the phenomenon have postulated that (1) these individuals have an unusual capacity for eidetic imagery; (2) the skill represents a mechanism utilizing memory and repetition as a substitute compensation for normal learning; (3) there is a specialized computer-like mechanism in the brains of these individuals. No theory has yet sufficed to account for the diversity of phenomena described nor for the fact that these unusual skills are seen almost exclusively in males. The current concepts are that the human organism, motivated to achieve his capabilities through constant practice and use of his skilled memory and eidetic imagery, develops his special talents; that if any normal individual would be forced to do nothing but indulge in these memory skills he probably could accomplish the equivalent.

The present case report of identical twins, Charles and George, 24-year-old male calendar calculators, shows many of the features of cases reported in the literature as well as certain unique features. These twins are self-taught with I.Q's in the 60–70's; they have an uncanny memory for dates not reflected in other aspects of learning. They can recall almost any day and can state accurately whether it was cloudy, sunny or rainy. Their calendar calculations go far beyond the range of any hitherto reported. Although Charles is completely accurate only for this century, George can project his calendar identifications to centuries before and centuries beyond our present perpetual calendars. With equal facility, George can identify instantaneously the 15th of February 2002 as a Friday, or August 28th, 1591 as a Wednesday. They do not know the difference between the Gregorian and Julian calendars

Reprinted by permission from *The American Journal of Psychiatry*, **121**, pp. 1075–1079, 1965. Copyright © 1965 by The American Psychiatric Association.

Read at the 120th annual meeting of The American Psychiatric Association, Los Angeles, Calif., May 4–8, 1964.

The authors wish to express their thanks to Dr. W. Edwards Deming and Mr. Robert Winter for their help in testing the "calendar calculating" phenomenon of the twins. Further work attempting to determine the mental mechanisms involved is, as yet, in progress and the data will be presented in the near future.

The authors should also like to thank Dr. Isaac N. Wolfson, Director at Letchworth Village, and Dr. George A. Jervis, Director of Psychiatric Research, Letchworth Village, Thiells, N.Y., for providing them with the opportunity of studying these twins.

(the change-over was in the year 1582), but when they identify dates before 1582, if one allows for the 10-day difference between the calendars, George is invariably right, Charles usually so. George has a range of at least 6000 years. Other facets of their calendar calculating serve to compound the riddle of their inexplicable skill. For example, when asked in what years April 21st will fall on a Sunday, each will answer correctly 1968, 1957, 1963, 1946, etc. When encouraged, George can continue as far back as 1700. When asked in what month of the year 2002 does the 1st fall on a Friday, George gave March, February and November—correct answers. They can also tell you correctly that the 4th Monday in February, 1933 is the 22nd or that the 3rd Monday in May, 1936 was the 18th. This is even more impressive when we note that like many other calendar calculators reported, George and Charles cannot add, subtract, multiply or divide simple single digit numbers. For example, the product of 3 × 6 might be given as 8. Although they cannot add up to 30, when given your birth date, they can accurately tell you it is 30 weeks until your next birthday or 13 weeks since you last had a birthday. George can tell you the year a particular famous man in history—for example, George Washington was born and how old he would be if he were alive today.

The twins' background is of some interest. The father, a self-made successful businessman, died at the age of 58 of cancer of the lung. He was a chronic alcoholic who had been tied to his mother and married late. It was said he never drank on the job, but on the way home from work he would often drink, become enraged, abusive and aggressive and would strike his wife and children. The mother is alive, age 64, and is given to mild mood swings. She had 3 normal pregnancies. The first child died at 13 months reportedly following convulsions. The next two were healthy girls, both trained as nurses and now married. One of them had been given to depressions. Our twin patients are from the 4th pregnancy, which occurred during the period of their father's excessive drinking and abusive behavior. The mother was upset and vomited frequently throughout this pregnancy. At 6 months she hemorrhaged, was rushed to a hospital and gave birth by caesarian section to triplets— two boys and a girl. The girl died within 12 hours. The boys, Charles and George were kept in incubators for 2 months. It is noted in the history that both had convulsions when removed from the incubators, but none since. Throughout the twins' childhood the home life was tempestuous; the parents fought and there was talk of divorce. The twins were "good babies" whose early health was good except for ear infections. George held his head up at 6 months, sat at 9 months but did not walk or talk until 2½ years. Charles, the first-born, lagged behind George. They were not difficult to manage until they began to walk. As soon as they walked they ran. There was head banging, biting of their hands, spilling water, destroying things in the house, etc. At 3 the mother was told by the pediatrician they were retarded and that they could not be enrolled in school. She did not know what the word "retarded" meant and the pediatrician explained the boys would never be mathematicians. The mother's reaction was frequently expressed as "thank goodness Mary died; otherwise there would be 3." She repeatedly said she wanted to kill herself and take the boys with her. Both parents were ashamed of the twins, but the mother and sisters would try to teach them letters, numbers, etc., for the few minutes that they could hold the twins' attention.

The development of George's special talent was observed at age 6—it had been noted that he would spend hours poring over an almanac which contained a perpetual calendar. From what has gone before it comes as a distinct surprise that George *could* or would pore over the almanac at 6 years, but the fact is George could decipher the almanac. The parents felt this talent was a compensation from God and the father later got a silver perpetual calendar that George played with for hours and hours. He made no errors from the beginning. A paternal aunt, a legal secretary, used to call to check dates of documents with him. The father praised George—calling him a smart boy. This pleased George, who frequently asked why he was different from the sisters. Charles, who was always slower in both physical and mental development, did not play with the almanac and initially showed no interest in dates. He and George had no close relationship until they were institutionalized at Letchworth Village at age 9. At that time George and Charles became inseparable. Charles became interested in telling dates but was noted to go through a period in which he made many mistakes. Both were only interested in this one activity, although they were capable of learning other things; for instance George can pick out tunes on the piano and knows the Greek alphabet.

At 9 they were taken to Letchworth Village and have been there for the past 15 years. The records at Letchworth are replete with notes of fighting, biting, destructiveness, *etc.* They spent about a year at school in Letchworth, but their behavior was difficult. They were transferred to Psychiatric Institute in April, 1963 for further study and there has been considerable improvement in their behavior. They have been cooperative and are willing, with some satisfaction, to exhibit their prowess. At first the other patients seemed frightened, but now the twins are the pets on the ward. They both are now able to wear plastic glasses; both are severely myopic, but they do not have retrolental fibroplasia, first suspected because of their having been in incubators for 2 months.

Of the twins, Charles seems to have more impairment than George. He has a left strabismus, horizontal and vertical nystagmia, some retinal changes in one eye as well as vitreous opacities. They both have rocking and swaying movements. Clinically both seem hyperosmic; frequently both go up to people sniffing and smelling. Although each can pick out his own shoes and bedroom slippers by smell, on quantitative smell tests neither performed better than average. EEG's here and previously at Letchworth have been normal.

Chromosome studies have shown normal karyotypes. The initial chromosome examinations suggested "mosaicism" with some cells of 45, 46, and 47 chromosomes. When this was repeated in our own laboratory and in the more experienced laboratory of Dr. M. Grumbach at Presbyterian Hospital, this finding was not confirmed. From a genetic standpoint they are now considered normal males. The similarity method of zygosity diagnosis, fingerprint examination and blood groups (O, N, Rh_1-DCc positive, E negative-Duffy positive, Kell negative) strongly suggest monozygosity. Other pertinent laboratory tests have been non-contributory so far. Ferric chloride, for phenyl pyruvic acid, dinitro phenyl hydrazine for keto acids, serum for ceruloplasmin, serum protein partition and P.B.I. are all normal. Urine amino acid fractions and 17 keto and hydroxy steroids are being studied.

Since their admission to our hospital, with a reduction in their fears and acceptance by our staff and patients, their behavior has improved and their I.Q.'s have risen. They now test between 60 and 70 in comparison to 40–50 range in previous years.

The problem raised by this pair of identical twins remains inexplicable. Although other cases of calendar calculators in mentally deficient people are not rare, this is the first pair of identical twins where each has a skill of calendar calculation beyond the range of known perpetual calendars. This feature casts doubt on explanations previously offered, namely that the skill developed is merely a hypertrophied repetition of a memory function or an extended eidetic imagery that allows for visual recall of previously learned experiences. Another explanation is that such individuals have a defect of abstract capacity along with an endowed talent that continues to be exercised because only through this performance can the limited individual come to terms with his environment. As long as the performance ranged within the limits of what could be memorized, learned or recalled, such explanations were plausible and had previously been accepted. However, our twins demonstrate their ability in areas where memory, learning and recall are not available to them. In addition, they operate so rapidly that it is obvious they use no formula even if they were capable of learning one. They operate in a range of calendar calculation far before and beyond our usual 200–400-year perpetual calendar. The longest known perpetual calendar extends to about the year 2400 and one of the twins can reach beyond the year 7000. Furthermore, they can calculate dates for which no formal calendar exists such as the years in which a certain day in a certain month falls on a Sunday, *etc.*, or which month in a certain year will the first fall on a Friday, *etc.* It is possible that motivational factors have extended the range of their unique skill, but this does not account for the basic structure of the skill. They do not have even a remote idea how they perform—saying "I know," or "It's in my head." After exploring their abilities with various people in different learned fields—psychiatrists, psychologists, internists and mathematicians, *etc.*, we must candidly admit that we have no better explanation. By showing that previous explanations really must again be questioned, we hope to indicate that other factors, probably beyond our present knowledge, must be understood before we have a better explanation than do our Identical Twin-Idiot Savants.

DISCUSSION

Arthur P. Holstein

It seems to work out as a general rule, that individuals who have gross chromosomal deformities in either size, shape, form, or number are grossly deformed individuals in other respects, and can be easily characterized clinically by many physical stigmata, for example, the Mongol and the Klinefelter's and Turner's Syndrome. George and Charles have no chromosomal defect and in a general fashion they are not grossly deformed individuals.

The Idiot-Savant seems to constitute a distinct syndrome; the general characteristics of which are as follows: first, their I.Q. is very low, most of them being around 50 or lower, one case reported had an I.Q. of 8. George's and Charles' I.Q. have been in this range. In contract to this exceedingly low I.Q., there is usually associated a marked increase in certain specific mental abilities. These are usually associated with calculation, and frequently with calendar calculations. The twins demonstrate this adequately. Other aspects of their problem-solving ability are more in line with their low I.Q. It is especially noted that the ability to function in abstract fashion seems to be lacking. George and Charles can subtract apples but not dollars. The age of onset is usually in childhood, and the approximate age of 7 years is noted in several protocols. Curiously enough, most of the people involved have been men although there are a few women noted who apparently have these abilities. The protocols in the literature are abbreviated and whether or not the men show differences in abilities from the women cannot be ascertained. However, raising the question of a sex-linked characteristic seems appropriate at present. Many of them seem to have music abilities which are somewhat better than one might expect from a person with a low I.Q. They are able to play musical instruments by ear. However, they are unable to learn to play these instruments in the usual fashion and cannot be taught to read music. Also to be noted is the fact that they enjoy listening to music. George and Charles have these abilities. Frequently it is mentioned that the person with this ability has an associated degree of interest in art and mechanical skills, which are well beyond those of the usual mentally retarded or normal person. Tredgold's original case is certainly a fine example of this. Scheerer notes that the Idiot-Savant frequently has an acutely perceptive sensory sensitivity. George and Charles can identify their shoes by smelling them. The reports do not clearly differentiate the various types of retardation occurring in the individuals reported on, however, it does appear that there is no specific type of retardation associated with the ability to calculate. For example, one young woman developed the ability following a case of typhoid encephalitis at the age of 17. Another young man who had the extremely low I.Q. of 8 was a spastic paraplegic from birth injury and though unable to talk had a phenomenal calendar memory somewhat approaching the abilities of the twins. The twins themselves have a type of mental retardation which is associated with their ocular defect of chorio retinitis and is transmitted as a mendelian recessive. This variation of cause should rule out that the Idiot-Savant is an autistic child grown up.

In considering the abilities of the twins (and Dr. Horwitz assures me that their identicalness extends through their blood types) the skill is not developed comparably in each. George developed it first and has more of the ability than Charles. Significantly he is the taller and dominant member of the pair. He is also the youngest. The fact that identical twins can develop differently in some aspects of their appearance and personality is not unusual and has been recorded in numerous instances. For example, Shields, in his book on *Monozygotic Twins, Brought Up Apart and Brought Up Together,* documents this many times. Rosenthal, writing about the Genain Quadruplets, has gathered together a significant amount of material on 4 monozygotic sisters who similarly show personality differences which are easily observed.

It is interesting to speculate that perhaps the phenomenon of a type of memory which Idiot-Savants have represents memory which in some fashion has developed separately from general intellectual ability as a part of the personality. This notion is not unusual since paranoid schizophrenics have an exquisite memory, and in a general way they incorporate their memory ability into their personality. At any rate, the qualities of memory that George and Charles and the others exhibit are apparently not associated with any aspects of mental functioning associated with their intelligence of which they are impoverished.

The importance, then, of the Idiot-Savant lies in our inability to explain him; he stands as a landmark of our own ignorance and the phenomenon of the Idiot-Savant exists as a challenge to our capabilities.

REFERENCES

1. Tregold, A. F.: Mental Deficiency. Baltimore: Wood, 1937.
2. Masland, R. L., Sarason, S. B., and Gladwyn, T.: Mental Subnormality. New York: Basic Books, 1958.

UNIT FIVE | DISCUSSION QUESTIONS

13 | HOW DIFFERENT ARE THEY?

Discuss how a revision of ideas concerning the proper sex role will improve our society.

What are some of the early differences between boys and girls in learning ability?

14 | INDIVIDUAL DIFFERENCES IN BEHAVIOR AND AUTONOMIC ACTIVITY IN NEWBORN INFANTS

What effects of the environment affect temperamental differences?

Give examples of maternal behavior that affects temperamental differences in young babies.

15 | THE XYY AND THE CRIMINAL

The legal implications of the double-Y "criminal" syndrome are currently being debated. In light of the evidence presented in this article, support your thesis in this issue.

Speculate about the viewpoints of the following concerning the XYY and the criminal: the lawyer, the penologist, the philosopher.

16 | IDENTICAL TWIN—"IDIOT SAVANTS"—CALENDAR CALCULATORS

Discuss the theories attempting to explain the phenomenon of the "idiot savant" according to this report.

What are some of the characteristics of the "idiot savant" as delineated in this article?

UNIT SIX
EVALUATING AND MEASURING BEHAVIOR

The fact that employers generally ask job applicants for references or past employment records is an indication that employers attempt to predict future performance on the basis of past behavioral patterns. Many colleges and universities require prospective students to submit the high-school grade point averages they have attained and the results of certain psychological test scores they have taken. This is an indication that probable academic success is also predictable on the basis of past performance. Even at race tracks people buy racing forms on the assumption that future expectations of horses and dogs can be determined by their past track records. Installment-buying customers are evaluated by their past payment records. All these examples are indications that prediction is an integral part of our way of life.

Approximately 200 years ago astronomers discovered that seemingly inaccurate recordings of astronomical events were in reality individual differences in reaction timing. Wundt's laboratory of the late 1800's concentrated on behavioral differences found in human beings. Ruby Yoshioka's *What Can We Predict?* is a knowledgeable discussion of the history of probability theory, which was founded on a gambler's curiosity.

During the first decade of this century, the French government solicited the services of two psychologists, Binet and Simon, to devise a method that would identify intellectual differences among Paris youngsters. The American revision of this test in 1916 ushered in an era that was destined to make the United States the leading proponent of psychological testing.

Both evaluation and measurement of human behavior are based on the assumption that heredity imposes certain limitations on one's intellectual abilities as well as on his physical skills. That these limits are affected by environmental factors has led to many classical studies illustrating the effects of heredity and environment upon intelligence and other abilities. The Psychological Corporation's *Methods of Expressing Test Scores,* which presents the meaning of test scores in relation to sampling and norm models, stands as an outstanding reference in psychometry.

Grace Rubin-Rabson discusses the limitations and difficulties facing the behavioral scientist in his quest for precision measurement. In her *Behavioral Science Versus Intelligence,* she emphasizes the uniqueness, as well as the complexity, of individuals that is encountered in the process of scientific evaluation.

Since Hermann Rorschach, the Swiss psychiatrist, published a set of inkblots, personality testing has also become a popular aspect of psychological evaluation. Rorschach died in 1922 at the age of 37 and he had barely begun to extend the application of his tests from mental patients to normal subjects. However, since that time, individual and group personality testing has become widespread. An appendix to William Whyte's book, *The Organization Man,* is the subject of the final article in this unit. Whyte's *How To Cheat on Personality Tests* is reprinted to illustrate how some observers have viewed this aspect of psychological testing.

17 | WHAT CAN WE PREDICT?

Ruby Yoshioka

A mathematical system which was born in order to predict the probable winnings of gamblers is now helping man predict the path of atomic particles, the color of a hybrid flower, the odds against quintuplets or whether an eel will swim to America or to Europe.

Aside from gambling, our daily lives are full of probabilities. Will it rain? Will I pass the science exam? Will a surgical operation be successful? At best what we decide will or will not happen is based on some previous experience or just a guess as to the outcome or a "feeling" of what probably will take place. This is the common conception of probability.

But for mathematicians and statisticians, probability is more than a guess or intuition. They have devised mathematical systems, some of which are very complex, whereby the chances of an event occurring can be predicted.

HOW THEORY AROSE

The theory of mathematical probability arose from the studies of games of chance, early in the 17th century. Blaise Pascal, a French mathematician, scientist, and philosopher, and creator of the famous Pascal triangle based on the binomial theorem, was asked by a gambler friend, who was interested in the "why" of gambling chances, to figure out why certain odds were more favorable to a gambling house than other odds. This Pascal undertook with the help of Pierre Fermat, another French mathematician, and developed probability theory.

Since that time, probability theory has become increasingly important and many mathematicians have contributed to its advancement.

Probability theory today has applications in virtually every field from atomic physics and biology to social science.

Predictions of weather, population increase, the number of accidents that may occur during a holiday weekend and the probable outcome of elections are all examples of the application of mathematical probability, as are the estimation of insurance rates.

The classic example to explain probability theory is in tossing coins. If a coin is flipped, what is the chance that it will turn up heads? Since it must turn up either heads or tails, the probability is ½; in 100 throws the probability is 50 heads and 50 tails in an ideal situation.

This does not mean that if heads shows in the first throw, tails will turn up in the next. Each throw is independent of the previous throw, since coins do not have

From *Science News,* **85,** 139, 1964. Reprinted by permission of *Science News,* weekly summary of current science. Copyright © 1964 by Science Service, Inc.

a memory. However, in the long run, that is, after many tosses, say 100,000, the ratio of heads to tails tends to be 1 to 1.

Thus, if in 100 throws, there are 45 heads, heads could turn up about 450 times in 1,000 throws. It would be most unusual and highly improbable that in 1,000 throws the number of heads would be only 45. Actually tossing the coin and recording the result would show this to be true.

Taking another example, if a die is thrown, the chances of any one of the numbers, 1 through 6, appearing is $\frac{1}{6}$. This means that after many throws, or in the long run, any single number, say 3, will appear in $\frac{1}{6}$ of the throws.

If you throw two dice, one blue and one white, the chance of 3 appearing on a blue dice is $\frac{1}{6} \times \frac{1}{6}$ or $\frac{1}{36}$, but a sum of 3 can be produced in two ways, with a 2 and 1, both equally likely. Thus its probability is $\frac{2}{36}$, or $\frac{1}{18}$, so a sum of 3 may be expected to occur once in every 18 throws.

As the number of throws increases, the chances of occurring at this ratio increase.

MORE COMPLEX PROBLEMS

These simple applications of probability theory as shown in the tossed coins and the throwing of dice have been applied to more complex problems of probability. James Bernoulli, later in the 17th century, clearly defined probability theory in relationship to large numbers of cases, applying the same mathematical equation.

As a result of Bernoulli's law and subsequent related laws, the central limit theorems were derived. These theorems state that as the number of trials increases, the predictions made by probability theory can be more and more closely satisfied.

For example, taking coins again, the ratio of heads to tails tends to come closer to 1 to 1 as the number of throws is increased. However, an interesting point is that the actual numerical difference between heads and tails tends to become greater with the greater number of trials. In 100 throws, if tails show 45 times and heads 55 times, the difference is 10. But, if 1,000 throws are made and the ratio is 450 to 550, the numerical difference is 100.

WHY GAMBLERS LOSE

Thus, the best lesson a gambler can learn from probability theory is that if he continues to play, he will always lose. Mathematicians have shown, since the time of Bernoulli, that the chances of loss become greater and greater as the gambler continues to play and the resources of the house increase compared to those of the gambler.

This is also true in a slot machine. The more quarters a player puts into the machine, the slimmer become his chances of becoming a winner.

A curve can be drawn from a table of the various ways in which an event may happen, such as the tossing of coins. The probability distribution curve is bell-shaped and is known as the normal distribution curve, or Gaussian curve after Karl Friedrich Gauss.

The normal curve is used extensively in many applications, for example, in showing the variations of I.Q. in a certain age group or the heights of different races. Where natural phenomena can be measured, such as the number of peas in a pod or the weight of children of a certain age, the normal probability distribution is closely followed.

In genetics, the Mendelian theory of the transmission of traits can be predicted by probability theory.

If a red flower is crossed with a white flower, the red gene will unite with the white gene to form a pink flower. If two pink flowers are then crossed, the next generation will produce one red, one white and two pinks, following the pattern of the probability distribution of heads and tails when two coins are tossed.

This ability to predict offspring of plants is most useful to agriculturists and botanists in hybridizing and improving plants and animals.

RANDOM SAMPLING

It is often desirable to know how a population will vote or how well a machine is turning out a product. A system of random sampling has been devised.

The straw vote taken before an election is an example of random sampling. From such a vote, the trend of the election can be predicted.

If the product of a new machine is to be tested, samples selected at random can give the manufacturer an indication of the quality of the whole.

Sampling is a convenient and oftentimes the only method by which a study of large groups can be made.

In physics the behavior of atoms and molecules and the paths of electrons and protons are determined probabilistically. Since it is impossible to determine the exact position or exact motion of an electron at a particular moment, its position or direction of movement must be based on probability and must be estimated.

Most physicists believe that probability behavior governing electrons must also apply to the universe, but the late Prof. Albert Einstein, among other scientists, believed there is an underlying order in the universe that does not involve probability.

Astronomers apply probability statistics when determining the position of stars and space scientists calculate travels in outer space on a probabilistic basis.

NEW METHOD OF CALCULATING

A new method of calculating probability that uses only existing factors rather than previous events has been recently devised by Prof. Marcel Neuts of Purdue University, Lafayette, Ind.

Prof. Neuts reported that his method can be applied to actual biological and physical phenomena as well as purely theoretical mathematical problems.

The concept of mathematical probability is far reaching and enters into virtually all phases of our lives, from birth rates to death rates, with all the probabilities and statistics that can happen in between.

Since this is so, an early introduction to the concept of probability and statistical methods would be extremely valuable to students in almost every field of study. To help make this important step in the introduction of probability theory to younger students, SCIENCE SERVICE has issued a THINGS of science kit on probability containing problems and explanations of elementary mathematical probability and the materials necessary to perform the experiments. The unit is available at 75¢ each from SCIENCE SERVICE, Washington, D.C. 20036.

18 | METHODS OF EXPRESSING TEST SCORES

The Psychological Corporation

An individual's test score acquires meaning when it can be compared with the scores of well-identified groups of people. Manuals for tests provide tables of norms to make it easy to compare individuals and groups. Several systems for deriving more meaningful "standard scores" from raw scores have been widely adopted. All of them reveal the relative status of individuals within a group.

The fundamental equivalence of the most popular standard score system is illustrated in the chart on the next page. We hope the chart and the accompanying description will be useful to counselors, personnel officers, clinical diagnosticians and others in helping them to show the uninitiated the essential simplicity of standard score systems, percentile equivalents, and their relation to the ideal normal distribution.

Sooner or later, every textbook discussion of test scores introduces the bell-shaped normal curve. The student of testing soon learns that many of the methods of deriving meaningful scores are anchored to the dimensions and characteristics of this curve. And he learns by observation of actual test score distributions that the ideal mathematical curve is a reasonably good approximation of many practical cases. He learns to use the standardized properties of the ideal curve as a model.

Let us look first at the curve itself. Notice that there are no raw scores printed along the baseline. The graph is generalized; it describes an idealized distribution of scores of any group on any test. We are free to use any numerical scale we like. For any particular set of scores, we can be arbitrary and call the average score zero. In technical terms we "equate" the mean raw score to zero. Similarly we can choose any convenient number, say 1.00, to represent the scale distance of one standard deviation.[1] Thus, if a distribution of scores on a particular test has a mean of 36 and a standard deviation of 4, the zero point on the baseline of our curve would be equivalent to an original score of 36; one unit to the right, $+1\sigma$, would be equivalent to 40, $(36 + 4)$; and one unit to the left, -1σ, would be equivalent to 32, $(36 - 4)$.

The total area under the curve represents the total number of scores in the distribution. Vertical lines have been drawn through the score scale (the baseline) at zero and at 1, 2, 3, and 4 sigma units to the right and left. These lines mark off subareas of the total area under the curve. The numbers printed in these subareas are per cents—*percentages of the total number of people.* Thus, 34.13 per cent of all cases in a normal distribution have scores falling between 0 and -1σ. For practical purposes we rarely need to deal with standard deviation units below -3 or above $+3$; the percentage of cases with scores beyond $\pm 3\sigma$ is negligible.

From *Test Service Bulletin*, **48**, January 1955. Reprinted courtesy of *Test Service Bulletin* of The Psychological Corporation.

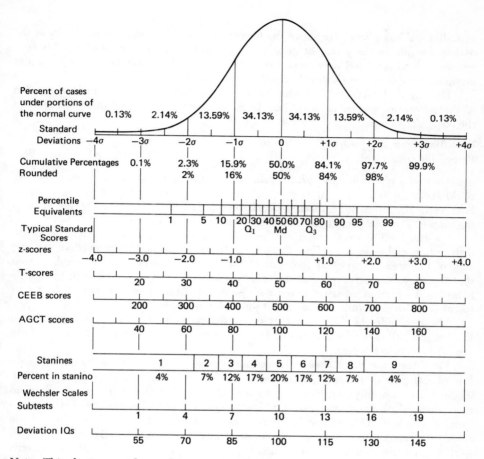

Percent of cases under portions of the normal curve	0.13%	2.14%	13.59%	34.13%	34.13%	13.59%	2.14%	0.13%	
Standard Deviations	−4σ	−3σ	−2σ	−1σ	0	+1σ	+2σ	+3σ	+4σ
Cumulative Percentages Rounded	0.1%	2.3% 2%	15.9% 16%	50.0% 50%	84.1% 84%	97.7% 98%	99.9%		

Percentile Equivalents
1 5 10 20 30 40 50 60 70 80 90 95 99
Q₁ Md Q₃

Typical Standard Scores

z-scores
−4.0   −3.0   −2.0   −1.0   0   +1.0   +2.0   +3.0   +4.0

T-scores
20   30   40   50   60   70   80

CEEB scores
200   300   400   500   600   700   800

AGCT scores
40   60   80   100   120   140   160

Stanines
1   2   3   4   5   6   7   8   9

Percent in stanine
4%   7% 12% 17% 20% 17% 12% 7%   4%

Wechsler Scales Subtests
1   4   7   10   13   16   19

Deviation IQs
55   70   85   100   115   130   145

Note: This chart cannot be used to equate scores on one test to scores on another test. For example, both 600 on the CEEB and 120 on the AGCT are one standard deviation above their respective means, but they do not represent "equal" standings because the scores were obtained from different groups.

The fact that 68.26 per cent fall between ±1σ gives rise to the common statement that in a normal distribution roughly two-thirds of all cases lie between plus and minus one sigma. This is a rule of thumb every test user should keep in mind. It is very near to the theoretical value and is a useful approximation.

Below the row of deviations expressed in sigma units is a row of per cents; these show *cumulatively* the percentage of people which is included *to the left* of each of the sigma points. Thus, starting from the left, when we reach the line erected above −2σ, we have included the lowest 2.3 per cent of cases. These percentages have been rounded in the next row.

Note some other relationships: the area between the ±1σ points includes the scores which lie above the 16th percentile (−1σ) and below the 84th percentile (+1σ)—two major reference points all test users should know. When we find that an individual has a score 1σ above the mean, we conclude that his score ranks at the 84th percentile in the group of persons on whom the test was normed. (This conclusion is good provided we also add this clause, at least subvocally: *if this particular group reasonably approximates the ideal normal model.*)

The simplest facts to memorize about the normal distribution and the relation of the *percentile* system to deviations from the average in sigma units are seen in the chart. They are

Deviation from the mean	-2σ	-1σ	0	$+1\sigma$	$+2\sigma$
Percentile equivalent	2	16	50	84	98

To avoid cluttering the graph reference lines have not been drawn, but we could mark off ten per cent sections of area under the normal curve by drawing lines vertically from the indicated decile points (10, 20, . . . 80, 90) up through the graph. The reader might do this lightly with a colored pencil.

We can readily see that ten per cent of the area (people) at the middle of the distribution embraces a smaller *distance* on the baseline of the curve than ten per cent of the area (people) at the ends of the range of scores, for the simple reason that the curve is much higher at the middle. A person who is at the 95th percentile is farther away from a person at the 85th percentile in units of *test score* than a person at the 55th percentile is from one at the 45th percentile.

The remainder of the chart, that is the several scoring scales drawn parallel to the baseline, illustrates variations of the *deviation score* principle. As a class these are called *standard scores.*

First, there are the *z-scores*. These are the same *numbers* as shown on the baseline of the graph; the only difference is that the expression, σ, has been omitted. These scores run, in practical terms, from -3.0 to $+3.0$. One can compute them to more decimal places if one wishes, although computing to a single decimal place is usually sufficient. One can compute z-scores by equating the mean to 0.00 and the standard deviation to 1.00 for a distribution of any shape, but the relationships shown in this figure between the z-score equivalents of raw scores and percentile equivalents of raw scores are correct only for normal distributions. The interpretation of standard score systems derives from the idea of using the normal curve as a model.

As can be seen, *T*-scores are directly related to z-scores. The mean of the raw scores is equated to 50, and the standard deviation of the raw scores is equated to 10. Thus a z-score of $+1.5$ means the same as a *T*-score of 65. *T*-scores are usually expressed in whole numbers from about 20 to 80. The *T*-score plan eliminates negative numbers and thus facilitates many computations.[2]

The College Entrance Examination Board uses a plan in which both decimals and negative numbers are avoided by setting the arbitrary mean at 500 points and the arbitrary sigma at another convenient unit, namely, 100 points. The experienced tester or counselor who hears of a College Board SAT-V score of 550 at once thinks, "Half a sigma (50 points) above average (500 points) on the CEEB basic norms." And when he hears of a score of 725 on SAT-M, he can interpret, "Plus $2\frac{1}{4}\sigma$. Therefore, better than the 98th percentile."

During World War II the Navy used the *T*-score plan of reporting test status. The Army used still another system with a mean of 100 and a standard deviation of 20 points.

Another derivative of the general standard score system is the *stanine* plan, developed by psychologists in the Air Force during the war. The plan divides the norm population into nine groups, hence, "standard nines." Except for stanine 9, the top, and stanine 1, the bottom, these groups are spaced in half-sigma units. Thus, stanine 5 is defined as including the people who are within ±0.25σ of the mean. Stanine 6 is the group defined by the half-sigma distance on the baseline between +0.25σ and +0.75σ. Stanines 1 and 9 include all persons who are below −1.75σ and above +1.75σ, respectively. The result is a distribution in which the mean is 5.0 and the standard deviation is 2.0.

Just below the line showing the demarcation of the nine groups in the stanine system there is a row of percentages which indicates the per cent of the total population in each of the stanines. Thus 7 per cent of the population will be in stanine 2, and 20 per cent in the middle group, stanine 5.

Interpretation of the Wechsler scales (W-B I, W-B II, WISC, and WAIS) depends on a knowledge of standard scores. A subject's raw score *on each of the subtests* in these scales is converted, by appropriate norms tables, to a standard score, based on a mean of 10 and a standard deviation of 3. The sums of standard scores on the Verbal Scale, the Performance Scale, and the Full Scale are then converted into IQs. These IQs are based on a standard score mean of 100, the conventional number for representing the IQ of the average person in a given age group. The standard deviation of the IQs is set at 15 points. In practical terms, then, roughly two-thirds of the IQs are between 85 and 115, that is ±1σ.[3] IQs of the type used in the Wechsler scales have come to be known as *deviation IQs,* as contrasted with the IQs developed from scales in which a derived mental age is divided by chronological age.

Users of the Wechsler scales should establish clearly in their minds the relationship of subtest scaled scores and the deviation IQs to the other standard score systems, to the ordinary percentile rank interpretation, and to the deviation units on the baseline of the normal curve. For example, every Wechsler examiner should recognize that an IQ of 130 is a score equivalent to a deviation of +2σ, and that this IQ score delimits approximately the upper two per cent of the population. If a clinician wants to evaluate a Wechsler IQ of 85 along with percentile ranks on several other tests given in school, he can mentally convert the IQ of 85 to a percentile rank of about 16, this being the percentile equal to a deviation from the mean of −1σ. Of course he should also consider the appropriateness and comparability of norms.

Efficiency in interpreting test scores in counseling, in clinical diagnosis, and in personnel selection depends, in part, on facility in thinking in terms of the major interrelated plans by which meaningful scores are derived from raw scores. It is hoped that this graphic presentation will be helpful to all who in their daily work must help others understand the information conveyed by numerical test scores.

NOTES

1. The mathematical symbol for the standard deviation is the lower-case Greek letter sigma or σ. These terms are used interchangeably in this article.

2. *T*-scores and percentiles both have 50 as the main reference point, an occasional source

of confusion to those who do not insist on careful labelling of data and of scores of individuals in their records.

3. Every once in a while we receive a letter from someone who suggests that the Wechsler scales ought to generate a wider range of IQs. The reply is very simple. If we want a wider range of IQs all we have to do is to choose a *larger arbitrary* standard deviation, say, 20 or 25. Under the present system, $\pm 3\sigma$ gives IQs of 55 to 145, with a few rare cases below and a few rare cases above. If we used 20 as the standard deviation, we would *arbitrarily* increase the $\pm 3\sigma$ range of IQs from 55–145 to 40–160. This *is* a wider range of numbers! But, test users should never forget that adaptations of this kind do not change the responses of the people who took the test, do not change the order of the persons in relation to each other, and do not change the psychological meaning attached to an IQ.

---

19 | BEHAVIORAL SCIENCE VERSUS INTELLIGENCE

Grace Rubin-Rabson

The physical scientist can with certainty predict the conditions under which water will boil, but a man's boiling point is not so readily determined. So complex is the behavior of a living thing, so intertwined the reaction of subject and investigator that one wonders whether the behavioral scientist can ever achieve the precision, the validity (the agreement between a score or measure and the thing it reputedly measures), or the replication (re-examination under identical conditions) available to the physical sciences.

Still, he must persist. When his work with people effects public policy, the behavioral scientist bears enormous responsibility. In these circumstances, since publication in a professional journal does not in itself guarantee merit nor the validity of conclusions, an objective review of the work's premises, its design, the raw data, the manner and accuracy of procedure and computations and the statistical techniques employed is in order.

Each human being is unique; there is no other in the world like him. Approach one for study and, like the chameleon under changing light, he reflects the con-

From *The Wall Street Journal*, July 1, 1969. Reprinted by permission of *The Wall Street Journal*.

frontation and is no longer the same. Approach more than one, sum up the results in neat statistical arrays and the averages describe no particular individual in the group. Design tests to analyze his abilities, his interests and aptitudes, and he is subjected to a mass-standardized procedure that, like mass-designed furniture, fits everyone to a degree and no one exactly. Devise skillful experimental techniques to test some aspects of his behavior under social pressure—and it must be some small aspect that can be clearly isolated—and a hopefully valid conclusion can be drawn about this small aspect. But these are again group findings, not necessarily true of every individual in the group.

DESPAIR?

Nor is human behavior a composite of bits pieced together in a simplified and artificial laboratory staging, but the response to a complex situation of a whole being prompted and defined at any moment by his entire intellectual and emotional experience.

Faced with this obstacle, the experimentalist might well throw up his hands in despair. Contrasted with him, his colleague practising psychotherapy does not despair, but goes blithely on his loving and persuasive way, unconcerned about the validity of his constructs, content that, for whatever reason, his patient improves. Truly it has been said: The psychotherapist uses important concepts that he cannot validate while the experimental psychologist validates unimportant concepts that he cannot use.

The behavioral scientist is himself a complicating factor, for he is human too, expressing his own needs in his choice of profession and specialized area; the problem he selects to investigate, the methods and materials he organizes for the investigation. Despite his careful conscious objectivity, it follows from his choice of problem that he may be unconsciously biased toward a particular outcome and, by subtle cues —perhaps heightened enthusiasm in his voice and gestures—convey the desired responses to his subjects or his co-workers. There is no fraud here, only a fairly obvious example to suggest the hazards inherent in keeping the experiment free of the experimenter.

In the early, quieter years of this century, American psychologists became interested in the area of intelligence testing. Little was known then about intelligence, little is known now, though the study of its theoretical and biopsychological structures has begun. A British psychologist, Liam Hudson, says of this somewhat overextolled attribute, recognized by everyone but acceptably defined by no one: "The field is still in its pre-Copernican state: The classical experiments have yet to be done, and the while, our research grows in on itself, and becomes encapsulated. What good ideas there are are stumbled on in true somnambulistic fashion; and only occasionally recognized as good."

So routine is intelligence testing now that the "I.Q. test" has become an accepted part of the school and clinical scene; so entrenched its use, the testers have ceased to question its validity, if ever they did.

The test result is a composite, dependent on natural endowment, in a measure on school skills, on the confidence engendered by success in school and extra-school skills. School skills, in turn, depend on natural endowment plus adequate learning.

From a poor start of faulty learning and cumulative confusion, the inevitable lack of skills and self-confidence pervades the test itself. The added handicaps then further obscure the natural endowment factor in the test result.

THE ALL-IMPORTANT IQ

The "intelligence-quotient" is a source of joy and obligation when high, of a dragging sense of mediocrity when centered around the average, of bitter and permanent pain when low, affecting an entire life. Instances of all three have appeared in the press within this year.

The first reports a "girl genius" with an I.Q. of 154–201, depending on the test. Even for an imprecise measure of an elusive concept, this is a range to give one pause. Is this genius an equal among college professors, or is she a genius destined for history? Which score goes down on her record? Does it make any difference? If these wide-ranging scores show a consistent upward trend, either the successive tests were easier, or this mathematics wizard, with sufficient practice, finally broke the code. Intelligence tests have a basic similarity, and test scores tend to increase with exposure to testing. On a second use of the same test, some test-item responses, failed the first time, will be available, not through increased intelligence, simply through investigation.

Another instance, one hard to believe, is the hurtful misuse of testing in evaluating small Mexican-American children in two California school districts. As reported in the press, on the basis of a Binet test administered in English, with a cut-off point of 70, certain of these children qualified for the Educable Mentally Retarded group. But when, some time later, the test was administered in Spanish, scores increased as much as 28 points, an average of 13.

To the horror of the humiliation of these children and their families, and the demoralizing effects of remaining in a slow group, add the lingering barbarism of a cut-off point on a test standardized on middle-class, English-speaking American children, and for this reason, unsuitable to these children, to Puerto Ricans newly arrived, to Negroes of the Deep South, to Indians isolated on reservations, though all of them, presumably, are attending some kind of American school.

A well-designed "culture-free" test may avoid the problem of cultural unsuitability, though it shares with the "culture-associated" test the fundamental drawback, as Hudson says, that classical experiments have yet to be done. Moreover, the tests predominantly used in schools and clinics are culture-associated.

Intelligence is not measurable to a point; should the tests be far more reliable than they currently are, the individual intelligence could be located only in a broad zone, a zone five to ten points on either side of the resulting I.Q. Depending on the quality of the test itself, on the examiner, on rapport, on physiological state, on anxiety, on test practice, on errors in administration and scoring, among an assortment of influences, a considerable variation can be taken for granted. How then, at any specific moment, whether for these or any other children, can one decide that the I.Q. of 69 goes to the retarded class and that the I.Q. of 70 remains with the normal class? Uneasy lies the head of the examiner who must make these decisions.

More uneasy still lie the heads of the expert witnesses at the Sirhan trial. The concepts now available to the psychology professions clearly proved inadequate for a decision in a life and death situation, however helpful such concepts may be in the clinic. Confused and contradictory as they were, a "third ear" might have heard an alert defense's briefing, gleaned from the textbooks, on persuasively aberrant responses and courtroom capers. The psychology professions are still young, and though precocious, perhaps not yet ready for the role of expert witness.

Sirhan, an example of the mid-range I.Q., seems to have been tested twice, with an earlier score of 89 and a later 109. Does he, then, barely belong to the average group and at the same time to the group superior to 75% of the population? If the two tests were different, then this is one more instance of large discrepancies in measures of the same thing; if the same test was used twice, then some of the possible reasons mentioned earlier apply. Were the tests suitable for an Arab boy brought up in another milieu even though attending an American school?

Teachers, being human too, are influenced by I.Q.s., and for this reason alone such designations might be dropped. Teacher expectations depend on scores, and these expectations are reflected in pupil response. In the experiment of Rosenthal and Jacobson a group of randomly selected children, assigned to a teacher initially led to believe the group superior, showed large increases in the intelligence quotient, one more example of the self-fulfilling prophecy. Long ago, without the extensive labors involved in such a study, the poet Goethe observed: "If one treats a person as if he were what he ought to be and could be, he will become what he ought to be and could be."

Will not the reverse hold equally true? If an individual is stigmatized as "low I.Q." or "mentally retarded," will not his unhappy family, his teachers and everyone around him consistently treat him as such, thus condemning him for life and confirming once more the self-fulfilling prophecy?

By coincidence, two reports involving the genetic factor in intelligence came to public attention at the same time. One implies a superior, the other an inferior, gene for intelligence in two ethnic groups. Lord Snow, the English writer, gracious to the people honoring him, flatteringly but unscientifically ascribed high Jewish achievement to superior intellectual genes. To this the Jews replied, realistically, "Poppycock." Traditional among Jews, they said, is the love of learning; with Maimonides, they believe the goal of life to be the accumulation of knowledge and the perfection of the human mind. These are social, not genetic, influences; motivation and striving in terms of this tradition account adequately for achievement in a permissive environment. When the young know that achievement is possible, they are motivated to achieve. In any case, Jews, like all people who have moved about the earth's surface, are not genetically pure, but mixed.

The other, somewhat over-publicized report of Dr. Arthur Jensen, while making several important points, concludes that lower average intelligence and scholastic performances of Negroes may involve genetic as well as social factors. His proposal that education be revised for children of lower intelligence, regardless of race, is strongly to be seconded. When the encrusted barnacles on American education are at length scraped off, may the mass procedures now employed for all children, irrespective of individual talent, finally give way to approaching the individual child in terms of his unique gifts and perceptions.

In addition, Jensen warns, with a higher birth rate among lower class Negroes (he does not mention the accompanying higher death rate) than among the comparable white group, the intellectual gap will widen, making an increasing proportion of Negroes unemployable except at unskilled labor. His proposal that Negro leaders advocate control of the birth rate can also be warmly seconded—for all people, world-wide.

MIXED GENES

The American Negroes, too, are a mixed people. Few of them are now pure blacks. Under many black skins lie white genes; and under nearly a quarter of white skins (as of 1960) lies an African element in the inherited biological background. In these circumstances, and until more is known about it, the attribution to any group of superior or inferior genes for intelligence seems untenable. Such attention is, in any case, socially unproductive.

Certainly the genetic factor is basic in intelligence and determines the upper limits of its growth. However, as in every other biological aspect, intellectual growth depends on other factors for its development: Adequate physical nourishment, especially in pregnant women and young children, and a stimulating environment. The stimulating environment must include not only the contributions of home and formal education, but a psychological ambience assuring equality, full acceptance and a realistic expectation of achievement. When, after some decades, these conditions truly exist for the Negro, one can consider comparing him with other groups. By then, no one will.

Philip Vernon, a British psychologist, in his recent book, "Intelligence and Cultural Environment," stresses social influences in the development of intelligence: "Clearly, the major barrier to the fuller realization of human potential lies in the realm of adult values and child-rearing practices." And, to quote Dr. Hudson once more: "The intelligence of young children grows, it seems, into the spaces that parents and teachers allot it. What we expect of them, children tend to become."

In an atmosphere of protest, an old world dies, a new one lies aborning: New insights, new curricula, new teaching methods, particularly for handicapped learners, wherever they come from, whatever the reasons for the handicap. Each contributes his talents; each must be served accordingly to his needs. What difference do a few points in a questionable test-score make? Invidious comparisons, in the world community, as in the family community, only arouse ill-will.

Let us move into more constructive areas.

20 | HOW TO CHEAT ON PERSONALITY TESTS

William H. Whyte, Jr.

The important thing to recognize is that you don't win a good score: you avoid a bad one. What a bad score would be depends upon the particular profile the company in question intends to measure you against, and this varies according to companies and according to the type of work. Your score is usually rendered in terms of your percentile rating—that is, how you answer questions in relation to how other people have answered them. Sometimes it is perfectly all right for you to score in the 80th or 90th percentile; if you are being tested, for example, to see if you would make a good chemist, a score indicating that you are likely to be more reflective than ninety out of a hundred adults might not harm you and might even do you some good.

By and large, however, your safety lies in getting a score somewhere between the 40th and 60th percentiles, which is to say, you should try to answer as if you were like everybody else is supposed to be. This is not always too easy to figure out, of course, and this is one of the reasons why I will go into some detail in the following paragraphs on the principal types of questions. When in doubt, however, there are two general rules you can follow: (1) When asked for word associations or comments about the world, give the most conventional, run-of-the-mill, pedestrian answer possible. (2) To settle on the most beneficial answer to any question, repeat to yourself:

a) *I loved my father and my mother, but my father a little bit more.*
b) *I like things pretty well the way they are.*
c) *I never worry much about anything.*
d) *I don't care for books or music much.*
e) *I love my wife and children.*
f) *I don't let them get in the way of company work.*

Now to specifics. The first five questions in the composite test (Table 1) are examples of the ordinary, garden variety of self-report questions.[1] Generally speaking, they are designed to reveal your degree of introversion or extroversion, your stability, and such. While it is true that in these "inventory" types of tests there is not a right or wrong answer to any *one* question, cumulatively you can get yourself into a lot of trouble if you are not wary. "Have you enjoyed reading books as much as having company in?" "Do you sometimes feel self-conscious?"—You can easily see what is being asked for here.

TABLE 1

Composite Personality Test

Self-Report Questions

1. Have you enjoyed reading books as much as having company in?
2. Are you sometimes afraid of failure?
3. Do you sometimes feel self-conscious?
4. Does it annoy you to be interrupted in the middle of your work?
5. Do you prefer serious motion pictures about famous historical personalities to musical comedies?

Indicate whether you agree, disagree, or are uncertain:

6. I am going to Hell.
7. I often get pink spots all over.
8. The sex act is repulsive.
9. I like strong-minded women.
10. Strange voices speak to me.
11. My father is a tyrant.

Hypothetical Questions—Dominance Type

12. You have been waiting patiently for a salesperson to wait on you. Just when she's finished with another customer, a woman walks up abruptly and demands to be waited upon before you. What would you do?
    a) Do nothing.
    b) Push the woman to one side.
    c) Give her a piece of your mind.
    d) Comment about her behavior to the salesperson.

Opinion Questions: Degree of Conservatism

Indicate whether you agree or disagree with the following questions:

13. Prostitution should be state supervised.
14. Modern art should not be allowed in churches.
15. It is worse for a woman to have extramarital relations than for a man.
16. Foreigners are dirtier than Americans.
17. "The Star-Spangled Banner" is difficult to sing properly.

Word Association Questions

Underline the word you think goes best with the word in capitals:

18. UMBRELLA (rain, prepared, cumbersome, appeasement)
19. RED (hot, color, stain, blood)
20. GRASS (green, mow, lawn, court)
21. NIGHT (dark, sleep, moon, morbid)
22. NAKED (nude, body, art, evil)
23. AUTUMN (fall, leaves, season, sad)

Hypothetical Situations—Judgment Type

24. What would you do if you saw a woman holding a baby at the window of a burning house:
    a) Call the fire department.
    b) Rush into the house.

    c) Fetch a ladder.

    d) Try and catch the baby.

25. Which do you think is the best answer for the executive to make in the following situation:

Worker: "Why did Jones get the promotion and I didn't?"

Executive:

    a) "You deserved it but Jones has seniority."

    b) "You've got to work harder."

    c) "Jones's uncle owns the plant."

    d) "Let's figure out how you can improve."

Opinion Questions: Policy Type

26. A worker's home life is not the concern of the company.

    Agree........ Disagree......

27. Good supervisors are born, not made.

    Agree........ Disagree........

28. It should be company policy to encourage off-hours participation by employees in company-sponsored social gatherings, clubs, and teams.

    Agree........ Disagree........

Opinion Questions: Value Type

29. When you look at a great skyscraper, do you think of:

    a) our tremendous industrial growth?

    b) the simplicity and beauty of the structural design?

30. Who helped mankind most?

    a) Shakespeare

    b) Sir Isaac Newton

STAY IN CHARACTER

The trick is to mediate yourself a score as near the norm as possible without departing too far from your own true self. It won't necessarily hurt you, for example, to say that you have enjoyed reading books as much as having company in. It will hurt you, however, to answer every such question in that vein if you are, in fact, the kind that does enjoy books and a measure of solitude. Strive for the happy mean; on the one hand, recognize that a display of too much introversion, a desire for reflection, or sensitivity is to be avoided. On the other hand, don't overcompensate. If you try too hard to deny these qualities in yourself, you'll end so far on the other end of the scale as to be rated excessively insensitive or extroverted. If you are somewhat introverted, then, don't strive to get yourself in the 70th or 80th percentile for extroversion, but merely try to get up into the 40th percentile.

    Since you will probably be taking not one, but a battery of tests, you must be consistent. The tester will be comparing your extroversion score on one test with, say, your sociability score on another, and if these don't correlate the way the tables say they should, suspicion will be aroused. Even when you are taking only one test, consistency is important. Many contain built-in L ("lie") scores, and woe betide you if you answer some questions as if you were a life of the party type and others as if you were an excellent follower. Another pitfall to avoid is giving yourself the benefit of the doubt on all questions in which one answer is clearly preferable to another, viz.: "Do you frequently daydream?" In some tests ways have been worked out to penalize you for this. (By the same token, occasionally you are given credit for excessive frankness. But you'd better not count on it.)

BE EMPHATIC TO THE VALUES OF THE TEST MAKER

Question five asks:

"Do you prefer serious motion pictures about famous historical personalities to musical comedies?" If you answer this question honestly you are quite likely to get a good score for the wrong reasons. If you vote for the musical comedies, you are given a credit for extroversion. It might be, of course, that you are a very thoughtful person who dislikes the kind of pretentious, self-consciously arty "prestige" pictures which Hollywood does badly, and rather enjoy the musical comedies which it does well. The point illustrated here is that, before answering such questions, you must ask yourself which of the alternatives the test maker, not yourself, would regard as the more artistic.

CHOOSE YOUR NEUROSIS

When you come across questions that are like the ones from 6 to 11—"I often get pink spots all over"—be very much on your guard. Such questions were originally a by-product of efforts to screen mentally disturbed people; they measure degrees of neurotic tendency and were meant mainly for use in mental institutions and psychiatric clinics.[2] The Organization has no business at all to throw these questions at you, but its curiosity is powerful and some companies have been adopting these tests as standard. Should you find yourself being asked about spiders, Oedipus complexes, and such, you must, even more than in the previous type of test, remain consistent and as much in character as possible—these tests almost always have lie scores built into them. A few mild neuroses conceded here and there won't give you too bad a score, and in conceding neuroses you should know that more often than not you have the best margin for error if you err on the side of being "hypermanic"—that is, too energetic and active.

DON'T BE TOO DOMINANT

Question 12, which asks you what you would do if somebody barged in ahead of you in a store, is fairly typical of the kind of questions designed to find out how passive or dominant you may be. As always, the middle course is best. Resist the temptation to show yourself as trying to control each situation. You might think companies would prefer that characteristic to passivity, but they often regard it as a sign that you wouldn't be a permissive kind of leader. To err slightly on the side of acquiescence will rarely give you a bad score.

INCLINE TO CONSERVATISM

Questions 13 through 17, which ask you to comment on a variety of propositions, yield a measure of how conservative or radical your views are.[3] To go to either extreme earns you a bad score, but in most situations you should resolve any doubts you have on a particular question by deciding in favor of the accepted.

Similarly with word associations. In questions 18 through 23, each word in capitals is followed by four words, ranging from the conventional to the somewhat unusual. The trouble here is that if you are not a totally conventional person you may be somewhat puzzled as to what the conventional response is. Here is one tip: before examining any one question closely and reading it from left to right, read vertically through the whole list of questions and you may well see a definite pattern. In making up tests, testers are thinking of ease in scoring, and on some test forms the most conventional responses will be found in one column, the next most conventional in the next, and so on. All you have to do then is go down the list and pick, alternately, the most conventional, and the second most conventional. Instead of a high score for emotionalism, which you might easily get were you to proceed on your own, you earn a stability score that will indicate "normal ways of thinking."

DON'T SPLIT HAIRS

When you come to hypothetical situations designed to test your judgment, you have come to the toughest of all questions.[4] In this kind there are correct answers, and the testers make no bones about it. Restricted as the choice is, however, determining which are the correct ones is extremely difficult, and the more intelligent you are the more difficult. One tester, indeed, states that the measurement of practical judgment is "unique and statistically independent of such factors as intelligence, and academic and social background." He has a point. Consider the question about the woman and the baby at the window of the burning house. It is impossible to decide which is the best course of action unless you know how big the fire is, whether she is on the first floor or the second, whether there is a ladder handy, how near by the fire department is, plus a number of other considerations.

On this type of question, let me confess that I can be of very little help to the reader. I have made a very thorough study of these tests, have administered them to many people of unquestioned judgment, and invariably the results have been baffling. But there does seem to be one moral: don't think too much. The searching mind is severely handicapped by such forced choices and may easily miss what is meant to be the obviously right answer. Suppress this quality in yourself by answering these questions as quickly as you possibly can, with practically no pause for reflection.

The judgment questions from 25 through 28 are much easier to answer.[5] The right answers here are, simply, those which represent sound personnel policy, and this is not hard to figure out. Again, don't quibble. It is true enough that it is virtually impossible to tell the worker why he didn't get promoted unless you know whether he was a good worker, or a poor one, or whether Jones's uncle did in fact own the plant (in which case, candor could be eminently sensible). The mealy-mouthed answer d)—"Let's figure out how you can improve"—is the "right" answer. Similarly with questions about the worker's home life. It isn't the concern of the company, but it is modern personnel dogma that it should be, and therefore "agree" is the right answer. So with the question about whether good supervisors are born or made. To say that a good supervisor is born deprecates the whole apparatus of modern organization training, and that kind of attitude won't get you anywhere.

KNOW YOUR COMPANY

Questions 29 and 30 are characteristic of the kind of test that attempts to measure the relative emphasis you attach to certain values—such as aesthetic, economic, religious, social.[6] The profile of you it produces is matched against the profile that the company thinks is desirable. To be considered as a potential executive, you will probably do best when you emphasize economic motivation the most; aesthetic and religious, the least. In question 29, accordingly, you should say the skyscraper makes you think of industrial growth. Theoretical motivation is also a good thing; if you were trying out for the research department, for example, you might wish to say that you think Sir Isaac Newton helped mankind more than Shakespeare and thereby increase your rating for theoretical learning. Were you trying out for a public relations job, however, you might wish to vote for Shakespeare, for a somewhat higher aesthetic score would not be amiss in this case.

There are many more kinds of tests and there is no telling what surprises the testers will come up with in the future. But the principles will probably change little, and by obeying a few simple precepts and getting yourself in the right frame of mind, you have the wherewithal to adapt to any new testing situation. In all of us there is a streak of normalcy.

NOTES

1.   Leading tests of this type include:

The Personality Inventory by Robert G. Bernreuter. Published by The Stanford University Press, Stanford, California. Copyright 1935 by The Board of Trustees of Leland Junior University. All rights reserved. *125 questions.* Measures several different things at once; scoring keys available for neurotic tendency; self-sufficiency; introversion-extroversion; dominance-submission; self-confidence; sociability.

Thurstone Temperament Schedule by L. L. Thurstone. Copyright 1949 by L. L. Thurstone. Published by Science Research Associates, Chicago, Ill. *140 questions.* Measures, at once, seven areas of temperament: to wit, degree to which one is active, vigorous, impulsive, dominant, stable, sociable, reflective. "The primary aim of the Thurstone Temperament Schedule . . . is to evaluate an individual in terms of his relatively permanent temperament traits. One of the values of the schedule is that it helps provide an objective pattern, or profile, of personal traits which you can use to predict probable success or failure in a particular situation."

Minnesota T-S-E Inventory by M. Catherine Evans and T. R. McConnell. Copyright 1942 by Science Research Associates, Chicago, Illinois. *150 questions.* Measures three types of introversion-extroversion—thinking, social and emotional.

The Personal Audit by Clifford R. Adams and William M. Lepley, Psycho-Educational Clinic, Pennsylvania State College. Published by Science Research Associates, Chicago, Ill. Copyright 1945 by Clifford R. Adams. All rights reserved. *450 questions.* Nine parts, of 50 questions each. Each part measures "a relatively independent component of personality." Extremes of each trait listed thus: seriousness-impulsiveness; firmness-indecision; tranquillity-irritability; frankness-evasion; stability-instability; tolerance-intolerance; steadiness-emotionality; persistence-fluctuation; contentment-worry.

2. Outstanding example is the *Minnesota Multiphasic Personality Inventory,* Revised Edition, by Starke R. Hathaway and J. Charnley McKinley. Published by The Psychological Corporation, N.Y. *495 questions.* This yields scores on hypochondriasis, depression, hysteria, psychopathic deviation, masculinity and femininity, paranoia, psychoasthenia, schizophrenia, hypomania. It also yields a score on the subject's "test-taking attitude," with a score for his degree of "defensiveness-frankness." If the subject consistently gives himself the benefit of the doubt, or vice versa, the scoring reveals the fact. This is not a test for the amateur to trifle with.

3. An example of this kind of testing is the *Conservatism-Radicalism Opinionaire* by Theodore F. Lentz and Colleagues of The Attitude Research Laboratory. Published by Character Research Association, Washington University, St. Louis, Mo., Dept. of Education. Copyright 1935. 60 statements are given; the subject indicates whether he tends to agree or disagree. His score is obtained by checking the number of times he sides with the conservative statement side vs. the radical one.

4. Two tests of this type are:

Test of Practical Judgment by Alfred J. Cardall, N.B.A., Ed.D. Published by Science Research Associates, Inc., Chicago, Ill. Copyright 1942, 1950 by Science Research Associates, Inc. All rights reserved. *48 Forced-choice questions* "designed to measure the element of practical judgment as it operates in everyday business and social situations." How were the "best" answers chosen? "Rigorous statistical analysis was supplemented by consensus of authority. . . ."

Practical Social Judgment by Thomas N. Jenkins, Ph.D. Copyright 1947. All rights reserved. Executive Analysis Corporation, N.Y. *52 questions* about hypothetical situations; subject must choose the "best" and the "poorest" of given answers.

5. An example of this kind of test is *How Supervise?* by Quentin W. File, edited by H. H. Remmers. Published by The Psychological Corporation, N.Y. Copyright 1948, by Purdue Research Foundation, Lafayette, Indiana. 100 questions on management policy and attitudes.

6. A *Study of Values,* Revised Edition, by Gordon W. Allport, Philip E. Vernan, and Gardner Lindzey. Copyright 1951, by Gordon W. Allport, Philip E. Vernan, and Gardner Lindzey. Copyright 1931 by Gordon W. Allport and Philip E. Vernan. Published by Houghton Mifflin Co. *45 forced-choice questions.* Answers are scored to give a measure of the relative prominence of six motives in a person: theoretical, economic, aesthetic, social, political, and religious. A profile is charted to show how he varies from the norm on each of the six.

UNIT SIX | DISCUSSION QUESTIONS

17 | WHAT CAN WE PREDICT?

Discuss in what ways modern science has used "probability" theory. Be specific in your examples.

If it is a fact that the gambler will eventually lose, why is the gambling profession so tempting to many people?

18 | METHODS OF EXPRESSING TEST SCORES

Discuss how information gained from the "bell-shaped" curve can be utilized in fields other than testing.

Discuss the meaning of "norms," "standardization," and "central tendency." Give examples in your discussion.

19 | BEHAVIORAL SCIENCE VERSUS INTELLIGENCE

Discuss the meaning of the intelligence quotient and how it relates to one's native intelligence.

The author refers to Arthur Jensen's research. What was his finding? What are your feelings regarding these findings?

20 | HOW TO CHEAT ON PERSONALITY TESTS

What do you think is the general public's opinion regarding personality tests?

Support your reasoning as to whether or not personality tests should be useful in personnel hiring.

UNIT SEVEN
STATES OF CONSCIOUSNESS

Responses do not occur without stimulation; a stimulus triggers the specific receptor activity that produces sensation. Sense modalities include: vision, hearing (audition), smell (olfaction), taste (gustation), pressure, temperature, pain, kinesthesia (stretching of muscles and joints), and equilibrium (balance). Parapsychology investigates the possibility that some individuals can be aware of events or capable of influencing physical objects without the use of known senses. Parapsychology studies these forms of perception known as "extrasensory perception (ESP)." Mental telepathy (communicating by thought transference), clairvoyance (perception without sensory knowledge), precognition (foretelling the future), and psychokinesis (influencing physical objects by mental powers) are forms of ESP.

Critical evaluations of collected data are being made and there is little doubt that some demonstrations of ESP are genuine. Nevertheless, many scientists refuse to accept the existence of ESP because it appears to be contrary to the basic laws of science. Yet mounting evidence makes it increasingly difficult to ignore the validity of ESP. R. A. McConnell's evaluation of this exciting possibility is entitled *ESP and Credibility in Science*. McConnell presents interesting evidence to support the existence of this phenomenon. The author presents the question raised by the marked absence of adequate ESP coverage in most psychology textbooks: "Why are psychologists not interested in ESP?"

Reports of sensory stimulation, involving the interpretation of fast exposures flashed on a theater screen, is the subject matter of Ann Anastasi's *Subliminal Perception*. Since 1957 many experiments evaluating subliminal perception have been conducted. This brief analysis is an accumulation of the reported results.

The phenomenon of "dermo-ocular vision," the ability to detect color in the dark with the fingertips, was reported by Russian scientists in 1963. A Russian housewife had the ability to run her fingers over printed text and "read" a newspaper! In November, 1964, a housewife in Flint, Michigan proved to Barnard College psychologists that she, too, had the same ability. Scientists in many countries are working to evaluate this strange and interesting ability. *Dermo-optical Perception: A Peek Down the Nose* by Martin Gardner is a discussion concerning the validity of this ability. The author supports the belief that recent tests, offered as confirming evidence, lack sufficiently tight controls to rule out trickery.

Since Sigmund Freud wrote his treatise on *Interpretation of Dreams* in 1900, scientists as well as laymen have been concerned with understanding the mystery of dreams. Dreaming is behavior, and there is little doubt that it can be motivated by unconscious material. *The Effect of Dream Deprivation* by William Dement outlines recent experiments on the need for a certain amount of dreaming each night.

Although hypnosis has been known and practiced since ancient times, it still escapes exact definition; however, most scientists agree that it is an extreme state of suggestibility. Hypnosis is used in a variety of professional fields. *Current Uses of Hypnosis* by C. Scott Moss explores these various professional uses. Moss not only discusses the needed professional training but also the limitations and dangers of hypnosis.

---

21 | ESP AND CREDIBILITY IN SCIENCE

R. A. McConnell

In discussing extrasensory perception (ESP) before psychology students, it is not uncommon to stress the credulity of the public. Perhaps, instead, we ought to examine the credibility of scientists—including those on both sides of the controversy.

In ESP research whom shall we trust? One can rather easily imagine experimental precautions to keep participating subjects from cheating. But how do we know whether the experimenter is deliberately deceiving us? And in a world where people believe all kinds of nonsense, how can we be sure that the experimenter is not deceiving himself?

Let us suppose that 10 experimenters independently get the same result. Can we accept it? Ten is not a large number. There are about 150,000 names in *American Men of Science*. We may reasonably assume that at least 10,000 of these hold beliefs about the nature of reality that the majority of scientists would regard as wholly without foundation. Thus, on a subject like ESP, where there are no recognized authorities, why should we accept the word of 10 experimenters—or, for that matter, a thousand? Are we not, all of us, creatures of our culture? Is there any way we can be sure that a scientist in any field is as rational as he pretends to be?

Questions concerning the credibility of scientists are rarely asked in our classrooms. I have wondered why. Perhaps it makes us uncomfortable to consider the possibility of incompetence, dishonesty, or mental illness among professional people. Whatever the reason, this is forbidden territory for study.

R. A. McConnell, "ESP and Credibility in Science," American Psychologist, **24**, May 1969, No. 5, pp. 531–538. Copyright © 1969 by the American Psychological Association, and reproduced by permission of the publisher and the author. The selection was originally delivered as an invited lecture to the introductory psychology classes at Carnegie-Mellon University, December 18 and 19, 1967.

The figures which comprise Examples 1 through 11 are from Upton Sinclair, *Mental Radio*, Charles C. Thomas, Springfield, Ill., 1962, and are reproduced by permission.

Once in a long while, these embarrassing ideas do come to the surface. Someone, a little bolder or a little more eccentric than the rest of us, may write an article that slips by the editorial censor. When that happens, we have a chance to learn what people really think.

When I accepted this invitation to talk to you, I was told I could give you an advance reading assignment. I asked that you read an eight-page article on ESP by G. R. Price (1955) that appeared in *Science* together with several letters to the editor (Soal; Rhine; Meehl & Scriven; Bridgman; Price; Rhine, 1956) written in reply to Price. These papers are currently available as part of the Bobbs-Merrill reprint series that is widely used for teaching psychology, and they have thus acquired a quasi-official status as source documents to which the very young may be exposed.

I also suggested that you read an analysis of Price's article (McConnell, 1955) that appeared in the *Journal of Parapsychology* and that was not included in the Bobbs-Merrill series. I hope that most of you have had a chance to study these references, which I shall now discuss briefly.

Price, a chemist by profession, presented a well-supported argument showing that existing experimental evidence constitutes conclusive proof of ESP if one accepts the good faith and sanity of the experimenters. But he went on to say that all of the otherwise convincing evidence for ESP can be easily explained away if one assumes that experimenters, working in collaboration with their witnesses, have intentionally faked their results.

Perhaps the most interesting thing about this unsubstantiated suggestion of fraud is that it was published on the first page of the most influential scientific journal in the United States. I will not say whether Price intended what he wrote as a joke. That is a riddle that I leave to you to answer. The important question is not whether Price took himself seriously, but whether you and I ought to do so.

I believe, as apparently does Price, that all kinds of fraud, even by highly placed scientists, are possible and that it is conceivable that there might be collaboration between two scientists in perpetuating a scientific hoax. Nevertheless, I think that those who accept Price's argument fail to understand two important things about science as a social enterprise.

First, they fail to realize that the way to tell whether a number of scientists are collaborating in a hoax is to consider the intricate web of public and private motivation, belief, and retribution that determines the behavior of professional people in our culture. Price suggested that scientists, university teachers, medical doctors, and intellectually prominent persons who have assisted in the investigation of ESP may have engaged in conscious collusive fraud. Price answered the question of how one might get such people to become willing accomplices by saying: "In recruiting, I would appeal not to desire for fame or material gain but to the noblest motives, arguing that much good to humanity could result from a small deception designed to strengthen religious belief." An experienced lawyer or even a politician would laugh at this explanation of a supposed conspiracy among well-educated and fully engaged members of our society, but evidently quite a few scientists find it plausible.

Second, those scientists who take Price seriously do not understand scientific method. Price suggested that the way to establish the scientific truth of ESP is to carry out a fraudproof experiment. In his words: "What is needed is one completely convincing experiment." He described in specific detail how this might be done by using prominent scientists and stage magicians as witnesses, backed up by motion pictures of the entire proceedings, plus photomicrographs of welded seals, and so on. This is nonsense because it assumes that scientific proof is of the same nature as legal proof. On the contrary, the acceptance of a scientific principle does not, and never can, depend upon the honesty of individual scientists.

I wish I had time to pursue with you the subtle psychological question of the nature of scientific proof and of how the method of science deals with individual experimenter error as well as mass irrationality. Those of you who are especially interested may wish to read a book by T. S. Kuhn (1962) titled *The Structure of Scientific Revolutions*.[1] Here today, I can only say that in my opinion, wittily or unwittingly, Price's article is a hoax about hoaxes and about the nature of science.

If you were to ask: "What does it signify that Price successfully placed his article in our most important journal of science?" I would answer as follows: There is a facade of respectability and belief that covers all of the activities of society and makes it possible for men to work together and for society to exist. Most people—including those who are well educated—are unaware of this false front and lose their equilibrium when they are forced by circumstances to penetrate behind it. On the other hand, those of you who are intellectually alienated from our culture understand quite well that this pretense exists. I hope that some day you will also understand why it is necessary and that it is not the contrivance of a group of evil men, but reflects what existential philosophers refer to as "the human condition."

This curtain of propriety and convention exists in science also, where it allows us to believe that all is well with our knowledge system. ESP or any other revolutionary discovery may seem to threaten science. From time to time, when such a challenge is offered, the stagehands nervously fumble, the curtain slips, and we see a little of the normally concealed machinery. We get a glimpse of underlying reality, a glimpse of the ignorance and fears that govern the inner affairs of the mind of man. Such was the case when *Science* published Price's critique of ESP. That is why his article is important.

EVIDENCE AND BELIEF

Then, what about ESP? If laboratory scientists lack sophistication about human nature and even about the methodology of science, how do we decide for ourselves whether ESP is real or imaginary, true or false?

Before we try to answer so difficult a question, let us go back to the beginning. I shall give you an operational definition of ESP that you may find a bit confusing. Then I shall describe a test for ESP that I hope will make the matter clear to you.

The definition goes this way: "Extrasensory perception is a response to an unknown event not presented to any known sense." I shall not try to explain it. Instead, let me describe the test.

I have brought with me a deck of ESP cards. These cards have five different kinds of symbols printed on them: a circle, a square, a plus, a star and wavy lines. Altogether, there are 25 cards, 5 of each kind.

Suppose I shuffle these cards, hide them, and ask you to guess them. By the theory of chance probability, the number you would most often get right is five.

Sometimes you would get four or six or seven. Only once in a long while would you get 15 right out of 25. In fact, if you got more than 10 right very often, you would begin to suspect that it was not just good luck. It might even be ESP.

Of course, you could not be sure. It might be luck—or it might be something else. If you look closely at the backs of these cards, sometimes you can see the symbol showing through. Perhaps in this way you recognized some of the cards when I shuffled them. Or again, every time I asked whether you were ready for your next guess, perhaps I gave you a hint without knowing it. Perhaps, unconsciously, I raised the tone of my voice just a little when I came to each star—because I think of stars as being "higher" than the other symbols, or for some other trivial reason.

You can see that there are many subtle ways for information to leak through by sight or by sound. No serious scientist would try to conduct an ESP experiment in this fashion. My only purpose in showing you these cards is to let you know how some of the early tests for ESP were done at Duke University 35 years ago. I regard these cards as a museum piece, although they are a lot of fun and can be used in preliminary testing.

The experiments that are carried out today are often so complex that one cannot evaluate them without advanced training in statistics, physics, and psychology. For this reason, and because the field is too large to describe in one lecture, I have prepared a list of reading materials. Some of these are intended to show the scope of the subject (Heywood, 1964; Langdon-Davies, 1961; McConnell, 1966; Murphy & Dale, 1961); others are experimental reports (Anderson & McConnell, 1961; McConnell & Forwald, 1967a, 1967b, 1968; McConnell, Snowdon, & Powell, 1955; Sinclair, 1962; Soal & Bateman, 1954).

You will notice that I have listed only my own journal articles. For this I offer my apology along with the following explanation. In any frontier field of science there are experimental hazards. If someone questions the soundness of what I recommend to you as evidence, I can probably do a better job of explaining if I have chosen research with which I am most familiar. I also want to convey the idea that there has been a large amount of work done in this field. If you study my papers and cannot find anything wrong with them, you ought to remember that there have been perhaps a hundred other investigators who have found substantial evidence for ESP under controlled experimental conditions.

ESP is a controversial idea in psychology. Nevertheless, the psychologists whom I know personally agree with me on many things. I am sure we agree on what constitutes good quality experimental laboratory research. We also agree that there is a sizable body of high-grade evidence for ESP in the literature.

In 1947 I visited Duke University in North Carolina where a man by the name of Rhine was doing experiments on ESP. I wanted to get acquainted with Rhine and with the people who were working under him. Even more important, I wanted to talk to those faculty members who rejected Rhine's work. I rented a dormitory room, and during four weeks I interviewed everyone I could, beginning with the President of the University and working down to assistant professors in various departments. I shall not have time to describe that adventure, but I will tell you what I was told by one professor of psychology in a private interview.

He said that he was familiar with the experimental literature of ESP and that, in his opinion, if it were anything else *but* ESP, one-tenth of the published evidence would already have established the phenomenon. He also explained that he would not accept ESP himself because, as he put it, he found "a world without ESP a more comfortable place in which to live."

That trip to Duke University was part of a larger investigation that made me decide to leave engineering electronics, in which I had acquired some experience, and to devote my life to the investigations of ESP and related effects.

That was 20 years ago. What has happened in this field since then? Among other things, there has been time to publish 20 more volumes of the *Journal of Parapsychology*. That comes to about 4,000 pages of research. There have been several thousand additional pages in the *Journal of the American Society for Psychical Research* and in the English and Continental journals. You might think that the argument would be settled by now.

Only recently, a brilliant young psychologist, who is here on your campus, gave a lecture on ESP in which he said "I tend to believe the evidence is as good as it is for many of our other psychological phenomena." He also said that "Psychologists will not be interested in ESP until there is a repeatable experiment."

Where my psychologist friends and I disagree, is that I believe that the available evidence for ESP is sufficient to establish its reality beyond all reasonable doubt. My psychologist friends think that the evidence is not yet conclusive. I do not regard this difference of opinion as very important. I am happy to allow anyone the privilege of doubt.

How else does the position of professional psychologists whom I know differ from my own? Perhaps the main difference—the really important difference—lies in our interpretation of the history and methodology of science—in what today we call the philosophy of science.

For one thing, my friends seem to believe that the only good evidence for ESP must come from controlled experimentation in a laboratory. My own belief is that all available evidence must be weighed, taking into account its source and the conditions under which it was gathered.

Perhaps it will clarify the problem if I say that there are only two important kinds of scientific evidence in this world: our own evidence and someone else's. Since most of us are not in a position to gather evidence of ESP, my remarks apply especially to other people's evidence.

The first thing to remember is that, no matter how reputable the scientific journal, someone else's evidence is always suspect. And if the matter is important, we ought to be *aggressively* skeptical about it.

Whether we are listening to a tale of a ghost in a haunted house or reading the tightly edited *Journal of Experimental Psychology*, we have to concern ourselves with two questions: what is the content of the report and what are the competence and motivation of the observer?

What I am suggesting is that our attitude toward *all* supposedly scientific reports must be that of the psychologist in receiving an introspective account from a human subject in a laboratory experiment—for it must be remembered that, as far as the reader is concerned, a journal article by a distant scientist is in some ways even less dependable than what psychologists, often condescendingly, refer to as a "verbal report."

From a study of the history of science, I have come to two conclusions in this connection: (*a*) the evidence presented in scientific journals by professional scientists for all kinds of ordinary phenomena is not as good as commonly supposed, and (*b*) on a controversial subject where the professionals do not agree, the evidence of the layman may have considerable scientific value. As corollaries, I suggest that the textbooks of science are often wrong and that contrary popular opinion is sometimes right. Let us examine these ideas.

STOREHOUSES OF KNOWLEDGE?

Textbooks are the storehouses of man's knowledge. They are presumed to contain all of the things we know to be true. If you are becoming a scientist, you will spend at least 18 years studying from books. It would not be entirely unfair to call most of this training a "brainwashing" process. Nearly everything you learn as factual reality must be accepted upon the word of some recognized authority and not upon your own firsthand experience. It should be a matter of concern to you whether you have been told the truth for those 18 years. Just how bad are the textbooks we use? Let me take an example from the field of geology.

Did you know that until the year 1800 the highest scientific authorities thought that there was no such thing as a meteorite? After all, there are no stones in the sky; so stones cannot fall out of the sky. Only a superstitious person would believe in meteorites.

Many of you are familiar with the work of Lavoisier. He was the founder of modern chemistry. He discovered that burning is the combining of oxygen with other things, and he helped to show that the formula for water is H_2O. He was one of the great scientists of all time.

In 1772 Lavoisier signed a report to the French Academy of Science in which he said he had examined a stone that was believed to have fallen from the sky in a great blaze of light. Lavoisier said in his report that this was just an ordinary stone that had been struck by lightning and had melted partly into glass while lying on the ground.

Eventually, of course, the leaders of science decided that meteorites do come from outer space, and they revised the textbooks accordingly. But in doing so, they forgot to mention that there had ever been any argument about the matter. So here we are, living in the space age, without realizing how hard it is to discover the truth about even a simple thing like meteorites, which can be seen as meteors in the sky on any clear night, and which have been found upon the surface of the earth since the dawn of history.

Even worse, as students, we have no way of estimating how many arguments are still going on in science and how many mistakes—truly serious mistakes—there are in the textbooks from which we study. It is my guess that we can safely believe nearly all of what is said in the physics and chemistry books. But we ought to believe only half of the ideas in the biological sciences—although I am not sure which half. And we should accept as final very little in the social sciences, which try to explain why groups of people behave as they do.

Our subject today is extrasensory perception, which belongs in psychology, one of the biological sciences. ESP is something about which the "authorities" are in error. Most psychology textbooks omit the subject entirely as unworthy of serious attention. But these books are mistaken, because ESP is a real psychological phenomenon.

Of course, I am only giving you my individual opinion about ESP. I do not want you to base your belief upon what I tell you. When you have studied advanced psychology and statistics, and when you come to realize that your professors cannot be expected to teach you everything you wish to know, then I hope you will go to the scientific journals and study the experiments that have been done and decide for yourself.

MENTAL RADIO

I have already discussed the credibility of experts and the errors we find in science textbooks. I would like to turn next to the other half of my thesis, namely, that evidence from a layman may sometimes have scientific value.

Most of you are familiar with the name Upton Sinclair, who was a socialist reformer and a writer active in the first half of the twentieth century. He died in 1968 at the age of 90. In his time he wrote nearly 90 books. One of the best known of these, published in 1906, was called *The Jungle*. It told about the cruel and unsanitary conditions in the processing of beef in the Chicago stock yards. As a result of that book, laws were passed, and today the situation is much improved. In a very real sense, all of us are indebted to this man.

Sinclair discovered that his wife had an unusual amount of what was then known as "psychic ability." (That was before the beginning of the ESP controversy.) After three years of serious experimentation, he wrote a book about it: *Mental Radio* (1962, orig. publ. 1930).

In his experiments, Sinclair, or someone else, would draw a secret picture and ask Mrs. Sinclair to draw another picture to match it. Some of the pairs of pictures are presented in the following examples. The one on the left is always the original picture, and the one on the right is what Mrs. Sinclair got by ESP.

Sometimes the pictures were made as far apart as 40 miles. At other times the target picture was held by Mrs. Sinclair in her hand—without looking, of course—while she concentrated before drawing her matching picture. The degree of success did not seem to depend upon distance.

Example 1

Let us examine some of the pictures. In Example 1 we see an almost perfect ESP response. It is a knight's helmet. Notice that for every important line in the left-hand picture there is a corresponding line on the right.

Example 2

Compare that with Example 2. Here, the response on the right is not quite the same as the target on the left, but the idea is the same.

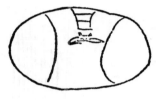 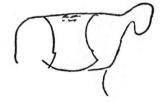

Example 3

The next slide is Example 3. Sinclair drew a football as a target. Mrs. Sinclair made the drawing on the right, but she thought it was "a baby calf with a belly band." Why did her ESP make this mistake? We cannot be sure, but we think it had something to do with the fact that in her childhood she had known a queer old man who raised calves as parlor pets and dressed them in embroidered belly bands.

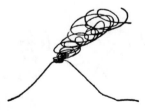 

Example 4

Example 4 is another instance of the right shape with a wrong interpretation. Upton Sinclair drew a volcano, and Mrs. Sinclair drew what she called a black beetle. The beetle is upside down. If you turn the example over, you can more easily recognize its antennae and legs.

Example 5

In Example 5 Sinclair drew a fish hook, which turned into two flowers.

Example 6

Example 6 shows a fragmentary response. Sinclair drew a balloon. The response on the right is what his wife received by "mental radio." She was not sure what it was, so she wrote beside the picture: "Shines in sunlight, must be metal, a scythe hanging among vines or strings."

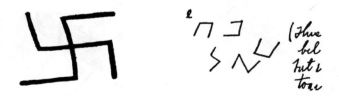

Example 7

Example 7 on the left is a swastika. Mrs. Sinclair drew the response on the right. She did not know what it meant, but she wrote beside it, "These things somehow belong together, but won't get together." You can see some of her words which were accidentally included when the printer made the book. Here is the beginning of "These" and "belong" and "but won't" and "together."

 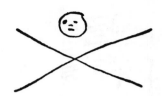

Example 8

Example 8 is a pair of drawings in which a stick man became a skull and cross-bones.

Example 9

Notice that in Example 9, Mrs. Sinclair left out some of the stars and added a moon instead.

Example 10

In Example 10 Sinclair drew an umbrella. His wife responded with this curious picture, which she described in writing beside it as follows: "I feel that it is a snake crawling out of something—vivid feeling of snake, but it looks like a cat's tail." I might mention that she had a special fear of snakes, having grown up on a plantation in a Mississippi swamp.

Example 11

The last example is the American flag and a response to it that could hardly be called a chance coincidence (Example 11).

You have seen a selection of 11 pictures out of a total of 290 trials made by Mrs. Sinclair. Perhaps 4 of the 11 would be called direct target hits. The rest are partial hits. Out of the 290 tries, 23% were rated by Upton Sinclair as hits, 53% were partial hits, and 24% were failures.

Of course, before you can be sure that these pictures were made by ESP, many questions must be answered. Because Upton Sinclair and his wife were laymen, you will have to pay particular attention to their competence and motivation. On the other hand, one important feature of Sinclair's book is that you do not have to be a scientist to understand it. Even though you may not have studied statistics and psychology, you can read the book yourself and make up your mind as to its value on the basis of common sense. When you do, I think you will arrive at the same conclusion that many scientists have reached by entirely different kinds of experiments. I think you will decide that extrasensory perception is a reality regardless of the skepticism of the psychological profession.

A MATTER OF INTEREST

I have been told by my friends that psychologists will not be interested in ESP until someone discovers a repeatable experiment. Upton Sinclair repeated his experiments over a period of three years. In London, a mathematician by the name of Soal (Soal & Bateman, 1954) repeated certain card-guessing experiments again and again over a period of six years using two subjects and many different witnesses. What do psychologists mean by a repeatable experiment?

Evidently, they mean an experiment that is "repeatable by prescription." They want a standard experimental procedure that can be described on paper by which any qualified person—or at least some qualified persons—can guarantee to produce ESP upon demand. I must confess that we have not yet reached that stage in ESP research. And, until we do, I can sympathize with my skeptical friends. I can see why they, as busy individuals with other interests, are unwilling to reach a firm position about the reality of ESP.

What I cannot understand is why they say: "Psychologists will not be *interested* in ESP until there is a repeatable experiment."

It is a statement of fact that psychologists are *not* interested in ESP. Recently, I had occasion to examine a number of psychology textbooks. Only one of them mentioned ESP—that book, by Hilgard and Atkinson (1967). After reading the four pages which these authors devote to ESP, I have only two minor critical observations to offer.

The first is that the authors have given too much space to finding fault with unimportant papers. They go back 25 years to a journal article in which they accuse an ESP experimenter of over-analyzing his data. I am sure that comparable examples of weak statistical method could be found in any one of the quantitative journals of the APA—and we would not need to go back a generation in time to do it.

My second comment is that Hilgard and Atkinson may have tended to damage their own scholarly reputations by recommending as a "scholarly review" a book by C. E. M. Hansel (1966) titled *ESP: A Scientific Evaluation*. This book has been reviewed by S. S. Stevens of Harvard, who regards ESP as a Rabelaisian joke and who gave Hansel his unqualified approval. If you like amusing book reviews, I suggest that you read Stevens (1967). I regret that I do not have time here today to document for you the basis of my unfavorable opinion of Hansel's book.[2]

I have wandered over many facets of ESP. I shall now summarize what I think are the most important ideas. Since the scientific study of ESP was begun by the London Society for Psychical Research in 1882, there have been hundreds and perhaps thousands of experiments done with a care typical of the journals of the APA. Many psychologists of high repute admit that the evidence is as good as that for other phenomena that are accepted by their profession.

Surprising though it may seem, most of this research on ESP has been done by people who were not psychologists. From this fact and from the usual psychology textbook treatment of the subject as well as from private discussion, we know that psychologists are *not* interested in ESP. This raises a question—a very mysterious question that I invite you to try to answer: Why are psychologists not interested in ESP?[3]

NOTES

1. For a condensation of this book see McConnell (1968b).
2. This has since been done. See McConnell (1968a).
3. Those who wish to answer this question might start their odyssey by visiting Clark et al. (1967) and Linder (1967).

REFERENCES

Anderson, M. L., & McConnell, R. A. Fantasy testing for ESP in a fourth and fifth grade class. *Journal of Psychology*, 1961, **52**, 491–503.

Clark, K. E., *et al.* The scientific and professional aims of psychology. *American Psychologist*, 1967, **22**, 49–76.

Hansel, C. E. M. *ESP: A scientific evaluation.* New York: Scribner's, 1966.

Heywood, R. *ESP: A personal memoir.* New York: Dutton, 1964.

Hilgard, E. R., & Atkinson, R. C. *Introduction to psychology.* New York: Harcourt, Brace & World, 1967.

Kuhn, T. S. *The structure of scientific revolutions* (Vol. II, No. 2, of the *International Encyclopedia of Unified Science*). Chicago: University of Chicago Press, 1962.

Langdon-Davies, J. *On the nature of man.* New York: New American Library Corporation, 1961.

Linder, R. Light one candle. *American Psychologist*, 1967, **22**, 804–805.

McConnell, R. A. Price in *Science*. *Journal of Parapsychology*, 1955, **19**, 258–261.

McConnell, R. A. ESP research at three levels of method. *Journal of Parapsychology*, 1966, **30**, 195–207.

McConnell, R. A. The ESP scholar. *Contemporary Psychology*, 1968, **13**, 41. (a).

McConnell, R. A. The structure of scientific revolutions: An epitome. *Journal of the American Society for Psychical Research*, 1968, **62**, 321–327. (b)

McConnell, R. A., & Forwald, H. Psychokinetic placement: I. A re-examination of the Forwald-Durham experiment. *Journal of Parapsychology*, 1967, **31**, 51–69. (a)

McConnell, R. A., & Forwald, H. Psychokinetic placement: II. A factorial study of successful and unsuccessful series. *Journal of Parapsychology*, 1967, **31**, 198–213. (b)

McConnell, R. A., & Forwald, H. Psychokinetic placement: III. Cube-releasing devices. *Journal of Parapsychology*, 1968, **32**, 9–38.

McConnell, R. A., Snowdon, R. J., & Powell, K. F. Wishing with dice. *Journal of Experimental Psychology*, 1955, **50**, 269–275.

Murphy, G., & Dale, L. A. *Challenge of psychical research*. New York: Harper, 1961.

Price, G. R. Science and the supernatural. *Science*, 1955, **122**, 359–367.

Sinclair, U. *Mental radio*. Springfield, Ill.: Charles C. Thomas, 1962.

Soal, S. G., & Bateman, F. *Modern experiments in telepathy*. London: Faber & Faber, 1954.

Soal, S. G.; Rhine, J. B.; Meehl, P. E., & Scriven, M.; Bridgman, P. W.; Price, G. R.; Rhine, J. B. (Letters to the editor in rejoinder to G. R. Price.) *Science*, 1956, **123**, 9–19.

Stevens, S. S. The market for miracles. *Contemporary Psychology*, 1967, **12**, 1–3.

22 | SUBLIMINAL PERCEPTION

Ann Anastasi

In the fall of 1957 widespread public alarm was aroused by the announcement of an "experiment" conducted by a commercial firm in a New Jersey motion-picture theater. During the showing of the regular film, the words "Eat Popcorn" and "Drink Coca-Cola" were flashed alternately on the screen every 5 seconds for 1/3,000th of a second. Because of the extremely brief exposure, these stimuli were described as "subliminal," that is, below the limen, or threshold, of perception. Nevertheless, the firm claimed that over the six weeks when this procedure was followed the sale of popcorn from the lobby refreshment stand rose 57.5 per cent and that of Coca-Cola rose 18.1 per cent. The report of these results aroused widespread comment in the popular press. This type of advertising was variously described as "the super-soft sell," "the invisible sell," and "the little ad that wasn't there." Dismal pictures were painted of a nation of robots whose behavior could be controlled by suggestions of which they were not even aware. The protests and charges soon reached such proportions as to come before the United States Congress and the Federal Communications Commission.

The specific claims made regarding the New Jersey motion-picture demonstration could not be evaluated because of the refusal of the commercial organization to reveal the necessary details of procedure and results. Without such knowledge it is impossible to determine whether the reported increase in sales resulted from the subliminal advertising or from other uncontrolled factors. We would need to know, for instance, whether the size and nature of the audience were in any way unusual during the experimental period. Because of weather conditions, time of year, or the particular films shown, the audience might be larger than usual or might include a larger proportion of teen-agers, who are more likely to buy popcorn and Coca-Cola. Similarly, any changes made in the display of merchandise or in the operation of the sales booth itself would need to be investigated. It would also help to have more direct information on the buying behavior of the audience. Was there an increase in purchases made on the way in, before exposure to the subliminal advertising? How many customers made their purchases during the film showing and how many on the way out?

In the absence of adequate information on the above demonstration, we may turn to some recent well-controlled investigations. Designed to test specific claims about the subliminal control of behavior, these experiments have yielded largely negative results. In one study, two groups of students watched the same 30-minute instructional film. During the showing of this film, a slide was projected on the screen for .01 second at 10-second intervals. The slide used in the experimental group showed a spoon of rice with the words "Wonder Rice" printed below it; the slide used in the control group contained only four lines arranged in a meaningless way.

At the conclusion of the film, all subjects were shown a picture of the spoon of rice without the name and were asked whether they had ever seen it in a rice advertisement. A few individuals in both groups said they had seen it, but the proportion did not differ significantly in the two groups—in fact, it was slightly *higher* in the control group. Regardless of their answer to the first question, all subjects were asked which of two brands (Monarch or Wonder) they believed was more likely to be associated with the picture. Both groups chose Monarch much oftener than Wonder, but the difference between the groups was insignificant. Thus the experimental subjects' subliminal exposure to the words "Wonder Rice" failed to increase the probability of their associating this brand name with the picture.

In another experiment, the word "beef" was superimposed on a classroom film in flashes of 1/200th of a second every 7 seconds. The control group was shown only the film, with no additional stimuli. After viewing the film, the experimental and control groups showed no significant differences in their references to beef in sentence completion and word-association tests. Nor was there a significant difference in reported preferences for roast beef sandwiches, out of a given list of five common types of sandwiches. The experimental subjects, however, rated themselves as significantly more hungry than did the control group, even when time of day and interval since last meal were equated. Three of the original 108 subjects were eliminated from the analysis of results because when questioned they said they had seen a word on the screen. But it is interesting to note that only one saw "beef"; the other two perceived the word as "beer."

In still another experiment, subliminal perception was found to have no significant effect upon the subject's choice of "right" or "left" circles when required to guess which was correct in each trial. Unknown to the subjects, the words "Choose right" and "Choose left" were exposed tachistocopically for durations of .01, .02, and .03 seconds in different parts of the experiment. The only subjects whose individual performance was better than chance later reported that they had seen the words and had followed the suggestion deliberately. In a learning experiment, performance in two different learning tasks was not significantly affected by the subliminal exposure of either correct or incorrect suggestions. In this experiment, the duration of subliminal exposure was based on an individually determined threshold for each subject.

Quite apart from its use in advertising and its potential dangers as a devious means of "behavior control," subliminal perception has been extensively studied in the psychological laboratory. Research on subliminal perception dates back fully 100 years. Many experiments have demonstrated that subjects do respond in various ways to stimuli of which they report no awareness. Stimuli may fall below the "awareness" threshold because of low intensity, brief duration, or other characteristics. To understand the subject's reaction to such stimuli, it is essential to consider the nature of a sensory threshold. There is no single intensity such that stimuli above it are always perceptible and those below it always imperceptible. Sensitivity varies along a continuum; the transition from perceptible to imperceptible is gradual.

The specific threshold established for a given subject depends in part upon the *standard of accuracy*. If the subject must give a correct response 75 per cent of the time, he needs a more intense stimulus than he would need to give 50 per cent correct responses. The threshold also depends upon the nature of the *response indicator*. For instance, a stimulus may be too weak for the subject to report awareness of it.

Nevertheless, if he is told to guess its location, he may be right significantly more often than by chance. Even weaker stimuli may lead to autonomic responses, such as a galvanic skin reaction to a word previously conditioned to an electric shock. Flashing such a word on a screen may evoke the conditioned galvanic response even when the word is too faint to be perceived in terms of other response indicators.

The problem of so-called subliminal perception thus reduces to that of threshold differences found with different response indicators. Reported awareness is a relatively crude and unreliable indicator. Such an awareness threshold will vary with the kind of directions given to subjects, the number and nature of available response categories, the serial position of stimuli, and other extraneous factors. This irrelevant variance tends to raise the threshold. An analogy may help to clarify the relationship among thresholds. Suppose you weigh yourself on an ordinary scale and find your weight to be 118 pounds. If you weigh yourself ten times during the day on such a scale, your weight will probably remain at 118 pounds. But repeated weighings on a highly sensitive laboratory scale will reveal systematic weight changes in the course of a 12-hour period. The latter could be described as "subliminal weight changes," which can be detected only with a delicate indicator.

By modifying the relative sensitivity of the two response indicators employed in a perception experiment, an investigator may artificially vary the extent of "subliminal perception" he finds from zero to any desired amount. It can thus be seen that subliminal perception is not a special phenomenon but a methodological artifact. It is not a mysterious technique for "beaming ideas directly into the mind" while by-passing the individual's conscious defenses. Research on so-called subliminal perception can be more accurately described as the study of diverse responses to *weak stimuli*. So far there is no evidence to suggest that weak stimuli exert more influence on behavior than do strong stimuli. In fact, the reverse is generally found to be true.

With regard to the use of subliminal stimulation in advertising, it should also be noted that individuals vary in their sensory thresholds. Hence a word flashed on a motion-picture screen may fall well above the awareness threshold of some persons and may be clearly read by them; for others, it may be totally imperceptible in terms of all response indicators; and for still others it may fall in the desired intermediate, or subliminal, zone. These thresholds also vary within the same person from time to time. When weak stimuli are employed, moreover, the probability of *misperception* increases. Remember the students who saw "beer" instead of "beef." The advertiser who hopefully flashes the words "Buy Tasty Tea" on a motion-picture screen may find that many subjects actually perceive "Burn Trashy Ties"—a suggestion they may feel strongly tempted to accept when opening Christmas packages.

If at some future time it should be adequately demonstrated that subliminal stimulation can seriously influence a person's actions, then psychologists should look to their code of professional ethics to make sure that they will use these techniques for the benefit of the individual and not for ulterior gains. Under such circumstances, too, legal controls should be instituted against misuse of the techniques by unscrupulous persons. But, in our present state of knowledge, subliminal perception does not constitute a social threat.

23 | DERMO-OPTICAL PERCEPTION: A PEEK DOWN THE NOSE

Martin Gardner

Science reporting in United States newspapers and mass-circulation magazines is more accurate and freer of sensationalism than ever before, with pseudoscience confined largely to books. A reverse situation holds in the Soviet Union. Except for the books that defended Lysenko's theories, Soviet books are singularly free of pseudoscience, and now that Lysenko is out of power, Western genetics is rapidly entering the new Russian biology textbooks. Meanwhile, Russian newspapers and popular magazines are sensationalizing science much as our Sunday supplements did in the 1920's. The Soviet citizen has recently been presented with accounts of fish brought back to life after having been frozen 5000 years, of deep-sea monsters that leave giant tracks across the ocean floor, or absurd perpetual-motion devices, of extraterrestrial scientists who have used a laser beam to blast an enormous crater in Siberia, and scores of similar stories.

By and large, the press in the United States has not taken this genre of Soviet science writing seriously. But in 1963 and 1964 it gave serious attention to a sudden revival, in Russia's popular press, of ancient claims that certain persons are gifted with the ability to "see" with their fingers.

The revival began with a report, in the summer of 1932, in the Sverdlovsk newspaper *Uralsky Rabochy*. Isaac Goldberg, of First City Hospital in Lower Tagil, had discovered that an epileptic patient, a 22-year-old girl named Rosa Kuleshova, could read print simply by moving a fingertip over the lines. Rosa went to Moscow for more testing, and sensational articles about her abilities appeared in *Izvestia* and other newspapers and popular magazines. The first report in the United States was in *Time,* 25 January 1963.

When I first saw *Time*'s photograph of Goldberg watching Rosa, who was blindfolded, glide her middle finger over a newspaper page, I broke into a loud guffaw. To explain that laugh, I must back up a bit. For 30 years my principal hobby has been magic. I contribute to conjuring journals, write treatises on card manipulation, invent tricks, and, in brief, am conversant with all branches of this curious art of deception, including a branch called "mentalism."

For half a century professional mentalists—performers, such as Joseph Dunninger, who claim unusual mental powers—have been entertaining audiences with "eyeless vision" acts. Usually the mentalist first has a committee from the audience

From *Science,* 151, 11 February 1966, pp. 654–657. Copyright © 1966 by the American Association for the Advancement of Science.

Reading with fingertips. A neuropathologist observes Rosa Kuleshova reading newspaper with the help of her fingers. (*Novosti Photo Service, Moscow*)

seal his eyes shut with adhesive tape. Over each eye is taped something opaque, such as a powder puff or a silver dollar. Then a large black cloth is pulled around the eyes to form a tight blindfold. Kuda Bux, a Mohammedan who comes from Kashmir, is perhaps the best known of today's entertainers who feature such an act. He has both eyes covered with large globs of dough, then many yards of cloth are wound like a turban to cover his entire face from the top of his forehead to the tip of his chin. Yet Kuda Bux is able to read books, solve mathematical problems on a blackboard, and describe objects held in front of him.

Now I do not wish to endanger my standing in the magic fraternity by revealing too much, but let me say that Kuda Bux and other mentalists who feature eyeless vision do obtain, by trickery, a way of seeing. Many ingenious methods have been devised, but the oldest and simplest, surprisingly little understood except by magicians, is known in the trade as the "nose peek." If the reader will pause at this point and ask someone to blindfold him, he may be surprised to discover that it is impossible, without injury to his eyes, to prepare a blindfold that does not permit a tiny aperture, on each side of the nose, through which light can enter each eye. By turning the eyes downward one can see, with either eye, a small area beneath the nose and extending forward at an angle of 30 to 40 degrees from the vertical. A sleep-mask blindfold is no better; it does not fit snugly enough around the nose. Besides, slight pressure on the top of the mask, under the pretense of rubbing the forehead, levers out the lower edge to permit even wider peeks. The great French magician Robert-Houdin (from whom Houdini took his name), in his memoirs[1] tells of watching another conjuror perform a certain card trick while blindfolded. The blindfold, Robert-Houdin writes, "was a useless precaution . . . for whatever care may be taken to deprive a person of sight in this way, the projection of the nose always leaves a vacuum sufficient to see clearly." Pushing wads of cotton or cloth into the two apertures accomplishes nothing. One can always, while pretending to adjust the blindfold, secretly insert his thumb and form a tiny space under the wadding. The wadding can actually be an asset in maintaining a wider aperture than there would be without it. I will not go into more subtle methods currently used by mentalists for overcoming such apparent obstacles as adhesive tape criss-crossed over the eyelids, balls of dough, and so on.

If the mentalist is obtaining information by a nose peek (there are other methods), he must carefully guard against what has been called the "sniff" posture. When the head of a blindfolded person is in a normal position, the view down the nose covers anything placed on the near edge of a table at which the person is seated. But to extend the peek farther forward it is necessary to raise the nose slightly, as though one is sniffing. Practiced performers avoid the sniff posture by tilting the head slightly under cover of some gesture, such as nodding in reply to a question, scratching the neck, and other common gestures.

One of the great secrets of successful blindfold work is to obtain a peek in advance, covered by a gesture, quickly memorize whatever information is in view, then later—perhaps many minutes later—to exploit this information under the pretense that it is just then being obtained. Who could expect observers to remember exactly what happened 5 minutes earlier? Indeed, only a trained mentalist, serving as an observer, would know exactly what to look for.

Concealing the "sniff" demands much cleverness and experience. In 1964, on a television show in the United States, a girl who claimed powers of eyeless vision was asked to describe, while blindfolded, the appearance of a stranger standing before her. She began with his shoes, then went on to his trousers, shirt, and necktie. As her description moved upward, so did her nose. The photograph in *Time* showed Rosa wearing a conventional blindfold. She is seated, one hand on a newspaper, and sniffing. The entire newspaper page is comfortably within the range of a simple nose peek.

OTHER DOP CLAIMANTS

After the publicity about Rosa, Russian women of all sorts turned up, performing even more sensational feats of eyeless vision. The most publicized of these was Ninel Sergyeyevna Kulagina. The Leningrad newspaper *Smena,* 16 January 1964, reported on her remarkable platform demonstration at the Psychoneurological Department of the Lenin-Kirovsk District. The committee who examined Ninel's blindfold included S. G. Fajnberg (Ninel's discoverer), A. T. Alexandrov, rector of the University of Leningrad, and Leonid Vasiliev, whose laboratory at the University is the center of parapsychology research in Russia. No magicians were present, of course. While "securely blindfolded," Ninel read from a magazine and performed other sensational feats. Vasiliev was reported as having described her demonstration as "a great scientific event."

There were dozens of other DOP claimants. The magazine *USSR* (now *Soviet Life*), published here in English, devoted four pages to some of them in its February 1964 issue[2]. Experiments on Rosa, this article said, made it unmistakably clear that her fingers were reacting to ordinary light and not to infrared heat rays. Filters were used which could block either light or heat. Rosa was unable to "see" when the light (but not heat) was blocked off. She "saw" clearly when the heat rays (but not light) were blocked off. "The fingers have a retina," biophysicist Mikhail Smirnov is quoted as saying. "The fingers 'see' light."

Accounts of the women also appeared in scientific publications. Goldberg contributed a report on his work with Rosa to *Voprossy Psikhologii* in 1963[3]. Biophysicist N. D. Nyuberg wrote an article about Rosa for *Priroda,* May 1963[4]. Nyuberg reports that Rosa's fingers, just like the human eye, are sensitive to three color modes, and that, after special training at the neurological institute, she "succeeded in training her toes to distinguish between black and white." Other discussions of Rosa's exploits appeared in Soviet journals of philosophy and psychology.

Not only did Rosa read print with her fingers, she also described pictures in magazines, on cigarette packages, and on postage stamps. A *Life* correspondent reported that she read his business card by touching it with her elbow. She read print placed under glass and cellophane. In one test, when she was "securely blindfolded," scientists placed a green book in front of her, then flooded it with red light. Exclaimed Rosa: "The book has changed color!" The professors were dumbfounded. Rosa's appearance on a TV program called "Relay" flushed out new rivals. *Nedelya,* the supplement of *Izvestia,* found a 9-year-old Kharkov girl, Lena Bliznova, who staggered a group of scientists by reading print ("securely blindfolded") with fingers held a few inches *off* the page. Moreover, Lena read print just as easily with her toes and shoulders. She separated the black from the white chess pieces without a single error. She described a picture covered by a thick stack of books (see my remarks above about exploiting previously memorized information).

In the United States, *Life* (12 June 1964) published a long uncritical article by Albert Rosenfeld[5], the writer whose card Rosa had read with her elbow. The Russian work is summarized and hailed as a major scientific breakthrough. Colored symbols are printed on one page so the reader can give himself a DOP test. Gregory Razran, who heads the psychology department at Queens College, New York, is quoted as saying that perhaps "some entirely new kind of force or radiation" has been detected. Razran expected to see "an explosive outburst of research in this field. . . . To see without the eyes—imagine what that can mean to a blind man!"

Let us hope that Razran, in his research, will seek the aid of knowledgeable mentalists. In a photograph of one of his DOP tests, shown in the *Life* article, the subject wears a conventional sleep-mask, with the usual apertures. She is reaching through a cloth hole in the center of an opaque partition to feel one of two differently colored plates. But there is nothing to prevent her from reaching out with her other hand, opening the cloth a bit around her wrist, then taking a nose peek through the opening.

The most amusing thing about such experimental designs is that there is a simple, but never used, way to make sure all visual clues are eliminated. A blindfold, in any form, is totally useless, but one can build a light-weight aluminum box that fits over the subject's head and rests on padded shoulders. It can have holes at the top and back for breathing, but the solid metal must cover the face and sides, and go completely under the chin to fit snugly around the front of the neck. Such a box eliminates at one stroke the need for a blindfold, the cumbersome screen with arm holes, various bib devices that go under the chin, and other clumsy pieces of apparatus designed by psychologists unfamiliar with the methods of mentalism. No test made without such a box over the head is worth taking seriously. It is the only way known to me by which all visual clues can be ruled out. There remain, of course, other methods of cheating, but they are more complicated and not likely to be known outside the circles of professional mentalism.

In its 1964 story *Life* did not remind its readers of the three pages it had devoted, in 1937, to Pat Marquis, "the boy with the X-ray eyes"[6]. Pat was then 13 and living in Glendale, California. A local physician, Cecil Reynolds, discovered that Pat could "see" after his eyes had been taped shut and covered with a blindfold. Pat was carefully tested by reporters and professors, said *Life*, who could find no trickery. There are photographs of Pat, "securely blindfolded," playing ping-pong, pool, and performing similar feats. Naturally he could read. Reynolds is quoted as saying that he believed that the boy "saw" with light receptors in his forehead. Pat's powers were widely publicized at the time by other magazines and by the wire services. He finally agreed to being tested by J. B. Rhine, of Duke University, who caught him nose peeking[7].

The truth is that claims of eyeless vision turn up with about the same regularity as tales of sea serpents. In 1898 A. N. Khovrin, a Russian psychiatrist, published a paper on "A rare form of hyperaesthesia of the higher sense organs"[8], in which he described the DOP feats of a Russian woman named Sophia. There are many earlier reports of blind persons who could tell colors with their fingers, but "blindness" is a relative term, and there is no way now to be sure how blind those claimants really were. It is significant that there are no recent cases of persons known to be totally blind who claim the power to read ordinary print, or even to detect colors, with their fingers, although it would seem that the blind would be the first to discover and develop such talents if they were possible.

JULES ROMAINS' WORK

Shortly after World War I the French novelist Jules Romains, interested in what he called "paroptic vision," made an extensive series of tests with French women who could read while blindfolded. His book, *Vision Extra-Rétinienne*[9] should be read carefully by every psychologist tempted to take the Russian claims seriously, for it describes test after test exactly like those that have been given to today's Russians. There are the same lack of controls, the same ignorance of the methods of mentalism, the same speculations about the opening of new scientific frontiers, the same unguarded predictions about how the blind may someday learn to "see," the same scorn for those who remain skeptical. Romains found that DOP was strongest in the fingers, but also present in the skin at any part of the body. Like today's Russian defenders of DOP, Romains is convinced that the human skin contains organs sensitive to ordinary light. His subjects performed poorly in dim light and could not see at all in total darkness. Romains thought that the mucous lining of the nose is especially sensitive to colors, because in dim light, when colors were hard to see, his subjects had a marked tendency to "sniff spontaneously."

The blindfolding techniques Romains used are similar to those used by the more recent investigators. Adhesive tape is crossed over the closed eyes, then folded rectangles of black silk, then the blindfold. At times cotton wool is pushed into the space along-side the nose, at times a projecting bib is placed under the chin. (Never a box over the head.) Anatole France witnessed and commented favorably on some of Romains' work. One can sympathize with the novelist when he complained to a U.S. reporter[10] that both Russian and American psychologists had ignored his findings and had simply "repeated one twentieth of the discoveries I made and reported."

It was Romains' book that probably aroused magicians in the United States to devise acts of eyeless vision. Harlan Tarbell, of Chicago, worked out a remarkable act of this type which he performed frequently[11]. Stanley Jaks, a professional mentalist from Switzerland, later developed his method of copying a stranger's signature, upside down and backward, after powder puffs had been taped over his eyes and a blindfold added[12]. Kuda Bux uses still other techniques[13]. At the moment, amateurs everywhere are capitalizing on the new wave of interest in DOP. In my files is a report on Ronald Coyne, an Oklahoma boy who lost his right eye in an accident at the age of 7. When his left eye is "securely blindfolded," his empty right eye socket reads print without hesitation. Young Coyne has been appearing at revival meetings to demonstrate his miraculous power. "For thirteen years he has had continuous vision where there is no eye," reads an advertisement in a Miami newspaper for an Assembly of God meeting. "Truly you must say 'Mine eyes have seen the glory of God.' "[14]

TESTS IN THE UNITED STATES

The most publicized DOP claimant in the United States is Patricia Stanley. Richard P. Youtz, of the psychology department at Barnard College, was discussing the Soviet DOP work at a faculty lunch one day. Someone who had taught high school in Owensboro, Kentucky, recalled that Patricia, then a student, had astounded everyone by her ability to identify objects and colors while blindfolded. Youtz traced Patricia to Flint, Michigan, and in 1963 he made several visits to Flint, tested her for about 60 hours, and obtained sensational results. These results were widely reported by the press and by such magazines of the occult as *Fate*[15]. The soberest account, by science writer Robert K. Plumb, appeared in the New York *Times*, 8 January 1964[16]. Mrs. Stanley did not read print, but she seemed able to identify the colors of test cards and pieces of cloth by rubbing them with her fingers. Youtz's work, together with the Russian, provided the springboard for Leonard Wallace Robinson's article "We have more than five senses" in the New York *Times Magazine*, Sunday, 15 March.

Youtz's first round of tests, in my opinion, were so poorly designed to eliminate visual clues that they cannot be taken seriously. Mrs. Stanley wore a conventional sleep-mask. No attempt was made to plug the inevitable apertures. Her hands were placed through black velvet sleeves, with elastic around the wrists, into a lightproof box constructed of plywood and painted black. The box could be opened at the other side to permit test material to be inserted. There was nothing to prevent Mrs. Stanley from picking up a test card or piece of colored cloth, pushing a corner under the elastic of one sleeve, and viewing the exposed corner with a simple nose peek. Youtz did have a double sleeve arrangement that might have made this difficult, but his account[17] of his first round of tests, on which Mrs. Stanley performed best, indicate that it was attached only on the rare occasions when a photo-multiplier tube was used. Such precautions as the double sleeve, or continuous and careful observation from behind, seemed unnecessary because Mrs. Stanley was securely blindfolded. Moreover, there was nothing to prevent Mrs. Stanley from observing, by nose peeks, the test material as it was being placed into the light-tight box.

Here is a description of Mrs. Stanley's performance by the New York *Times* reporter who observed her: "Mrs. Stanley concentrates hard during the experiments. . . . Sometimes she takes three minutes to make up her mind. . . . She rests her forehead under the blindfold against the black box as though she were studying intently. Her jaw muscles work as she concentrates."[18] While concentrating, she keeps up a steady flow of conversation with the observers, asking for hints on how she is doing.

Youtz returned to Flint in late January 1964 for a second round of tests, armed with more knowledge of how blindfolds can be evaded (we exchanged several letters about it)[19] and plans for tighter controls. I had been unsuccessful in persuading him to adopt a box over the head, but even without this precaution, results of the second round were not above chance expectations. These negative results were reported by the New York *Times*,[18] but not by any other newspaper or news magazine that had publicized the positive results of the first round of tests. Youtz was disappointed, but he attributed the failure to cold weather.[20]

A third series of tests was made on 20 April for an observing committee of four scientists. Results were again negative. In the warm weather of June, Youtz tested Mrs. Stanley a fourth time, over a 3-day period. Again, performance was at chance level. Youtz attributes this last failure to Mrs. Stanley's fatigue.[20] He remains convinced that she does have the ability to detect colors with her fingers and suspects that she does this by sensing delicate differences in temperature.[21] Although Russian investigators had eliminated this as an explanation of Rosa's powers, Youtz believes that his work with Mrs. Stanley, and later with less skillful Barnard students, will eventually confirm this hypothesis. He strongly objects to calling the phenomenon "vision." None of his subjects has displayed the slightest ability to read with the fingers.

NINEL IS CAUGHT CHEATING

In Russia, better-controlled testing of Rosa has strongly indicated nose peeking. Several articles have suggested this, notably those by L. Teplov, author of a well-known book on cybernetics, in the 1–7 March 1964 issue of *Nedelya*, and in the 25 May issue of the Moscow *Literaturnaya Gazeta*. Ninel Kulagina, Rosa's chief rival, was carefully tested at the Bekhterev Psychoneurological Scientific Research Institute in Leningrad. B. Lebedev, the institute's head, and his associates summarized their findings as follows:[22]

In essence, Kulagina was given the same tasks as before, but under conditions of stricter control and in accordance with a plan prepared beforehand. And this was the plan: to alternate experiments in which the woman could possibly peek and eavesdrop with experiments where peeking would be impossible. The woman of course did not know this. As was to be expected, phenomenal ability was shown in the first instance only. In the second instance [under controls] Kulagina could distinguish neither the color nor the form. . . .

Thus the careful checking fully exposed the sensational "miracle." There were no miracles whatever. There was ordinary hoax.

In a letter to *Science*,[23] Joseph Zubin, a biometrics researcher at the New York State Department of Mental Hygiene, reported the negative results of his testing of an adolescent who "read fluently" after blindfolds had been secured around the edges with adhesive tape. Previous testing by several scientists had shown no evidence of visual clues. It became apparent, however, that the subject tensed muscles in the blindfold area until "a very tiny, inconspicuous chink appeared at the edge. Placing an opaque disk in front of the chink prevented reading, but not immediately. The subject had excellent memory and usually continued for a sentence or two after blocking of the reading material." Applying zinc ointment to the edges of the adhesive proved only temporarily effective, because muscle tensing produced new chinks (made easier to detect by the white ointment). A professional magician, Zubin reports, participated in the investigations.

The majority of psychologists, both here and in the Soviet Union, have remained unimpressed by the latest revival of interest in DOP. In view of the failures of subjects to demonstrate DOP when careful precautions were taken to rule out peeks through minute apertures, and in view of the lack of adequate precautions in tests that yielded positive results, this prevailing skepticism appears to be strongly justified.

REFERENCES AND NOTES

1. Robert-Houdin, J. E. *Confidences d'un Prestidigitateur* (Blois, 1858), chap. 5; English translation, *Memoirs of Robert-Houdin: Ambassador, Author, and Conjuror* (London, 1859); reprinted as *Memoirs of Robert-Houdin: King of the Conjurers* (Dover, New York, 1964).
2. *USSR* 89, 32 (1964).
3. For English translation, see I. Goldberg, *Soviet Psychol. Psychiat.* 2, 19 (1963).
4. For English translation, see N. D. Nyuberg, *Federation Proc.* 22, T701 (1964).
5. Rosenfeld, A. "Seeing color with the fingers," *Life* 1964, 102–13 (12 June 1964).
6. "Pat Marquis of California can see without his eyes," *Life* 1937, 57–59 (19 Apr. 1937).
7. Rhine, J. B. *Parapsychol. Bull.* 66, 2–4 (Aug. 1963).
8. Khovrin, A. N., in *Contributions to Neuropsychic Medicine* (Moscow, 1898).
9. Romains, J. *Vision Extra-Rétinienne* (Paris, 1919); English translation, *Eyeless Vision*, C. K. Ogden, transl. (Putnam, New York, 1924).
10. Davy, J. *Observer*, 2 Feb. 1964.

11. See H. Tarbell, "X-ray eyes and blindfold effects" in *The Tarbell Course in Magic* (Tannen, New York, 1954) vol. 6, pp. 251–261. Tarbell speaks of his own works in this field as a direct result of his interest in Romains' work, and briefly describes an eyeless vision act by a woman who performed under the stage name of Shireen in the early 1920's.

12. See M. Gardner, *Sphinx* 12, 334–337 (Feb. 1949); *Linking Ring* 34, 23–25 (Oct. 1954); also G. Groth, "He writes with your hand," in *Fate* 5, 39–43 (Oct. 1952).

13. A description of an early eyeless vision act by Kuda Bux will be found in H. Price; *Confessions of a Ghost-Hunter* (Putnam, New York, 1936), chap. 19.

14. For the story of Ronald Coyne, born 1943 at Chouteau, Oklahoma, see the 77-page booklet, *When God Smiled on Ronald Coyne*, by R. R. Coyne, 1952 (revised 1965), published by Ronald Coyne Revivals, P. O. Box 1265, Tulsa, Oklahoma. [Ed.]

15. Saltzman, P. *Fate* 17, 38–48 (May 1964).

16. Plumb, R. K. "Woman who tells color by touch mystifies psychologist," in New York *Times*, 8 Jan. 1964; see also Plumb's follow-up article, "6th Sense is hinted in ability to 'see' with fingers," *ibid.*, 26 Jan. 1964. The *Times* also published an editorial, "Can fingers 'see'?" 6 Feb. 1964.

17. Youtz, R. P. "Aphotic Digital Color Sensing: A Case under Study," photocopied for the Bryn Mawr meeting of the Psychonomic Society, 29 Aug. 1963.

18. "Housewife is unable to repeat color 'readings' with fingers," New York *Times*, 2 Feb. 1964.

19. For an exchange of published letters, see M. Gardner, New York *Times Magazine*, 5 Apr. 1964, and R. P. Youtz, *ibid.*, 26 Apr. 1964.

20. Youtz, R. P. "The Case for Skin Sensitivity to Color; with a Testable Explanatory Hypothesis," photocopied for the Psychonomic Society, Niagara Falls, Ontario, 9 Oct. 1964.

21. See R. P. Youtz, letter, *Sci. Amer.* 212, 8–10 (June 1965).

22. Lebedev, B, *Leningradskaya Pravda*, 15 Mar. 1964; translated for me by Albert Parry, department of Russian studies, Colgate University.

23. Zubin, J. *Science* 147, 985 (1965).

24 | THE EFFECT OF DREAM DEPRIVATION

William Dement

About a year ago, a research program was initiated at the Mount Sinai Hospital which aimed at assessing the basic function and significance of dreaming. The experiments have been arduous and time-consuming and are still in progress. However, the results of the first series have been quite uniform, and because of the length of the program, it has been decided to issue this preliminary report.

In recent years, a body of evidence has accumulated which demonstrates that dreaming occurs in association with periods of rapid, binocularly synchronous eye movements.[1,2,3] Furthermore, the amount and directional patterning of these eye movements and the associated dream *content* are related in such a way as to strongly suggest that the eye movements represent scanning movements made by the dreamer as he watches the events of the dream.[3] In a study of undisturbed sleep,[4] the eye-movement periods were observed to occur regularly throughout the night in association with the lightest phases of a cyclic variation in depth of sleep, as measured by the electroencephalograph. The length of individual cycles averaged about 90 minutes, and the mean duration of single periods of eye movement was about 20 minutes. Thus, a typical night's sleep includes four or five periods of dreaming, which account for about 20 percent of the total sleep time.

One of the most striking facts apparent in all the works cited above was that a very much greater amount of dreaming occurs normally than had heretofore been realized—greater both from the standpoint of frequency and duration in a single night of sleep and in the invariability of its occurrence from night to night. In other words, dreaming appears to be an intrinsic part of normal sleep and, as such, although the dreams are not usually recalled, occurs every night in every sleeping person.

A consideration of this aspect of dreaming leads more or less inevitably to the formulation of certain rather fundamental questions. Since there appear to be no exceptions to the nightly occurrence of a substantial amount of dreaming in every sleeping person, it might be asked whether or not this amount of dreaming is in some way a necessary and vital part of our existence. Would it be possible for human beings to continue functioning normally if their dream life were completely or partially suppressed? Should dreaming be considered necessary in a psychological sense or a physiological sense or both?

The obvious attack on these problems was to study subjects who had somehow been deprived of the opportunity to dream. After a few unsuccessful preliminary

From *Science*, **131**, 10 June 1960, pp. 1705–1707. Copyright © 1960 by the American Association for the Advancement of Science.

trials with depressant drugs it was decided to use the somewhat drastic method of awakening sleeping subjects immediately after the onset of dreaming and to continue this procedure throughout the night, so that each dream period would be artificially terminated right at its beginning.

SUBJECTS AND METHOD

The data in this article are from the first eight subjects in the research program, all males, ranging in age from 23 to 32. Eye movements and accompanying low-voltage, nonspindling electroencephalographic patterns[4] were used as the objective criteria of dreaming. The technique by which these variables are recorded, and their precise relationship to dreaming, have been extensively discussed elsewhere.[2,4] Briefly, the subjects came to the laboratory at about their usual bedtime. Small silver-disk electrodes were carefully attached near their eyes and on their scalps; then the subjects went to sleep in a quiet, dark room in the laboratory. Lead wires ran from the electrodes to apparatus in an adjacent room upon which the electrical potentials of eye movements and brain waves were recorded continuously throughout the night.

Eye movements and brain waves of each subject were recorded throughout a series of undisturbed nights of sleep, to evaluate his base-line total nightly dream time and over-all sleep pattern. After this, recordings were made throughout a number of nights in which the subject was awakened by the experimenter every time the eye-movement and electroencephalographic recordings indicated that he had begun to dream. These "dream-deprivation" nights were always consecutive. Furthermore, the subjects were requested not to sleep at any other time. Obviously, if subjects were allowed to nap, or to sleep at home on any night in the dream-deprivation period, an unknown amount of dreaming would take place, offsetting the effects of the deprivation. On the first night immediately after the period of dream deprivation, and for several consecutive nights thereafter, the subject was allowed to sleep without disturbance. These nights were designated "recovery nights." The subject then had a varying number of nights off, after which he returned for another series of interrupted nights which exactly duplicated the dream-deprivation series in number of nights and number of awakenings per night. The only difference was that the subject was awakened in the intervals between eye-movement (dream) periods. Whenever a dream period began, the subject was allowed to sleep on without interruption, and was awakened only after the dream had ended spontaneously. Next, the subject had a number of recovery nights of undisturbed sleep equal to the number of recovery nights in his original dream-deprivation series. Altogether, as many as 20 to 30 all-night recordings were made for each subject, most of them on consecutive nights. Since, for the most part, tests could be made on only one subject at a time, and since a minute-by-minute all-night vigil was required of the experimenter to catch each dream episode immediately at its onset, it can be understood why the experiments have been called arduous and time-consuming.

Table 1 summarizes most of the pertinent data. As can be seen, the total number of base-line nights for the eight subjects was 40. The mean sleep time for the 40 nights was 7 hours and 2 minutes, the mean total nightly dream time was 82 minutes, and the mean percentage of dream time (total dream time to total sleep time

× 100) was 19.4. Since total sleep time was not held absolutely constant, percentage figures were routinely calculated as a check on the possibility that differences in total nightly dream time were due to differences in total sleep time. Actually, this is not a plausible explanation for any but quite small differences in dream time, because the range of values for total sleep time for each subject turned out to be very narrow throughout the entire study. When averaged in terms of individuals rather than nights, the means were: total sleep time, 6 hours 50 minutes; total dream time, 80 minutes; percentage of dream time, 19.5; this indicates that the figures were not skewed by the disparate number of base-line nights per subject. The remarkable uniformity of the findings for individual nights is demonstrated by the fact that the standard deviation of the total nightly dream time was only plus or minus 7 minutes.

PROGRESSIVE INCREASE IN DREAM "ATTEMPTS"

The number of consecutive nights of dream deprivation arbitrarily selected as a condition of the study was five. However, one subject left the study in a flurry of obviously contrived excuses after only three nights, and two subjects insisted on stopping after four nights but consented to continue with the recovery nights and the remainder of the schedule. One subject was pushed to seven nights. During each awakening the subjects were required to sit up in bed and remain fully awake for several minutes. On the first nights of dream deprivation, the return to sleep generally initiated a new sleep cycle, and the next dream period was postponed for the expected amount of time. However, on subsequent nights the number of forced awakenings required to suppress dreaming steadily mounted. Or, to put it another way, there was a progressive increase in the number of attempts to dream. The number of awakenings required on the first and last nights of deprivation are listed in Table 1. All the subjects showed this progressive increase, although there was considerable variation in the starting number and the amount of the increase. An important point is that each awakening was preceded by a minute or two of dreaming. This represented the time required for the experimenter to judge the emerging record and make the decision to awaken the subject after he first noticed the beginning of eye movements. In some cases the time was a little longer, as when an eye-movement period started while the experimenter was looking away from the recording apparatus. It is apparent from this that the method employed did not constitute absolute dream deprivation but, rather, about a 65- to 75-percent deprivation, as it turned out.

NIGHTLY DREAM TIME ELEVATED AFTER DEPRIVATION

The data on the first night of the dream deprivation recovery period are summarized for each subject in Table 1. As was mentioned, one subject had quit the study. The mean total dream time on the first recovery night was 112 minutes, or 26.6 percent of the total mean sleep time. If the results for two subjects who did not show marked increases on the first recovery night are excluded, the mean dream time is 127 minutes or 29 percent, which represents a 50-percent increase over the group base-line mean. For all seven subjects together, on the first recovery night the increase in percentage of dream time over base-line mean (Table 1, col. 3, mean percentage

TABLE 1 Summary of experimental results. TST, total sleep time; TDT, total dream time.

	Mean and range, base-line nights			Dream-deprivation nights (No.)	Awakenings (No.)			Dream-deprivation recovery nights					
								First night			First control recovery		
	TST	TDT	Percent		First night	Last night	No.	TST	TDT	Percent	TST	TDT	Percent
Subject W. T. (4 base-line nights)	6h36m 6h24m–6h48m	1h17m 1h10m–1h21m	19.5 17.0–21.3	5	8	14	1	6h43m	2h17m	34.0	6h50m	1h04m	15.6
Subject H. S. (5 base-line nights)	7h27m 7h07m–7h58m	1h24m 1h07m–1h38m	18.8 15.4–21.8	7	7	24	2	8h02m	2h45m	34.2	8h00m	1h49m	22.7
Subject N. W. (7 base-line nights)	6h39m 5h50m–7h10m	1h18m 1h11m–1h27m	19.5 17.4–22.4	5	11	30	5	6h46m	1h12m	17.8	7h10m	1h28m	20.2
Subject B. M. (6 base-line nights)	6h59m 6h28m–7h38m	1h18m 0h58m–1h35m	18.6 14.8–22.2	5	7	23	5	7h25m	1h58m	26.3	7h48m	1h28m	18.8
Subject R. G. (10 base-line nights)	7h26m 7h00m–7h57m	1h26m 1h13m–1h46m	19.3 16.9–22.7	5	10	20	5	7h14m	2h08m	29.5	7h18m	1h55m	26.3
Subject W. D. (4 base-line nights)	6h29m 5h38m–7h22m	1h21m 1h08m–1h32m	20.8 17.8–23.4	4	13	20	3	8h53m	2h35m	29.0			
Subject S. M. (2 base-line nights)	6h41m 6h18m–7h04m	1h12m 1h01m–1h23m	17.9 16.2–19.3	4	22	30	6	5h08m 6h32m	1h01m 1h50m*	19.8 28.1*	6h40m	1h07m	16.8
Subject W. G. (2 base-line nights)	6h16m 6h08m–6h24m	1h22m 1h17m–1h27m	20.8 20.7–20.9	3	9	13							

*Second recovery night (see text).

figures; col. 10, first recovery night percentages) was significant at the $p < .05$ level in a one-tail Wilcoxin matched-pairs signed-ranks test.[5]

It is important to mention, however, that one (S.M. in Table 1) of the two subjects alluded to above as exceptions was not really an exception because, although he had only 1 hour 1 minute of dreaming on his first recovery night, he showed a marked increase on *four* subsequent nights. His failure to show a rise on the first recovery night was in all likelihood due to the fact that he had imbibed several cocktails at a party before coming to the laboratory so that the expected increase in dream time was offset by the depressing effect of the alcohol. The other one of the two subjects (N.W. in Table 1) failed to show a significant increase in dream time on any of five consecutive recovery nights and therefore must be considered the single exception to the over-all results. Even so, it is hard to reconcile his lack of increase in dream time on recovery nights with the fact that during the actual period of dream deprivation he showed the largest build-up in number of awakenings required to suppress dreaming (11 to 30) of any subject in this group. One may only suggest that, although he was strongly affected by the dream loss, he could not increase his dream time on recovery nights because of an unusually stable basic sleep cycle that resisted modification.

The number of consecutive recovery nights for each subject in this series of tests was too small in some cases, mainly because it was naively supposed at the beginning of the study that an increase in dream time, if it occurred, would last only one or two nights. One subject had only one recovery night, another two, and another three. The dream time was markedly elevated above the base-line on all these nights. For how many additional nights each of these three subjects would have maintained an elevation in dream time can only be surmised in the absence of objective data. All of the remaining four subjects had five consecutive recovery nights. One was the single subject who showed no increase, two were nearing the base-line dream time by the fifth night, and one still showed marked elevation in dream time. From this admittedly incomplete sample it appears that about five nights of increased dreaming usually follow four or five nights of dream suppression achieved by the method of this study.

EFFECT NOT DUE TO AWAKENING

Six of the subjects underwent the series of control awakenings—that is, awakenings during non-dream periods. This series exactly duplicated the dream-deprivation series for each subject in number of nights, total number of awakenings, and total number of awakenings per successive night. The dream time on these nights was slightly below base-line levels as a rule. The purpose of this series was, of course, to see if the findings following dream deprivation were solely an effect of the multiple awakenings. Data for the first recovery nights after nights of control awakenings are included in Table 1. There was no significant increase for the group. The mean dream time was 88 minutes, and the mean percentage was 20.1. Subsequent recovery nights in this series also failed to show the marked rise in dream time that was observed after nights of dream deprivation. A moderate increase found on four out of a total of 24 recovery nights for the individuals in the control-awakening group was felt to be a response to the slight reduction in dream time on control-awakening nights.

BEHAVIORAL CHANGES

Psychological disturbances such as anxiety, irritability, and difficulty in concentrating developed during the period of dream deprivation, but these were not catastrophic. One subject, as was mentioned above, quit the study in an apparent panic, and two subjects insisted on stopping one night short of the goal of five nights of dream deprivation, presumably because the stress was too great. At least one subject exhibited serious anxiety and agitation. Five subjects developed a marked increase in appetite during this period of dream deprivation; this observation was supported by daily weight measurements which showed a gain in weight of 3 to 5 pounds in three of the subjects. The psychological changes disappeared as soon as the subjects were allowed to dream. The most important fact was that *none* of the observed changes were seen during the period of control awakenings.

The results have been tentatively interpreted as indicating that a certain amount of dreaming each night is a necessity. It is as though a pressure to dream builds up with the accruing dream deficit during successive dream-deprivation nights—a pressure which is first evident in the increasing frequency of atempts to dream and then, during the recovery period, in the marked increase in total dream time and percentage of dream time. The fact that this increase may be maintained over four or more successive recovery nights suggests that there is a more or less quantitative compensation for the deficit. It is possible that if the dream suppression were carried on long enough, a serious disruption of the personality would result.[6]

REFERENCES AND NOTES

1. Aserinsky, E., and Kleitman, N. *J. Appl. Physiol.* **8**, 1 (1955); W. Dement and E. Wolpert, *J. Nervous Mental Disease* **126**, 568 (1958); D. Goodenough, A. Shapiro, M. Holden, L. Steinschriber, *J. Abnormal Social Psychol.* **59**, 295 (1959); E. Wolpert and H. Trosman, *A.M.A. Arch. Neurol. Psychiat.* **79**, 603 (1958).
2. Dement, W. *J. Nervous Mental Disease* **122**, 263 (1955).
3. _____ and Kleitman, N. *J. Exptl. Psychol.* **53**, 339 (1957); W. Dement and E. Wolpert, *ibid.* **55**, 543 (1958).
4. Dement, W., and Kleitman, N. *Electroencephalog. and Clin. Neurophysiol.* **9**, 673 (1957).
5. Siegel, S. *Nonparametric Statistics for the Behavioral Sciences* (McGraw-Hill, New York, 1956).
6. The research reported in this paper was aided by a grant from the Foundations' Fund for Research in Psychiatry.

25 | CURRENT USES OF HYPNOSIS

C. Scott Moss

Despite the many unanswered questions that exist, several thousand physicians and dentists regularly employ hypnosis in the exercise of their professions, and many more have dallied with it at some time in their careers. While the use of hypnosis in any context inevitably stimulates nagging questions concerning the nature of the phenomenon, American medicine is generally pragmatic, being charged with a concern for urgent problems demanding fairly immediate solution, and the average practitioner tends to isolate practice from the more weighty theoretical and conceptual considerations.

MEDICAL USES OF HYPNOSIS

Proponents claim hypnosis as a potent medical tool. Dentists have extolled the use of hypnotic suggestion in the control of capillary bleeding, saliva flow, vomiting, and gagging. Physicians have reported success with a myriad of ailments and troublesome conditions: headaches can be relieved, fractures set, surgery performed, and bad habits like thumb sucking or bed wetting, insomnia, obesity, and excessive smoking counteracted. Such examples could be multiplied almost infinitely and the literature is replete with reports of the applicability of hypnosis in the fields of internal medicine, surgery, anesthesiology, obstetrics and gynecology, dermatology, and of course, psychiatry.

The best publicized use of hypnosis in medical practice is as an adjunct to surgical treatment. Hypnosis has undoubted value in the control and elimination of pain. A hundred years ago J. Esdaile, working in India, performed over 3,000 well-documented operations, many of them involving major amputations. Yet the mechanism involved remains so little understood (it is so incredible that "just talk" could effect such startling results) that today when an operation or childbirth is performed using hypnosis it still receives sensational publicity.

It is now recognized that at best hypnosis as the sole analgesic or anesthetic agent is effective with only a limited proportion of surgical patients. Instead, the primary value may be as a sedative or tranquilizer in allaying the anxiety and apprehension that accompanies every illness. The use of hypnosis to reduce preoperative fear and postoperative discomfort can be of value in effecting a significant reduction in the amount of medication used. Fetal anoxia is a leading cause of death during delivery, for example, and in many cases hypnosis can reduce the quantity of drugs required; similarly, patients are often given medication to relax them prior to an operation, and when a general anesthetic is added, this can contribute to respiratory failure. In addition, many diseases have a strong functional or psychosomatic component—that is, they originate from or are aggravated by emotional reactions to continued stress, such as in functional hypertension or some types of ulcerous conditions, and there is obvious value in training such patients in methods of self-relaxation.

It perhaps needs further emphasis that hypnosis is not a panacea and for manifest reasons will never replace chemoanesthesia. Many patients are refractory to this approach, it can be expensive in terms of the time and energies of the physician, and high-level competence is a difficult skill to acquire. On the other hand, the main value of the employment of hypnosis in medical practice may well be that it serves as a constant reminder to look on the patient as a whole person, not merely the embodiment of a particular disease. The fundamental step in the recovery process has always been to instill hope and encouragement in the patient. As Hippocrates stated, "It is more important to know what kind of a person has a disease than to know what kinds of a disease a person has."

Shor (1962) reviewed major experiments concerning the physiological effects of painful stimulation during hypnotic analgesia, and further presented the results of a study designed to identify the influence of anxiety on pain reactions. He concluded on the basis of his experiment that hypnosis can be an effective agent in reducing the subjective experience of pain, but that anything else which minimizes the anxiety component of the total experience could have a similar effect.

Barber (1963), in a critical review of experimental and clinical findings, arrived at a compatible conclusion. His review also suggested that hypnosis quite probably produces a diminution in anxiety and pain; however, some of the reported results may be attributable to either the subject's unwillingness to confess that pain was experienced or an amnesia for the pain experience. Consistent with his established theoretical position, Barber does not discount the possibility that similar results could be effected in waking subjects of comparable native suggestibility.

HYPNOSIS AND PSYCHOTHERAPY

Freud's rejection of hypnosis doubtlessly contributed to a reluctance to consider its use in psychoanalysis, but medical men in general shared in the age-old attitude of superstitious awe, fear, and antagonism toward hypnosis, and they held similar reservations concerning its employment in all forms of psychotherapy. It was not until World War II, when psychiatrists were confronted with the need to treat large numbers of acute combat disturbances, that they reevaluated the potentialities inherent in hypnosis. Present-day advocates report that hypnosis has been utilized in the successful treatment of a broad spectrum of psychopathology, ranging from the neuroses and psychoses to alcoholism, drug addiction, psychosomatic disorders, and even organic conditions.

An extensive variety of specialized hypnotic techniques are available to psychotherapists today, and it is noteworthy how often clinicians devise new techniques to meet the exigencies of a case. The current period in hypnosis begins with the work of such important investigators as Hull, Williams, Wells, LeCron, Guze, Kline, Weitzenhoffer, Pattie, White, Brenman, Gill, Wolberg, Raginsky, Eysenck, Rosen, Schneck, and Watkins, Milton Erickson was among the first to make extensive therapeutic application of specialized hypnotic techniques, which he skillfully devised and tailored to the unique and individual needs of his patients, and he is often considered the father of the present era in hypnotherapy.

The modern-day hypnotheropist utilizes such glamorous-sounding techniques as free and directed associations, age regression, abreaction through revivification, automatic writing and drawing, experimentally implanted conflicts, symptom substitution and transformation, visual and auditory hallucinations, scene visualization through crystal gazing, time distortion, suggested dreams, relaxation through autohypnosis, and even simulated electro shock. These techniques are used to directly reduce or eliminate annoying symptoms, promote catharsis or abreaction (release of the emotions believed to support neurotic symptom formation), desensitize or recondition a patient to a traumatic experience, and to uncover the meaning behind his symptoms (insight).

Hypnosis has now been adapted by exponents of almost every school or doctrine of psychotherapy, and in recent years even some analytically oriented psychotherapists have displayed a disposition to incorporate hypnotic techniques within the principles and practice of psychoanalysis. When hypnotherapy is conducted by a psychoanalyst it is termed hypnoanalysis. The therapist first trains the patient as a hypnotic subject and then employs the usual psychoanalytic procedures until severe resistances (verbal blocks) are encountered, whereupon the patient is quickly hypnotized and specialized hypnotic techniques are used to obtain the suppressed material.

The more objective case studies report inexplicable successes and failures in the employment of hypnotherapy; nevertheless, favorable results occur with sufficient frequency to sustain the tantalizing prospect that hypnosis may yet provide a means for reducing the extended duration of psychotherapy. Hypnotherapy continues to have many vociferous critics among professional psychotherapists, and differences of opinion often reach vitriolic intensity. If its advocates are hard pressed to prove the special efficacy of their technique, and to many the value seems self-evident, they can at least take some measure of consolation in the fact that there is little experimental evidence that one form of psychotherapy is superior to any other or, for that matter, that psychotherapy works at all (Frank, 1961). (Refer to papers by Erickson [1954a] and Moss [1965] for a description of special techniques of brief hypnotherapy; for more extended accounts, read Wolberg [1945] and Brenman and Gill [1947].)

LIMITATIONS AND DANGERS OF HYPNOSIS

It should come as no surprise that the experts are as sharply divided on the question of the alleged dangers of hypnosis as they are on every other aspect of this controversial subject. As we have seen, some authorities attribute enormous power to hypnosis, while others dismiss it as a fraud or an illusion. Some of its detractors perceive only a negative or morbid connotation, while denying any possible virtue; conversely, many practitioners assert that hypnosis is a powerful instrument, but that no real danger inheres because the subject retains an ability to protect himself from its improper application.

Harold Rosen, Chairman of the Committee on Hypnosis of the Council on Mental Health of the American Medical Association, is generally recognized as the leading public spokesman for those who, while representing hypnosis as a potent medical tool, have emphasized that great harm can and has been done with hypnosis by the psychiatrically untrained. Rosen has repeatedly charged that hypnosis can endanger the patients' physical and emotional health and life, through serious adverse sequelae, such as incapacitating substitute symptoms, suicidal depressions, and psychotic episodes. In contrast, many qualified medical hypnotists have taken issue with this contention, maintaining that the dangers have been grossly exaggerated. A thoughtful article on the subject has been written by Meares (1961), who discusses nine possible danger areas.

1. Perverse motivation: either the patient or physician may misuse the situation to satisfy ulterior needs.
2. Untoward personality effects: hypnosis can increase a subject's suggestibility and overdependence; conversely, continued use of hypnosis may exaggerate unfortunate facets of the physician's own personality.
3. Traumatic insight: sudden confrontation with repressed material intolerable to the subject.
4. Precipitation of a psychosis.
5. Development of disabling substitute symptoms when the original symptoms have been removed by hypnotic suggestion.
6. Sudden panic reactions occasioned by the experience of hypnosis itself.
7. Complications arising from misunderstandings of communication.
8. Possible unscrupulous use of hypnosis.
9. Difficulty in waking a subject and unfortunate effects of incomplete waking.

It is Meares' conclusion that the use of hypnosis by an unskilled person can represent a real danger "but the dangers to the patient in the hands of an adequately trained physician are very small indeed."

It should further be apparent that most of the identified dangers are by no means unique to the use of hypnosis, being intrinsic to the intimate interpersonal relationship that develops in any form of psychotherapy. The absence of definitive evidence on the subject notwithstanding, it behooves the practitioner to exercise caution, if for no other reason than that engrained public and professional prejudices will single out the employment of hypnosis as the most blameworthy cause in the event of unfortunate complications.

PROFESSIONAL TRAINING IN HYPNOSIS

Until a few short years ago, hypnosis retained its aura of dark mystery, and practitioners were regarded as charlatans and quacks, which they too often were. Recently, hypnosis has gained a degree of scientific respectability through recognition and acceptance by the major medical and psychological professional organizations. In 1958 the Council on Mental Health of the American Medical Association issued a report legitimizing the use of hypnosis in the practice of medicine. In 1960, the AMA sponsored a conference on standards for training in hypnosis, and in 1961 the American Psychiatric Association issued an official policy statement affirming that hypnosis is a specialized psychiatric procedure.

Meanwhile, the Council of Representatives of the American Psychological Association voted in 1960 to recognize the efforts of the Society for Clinical and Experimental Hypnosis, one of the two national professional organizations concerned with hypnosis, to elevate standards of competency. The APA annual directory now lists diplomates of the SCEH sponsored American Board of Examiners in Psychological Hypnosis (there are also boards in medical and dental hypnosis).

Yet another indication of a more serious regard for hypnosis is the fact that at this writing sixteen states have enacted laws restricting the use of this technique, and several other states have legislation under consideration. While existing laws leave much to be desired, many of them do attempt to restrict the employment of hypnosis to physicians, dentists, and psychologists in their professional capacities.

Both the British Medical Association and the American Medical Association have defined hypnosis as a temporary condition of altered attention, induced in the subject by a hypnotist and characterized by the usual phenomena. Seen in its proper perspective, hypnosis is recognized as only one, albeit important, aspect of the doctor-patient relationship, but a technique which has an enhanced potential for treatment or harm. For this reason, the AMA and the American Psychiatric Association have recommended that training should be provided through departments of psychiatry in medical schools, teaching hospitals, and psychiatric training centers.

It has been lamented that the induction of hypnosis requires little or no technical skill or training and it is widely recognized that mere ability to hypnotize does not qualify anyone to treat patients with hypnosis. Hypnosis is only one important tool in the medical armamentarium, and judicious use requires a breadth of knowledge about human dynamics and psychopathology. The AMA recommends that the physician who wishes to employ hypnosis have additional training in basic psychiatry beyond that now included in the present undergraduate medical school curriculum (Rosen and Bartemeier, 1961). General practitioners in increasing numbers have requested training in the technique, as have their colleagues in various medical specialties. Both the AMA and the APA maintain that training in all aspects of hypnosis should be made available to physicians requesting it. There are at this time, however, only a limited number of personnel competent to conduct this instruction, and a dearth of proper facilities where such training can be received.

In earlier days, the interested professional person relied primarily on self-instruction through reading of the limited professional literature and the more accessible but often highly distorted sensationalized commercial accounts, in combination with his own trial-and-error applications. Since 1950, a number of physicians, dentists, and psychologists have attended seminars, lectures, and symposia of two or three days' duration. The question has been raised as to whether this limited training really was better than none at all, but it was the only resource available. More adequate facilities only now are being planned and established.

A report of the AMA Committee on Hypnosis (Rosen *et al.*, 1962) discusses the problems associated with training in medical hypnosis, presents (as a critique of available instruction) a rationale for the establishment of adequate training, and proposes for consideration the structure and content of a model course in hypnosis. According to this report, only one medical school in the United States offers adequate training in hypnosis to practicing physicians, although several were projecting courses based on recommendations of the report. In addition, several other medical schools provide some degree of formal course instruction in hypnosis for medical students and residents.

The reprint of a paper by Moss *et al.* reports on the current status of psychological training and research in hypnosis. Results of a recent survey indicate that only eight of fifty-five psychology departments approved for graduate training programs in clinical psychology by the American Psychological Association have courses in hypnosis. The article elucidates some of the reasons for opposition to inclusion of this type of training in the curriculum and raises doubt that any sizable number of psychology departments will institute such courses in the near future.

A somewhat paradoxical attitude expressed by department chairmen was that while they oppose the practice of hypnosis by the untrained, they do not favor inclusion of the necessary instruction in the graduate-school curriculum. This opinion is consistent with the prevalent attitude among many faculty that specialized clinical techniques are best acquired on a postgraduate level, although it is recognized that the opportunity for intensive training at this stage in professional development is decidedly limited. In recognition of this problem, for several years now the American Psychological Association has sponsored postdoctoral institutes on hypnosis in conjunction with its annual national meeting.

HYPNOSIS AND RESEARCH

"Considering the long history of investigations of hypnotic behavior, it may seem surprising to some that our knowledge today—or lack of knowledge—is probably not much advanced over our knowledge of 100 years ago . . . we find ourselves generally preoccupied with many of the same problems now that haunted our forefathers." Fisher (1962, p. 109) wrote this in his excellent article on hypnotic research, and he went on to identify as basic unresolved issues many of the same problems that have concerned us thus far in this book: relations between personality characteristics and hypnotic susceptibility; the range of pathology susceptible to hypnotic intervention; establishment of the limits of hypnotic control over psychological and physiological functions; the so-called "genuineness" of various hypnotic phenomena; and the many competing theories concerning the nature of hypnosis. What are some of the paramount reasons for the unsatisfactory status of scientific knowledge in this area? Fisher points out there is increasing use of hypnosis as a research tool, but that such experiments are based on numerous implicit and unproven assumptions about the nature of hypnotic behavior. "In hypnotic research we are plagued with both a lack of generalizable facts and a plethora of questionable interpretations."

As Reyher (1962) states, hypnotic research can be broadly characterized as having either an intrinsic or instrumental orientation. Intrinsic research is concerned with the phenomena and nature of hypnosis itself, whereas instrumental research employs hypnosis as a tool in the study of personality, psychopathological, or psychophysiological alterations. Proponents of the instrumental approach contend that hypnosis provides unique possibilities for furthering psychological research. They advocate the use of hypnosis to control such important psychological variables in the experimental situation as interest and motivation and thus insure the focusing of attention and elimination of distractions. More than that, they believe that hypnosis can be employed to produce the conditions that are to be the object of study, as for example, hypnotically induced emotional fluctuations (depression, elation, anger) in validation studies of personality tests, or the hypnotic stimulation of neurotic conflicts in investigations of ego-defense mechanisms (repression, displacement, rationalization) or evaluations of the efficacy of different types of psychotherapy.

Hundreds of such studies have not been reported; however, Reyher observes, "Despite its ability to command enduring interest, instrumental hypnotic research has remained relatively inconsequential and isolated. One of the principal reasons for this state of affairs is the lack of criteria for determining the relevance of hypnotically induced behavior to clinical or natural behavior" (p. 344). In other words, psychologists have largely ignored results of this kind of hypnotic research because they remain unconvinced that hypnotically induced behavior is comparable enough to its natural counterpart to provide valid evidence. Because so few unequivocal facts have been established about hypnosis *per se*, investigators who employ hypnosis as a research instrument are in the vulnerable position of studying one unknown (the subject of experiment inquiry) by means of a second unknown (hypnosis). Many psychologists maintain that the only defensible position is an intrinsic orientation—that is, interested investigators first must resolve many of the crucial issues concerning the nature of hypnosis itself.

While some of the problems involved in the creation of adequate research designs for the evaluation of hypnotic research are peculiar to this phenomenon, the majority of problems are similar to those encountered in the evaluation of any other form of behavior. Well-controlled studies, with adequate sampling, valid and reliable criterion measures, and full reporting of negative and positive results are necessary in the objective evaluation of any psychological manifestation. The hugely complicating factor in hypnosis research is the seeming hypersuggestibility of the subject. In any experimental situation the investigator exercises extreme care that his personal biases do not influence the behavior of the subject. In hypnosis research, the investigator either deliberately trades upon the subject's increased suggestibility in order to effect a certain outcome or result, or when the experimenter attempts to hide his wishes or expectations, the exquisite sensitivity of the subject introduces the likelihood that he will ferret out these expectations and behave in a manner to demonstrate their validity.

The minimum safeguards that must be incorporated into any hypnosis experiment have been carefully outlined in recent articles by Fisher, Sutcliffe (1960), and Barber (1962b). A major requirement if causation is to be attributed to hypnosis is that hypnotic behavior must be compared with normal waking behavior. It may appear obvious to use waking control subjects, but surprisingly few studies have done so. Some studies have used subjects as their own control; however, where one subject is asked to perform the same task in the waking and trance states there is the general problem of learning or transfer effects, and a further problem unique to hypnosis—namely, that the good hypnotic subject may purposely give his best performance under the hypnotic condition. A very few studies have used independent waking controls, but too frequently the hypnotic or experimental group has been carefully selected, while haphazardly chosen subjects are assigned to the control group. Sutcliffe and Barber have recommended that, in order to control for subject variables, both experimental and control groups be drawn at random from a population of good hypnotic subjects or from an unrated population.

In a test of the hypothesis that hypnotic behavior is a function of a subject's concept of how a hypnotized subject should act, Orne (1959) gave identical lectures on hypnosis to two psychology class sections, except that in one catalepsy of the dominant hand was misrepresented as a common feature of trance behavior. Later, as was predicted, this "typical" behavior was found to spontaneously occur only in volunteer hypnotic subjects from the class which had observed the demonstration of catalepsy. Orne believes that in all psychological experiments, not just those involving hypnosis, the subject strives to behave in accordance with his perception of the experimenter's expectations. The totality of cues, verbal and nonverbal, which communicate the hypotheses or wishes of the investigator, he has termed the *demand characteristics* of the experimental situation. It is clear that the demand characteristics may be a major determinant of a subject's behavior, and much of Orne's work, therefore, has been concerned with the development of techniques which permit the study and isolation of these factors. One such method in hypnotic research involves the employment of simulators.

Orne believes that the unconvincing performance of many waking control subjects may be attributed to their knowledge that the experimenter knows they are just playing a role. His simulators are often chosen for their role-taking ability, carefully rehearsed, and instructed to try and fool the investigator who is "blind" to the true status of the subject (whether he is hypnotized or not). It is hoped in this manner to motivate the subject to an optimal performance and to insure that subtle nonverbal communications emanating from the hypnotist remain constant for both experimental and control groups. Simulators naturally do not have the subjective experiences that presumably distinguish the hypnotic state, and must of necessity guide their behavior by the demand characteristics of the situation. Orne and his colleagues report that well-motivated simulators are able to manifest a pattern of behavior almost indistinguishable from a real hypnotic performance.

Still other complications exist in regard to sample bias. All hypnosis studies are perforce conducted on volunteer samples, and the very real possibility exists that people who volunteer may not be representative of the general population. Thus, it is quite impossible to generalize about the distribution of hypnotic susceptibility to include that sizable segment of the population who refuse to participate. It is more than likely that any method that depends upon the subject's initiative in volunteering will oversample the more susceptible, although willingness is a necessary but not sufficient condition to being hypnotized. More importantly, it is entirely possible that important differences exist in the attitudes and traits of people who are willing or unwilling to be hypnotized, and while these can be determined, it remains impossible to establish the relationship between susceptibility and character among members of the non-volunteer group.

Even more lamentable, because it could be avoided, investigations of hypnosis share in a critical shortcoming of a great many current psychological studies, a dependence on *volunteer undergraduate (mostly male) college students*—a sample that by no stretch of the imagination can be regarded as representative of the general population. This source of sample bias is purely attributable to expediency—that is, the ready accessibility of such subjects for study. There is only one real exception to this criticism: a number of investigations have used psychiatric patients as the subject population, so that even our tentative conclusions to date are largely applicable to the emotionally disturbed or freshman college students.

Another source of error resides in the preferential treatment often accorded the experimental or hypnosis group. In many experiments the hypnosis group receives a careful preliminary rehearsal in the role he is expected to assume (many experts maintain that to be effective, induction methods must be flexible and individualized, ideas must be presented to subjects in a meaningful fashion, and subjects must be allowed sufficient time to achieve the desired results). These preliminary sessions allow subjects an opportunity to familiarize themselves with the general experimental situation and even to receive specific practice on the criterion tasks. These "training" sessions also may have the effect of establishing a close interpersonal relationship with the experimenter, with the result that the hypnotic group is more highly motivated and more inclined to comply with his wishes or suggestions.

It is also recognized that the mere structuring of the situation as an experiment in hypnosis may be an important factor in arousing enhanced interest and motivation. The fact that a situation is defined as hypnosis implies that the subject is expected to carry out all suggested acts to the best of his ability, and that the experimenter accepts responsibility for the consequences of the behavior he asks the subject to perform. Variables of this nature emphasize the importance of treating the experimental and control groups as nearly identically as possible.

The hypnotist himself may be a source of systematic error in these experiments. Despite the best of intentions and precautions, his investment in a given experimental outcome may be implicitly communicated to the subject, so that the outcome is unwittingly predetermined. Replication of experiments with independent investigators is desirable, just as this is a requirement in all scientific experiments. It is necessary to build into experimental designs a sample of investigators in order to parcel out the effect of experimenter bias. What may eventually be required is a closely coordinated program of research in which "we might hope that different experimenters in different laboratories could jointly attack a central problem . . . instead of multiple investigators each working on his own pet theories" (Fisher, 1962, p. 125).

There are, of course, many other sources of experimental error in hypnosis research, but these should serve to introduce the reader to some of the complications that confront serious investigation. Sutcliffe (1960) concluded that it is not by chance alone or even the aforementioned difficulties that account for the lack of methodological rigor characteristic of studies of hypnosis. He accuses a large proportion of experts of possessing what he calls a "credulous" view—they take the validity of hypnotic phenomena on faith. In contrast, there are those who doubt the genuineness of hypnotic behavior and contend that the hypnotic subject is "acting" in conformity with the suggestions of the hypnotist. This Sutcliffe has termed the skeptical point of view. In his paper he reviews evidence from published studies of hypnotically produced aesthesias; auditory, visual, and temporal hallucinations; regression; and antisocial behavior. His general conclusion is that the occasional well-designed study can be said to directly support or be consistent with the "skeptical" point of view, although many studies need to be replicated with proper controls to achieve unequivocal conclusions.

Weitzenhoffer (1963 and 1964) was so sufficiently stung by Sutcliffe's thesis that he felt impelled to take sharp issue and to examine in detail the evidence presented in support of it. Readers are enjoined to read Weitzenhoffer's well-considered defense of the genuineness of hypnotic behavior, his support of the experimental work of Erickson and others (whom Sutcliffe ranked as a leader among the "credulous"), and his penetrating critical analysis of the positions of Pattie, Orne, Barber, and others whom Sutcliffe had classified as representatives of the "skeptical" point of view. The author is well aware that Weitzenhoffer's article may serve as a desirable and articulate counterbalance to some of the unintentional and yet unavoidable biases, prejudices, and predilections he may have interpolated in this text.

There is space to paraphrase only a few representative but topical comments made by Weitzenhoffer on the use of simulators as controls. He acknowledges the possibility that simulators can be found who can closely duplicate the behavior of hypnotized subjects, but contends that one cannot logically invalidate the reality of hypnotic behavior by showing that some individuals can imitate it by acting. He particularly objects to rehearsal of the simulator or allowing him to observe hypnotized subjects in action. It is Weitzenhoffer's position that the control subject should have no more and no less information than has the hypnotized subject, and the simulator should simply be instructed to behave as he thinks he would if he were hypnotized. The use of simulators is characterized as a weak tool, hardly worth the trouble, but one that has strong appeal to those convinced that the hypnotic subject is bent on deceiving the investigator. He asks: Is it really surprising that they find what they already "know" to be a fact—namely, that hypnotic behavior is not genuine?

It is on this note of high controversy, so typical of the present state of affairs in this field, that we shall close. It is hoped that if the reader has been frustrated by the absence of definitive answers, some of his preconceptions have been challenged and his intellect has been excited by this brief excursion into hypnosis. If this is so he will share in the sense of adventure that compels some professional persons to persist in investigation of a fascinating but elusive phenomena. Perhaps a few readers will continue into professional careers where they will be in a position to join in contributing badly needed research data. Clark Hull said it best in the closing pages of his classic text, written more than thirty years ago:

Too many of the works on the subject in the past have fallen short of the scientific ideal. Doubtless many things have contributed to this weakness, but surely a major factor must be the inherent difficulty of the problems involved, the fundamental elusiveness of the phenomena, and the consequent subtlety necessary in the experimental controls. These difficulties are so great that to enter seriously on a program of investigation in this field is a little like tempting fate; it is almost to court scientific disaster. Small wonder that orthodox scientists have usually avoided the subject! Yet each generation may be expected in the future, as in the past, to produce a very few rash souls who will not only risk the dangers of making scientific errors but will also have the courage to brave the semi-superstitious fears of the general public and the uneasy suspicions of their orthodox scientific brethren. It is to them that the present work is really addressed [p. 403].

UNIT SEVEN | DISCUSSION QUESTIONS

21 | ESP AND CREDIBILITY IN SCIENCE

Do you support McConnell's views concerning the credibility of ESP? Discuss and give examples.

Why has the response of many psychologists to the credibility of ESP been negative? (See Hebb's article (7) in this book.)

22 | SUBLIMINAL PERCEPTION

Discuss the origin of the term "subliminal." Does this term refer primarily to vision?

Discuss the main difficulties in subliminal advertisement as a bona-fide technique of advertisement and communication.

23 | DERMO-OPTICAL PERCEPTION: A PEEK DOWN THE NOSE

Discuss Gardner's hypothesis concerning the evidence for DOP.

In what ways do you account for the reported cases of "extra-ocular vision" in sighted people?

24 | THE EFFECT OF DREAM DEPRIVATION

Discuss the behavioral changes that occur during a period of dream deprivation.

Discuss why dreams are important (or not important).

25 | CURRENT USES OF HYPNOSIS

Should hypnosis be a form of nightclub entertainment? What are the advantages and/or disadvantages?

How do you explain why hypnosis is not used more often by scientists in the treatment of human problems?

As our society becomes increasingly complex and demanding, the problems of group living likewise increase. Strikingly different, strange, and unorthodox methods of coping with the environment are likely to be considered as abnormal behavior. When an individual's methods of adjustment are inefficient, he may have what is called a neurosis. A *neurosis* is a condition in which the patient does not require hospitalization; nevertheless he fails to operate at full efficiency. The condition is similar to that of an automobile with a poorly adjusted carburetor: The engine is operative, but it fails to perform at full efficiency. If the specific problem is not attended to, the engine, as a whole, suffers and the problem is magnified. So, too, when the neurotic person fails to operate at maximum efficiency, his interaction with others is affected. (The terms *psychoneurosis* and *neurosis* are used interchangeably by many psychologists.) *Anxiety reaction* (extreme uneasiness in situations that are not dangerous), *phobia* (irrational fear), *amnesia* (loss of identity), and *obsessions* and *compulsions* (recurrent irresistible ideas and acts) are the examples of neurosis most frequently encountered.

On the other hand, a *psychosis* is a condition in which the maladjustment is so severe that hospitalization is often necessary. The distinction between neurosis and psychosis is easier to make in theory than in practice because many of the symptoms and conditions are undefined and borderline. A humorous distinction has been made between the psychotic and the neurotic: "To the psychotic, 2 and 2 make 5; to the neurotic, 2 and 2 make 4, but he's unhappy about it!"

Schizophrenia (various reactions characterized by fundamental disturbances in reality relationships), *manic-depressive* (marked emotional oscillation), and *paranoia* (delusions) are the most prevalent examples of psychosis. Of all the psychotic disorders, schizophrenia makes up the largest group. The National Institute of Mental Health (NIMH) reports that 73% of all psychotics admitted to U.S. public mental hospitals were classified as schizophrenics.

In the first reading, *One of the Great Mystery Stories of Medicine,* Lawrence Galton presents two theories concerning schizophrenia: (1) schizophrenia does not have an organic base and is considered to be a functional disorder, and (2) schizophrenia is an organic-based disorder and is necessarily considered to be organic. Recent experiments and therapeutic measures are also discussed.

Thomas S. Szasz' *Mental Illness Is a Myth* presents an argument for the case that mental disorder should not be thought of as an "illness," but rather it should be considered as part of an individual's pattern of "personal conduct." His viewpoint has been the center of current controversy among many behavioral scientists.

In the third article by Karl Menninger, *Psychiatrists Use Dangerous Words,* the author examines some of the concepts and terms used to describe abnormal mental conditions; e.g., manic-depressive, schizophrenic, and psychotic. Menninger suggests healthier, and more useful, ways of viewing and discussing what he calls "human problems."

The involvement of behavioral scientists as "expert witnesses" has become a vital part of America's judicial procedures and the question of legal insanity is one of considerable debate in the courtroom as well as in the classroom. *The Psychologist as an Expert Witness on the Issue of Insanity* by Ray Jeffery, the final reading in this unit, presents excerpts from two federal court hearings in which psychologists testified. In each case, actual quotations are given to illustrate the impact of cross-examination between the psychologists and the government attorneys.

---

26 | ONE OF THE GREAT MYSTERY STORIES OF MEDICINE

Lawrence Galton

"Surely no other term in medicine rivals schizophrenia in the amount of confusion and despair it provokes. One of the great mystery stories of modern medicine, it is full of clues, rich in suspects, littered with victims, and with as yet no solution. The police as usual are busy but not impressive. . . ."

So, not long ago in the Journal of the American Medical Association, wrote Dr. Leston L. Havens of the Department of Psychiatry of Harvard Medical School.

And as if to exemplify the confusion and frustration involved in the policework—in the research into schizophrenia—almost simultaneously with the publication of Dr. Havens's observation, a Canadian researcher at a New York scientific meeting was reporting, hopefully, the finding of a chemical, called NAD, which seemed able to erase the symptoms of the disease. But, a few months later, when a group of U.S. investigators tried NAD they got no results.

There have been two theories about schizophrenia. One—the still-prevailing—is that it is primarily psychological in nature, a matter of inadequate personality finally succumbing to some environmental stress.*

---

* See cover illustration showing paintings produced by one patient at successive stages of schizophrenic disintegration.

The other is that schizophrenia is physical—basically, a disorder of body chemistry. As proponents of this theory—the schizochemists, they are sometimes called—explain: "Before anyone can get schizophrenia, his body 'factory' must be different from that of a normal person; it must have the capacity to go out of order and set biochemical changes in motion. It may be triggered into going out of order by environmental stresses—but the physiological weakness must be there first."

The ranks of the schizochemists are growing. They include distinguished biologists, geneticists and psychiatrists. Recently, many joined to establish the American Schizophrenia Foundation, aimed at intensification of biochemical research. They see the psychological approach as sterile. They believe that, although there is as yet no definitive proof of a biochemical factor, there is growing evidence in favor, and that, despite difficulties and setbacks, it is in the biochemical search that the hope lies, perhaps not too remotely, for making understandable and manageable—as much so as diabetes, for example—one of the most widespread and devastating of illnesses.

Schizophrenia accounts for more than half of the mentally ill patients who fill more than half the hospital beds in this country. According to some estimates, it affects two million people in this country and Canada—and one of every 100 persons in the world today has, has had, or will have the disease. The 1 per cent incidence seems to prevail in all societies, cultures, racial and ethnic types and social classes.

Though it can develop at any time—even early in childhood—typically it overtakes people in the 16 to 30 age group.

Often it maims them for life. Although tranquilizing drugs have helped in many ways, they do not appear to have greatly changed the over-all recovery rate. According to Dr. Don D. Jackson of the Stanford University School of Medicine, a schizophrenic entering a state hospital has little better than an even chance of ever returning to society as a functioning member.

With or without treatment, according to the American Schizophrenia Foundation, about one-third of patients recover, a third remain totally disabled, and another third are discharged into the outside world "not sick enough to be institutionalized, not well enough to live healthy, happy lives."

Many of the last group, the foundation reports, will take their own lives to escape their pain and suffering. Schizophrenia is one of the reasons that suicide has become a major problem in the United States.

The symptoms of the disease are diverse. To the schizophrenic, the world may appear as though he were viewing it through a distorted looking glass; colors may assume unnatural brilliance or lose their brilliance; three-dimensional objects may look flat. Often the schizophrenic has illusions: A coat hanging in a closet may become a bear; a child may see a playmate turn temporarily into a lion. Frequently, there are auditory hallucinations: voices in the head—singing, or accusing or commanding. There may be changes in other senses—smell, taste, touch. Schizophrenics sometimes appear insensitive to pain yet may complain of bizarre sensations such as worms crawling under their skins.

There are disturbances in thought and thought content. Some victims experience a slow-down in the thinking process so that logical thinking becomes difficult or impossible. Others complain their minds are racing away from them. Some develop delusions of being persecuted; others, of being in positions of high authority. Sudden fear—nameless and overwhelming—is common; so, too, is deep depression.

In the 19th century, Emil Kraepelin, a European psychiatrist, distinguished four major subclasses of schizophrenia. His classification system is still in use:

In what Kraeplin called "hebephrenic" schizophrenia, silliness, abnormal pleasure in pranks and gaudy adornment and hypochondria are among predominating symptoms.

The "catatonic" schizophrenic is mute, stuporous, withdrawn; and often assumes strange, uncomfortable positions he may maintain for long periods.

In "paranoid" schizophrenia, there are embittered, suspicious attitudes and feelings of persecution.

The "simple" type of schizophrenic reaction, gradual in onset, is marked by apathy and indifference, withdrawal, confusion and secret grandiosity.

One investigator, Dr. Robert S. de Ropp, has graphically described extreme cases of schizophrenia. A 28-year-old catatonic woman had been in a disturbed ward for eight years. "We find her huddled in a corner of a wooden bench, completely motionless, her knees drawn up under her chin and her thin arms clasped about her legs . . . her body so thin bones are visible through the flesh. . . . Most of the time she remains motionless, not moving even to satisfy calls of nature or take food. If you move her arm, it remains in any position in which you happen to place it. . . . The attendants have come to regard her as virtually an inanimate object, like a piece of furniture. Her husband has [divorced her and] married again. Her children do not remember her. Her illness began when she was 20. She may live on into her 60's. For all those 40 years she must be cared for—a living corpse, denied even the privilege of burial."

A second patient, a paranoid, is a man of 28, "very active, but his activity has no connection with the realities of the world. . . . Everything he sees, hears, touches, even the food he eats, becomes endowed . . . with sinister, malignant significance. . . . The glance of an attendant, even a casual gesture by one of his fellow inmates, is interpreted as a threat. . . . He pushes food away . . . when they try to feed him by force he fights and screams and struggles. . . . He [too] may live for another 40 years, alone as only the mad can be alone, a curse to himself, a burden to those who care for him."

But if the disease can be totally disabling, it can also be mild and fleeting. Abraham Lincoln is believed to have experienced a schizophrenic breakdown as a young man. Kierkegaard, August Comte, Rousseau—many noted artists, writers, philosophers and scientists—suffered from time to time with schizophrenia.

A long-prevalent theory, as already noted, has been that it is an environmental-personality disorder—and that the stage may be set for it by a defective mother-child relationship. The child fails to develop normally. At some point, as the result of personality deficiency, he may become schizophrenic when life introduces a critical situation.

Recently, studies of sensory deprivation have led some investigators to postulate a mechanism through which schizophrenic symptoms may be brought on. The human organism appears to need a certain rate of sensory input. When the input is lowered—as in sleep, for example—dreams occur, and dreaming appears to be essential to physical well-being. In experiments, volunteers subjected to sensory deprivation—by being confined separately in rooms with hands isolated in special cuffs, eyes masked, sounds barred—have, in most cases, experienced hallucinations and psychosislike reactions after short periods. It has been suggested that schizophrenia may be triggered when the victim, experiencing severe anxiety, manages to reject the input of sensory experience from the environment that has provoked his anxiety —and then suffers hallucinations and the build-up of a delusional system.

Lately, going beyond mother-child interaction as the root cause of schizophrenia, some investigators have become convinced that an understanding of the disorder must be based on knowledge of total family interactions and behavior. They believe, for example, that the father's role is as important as the mother's in child development. One bit of evidence: research indicating that the highest probability of recovery in schizophrenics comes from homes in which the father had the dominant role.

There have been studies, too, indicating that, in some cases, the family system operates only at the expense of the schizophrenic's ill health. "Ulcers, heart attacks, gall-bladder disfunction and other disorders," observes Dr. Jackson of Stanford, "appear to afflict other members of the family with suspicious frequency just at that time in conjoint family therapy when the patient makes a significant change for the better."

But there is impressive evidence that heredity operates in schizophrenia—and a heredity factor suggests physical disorder. The classic study was done 20 years ago with identical twins by Dr. Franz J. Kallmann of the Columbia University College of Physicians and Surgeons. Dr. Kallmann was able to demonstrate that if one identical twin is in a state hospital suffering from schizophrenia, there is an 85 percent likelihood that the other twin will be found to have the disorder.

In 1964, Dr. David Rosenthal of the National Institute of Mental Health was able to report on four young women, identical quadruplets now in their 20's, who constitute the first recorded case of quadruple schizophrenia. For three years, a team of 60 physicians and other specialists studied the girls, their upbringing and their genetic make-up, seeking an answer to the question of whether heredity or environment causes mental illness.

They found evidence of a single gene that might have been initially responsible. They found an abnormal brain-wave pattern shared in common by the quads—and by their father. And they found a mental-illness pattern in the father's family.

They also found abnormal environmental influences. The quads' parents were suspicious and would not allow them to have friends. The father drank heavily, and abused and frightened them.

Major conclusion of the study: schizophrenia results from an interplay of hereditary and environmental factors. Dr. Rosenthal reported: "In most cases, an inherited factor needs to be present for schizophrenia to develop. However, without severe environmental stresses the illness may not appear in those who have a predisposition to it."

If there is an inherited, or genetic, factor, it could very well manifest itself in a biochemical aberration. Sigmund Freud himself had mentioned the possibility of a biochemical answer to mental illness.

The ability of genetic errors to produce mental disease through physical mechanisms has become very clear in recent years. Phenylketonuria, or PKU, is one example. The child with PKU, once doomed to mental retardation, has lacking in the genetic blueprints in his cells the instructions to synthesize a specific chemical, a digestive enzyme—phenylalanine hydroxylase. Without the enzyme, his body is unable to metabolize phenylalanine, a constituent of many foods. The material builds up to abnormal levels in body and brain. Today, a widely used chemical test can spot the disorder in infants and, by special diet, retardation can be avoided.

Attempts to discover some biochemical defects in schizophrenics date back more than half a century. At one point, investigators observed that administration of thyroid-gland extract seemed to benefit some schizophrenics, and there was a feeling that thyroid derangement might be the key to the problem. It was not. Other investigations got nowhere.

Then, in 1943, the "chemistry of madness" search received a shot in the arm. Dr. Albert Hofmann, a scientist with the Swiss-based pharmaceutical firm, Sandoz, accidentally discovered that LSD—a chemical derivative of ergot, a fungus that grows on wheat—produced hallucinations resembling those experienced in schizophrenia. Ever since, entirely apart from the sociological implications of LSD, a growing corps of investigators has become increasingly sanguine about the biochemical hypothesis.

One startling fact about LSD was the tiny amount—less than one-70-millionth of a man's body weight—needed to distort ordinary perceptions. That made it seem not unreasonable to assume that naturally occurring materials, in extremely minute quantities, might also produce disturbances, and that chemical and other tests available in the past for detecting such materials had not been nearly fine enough.

LSD led Dr. D. W. Woolley of Rockefeller University to formulate what is known as the serotonin hypothesis. Serotonin is a chemical originally discovered in the lining of the intestine, and found to influence functioning of intestinal and other smooth muscle—the type not under voluntary control. Later, serotonin also was found in the nervous system and brain where, some investigators believe, it may act as an important hormone, or chemical messenger.

When, in a laboratory experiment, Dr. Woolley took a strip of smooth muscle and treated it with LSD, it went into contraction. But when serotonin had been applied to the muscle first, the muscle did not contract. Possibly then, LSD produced its bizarre behavioral effects because it antagonized or competed with serotonin in the nervous system. If this were so, schizophrenia might be caused by some disturbance in body chemistry which upset serotonin action.

Favoring the concept was research indicating that some tranquilizing agents and stimulating drugs, when they produced changes in behavior, also produced changes in the levels of serotonin. The serotonin hypothesis is being actively explored today.

Generally, in searching for biochemical clues, investigators have tried to find something unusual in the blood, urine or spinal fluid of schizophrenics—abnormal quantities of some natural substances, or something not present at all in normal people. They have tried to identify it, see if it causes temporary schizophrenic symptoms when given to normal volunteers, figure out why it is formed, where in the body chemical system something may have gone wrong, what might be done to correct the fault.

In the past 20 years, there have been many false leads. Often investigators at some one institution have turned up what seemed to be an abnormality in their patients but investigators at other institutions have not been able to find it in theirs. In some instances, abnormal urine or other findings have been traced to the poor diets of schizophrenics.

But out of such research have come a number of promising leads. About 10 years ago, Dr. Robert Heath and associates at Tulane University found evidence of a distinctive abnormality in one portion of schizophrenic blood. More than half of blood is plasma, a fluid that carries the red and white blood cells. Plasma also contains globulins, complex chemicals which serve such functions as controlling blood clotting and combating disease organisms. Something was wrong in one of the globulins in schizophrenics. When that globulin, taken from their blood, was injected into normal volunteers, it produced transient psychotic episodes. To the abnormal material in the globulin—still not clearly identified—the Tulane workers gave the name of taraxein.

The finding was greeted skeptically as one more false lead. When, at a national meeting of psychiatrists, Dr. Heath showed movies of the disorienting effects of taraxein on prisoner volunteers, one comment in the audience was: "The volunteers must have been crazy to begin with."

But by 1962, Drs. Jacques Gottlieb and Charles Frohman of the Lafayette Clinic in Detroit were reporting independent work with a factor in schizophrenic globulin, possibly the same factor as Heath's. The Detroit research indicated that the factor could modify the chemical reactions by which simple sugars are made to produce energy. If such a disturbance in energy production took place in the cells of the nervous system, message transmission might be altered. The altered transmission might account for the strange sights and sounds in schizophrenia. Conceivably, as a result of altered transmission, the message received in the brain of a catatonic might not be stimulating or seem important, leaving the victim stuporous, almost inanimate.

Meanwhile, Dr. Hudson Hoagland and associates at the Worcester Foundation for Experimental Biology also were studying a suspect globulin factor. They trained rats to climb a rope for a food reward. When they injected them with globulin samples from either hospitalized schizophrenic patients or nonpsychotic control donors, the rats became confused and took longer to climb the rope. But the injections from the schizophrenic patients produced twice the climbing time delay.

Through a series of complex tests, the Worcester workers were able to establish some evidence that the factor may be an amine—one of a group of highly potent body chemicals. Amines, which are known to occur in brain areas concerned with mood and emotion, include among their number the hormone adrenalin, which is involved in the body's response to stress.

Almost at the same time, researchers elsewhere turned up an abnormal amine substance in the urine of schizophrenic patients but not in that of normal persons, and found that it was derived from the same material used in forming adrenalin. Worcester workers have reported that preliminary tests in their laboratories showed that the abnormal amine disturbs trained rat performance in much the same way as the factor from the blood of schizophrenics, and investigations are continuing.

Meanwhile, since 1952, the possibility that an adrenalin disturbance might have something to do with causing schizophrenia has been under study in Saskatchewan, Canada, by Drs. Abram Hoffer and Humphrey Osmond.

It was the late Aldous Huxley who, after taking mescaline, a prime hallucinatory drug derived from a Mexican cactus plant, commented that the "schizophrenic is like a man permanently under the influence of mescaline."

Before going to Saskatchewan in 1951, Dr. Osmond had experimented in London with mescaline, which has a chemical structure similar to adrenalin's. One day, while Osmond was playing back a recording of effects produced by mescaline in a volunteer during an experiment, it was overheard by a colleague, a severe asthmatic, who remarked that sometimes when he took very large doses of adrenalin for his asthma he experienced similar effects—feelings of unreality and colored visions.

Osmond and Hoffer had picked up the clue—especially after learning from a Canadian physician that during the war, for lack of adequate supplies of normal adrenalin, a pinkish kind sometimes had to be used during anesthesia and then when patients recovered they had hallucinations and other disturbances.

Adrenochrome is a chemical derived from adrenalin. When adrenalin decomposes, it may form adrenochrome. Perhaps adrenochrome was the hallucinogen in pink adrenalin. If so, it might be that under normal circumstances in the body adrenalin decomposition goes through an adrenochrome stage of very brief duration, but that in schizophrenics the stage might be prolonged because of a metabolic defect. That is, the schizophrenic may not have the proper body chemicals to dispose of the poison rapidly enough to prevent intoxication and bizarre symptoms.

Osmond became a guinea pig. Ten minutes after taking an injection of adrenochrome, he noticed the ceiling in the laboratory changing color. Outside, he found the corridors "sinister and unfriendly," and was unable to relate distance and time. After a second injection, he reported: "I felt indifferent toward humans and had to curb myself from making unpleasant remarks." In subsequent experiments with volunteers, Hoffer and Osmond found several becoming temporarily psychotic after receiving adrenochrome.

Assuming that adrenochrome might be the culprit in schizophrenia, the two investigators began to look for some method of treatment. Reasoning that something capable of slowing down formation of adrenalin might help, they thought of nicotinic acid, also known as Vitamin B3, which in large amounts might latch onto some chemical constituents needed to build adrenalin.

Results have been gratifying, according to reports published by Dr. Hoffer, who is director of psychiatric research for the Saskatchewan Department of Public Health, and Dr. Osmond, now director of the Bureau of Research in Neurology and Psychiatry at the New Jersey Neuro-Psychiatric Institute in Princeton. In comparison studies covering hundreds of patients, 30 per cent of those who did not receive the vitamin eventually recovered; of those treated with nicotinic acid, 75 per cent recovered. When the vitamin was used within a year after the onset of schizophrenia, symptoms often disappeared after a few months of treatment. For long-term schizophrenia several years of treatment were needed.

Some researchers in the field believe that use of the vitamin is worth further investigation, but that the studies done so far cannot be considered conclusive. For example, some patients who benefited after the vitamin therapy had also received other treatment—such as electro-shock, sedation or psychotherapy. Skeptics see a need for studies in which the vitamin would be used in large groups as sole treatment, to establish its effect clearly.

While this debate has been building up, Dr. Hoffer, at that aforementioned symposium in New York, reported early results of another new treatment. Late in December, 1965, NAD, a compound related to nicotinic acid, had become available. When he tried it with 17 patients, it appeared to melt away the disease in 13.

One patient had been hospitalized for almost 30 years, and had shown only minor response to tranquilizer treatment. Eventually, the tranquilizer had to be discontinued because it had begun to produce ill effects. At that point, treatment with nicotinic acid was started. After a year, there had been some improvement. After two weeks of NAD, the patient could contact relatives and leave the hospital. Another patient had been hospitalized 8 years and had not responded to tranquilizers, shock treatment and psychotherapy. Three days after NAD treatment was begun, she had almost completely recovered.

He was, Dr. Hoffer emphasized, making only a very preliminary report about NAD. The number of patients treated was small, the time short, but the results seemed impressive enough for a report so other investigators could try the chemical and study its possibilities.

How might NAD work? "NAD is the active form of nicotinic acid," Dr. Hoffer explained to this writer. He had an idea that schizophrenia might result from a defect in production of NAD, which the body normally makes from nicotinic acid, the vitamin coming in from food. With NAD lacking, too much adrenalin might be changed to adrenochrome. "As a result, electric transmission across the synapses [the points of connection between cells in the nervous system] is partially blocked and parts of the brain thrown out of phase. Perception becomes distorted; the subject believes he still perceives normally and, responding normally to abnormal perception, is judged abnormal."

But almost immediately after Hoffer's report, a group of workers in the United States set out to try NAD and found themselves unable to duplicate his results. At Rockland State Hospital, Orangeburg, N.Y., Dr. Nathan S. Kline and a team of investigators divided 20 male chronic schizophrenics into 10 matched pairs. They gave one patient of each pair NAD; the other, sugar pills prepared to resemble the drug. All were carefully evaluated before—and again after 15 days of treatment—through interviews, sound films of their behavior and psychiatric rating scales. No significant difference could be found between those receiving NAD and those getting the sugar pills.

As yet, there is no clear explanation of the striking results in Canada and the failure in New York. Although NAD apparently was not responsible for the improvement in Dr. Hoffer's patients, Dr. Kline has suggested, something else the Canadian psychiatrist may have done in the course of treatment—without realizing its importance—could have helped.

Dr. Kline, president-elect of the American College of Neuropsychopharmacology, remains, he has said, "as convinced as ever that a metabolic disorder is involved" in schizophrenia, and that drug treatment "is a major part of the answer," even though NAD apparently is not the right drug.

Meanwhile, another avenue is being explored. It, too, relates to mescaline and adrenalin. Two years ago, Dr. Arnold Friedhoff of New York University discovered a chemical, DMPE, in the urine of 15 out of 19 schizophrenics but not in 14 other subjects. It shows up as a pink spot when urine is put through a special analytical test. Its chemical structure is similar to that of mescaline, which is also similar to that of adrenalin. In animals, DMPE proved to have potent mind-altering properties.

At first, there was some tendency to regard it as another possible red herring. But late in 1965, Dr. Cyril A. Clarke and associates at the University of Liverpool reported hunting for pink spots in the urine of more than 800 individuals—schizophrenic, otherwise mentally ill and normal. They found a "clear-cut association" of pink spots with schizophrenia.

This past spring, Dr. John R. Smythies of the Edinburgh University Department of Psychiatry made another report to the annual conference of the National Association for Mental Health in London. Not only are DMPE and mescaline much alike chemically and closely related to adrenalin; the difference between the first two and adrenalin lies largely in certain added-on groups of atoms—methyl groups. Adrenalin does not have them; the other two do. Thus, a single faulty step in body chemistry—in the handling of methyl groups—might be enough to turn adrenalin into an agent, such as DMPE, that might be responsible for schizophrenia. It was time, Smythies declared, to look for possible new therapeutic agents that could correct the methyl-handling error, and perhaps overcome schizophrenia.

If, as of now, the biochemistry of schizophrenia still seems murky, it is hardly surprising. In few areas of scientific investigation are there so many difficulties. Much of the research has had to be carried out with patients long institutionalized, often under conditions of overcrowding which may allow chronic infections, especially of the digestive tract, to produce or spread metabolic changes that could be mistakenly attributed to the mental disease.

Many schizophrenics, too, have been exposed to multitudinous drugs and other treatments which may produce metabolic changes that could be attributed to the disease. Also, disturbances in behavior and activity in schizophrenia could possibly cause deviations from normal in many biochemical and metabolic measures.

Far from being discouraged, investigators are optimistic. They note that it took 25 years from the suspicion that the key to diabetes might lie in the pancreas to actual isolation of the key—insulin.

They believe that many of the findings of recent years in schizophrenia research point in the right direction. They see some likelihood that, with further studies, many of the seemingly unconnected findings—taraxein, adrenochrome, DMPE and others —may yet be fitted together to form a comprehensible pattern. Conceivably, for example, taraxein could act to sensitize the nervous system to such substances as adrenochrome.

Some of the more sanguine believe that, with intensified research, a clear biochemical understanding of schizophrenia could emerge within a decade, and that with it could come the means for making the disease not only a quickly remediable but also, quite likely, a preventable one.

27 | MENTAL ILLNESS IS A MYTH

Thomas S. Szasz

On Feb. 28, 1966, the United States Court of Appeals for the Second Circuit handed down a decision which displaced the time-honored M'Naghten Rule as a test of criminal insanity, and substituted for it a new rule recommended by the American Law Institute.

The M'Naghten Rule dates from 1834, when one Daniel M'Naghten shot and killed a man named Drummond, the private secretary of Sir Robert Peel, whom M'Naghten had intended to kill. At M'Naghten's trial, evidence was introduced showing that he "was laboring under an insane delusion" of being hounded by enemies, among them Peel. The jury found him "not guilty, on the ground of insanity."

De jure, M'Naghten was acquitted; *de facto,* he was sentenced to life imprisonment in an insane asylum. He died in 1865, having been incarcerated for the last 22 years of his life.

The new ruling (binding on Federal courts in New York, Connecticut and Vermont) provides that: "A person is not responsible for criminal conduct if at the time of such conduct as a result of mental disease or defect he lacks substantial capacity either to appreciate the wrongfulness of his conduct or to conform his conduct to the requirements of law."

Both of these tests—and others, whatever their semantic differences—rest on the premise that the human mind may become "diseased," and that a person who has a "diseased mind" may, because of it, commit criminal acts unintentionally, not know the difference between right and wrong, or be unable to restrain himself from engaging in conduct prohibited by law. The value of all psychiatric tests of criminal responsibility thus hinges on the soundness of this underlying concept of "mental disease."

But what exactly is mental disease? If it is an illness, what kind is it? And if it is not an illness, why is it called an illness? Because of the frequency with which issues of mental health and illness arise not only in criminal cases but in matters of everyday life, it is important that we ask these questions and intelligently debate various possible answers to them.

I submit that mental illness is a myth. Bodies are physical objects; minds, whatever they may be, are not physical objects. Accordingly, mental diseases (such as depression or schizophrenia) cannot exist in the sense in which bodily diseases (such as broken bones or ulcerated skins) exist.

My disbelief in mental illness does not mean that I reject any facts of human behavior. "A myth," says the British philosopher Gilbert Ryle, "is not a fairy story.

It is the presentation of facts belonging in one category in the idiom belonging to another. To explode a myth is accordingly not to deny facts, but to reallocate them." To say that mental illness is a myth is therefore not to *deny* facts (such as sadness or fear) but to *reallocate* them (from the category of mental illness to the category of personal conduct). Insofar as men are human beings, not machines, they always have some choice in how they act—hence, they are always responsible for their conduct. There is method in madness, no less than in sanity.

As long ago as the early nineteen-twenties, George H. Mead formulated the thesis that social situations—and human behavior in them—are analogous to games which must be played by certain "rules." In life, the games are infinite. As social conditions undergo rapid change, old games are constantly scrapped and new ones started. But most people are totally unprepared to shift from one type of game playing to another. They have early in life learned one set of rules—or, at most, a few—and find themselves forced to play new games by the old rules. This fundamental conflict leads to various problems in living—some severe enough to be commonly diagnosed as "mental illness" or "disease." It is these problems in living that the psychiatrist is usually called on to treat.

"But surely," someone might say, "a dope fiend, a rapist, or a Lee Harvey Oswald is not a *normal* person. What difference does it make whether we call him sick or something else?"

It makes, of course, all the difference in the world, for what we call things, and especially people, will shape our attitudes and justify our actions toward them. For example, when socially threatening behavior is called "witchcraft," it is handled by means of theological sanctions; when it is called "crime," it is handled by means of judicial sanctions, and when it is called "mental illness," it is handled by means of psychiatric sanctions.

The practices of modern American psychiatrists originate from two principal sources: hospital psychiatry and psychoanalysis.

Institutions for the care of the insane have existed since antiquity. However, the systematic confinement of madmen in buildings labeled "hospitals" did not begin until the middle of the 17th century. For about 250 years, from 1650 to 1900, the psychiatrist worked almost exclusively in the mental hospital. The alienist, as he was then called, was employed by an institution—a private or, more often, a public insane asylum.

The historical model and social prototype of the modern mental hospital is the French Hôpital Général. According to the distingished medical historian George Rosen, the purposes of this institutional system were threefold: "In part they were economic: to increase [the] manufacture [of goods], provide productive work for the able-bodied, and to end unemployment; in part social: to punish willful idleness, restore public order, and rid Paris of beggars; and in part, religious and moral: to relieve the needy, the ill and suffering, to deal with immorality and antisocial behavior, and to provide Christian instruction."

A few years after its foundation, the Hôpital Général of Paris alone contained 6,000 persons, or about 1 per cent of the population. Who were these "mentally ill" people? According to regulations issued in 1680, "children of artisans and other poor inhabitants of Paris up to the age of 25 . . . girls who were debauched or in evident danger of being debauched . . . [and] wayward children . . ." were among those listed as proper subjects for confinement. In addition, old people, persons with venereal diseases, epileptics, vagrants, prostitutes—in brief, all of society's *"misérables"*—were incarcerated in the Hôpital Général. Michel Foucault, a French student of psychiatric history, thus concludes: "The Hôpital Général is not a medical establishment. It is rather a sort of semijudicial structure, an administrative entity which, along with already constituted powers, and outside the courts, decides, judges and executes."

The facts I have cited are important in showing us one of the roles of the psychiatrist—indeed, his traditional role: He is a physician working in a mental hospital, employed, as a rule, by the state, and charged with the task of confining and "treating" people who are considered "insane." Although some of his methods have changed, the social role of the institutional psychiatrist has remained what it has always been.

Nor is its importance diminished. At the present time in the United States, approximately 750,000 persons are incarcerated in mental hospitals—90 per cent of them against their will. This is about three times the number of persons imprisoned in jails.

The mental hospital is also important for the psychiatrist: Of 15,200 practicing psychiatrists in the United States, approximately 50 per cent are in institutional practice, most of them in mental hospitals, or in related administrative positions.

I do not imply that the hospital psychiatrist does not try to help his patient, but rather that his interpretation of "helping" is different from the patient's. If one person has the power to confine another, and uses it, it seems inevitable that the confined person will consider the other his jailer. This point of view, often held by mental patients, was expressed by Valentine Alamazov, the protagonist of Valeriy Tarsis's autobiographical novel, "Ward 7." Finding himself incarcerated in a mental hospital, Alamazov had this to say to his psychiatrist:

"I don't regard you as a doctor. You call this a hospital, I call it a prison. . . . So, now, let's get everything straight. I am your prisoner, you are my jailer, and there isn't going to be any nonsense about my health . . . or about examination and treatment."

It was Sigmund Freud who created the second major form of contemporary American psychiatric practice—psychoanalysis.

In the eighteen-eighties, when Freud was a young physician, to be a psychiatrist was to be an alienist or hospital psychiatrist. Traditionally, the psychiatrist was called in by a "mentally healthy" member of the family to treat one of its "mentally sick" members; often this meant removing the sick member from the family and putting him in a mental hospital as a "patient."

Freud departed from this traditional approach. Instead of acting as the agent of the family—ostensibly caring for the patient, but actually protecting the family from him—Freud created a new professional role—the agent of the patient.

He did not accept the situation as it was presented to him, usually by the patient's family. Instead, he listened at length to the patient to ascertain how he perceived his problem; and he tried to help him realize his own aspirations and goals, even if these brought the patient, or Freud himself, into even greater conflict with the family or with society.

Thus, ethically, Freud acted like other physicians, but unlike other psychiatrists: He tried to help his patient, not someone else. By systematically refusing to "treat" patients who did not want to be treated by him, Freud departed from the accepted psychiatric methods of his day. Many psychoanalysts still adhere to this principle in treating patients. Most hospital psychiatrists do not.

It is important to note also that Freud characterized psychoanalytic treatment in humanistic and pedagogic terms and did not regard his work as medical. Psychoanalysis was never intended to make "sick" people "well" again. The analyst's task, in Freud's words, was "to serve the patient . . . as a teacher and educator."

Freud was emphatic that the analyst—and hence also the psychotherapist who only listens and talks and uses no "medical" methods—does not cure disease. Indeed, although the three great pioneers of psychoanalysis—Freud, Adler and Jung—had little good to say about one another's doctrines and methods in later years, they all agreed on one thing: that psychological methods of therapy are *not* medical procedures.

We are now ready to reconsider the question: What is mental illness? In order to do this, it is necessary to understand the principal uses of the concept of mental illnesses and their social consequences.

First, the term "mental illness" is used to refer to certain types of bodily diseases —that is, to diseases of the brain whose predominant symptoms are abnormalities of behavior (for example, neurosyphilis). According to one school of psychiatric thought, all mental diseases are of this type. Those who hold this view assume that some metabolic, genetic or neurological defect—perhaps a very subtle one—will ultimately be found to explain all disorders of thinking and behavior now called "mental illness."

No one would deny that, like any other part of the body, the brain may be injured or become diseased. Nor are there, to my knowledge, any psychiatrists who would deny that some of the people nowadays diagnosed as mentally ill (and free of demonstrable organic disease) might actually be suffering from the effects of as yet undiscovered neurologic or metabolic disease processes. But for those who regard mental illness as a type of brain disease, the concept of mental illness is unnecessary and misleading. If they mean that people labeled mentally ill suffer from diseases of the brain, it would seem better for the sake of clarity to say that and not something else.

The second major use of the term "mental illness" is to denote a "functional" or "psychological" disorder. Proponents of this view admit that patients called "mentally ill" do not suffer from bodily diseases, but they maintain that such individuals exhibit defects or deformations of their personalities so severe as to justify calling them "ill."

When physicians (or others) label people as "sick" merely because their actions differ from those of their fellows, they speak metaphorically—as poets, not scientists. To be sure, this kind of metaphoric use of the term "sick" is not limited to psychiatry: People also say that our economy is "sick," that a joke is "sick" or that someone they dislike makes them "sick." Yet only in connection with mental illness do we systematically act as if figure of speech were fact. No one believes that "sick economies" require medical help, but nearly everyone believes that "sick minds" do.

The power to name, or to classify, is the basis for the third use of the term "mental illness"—that is, to denote a deviant social role. For our purposes it is necessary only to distinguish between two types of social roles: those that are assumed voluntarily, such as husband or graduate student, and those that are ascribed to a person against his will, such as draftee or convicted criminal.

Roles are social artifacts. Role deviance, therefore, has meaning only in the context of specific social customs and laws. The criminal is deviant because he breaks the law; the homosexual because most people are heterosexuals; the atheist because most people believe—or say they believe—in God. In the same way, the so-called "potential killer" (who, however, has not yet killed anyone) is considered deviant because he appears to be more dangerous than most people; and so is the chronically withdrawn mental-hospital patient, because most people are—and are expected to be—socially more responsive. (I shall say more about the problems that such persons pose for those about them, and for society in general, later on.)

But which kinds of social deviance constitute "mental illness"? The answer is: that conduct which deviates from psychiatrically defined rules of mental health.

However obvious this may be, its implications for our understanding of mental illness seem to be vastly unappreciated. The fact is that every time psychiatrists formulate a new rule of mental health they create a new class of mentally sick individuals. For example, the proposition that prejudice against Jews or Negroes is a manifestation of psycho-pathology—one of many instances in the contemporary inflation of the concept of mental illness—is nothing but an attempt to expand the category of people who can be legitimately classified as psychologically sick.

Since the consequences of being labeled mentally ill include such penalties as personal degradation, loss of employment, loss of the right to drive a car, to vote, to make valid contracts or to stand trial—and, last but not least, incarceration in a mental hospital, possibly for life—the expansion of the category of people who can be so designated is useful for the increased employment of psychiatric methods of social control.

Labeling someone mentally ill is a special kind of name-calling. In other fields name-calling may constitute libel, but calling someone "mentally sick" does not. The main reason for this is that the psychiatrist who makes a diagnosis of mental illness (especially on an involuntary patient) has more social power than the person he diagnoses.

The role of power in the psychiatric diagnostic process becomes obvious only when the potential patient is a Very Important Person. When someone like Secretary of Defense Forrestal disturbs people by his ideas and actions, it is difficult to get a psychiatrist to label him mentally ill. The reason for this is that by casting the individual in a socially deviant role the psychiatric diagnostician imparts a negative, debased identity to that person. This he cannot do if his intended "patient" is socially more powerful than he is. When a mental-hospital superintendent in Louisiana tried to incarcerate and "treat" Gov. Earl Long, the Governor fired the doctor—and walked out of the hospital.

One of the traditional problems of legal psychiatry, as we saw at the outset, is the determination of criminal insanity. Lawyers and psychiatrists persist in trying to distinguish between "sane" and "insane" criminals, and in finding a "scientific" basis for determining which offenders ought to be "punished" with imprisonment and which "treated" with involuntary mental hospitalization.

I submit that criminal insanity is a metaphorical and strategic concept just as civil insanity is. The effort to distinguish, by psychiatric methods, among different classes of criminals is really an exercise in second-order classification: Having labeled some persons as "criminals," we have the option of labeling them also as "mentally healthy," and dealing with them by means of penal sanctions, or as "mentally ill" (that is, as "criminally insane"), and dealing with them by means of psychiatric sanctions.

I do not believe that insanity should be an "excusing condition" for crime. Law-breakers, irrespective of their "mental health," ought to be treated as offenders.

Another classic dilemma of psychiatry is the problem of what society should do with its "insane" citizens who, while having committed no crime, lack "insight" into their "illness" and hence do not seek "treatment." Here we should distinguish between two fundamentally different types of psychiatric practice. The person who decides to consult a psychiatrist and pays him for his services is like a graduate student pursuing a course of study: he assumes the role of mental patient (if we wish so to label his role) *voluntarily* and is free to cast it off. By contrast, the person who is coerced into psychiatric treatment by his relatives or by the law, and who does not pay the psychiatrist for his services, is like a prisoner sentenced to a term of servitude; he is placed in the role of mental patient *against his will* and is not free to cast it off.

The psychiatrist thus has a choice between doing something *to* his patient and doing something *for* him. One of the things the psychiatrist can do to his patient is to prescribe certain life games, with the expectation that these will pacify the patient's family and social environment—and perhaps also "help" the patient. Since this kind of treatment is carried out against the wishes of the patient, it requires coercion.

One of the things the psychiatrist can do for his patient is to analyze his life games, with the expectation that this understanding will help the client to lead a life more free and responsible. To do this, however, requires a voluntary, cooperating client. Coercion has no place whatever in this type of psychiatric work. Such a psychiatrist aspires to be on tap, not on top.

The reader who finds this thesis persuasive might wonder about its practical application. If we look upon mental illness as a metaphor and a social role, rather than as a disease, how will this affect what we *do?*

For work with voluntary clients the consequences would be mainly professional and economic: The humanistic view of mental illness would open opportunities for training nonmedical persons (psychologists, social workers and others) in psychotherapy and psychoanalysis, and would eliminate the rationale for preventing such persons from engaging in the independent practice of these skills.

For work with involuntary clients the consequences would be mainly legal and social: The humanistic view of mental illness would remove the justification for involuntary mental hospitalization and treatment; accordingly, it would require the mobilization of fresh personal efforts and social resources to cope with problems now dealt with by means of traditional psychiatric methods.

It would be impossible suddenly to empty out our mental hospitals and to stop all commitments—though, to be sure, I consider these desirable goals. To attain them, however, we must provide suitable alternatives to the present social functions of involuntary mental hospitalization. I must limit myself here to mentioning only a few such alternatives, each directed toward ameliorating a specific type of human problem.

The usual justification for commitment is that the person whose confinement is sought is "dangerous to himself or others." My position is based on a principle enunciated more than 100 years ago by John Stuart Mill: "The only purpose for which power can be rightfully exercised over any member of a civilized community, against his will, is to prevent harm to others. His own good, either physical or moral, is no sufficient warranty."

Suicide, for example, should be recognized as a basic human right. The threat of suicide, or an attempt at suicide, should not be ground for involuntary mental hospitalization. (This does not mean that a physician should not treat a person who, say, is unconscious as a result of an overdose of barbiturates. It does mean that, after the patient has regained consciousness, he should not be confined in a hospital against his will.)

While being "dangerous to oneself" should never be considered a legitimate reason for depriving a person of his liberty, being "dangerous to others"—if it involves breaking the law—is the best reason for doing so. One of the main functions of society is to prevent violence among its members. Thus, if individuals commit violence, or threaten to do so, they should be treated for what they are—law-breakers.

Judicial sentencing of lawbreakers does not deprive us of the opportunity of also trying to help them. If we truly believe that some lawbreakers are "mentally ill," we could offer them psychiatric help in prison. As always, the clients ought to be free to accept or reject such help.

The social control, by means of psychiatric sanctions, of dangerous behavior is complicated by the fact that people often disagree on what constitutes "dangerousness," and, even if they agree on it, on how such "dangerousness" is to be established. Thus, one group of persons now often committed is composed of individuals who manage their lives more or less adequately, but who break certain laws or social customs, and are therefore considered "dangerous" and treated as involuntary patients.

If we wish to avoid using coercive psychiatric measures against persons of this type, we have two basic options. Instead of constantly proliferating legislation prohibiting various kinds of personal conduct not directly injurious to others (as we now do), we might consider repealing and eschewing such legislation. We would thereby eliminate many types of "crime," and hence the need to define such criminals (as "dope addicts," "homosexuals" and so forth) as mentally sick. Or, if we wish to persist in our efforts to control private behavior by means of criminal sanctions, we might decide that it is more humane to punish persons who transgress these prohibitions by means of penal rather than psychiatric sanctions; the result would be the jailing of many individuals now committed to mental hospitals. (The desirability of confining lawbreakers in mental hospitals rather than in prisons is sometimes advocated on the allegedly humanitarian ground that conditions in mental hospitals are better than in jails. Even if this were true—and as a rule it is not—it would not justify redefining lawbreakers as patients. The proper remedy for inadequate prisons is prison reform.)

In addition to persons whose dangerousness is actual, established by what they have done, there are those whose dangerousness is potential, who are feared for what they might do. We often hear of "potential trouble-makers" who, however, have broken no laws, and hence could not be convicted of crime, but whom many would like to "diagnose" as "deranged" and restrain in mental hospitals.

We cannot eat our cake and have it, too: we cannot have a free society and imprison—in jails or mental hospitals—people who have broken no law. This does not mean that some people might not be "potentially" dangerous to others (indeed, many, like drunken drivers, are very dangerous); it means only that we cannot restrain such people through our mental-hygiene laws without gravely injuring the entire fabric of our society.

Another large group of persons confined involuntarily in mental hospitals is the aged; in some public mental hospitals as many as one-third of the inmates fall into this group. Yet, even hospital psychiatrists admit that many of these patients do not need mental-hospital care. "Only 50 per cent of the [elderly] patients . . . hospitalized required hospitalization in a mental institution," testified Dr. Dale C. Cameron, superintendent of St. Elizabeth's Hospital in Washington, before a House committee. "For many older patients," he added, "the primary need was found to be for physical rather than psychiatric care."

The fact that public mental hospitals accept geriatric patients—whose "mental illness" is so clearly a strategic concept designed to justify their forcible removal to places of custody—diminishes the pressure on society to provide suitable accommodations for them.

Still another group of involuntarily hospitalized patients is composed of individuals who present so-called psychiatric emergencies. Examples are the young man who becomes uncommunicative, does not leave his room, refuses to eat, perhaps even soils himself; or the young woman who faints and thereafter remains unresponsive and acts as if she were unconscious.

Patients of this type do not object to being hospitalized or to receiving medical care. Moreover, some of them suffer from bodily illness—brain tumor, head injury, uncontrolled diabetes. Others develop medical problems as a result of their behavior —severe dehydration because of failure to eat and drink, for example. Such patients should therefore be hospitalized in medical, not mental, hospitals, and should be treated as medical emergencies. Consent for hospitalization and treatment should be given by relatives, and confinement should last only until the patient has regained his powers.

The application of these principles to the care of chronic mental patients would help us to avoid coercion in their care as well. Regardless of the cause—subtle malfunctions of the brain, the effect of prolonged institutionalization or flight from communal existence into a world of private dreams—people who are almost completely unable to cope with their problems of living will no doubt always be with us. Such "nondangerous" but gravely disabled individuals could be dealt with by offering them care—good and attractive enough so that they would willingly accept it—while leaving them free to make other choices.

In short, the abolition of involuntary mental hospitalization and treatment would mean that psychiatric help, like medical, would (on the whole) have to be restricted to voluntary clients. Furthermore, some persons who are now cast in the role of involuntary mental patients would, if they broke laws, have to be dealt with as offenders, not as patients.

The nominal aim of psychiatry is the study and treatment of mental disorders. The consequences of subscribing to this apparently harmless, conventional definition of "mental health" work are, in our present age, momentous. Accepting the existence of a class of phenomena called "mental diseases," rather than inquiring into the conditions under which some persons may designate others as "mentally ill," has been the decisive step in embracing what I call the mental-health ethic. In so doing, the study of a large part of human behavior is subtly transferred from ethics to psychiatry, from the free marketplace of ideas to the closed wards of the mental hospital.

The psychiatrist deals with moral and social problems, not with medical diseases. Hence he cannot help being embroiled in the moral conflicts of his patient and of his society. The psychiatrist's role as moral legislator and social engineer is obscured, however, by the rhetoric of mental health and illness which makes his work appear as a species of medical therapy. This evasion of ethical judgments and choices may be reassuring to the laity and comforting to the profession. But can we, as individuals, afford it?

The individual can never escape the moral burden of his existence. He must choose between obedience to authority and responsibility to himself. Moral decisions are often hard and painful to make. The temptation to delegate this burden to others is therefore ever-present. Yet, as all history teaches us, those who would take from man his moral burdens—be they priests or warlords, politicians or psychiatrists —must also take from him his liberty and hence his very humanity.

A humanistic psychiatry must, therefore, repudiate its seemingly therapeutic mandate, the pursuit of which often results, intentionally or unwittingly, in moral tranquility gained at the expense of freedom and responsibility. Instead of trying to diminish man's moral burdens, such a psychiatry must aim at increasing his powers and so making him equal to his task.

And what is this task? No one has stated it better than Albert Camus when he wrote: "The aim of life can only be to increase the sum of freedom and responsibility to be found in every man and in the world. It cannot, under any circumstances, be to reduce or suppress that freedom, even temporarily."

---

28 | PSYCHIATRISTS USE DANGEROUS WORDS

Karl Menninger, M.D.

Every profession has its own jargon, and we psychiatrists have ours. But while the strange terms a lawyer or an archaeologist uses are harmless enough—the worst they do is mystify outsiders—the terms psychiatrists use can hurt people and sometimes do. Instead of helping to comfort and counsel and heal people—which is the goal of psychiatry—the terms often cause despair.

From *Saturday Evening Post,* April 25, 1964. Reprinted by permission of The Curtis Publishing Company and the author.

Words like "schizophrenia" and "manic-depressive" and "psychotic," for example, frighten patients and worry their anxious relatives and friends. The use of these alarming terms also affects us psychiatrists. They lead us back into the pessimism and helplessness of the days when mental illness was thought to be made up of many specific "diseases," and when each "disease" bore a formidable label and a gloomy prognosis.

Mental illness is not simple, but neither is it esoteric, weird and unhuman. We all know what it is from our own experience. We've all "had it"; we've all suffered from spells of mental illness of varying intensity and duration.

Occasionally they strike hard or last long. They may impel us to make serious mistakes and even do dreadful things. More often they only confuse or paralyze or frighten us; we become a bit demoralized. We fight against it and do the best we can. What we need from the outside world during our struggle is help. Not a "label" but *help*.

Psychiatrists are sometimes called "talking doctors," as opposed to "pill-prescribing doctors" and "baby-delivering doctors." In treating a patient we rely heavily upon his reactions to what we *say* to him. There is more to psychiatric treatment than talking, of course, but talking is a considerable part of it, and the psychiatrist's language must be carefully chosen. Nuances and implications that would be of no consequence in a discussion of surgical procedures may be of critical importance in dealing with a case of mental illness. A single wrong word might ruin a recovery.

Every psychiatrist has had patients come to him with stories something like this: "I got upset and went to see a psychiatrist. He talked with me a couple of times and I felt better. But he told my parents that I had schizophrenia. And after that they seemed to think there was no use trying. I was in the hospital for a while, and now again I'm worried and depressed. Is this what you call 'schizophrenia'? Do I have it? Am I hopeless? Isn't suicide my only way out?"

In such a case—and there are many of them—the label applied to the illness becomes almost as damaging as the illness itself. The patient learns that he has "schizophrenic tendencies" (or "incipient schizophrenia," or some such malady) and assumes, with everyone else, that he has an incurable mental disease, one that will probably grow continually worse.

A label can blight the life of a person even after his recovery from mental illness. A young doctor I knew suffered for a time from some anxiety and indecision. He consulted a psychiatrist and soon recovered. Unfortunately, a "tentative" diagnosis of schizophrenia got abroad—I don't know how—and the young doctor's professional career was seriously impaired. He was injured, not by mental illness but by a word.

Certainly there are behavior patterns which can be described as schizophrenic, provided one defines the adjective. But schizophrenia is no more a clear-cut disease than "the falling sickness" or "biliousness" or "chronic endogenous indurative myelomalacia." I don't know what these names mean, but I don't know what schizophrenia really means either, because it means widely different things to different people and in different countries. The same can be said of terms like "neurotic," "extroversion," "catalepsy," "psychopathic" and many others.

Science in general and psychiatry in particular have come a long way since these words were coined. They no longer mean what they once did. "Dementia" and "demented," for example, used to mean literally the loss of one's mind, and "dementia praecox" was a supposed disease in which this "loss of mind" occurred precociously

—that is, in young people, as compared with "dementia senilis," which occurred in old people. But gradually we came to realize that people didn't "lose" their minds, and that this was a misleading figure of speech. So another figure of speech was coined: splitting of the mind. And dementia praecox began to be called schizophrenia. It developed the same bad reputation, however, and the barest hint that someone was afflicted with this dreadful condition was enough to throw his loved ones into frantic despair, even though, as we now know, the collective symptoms called schizophrenia usually disappear.

I avoid using words like schizophrenia just as I avoid using words like "wop" and "nigger." I know what people mean by these names, but I dispute their specificity; they chiefly denote an attitude of the speaker toward skin color or foreign birth, and their use can do great harm.

I must frankly admit that many of my colleagues disagree with me. The American Psychiatric Association, in its official classification, lists only "schizophrenic reaction," but while some of us understand this to refer to one familiar pattern of behavior shown by an individual over a period of time, many others consider this a specific, well-defined *disease*, not a reaction or a pattern.

Those of us who use the outmoded terminology do so partly out of habit; it's easy to lapse into the established jargon. But it really comes down to one's attitude, or rather his conception of the nature of mental illness. I do not agree with certain writers that there is no mental illness. I would say rather that there is a great deal of mental illness. I agree with the American Medical Association and with the Joint Commission on Mental Illness and Health that mental illness is our No. 1 health problem. I do not think we help that problem by calling it a myth. But neither do I think we help it by persisting in obsolete terminology. Not only do these terms panic the patient but they discourage the doctor and permit him to justify a program of indifference and neglect.

In *The Vital Balance,* a book I wrote in collaboration with Drs. Martin Mayman and Paul Pruyser, we suggest that mental illness is not a "thing"—like a specimen in a museum—for which a label must be found. It is rather a state of functioning, a way of behaving. An individual having unusual difficulties in coping with his environment struggles and kicks up the dust, as it were. I once used the figure of a fish caught on a hook; his gyrations must look peculiar to other fishes that don't understand the circumstances. His splashings are not a *disease;* they are not the affliction. They are his efforts to get rid of the affliction. And as every fisherman knows, these efforts may succeed. To concentrate on patterns of splashing is an old-fashioned emphasis in psychiatry that is rapidly passing, although some still hold to it.

"What would you substitute?" I am sometimes asked. "What do you want to call these people—or these conditions?" Such questioners obviously have not caught my point. I wouldn't call them anything. I want us to emerge from the name-calling stage. Psychiatry should repudiate it. Some angry people don't call their opponents liars or skunks any more; they call them psychiatric names like "psychotics" or "psychopaths." Why? Because these technical words have become pejorative. They no longer mean merely psychiatric illness; they mean something despised.

These damning words were a great handicap to my brother William in World War II when, as assistant to the surgeon-general of the Army, he undertook to reduce the enormous manpower losses from mental illness. He found that many good soldiers were discharged after being labeled with old-fashioned designations implying incurable mental illness and personality disorder. With the aid of many colleagues over the country, Doctor Will radically revised and improved the Army classification of mental illness. (His revision was later adopted, in essence, by the U.S. Navy, the Veterans Administration and the American Psychiatric Association.)

"But," my questioner may continue, "if you are not going to call these conditions anything, how are you going to refer to them?" I think the answer is quite simple: How does the patient himself refer to his problem? "Oh, he says he is upset, he says he is nervous, and feels as if he were going to pieces. But these are lay terms; they are not scientific."

True, these are subjective expressions. They seem to be figures of speech. However, many psychiatric terms are figures of speech. Can a mind be split like a log of wood as the term schizophrenia implies? Actually the expressions coming from everyday life are often more accurate than the technical words and don't have the same dreadful or false implications. Some of them, like "going to pieces," imply those essential qualities of integration and steadiness which are the basis of our concept of the "vital balance." Things may happen today that so increase my tension that I feel as though I might explode. This tension is released in various ways—a game of cards, a concert or just a good night's rest. If these outlets don't restore the vital balance—if I can't listen to music, if I can't sleep—the threat of disintegration may increase, and I will feel worse and try harder to recover my equilibrium. I may even ask for help.

Any particular instance of such imminent "going to pieces" can be described scientifically—quantitatively and then qualitatively. We can say that a certain patient who has asked to be examined is indeed partially disorganized. This disorganization can be identified by anyone who has had experience in such things as being of severe degree, or moderately severe, or only slight.

But the most important thing the psychiatrist will try to do is to identify the factors in the environment and in the patient which combine to produce this picture of disturbance and distress. Where is the fishhook? Where does the shoe pinch? Where are the weak spots? And what are the forces bearing so heavily upon this individual as to get him out of line? This is psychiatric diagnosis in a new key—it includes prescriptions for treatment and it expects recovery. It may sound deceptively simple, but I prefer it to labels and concepts which sound deceptively complex.

To illustrate, let me cite the case of Helen D., the daughter of superior and ambitious parents. Even after careful study I do not know of anything they "did wrong." They were, like most parents, merely earnest, often puzzled, not perfect but trying hard. And Helen did well during her growing years. She was pretty and popular, studious and athletic. All was very promising, with a few minor, very human exceptions, until her senior year at college. Her letters home began to be irregular and infrequent. On the telephone she sounded preoccupied. She wrote her older brother that neither he nor their parents were aware of "the danger we are all in." She asked him why he did not love his country enough to join the John Birch Society or the Peace Corps. She missed classes; her grades declined. Her counselor referred her to the college psychiatrist who . . .

I stop in the middle of a sentence purposely. What do you want to read? What do you hope he did? Of course he recognized that she was confused and frightened and depressed and "morbidly preoccupied." Of course he prescribed temporary interruption of her schooling and intensive treatment.

But what did he tell her parents was "the matter" with her? Did he say she was afflicted with a "psychosis"? Did he call her affliction malignant and probably progressive? Did he diagnose it "manic-depressive" or "borderline"? Or did he describe it as a moderately severe personality disorganization related to certain excessive stresses, with such-and-such features amenable to treatment?

Fortunately he did the latter. Treatment was promptly instituted and she re-entered college the following fall to graduate with honors a year later.

BRANDED AS INSANE

But suppose she had been officially labeled. Would her treatment have been so vigorously and expectantly pushed? More likely the parents and the college authorities would have reconciled themselves to the probability that this girl would never return to college. And even if she had been able to return, the college would probably have been reluctant to readmit her. And if she had been readmitted, it would have taken extraordinary courage for her to face her comrades as a "schizophrenic."

Contrast this with those who were not labeled and who this very minute can bravely say to their friends, "I had a severe spell of illness; I was quite depressed, but I got it straightened out. I'm fine now, and I think I learned a great deal from the whole experience."

To sum up, I think many words psychiatrists use are dangerous. They misrepresent mental illness and permit the public and even psychiatrists to entertain a pessimistic view of mental illness.

The widespread pessimism about mental illness may explain why so little is done about it. How shocking it is that for all the emphasis given the subject—by the late President Kennedy, for example, and by the A.M.A.—only about one fifth of the state hospitals for the mentally ill give patients any treatment.

In the past 10 years my brother, Doctor Will, has spoken earnestly to the legislatures of many states. What has he told them? Simply that mental illness is our No. 1 health problem; that the mentally ill can be helped and most of them cured; that it is more humane and less expensive to treat them scientifically than to confine them despairingly.

Why is this so hard for the public to believe? Why is the public so willing to retain its pessimism and cling to the ancient superstition that mental illness is incurable? For the mentally ill *can* be saved, most of them. They can be cured, but they need help. Their symptoms are a cry for help. We cannot plead ignorance to excuse our neglect, for we know what to do. It is not our helplessness that has deterred us so long but our hopelessness—and perhaps, in part, our dreadful vocabulary.

29 | THE PSYCHOLOGIST
AS AN EXPERT WITNESS
ON THE ISSUE OF INSANITY

Ray Jeffery

Recent discussions of psychology and law have been concerned with certification, privileged communication, and the like, but there are little data on the subject of the psychologist as an expert on criminal cases involving the issue on insanity.

The Code of Ethics urges psychologists to behave in a responsible manner with regard to interpretation of test data. The author is aware of the fact that the interpretation of many psychological tests and reports is open to differences of opinion, that they are by no means settled issues, and that considerable research is currently going on in the area.

Nevertheless, some psychologists have behaved in the courtroom as though the issues were settled. They have made assertions that do not have the blessings of the entire professional psychological community, and these assertions have brought court opprobrium to them, and perhaps to the psychologist in general. On one occasion, following such testimony, the presiding judge literally threw a deck of projective cards onto the floor. The defense attorney then requested that the court record show that the judge had expressed his feelings toward the testimony of this expert witness, to which the judge replied that the record would also show that he (the judge) was going even further in that he was throwing out all of the testimony of this psychologist. Quite obviously, testimony which can arouse such a reaction in a reputable court of law is, or should be, of concern to psychologists interested in the contribution they can make to society, and in the role of their professional image in the acceptance or rejection of such contributions. The data to be presented were gathered in the District Court of the District of Columbia, and the impression created in the court was that the psychologists were not poor representatives of their profession, since in the words of the Government attorney, they were men "with more degrees than a thermometer."

The testimony may also serve the function of providing psychologists who rely on projective tests with information on how such evaluations may be treated by an opposing and often hostile attorney, or how they may be interpreted in a court of law which permits cross-examination of witnesses, including expert witnesses.

The writer is a sociologist who recently was a coinvestigator on a National Institute of Mental Health project concerning the operation of the insanity defense in the

Ray Jeffery, "The Psychologist as an Expert Witness on the Issue of Insanity," *American Psychologist*, **19**, 1964, pp. 838–843. Copyright © 1964 by the American Psychological Association, and reproduced by permission.

District of Columbia. He had occasion to observe psychologists in the courtroom, and to examine in detail court transcripts of over 25 cases in which insanity was an issue. Testimony by psychologists was given in 2 of the cases, relevant excerpts from which are presented below. The other trials involved psychiatric testimony exclusively.

The writer is not an expert on personality assessment and diagnosis, and he will leave it to the psychological community to evaluate the testimony herein presented. It should be noted that the transcripts become public records open for public inspection. As will be evident from these transcripts, attorneys have available such public records as research reports on psychological tests—and may read them, even if psychologists do not. This is in contrast to hospital hearings, where the records are private and confidential.

UNITED STATES V. KENT[*]

PSYCHOLOGIST A: DEFENSE

Psychologist A testified that she had administered the following tests to Kent: the Wechsler Memory Scale, the Bender-Gestalt, the Rorschach, the Thematic Apperception Test, the House-Tree-Person Test, and the Szondi Test. From this evidence she diagnosed the defendant as schizophrenic, chronic undifferentiated type, characterized by abnormal thoughts, difficulty with emotional control, deficient in common-sense judgment, and lacking in close relationships with other people. She considered these as indicative of psychosis, and that the crimes of housebreaking, robbery, and rape, of which the defendant was accused, were products of the mental disease.

CROSS-EXAMINATION BY GOVERNMENT

Q[uestion]. What did the House-Tree-Person Test reveal?
A[nswer]. The major finding was a feeling of withdrawal, running away from reality, feelings of rejection by women.
Q. And the results of the Szondi?
A. This showed a passive, depressed person who withdrew from the world of reality, with an inability to relate to others.
Q. Wasn't the Szondi Test made up around 1900, or the early 1900 period? And wasn't it made up of a number of pictures of Europeans who were acutely psychotic?
A. Yes, that is true.
Q. And this tells you something about his personality?
A. Yes, you can tell something about the person from his responses to the photos.
Q. And the House-Tree-Person Test—you handed the defendant Kent a pencil and a blank piece of paper, is that right, Doctor?
A. That is correct.
Q. And you asked him to draw a house?
A. Yes.

---

[*]   Criminal No. 798–61, District Court for the District of Columbia.

Q. And what did this tell you about Kent?

A. The absence of a door, and the bars on the windows, indicated he saw the house as a jail, not a home. Also, you will notice it is a side view of the house: he was making it inaccessible.

Q. Isn't it normal to draw a side view of a house? You didn't ask him to draw a front view, did you?

A. No.

Q. And those bars on the window—could they have been Venetian blinds and not bars? Who called them bars, you or Kent?

A. I did.

Q. Did you ask him what they were?

A. No.

Q. What else did the drawing reveal about Kent?

A. The line in front of the house runs from left to right. This indicates a need for security.

Q. This line indicates insecurity! Could it also indicate the contour of the landscape, like a lawn or something?

A. This is not the interpretation I gave it.

Q. And the chimney—what does it indicate?

A. You will notice the chimney is dark. This indicates disturbed sexual feelings. The smoke indicates inner daydreaming.

Q. Did I understand you correctly? Did you say dark chimneys indicate disturbed sex feelings?

A. Yes.

Q. You then asked Kent to draw a tree. Why?

A. We have discovered that a person often expresses feelings about himself that are on a subconscious level when he draws a tree.

Q. And what does this drawing indicate about Kent's personality?

A. The defendant said it was a sequoia, 1500 years old, and that it was diseased. This indicates a feeling of self-depreciation. Also, the tree has no leaves and it leans to the left. This indicates a lack of contact with the outside world—the absence of leaves.

Q. Don't trees lose their leaves in winter, Doctor? If you look out the window now, in Washington, do you see leaves on the trees? Perhaps the defendant was drawing a picture of a tree without leaves, as they appear in the winter.

A. The important thing is, however, why did the defendant select this particular tree. He was stripped of leaves, of emotions.

Q. You then asked him to draw a person?

A. Yes.

Q. And he drew this picture of a male?

A. Yes.

Q. And what does this drawing indicate about Kent?

A. The man appears to be running. This indicates anxiety, agitation. He is running, you will notice, to the left. This indicates running away from the environment. If he had been running to the right this would indicate entering the environment.

Q. How about the hands?

A. The sharp fingers may indicate hostility.

Q. Anything else?

A. The head and the body appear to be separated by a dark collar, and the neck is long. This indicates a split between intellect and emotion. The dark hair, dark tie, dark shoes, and dark buckle indicate anxiety about sexual problems.

Q. You then asked Kent to draw a person of the opposite sex. What did this picture indicate?

A. The dark piercing eyes indicated a feeling of rejection by women, hostility toward women.

Q. Are you familiar with the occasion upon which a Veterans Administration psychologist gave this House-Tree-Person Test to 50 psychotics, and then gave 50 normal subjects the same test, and then had a group of psychologists rate them?

A. No, I am not familiar with that research.

PSYCHOLOGIST B: DEFENSE

Psychologist B testified that he administered the Wechsler-Bellevue, the Graham Kendall, the Rorschach, and the Symonds Picture Story Tests. He also testified that he had diagnosed the defendant as schizophrenic, undifferentiated type, and that mental illness had produced the alleged crimes.

CROSS-EXAMINATION BY GOVERNMENT

Q. Did you administer the Szondi Test, Doctor?

A. No. I don't happen to think much of it. The test assumes a schizophrenic looks a certain way, and we have evidence this isn't so.

Q. What responses did you receive from Kent on the Rorschach, the ink-blot test?

A. Wolf, butterfly, vagina, pelvis, bats, buttocks, etc.

Q. And from this you concluded the defendant was schizophrenic?

A. Yes, that and other things.

Q. You gave him the Wechsler Adult Scale?

A. Yes.

Q. On the word-information part of the test, the word "temperature" appears. What question did you ask the defendant?

A. At what temperature does water boil.

Q. You gave him a zero. Why?

A. Because he answered 190° and that is the wrong answer. The right answer is 212° F.

Q. What question did you ask about the Iliad?

A. I am not sure: I believe I asked him to identify the Iliad or who wrote the Iliad.

Q. And he answered "Aristotle"?

A. Yes.

Q. And you scored him zero?

A. That's correct.

Q. Now you asked the defendant to define blood vessels, did you not?

A. Yes.

Q. And his answer was capillaries and veins. You scored him zero. Why? Aren't capillaries and veins blood vessels?

A. I don't know. The norms don't consider that answer acceptable.

Q. What norms?

A. You see, these tests are scored on the basis of norms secured by administering the test to thousands of people.

Q. On the comprehension section you asked Kent: "If you found a sealed, addressed, stamped envelope on the street, what would you do with it?" and he answered "Turn it in." Why did you give him a 1? Why not a 2?

A. Because of the norms. A 2-answer would require more—something like "Mail it" or "Take it to the post office."

Q. You asked Kent: "What does the phrase 'Strike when the iron is hot' mean?" What was his answer?

A. "Strike when it is best to strike." I gave him a zero.

Q. Why? Doesn't "Strike when the iron is hot" mean to strike when the opportunity presents itself?

A. In terms of the norms it is not an acceptable answer.

Q. You asked Kent: "What is similar about the eye and the ear?" and he said "They are organs." You gave him a 1. Why?

A. Because a 2-answer is more precise such as "organs of perception."

Q. You asked him: "What is winter?" and he stated "A season of the year." You gave him a 1—why not a 2? Isn't winter a season of the year, Doctor?

A. Well, again it is a matter of the norms. A 2-answer would include a "cold season of the year."

Q. You asked him: "What is a slice?" and he said "to cut." What is wrong with that. You gave him a 1.

A. A 2-answer would include "to slice thin" or "cut into thin pieces."

Q. You asked him to define "conceal" and he said "to get rid of." What score did you give him?

A. A zero.

Q. You asked him to define "sentence" and he said: "A group of words, as a noun and a verb." Why did you give him a 1?

A. A 2-answer would include the notion that a sentence expresses an idea.

Q. You asked him "What is a sanctuary?" and he said "Protection." Why did you give him a 1?

A. According to the norms, a 2-answer includes the notion of a place or a building.

Q. You asked Kent to define "calamity," and he said "a bad thing." You gave him a zero. Isn't a calamity a bad thing, Doctor?

A. Bad is not an acceptable answer in terms of the norms.

PSYCHOLOGIST C: DEFENSE

The witness testified he administered the Wechsler Intelligence Scale, the Rorschach, the Human Figure Drawing, the Kohn, the Porteus Maze, and the Thematic Apperception Tests.

CROSS-EXAMINATION BY GOVERNMENT

Q. You asked the defendant to draw a human figure?

A. Yes.

Q. And this is the figure he drew for you? What does it indicate to you about his personality?

A. You will note this is a rear view of a male. This is very rare, statistically. It indicates hiding guilt feelings, or turning away from reality.

Q. And this drawing of a female figure, does it indicate anything to you, and, if so, what?

A. It indicates hostility towards women on the part of the subject. The pose, the hands on the hips, the hard-looking face, the stern expression.

Q. Anything else?

A. The size of the ears indicates a paranoid outlook, or hallucinations. Also, the absence of feet indicates feelings of insecurity.

Q. On the Wechsler, you asked him: "What would you do if you found a sealed, addressed, stamped envelope?" and he answered: "Open it and find out who it belongs to. I will show you I know right from wrong." [This is the same subject who answered "Turn it in" to the previous psychologist.]

PSYCHOLOGIST D: DEFENSE

Psychologist D testified he saw the subject once at jail or the receiving home for an hour and a half; that he administered the Rorschach and started the Human Figure Drawing Test. The testing was interrupted when the defendant's father was announced, and Kent became very upset, highly emotional.

He diagnosed the defendant as schizophrenic, undifferentiated type. He thought productivity existed; that is, the schizophrenia produced the housebreakings, robberies, and rapes. The test showed severe thinking disturbance, an inability to control impulses, and disturbed sexual feelings.

CROSS-EXAMINATION BY GOVERNMENT

Q. Why did you see the defendant Kent?

A. Because of a call from Mr. Arens.

Q. Are you a member of the Washington School of Psychiatry?

A. No.

Q. The defendant made one drawing for you, right, Doctor?

A. Yes, that is right.

Q. After the announced arrival of his father?

A. Yes.

Q. Do you use the House-Tree-Person Test?

A. Never.

Q. Does it have validity?

A. Yes.

Q. Do you use the Szondi?

A. Five or six times.

Q. When did you stop using it?

A. At the fifth administration, about nine years ago.

Q. What does this drawing that Kent made for another psychologist indicate to you?

A. The transparency of the picture—that is, seeing through the figure to something beneath—suggests pathology.

Q. Do you usually use an extensive battery of tests before reaching a diagnosis?

A. Yes.

Q. Do you usually arrive at the diagnosis on the basis of one Rorschach administered twice within an hour?

A. Frequently.

Q. What else in the drawing is significant psychologically?

A. The irregularity or sketchiness of the lines may suggest tension and anxiety. The attention paid to details—to the belt-bow-tie, and pockets—indicate a little-boy-like quality about the defendant.

Q. Is it significant that the figure is running to the left, and not to the right?

A. To some people, yes. I don't place any significance on it.

Q. What about this drawing, made by Kent for another psychologist? What is significant about it?

A. The minimization of the breasts and the three lines across the genital area indicate tension in the sexual area. Breasts are symbolic of motherhood and early infant experiences. By minimizing the breasts the defendant indicates he has not received the satisfaction from women he had hoped to.

Q. Now, I will show you the picture Kent drew for you on September 9, 1961. What is significant about it?

A. The overemphasis of the breasts indicates how upset the defendant was because his father had been announced.

Q. You showed the defendant a series of Rorschach cards, right? And what responses did you get to Card 1, Card 2, etc.?

A. Cat, flying bird, a house, people, crab, wolf, pinchers, wings, clouds, blood, "like a vagina," menstrual blood, buckets, hip-bones, breast, apes, butterflies, jet airplane.

Q. On the basis of these responses, you concluded the defendant was a schizophrenic?

A. Yes.

UNITED STATES V. JENKINS*

PSYCHOLOGIST A: DEFENSE

Psychologist A testified that he had administered the following tests to the defendant: Wechsler Adult Intelligence Scale, Bender-Gestalt, Rorschach, and Szondi. The IQ rating was 74, a dull normal.

DIRECT EXAMINATION BY DEFENSE

Q. Why do you give these tests?

A. To get a personality functioning—to get a sample of behavior. It is assumed that the sample is representative of how a person deals with other life situations.

COURT. Do you say you can conclude that a person is suffering from schizophrenia from answers to a Rorschach?

A. Yes. For example, if somebody looked at this card and described it as a church with a steeple with three men standing there and the Virgin Mary descending, with the Devil hiding behind the house, I would feel confident in thinking that person is suffering from disordered thinking.

---

* Criminal No. 614–59, District Court for the District of Columbia.

Q. As a result of your tests, what is your diagnosis?

A. Schizophrenia.

Q. And productivity?

A. I cannot fail to see how a man's mental condition is unrelated to his behavior. I would expect there is a relationship, yes. I cannot say definitely that one thing is a product of another.

CROSS-EXAMINATION BY GOVERNMENT

Q. Doctor, do you agree with this statement: "It is well established that psychiatrists and psychologists freely concede there is no absolute accuracy and reliability of tests in the measurement of intelligence."

A. I do not agree.

Q. How about this statement: "Two persons of substantially the same mental capacity may test with materially different scores or rating depending on education, training, environment, etc."

A. Well, environment includes so much that I would think this would affect the performance on intelligence tests.

Q. You can tell from responses to Rorschach cards what his personality is like?

A. From a global picture.

Q. What response did he give to Card 4?

A. He saw a frog.

Q. And what significance do you attach to this answer, Doctor?

A. This is not the response normal people give. People often see two boots.

Q. And Card 5?

A. He saw a butterfly. This is a perfectly acceptable response. Many normal people see butterflies in this card.

Q. Card 6?

A. He said: "Don't see nothing—don't look like nothing."

Q. What things about the defendant's responses to the Rorschach led you to your diagnosis of schizophrenia?

A. The poor quality of his responses, the lack of seeing other kinds of responses, more typical responses you would expect from an adult.

Q. You also administered the Draw-a-Person test?

A. Yes.

Q. And what did it indicate?

A. The defendant drew the figure on the upper left-hand corner of the page. This indicated explosive feelings, insecurity, in a sense, holding onto the edges of the paper. This indicates anxiety and insecurity.

Q. What if he had placed the drawing in the middle of the page—what would that indicate?

A. It would mean he is a little less insecure.

Q. Do you believe in free will?

A. I believe it means complete control over one's actions and thoughts. I believe one's environment and heredity affect one's ability to exercise choice. Man has ability to make choices, but this is affected by other factors.

Q. Do you come from the so-called behavioristic school?

A. No, I am an eclectic.

Q. Do you believe all crime is a product of mental illness?
A. No.
Q. Any category of crimes?
A. I would expect bizarre crimes are often a product of mental illness.
Q. On the Wechsler, you asked him, "What color is the flag?" What did the defendant answer?
A. He answered, "Red, white, blue"—a 1, or perfect score. The test is scored 1–0.
Q. The second question?
A. "What shape is a ball?" He answered, "Round"—a 1 response.
Q. The fifth question?
A. "What does rubber come from?" His answer was "wood." I gave him a zero.
Q. Why a zero—aren't trees wood?
A. Yes, but it doesn't follow that rubber comes from wood.
COURT. You know where we get wood other than trees?
A. No.

[Other questions, similar to Kent material used, not recorded here because of repetition.]

Q. Why do you use pictures of insane people on the Szondi? Why not normal subjects?
A. We know penicillin works; we don't know why it works. It's the same thing here. We know that certain kinds of tests work; we don't understand why they work.
Q. You stated he was a chronic, undifferentiated schizophrenic. Can he also be an undifferentiated psychotic?
A. No. Undifferentiated psychosis is not a recognized classification.
Q. Do you know whether or not these schizophrenia symptoms were in remission on June 10, 1959?
A. No, I do not.
Q. You cannot state an opinion as to whether or not the schizophrenia caused the crime?
A. Yes, that is right.

PSYCHOLOGIST B: DEFENSE

This psychologist testified that she gave one part of the Szondi Test. She made a diagnosis of schizophrenia on the basis of the increase in the IQ scores.

DIRECT EXAMINATION BY DEFENSE

Q. What background factors confirmed your diagnosis of schizophrenia?
A. He was a withdrawn person who had few friends. He didn't associate with other children. He couldn't control his behavior.

CROSS-EXAMINATION BY GOVERNMENT

Q. What do you mean by adequate controls?
A. When the tensions build up in him to a state of anxiety, anger, frustration, his emotions explode into behavior over which he has no control.

Q. Do you believe in free will?

A. That is a philosophic, not a psychological, problem. Free will is an arbitrary, sudden explosion without cause. I don't believe that. If I am free to choose, why is it I choose one thing and you choose another? It is because of the structure of the nervous system, and the influence of the environment.

Q. You believe in God?

A. Yes, certainly.

COURT. You believe in free will, don't you?

A. I believe I can make a free choice, based on what I am.

COURT. Any individual is free to make a choice, isn't he?

A. Yes.

Q. Why did you use photographs of mentally ill persons—why not normal persons?

A. Because photographs of mentally ill persons are supposed to accentuate the needs or drives or deprivations or frustrations that human beings experience. Normal people have managed to resolve their frustrations. I don't know why it works. It is something underneath. It is difficult to explain and understand. Doctors use digitalis for heart disease without knowing why it acts as it does.

[On questioning concerning the Szondi Test, the witness testified that a psychologist could diagnose illness by the pictures a subject selected as those he liked or disliked. At this point the judge threw the cards down. At a Bench conference the defense attorney asked: "May the record reflect that after the last question the Court slammed the cards down?"

COURT. The record may reflect it but the record may show I am throwing it all out. That will take care of that session.

UNIT EIGHT | DISCUSSION QUESTIONS

26 | ONE OF THE GREAT MYSTERY STORIES OF MEDICINE

Discuss whether schizophrenia is an organic or environmentally-based disorder. Quote references to support your thesis.

List and define three types of schizophrenia.

27 | MENTAL ILLNESS IS A MYTH

The author feels that restraining individuals in mental hospitals is a risk to our society. Why?

Define and discuss the term "mental illness."

28 | PSYCHIATRISTS USE DANGEROUS WORDS

Compare Menninger's view of mental illness with Szasz's views in the preceding article.

What are the difficulties in using descriptive terms to define mental illness?

29 | THE PSYCHOLOGIST AS AN EXPERT WITNESS

Discuss some of the methods the government used to cross-examine the validity of psychological testing instruments.

How well do you think the psychologists in the case reported their findings? Give reasons.

UNIT NINE
DRUGS AND BEHAVIOR

Man has used various drugs and alcohol for many years. As far back as we have a record of his fears and fancies, we know that he has always believed in secret potions and magic charms to ward off evil spirits and cure him of unwelcomed illness. It was later believed that only criminals, degenerates, and other undesirables were addicts. Today, we recognize that drug addiction and alcoholism know no class boundaries and are psychological, as well as physiological and social, problems.

Recently much discussion has been centered around LSD and drug usage. Newspapers, magazines, TV documentaries, lectures, and classroom discussions have contributed to the impression that the problem is rampant among America's youth. A 1970 report of the San Mateo County (Calif.) Narcotics Advisory Committee showed that 20.2% of ninth-grade boys had used marijuana 10 times or more in 1969 compared to 14.3% in a report made a year ago. A closer view of the commission's statistics reveals an increase in use of LSD and amphetamines, as well as marijuana. Although this sampling is not a valid assessment of the total population, it illustrates the magnitude of this growing problem.

Addiction is one of this country's major medical, social, and economic problems. It affects males as well as females, in urban as well as rural communities, without regard for educational, religious, cultural, or financial status. The first reading, *Ours Is the Addicted Society* by Leslie H. Farber, presents a timely discussion of drug and alcohol use in this country. In examining the causes and effects of various kinds of addiction, the author includes a consideration of some of the special problems that are created.

In *Marijuana and Behavior; the Unfilled Gaps,* Lawrence Massett gives a report of the drug studies currently being conducted to evaluate claims that marijuana leads to the use of more dangerous drugs like heroin. Another much-debated contention that marijuana can trigger mental breakdowns in otherwise healthy individuals is discussed in this article. Sidney Cohen's *Pot, Acid, and Speed* is a brief coverage of the historical background of drug use, the chemical effects of drug-taking, and the pattern of certain drug abuse. Finally, Stanley F. Yolles' *Recent Research on LSD, Marijuana, and Other Dangerous Drugs* brings up the controversial topics of chromosome damage and birth defects, in addition to relating the research goals of other drug studies now in progress. His recommendations on prevention and education programs of the National Institute of Mental Health (NIMH) conclude the report.

30 | OURS IS THE ADDICTED SOCIETY

Leslie H. Farber

This has been called the "Age of Anxiety." Considering the attention given the subject by psychology, theology, literature, and the pharmaceutical industry, not to mention the testimony from our own lives, we could fairly well conclude that there is more anxiety today, and, moreover, that there is definitely more anxiety about anxiety now than there has been in previous epochs of history. Nevertheless, I would hesitate to characterize this as an "Age of Anxiety," just as I would be loath to call this an "Age of Affluence," "Coronary Disease," "Mental Health," "Dieting," "Conformity," or "Sexual Freedom," my reason being that none of these labels, whatever fact or truth they may involve, goes to the heart of the matter.

Much as I dislike this game of labels, my preference would be to call this the "Age of the Disordered Will." It takes only a glance to see a few of the myriad varieties of willing what cannot be willed that enslave us: We will to sleep, will to read fast, will to have simultaneous orgasm, will to be creative and spontaneous, will to enjoy our old age, and, most urgently, will to will.

If anxiety is more prominent in our time, such anxiety is the product of our particular modern disability of will. To this disability, rather than to anxiety, I would attribute the ever-increasing dependence on drugs affecting all levels of our society. While drugs do offer relief from anxiety, their more important task is to offer the illusion of healing the split between the will and its refractory object. The resulting feeling of wholeness may not be a responsible one, but at least within that wholeness —no matter how perverse the drugged state may appear to an outsider—there seems to be, briefly and subjectively, a responsible and vigorous will. This is the reason, I believe, that the addictive possibilities of our age are so enormous.

Let me be more specific about the addictive consequence of this disability of will which, in varying degree, affects us all. Increasingly, I believe we are addicted to addiction. This is to say that, with few exceptions, we subscribe to the premise— whether implicit or explicit—that this life cannot be lived without drugs. And those who would repudiate this unpleasant premise by living without drugs are still more or less captive to it, in that so much of their consciousness must be given over to withstanding the chemical temptations that beset them. Withstanding is a lesser evil than yielding, but it is no escape from the issue of addiction, so that I would have to characterize the predicament as one of being addicted to not being addicted. I do not mean to suggest that we choose one course or the other, but rather that both the premise and its negative variation exist in all of us. Even the most debilitated heroin addict retains his pride in the few items to which he has not become addicted.

From *The New York Times Magazine,* December 11, 1966. © 1966 by The New York Times Company. Reprinted by permission.

Not many years ago, we had best remind ourselves, the problem of addiction seemed confined to a few chemicals—narcotics, alcohol and, perhaps, barbiturates —and it was then possible to make fairly clear distinctions between addiction and habituation, based mainly on the presence or absence of physiological withdrawal symptoms. However, today even the well-publicized and allegedly extreme agonies of heroin withdrawal have been disputed by the Lazaruses who came back. Recently, a member of Synanon expressed to a reporter his disagreement with the fictional clichés which have acquired the status of scientific fact, remarking: "Kicking the habit is easy. It's not like that Frank Sinatra movie, crawling all over the walls. Sure, it's tough for a couple of days, but it's more like getting over a bad cold."

Fearing this view might be as extravagant in one direction as Nelson Algren's violent imaginings were in another, I checked with a friend who had been a staff member at Lexington. He thought the "bad-cold" analogy an accurate one, and added: "We had far more trouble with withdrawal symptoms in barbiturate users."

Our appropriation of the drug-user's vocabulary for our own purposes shows the extent to which the problem of addiction has invaded our daily existence. When our absorption with not only a chemical but a person, an activity, a distraction, an ideology seems to have more weight than is warranted, we say we are "hooked," meaning either that we wish we could be cured of our vice or else that we value the passion contained in our infatuation.

If someone or something excites us pleasurably, we say he or it "turns us on," but if our response is indifference or boredom, we are "turned off." Our extension of these terms for our own purposes is, to some degree, a fashionable reaction to the notoriety drugs have earned in the mass media. However, my own belief is that we resort to the junkie vocabulary because it expresses a metaphysical or addictive shift in our existence that the older vocabulary did not quite account for—at least in ordinary usage.

Even if we try to restrict ourselves to drug-taking, statistics about the extent and degree of addiction are hard to come by. Certainly we are no longer surprised to learn of the growing proportion of college students who resort to such drugs as marijuana, amphetamines, barbiturates, LSD, tranquilizers. One expert is quoted in The New York Times to the effect that about 40 per cent of the students at the University of California use drugs from time to time. This figure falls somewhat short of Timothy Leary's immoderate proclamation: "Today, in the molecular age, the issue is not what books you read or which symbols you use, but which chemicals are part of your life and your growth."

Numerical estimates notwithstanding, on the theory that convicts tend to riot for those privileges society deems essential, such as humane treatment, recreation, adequate food, civil rights, I am more persuaded by this news release:

WALPOLE, MASS., Aug. 13 (AP)—*Inmates rioted outside a medication dispensary at the Massachusetts State Prison in an attempt to steal drugs late last night, injuring nine guards. . . Two guards were stabbed and five others beaten as the inmates pushed their way into the 'pill' room, yelling, thrashing and literally gobbling down as many pills as they could at one time . . . State Police Cpl. James Dunne, who led the squad equipped with 12-gauge shotguns, gas masks and crash helmets, said about 18 of the inmates were reeling 'on Cloud Nine' when he arrived . . .*

And from industry, where access to drugs is sufficiently relaxed not to require riots, I offer this item:

LOS ANGELES, Oct. 9 (Los Angeles Times)—*Use of illegal drugs in industry, especially among production-line workers, is so common that to arrest everybody who sold or used them would mean some plants would have to hire whole new shifts of employees, according to a police narcotics specialist. The drugs most commonly used are amphetamine sulfate compounds and barbiturate derivatives, which keep workers awake, or put them to sleep. . .*

Since it is forbidden to peddle or "push" most drugs, including whisky, on television, Madison Avenue has responded to the double dilemma of addiction by advertising aspirin as though it were *the* drug for every tribulation we must undergo. On television we are shown scenes in which mothers snap at their children, employers lose their tempers with employes. With only an awkward swipe at the questionable ethics of permitting this poor old headache remedy to carry such a heavy burden, advertisers show these embattled and suffering creatures putting one hand to their heads while a kindly neighbor advises them that this new aspirin combination is the perfect cure for "tension." The happy scenes following their use of the drug are deliberate efforts to imitate the style in which the pharmaceutical companies persuade physicians of the virtues of their products.

Most touching are aspirin commercials in which an aging movie star, long past his prime and no longer regularly employed, sits thoughtfully in his well-appointed study, telling the television audience that movie-making is a hectic and demanding affair. To avoid tension and headache, intrinsic to such activity, he has always resorted to this particular remedy.

Although probably unintentional, such a commercial goes to the heart of addiction, for we must contemplate the pathos of this formerly glamorous creature whose powers have so dwindled that he is reduced to doing headache commercials in which, fooling no one, he pretends nothing has changed. As he holds his bottle of pills to the audience, he seems to say life is really impossible without these pills. But we know, and he knows, that aspirin is not enough; for the vast restitution he demands of life, more powerful drugs are needed.

Should he seek them, he will not have to resort to any illicit drug traffic. He will have no trouble finding a physician who will prescribe amphetamines or psychic energizers to brighten his mood as he waits for calls from his agent. And if the phone refuses to ring, one or several of the many tranquilizers can be prescribed so that he can endure the waiting. Whatever insomnia may have originally been his lot will now be painfully exacerbated by his drug-taking so that other sedatives, fortified often by alcohol, will insure his sleeping. As he moves from one drug to another, mixing and testing the chemicals he believes his state requires and countering their disagreeable effects with still other chemicals, from time to time the sheer immodest scope of his undertaking will strike him; he has become a deranged chemist, his only laboratory his own poor body.

No matter how haggard that body becomes, he must unfortunately depend on it for fresh chemical inspiration. And, if everything else fails, there is LSD for instant revelation, if not wisdom, about the pretentious games that have brought him to this impasse, allowing him the death and rebirth that are now accepted pieties of the LSD mystique.

While it is true that the medical profession and the pharmaceutical industry together are the largest and most powerful group of pushers for the new drugs, I see no conspiracy on their part to make addicts of us all. It has long been common knowledge that physicians are the most devoted users of the drugs they prescribe, unlike the more disreputable pushers whose livelihood depends on abstaining from the drugs they peddle. The men who devise and merchandise these pills and the physicians who dispense them are, by and large, decent human beings who share the same disability of will that afflicts everyone.

Believing, as we do, that we should be able to will ourselves to be calm, cheerful, thin, industrious, creative—and, moreover, to have a good night's sleep—they simply provide the products to collaborate in such willing. If the satisfactions turn out to be short-lived and spurious and if their cost in terms of emotion, intellect and physical health is disagreeable, these scientists are ready to concoct new drugs to counter this discomfort. In other words, they offer us always new chances—virtually to the point of extinction—to will away the unhappiness that comes from willing ourselves to be happy.

Recently, Dr. Carroll L. Witten, president-elect of the American Academy of General Practice, was quoted in the press as being in agreement with a report issued this year by the United Nations Commission on Narcotics which expressed concern over "the alarming rise in the sale of barbiturates, tranquilizers and amphetamines."

The report suggested further that the "explosive expansion of the use of drugs . . . was most likely a result of their being used less as medication than as agents for producing sleep, a sense of happiness and relaxation." Dr. Witten declared:

I believe these drugs are not only used wrongly, to excess and without adequate indication, but that in many cases their indiscriminate use has led to dependency, habituation and addiction, with all of the consequent results thereof.

Dr. Witten said he was referring specifically to the non-narcotic drugs used as "psychic energizers, stimulators, activators, deactivators, depressants, alleviators, levelers, elevators or in whatever imaginative category one might place them. One must note with a great deal of alarm," he declared, "that the vast majority of cases first obtained their drugs through the prescription of a physician."

If willing what cannot be willed has led us to being addicted to addiction, it would seem that our addictive appetite will always be more than a match for the ever-mounting number of chemicals that are fashioned to gratify the appetite. And even if we eliminate actual drugs from our consideration, the addictive possibilities are endless: cigarettes, chocolate, detective and spy stories, football on television, psychoanalysis—to mention only a few of my own excesses, which I would unhesitatingly characterize as addictive. Everyone, I am convinced, has his own list, as well as another more prideful list of those objects and activities whose addictive claims he has successfully withstood.

If the term is not to be altogether meaningless, some distinction must now be made between one addiction and another. Concretely, when it comes to putting myself to sleep, how shall I distinguish between detective stories and sleeping pills? Or between watching football on TV and enduring my Sunday with tranquilizers? Or completing a tedious chore on amphetamines and procrastinating as usual?

The first generalization I would make about these sets of alternatives is that in an immediate sense drugs are clearly more effective. Detective stories, for me at least, are not entirely reliable as sedatives. If the story is so poor as to outrage or challenge my diminished sensibilities, I am in trouble, whereas I can always take another sleeping pill.

Watching even an exciting, well-played football game on TV, I cannot entirely obliterate from my awareness the perception that there are other ways in which I could more profitably spend my time. And if the game is inept and boring and still I do not turn the set off, my view of my condition is grim indeed. On the other hand, with tranquilizers, I could achieve a state of not unpleasant relaxation, unruffled by the sort of nagging self-concern which interrupts my absorption with even a good football game.

It is the last set of alternatives that will prove the most troublesome. If I have a group of evaluations of psychoanalytic candidates to write, I am inclined to put it off. The reasons and/or rationalizations for my procrastination will be various: I don't feel well; such reports are too tedious to be endured; I resent the bureaucratic rule requiring these reports; I am reluctant to set myself up as a judge of the performance of these young men; I am convinced I am not equal to the imaginative discrimina-tions that would do these human beings justice.

With a dose of amphetamine, however, my self-concern, with its associated fatigue and hesitations and doubts, will vanish, so that in a single-minded way I shall vigorously engage my task. Within a few hours all the evaluations will be completed. Like a schoolboy who has at the last minute finished his term paper, I shall feel relieved and virtuous to have at long last done what my organization demands of me.

Reading over my reports after I have recovered from the drug, I may be cha-grined to note a breathless, assertive and yet self-indulgent quality to my writing that did not trouble me at the time. But I can counter my dissatisfaction by assuring myself these deficiencies matter very little, since I have done all that was asked of me. It was my own sin of pride that initially led me to regard my task as such an intricate and demanding responsibility. Besides, I will tell myself, wasn't it a choice between doing nothing and doing something, however imperfectly?

Thus will my mood of accomplishment prevail, helping me to disown my self-criticism and perhaps persuading me, since I won't have to read these reports again, that I had indeed been discriminating in preparing them. And my earlier doubts as to whether these evaluations should have been written at all can be postponed for another time.

The sensation of being a going, if unquestioning, member of society should not be slighted, because it is hard to come by these days. Nevertheless, we must con-cede that while the drugs in these sets of alternatives may be more effective, their effectiveness is largely dependent on the chemical deadening of important imagina-tive and critical capacities, whose privileges are admittedly problematic. Practically every drug invented, from opium to LSD, has had its champions in both science and the arts who insisted that their particular brew was not only reductive but was ac-tually heightening of human potentiality.

The objective evidence for their claims, however, has always been depressing, and of the same order as my own reports, whether it be the music played under marijuana or heroin, the pictures painted and the poetry composed under LSD, the deadlines met by means of amphetamines, or even—perhaps especially—the percep-tions and insights granted by drugs.

At this point, the question must be raised: aren't other addictions—nondrug addictions—also reductive? The answer has to be a qualified affirmative. The friend watching me glued for hours to the television set, isolated from all intelligible life, impervious to the claims of my children who have waited all week to have a few moments with me, has to find my human condition bizarre, to say the least.

Far more seriously incapacitating, of course, are those nondrug addictions that involve ideas and habits of thought. Those who over the years develop an addiction to shopworn ideologies—religious, scientific, political, esthetic, psychological—in a sense forfeit, in willful dedication, the very capacities of spirit and intellect that might set them free.

Nevertheless, there is a difference between drugs and no drugs. While disdain and denial of these capacities will cause them to shrivel and grow even more paralyzed as years go by, there remains the possibility of a response, however minimal at first, to some human claim. Chemical deadening, on the other hand, if pursued, will, by its very nature, render such capacities eventually heedless to any call.

But to return to my evaluations of those psychoanalytic candidates—my will, with the help of amphetamine, has had its undiscriminating way in my reports, without the reflective give-and-take between me and my writing that could be called dialogic, causing this enterprise to resemble other headstrong monologic sprees in which the speaker is deaf and blind to those about him at the same time that he is convinced of a singular openness and freedom and mutuality to the exchange.

The nonuser has a dispiriting effect on groups enthusiastically consolidated by such convictions, so that they would prefer him to find his own sober companions. And his response to them will be marked by his discouraged observation that, despite the cries of mutual congratulation, all he can hear are colliding monologues, breathlessly composed so that each participant gives in to his own worst headstrong and literal-minded inclinations.

The person who ordinarily must guard against his habit of vast abstraction now becomes even more abstract in his theoretical pronouncements. The person top-heavy with esthetic sensibility becomes even more indulgent to that side of himself, abdicating his ability to temper such estheticism with moral and psychological discriminations.

The most blatant examples of the literal-minded aspect of the drugged state comes from the public writings on LSD, but it is by no means restricted to this particular drug. Under LSD, it would seem one is at the mercy of any fancy that strikes him, much like the hypnotic subject responding to the commands of the hypnotist. Should he note that his hand is ugly, that hand becomes literally swollen and grotesque. Should the thought strike him that he is alone in the world, he will quickly and literally find himself as one small mortal in the midst of an endless desolate landscape. In each instance, what properly should be no more than a beginning metaphor has been exalted, at the behest of the will, into physical reality. Similarly, the death undergone with LSD can be regarded as more deathly than death itself. In a section, jarringly titled "Running Smack Into Your Essence," of "LSD: The Acid Test," published in *Ramparts,* one evangelist, Donovan Bess, wrote:

The psychedelic death is especially lonely—lonelier, perhaps, than for the soldier who physically dies in a Vietnamese field hospital. He at least has the comfort of cuddling up in the image of his mother. Under LSD you have no such bourgeois comfort; you have no familial figure at all. You die grown up. If you can hang onto that, afterward, you can offer society some adult values. You came to this point in a rite of passage as explicit, as terrible and as meaningful as those rites used in aboriginal Australia.

In considering the addictive state which may result from drugs, narcotic and non-narcotic, I must of course neglect the specific effects each drug has or purports to have on the central nervous system. An unfortunate consequence of such neglect will be to give the false impression that my own addiction to nonaddiction has led me to advocate an impossibly ascetic life, requiring abstention from all chemical assistance, come what may. Let me quickly insist that all the drugs I have mentioned may be taken in nonaddictive ways for reasons that are appropriate to the effects of the particular drug. This is to say, there are times when prolonged sleeplessness can and should be interrupted by sedatives, just as there are painful occasions when morphine is the only answer. Even amphetamines may allow the completion of a low-level chore.

The difficulty, however, here, as indicated earlier, is that the mood of accomplishment may persuade us to disregard the quality, or lack of quality, of our performance, not to mention the disagreeable drug side-effects, so that we turn to the drug in situations that require more of our wits and equanimity than amphetamines will allow. Perhaps a greater danger, as the use of amphetamines becomes more widespread, is that the deadlines asked of us are increasingly determined by the amphetamine intoxications of those who ask. (Another illustration of the manner in which the drugged state influences social values is suggested by the aspirin commercials referred to in this article. The writers of these advertisements seem to be selling not only aspirin but also their conviction—possibly arrived at through their own experience with tranquilizers—that our ordinary difficulties, since they are only subjective and therefore not worth contending with, are best erased with drugs. Thus, an advertisement for meprobamate, addressed to physicians, shows a picture of an overwrought mother with a child, the caption reading: "Her kind of pressures last all day . . . shouldn't her tranquilizer?")

For the sake of completeness, alcohol and marijuana are two drugs whose object is explicitly pleasure, and which may be used nonaddictively. However, too much has been made recently by the younger generation of the nonaddictive properties of marijuana simply because its physical effects are less dramatic than those of alcohol and other drugs. More dramatic is its effect upon relation: the pleasures of monologue experienced as dialogue under the drug, persist as a habit of tolerance for such illusion—which in a sense is the very issue of addiction.

Let us consider briefly the addictive course—from initial pleasure to ultimate disaster—that will result from prolonged and excessive use of any of the drugs I have mentioned, singly or in combination.

The first subjective experience of wholeness and the pleasure accompanying it will acquire its intensity partly through contrast with the discomfort which preceded the use of the drug and partly through the manner a particular drug answers a particular person's need at a particular time. Thus, users are labeled according to their preferences as "Up-Heads" or "Speed-Heads," "Down-Heads," "Acid-Heads," "Pot-Heads," "Lushes," "Junkies."

With further sophistication and availability, and the cooperation of the medical profession, drug-users already are specializing less and availing themselves more of

other products and mixtures of products. But the initial feeling of well-being is difficult to duplicate precisely, regardless of the ingenuity of the user. As the drug and
the state associated with it begin to wear off, the user returns to a world which has
lost none of its oppressiveness and with which, in the midst of the drug hangover, he
feels less able to cope.

The distance between himself and the wholeness he sought has grown somewhat,
so that he is now vulnerable to the beginning belief that the relief the drug afforded
is an extraordinary sort of transcendence which his usual life with others cannot
provide, except in the occasional unpredictable and surprising manner in which such
moments arise. In other words, he has been burned by the demonic and addictive
notion that he need not wait on life for the transcendence he seeks, that he may
invoke it whenever he so decrees or wills by returning to the drug or drugs which
first allowed him this remarkable feeling.

With this seeming triumph of his will, he will be more impatient of the often
frustrating give-and-take of life without drugs, willfully demanding his well-being
of those about him and thereby suffering even more the penalties of such willing. In
a sense he insists futilely that life now be his drug.

Needless to say, his mounting impatience will be inimical to the exercise or development of such qualities as imagination, judgment, humor, tact. And should he
glimpse, however dimly, his impoverishment, he may wish to believe these qualities
at least can return with drugs, disowning the evidence accumulating to the contrary.
However, without these qualities he is more and more confined to the exigencies of
the moment, for he can no longer really remember his drug experience in the past nor
can he imagine what may follow. As his intolerance for life without drugs increases,
his competence for such life diminishes, so that with every return to the drug he is,
in the spirit of Heraclitus, a different and lesser person who attempts to cross the
same stream twice.

What seemed the feeling of transcendence at the beginning has long since been
abandoned as his drug goal in favor merely of getting from one moment to the next,
in favor of mindlessly and minimally staying alive. What began with his will to de-
cree well-being for himself without having to wait on life now culminates in almost a
paralysis of will for every trivial action, even getting dressed or feeding himself. It is
as though all the taken-for-granted stream of activity had disintegrated into a swarm
of tiny yet insurmountable enterprises for his will, every one seeming to require
further drugs for its accomplishment.

As a result of the bombardment of his body by such large dosages of drugs, his
physical debilitation grows extreme. Yet even his bodily exhaustion and derangement
offers a last resort to the will which is now unequal to practically every small movement in his world. Unlike other depleting illnesses that mysteriously overtake us, this
one has been induced by himself and seems to be within his control. That is, he may
try to assuage his agonies with more chemicals or he can withdraw the noxious agent
so that his body can slowly recover its strength.

All other dramas in which his will has been involved have given way now to the
one small immediate drama of whether he shall live or die to this world. It is a far
cry from the transcendence he sought originally, but every addict knows the drama
of his failing body is the last plot his will must confront. Unlike the proponents of
LSD, he is beyond metaphysical conceits about the meaning of dying to this world,
nor will he glamorize recovery, to whatever degree it may occur, as spiritual rebirth.

Nietzsche, I believe, was not as interested in theological argument about the disappearance of the divine will in our lives as he was in the consequences of its disappearance. Today, the evidence is in. Out of disbelief we have impudently assumed that all of life is now subject to our own will. And the disasters that have come from willing what cannot be willed have not at all brought us to some modesty about our presumptions. Instead, we have turned to chemicals, which seem to enhance our willful strivings. It was only a question of time before man, in his desperation, would locate divinity in drugs and on that artificial rock build his church.

31 | MARIJUANA AND BEHAVIOR;
THE UNFILLED GAPS

Lawrence Massett

Although the drug bill now working its way through Congress reduces the penalties for marijuana possession (SN: 1/24, p. 102), neither Congress nor the Administration regards the bill as a final settlement of the proper legal status for marijuana.

Scientific research into the effects of marijuana on human behavior has so far provided few definitive answers to the questions figuring in public controversy over the drug. True, there is now agreement among the scientific community that marijuana is not a physically addictive drug like the narcotics; this agreement is reflected in the proposed drug bill, which will remove marijuana from its former legal classification alongside heroin. Yet there remain many questions that must be answered before a completely adequate scheme of Federal regulation for marijuana, or sound public attitudes toward it, can be developed.

It is often held, for example, that marijuana leads to the use of more dangerous drugs like heroin and propels smokers into crime, insanity and social apathy. Harry J. Anslinger, for years head of the U.S. Bureau of Narcotics and presently the United States representative to the United Nations Commission on Narcotic Drugs, recently characterized marijuana as a "scourge that undermines its victims and degrades them mentally, morally and physically."

From *Science News*, **97**, February 7, 1970. Copyright © 1970 by Science Service, Inc. Reprinted by permission.

The public defenders of marijuana, equally outspoken, deny the existence of any such link between marijuana and personal or social debilitation, and claim, as does the popular philosopher Alan Watts, that smoking marijuana can be "a profound religious experience."

Because the controversy remains vehement and unresolved in spite of its long history, the Government is relying heavily on future research to settle the disputed questions. Perhaps the most important feature of the new drug bill is an Administration-sponsored provision that will enable the Attorney General to revise Federal marijuana regulations at a later date, as scientific evidence accumulates.

To furnish the necessary evidence, the National Institute of Mental Health has begun funding more than 20 research projects into the behavioral effects of marijuana. Many of the questions at which the research is aimed have been investigated before, but in a way that has failed to produce unambiguous conclusions.

The question of whether marijuana smoking is a first step on the road to narcotic addiction, for example, has been the subject of numerous research projects. The most notable recent study, published in 1968 by Drs. John G. Ball and Carl D. Chambers of the Addiction Research Center of the National Institute of Mental Health in Lexington and Dr. Martin J. Ball of the University of Kentucky Medical School, consists of a survey of some 2,000 opiate addicts.

Most of the addicts who came from states bordering Mexico or the Gulf of Mexico or from the metropolitan belts of the East and Midwest had been marijuana smokers, the survey found. On the other hand, most of the opiate addicts from 12 states in the South did not use marijuana.

These equivocal results demonstrate no causal link between opiates and marijuana, although they do not rule out the possibility that such a link might exist. Social environment, for instance, might enter the picture.

Drs. Ball, Chambers and Ball speculate that in metropolitan centers the easy availability of marijuana involves novice smokers in a drug underworld where peer-group influences draw them toward heroin. Although the speculation is not contradicted by the results of their study, no survey to date has been able to pinpoint the exact connection, if there is any, between marijuana and heroin use.

Consequently, one of the research projects currently funded by NIMH is a long-term study, under the direction of Dr. Stanley E. Grupp at Illinois State University, into marijuana use among various social groups, with an emphasis on isolating the factors that might cause a marijuana smoker to turn to addicting drugs. "Many of the marijuana smokers we're studying have had opportunities to use heroin but haven't done so," says Dr. Grupp. "So far, we don't know why."

Other controversial allegations about marijuana stand in similar need of further research. Claims that marijuana can induce mental deterioration, criminal behavior and passivity have not so far been supported by any research in the United States. Yet the scientific literature from foreign countries, such as India, Egypt and Indonesia, contains reports of investigations supporting such claims.

In these countries, research indicates, criminals and mental patients are often found to have been habitual users of cannabis. Whether there is any causal connection is a moot question. Most American investigators feel that scientists abroad have failed to distinguish adequately the effects of cannabis from the possible effects of poverty, malnutrition and other deteriorating factors. Dr. William H. McGlothlin, a psychologist at the University of California at Los Angeles, is using part of his NIMH grant to prepare a systematic evaluation of the world-wide literature on cannabis. So far he finds that all the foreign studies "can be criticized on methodological grounds."

Nevertheless, he adds, the observations of foreign investigators should not be entirely rejected. The possibility that chronic cannabis users tend to become social dropouts Dr. McGlothlin finds quite plausible. "Chronic users of any drug, including alcohol, are liable to drop out," he says. In fact, it has been suggested (by the Council on Mental Health of the American Medical Association, among others), that the increasing popularity of marijuana in the United States may result in a serious social problem, principally because large numbers of people may wind up centering their lives around the smoking of marijuana, just as alcoholics focus their existence upon drinking.

Recently Dr. McGlothlin, together with two sociologists, Dr. David O. Arnold of the University of California at Santa Barbara and Paul K. Rowan of California State College at Los Angeles, two more NIMH grantees, conducted a survey bearing on the question. They studied a group of adults who typically had been introduced to marijuana in the 1940's. The adults surveyed were interested in psychotherapy, yoga, Zen meditation and other techniques of exploring consciousness and were willing to try almost any psychotropic drug. A few of the adults had tried heroin, but the drug they favored most, other than marijuana, turned out to be alcohol.

Dr. McGlothlin, Dr. Arnold and Rowan concluded that "marijuana abusers would be drawn from the population who do, or would, use alcohol in excess." If potential alcoholics and potential marijuana abusers are roughly the same people, they suggest, it follows that the legalizing of marijuana might not increase the level of drug abuse in America. Such a conclusion, however, is highly tentative, since the survey included only 29 persons, who may very well not be representative of the sorts of people who have begun smoking marijuana in recent years.

Another much-debated contention supported by some of the foreign evidence, that marijuana can trigger mental breakdowns in otherwise healthy individuals, is not thus far supported by American research. Dr. McGlothlin points out that cannabis preparations used in the Middle East and India, from where most of the foreign research comes, are considerably more potent than the marijuana available in the United States; hence foreign research and American research on this question are not directly comparable.

Researchers in this country, nevertheless, are gradually amassing evidence that indicates the American variety of marijuana is a comparatively mild drug. More than 30 years ago, the Mayor's Committee on Marijuana in New York performed a prototypical series of clinical tests on subjects under the influence of marijuana and concluded that "the basic personality structure of the individual does not change" as a result of smoking marijuana.

Most of the subjects, the committee reported, were quiet and generally euphoric after taking the drug. On tests of intelligence and cognitive functioning, marijuana appeared to produce a transitory adverse effect of the subjects' performance. But the effect was slight for those subjects who were experienced users. A few subjects, judged to be prepsychotic or severely disturbed, showed anxiety reactions or psychotic-type reactions to the drug.

Clinical research since the 1930's has confirmed and amplified the findings of the Mayor's Committee. Recently Dr. Andrew Weil of the National Institute of Mental Health, Dr. Norman Zinberg of Harvard University and Judith M. Nelsen of the Boston University School of Medicine performed tests of muscular and mental coordination on a small group of marijuana smokers. The impairment in performance on the tests evidenced by their subjects was, they noticed, closely related to the strength of the marijuana dosage administered.

At normal dosage levels, the performance of experienced users in some cases "appears to improve slightly after smoking marijuana," the experiments showed. Dr. Weil believes further experiments he plans under the NIMH effort may demonstrate that marijuana interferes with short-term memory (memory of the immediately preceding seconds and minutes) for neophyte smokers. This hinders a subject's efforts to carry out a complex train of thought or to maintain the thread of a conversation. Experienced marijuana users, he speculates, somehow learn to overcome such hindrances, or even to improve their performance, unless they have received a high dose.

Dr. Reese T. Jones, a psychiatrist in charge of a NIMH-supported marijuana research program at the Langley Porter Neuropsychiatric Institute in San Francisco, reports similar findings about the importance of dosage level in marijuana experiments. When the dosage level is maintained at or below the level present in the marijuana normally available in this country, "adverse reactions are rare," he says. At high dosage levels, anxiety reactions often occur.

In the next few years, it is expected, scientists will have collected far more precise information about the effects of marijuana on behavior. Whether such information will succeed in resolving the public controversy over marijuana remains to be seen, since much of the research will inevitably be open to methodological criticism.

Long-term sociological research into the effects of marijuana, for instance, may be criticized on the grounds that the persons surveyed might not be representative subjects. "Since the drug is illegal in the United States," says Dr. Helen Nowlis, a psychologist at Rochester University, "researchers who want to study the use of marijuana over a number of years have to work with subjects willing to admit that they regularly break the law. These subjects may not be typical marijuana smokers."

Studies performed by clinical psychologists are subject to other criticisms related to the selection of subjects, the method of administering marijuana and the choice of drug used as a placebo for control purposes. Dr. Nowlis points out, for example, that cognitive-functioning tests and simulated driving experiments in laboratories may tell very little about the performance of a marijuana user in a real car in the outside world. "I cannot," she says, "conceive of a research design that could provide definitive answers."

Most scientists engaged in studying the behavioral effects of marijuana, however, feel that future research will show marijuana to be neither as harmful nor as beneficial as popularly claimed. "Drug studies are always fuzzy," Dr. Jones notes, "and people will be able to pick out the points they like and ignore the rest." On the basis of the evidence so far, he states, it would nonetheless be reasonable to conclude that marijuana is a rather mild drug.

At ordinary dosage levels, Dr. Jones says, marijuana "doesn't look so different from other psychotropic drugs." In fact, he adds, "I suspect marijuana will turn out to look more like alcohol than it does different."

In any case, many researchers feel that the public controversy over marijuana is not so much a debate over the scientific evidence as a quarrel over social values.

"The generation gap, the Vietnam War, and all kinds of political and social attitudes are involved," says Dr. Nowlis.

As social attitudes change and as scientific knowledge about marijuana accumulates, the present dispute may come to seem ridiculous, Dr. Grupp believes. "Maybe 30 years from now we might look back on this controversy," he says, "as one big put-on."

---

32 | POT, ACID, AND SPEED

Sidney Cohen

Does it seem to you that the news media are full of drug happenings? Why are we witnessing a drug abuse explosion? Why so many "heads"—potheads, pillheads, hopheads, acidheads and rumheads? Is this the age of chemical escape? Have we finally arrived at the portal of the Brave New World?

Certain aspects of the current bedrugged scene are new. Our psychochemists are now capable of synthesizing highly potent mind-shaking chemical structures. A minute speck of d-lysergic acid diethylamide (LSD, acid) can propel one into an orbit far beyond the range of the older psychedelic vegetables. It is probably the most potent of all drugs, certainly the most powerful psychedelic.

Comparative strengths of LSD and other hallucinogens (approximate)

Drug	Chemical breakdown	Dosage
Marijuana	leaves and tops of *Cannabis sativa*, swallowed	30,000 mg
Peyote buttons	*Lophophora williamsii*	30,000 mg
Nutmeg	*Myristica fragrans*	20,000 mg
Hashish	resin of *Cannabis sativa*	4,000 mg
Mescaline	3,4,5,-trimethoxyphenylethylamine	400 mg
Psilocybin	4-phosphoryltryptamine	12 mg
STP	2,5-dimethoxy-4-methyl-amphetamine	5 mg
LSD	d-lysergic acid diethylamide tartarate	0.1 mg

From *Medical Science*, **19**, 1968. Copyright © J. B. Lippincott and reprinted by permission.

Some aspects of drug overuse are quite old—even for North America. A century ago Americans drank more distilled spirits per capita than they do today. Opium or its alkaloids were consumed regularly by as many as 4 per cent of our citizenry. Today, the number of users is estimated at .01 per cent. In those days, 100 years ago, many physically or spiritually ailing people were devoted consumers of proprietary cough cures, painkillers and soothing syrups which contained opium in the bottle but not on the label. Then, too, the hypodermic syringe had just been invented, and large amounts of morphine were injected, especially during the Civil War. Morphinism came to be known as the "Soldier's disease." To add to the substantial population of opiate users, the immigrant Chinese brought their custom of opium smoking to the West, where it spread to a number of the natives. Just 70 years ago, heroin, a cure for opium and morphine addiction, was introduced—a sad example of scientific error prevailing over scientific fact.

During the 19th century many other drugs were misused: cocaine, bromides, chloral and chloroform. Even before ether was discovered to have anesthetic properties, it was sniffed by college students to alter their consciousness. The prime psychedelic of the 19th century was nitrous oxide, popularly called "laughing gas" because it evoked hilarity and delight. It provided more than a "high," it revealed enormous insights and universal truths. Sir Humphrey Davy, who later suggested its use in anesthesia, tried it in a self-experiment. As he was going under he discovered the final secret of the universe and scrawled it on a pad so that it would not be forgotten. After he recovered he immediately searched for the note, which read: "Gad, the stench is awful." It may be that in the years to come the psychedelic enlightenments of today will be judged to be equally revealing.

POT

It is astonishing to recall that Fluidextracts of Cannabis were on every apothecary's shelf in bygone days, yet the preparation did not find its way into the stomachs of more than one or two venturesome citizens. The most frequent use of this high-powered "pot" was as a green coloring agent for corn remedies.

It was not until the Mexican laborers came to work in the fields of the Southwest in the 1930's, and ships brought pot into the port of New Orleans, that marijuana took hold in this country. At first it was an item for jazz musicians. Then Mezz Mezzrow spread it around Harlem, and it became a favorite of minority groups. During the past decade it has extended to the campus, the arty set, and beyond. Today, it is the most popular of the illegal drugs.

According to law, it is grouped with the narcotics and cocaine. All activities involving marijuana, including possession or use, are felonious. Even knowingly being in a place where the pot is used or kept may be subject to penalty. Pharmacologically, it is a mild hallucinogen, the variety grown in the United States being particularly mild. Well-cultivated Mexican or North African material is much stronger. A small amount of the resin of Indian hemp, hashish, is sometimes available, and it is five or six times stronger than the American product.

Marijuana contains a variety of tetrahydrocannabinols which are unstable. The instability of the active ingredient has retarded research, but a reliable, synthetic cannabinol is now available for investigative purposes.

The drug is not addicting in that physical withdrawal symptoms are not seen following sudden withdrawal. Psychological dependence is well known. Tolerance of any degree does not occur.

In this country smoking is the mode of use. The smoker acquires the habit of retaining the deeply inhaled smoke as long as possible in order to enhance absorption across the alveolar capillary bed. Some smokers perform a modified Valsalva maneuver before exhaling. The marijuana cigarette is often irritating, and can produce a "cigarette cough" and conjunctivitis. Whether pulmonary emphysema may result from many years of the unphysiologic way that marijuana is inhaled is not known. Little or no smoke may be exhaled if the technique employed is correct. The absorbed material is carried from the lungs directly to the brain, and the effects are perceived immediately. Pot smokers who do not inhale may notice little or nothing from their reefers. The effects from a puff or two of moderately-good-quality marijuana may last for a few hours. Naturally, one can get "stoned" by increasing the dose. We have no evidence that carcinogens are present in marijuana.

What most users seek is a feeling of relaxation with a dissolution of the tensions and the frustrations of the day. Sometimes drowsiness is noted, especially during the first few trips. Time is often slowed and perceptual distortions are mentioned. Hunger may be experienced; this, presumably, is due to a hypoglycemic effect. Fantasy-type mentation and a euphoric mood are sought and relished. Since ordinary controls are partially in abeyance, paranoid notions can supervene. Ideas of reference, suspiciousness or strong feelings of grandiosity are known. An overestimate of one's own capabilities is not infrequent. Often mental productions are not as highly assessed when they are later examined in the sober state.

It is difficult to assume an intelligent position about marijuana since some of the information we possess is inaccurate, and important data are not yet available. The following statements can be made even at our present level of knowledge.

1. Pot can make you a felon. Mezz Mezzrow, the founder of the pot cult, said, some time before his death, "I laid off five years ago, and if anyone asks my advice today, I tell him to steer clear of it because it carries a rap. That's my final word to all you cats: today I know of one very bad thing the tea can do—it can put you in jail."

2. The occasional use by curious individuals is rarely associated with difficulties. It is true that people trying pot for the first time may lose control and engage in antisocial activities. This is analogous to the person who becomes drunk for the first time. More experienced users of drink and pot often learn how to handle their disinhibiting agent. However, both drugs are known to be associated with crimes of violence and the inefficient operation of vehicles.

3. The person who regularly smokes a number of reefers daily, the "pothead," is in the position of his alcoholic equivalent, the "rumhead." In both instances a chemical has become the central theme of existence. In both instances emotional growth and development are impeded because problem solving is not accomplished. Rather, the alcohol or the pot becomes a universal solution.

4. The advocates for the legalization of pot do not seem to recognize that even if it were to become a legal item, its use by minors, or "potted" drivers, would be

against the law. Legalization is not as simple as the enthusiasts assume. This country is a co-signer of a United Nations treaty regarding marijuana, which would have to be abrogated. In this regard it is interesting that almost every country has laws against cannabis use, a few more stringent than ours. In Egypt and Nigeria the death penalty could be invoked for its growth and distribution. This peculiar taboo, then, is not a product of our competitive Western culture or Puritan ethic, or a plot of the whiskey or tobacco interests. Instead, it seems to result from a fairly general impression that prolonged use (especially of the stronger preparations) can be harmful. In those countries where hashish is used most widely, namely among the Mohammedan peoples of the Middle East and India, reports continue to appear about the psychotic or demented states of long-term, heavy users. The question that remains is the accuracy of these observations.

Consideration should be given to reducing the penalties for *possession* and *use* of marijuana. This is suggested not in response to any pressure group's exhortations. It is a matter of logical consistency. If we were to remove marijuana from the narcotic category, it should be placed on the dangerous drug list. It is illogical to impose lesser penalties for a strong psychedelic like acid than for a minor psychedelic like pot.

5. Marijuana will not solve the most serious problems we have with drugs—alcohol. The 5 per cent of the drinking population who misuse alcohol to their detriment would not become abstinent if the marijuana restrictions were eliminated. Instead, we would add an unknown number of chronic potheads. In those countries where alcohol is forbidden, skid rows based on pot exist.

6. Whether marijuana use directly causes escalation to heroin is unlikely. What probably happens in those instances where pot has been used prior to heroin involvement is that personality and social factors determine the misuse of both drugs. It is conceivable that when any illegal drug is used, it may permit more serious drug abuse to occur at a later date.

Today, we may be observing a novel phenomenon. Drug subcultures composed, in the main, of young people, exist in our cities. The ordinary taboos against drug abuse do not exist in these subgroups. Many of them will try anything and everything. We have recent evidence of the "joy popping" of heroin and the "mainlining" of cocaine by a few of these youngsters. No doubt, a small number of them will find themselves hooked on the narcotics. In that sense it may be said that their original use of one culturally-alien drug like marijuana made their initiation into the stronger agents easier.

ACID

It is but a quarter century since the strange psychological effects of d-lysergic acid diethylamide (LSD, acid) were discovered by the serendipitous Swiss biochemist, Albert Hofmann. Since that time the LSD story has changed frequently and rapidly. Originally, the compound was a research tool used to study experimental psychoses, and investigators called it an hallucinogen or a psychotomimetic. The mental and biochemical effects induced, and its psychotherapeutic potential, were studied scientifically. Later, it was noted that not all LSD experiences were disorganizing states of psychosis. Some subjects described alterations of consciousness which were highly euphoric, visually fascinating or even insightful. This self-transcendent state, chemically produced, was also studied by a few investigators. Today, all research efforts have diminished markedly, and few projects are under way.

Part of the reason for the decrease in investigational activity was the spilling of the drug onto the black market a half dozen years ago. A few professors at Harvard had taken LSD and were so overwhelmed by the experience that they proclaimed it as a cure for everyone's psychological problems. Indeed, even our world problems could be solved if only everyone turned on. This seductive message was widely transmitted via the news media. Many were anxious to achieve instant Nirvana via psychedelics, a word presumed to mean "mind manifesting." Large numbers of people have tried LSD during the past few years. In general, they are young middle- or upper-class persons.

During the past two years "hip" colonies based upon "acid" and "pot" use have evolved in a number of our large cities. In contrast to the majority of LSD imbibers who have tried the drug once or a very few times, the acidhead has made it a central theme of his existence. Perhaps he has dropped out, left school or work, and is preoccupied with obtaining, using and talking about psychedelics. Other regular users are able to keep functioning while spending LSD weekends at home or in Hippyland.

During the past year a number of developments have occurred which reflect the swirling countercurrents of the LSD scene. Certainly, when new users are encountered, they are often of high school, even junior high school age. They often openly state that their use of "acid" is for a "blast." Occasionally, the contents of the capsule or the sugar cube are "mainlined." They appear to be trying to avoid their customary "low," consisting of boredom and frustration, as much as seeking a "high." Many seem emotionally deprived, have difficulty relating, and are unable to enjoy the sober state. On the other hand an impression exists that less LSD is being used today than a year ago. Not only are users stopping because of bad trips or prolonged adverse reactions, but a movement away from LSD by some of its more devout adherents is discernible. These few are slowly coming to realize the illusory nature of most chemical Enlightenments. A number have gone over to meditation and similar non-drug techniques which they are finding more valuable and sustaining.

Unfortunately, another trend is developing in the residual group of "acid" swallowers. Some are trying a wide variety of chemicals, apparently in the search for novel "highs." Deliriants like Asthmador and Jimson weed, intoxicants like airplane glue and nutmeg, stimulants and sedatives, even the strong narcotics, are being sampled. This multiple chemical consumption is unfortunate because of the known and unknown hazards. Furthermore, it exemplifies the thoughtless, hedonistic pursuit of a bedrugged dissociation.

Some of the pharmacology of LSD is unusual. It is active in an amount which is almost invisible, 25 micrograms, 1/40,000th of a gram. The average dose is 100 mcg, and up to 10,000 mcg has been taken with recovery. The lethal dose for man may be about 15,000 mcg. Tolerance occurs within days and is lost just as rapidly. No withdrawal symptoms are evident. It has a central sympathetic effect, dilating and partially paralyzing the iris, increasing body temperature and increasing blood pressure and blood sugar slightly.

It is the psychological effects, which can last 6–12 hours following an average dose, that are most remarkable. The strange changes in time-space perception are astounding. The reversion from rational and logical thought to a fantastic reverie sort of mentation, is attractive to those who seek freedom from problems. States varying from pleasure to ecstasy are often seen; these are the good "trips" sought after by those unable to enjoy "the sober certainty of waking bliss." Less frequent are the "bum trips" or "freakouts" which are horrendous encounters with madness. What is relished by some and intensely disliked by others is the loss of ego integrity. It may be partial, with peculiar changes in body image, or total with depersonalization and a complete dissolution of ego intactness. This can be called "ego death" and has certain correlates with the spontaneously-occurring transcendental state. Alternatively, it can be an experience of insanity (the older name was model psychosis) and be accompanied by terror and panic.

Much research has been done with LSD; much remains undone. Its therapeutic potential has been studied, but it still remains unestablished and investigational.

The possible adverse effects of one or more LSD exposures are many. Under research conditions these can be prevented or minimized. It has been during the past five years of its other-than-medical use that the complications have been seen in growing numbers. During the course of LSD activity panic or paranoid reactions are possible. These can lead to injury or death. After recovery from the acute effects, flashbacks, or transient recurrences of LSD-like sensations have occurred in some people. The cause of these recrudescences is obscure: LSD is not retained in the organism, and a psychological hypothesis is more attractive than a pharmacological one. The prolonged untoward reactions consist of anxiety states and psychotic breaks. Both are amenable to treatment, with the exception of an occasional psychotic who slips into a chronic schizophrenia. The young person whose attitude toward his life and value system changes so markedly that he drops out is also a casualty—a victim of the delusion that the way to live this life is to leave it. The incidence of these complications is undetermined. The great majority of them remain unreported in the literature, and the actual incidence of LSD taking is quite unknown.

The significance of the chromosomal malformations that have been found remains obscure. That structural alterations of genetic material reflect functional changes in protein manufacture is certainly likely. We do not know today what they represent in the adult exposed to moderate or large amounts of LSD, nor in the offspring of acidhead mothers who also exhibit similar disruptions of chromosomal pattern. No clinical disease is apparent, but it may require time or an environmental stressor to make the genetic defect manifest.

Likewise, the question of brain damage in acidheads cannot be answered definitely at our present level of information. Results of some preliminary work in our laboratory indicate that certain changes in organic brain cell functioning occur, but this is preliminary and further study is necessary.

Just what the future of LSD will be is uncertain. A fair possibility is that the crest of enthusiasm has passed, and acid use may go into a decline in the coming years. Some will continue its use, no doubt. Other, similar drugs might come forth. Agents like LSD, STP (2,5-dimethoxy-4-methyl-amphetamine), and DMT (dimethyltryptamine) are so powerful that it is not likely that they will remain popular potions indefinitely.

SPEED

During the past year methamphetamine (methedrine, "speed," "crystal") has risen to surprising prominence in the hierarchy of abused drugs. The misuse of amphetamines is hardly new. The Japanese post-World War II experience with their epidemic of stimulant overuse is well known. An occasional truck driver will keep driving on pills which enhance alertness but reduce judgment. A few women will enjoy the lift of their weight-reducing medication and proceed to escalate the dosage. The fatigued housewife may find sufficient relief in amphetamines that she will become dependent upon them.

The picture changed about a year ago. The hippies discovered the "pep pill." At first, it was used to enhance and intensify the LSD "high." Soon, however, the word spread that if sufficient "speed" were taken, it was a charge in its own right. "Speed" was so great that a few gave up the "acid" to concentrate their drug-taking careers on meth. They ate the "jolly beans" by the handful. In the natural history of drug abuse a law seems to hold which may be expressed as: "Stronger and more rapidly-acting drugs tend to drive out weaker and slower-acting ones." The mode of use of speed was soon converted to sniffing a concentrated liquid, and then to its intravenous injection. The "mainlining" of "speed" probably will remain the ultimate until some enterprising hippie discovers the spinal route. At any rate mainlining speed apparently produces as orgiastic a state as cocaine. "Methheads" and "speedfreaks" now inhabit East Village, Haight-Ashbury and Venice West, with a few of the old-fashioned hippies horrified with these bedazed, sometimes maniacal, often paranoidal creatures. Paranoid psychoses and organic syndromes are seen regularly in heavy "speedfreaks" who may inject 500 to 1000 mg at a shot. This is an impressive dose indeed to the physician who prescribes 10 mg of methedrine by mouth.

It is used by ineffectual couples to enhance the sexual interval. Orgasm is delayed or may not ensue. "Balling" speed is another way by which it is absorbed, via the genital mucosa.

Nor is it surprising that this euphoriant drug (and also some cocaine which is beginning to reappear on the American black market) has been the latest to arrive on the scene. The mindless search for pleasure requires ever stronger means to achieve some ultimate chemical joy. The next act will consist of a more precise method of achieving this end. It is not far off. The technology has been worked out. It will be a matter of implanting electrodes in the pleasure centers of the midbrain. Then, by pressing one of the buttons, we can have the choice of sexual ecstasy, the satisfaction of food satiation, or the pleasure of being relieved of a raging thirst. And if these specific pleasures are insufficient, we will have still another button which simply gives us an indescribable, transcendent glow.

The spectacle of drug abuse astonishes those physicians and pharmacologists who are well aware of the hazards of these agents. In some instances the potential dangers are hardly known at this time. The reward-danger ratio is too high a price to pay. It seems inevitable that the misuse will recede eventually, but not before many valuable people have been psychologically, physically or socially impaired.

33 | RECENT RESEARCH ON LSD, MARIJUANA, AND OTHER DANGEROUS DRUGS

Stanley F. Yolles

There has been considerable progress in elucidating the nature and extent of the LSD problem. Intensive research efforts have enabled us to obtain a better understanding of the short- and long-term implications of LSD use, particularly in regard to its psychologic and biologic effects.

The scope of research either funded by the NIMH, or utilizing LSD from the NIMH supplies, covers a wide range of activity from surveys and epidemiologic studies through basic biochemical and experimental psychopharmacologic research. Currently the NIMH is supporting a total of 58 studies and will have expended over $3.4 million in FY 1968 for research in the area of LSD and related hallucinogenic agents. This represents an increase of 20 projects and $1.7 million over the level of support in FY 1966.

During early 1967 there was considerable concern regarding the extent of the LSD problem in the United States, particularly in light of reports that the number of users was increasing at a very rapid rate. NIMH is continuing to support several studies designed to measure the extent and trends of LSD and other hallucinogenic use. Preliminary findings from these studies indicate that we have witnessed in the past year a significant decline in LSD use in the United States.

I am sure that there are a number of factors associated with this decline. Our evidence would indicate that a key factor in explaining this decline has been the availability of factual scientific information based on research findings which suggest that LSD can cause severe psychotic reactions and may cause chromosomal changes not only in the cells of the user but also, for women, in their children.

CONFERENCE ON TOXIC EFFECTS OF LSD

Five months ago, the NIMH convened a meeting of the country's leading research experts to evaluate the information then available regarding the toxic effects of LSD. I would like to discuss briefly some of the highlights of this conference.

The discussion indicated that with several exceptions the evidence for *persisting* psychologic damage from chronic LSD administration is minimal. One exception is the observation that chronic users (when not on LSD) showed uniformly lower thresholds to auditory stimuli. This suggests the possibility that sensory overload may be a problem for the chronic LSD user even when he is not ingesting this drug.

The above selection was originally presented as a Statement before the Subcommittee on Juvenile Delinquency of the Committee on the Judiciary, U.S. Senate, March 1968, and is reprinted by permission of the author.

In other words, these persons are more sensitive to sounds and might have difficulty in discriminating between low and high intensity sounds.

Several workers have described the phenomenon of recurring hallucinogenic experience without recurrent ingestion of the drug. In some instances users of LSD without taking the drug have recurrent paranoid episodes, at times accompanied by vivid hallucinations. The significance and extent of these reactions are not as yet fully known.

Though a continuing problem, admissions to psychiatric units of persons with so-called "bad trips" are *declining*. Dr. William Frosch, who reported in 1966 that there was a rapidly rising rate of such admissions to Bellevue Hospital in New York City, now informs us that the admission rate for such cases at his hospital has declined.

Some investigators in the past year had expressed concern about possible outbreaks of new forms of acute and/or chronic organic psychoses related to hallucinogenic drug use. The consensus of those present at the meeting was that there is not sufficient evidence to justify this concern. However, modification of the usual therapy for acute hallucinogen-caused psychoses is indicated. The results in terms of terminating the acute psychotic reactions are in most instances good.

CHROMOSOME DAMAGE

Considerable public attention has recently been focused on the relationship between LSD and chromosome damage. These reports are particularly alarming because of the association of chromosomal damage with leukemia-type syndromes and birth defects. The types of chromosomal changes noted in some LSD users have also been observed in survivors of the Hiroshima atomic blast and other persons exposed to high doses of ionizing radiation, all of whom have an increased likelihood of developing leukemia-type syndromes.

The initial report of the chromosome damage possible attributable to LSD by Dr. Maimon Cohen of the University of Buffalo School of Medicine sparked a flurry of research activity around the effects of hallucinogenic drugs on chromosomes *in vivo* and *in vitro* and upon the offspring of exposed human and animal subjects.

The NIMH is currently supplying LSD to 20 investigators engaged in research of this type. The initial report of Cohen referred to the production of chromosomal abnormalities in human white blood cells (lymphocytes) cultured with LSD. These changes were not observed when LSD was not present in the medium (although similar changes have not been observed when such cultures have been made with thorazine, aspirin and caffeine).

Dr. Cohen's findings were confirmed nearly immediately by Drs. Irwin and Egozcue of the University of Oregon School of Medicine. They additionally reported chromosomal abnormalities in the circulating lymphocytes of several "hippies" in the Portland area. Dr. Herman Lisco of Harvard University has reported identical changes in persons who had been exposed to psilocybin, another hallucinogen.

Similar human *in vivo* reports about LSD were made by Drs. Cohen, Frosch and Hirshhorn. Their findings, however, were not confirmed by several investigators at the University of California, by Dr. David Hungerford of the Cancer Research Institute in Philadelphia or by Dr. Albert Kurland's group at Spring Grove State

Hospital. In the several studies where chromosomes were examined before and after LSD administration in man, the Irwin and Cohen findings could not be replicated.

If LSD does in fact cause chromosomal abnormalities in man, the significance can only be learned over time. Similar changes occur after certain viral illnesses; but in these conditions the effects are short-term and are not associated with serious pathological consequences. Long lasting chromosomal damage of this type has, however, been reported in persons exposed to atomic radiation and other individuals considered highly vulnerable to leukemia. In considering the leukemia-causing potential of LSD we must consider that longitudinal studies in identified individuals are mandatory to determine whether such changes are long-term and a prelude to leukemia. Short-term chromosomal changes may not have any pathological significance.

BIRTH DEFECTS

Observations of chromosomal abnormalities also led to several studies to determine the effects of LSD on offspring in several animal species. In the mouse and the hamster, when LSD was administered early in pregnancy, there was a significant increase in the number of spontaneous abortions and birth defects. Contradictory reports have appeared about such findings in the rat. Experts in this field tell us that it is impossible to generalize from one species to another with regard to drug effects upon the fetus. Thalidomide, for example, failed in several animal studies to present birth defects across species lines although it did produce birth defects in man.

There have been a number of newspaper articles which have attempted to relate LSD to reported birth defects. One report in the *New York Times* of February 10 quotes Dr. William Frosch of New York University describing one child with retarded mental development. This investigator pointed out that there was no direct evidence that the drug was to blame. There has been one report from the University of Iowa which was reported in *Lancet* and purported to show that an offspring who had been exposed to the drug during the mother's 45th day of pregnancy showed findings similar to that of Thalidomide exposed infants. Dr. Hirshhorn has reported chromosomal breaks in 50 per cent of infants exposed to LSD *in utero*. There have been two reports of encephalocele, an unusual defect in which the brain herniated through an incompletely fused skull in fetuses who had been exposed to LSD early in the pregnancy and then were spontaneously aborted.

Evidence that hallucinogenic drugs can cause birth defects in exposed humans is at best presumptive at this time. Reports from animal studies and *in utero* chromosomal investigations suggest a possible link between some of the birth defects reported and maternal ingestion of LSD. These investigators themselves would be the first to argue that their findings are not definitive and that a reasoned and deliberate response is indicated.

At this time our information about the biologic hazards of LSD and other hallucinogenic drugs must be considered incomplete. However, in light of the preliminary findings, one should add to the usual warnings about LSD use particular emphasis on the possible hazards for women in the childbearing ages.

Additionally, the advisory committee was strongly supportive of continuing, refining and integrating research into the mechanism of action and the biological and psychological effects of LSD, because of its abuse, its unique nature, and its possible therapeutic potential.

SURVEYS OF LSD USE IN COLLEGES

I would now like to turn to a discussion of findings from several surveys of LSD use in college populations. Five percent of the college students polled admitted to using LSD with a range among individual colleges of 2–9 per cent. LSD users are much more likely to have also used marijuana as well as other drugs such as amphetamine and barbiturates. Conversely, only a small percentage of those who have used marijuana also use LSD. LSD users tended to be "experimenters" with only 30 per cent of the sample "serious" LSD users.

We have now some data about the characteristics of the student drug user. The academic standing of the occasional user was better than average, while the heavily involved drug users had lower than average scholastic grades. There is a relatively small group, perhaps 3–4 per cent of student drug users, for whom taking drugs is no longer a question of "just being in," but whose problem of drug abuse represents a complicated and severe psychiatric problem. There is a decline in the number of admissions to college health services of students with psychotic reactions secondary to LSD use paralleling the decrease at Bellevue noted earlier.

ONGOING RESEARCH

Research continues on the possible therapeutic usefulness of LSD particularly in the treatment of alcoholism and psychoneurosis. We currently have 12 studies and are spending this year over $1 million in this area.

I have already indicated what research results there are and I would now like to describe briefly some of the other research going on in this area and what we are hoping to find out.

There are currently a total of 93 studies being conducted which are using LSD supplied by this Institute. All requests for this drug are reviewed by a joint FDA-NIMH committee to establish the soundness of research designed and to guarantee that all necessary precautions are observed. A large number of these studies are devoted to elucidating the mechanism of action of LSD. This agent has been of great interest to neuropharmacologists and others studying the central nervous system because its actions appear to be related to the levels of serotonin and perhaps to catecholamine levels in the brain (serotonin and catecholamines are naturally occurring substances which appear to play a key role in the biochemical transactions of the brain).

Sixty per cent of studies are in animals, 16 per cent in humans and 24 per cent in isolated tissues. Most of the animal and tissue culture studies are devoted to elucidating the mechanisms of action of LSD. Recent reports by Dr. George Agahanjian and Dr. Daniel Freedman suggest that LSD may exert subtle chemical and/or electrical effects on the very area of the midbrain which is believed responsible for phase I R.E.M. sleep. This is particularly intriguing in view of reports of temporary psychosis in individuals who are specifically deprived of this type of sleep. Additionally, many psychotropic drugs specifically inhibit this phase of the sleep cycle.

Other investigators are studying the metabolism of hallucinogenic drugs. Research is also proceeding on the effects of LSD upon brain protein metabolism and nucleic acid synthesis in order to better understand the biochemical basis of learning and memory. These studies are all correlated with behavioral and learning studies in various animal species. It is clear that LSD is an extremely valuable research tool which has opened up broad vistas for basic research that would be impossible to develop without its ready availability to the research community.

Human studies are designed to test the therapeutic potential of LSD in alcoholism, psychoneurosis and other treatment-resistant psychiatric conditions. Additionally, LSD has some behavioral and subjective effects in man which cannot be derived from animal studies. As a tool to study perception, sensory integration and basic emotional mechanisms, LSD and other hallucinogenic drugs should continue to be available for human pharmacological studies.

MARIJUANA

I shall now turn to the subject of marijuana. The official name of the drug is cannabis. Basic research to uncover knowledge about the pharmacology and physiological activity of cannabis has been severely hampered by the lack of availability of adequate legitimate sources of a standardized natural product. The little research that has been done has utilized marijuana seized by the Federal Bureau of Narcotics and supplied to researchers. Unfortunately this material was relatively old and had lost much of its original potency.

PROBLEMS OF RESEARCH

A key problem in the field of research on cannabis is the lack of a standard product. For results of scientific investigation to be reproducible, researchers must have available agents whose chemical constituents and potency are identical. There is tremendous variability in black market cannabis. Seized materials may be adulterated with other plant or chemical materials, or may be mixtures of different varieties of cannabis. We know that the potency of cannabis varies according to its age and where it is grown. Until recently the only solution to this problem appears to be the development of a special facility for growing a standardized variety of cannabis. While this project still has high priority to facilitate scientific studies of natural cannabis the recent synthesis of a number of tetrahydrocannabinols, the chemically active constituents of cannabis, shows great promise in expediting research in the field.

The synthesis of the tetrahydrocannabinols and their increasing availability for research purposes now makes it possible for us finally to perform the vitally needed pharmacologic, biochemical, genetic, and behavioral research necessary to answer our questions about the mode of action and toxicity of cannabis. While there have been reports over the year from foreign countries about irreversible psychoses associated with marijuana use, in recent years responsible scientists in this and other countries have raised considerable question about the validity of these conclusions. For instance, many of these foreign studies were done on chronic institutionalized persons. We are well aware from our own research on institutionalized schizophrenics that after several years it is extremely difficult, if not impossible, to distinguish between the effects of the disease and the effects of institutionalization. Additionally, these foreign studies have dealt with populations with chronic physical diseases, malnutrition, etc., which make it extremely difficult to delineate which symptoms are due to chronic marijuana use and which are due to other factors.

PROPOSED RESEARCH

With the impending availability of adequate supplies of synthetic tetrahydrocannabinols we have developed and have given high priority to an intensive systematic plan of research to elucidate a number of basic facts. These studies will range from the investigation of long-range toxicity in animals through biochemical research and carefully controlled human studies. Additionally, we will expand our current program of social and psychological investigations of marijuana users. We have already begun negotiations to perform studies in these foreign countries where the "marijuana psychosis syndrome" has been described.

We estimate that studies of marijuana will cost approximately $5.25 million over the next three years. Though major gaps in our knowledge do exist, data from ongoing and past research have already given us some answers.

SURVEYS OF MARIJUANA USE IN HIGH SCHOOLS AND COLLEGES

Surveys of high school and college drug use indicate that approximately 20 per cent of the college students questioned reported some experience with marijuana. It is estimated that about two million high school and college students have had some experience with marijuana. Generally more men students reported involvement. Of those who reported having ever used marijuana, 65 per cent had used it less than ten times with "once or twice" the commonest response. It is of great interest that *fully 50 per cent of those who have tried marijuana experienced no effects.* This finding may be a function of at least four factors, (1) the agent may not have been potent, (2) frequently effects are seen only after repeated use, (3) the expectation of the user has a significant effect on what he experiences, (4) the social setting in which use takes place has an effect on the response.

Under NIMH contract support a survey instrument for more accurately assessing the prevalence of drug abuse in high school and college populations has been developed. On the basis of successful pilot studies with this instrument a grant proposal for a five-year study is pending review by the National Advisory Mental Health Council at its next meeting.

Our evidence would indicate that in contrast to the decreasing use of LSD, use of marijuana has been increasing.

The United Nations estimates that in 1950 there were 200 million users of marijuana in the world, mainly in India and in North Africa. In the United States, we are not quite sure of the exact extent of the problem. Estimates as high as 20 million have been made, but it is much more likely that in the neighborhood of 4 to 5 million persons have used it at least once.

EFFECTS OF CANNABIS

Little can be added to previous reports on the toxicity of marijuana. It is considered to be a mild hallucinogen, taken by the usual route of smoking, occasionally by ingestion. It may induce a mild euphoria and lead to heightened suggestibility and a faulty perception, really an exaggerated notion of thinking more clearly, profoundly and creatively. In addition, it is known to cause reddening of the membranes of the eyes, rapid heartbeat, muscular incoordination, unsteadiness, drowsiness, and distortion of time and space perception.

In acute intoxication, especially when ingested, it may also produce visual hallucinations, pronounced anxiety, paranoid reactions and transient psychoses lasting 4 to 6 hours. It generally tends to lessen inhibitions and creates for the user a false reality based on his wants, his motivations, or the set. In this respect it is similar to LSD but its effects are not as potent.

The muscular incoordination and the distortion of space and time perception commonly associated with marijuana use are potentially hazardous since the drug adversely affects one's ability to drive an automobile or perform other skilled tasks.

We still do not know enough about the long-term effects of marijuana use. As in the case of tobacco, it is possible that there are serious consequences of chronic use which will only become apparent through careful longitudinal studies.

One needs to be particularly concerned about the potential effect of a reality distorting agent on the future psychological development of the adolescent user. We know that normal adolescence is a time of great psychological turmoil. Patterns of coping with reality developed during the teenage period are significant in determining adult behavior. Persistent use of an agent which serves to ward off reality during this critical development period is likely to compromise seriously the future ability of the individual to make an adequate adjustment to a complex society.

While we have no data to indicate that marijuana can affect chromosomes, this possibility is being investigated.

PREVENTION AND EDUCATION

Prevention and education efforts in the area of hallucinogenic agents have a high priority for the NIMH. Efforts in this and other areas related to research are coordinated with the FDA through a mechanism by which the Chief of the FDA's Division of Drug Studies and Statistics has a joint appointment in the NIMH Center for Studies of Narcotic and Drug Abuse.

I would like to point out that prevention and education efforts aimed at the student population demand extremely careful preparation and implementation. Even high school students are extremely sophisticated about drugs. We are constantly impressed at speaking appearances before high school and college audiences about:

1. The extent of accurate knowledge mixed with misinformation about all drugs, not just LSD and marijuana, but barbiturates, amphetamines, etc; and

2. The suspicion with which students approach information supplied by "official sources."

"Scare" techniques are not only ineffectual, but are even detrimental to conveying needed information about the hazards of drug abuse. With the present incidence of marijuana use, many students have either experienced or observed first-hand the effects of this drug. They know that psychoses or other grave consequences are not an inevitable concomitant of smoking one marijuana cigarette.

It is clear that to be effective, a preventive educational effort must be carefully tailored to specific population groups and must be based on the best educational and scientific footing. The decrease in LSD use is, at least in part, I would suggest, a function of the degree to which users *will* respond to scientific evidence of potential danger.

Let me give you one example of how we have implemented this approach. In September 1966, the National Association of Student Personnel Administrators joined with FDA, NIMH and the Treasury Department in planning a program to provide student personnel and other college administrators with up-to-date, accurate information which would help them understand and cope with student drug use. Subsequently, FDA funded a contract to implement these plans. Under the direction of Dr. Helen H. Nowlis, Professor of Psychology and former Dean of Students at the University of Rochester, the National Association of Student Personnel Administrators' Drug Education Project was developed. In February and March 1967, over 1,400 persons participated in seven regional conferences for the purpose of acquiring and exchanging information about the problems of drug abuse on the campus.

The continuing demand for consulting services for professional groups and colleges planning drug education programs led to a continuation of the project on a part-time basis.

The NIMH is now developing a variety of materials as part of its education efforts. Films for television as well as small groups, film strips, pamphlets, etc., are being prepared. We have consulted with leading experts in the communications industry as well as educators so that our materials will be instructive, effective and scientifically sound.

ALIENATION

I think that it is critical to point out that in trying to understand scientifically the problem of drug abuse, one must look beyond the specific problems of such agents as LSD, marijuana, amphetamines and barbiturates to some of the underlying causes of widespread drug use and abuse. We live in a drug-oriented culture. From aspirin to sleeping pills, from tranquilizers to "the pill," Americans, of all ages, are ingesting drugs in greater variety and greater numbers than ever before. I think that if we are to get to the root of this problem of drug abuse, we must be prepared to investigate and identify the underlying problems which lead people to choose to distort or ward off reality with drugs.

One way of conceptualizing the problem is to view drug abuse in the student population in the broader context of the nature and extent of "casualties" of the educational system. Through our interest in school and college mental health, suicide prevention, and alcoholism, we have become increasingly aware that a fair percentage of our brightest and most competent youth are not "succeeding" in their encounter with the higher educational system.

Behavioral scientists use the term "alienation" in describing the cross-generational disease epitomized by the youth-coined term "don't trust anyone over 30." Alienation has been characterized as: "rebellion without a cause . . . rejection without a program . . . a refusal of what is without a vision of what should be."

Lapses in communication between generations were noted by Greek philosophers over 2,000 years ago, and more recently were manifested in American society by the so-called "lost generation" of the 1920's and the "silent generation" of the 1950's. However, the current problem of alienation in the United States is wider, deeper, and more diffuse than at any previous time in our history. It affects the rich and the poor, the college student and the school dropout, the urban and the rural youngster. The number of persons, both young and old, beset by alienation is far greater than that ever seen in any previous generation.

Because many alienated youngsters question the relevance of major societal values and institutions, they find themselves unable to learn from the various opportunities that presently are available to them. As Freedman and Brotman point out . . . "To ask one of the youngsters, as one of the authors did, 'Where's the action?' elicits a scornful answer: 'There's only action if you have a high.' The implication is clear; what is meaningful is the subjective state. If an undrugged state is defective, myopic, why not alter perception through drugs and create a new 'reality'? Some youngsters who feel helpless to accommodate to or change an unacceptable world, consciously choose to alter their own. . . . Their most frequent statement is that life is a 'drag.' It lacks meaning for there is no engagement; the future is unknown but certainly horrible. Since you cannot alter the world or determine the direction in which it will go, you must alter your state of consciousness and perception, that is, see the world and experience the world through 'a high.' Any alteration is acceptable, and thus, the barbiturate user can describe to you the joys of a 'drowsy high' and the amphetamine user will talk about the 'high' he gets on benzedrine—and likewise for the LSD, marijuana, and heroin abuser. All that is important is in one's subjective state. Perceptions and beliefs of the square world or the non-drug world are superficial, distorted, meaningless. . . ." This rejection of many goals of the society, the unwillingness to model themselves on any stable adult leaders and the inability to acquire the necessary attitudes and skills for responsible adult behavior, make urgent the development of new and innovative approaches to bridge the intergenerational gap.

If this is not done, there are serious dangers that large proportions of current and future generations will reach adulthood embittered towards the larger society, unequipped to take on parental, vocational and other citizen roles, and involved in some form of socially deviant behavior.

I would propose that if we are ever to solve the problem of drug abuse, it is critical for us to focus on and try to solve the root causes of alienation.

RECOMMENDED READINGS

BACKGROUND INFORMATION

Berg, D. "Studies and surveys of drug abuse." Unpublished charts. U.S. Department of Justice, Division of Drug Studies and Statistics, Arlington, Va., 1968.

Caruanta, S. " 'Drugs'—A Social, Medical or Educational Problem?," *The Health Education Journal*, Volume 25, November 1966, pp. 184–91.

Fort, J. "Comparison Chart of Major Substances Used for Mind-Alteration," Rochester: NASPA Drug Education Project, 1966.

Goldstein, R. *1 in 7: Drugs on the Campus*, New York. Walker, 1966.

Hollander, Charles (ed.). *Background Papers on Student Drug Involvement*, Washington, D.C.: United States National Student Association, 1967, p. 162.

"LSD, STP, and Marijuana." Reprint of Special Section from *American Journal of Psychiatry*, 125: 341–390, September 1968.

Masters, R. E. L. and Houston, Jean. *The Varieties of Psychedelic Experience*, New York: Holt, Rinehart & Winston, 1966, p. 326.

Metzner, R. "Pharmacology of Psychedelic Drugs, I: Chemical and Biochemical Aspects," *Psychedelic Review, 1* (1963), 69–115.
Nahum, L. H. "Psychedelic Drugs," *Connecticut Medicine,* 30 (March 1966), 162–65.
Simmons, J. L. and Winograd, B. *It's Happening,* Santa Barbara: Marc/Laird Press, 1966.

UNIT NINE | DISCUSSION QUESTIONS

30 | OURS IS THE ADDICTED SOCIETY

Discuss your views on the author's statement, "those who are addicted by not being addicted."

What are your views concerning the dangers in experimenting with drugs on an individual basis?

31 | MARIJUANA AND BEHAVIOR: THE UNFILLED GAPS

Based on the information stated in this article, discuss whether a causal link exists between opiates and marijuana.

What are your views concerning the argument that marijuana should be legal to individuals over 18 years of age?

32 | POT, ACID, AND SPEED

Are we witnessing a drug abuse explosion in this decade? Discuss.

Discuss the risks in the misuse of narcotics by people of college age.

33 | RECENT RESEARCH ON LSD, MARIJUANA, AND OTHER DANGEROUS DRUGS

Discuss the relationship between LSD and chromosome damage.

List and discuss some of the ongoing research on dangerous drugs.

UNIT TEN
RESOURCES FOR GROWTH
AND BEHAVIOR MODIFICATION

The 1960's witnessed a tremendous upsurge of individual and group-type activities directed toward the improvement of human relationships. Much of this voluntary activity was an attempt to meet the problems of everyday living. Personal growth and change not only enhances life's benefits, but it serves a preventative role as well. Prevention of mental illness is the cornerstone of mental hygiene. Historically, it was believed that demons and evil spirits were responsible for all mental disorders. Therefore, certain individuals believed to be endowed with mystical powers were encouraged to offer incantations and administer special potions to cure the mentally ill. For years efforts were devoted to exorcising witches and evil spirits from the mentally ill. As late as the 19th century, the abnormal behavior of mental patients was thought to be exhibited voluntarily. Therefore such patients were subjected to harassment and physical punishment designed to show them the error of their ways.

Today, behavioral scientists are involved not only in the search for the environmental and organic causes of mental illness but also in the application of preventative procedures. Psychotherapy, often referred to as "talk therapy," is concerned with psychological treatments used to help mentally distressed patients. Among the chief approaches are: psychoanalytic therapy, behavior therapy, family therapy, hypnotherapy, ego therapy, and client-centered therapy. Among the techniques used by behavioral scientists are: group therapy, play therapy, psychodrama, and hypnosis.

The roots of sensitivity training began about 20 years ago. The late 1960's saw a great momentum in this activity and many *institutes* were created to provide and service this demand formally. Participants in the group sessions are not psychotherapy patients, but "normal" people who wish to attain a greater degree of self-knowledge with an eye toward improving their ability to relate meaningfully to others. To clarify much of the misunderstanding of the group experience that has resulted from a lack of understanding about its organization, objectives, and techniques, James C. Coleman discusses two main kinds of groups: (1) sensitivity-training, and (2) encounter. *Sensitivity and Encounter Groups* outlines group formats, goals, and the group process. Advocates of sensitivity and encounter groups feel that it is valuable for the individual to know how others see and react to him. This requires critics of the groups to believe that it is harmful to expose oneself so openly. Other controversies exist concerning the training and qualifications of the "facilitators" of the groups. Martin Lakin in *Some Ethical Issues in Sensitivity Training* calls for a clear statement of standards of training, trainer preparation, and the publication of a code of ethics. Lakin outlines some of the ethical issues and evaluations in this article.

Man has attempted to control his behavior since the beginning of time. More recently, some behavioral scientists have begun to relate human behavior to other natural phenomena; that is, to view human behavior as being subject to natural laws. The extension of behavioral studies to lower animals has created a science of comparative psychology. Jack Michael and Lee Meyerson in *A Behavioral Approach to Human Control* present a concise summary of the important principles of a behavioral system.

Finally, Carl R. Rogers and B. F. Skinner debate *Some Issues Concerning the Control of Human Behavior.* The questions of ethics involved in the exercise of behavioral control bring up important issues that are aired in this exchange between Rogers and Skinner.

---

34 | RESOURCES FOR PERSONAL GROWTH AND CHANGE

James C. Coleman

INTENSIVE GROUP EXPERIENCE

The last two decades have seen a great deal of experimentation in the use of groups to increase the awareness and effectiveness of essentially normal people and to find pathways to enriched and more meaningful human relationships and "ways of being." This potent new cultural phenomenon is referred to as the *intensive group experience.* Groups vary considerably in goals and methods: a particular group may focus on training in human relations skills, on resolving personal problems, on developing creative imagination, or on other goals and may have an existential, humanistic, psychoanalytic, or other theoretical orientation. Groups have functioned in universities, industries, churches, clinics, and resort settings, and participants have been students, business executives, delinquents, priests, dancers, educators, philosophers, police officers, youth leaders, married couples, and entire families.

Despite their differences, most such groups are small and relatively unstructured, with the group having considerable freedom in choosing its goals and direction, and

---

with a nondirective leader whose main responsibility is usually to facilitate the expression of thoughts and feelings. And central to all is the focus of the intensive experience of interacting with each other under conditions which differ from those in ordinary life in the degree to which honest exploration of feelings is encouraged. Unlike most therapy, they do not attempt to help their members come to terms with the past but focus on the "here and now," trying to get people to confront what they are feeling and doing at the moment and to try out new ways of feeling and communicating.

In the present section we shall review the nature and functioning of the common types of intensive experience groups and then examine briefly some of their apparent effects. The two main kinds of groups that have developed are (1) sensitivity-training groups (also called T-groups) and (2) encounter groups. "Workshops" and "training laboratories," in which additional resources and activities are built around the common intensive group experience, are also common.

SENSITIVITY TRAINING (T-GROUPS)

Sensitivity training is an outgrowth of a research effort begun shortly after World War II by Kurt Lewin and his colleagues. They were concerned about the dangers of autocratic leadership and hoped, through research on group processes, both to identify the skills needed for effective democratic group functioning and to learn how these skills could be taught. The impetus of the original work led to the establishment of the National Training Laboratories at Bethel, Maine, associated with the National Education Association and now titled the NTL Institute for Applied Behavioral Science. The Institute and its affiliates continue to combine research aimed at establishing basic principles with practical help to various group through intensive group experience. These "training groups" have been nicknamed "T-groups." Such training has been directed especially toward groups of professionals concerned with helping people in various ways, such as clergymen, youth leaders, nurses, psychologists, teachers, and social workers.

"Labs" are held each year for various groups of professionals. Here lectures, problem-solving exercises, and other activities are added to the basic T-group experience. A main thrust has been with business groups, especially executives, in whom attempts are made to develop human relations skills and an awareness of the need for them. One popular annual session is a "Presidents' Conference" for presidents of businesses. Recently there has been increased emphasis on training for community leaders.

There continues to be considerable experimentation with both the format and the focus of T-groups. Training labs are now offered on organizational growth, relationships between (as well as within) groups, and "personal growth." A number of university institutes and other organizations also conduct T-groups for students. In some cases college courses in group dynamics are being taught as T-groups, meeting once or twice a week throughout the college term, reading case examples of human relations problems and other source materials as varied as existential theory and Golding's *Lord of the Flies*, and using their class time to analyze their interactions and discuss their reading and whatever else is of concern to them.

GROUP FORMAT AND GOALS. Sensitivity-training groups usually consist of 10 to 15 persons with one or two leaders called *trainers.** A group usually meets for a total time of 20 to 50 hours, either on consecutive days or spaced over a period as long as several weeks. Recently, two new approaches have been introduced: (1) the *marathon group*, which may meet for an entire weekend without breaking for sleep, and (2) a combination of spaced and massed approaches, in which the initial session may begin with a live-in weekend (often some distance away from home), continue with weekly meetings, and then conclude with a final live-in weekend.

The ultimate purpose of greater effectiveness in the participants' relations with others requires the achievement of several subgoals, including:

1. Increased awareness of what one is doing and how others are reacting to it, with an examination of the values and assumptions behind his actions.

2. Increased sensitivity to what others are thinking and feeling and to the subtle ways in which people communicate with each other by voice inflections, facial expressions, and bodily postures.

3. Increased awareness of how individuals affect groups and how groups affect individuals, of what behavior inhibits or facilitates group functioning, and of how subgroups form and conflict with each other.

4. Increased skill in identifying what is happening in a group and what is helping or interfering with openness.

---

* The NTL Institute and its affiliates have a well-worked-out procedure for training T-group leaders and issue certificates to those who have taken the training.

5. Increased competence in helping oneself and others achieve more effective interactions and in helping to make a group function more effectively in different kinds of situations.

Although these goals may be only partially achieved in the brief time a T-group meets, it is hoped that a direction will be established and new channels opened up for "learning how to learn." In essence, sensitivity-training groups are an institutionalized setting for social learning.

GROUP PROCESS. In the small face-to-face T-group there are usually no planned topics or activities, and the trainer does not take a leadership role. Often he simply specifies the amount of time the group will meet and points out that the major concern is to try to understand one's own behavior and that of other group members. The focus is kept on what is happening or being felt or communicated at the present moment, how the participants are portraying themselves to and affecting each other.

The lack of structuring often leads initially to feelings of frustration and expressions of hostility and discontent. Then, as the group interaction gets under way, the process of feedback becomes of crucial importance.

Given the unstructured group as the vehicle and the behavior emitted in the group as the principal topic of conversation, the success of the venture depends on the crucial process of feedback. Thus, the participants must be able to inform each other how their behavior is being seen and interpreted and to describe the kinds of feelings generated. This is the primary process by which the delegates 'learn.' They must receive articulate and meaningful feedback about their own behavior . . . and their efforts to interpret group processes. (Campbell & Dunnette, 1968, p. 76)

For the desired new learning to occur, it is considered necessary for a certain amount of tension or anxiety to be generated—particularly near the beginning (Campbell & Dunnette, 1968). This anxiety arises when the individual discovers that his previous role-bound methods of interacting are seriously deficient for functioning successfully in this new type of group. Anxiety may also be aroused when the individual's self-image and defense mechanisms come under scrutiny by the group. Such anxiety apparently helps to jar him loose from his preconceived notions and habitual ways of reacting so that the feedback can have maximal effect in helping him to learn new and more effective ways of perceiving and interacting. Unless such "unfreezing" occurs, the feedback he gets may be ineffectual (Schein, 1964).

To ensure effective feedback, there must be a climate of "psychological safety" (Bradford, Gibb, & Benne, 1964). Each member must feel that it is safe to drop his defenses, to express his feelings, and to try out new ways of interacting. Unless the group is nonevaluative and supportive concerning whatever is revealed, this feeling of safety cannot be achieved and group progress is likely to come to a halt.

The establishment of such a climate is largely the responsibility of the trainer. Although he makes it clear that the group members are responsible for setting their own goals and making their own analyses, he sets the pace by expressing his own feelings openly and honestly, by supporting the honest expression of feeling by others, and by serving as a helpful model in absorbing expressions of hostility and frustration without becoming defensive. He also gives—and encourages others to give—

descriptive rather than evaluative feedback: for example, not "You're being bossy" but "It made me uncomfortable when you said that."

The trainer may help the group to concentrate on either group-level or individual-level learnings. Thus he may raise questions about group factors, such as how the norms are being established or how decisions are being made, or he may call attention to feelings being expressed or perhaps being felt but expressed only in indirect and nonverbal ways. Through such a group experience, members can become much more aware of what they are really doing and how it is making other people feel, as well as what kinds of interactions are fostering or interfering with the functioning of the group. To a greater or lesser extent, depending on the trainer and the context, the experiences in awareness and in trying out new modes of interaction in the safety of the group may be supplemented by "cognitive handles" of theory and terminology.

ENCOUNTER GROUPS

Although some encounter groups are indistinguishable from sensitivity-training groups, others are considerably different in rationale, goals, and methods. Both are aimed at increased self-understanding, improved effectiveness in relating to others, and exposure to new channels of personal growth. In general, however, encounter groups put a greater emphasis on individual growth than on group interaction or group skills. Where the T-group member tends to direct his attention to how he is affecting others, the encounter-group member tends to focus on how others are affecting him and on the meaningfulness of an encounter between two human beings.

FORMAT AND GOALS. The basic encounter group is usually directed toward helping individual members gain insight into particular personal or social problems and learn to cope with them more effectively. For example, Stoller (1967) reports on the use of videotapes to help group members to see themselves in action:

In one group, a wife had spent considerable time complaining bitterly that her husband 'behaved like a child' with her. On video tape, I was able to show her that she used many of the mannerisms of a scolding mother with him—she would glare, shake her finger, and when pleased, pat his head. 'I couldn't believe it,' she said. 'It was worth a thousand words.' (p. 32)

There is even greater flexibility and experimentation in encounter groups than in T-groups, and a variety of formats have emerged. One interesting type is the workshop devoted to a particular topic or to personal or community problems. Of particuar interest here is the family workshop, in which three or four families remain together for several days—usually a weekend—with the goal of gaining insight into their interactions and relationships and finding new and more effective ways of family functioning.

A center at which leaders conduct many different kinds of encounter groups is the Esalen Institute at Big Sur, California. Body awareness, nonverbal communication, creative imagination, and numerous other topics have formed the focus of weekend or week-long workshops. The typical sequence of interaction in such workshops is summarized below.

Events in Encounter Groups

Rogers (1968) has delineated certain patterns which tend to occur in encounter groups. Although there is no clear-cut sequence in which one pattern ends and another begins, some patterns are likely to occur early and others later in the group process.

Milling around. As the leader makes it clear that the group is responsible for the direction of the group, there tends to be an initial period of confusion, frustration, awkward silences, and "cocktail-party talk"—polite surface interaction. Concern centers around such questions as "Who is responsible for us?" and "What is the purpose of the group?"

Resistance to personal expression or exploration. Initially it is the public self which members tend to present to each other. The individual is fearful and resistant to revealing his inner self and inner world. However, some members may reveal rather personal attitudes, which receive a very ambivalent reaction.

Expression of feelings. Despite doubts about the trustworthiness of the group and the risk of exposure, expression of feeling does begin to occur. Initially such feelings are likely to concern events outside the group, such as circumstances in a member's life situation which frustrate him; then gradually there is an expression of "here-and-now" feelings which often take the form of an attack upon the leader for insufficient guidance. Negative feelings usually predominate at first.

Expression and exploration of personally meaningful material. Criticism and anger having been expressed and accepted, a climate of trust begins to develop, and a member decides to gamble on revealing some deeper fact of himself to the group. Usually again, the information focuses on events outside the group.

The expression of immediate interpersonal feelings in the group. The next event is usually the expression of feelings being experienced toward each other. Such feelings may be negative or positive: "I like you less each time you speak out," or "I like the way you call a spade a spade." The attitudes underlying such feelings are explored in an increasing climate of trust.

The development of a healing capacity in the group. A fascinating aspect of the intensive group experience is the spontaneous way in which a number of group members are able to give help with a spirit of concern and caring that then helps other group members to reveal their true feelings.

Self-acceptance and the beginning of change. The individual comes to perceive himself as he really is and to feel that it is all right to be himself, with both strengths and weaknesses. As he learns to accept and be himself, he can drop his defenses, and he becomes more open to experience and to change.

The cracking of façades. One of the threads which overlaps and interweaves with what has gone before is the increasing impatience with defenses. The revealing of their deeper selves by some group members begins to make it clear that a more meaningful encounter is possible than one of surface interaction. Thus the group demands that each individual remove his mask, reveal his current feelings, and be himself—as the group strives toward the goal of a deeper and more basic encounter.

The individual receives feedback. In the interaction of group members, the individual receives a good deal of feedback concerning how he appears to others. In some instances the feedback is warm and positive; in others, it can be negative, as other members tell the individual what he does that annoys or irritates them. Through such feedback the individual may gain significant new insights.

Confrontation. The term confrontation is used when one member confronts another directly and "levels" with him. Such confrontation is a form of feedback and may be negative or positive in nature, but it is often an intensely emotional event. It is considered to be one of the most important and change-producing aspects of the intensive group experience.

The expression of positive feelings and closeness. As group sessions progress, there tend to be increasing feelings of warmth and group closeness; such feelings are considered to be of therapeutic value for the individual members.

Behavior changes in the group. Gestures and tonal inflections may change, the member may show greater ease and spontaneity in expressing his feelings, greater depth of feeling toward others, and so on. There may be increased understanding of oneself and others, new insight into problems, and the working out of more effective ways of relating to others.

A basic theme which runs through the group sessions is the concept of the basic encounter, in which members come into more direct and closer contact with each other than is customary in everyday life.

Another format for encounter groups is the marathon group which, as we have noted, usually stays together for a whole weekend without breaking for sleep. The events in a marathon encounter group that focused on the problem of racial discrimination are summarized below.

A Marathon Encounter Group*

The following excerpts are taken from the report of a marathon encounter group that focused on the problem of racial discrimination. The meeting was held at Esalen Institute on a July weekend in 1967 at a time when many of our cities were torn by riots in the ghetto areas. The group consisted of mixed-race, predominantly middle-class participants under the leadership of a Negro psychiatrist and a staff member (Leonard, 1968).

The first evening was devoted to preliminary exercises such as trying to communicate without words. Participants were told to expect that they would soon be relating on levels generally unknown in the outside community and were directed to try to be completely honest and open, relating on the level of present feelings, not theorizing or rationalizing, not escaping into past events or future worries—and forgetting about politeness.

The next morning the first confrontation occurred, not between black and white but among the blacks, with bitter name-calling and accusations. For a time there was

---

* Reprinted from *Education and Ecstasy* by George B. Leonard. Copyright © 1968 by George B. Leonard and used by permission of the publisher, Delacorte Press and the Sterling Lord Agency.

accusation but not encounter or change. Then a young Japanese-American named Larry, who had been cool and cynical, suddenly began to talk.

. . . *He had not realized how deeply he had felt racial prejudice or how much it had ruled his life. But now he knew he was a yellow man, a "Jap," and was ready to admit it. He declared himself to be a soul brother. With this declaration, all of his reserve collapsed and he "burst" into tears. The dikes were down then, and several of the Negroes poured out their hurt. "How many of you people can realize," a mother asked, "what it's like to send your children off to school and know they'll probably be called 'nigger' or spat on? And there's nothing, nothing you can do about it?"* (p. 204)

Soon after, Larry's Negro friend Cliff became locked in a bitter encounter with a beautiful young white schoolteacher named Pam:

She had told him she wanted his friendship, and he had responded scathingly, denouncing her "pitiful condescending" overtures. Now her eyes were filled with tears.

"Please. What can I do? I'm trying. Please help me." Cliff rocked his chair back and forth, looking across the room at her with contempt.

"No, baby, I'm not going to help you. I'm not going to take you off the hook. I want you to feel just what I feel. I want you to feel what I've felt for twenty-one years. Go on. Cry."

"Please," she begged. Tears streamed down her cheeks. Cliff kept rocking back and forth, his eyes fixed on hers. No one came to her aid. Somehow it seemed right that this interval in time should be fully realized by everyone in the room. The silence intensified, became in itself a powerful medium of communication. (pp. 204–205)

A number of different topics came up during the hours which followed but the main theme through dinner and later into the evening was the hurt and anger of the Negroes and their despair and absolute distrust of all whites. After darkness fell, the group was split into two sections for the night; and about this time an episode occurred that was to occupy one group for most of the night.

We had let a newcomer join the group at dinnertime. Chuck was in his early twenties, almost jet black, with a wary face and a body as taut as a steel spring. He began telling the group how he had successfully "transcended" the entire matter of race. He was utterly lacking in bad feelings against whites. He disliked the system, but not the man. He thought that racial incidents were extremely rare, especially in his own life. He never felt anger or hostility.

No one believed him. "It makes me nervous just to hear your voice," I told him. "That singsong way you have of talking, like there's no relation between what you're saying and what you feel. It puts me on edge. I feel like yelling at you." Someone suggested that I do so, and I did. Others followed me, cursing, yelling and cajoling as they expressed their feelings toward him and his professed attitude. But nothing moved Chuck. His face became a mask of stone. He had nothing but love for all mankind, the stone said. The group united in trying to get through to him. Black and white worked together. Cliff and Pam, the afternoon's bitterness forgotten, operated like a team. There was an unspoken accord among the eighteen people in the group that somehow no matter how long it took, we would get through to Chuck. . . . (p. 206)

At this point an incident occurred which struck the group as funny and the resulting laughter served to release the tension of group members and to take the pressure temporarily off Chuck. It may be pointed out here that if Chuck had asked the group to take the pressure off him, they would have; or he could simply have left the group which would have been considered an honest and appropriate response. However, Chuck seemed to be fascinated by the confrontation.

Another hour passed. At last, Chuck's voice was beginning to sound more natural. He was talking about his sexual prowess. "I could take any woman here," he said, his eyes flashing around the room.

"How would you take Pam?" I asked him.

"I'll tell you."

"Tell her."

He turned toward the teacher. "All right. First I'd rap you, then I'd take you."

"Rap?"

"Talk. You know, establish rapport. I'd rap you, then I'd take you."

Pam looked at him with scorn. "You'd never take me. I wouldn't let you touch me. Ever."

"I'd take you, all right, baby." A fury lay just beneath his words.

Voices broke out around the group as various women denied or affirmed his sexual attraction. The Negro house-wife leaned over toward him.

"You could never take me, and I'm going to tell you why." Something in her voice reduced us all to silence. "Because you're just a dirty little black nigger."

Chuck almost leaped from his chair. Clenching his fists on the armrests, he loosed his hidden fury in a savage and frightening tirade. Finally, he caught himself, looked around the room with dazed eyes and covered his face with his hands. He sat that way as members of the group comforted him. Then he looked up and smiled. His face was different.

A little later, after a surprisingly tender interchange, he said, "I want to thank all of you. I've learned more in the last two hours than in the last two years." (pp. 207–208)

The following morning—Sunday—the group took an unexpected turn in that the whites began revealing themselves and baring the most tragic and painful moments in their lives. After one particularly tragic revelation:

Almost everyone in the room was crying. We were unashamed of our tears. We were not Negroes or whites or Orientals. We were human beings joined in a very precious, fragile awareness of our common plight, of the waste and loss in every life, and of hope for something better. For many of us, that morning was transcendental, a space in life when ordinary objects seem to shimmer, when all faces are beautiful and time can be taken at the crest like a great onrushing wave. That was the way it was for me.

Noon came and passed, but we wouldn't leave. At one-thirty, the dining-room crew came and told us we would have to go. We rose and moved, without a word, to the center of the room in a mass, moist-eyed embrace. (p. 209)

GROUP PROCESS. In achieving group goals, emphasis is placed on the honest expression of thoughts and feelings, including anger and hostility, the breaking loose from habitual perceptions and role behaviors, and acceptance of responsibility for one's own acts and values. There is an encouragement of "constructive aggression" and a deliberate instigation of group pressures on individual members to change their behavior.

The intensity of the encounter group is at its height when the marathon format is used. This format is based on the view that the "opening up" process will be hastened by such intense, continuous contact, as well as by the lowering of inhibitions that comes with fatigue. Presumably also, there will be a more truthful expression of feelings since the participants are likely to be too tired to play games. Finally, being separated from any other environment for a sustained period of time, it is thought that they become more involved in the group experience and more susceptible to its pressures toward change.

The marathon encounter group has been called a "pressure cooker" because of the emotional tensions it builds up. And like a pressure cooker, it seems capable of compressing the amount of time required to do its work.

EFFECTS OF INTENSIVE GROUP EXPERIENCE

In both T-groups and encounter groups, a new reference group is established which exposes the individual to new norms concerning what is desirable, helpful, and authentic and supports him in his attempts to change in accordance with these new norms. In both instances, people have a chance to confront the degree to which they are playing rigid roles and doing what they think is expected of them—and hence have been blind to alternative ways of perceiving and meeting their problems. In such following of prescribed roles and expectations, labels are especially rigidifying:

When a person is labelled—neurotic, psychotic, executive, teacher, salesman, psychologist—either by himself or by others, he restricts his behavior to the role and even may rely upon the role for security. This diminishes the kind of experiences he is likely to have. Indeed, it is those groups whose members have shared labels—be it schizophrenic or executive—which are hardest to help move into intimate contact. (Stoller, 1967, pp. 29–30)

In the intensive group experience, people may discover with real shock the many rigidifying things they are doing to themselves. In the safety of the group they can begin to discard their façades and learn to become more honest and flexible in their perceptions and responses.

SOME OUTCOMES AND ISSUES. Expectation of change from T-groups or encounter-group experience rests on the assumption that most people lack adequate self-understanding and interpersonal competence at the start, that psychological freedom to "open up" can be achieved in a short time, even among strangers, that members can give each other the feedback they need for new learning, and that the behavior changes can transfer to the "back home" situation. Most of those who participate in such groups feel that the experience has changed them and has been useful and meaningful (Campbell & Dunnette, 1968). Objective data regarding behavioral changes have been harder to come by.

Most of the research concerning the outcome of intensive group experiences has centered on T-groups. In a comprehensive review of these research findings, Campbell and Dunnette (1968) have concluded that the evidence is reasonably convincing that T-group experience induces behavior changes which carry over to the "back home" setting. Rather than a "typical" effect of T-group training, however, it appears that individual participants are affected in different ways. Clear evidence is lacking on whether people who have been in a T-group tend to show a higher general level of "sensitivity" or increased accuracy in their interpersonal perceptions, as judged by others.

Intensive groups are not without risk. Among these are: (1) short-term change and subsequent discouragement; (2) the risk that the individual may in revealing himself become deeply involved in problems which are not worked through; (3) the revelation of marital tensions which have been kept under cover, placing an absent spouse at a disadvantage later; and (4) the development of loving feelings between group members which have a high degree of sexual involvement—which, if not worked through in the group, may pose a threat to participants' marriages (Rogers, 1968). Especially with immature or unstable participants or an untrained or unskillful leader, the hazards of such unsettling experiences are obvious.

HOW PARTICIPANTS FEEL ABOUT INTENSIVE GROUP EXPERIENCE

In one follow-up study in which 481 individuals were queried about the results of their basic encounter-group experience from two to twelve months later, Rogers (1968) obtained the following responses:

Per Cent	Result Reported
5	Mostly damaging, annoying, or confusing
4	Neutral
19	More helpful than unhelpful
30	Constructive in its results
45	A deeply meaningful experience

Per cents who found the experience damaging or neutral are approximations. The figures add up to more than 100 per cent because some respondents checked more than one answer.

It would appear that the long-term effects of intensive group experience depend on both the avenues to personal growth that are opened up in the group experience and the extent to which the individual continues to find support for his new ways of feeling and acting in the life setting to which he must return and in which he must function and perhaps earn his livelihood. An interesting development in this connection has been that whereas individuals were originally urged to come to T-groups and encounter groups without their associates, so as to be completely free of their usual role restrictions, work teams and family groups are now being encouraged to take training as groups so that they can continue to support each others' changes after the training session ends.

The need for a great deal more research on the effects of intensive group experience on both individuals and groups can hardly be overemphasized. Even though only a small per cent of participants appear to find the experience a damaging or negative one, it is an important concern if such an experience is potentially damaging to anyone. We need to know more about the effects of these groups on different kinds of people, more about the relation of such learning to other kinds of learning, and more about just what kinds of behavioral objectives can reasonably be expected from such experiences.

POTENTIAL OF INTENSIVE GROUP EXPERIENCE. Perhaps the most significant function of the intensive group experience is the unusual chance it offers members to explore new avenues to the greater realization of human potentials. For this reason, the various experimental formats utilizing intensive group experiences have been referred to collectively as the "human potential movement"; probably it is for the same reason that this movement has elicited the interest and often active participation of many distinguished clergymen, philosophers, writers, historians, educators, and scientists.

There is a widespread belief that in our preoccupation with scientific and technological advances we have glorified the development of intellect at the expense of emotional and social development—that we seem bent on achieving a society in which people are alienated from their own feelings, from each other, and from the broader society. The "human potential movement" has stemmed in part from concern over this trend. By providing a tool for humanizing education, government, and industry, it represents a counterforce in the direction of greater self-understanding, enriched emotional experiencing, and more intimate and fulfilling personal relationships.

As Rogers (1968) has pointed out, encounter groups also raise the final issue of the type of person we want to develop in our society:

It seems evident from our review of the group process that in a climate of freedom, group members move toward becoming more spontaneous, flexible, closely related to their feelings, open to their experience, and closer and more expressively intimate in their interpersonal relationships. If we value this type of person and this type of behavior, then clearly the group process is a valuable process. If, on the other hand, we place a value on the individual who is effective in suppressing his feelings, who operates from a firm set of principles, who does not trust his own reactions and experience but relies on authority, and who remains aloof in his interpersonal relationships, then we would regard the group process, as I have tried to describe it, as a dangerous force. (p. 275)

Although we might not all agree on the answer, most of us probably would agree on the importance of the issue.

35 | SOME ETHICAL ISSUES IN SENSITIVITY TRAINING

Martin Lakin

Sensitivity training, in its various forms, has evolved over the past two decades. It is a powerful form of experiential learning that includes self, interactional, and organizational understanding. It has its origins in the study of change and conflict resolution through attention to underlying as well as overt interactional processes. It has been widely used to reexamine managerial, pedagogic, and "helping relationships" from the factory to the classroom, from the community to the home. Typically, small groups of participants under the guidance of a "trainer" use the data of their own spontaneous interactions, and reactions to one another. The trainer functions to facilitate communication, to indicate underlying problems of relating, and to model constructive feedback. He keeps the group moving and productively learning about processes and persons and helps to avoid counterproductive conflict or unnecessary damage to participants. With the evolution of mutant forms of training, particularly over the past few years, and their growing popularity, examination of latent ethical questions has become urgent. This article is presented not to censure an obviously significant and often helpful growth in American psychology, but rather to open for discussion and scrutiny elements of it that affect public welfare and reflect on professional standards.

The number of persons who have experienced some form of training is rapidly growing. However named (training, encounter, human relations), the experience invariably involves emotional confrontations and even an implicit injunction to reconsider if not actually to change personal behavior patterns. Since participants are not self-avowed psychotherapy patients but "normal" persons, and because the trainers are presumably not concerned with reparative but with learning or personal enhancement, it is difficult to draw a firm line between it and other psychotherapeutic forms. Indeed, comparison inevitably forces itself upon us and suggests strongly what many of us realize so well, that a distinction between "normal" and "pathological" behavior is hazy at best. However, the comparison also compels one to consider ethical implications of the differences between the contractual relationships between participant and trainer, on the one hand, and those between patient and therapist, on the other. Concerns about the contractual implications have been only partially met by state-

Martin Lakin, "Some Ethical Issues in Sensitivity Training," *American Psychologist*, **24**, October 1969, No. 10, pp. 923–928. Copyright © 1969 by the American Psychological Association, and reproduced by permission.

This paper was presented at the meeting of the Southeastern Psychological Association, New Orleans, February 1969.

ments of differences in the goals of training from those of therapy and by the difference in self-definition of a participant from that of a patient, as well as by the avowed educational objectives of trainers. Also, formerly it could be argued that the trainer had little therapeutic responsibility because he initiated little; that interactions of the group were the resultant of collective interchange and give-and-take, and did not occur at his instance; that is, a participant "discloses" intimate details of his life or "changes" behavior patterns as a result of a personal commitment or a collective experience rather than because a trainer directs him to do so. Training groups evolved from a tradition of concern with *democratic* processes and *democratic* change. The generally accepted hypothesis was that the best psychological protection against unwarranted influence was individual and collective awareness that could forestall insidious manipulation by dominant leaders or conformist tyranny by a group.

Many people currently involved in the various forms of training are not as psychologically sophisticated or able to evaluate its processes as were the mainly professional participants of some years ago. The motivation of many present participants is cathartic rather than intellectual (e.g., seeking an emotional experience rather than an understanding). Particularly because training is increasingly used as a vehicle for achieving social change, it is necessary to explore its ethical implications—notwithstanding our as yet incomplete understanding of its special processes. There are ethically relevant problems in setting up a group experience, in conducting the group, and following its termination.

PREGROUP CONCERNS

A psychotherapeutic intention is clear by contrast with the training intention. Sophisticated therapists know that this clarity is not absolute; complex issues of values and commitment to specific procedures cannot really be shared with patients, despite the best intentions of a therapist to be candid. Nevertheless, the therapist's mandate is relatively clear—to provide a corrective experience for someone who presents himself as psychologically impaired. By contrast, participant expectancies and fantasies about training vary much more widely. By comparison with the therapist, the trainer's mandate is relatively ambiguous. For example, some trainers view the group experience primarily as a vehicle to produce increased awareness of interactional processes to be employed in social or organizational settings. However, currently, some others dismiss this goal as trivial in favor of an expressive or "existential" experience. Both approaches are similar in that they require a participant-observer role for the trainee. Yet, the emphasis upon rational and emotional elements differs in these approaches, and this difference makes for divergent experiences. The problem is that there is no way for a participant to know in advance, much less to appraise, intentions of trainers, processes of groups, or their consequences for him. It is not feasible to explain these because training, like psychotherapy, depends upon events that counter the participant's accustomed expectations in order to have maximum impacts. Since it is inimical to training to preprogram participant or process, the nature of the training experience depends more than anything upon the particular translations, intentions, and interventions the trainer makes. This makes it imperative for the trainer to be first of all clear about his own intentions and goals.

Training has begun to attract the participation of more psychologically disturbed persons in recent years—a higher proportion of more frustrated individuals seeking personal release or solutions. Correspondingly, there is a larger supply of inadequately prepared persons who do training. To my knowledge, only the National Training Laboratories—Institute of Applied Behavioral Science has given systematic consideration to the training of leaders, but even its accredited trainers are not all prepared to deal with the range of expectations and pathologies currently exhibited by some participants. Some people who are inadequately prepared are suggesting to other people what they feel, how to express their feelings, and interpreting how others respond to them. Some, equally poorly prepared persons, are engaged in applying training to social action and to institutions. Recently, it has come to my attention that there are inadequately prepared trainers who lead student groups on college campuses without supervision. Several eye-witness accounts of these groups suggest that highest value is placed upon intensity of emotionality and on dramatic confrontations. Screening of participants is virtually unknown and follow-up investigation of the effects of these groups is unheard of. Their leaders are usually individuals who have participated in only one or two experiences themselves. Most disturbing of all, there is no sign that these leaders are aware of or concerned about their professional limitations. I think it must be recognized that it will be difficult to restrain poorly prepared individuals from practicing training in the absence of a clear statement of standards of training, trainer preparation, and the publication of a code of training ethics. (An antiprofessional bias is very popular just now, as we all know, and training fits nicely the image of "participative decision making.") Unfortunately, accredited and competent trainers have done little to deter the belief that training requires little preparation and is universally applicable. I do not exempt the National Training Laboratories from responsibility in this regard.

"Adequate preparation" should be spelled out. One would wish to avoid jurisdictional protectionism, although a degree in a recognized educative or therapeutic discipline is certainly one index of responsible preparation. For work with the public, trainers should have had, in addition to a recognized advanced degree in one of the "helping professions," background preparation in personality dynamics, a knowledge of psychopathology as well as preparation in group dynamics, social psychology, and sociology. They should also have had an internship and extensive supervised experience.

It should be recognized that it is difficult, if not impossible, to do effective screening in order to prevent the participation of persons for whom training is inappropriate. One reason is that it is almost impossible to prevent false assertions about one's mental status on application forms. It is also true that it is difficult to assess the precise effects of training upon a particular individual. It could be argued that short-range discomfort might be followed by long-range benefits. Probably the most important step that could be taken immediately would be the elimination of promotional literature that suggests by implication that training is, indeed, "psychotherapy," and that it can promise immediate results. Why has such a step not been taken until now? I suggest that one reason is that currently many trainers do indeed view training as a form of therapy even though they do not explicitly invite psychologically troubled applicants. They do not wish to screen out those who do seek psychotherapy. But this reluctance to exclude such persons makes it almost certain that psychologically impaired individuals will be attracted in large numbers to training as a therapy.

More serious is the fact that there is little evidence on which to base a therapeutic effectiveness claim. To me it seems indefensible that advertising for training should be as seductive as it is in offering hope for in-depth changes of personality or solutions to marital problems in the light of present inadequate evidence that such changes or solutions do occur. Great candor is necessary about the needs that are being addressed by the newer training forms. A legitimate case could perhaps be made for the temporary alleviation of loneliness that is unfortunately so widespread in contemporary urban and industrial life, but the training experience as a palliative is neither learning about group processes nor is it profound personal change. Such candor is obviously a first requisite in face of the fact that some training brochures used in promotion literally trumpet claims of various enduring benefits. I suggest that immediate steps need to be taken to investigate these claims, to reconsider the implementation of screening procedures, set up and publicize accreditation standards, and monitor promotional methods in order to safeguard the public's interest and professional integrity.

ETHICAL QUESTIONS RELATED TO THE PROCESSES
OF TRAINING GROUPS

Being a trainer is an exciting role and function. Being looked to for leadership of one kind or another and being depended upon for guidance is a very "heady" thing as every psychotherapist knows. On the other hand, training, in its beginnings, was based on the idea that participation and involvement on the part of all the members of the group would lead to the development of a democratic society in which personal autonomy and group responsibility were important goals. The trainer had only to facilitate this evolution. Personal exertion of power and influence, overt or covert, was naturally a significant issue for study and learning in group after group. Evaluation of the trainer's influence attempts was crucial for learning about one's responses to authority. The trainer was indeed an influence, but the generally accepted commitment to objectification of his function made his behavior accessible to inquiry and even to modification. Correspondingly, experienced trainers have almost always been aware that the degree of influence they wield is disproportionately large; therefore they, themselves, tried to help the group understand the need for continual assessment of this factor. Awareness of this "transference" element has stimulated trainers in the past to emphasize group processes that would reveal its operations and effects.

However, with the advent of a more active and directing training function that includes trainer-based pressures upon participants to behave in specific ways, but without provision for monitoring of trainer practices, the "democratic" nature of the group interaction is subverted. More important is the fact that there is less possibility for participants to overtly evaluate the influences exerted upon them by the trainer. In some groups that emphasize emotional expressiveness, some trainers purposefully elicit aggressive and/or affectionate behaviors by modeling them and then by inviting imitation. Some even insist that members engage one another in physically aggressive or affectionate acts. Still others provide music to create an emotional experience. Such leadership intends to create certain emotional effects. It does so, however, without sufficient opportunity to work them through. Moreover, analytic or critical evaluation of such experiences would almost certainly be viewed as subversive of their aims.

It will be argued that participants willingly agree to these practices. The fact that the consumer seeks or agrees to these experiences does not justify them as ethically defensible or psychologically sound. It should be remembered that "the contract" is not between persons who have an equal understanding of the processes involved. It cannot be assumed that the participant really knows what he is letting himself in for. At the request of the trainer, and under pressure for group approval, some aggressive displays (e.g., slappings) or affectional displays (e.g., hugging) have occurred that some participants later came to view as indignities.

The question of group acquiescence involves a related point. A crucial element in the history of training was its stress upon genuine consensus. This emphasis was a deterrent to the domination of any single power figure or to the establishment of arbitrary group norms. Action and "decision" were painstakingly arrived at out of group interaction, consisting of increasingly candid exchanges. Influence could be exerted only under continuing group scrutiny and evaluation. Some trainers who are impelled to elicit expressiveness as a primary goal are also committed to democratic values; however, owing to their primary commitment to the significance of emotional expressiveness, they may employ their sensitivities and skills to achieving it in ways that are relatively subtle or even covert. When the participant is encouraged to experience and express strong emotions, the trainer's function in promoting these is often obscured. What is often *his* decision or initiative is presented as *group* initiative. In his recent book, Kelman (1968) has suggested that a group leader has the responsibility of making group members aware of his own operations and values. I find no fault with that suggestion; however, it is very difficult to accomplish this. It is made even more difficult, if I am correct, because some trainers may even have an interest in the group remaining *unaware* of their particular manipulations because they wish to sustain the illusion that it is the group's rather than their own personal decision that results in a particular emotional process. The intention may not be to deceive consciously. It is difficult for trainers to practice complete candor with their participants and yet to facilitate the process of training for reasons I suggested above. Nevertheless, in the light of these questions, trainers should reexamine their own activities. It might be that aroused concern will lead established trainers to take the necessary steps to educate aspirants for professional status to a new sensitivity to these issues.

LEARNING AND EXPERIENTIAL FOCUSES

There are genuine differences in point of view and in emphasis between trainers. Some regard the emotional-experiential as the primary value in training. Others uphold a more cognitive emphasis, while recognizing that a high degree of emotional engagement is a vital part of training. For their part, participants are, more often than not, so emotionally involved as to be confused about just what it is that they are doing, feeling, or thinking at a given point in time. We know that participants slide back and forth between cognitive and affective experiencing of training. The participant must partially depend upon external sources for confirmation or disconfirmation. He looks to other members, but most of all to the trainer himself, for clarification. Surely, dependency plays a huge role, but it will not be destroyed by fiat. It is the responsibility of the trainer to make as clear as he can his own activities, his own view of what is significant, and to encourage exchanges of views among participants so that all can have the possibility of differential self-definition and orientation during the training process. This would help prevent a situation where inchoate and inarticulated pressures push individual participants beyond their comprehension.

In training, as in any other society, there are pressures of majority upon minority, of the many upon the one. Scapegoating, where recognized, would be objected to as demeaning whether it occurs as a means of inducing conformity or to build self-esteem. When the focus is upon group processes, it is often brought into the open, discussed, and countered. Where, however, the emphasis is purely on personal expressiveness, the same phenomenon may be used as a pressure rather than exposed. The implicit demand for emotionality and emphasis upon nonverbal communication even makes it more difficult to identify scapegoating when it occurs in such groups.

ETHICAL ISSUES AND EVALUATIONS

Participants sometimes come to training under "threat" of evaluation. The implications of a refusal to participate by an employee, a subordinate, or a student have not been sufficiently studied. I recall one instance where an employee of a highly sensitive security agency was sent for training. His anxious, conflicted, and disturbed response to training norms of "trust" and "openness" were not only understandable but, in retrospect, predictable. True, the commitment to maintain confidentiality was honored; nevertheless, should his participation have been solicited or even permitted? Evaluation as a participant concern is unavoidable, despite protestations and reassurances to the contrary. Training of trainers should emphasize the professional's ethical responsibility in these matters, but it will not obviate these concerns. The increase in unaccredited and marginally prepared trainers must increase them. It is difficult for most people to monitor their own tendencies to gossip or inform. Especially if the trainer is also an evaluator of participants, he cannot really compartmentalize the impressions he gets of behavior in training, from other data that he has about the participants. Perhaps it would help to make everyone aware of this fact. At least the "risk" then becomes explicit from everyone's point of view.

A diminution of risk was thought to be one of the major advantages of "stranger" groups where time-limited contact was thought to encourage a degree of candor and interpersonal experiment that was nominally proscribed. Obviously, this cannot be the case in groups where participants are related, classmates, or involved in the same company or agency. It should be recognized that it is almost impossible to assure confidentiality under such circumstances or to prevent "out of school" reports. Trainers need to be especially sensitive to this in preparing other trainers. For example, where graduate students are involved in training groups and have social or other connections with one another, or with those they observe, numerous possibilities for teaching the importance of professional detachment present themselves. Trainees should learn how important it is to avoid irresponsible behavior in order to maintain the confidence of participants, how vital it is to inhibit a desire for personal contact when they have a professional role to play. Essentially, they have the same problem that faces the fledgling psychotherapist in inhibiting his own curiosity and social impulse in order to fulfill a professional function. The necessary detachment emphasized here is yet another significant and ethically relevant area that emotional expressiveness as an end in itself does not articulate. Responsibility is taught and modeled. It should be as consciously done in training as in any other helping relationship.

POSTTRAINING ETHICAL ISSUES

A strongly positive reaction to training more frequently than not impels the gratified participant to seek further training experiences. Unfortunately, almost as frequently he seeks to do training himself. After all, it appears relatively easy. The apparent power and emotional gratifications of the trainer seem very attractive. If steps in professional preparation in becoming a trainer are not better articulated, and closely wedded to the traditional helping professions, we shall soon have vast numbers of inadequate trainers who practice their newly discovered insights on others, in the naive conviction that they have all but mastered the skills involved in group processes and application to personal and social problems.

A final issue to which I wish to call your attention is that of posttraining contact with the participant. Participants are often dramatically affected by training. In some cases, trainer and group are mutually reluctant to end the group. In a recent case that came to my attention, my view is that the trainer was seduced, as it were, by the group's responsiveness to him. In turn, the participants were delighted by the trainer's continuing interest. Trainers must be aware of the powerful desire to sustain a relationship with them. Therefore, they must be clear at the outset what limits they propose for training. It is as important to be determinate about the termination point of training as about any other aspect of its conduct. Under the conditions of ambiguity and ambivalence of an "indeterminate" relationship, participants appear to be caught, as it were, midstream, uncertain as to the definition or possibilities of a relationship with this presumed expert upon whom they naturally depend for guidance and limit setting.

The questions that I have raised do not admit of a quick solution. They are ethical dilemmas. Steps to eliminate or ameliorate the grossest of them can be taken through awareness and self-monitoring. One practical step that I propose is the immediate creation of a commission by our professional organization to investigate training practices, standards of training preparation, and to recommend a code of ethics for accredited trainers. Research may help, but I doubt that it can come quickly enough to affect the increasing danger of the current and potentially still greater excesses in this area.

Sensitivity training is one of the most compelling and significant psychological experiences and vehicles for learning as well as a promising laboratory for the study of human relationships, dyadic, and group. It may be a superior device for personal and social change, even for amelioration or resolution of social conflict. However, it may also be abused or subverted into an instrument of unwarranted influence and ill-considered, even harmful, practices. The immediate attention of the profession is necessary to maintain its positive potential and correspondingly respectable standards of practice.

REFERENCE

Kelman, H. C. *A time to speak—On human values and social research?* San Francisco: Jossey-Bass, 1968.

36 | A BEHAVIORAL APPROACH
TO COUNSELING AND GUIDANCE

Jack Michael and Lee Meyerson

A behavioral approach to human control does not consist of a bag of tricks to be applied mechanically for the purpose of coercing unwilling people. It is part of a highly technical system, based on laboratory investigations of the phenomena of conditioning, for describing behavior and specifying the conditions under which it is acquired, maintained, and eliminated.

Much more knowledge of conditioning and its broad field of applicability to human behavior is available today than can be appreciated by those who have only vague recollections of the glandular and motor responses of the dogs studied by Pavlov.

It is the major purpose of this paper to describe, in a didactic way, a portion of the new knowledge that has been obtained. Starting from definitions of specialized concepts and terminology, mastery of which will permit further reading of the technical literature, an overview is given of a descriptive and explanatory system of behavior that has relevance for [many applied areas]. . . .

It is necessary to understand at the outset that the familiar characterization of behavior as a function of the interaction of hereditary and environmental variables is accepted, not with the lip service that is sometimes given before fleeing to hypothetical constructs of inner behavior determiners that are neither heredity nor environment, but with utmost seriousness.

The consequences of this orientation should be made explicit: Inherited genetic and constitutional determiners are not under the control of, or subject to, direct experimentation by behavioral scientists. This means that the only channel open . . . for influencing human behavior is through changes in the environment. Additionally, certain environmental manipulations, such as separating a person from his frontal lobes or administering drugs that have psychopharmacological effects, are not available to psychologists and educators. The phenomenon with which [we] deal, then, is behavior, and the independent variable which controls behavior must be the environment. A behavioral system attempts to specify, without reference to unobservable, hypothetical inner-determining agents, the conditions and the process by which the environment controls human behavior.

Reprinted by permission from *Harvard Educational Review*, 1962, **32**, 382–402.

A BEHAVIORAL SYSTEM[1]

RESPONDENT CONDITIONING

Certain physical events in the environment are related to certain human muscular and glandular activities in a relatively invariable way. A light shined in the eye elicits a constriction of the pupil. An acid solution placed on the tongue elicits secretion by the salivary gland. Such physical events are called stimuli and the muscular and glandular activities are called responses. Some of these stimulus-response relationships or reflexes are present at birth, and in humans most of them are involved in maintaining the internal economy of the body or protecting it against harmful external conditions.

A stimulus which is not a part of a reflex relationship becomes a *conditioned stimulus* for the response by repeated, temporal pairing with an *unconditioned stimulus* which already elicits the response. This new relationship is called a *conditioned reflex;* and the pairing procedure is called *respondent conditioning.*

In general, conditioning does not produce permanent effects. If the conditioned stimulus is presented frequently in the absence of the unconditioned stimulus, a procedure called *extinction,* it loses its eliciting properties.

The procedures for producing conditioning and extinction were first explored systematically by I. P. Pavlov, and respondent conditioning is an area of continued interest and active investigation.

However, if conditioning phenomena were limited in applicability to the transfer of eliciting effects from reflex stimuli to other stimuli, the field would be of little importance in understanding human behavior. Most of the behavior that is of interest to society does not fit the paradigm of the reflex. There is in general no identifiable eliciting stimulus for the broad class of "voluntary" activity called by B. F. Skinner *operant* behavior. The basic operation of respondent conditioning, however, the systematic temporal pairing of stimulus conditions, is of some significance since a portion of almost any kind of stimulus effect can be transferred to a new stimulus by the procedure of pairing the two stimuli.

OPERANT CONDITIONING

Whereas for reflexes and conditioned reflexes the event of critical explanatory importance is the eliciting stimulus preceding the response, for a large class of non-reflex behavior the critical events are the environmental consequences of the behavior. Such behavior can be said to "operate" on the environment, in contrast to behavior which is "respondent" to prior eliciting stimuli.

It is convenient to group the kinds of stimulus events which are consequences of acts into three major classes in terms of their effects on operant behavior.

POSITIVE REINFORCERS. These stimulus events are defined by the observation that the behavior which preceded them has a higher probability of occurrence under similar conditions in the future. Such events are often called rewards and described as pleasant. Some of these positive reinforcers are of biological significance to the organism such as food, water, sexual contact, and some are of acquired significance such as praise, affection, grades, money.

NEGATIVE REINFORCERS OR AVERSIVE STIMULI. These events are defined by the observation that behavior which preceded their removal is more likely to occur under similar conditions in the future. The common aversive stimuli are those we call painful or unpleasant such as extreme heat or cold, blows on the surface of the body, distortions of certain inner organs as in a stomach ache, very loud sounds or very bright lights. Another class of aversive stimuli are those whose properties are acquired during our lifetimes such as social disapproval, criticism, nagging, threat.

The operation of presenting a positive reinforcer contingent upon a response is called *positive reinforcement.* The operation of removing an aversive stimulus contingent upon a response is called *negative reinforcement.*[2] Both operations are called *operant conditioning* and both increase the future frequency of the response which preceded them.

NO CONSEQUENCE AND NEUTRAL STIMULI. Responses continue to occur if they receive either positive or negative reinforcement. They cease if followed by no consequence or by neutral stimuli. The procedure of allowing behavior to occur without reinforcement is called *operant extinction,* and can be contrasted with *respondent extinction* which is the procedure of allowing a conditioned stimulus to occur without pairing it with an unconditioned stimulus.

It should be noted that none of the above statements constitutes postulates, axioms, assumptions or issues of theoretical controversy. The definitions are simply descriptions of observed relationships. Some events serve as reinforcer and some do not. The determination of what constitutes a reinforcer for a particular organism is an empirical problem, although of course, it is often very helpful to have studied biologically similar organisms or those inhabiting similar environments. In the case of humans, the reinforcers of biological significance are apparently very similar to those of other mammals and are fairly well known. On the other hand, the specification of the events of acquired reinforcing value for an individual human requires either a contemporary investigation or considerable knowledge of his environmental history.

CONDITIONED REINFORCERS. Only a small proportion of the important consequences of human behavior are the unconditioned reinforcers attributable to biological characteristics. Other consequences, *conditioned reinforcers,* acquire their reinforcing properties as a function of experience. It appears that an event becomes a conditioned reinforcer in some degree simply by being paired with another reinforcer. However, most of the conditioned reinforcers that are important in human affairs are, in addition, stimuli in the presence of which further behavior is reinforced. In common sense terms, most conditioned reinforcers are means to an end which may be an unconditioned reinforcer or another conditioned reinforcer. For example, a match for a smoker will serve as a reinforcer for the behavior which procured it because it makes possible the further behavior of striking it and lighting the cigarette.

Some conditioned reinforcers are specific to particular unconditioned reinforcers as when signs regarding the serving of food, pictures of food, and menus, function as conditioned reinforcers for humans who are momentarily reinforceable with food. Some conditioned reinforcers, however, because they have been paired with many different unconditioned and conditioned reinforcers and because they have been means to many different ends almost become ends in themselves. Reinforcers that have this property, such as money, social approval, successful manipulation of the physical environment, affection, and others are called *generalized conditioned reinforcers.*

COMMON SENSE, AUTOMATICITY, AND SUPERSTITIOUS BEHAVIOR. It may seem that to emphasize the pleasant and unpleasant consequences of acts through "rewards and punishments" is nothing new. The effects described above have long been known and used in an intuitive way, but they also have long been misunderstood. The strengthening effect of a reward is commonly understood in terms of a rational process. It seems only natural that a person will repeat that which he can see will benefit him, and perform again those acts which he believes will terminate unpleasant conditions. However, the effect does not depend on a rational process at all. The foreseeing of consequences or the ability to state the relation between the consequence and the behavior which produced it is unnecessary. Any behavior which is followed by reinforcement—in all of the many species studied, and above all in man—is more likely to occur again in the same or a similar situation. This could be called the *automaticity* of the effect of reinforcement. To increase the occurrence of a particular class of behavior, it is necessary only to ensure that reinforcement occurs relatively soon after the behavior.

The automaticity effect is most drastically demonstrated in what is called "superstitious behavior." When reinforcement follows behavior, even though the behavior did not produce or in any sense cause the reinforcement, it is called *accidental reinforcement.* Behavior which is developed as a function of accidental reinforcement was whimsically referred to as superstitious behavior in a study with pigeons (Skinner, 1948a) and the term has become a quasi-technical term in the behavioral field. Humans, probably because of their more complex environment, provide many more examples of superstitious behavior than lower animals. The verbalizations and unique motor activities of gamblers and the unnecessary postures and movements seen in sports activities are examples of the effects of accidental contingencies of reinforcement.

SHAPING

Inasmuch as an operant response must first occur before it can be followed by reinforcement, one might suppose that operant conditioning cannot be used to produce new behavior. However, the detailed topography of a response—the particular muscle actions, including force and speed of various muscle components—varies from one occurrence to another. To produce new behavior then, or behavior that has not appeared in the response repertoire before, it is sufficient to selectively reinforce one of the variations in topography which resulted from the previous reinforcement, while allowing the other variations to extinguish. This has the effect of producing a further class of variations from which one may again differentially reinforce some and allow others to extinguish, and so on.

For example, in teaching a child to talk, his efforts to pronounce a particular word will at first be reinforced rather uncritically. Eventually, some of the variations will resemble accepted pronunciation more than others and receive selective reinforcement while other variations are allowed to extinguish. These events have the effect of producing a class of responses which come ever closer to the correct pronunciation than the last reinforced response, and the selective reinforcement can be applied again. This procedure for producing new behavior is called *shaping*. It is essentially the differential reinforcement of successive approximations to some complex form of behavior. It is the technique which animal trainers use to produce unusual and entertaining behaviors in their subjects, and it is the technique whereby humans acquire the complex response topographies of speech, athletic abilities and other motor skills.

STIMULUS CONTROL OF OPERANT BEHAVIOR

Although the emphasis in describing operant behavior has been on the reinforcement occurring subsequent to the response, stimulus control is implied in the phrase concluding the principle of operant conditioning—if an operant response is followed by reinforcement it is more likely to occur *under similar conditions* in the future. The simplest principle of stimulus control is that the future probability of response is highest when the stimulus conditions resemble most closely those existing at the moment of previous reinforcement. The expression "resemble most closely" must be analyzed in some detail, but first a description is needed of a typical experimental situation in which the effects of stimuli on operant behavior are studied. A lower animal rather than a human is described as the subject in this example because stimulus control in humans is confounded by their extensive training regarding the relevance of certain classes of stimuli (see "discrimination training" below). A food-deprived monkey is placed in a small chamber containing a movable foot pedal, and reinforced with food for pressing the pedal. Suppose that the chamber is illuminated by a relatively bright overhead light, a moderately loud tone of 1000 cycles per second plays constantly, and a small translucent disc above the pedal, at eye level, is illuminated from behind with a bright green light. Although none of these stimulus conditions can be said to elicit the response, they all come to exert some control over its probability, for if any of them is changed, the tendency to respond will be temporarily lowered. Of course, if we continue to reinforce in the presence of the changed stimuli, responding will recover and the class of stimulus conditions controlling the response will be broadened. If, instead of changing only one of the stimulus conditions, we change all of them, the tendency to respond will be very low. In brief, any change from the stimulus conditions that existed at the moment of reinforcement will reduce the tendency to respond, and the greater the change, the greater the reduction.

There is, however, a vagueness in this formulation. How can the extent to which a changed stimulus condition resembles the original one be evaluated? For example, can we predict for a specific monkey whether changing the tone will reduce his tendency to respond more than turning off the overhead light? We cannot. It is an empirical question. To some extent the similarity of different stimulus conditions will depend on the biological characteristics of the species. But in part, as in the case of reinforcers, the importance to the individual organism of the various aspects of the stimulus condition will depend on the previous history of that particular organism.

In the situation described above a change in color on the translucent disc would not be expected to change the tendency to respond very much because the disc color is only a small part of the total stimulus situation. By skilled use of the procedures of reinforcement and extinction, however, we can bring about the more precise type of stimulus control that is called *discrimination*. If we change the color from green to red, and in the presence of the red disc we do not reinforce the pedal response, it will become less frequent, i.e., extinguish. If we then restore the color and in its presence pedal pressing is again reinforced and so on, alternating the two conditions, the control of the disc color over the pedal response will become quite strong. This procedure is called *discrimination training*. If in the presence of a stimulus a response is reinforced, and in the absence of this stimulus it is extinguished, the stimulus will control the probability of the response in high degree. Such a stimulus is called a *discriminative stimulus*.

Almost all important human behavior is under the control of discriminative stimuli. Although part of the educational process involves extensive shaping, particularly for motor skills, the educator's major efforts are directed toward the development of *discriminative repertoires*, or in common terminology, knowledge. Many details regarding the building of discriminative repertoires have been discovered in the experimental laboratory, and these findings are now beginning to see systematic exploitation in the field of programmed instruction.

The development of effective discriminative repertoires for interpersonal behavior is also a topic of great importance for those dealing with the practical control of behavior, and although the principles of discrimination are the same when the stimuli to be discriminated are the behaviors of other people, the details of application remain to be worked out.

A beginning has been made in applying basic principles of discrimination to verbal behavior, language, and communication. This is presently seen to be a field composed of one discriminative repertoire under the control of the many features of the physical and social environment, with additional repertoires controlled by features of the first (Skinner, 1957b).

SCHEDULES OF INTERMITTENT REINFORCEMENT

Thus far discussion has centered on the role of reinforcement in simply making a response more likely to occur in the future, in shaping up novel topographies or forms of response, and in bringing a response under the control of a particular stimulus condition. But reinforcement does not lose its relevance once an adequate topography has been developed and the behavior is under proper stimulus control. It has additional effects that may be treated according to the schedule by which reinforcement is given.

An important characteristic of much behavior is that it is repeated, either because the appropriate stimulus conditions persist or because they recur. Having learned to ask a parent for a cookie a child can immediately ask for another, and another. This behavior must eventually cease because of temporary changes in the parent's disposition to provide the reinforcer, because the reinforcer loses its effectiveness by satiation, or for other reasons, but there will be other occasions for similar behavior to occur. If every occurrence of such a repeatable response is followed by reinforcement the behavior will continue until other variables exert control. On the other hand, if reinforcement is discontinued altogether the behavior will cease.

Between the extremes of *continuous reinforcement* where every relevant response is reinforced and *extinction* where there is no reinforcement there are many situations where responses are only occasionally reinforced. Such *intermittent reinforcement* might be expected to produce an effect intermediate between continuous reinforcement and extinction, but that is not the case. The situation is much more complex. A schedule of intermittent reinforcement is actually a way of arranging reinforcement contingencies regarding the passage of time, the number of responses, or both. The complexity arises from the varied and intricate ways in which these temporal and number contingencies can be combined and interrelated in natural and laboratory environments, and from the extreme sensitivity of the behavior of organisms to such conditions.

RATIO REINFORCEMENT. There is a large class of schedules involving solely a number contingency, and this is usually specified in terms of the ratio of responses to reinforcements. Industrial piecework pay is an example of ratio reinforcement, as is the pay-off schedule provided by the "one-armed bandit" of the gambling house. The principal characteristic of such schedules is that the more rapidly one works the more frequently one is reinforced. Behavior conforms to this kind of requirement by occurring at a high rate. Another feature of this kind of schedule is that very large amounts of work per reinforcement can be tolerated, but to avoid premature extinction the organism must approach such conditions gradually by first being exposed to less stringent requirements. A third feature is that simple ratio reinforcement does not have self-corrective properties. Any temporary reduction in the tendency to respond simply delays the ultimate reinforcement. Vicious circles can easily develop where the less one responds the less one gets, and therefore the less one responds in the future.

INTERVAL REINFORCEMENT. Another class of schedules involves only temporal contingencies. The most commonly studied arrangements are those where the probability of a response being reinforced increases as a simple function of the passage of time, and under these conditions the frequency of responding generally reflects the changing probability of reinforcement. An example from daily life is the behavior of telephoning someone who is not at home. One cannot hasten his return home by rapid re-dialing, as in ratio reinforcement, but the probability of making the connection and completing the call increases as time passes. If the interval varies randomly, response frequency is relatively constant over time. If the interval is constant, responding increases in frequency as the time for reinforcement approaches. In such schedules the rate of responding is directly related to the frequency of reinforcement. Only moderate response rates are generated by interval reinforcement but when the reinforcement is discontinued altogether, responding decreases in frequency very slowly compared with behavior which has been continuously reinforced. Resistance to extinction is high. In contrast to the ratio schedules described earlier, interval schedules in general are self-corrective. Any temporary reduction in response frequency is counteracted by receiving the next reinforcement after fewer unreinforced responses, and this restores the tendency to respond.

Much more complex arrangements of temporal and number contingencies occur in the human physical and social environment, and also in the behavior laboratory. Fortunately the field is somewhat systematized and it is becoming increasingly possible to predict the effects of new arrangements on the basis of what is known about their components.

INTERMITTENT REINFORCEMENT AND MOTIVATION. In addition to its general theoretical relevance in illuminating the effects of reinforcement contingencies, intermittent reinforcement is of considerable practical significance because of its relationship to the traditional field of motivation. The well-motivated person is one who works at some activity with persistence, even though his reinforcement is long delayed. He is also a person who can put out a very large amount of work with only an occasional reward. It is not evident, however, that these properties are *in* the person or that the behavior cannot be produced by manipulating the environment. Variable interval schedules generate great persistence in the face of non-reinforcement, and ratio schedules produce large amounts of work for the minimum number of reinforcements. Not only good motivation but the pathologically "driven" behavior that is said to characterize the gambler can be generated in the laboratory by programing the same kind of variable ratio schedule that acts on the gambler. Similarly when a child cries and begs his parents with great persistence and intensity to take him with them rather than leave him with a baby sitter, we are likely to say something like "he *wants* very much to go with them." The work on intermittent reinforcement tells us very clearly that just such a performance could be generated by acquiescing to the child's requests after only mildly intense and slightly persistent entreaties at first and then slowly raising the requirement. Whether any particular sample of behavior arose in this way is an empirical question.

DEPRIVATION AND SATIATION

Not all motivational problems fit the paradigm described above. Deprivation and satiation have two major effects on behavior which cannot at present be reduced to the effects of any of the biological or environmental variables discussed previously.

Food, water, sexual activity, activity in general, and some other similar unconditioned reinforcers will serve as reinforcers only if the organism has been deprived of them. Satiation weakens and deprivation strengthens the effectiveness of these reinforcers. This is one major effect of this variable. In addition, deprivation with respect to a reinforcer results in an increased likelihood of occurrence of all the behavior that has in the past been reinforced with it.

Stated in terms of food, for example, the first effect is that as deprivation time increases, food becomes a more powerful reinforcer. As eating continues, food loses its reinforcing capacity. The second effect is seen in that food-seeking behavior becomes more frequent as time since last eating increases, and less frequent as eating proceeds. This second effect cannot at present be reduced to the first, since the increase in food-seeking behavior can be observed even before reinforcement has been received.

The study of deprivation-satiation variables appears to come closest to the traditional field of motivation, but there are many cases where these variables are *not* relevant, but it is common to infer them. For example, one man may show strong persistent behavior directed toward socio-sexual relations with women, and another may show very little such behavior. The customary explanation is in terms of sex drive, with the implication that equivalent periods of deprivation affect the two men differently or that one is more deprived than the other. It is more likely in our culture that differences of this magnitude are due largely to different histories of intermittent reinforcement although again this interpretation would require independent evidence in any particular case. Laboratory studies with lower animals indicate quite clearly that variables such as frequency of reinforcement and kind of schedule can cause variations in frequency and persistence of behavior that are greater than the variations generated by deprivation.

It would also be a mistake to infer a history of specific deprivation from the knowledge that a particular event will function as a reinforcer. In the case of ordinary conditioned reinforcers this mistake would not usually be made—the fact that the sight of a telephone is reinforcing certainly doesn't suggest telephone deprivation, since a telephone is so obviously a means to an end. The generalized conditioned reinforcers, however, of affection, attention, money, because they are means to many different ends, erroneously might be assumed to be subject to the deprivation effect in themselves.

In summary then, deprivation and satiation are critical determiners of the momentary effectiveness of a number of reinforcers, and of the momentary strength of large classes of responses. But to pattern all "motivational" problems on this model would be to neglect other equally if not more important determiners.

EMOTION

It is customary to consider emotion as respondent behavior, but operant aspects of emotion can also be specified. Like deprivation, emotional variables offer a large class of operant responses. For example, a person who is ordinarily described as fearful not only shows the respondent effects such as a more rapid heart rate, moist palms and dry throat, but also he shows an increased tendency to engage in all those operant behaviors which have in the past been reinforced by escape from current or similarly difficult situations. Further, those aspects of his repertoire which ordinarily receive positive reinforcement in this situation are weakened. His tendencies to run away, to hide, to seek help from other individuals, are all increased, whereas his tendencies to eat, play, and engage in normal social behaviors are decreased. These phenomena presently are not well understood.

The operations which produce behavioral changes in respondent and operant repertoires under emotion have not yielded to efforts to develop a simple classification scheme. Furthermore, the class of responses which are altered by any particular operation contain such a large component of acquired behaviors that the similarities between different individuals are of little systematic value. However, although an empirical description and ordering of the responses which change with emotion presently are limited, the principles whereby already developed repertoires can be transferred from one stimulus condition to another are somewhat better understood. The operation of temporal pairing is relevant. Any stimulus which is systematically present during an emotional condition will produce some of the respondents and some of the change in the operant repertoire that characterize the emotional condition when it is presented alone. Practical use of principles in this field has been under investigation in the U.S.S.R. ever since the earliest work of Pavlov. More recently, however, a group of British investigators have made very successful deliberate applications of emotional conditioning principles to the treatment of abnormal behavior (Eysenck, 1960).

AVERSIVE CONTROL

ESCAPE AND AVOIDANCE. An environmental arrangement in which an organism's response can terminate an already present aversive stimulus is called an *escape* procedure. It is negative reinforcement, and operant conditioning of the response is the result. When behavior can prevent or delay the onset of the aversive stimulus the procedure is called *avoidance,* and this arrangement also will result in the development and maintenance of operant behavior. Avoidance cannot be considered as a simple case of negative reinforcement, however, since there is often no obvious stimulus termination immediately following the response. Turning off an alarm clock that has already begun to ring is an example of escape behavior, but pushing in the stop before it begins to ring is avoidance.

Examples of this kind of control are easily found in parent-child interactions. Children's cleanliness activities are often maintained as escape behavior where the aversive stimulus is the nagging verbal behavior of a parent. Sometimes these activities constitute avoidance behavior. Here the aversive stimulus is criticism, scolding, or being made to wash over again. Later, when children go to school their studying behavior is often maintained as avoidance behavior, where the aversive stimulus is again criticism, failing grades, or removal of privileges. The distinction between behavior for positive reinforcement and the avoidance paradigm is illustrated in the following not uncommon interchange between parent and child. The child is told to do something and asks "What will I get if I do?" whereupon the parent replies "You'll get something if you don't!"

Laboratory findings with avoidance behavior have indicated several characteristics of this kind of control which are closely related to behavior disorders of many kinds. In the first place, successful avoidance behavior will by its very nature prevent the discovery that the aversive stimulus has been discontinued, and when this is coupled with the extraordinary persistence of such behavior it suffices to explain many human activities that serve no current function.

Another finding relevant to behavior problems is the fact that occasional presentations of the aversive stimulus without respect to the organism's behavior will maintain the avoidance repertoire almost indefinitely. In this way, even though the bad thing that one is avoiding is no longer related to one's behavior, so long as it occurs once-in-a-while the avoidance repertoire may persist.

A final point concerns the conditions under which the escape or avoidance repertoire will occur. In escape behavior the presentation of the aversive stimulus produces immediate strength in the escape repertoire and the escape repertoire is not readily seen in the absence of the aversive stimulus. In avoidance, the presentation of stimuli which have in the past accompanied that or other aversive stimuli strengthen the avoidance repertoire, but an even stronger effect is seen when the aversive stimulus itself is presented momentarily. To maintain behavior in this manner it is necessary to maintain the threat of aversive stimulation.

PUNISHMENT. Technically, punishment refers to the operation of presenting an aversive stimulus contingent upon a response, or removing a positive reinforcer contingent upon a response.[3] It is widely used in our culture to reduce the frequency of behavior, and according to "common sense" psychology is often described as opposite in effect from reward. As rewards strengthen behavior, so punishments are believed to weaken it. Considerable experimental evidence is now available regarding the effects of this operation, which turn out to be quite complex.

One kind of complexity arises because whereas the strengthening effects of reinforcement can be studied in isolation, the weakening effects of punishment can only be studied by superimposing them on preceding or ongoing strengthening effects. This is not only a methodological problem. In practical affairs the question of the efficacy of punishment seldom arises except with respect to behavior that has at least moderate probability of occurrence.

It is difficult to generalize about this competition between reinforcement and punishment since the parameters of the positive reinforcement and the aversive stimulus used are critical, as is the availability of alternative responses which are reinforced and/or punished to varying degrees. However, it is probably safe to say that when no other response but the punished one can obtain positive reinforcement, and with positive reinforcers like food, it takes very severe punishment to effectively reduce the frequency of the behavior.

Added to this complication is the fact that an aversive stimulus may have some effects because it is aversive, but it also has other stimulus effects. By the principle of stimulus control mentioned earlier an aversive stimulus can reduce the frequency of responding if the stimulus constitutes a change from the conditions which existed during previous reinforcement, regardless of its aversive characteristics. And since reinforcement often occurs in the same situation as punishment, an aversive stimulus, as a result of some systematic relation to the reinforcement, can acquire even more complex stimulus properties, such as those of a discriminative stimulus, or even a conditioned positive reinforcer.

Finally, there is a complication in interpreting the effects of punishment in human interactions that is brought about by the fact that a person who punishes may for a time be less disposed to provide any ordinary positive reinforcement. If this is the case, punishment systematically precedes a period of extinction. This arrangement results in a reduction in some behavior—but not due to the aversive effects of the punishment. On the other hand, punishers sometimes show a greater disposition to provide positive reinforcement shortly after they have administered punishment. This results in a temporary increase in some kinds of behavior, and, under proper conditions, even a future increase in the punished behavior.

Any stimulus which is paired temporally with an aversive stimulus acquires some of its properties. Such stimuli are called *conditioned aversive stimuli* or conditioned negative reinforcers. Aversive stimuli and conditioned aversive stimuli, in addition to producing the effects described above are also classed as emotional variables, because of their respondent effects and their effects on large classes of operant responses. This emotional effect enters into and further complicates various kinds of aversive control. It also appears to be responsible for various deleterious changes in certain internal organs. Because of this, and for many other reasons, aversive control is in most cases socially undesirable although it is apparently not completely avoidable.

This concludes the presentation of the basic empirical principles of this behavior system. Of course, many details have been omitted, but the major relations have been covered. Further development of this system is proceeding along two lines: workers in experimental laboratories are constantly discovering new details, improving imprecise relations, and sometimes revealing new major principles; others working in applied settings are developing a behavioral technology based on these basic principles.

NOTES

1. The principles of the system presented here are based on data reported by a great many people. Most studies within the last 5 years were reported in the *Journal of the Experimental Analysis of Behavior*.

The statements about avoidance are based in large part on work done by Murray Sidman and his associates. Statements about punishment are based primarily on the work of N. H. Azrin and his associates. A more complete treatment of the material basic to this systematic presentation is available in J. G. Holland and B. F. Skinner, *The Analysis of Behavior* (New York: McGraw-Hill, 1961) and in B. F. Skinner's earlier work, *Science and Human Behavior* (New York: Macmillan, 1953). Similar material has been presented in several shorter papers, like the present one. . . . Two of these are especially valuable in their thoroughness and in their detailed discussion of practical applications of research findings. They are C. B. Ferster's "Reinforcement and punishment in the control of human behavior by social agencies," *Psychiatric Research Reports*, 1958, **10**, 101–118; and M. Sidman's "Operant techniques," in Arthur J. Bachrach (Ed.), *Experimental Foundations of Clinical Psychology* (New York: Basic Books, 1962).

2. Negative reinforcement should not be confused with punishment which is the presentation of an aversive stimulus contingent on a response.

3. Common sense usage often has punishment synonymous with what is referred to here as an aversive stimulus or, even more broadly, as aversive control.

37 | SOME ISSUES CONCERNING THE CONTROL OF HUMAN BEHAVIOR: A SYMPOSIUM

Carl R. Rogers and B. F. Skinner

I—SKINNER

Science is steadily increasing our power to influence, change, mold—in a word, control—human behavior. It has extended our "understanding" (whatever that may be) so that we deal more successfully with people in nonscientific ways, but it has also identified conditions or variables which can be used to predict and control behavior in a new, and increasingly rigorous, technology. The broad disciplines of government and economics offer examples of this, but there is special cogency in those contributions of anthropology, sociology, and psychology which deal with individual behavior. Carl Rogers has listed some of the achievements to date in a recent paper (1956). Those of his examples which show or imply the control of the single organism are primarily due, as we should expect, to psychology. It is the experimental study of behavior which carries us beyond awkward or inaccessible "principles," "factors," and so on, to variables which can be directly manipulated.

It is also, and for more or less the same reasons, the conception of human behavior emerging from an experimental analysis which most directly challenges traditional views. Psychologists themselves often do not seem to be aware of how far they have moved in this direction. But the change is not passing unnoticed by others. Until only recently it was customary to deny the possibility of a rigorous science of human behavior by arguing, either that a lawful science was impossible because man was a free agent, or that merely statistical predictions would always leave room for personal freedom. But those who used to take this line have become most vociferous in expressing their alarm at the way these obstacles are being surmounted.

Now, the control of human behavior has always been unpopular. Any undisguised effort to control usually arouses emotional reactions. We hesitate to admit, even to ourselves, that we are engaged in control, and we may refuse to control, even when this would be helpful, for fear of criticism. Those who have explicitly avowed an interest in control have been roughly treated by history. Machiavelli is the great prototype. As Macaulay said of him, "Out of his surname they coined an epithet for a knave and out of his Christian name a synonym for the devil." There were obvious reasons. The control that Machiavelli analyzed and recommended, like most political control, used techniques that were aversive to the controllee. The

From *Science*, **124**, 30 November 1956, pp. 1057–1066. Copyright © 1956 by the American Association for the Advancement of Science and reprinted by their permission and that of the authors.

threats and punishments of the bully, like those of the government operating on the same plan, are not designed—whatever their success—to endear themselves to those who are controlled. Even when the techniques themselves are not aversive, control is usually exercised for the selfish purposes of the controller and, hence, has indirectly punishing effects upon others.

Man's natural inclination to revolt against selfish control has been exploited to good purpose in what we call the philosophy and literature of democracy. The doctrine of the rights of man has been effective in arousing individuals to concerted action against governmental and religious tyranny. The literature which has had this effect has greatly extended the number of terms in our language which express reactions to the control of men. But the ubiquity and ease of expression of this attitude spells trouble for any science which may give birth to a powerful technology of behavior. Intelligent men and women, dominated by the humanistic philosophy of the past twenty centuries, cannot view with equanimity what Andrew Hacker has called "the specter of predictable man" (1954). Even the statistical or actuarial prediction of human events, such as the number of fatalities to be expected on a holiday weekend, strikes many people as uncanny and evil, while the prediction and control of individual behavior is regarded as little less than the work of the devil. I am not so much concerned here with the political or economic consequences for psychology, although research following certain channels may well suffer harmful effects. We ourselves, as intelligent men and women, and as exponents of Western thought, share these attitudes. They have already interfered with the free exercise of a scientific analysis, and their influence threatens to assume more serious proportions.

Three broad areas of human behavior supply good examples. The first of these —*personal control*—may be taken to include person-to-person relationships in the family, among friends, in social and work groups, and in counseling and psychotherapy. Other fields are *education* and *government*. A few examples from each will show how nonscientific preconceptions are affecting our current thinking about human behavior.

PERSONAL CONTROL

People living together in groups come to control one another with a technique which is not inappropriately called "ethical." When an individual behaves in a fashion acceptable to the group, he receives admiration, approval, affection and many other reinforcements which increase the likelihood that he will continue to behave in that fashion. When his behavior is not acceptable, he is criticized, censured, blamed, or otherwise punished. In the first case the group calls him "good"; in the second, "bad." This practice is so thoroughly ingrained in our culture that we often fail to see that it is a technique of control. Yet we are almost always engaged in such control, even though the reinforcements and punishments are often subtle.

The practice of admiration is an important part of a culture, because behavior which is otherwise inclined to be weak can be set up and maintained with its help. The individual is especially likely to be praised, admired, or loved when he acts for the group in the face of great danger, for example, or sacrifices himself or his possessions, or submits to prolonged hardship, or suffers martyrdom. These actions are not admirable in any absolute sense, but they require admiration if they are to be strong. Similarly, we admire people who behave in original or exceptional ways, not because such behavior is itself admirable, but because we do not know how to encourage original or exceptional behavior in any other way. The group acclaims independent, unaided behavior in part because it is easier to reinforce than to help.

As long as this technique of control is misunderstood, we cannot judge correctly an environment in which there is less need for heroism, hardship, or independent action. We are likely to argue that such an environment is itself less admirable or produces less admirable people. In the old days, for example, young scholars often lived in undesirable quarters, ate unappetizing or inadequate food, performed unprofitable tasks for a living or to pay for necessary books and materials or publication. Older scholars and other members of the group offered compensating reinforcement in the form of approval and admiration for these sacrifices. When the modern graduate student receives a generous scholarship, enjoys good living conditions, and has his research and publication subsidized, the grounds for evaluation seem to be pulled from under us. Such a student no longer *needs* admiration to carry him over a series of obstacles (no matter how much he may need it for other reasons), and, in missing certain familiar objects of admiration, we are likely to conclude that such *conditions* are less admirable. Obstacles to scholarly work may serve as a useful measure of motivation—and we may go wrong unless some substitute is found—but we can scarcely defend a deliberate harassment of the student for this purpose. The productivity of any set of conditions can be evaluated only when we have freed ourselves of the attitudes which have been generated in us as members of an ethical group.

A similar difficulty arises from our use of punishment in the form of censure or blame. The concept of responsibility and the related concepts of foreknowledge and choice are used to justify techniques of control using punishment. Was So-and-So aware of the probable consequences of his action, and was the action deliberate? If so, we are justified in punishing him. But what does this mean? It appears to be a question concerning the efficacy of the contingent relations between behavior and punishing consequences. We punish behavior because it is objectionable to us or the group, but in a minor refinement of rather recent origin we have come to withhold punishment when it cannot be expected to have any effect. If the objectionable consequences of an act were accidental and not likely to occur again, there is no point in punishing. We say that the individual was not "aware of the consequences of his action" or that the consequences were not "intentional." If the action could not have been avoided—if the individual "had no choice"—punishment is also withheld, as it is if the individual is incapable of being changed by punishment because he is of "unsound mind." In all these cases—different as they are—the individual is held "not responsible" and goes unpunished.

Just as we say that it is "not fair" to punish a man for something he could not help doing, so we call it "unfair" when one is rewarded beyond his due or for something he could not help doing. In other words, we also object to wasting *reinforcers* where they are not needed or will do no good. We make the same point with the words *just* and *right*. Thus we have no right to punish the irresponsible, and a man has no right to reinforcers he does not earn or deserve. But concepts of choice, responsibility, justice, and so on, provide a most inadequate analysis of efficient reinforcing and punishing contingencies because they carry a heavy semantic cargo of a quite different sort, which obscures any attempt to clarify controlling practices or to improve techniques. In particular, they fail to prepare us for techniques based on other than aversive techniques of control. Most people would object to forcing prisoners to serve as subjects of dangerous medical experiments, but few object when they are induced to serve by the offer of return privileges—even when the reinforcing effect of these privileges has been created by forcible deprivation. In the traditional scheme the right to refuse guarantees the individual against coercion or an unfair bargain. But to what extent *can* a prisoner refuse under such circumstances?

We need not go so far afield to make the point. We can observe our own attitude toward personal freedom in the way we resent any interference with what we want to do. Suppose we want to buy a car of a particular sort. Then we may object, for example, if our wife urges us to buy a less expensive model and to put the difference into a new refrigerator. Or we may resent it if our neighbor questions our need for such a car or our ability to pay for it. We would certainly resent it if it were illegal to buy such a car (remember Prohibition); and if we find we cannot actually afford it, we may resent governmental control of the price through tariffs and taxes. We resent it if we discover that we cannot get the car because the manufacturer is holding the model in deliberately short supply in order to push a model we do not want. In all this we assert our democratic right to buy the car of our choice. We are well prepared to do so and to resent any restriction on our freedom.

But why do we not ask *why* it is the car of our choice and resent the forces which made it so? Perhaps our favorite toy as a child was a car, of a very different model, but nevertheless bearing the name of the car we now want. Perhaps our favorite TV program is sponsored by the manufacturer of that car. Perhaps we have seen pictures of many beautiful or prestigeful persons driving it—in pleasant or glamorous places. Perhaps the car has been designed with respect to our motivational patterns: the device on the hood is a phallic symbol; or the horsepower has been stepped up to please our competitive spirit in enabling us to pass other cars swiftly (or, as the advertisements say, "safely"). The concept of freedom that has emerged as part of the cultural practice of our group makes little or no provision for recognizing or dealing with these kinds of control. Concepts like "responsibility" and "rights" are scarcely applicable. We are prepared to deal with coercive measures, but we have no traditional recourse with respect to other measures which in the long run (and especially with the help of science) may be much more powerful and dangerous.

EDUCATION

The techniques of education were once frankly aversive. The teacher was usually older and stronger than his pupils and was able to "make them learn." This meant that they were not actually taught but were surrounded by a threatening world from which they could escape only by learning. Usually they were left to their own resources in discovering how to do so. Claude Coleman has published a grimly amusing reminder of these older practices (1953). He tells of a schoolteacher who published a careful account of his services during 51 years of teaching, during which he administered: ". . . 911,527 blows with a cane; 124,010 with a rod; 20,989 with a ruler; 136,715 with the hand; 10,295 over the mouth; 7,905 boxes on the ear; [and] 1,115,800 slaps on the head. . . ."

Progressive education was a humanitarian effort to substitute positive reinforcement for such aversive measures, but in the search for useful human values in the classroom it has never fully replaced the variables it abandoned. Viewed as a branch of behavioral technology, education remains relatively inefficient. We supplement it, and rationalize it, by admiring the pupil who learns *for himself;* and we often attribute the learning process, or knowledge itself, to something *inside* the individual. We admire behavior which seems to have inner sources. Thus we admire one who *recites* a poem more than one who simply *reads* it. We admire one who *knows* the answer more than one who *knows where to look it up.* We admire the *writer* rather than the *reader.* We admire the arithmetician who can do a problem in his head rather than with a slide rule or calculating machine, or in "original" ways rather than by a strict application of rules. In general we feel that any aid or "crutch" —except those aids to which we are now thoroughly accustomed—reduces the credit due. In Plato's *Phaedrus,* Thamus, the king, attacks the invention of the alphabet on similar grounds! He is afraid "it will produce forgetfulness in the minds of those who learn to use it, because they will not practice their memories. . . ." In other words, he holds it more admirable to remember than to use a memorandum. He also objects that pupils "will read many things without instruction. . . [and] will therefore seem to know many things when they are for the most part ignorant." In the same vein we are today sometimes contemptuous of book learning, but, as educators, we can scarcely afford to adopt this view without reservation.

By admiring the student for knowledge and blaming him for ignorance, we escape some of the responsibility of teaching him. We resist any analysis of the educational process which threatens the notion of inner wisdom or questions the contention that the fault of ignorance lies with the student. More powerful techniques which bring about the same changes in behavior by manipulating *external* variables are decried as brainwashing or thought control. We are quite unprepared to judge *effective* educational measures. As long as only a few pupils learn much of what is taught, we do not worry about uniformity or regimentation. We do not fear the feeble technique; but we should view with dismay a system under which every student learned everything listed in a syllabus—although such a condition is far from unthinkable. Similarly, we do not fear a system which is so defective that the student must *work* for an education: but we are loath to give credit for anything learned without effort—although this could well be taken as an ideal result—and we flatly refuse to give credit if the student already knows what a school teaches.

A world in which people are wise and good without trying, without "having to be," without "choosing to be," could conceivably be a far better world for everyone. In such a world we should not have to "give anyone credit"—we should not need to admire anyone—for being wise and good. From our present point of view we cannot believe that such a world would be admirable. We do not even permit ourselves to imagine what it would be like.

GOVERNMENT

Government has always been the special field of aversive control. The state is frequently defined in terms of the power to punish, and jurisprudence leans upon the associated notion of personal responsibility. Yet it is becoming increasingly difficult to reconcile current practice and theory with these earlier views. In criminology, for example, there is a strong tendency to drop the notion of responsibility in favor of some such alternative as capacity or controllability. But no matter how strongly the facts, or even practical expedience, support such a change, it is difficult to make the change in a legal system designed on a different plan. When governments resort to other techniques (for example, positive reinforcement), the concept of responsibility is no longer relevant and the theory of government is no longer applicable.

The conflict is illustrated by two decisions of the Supreme Court in the 1930's which dealt with, and disagreed on, the definition of control or coercion (Freund, et al., 1954, p. 233). The Agricultural Adjustment Act proposed that the Secretary of Agriculture make "rental or benefit payments" to those farmers who agreed to reduce production. The government agreed that the Act would be unconstitutional if the farmer had been *compelled* to reduce production but was not, since he was merely *invited* to do so. Justice Roberts expressed the contrary majority view of the court that "The power to confer or withhold unlimited benefits is the power to coerce or destroy." This recognition of positive reinforcement was withdrawn a few years later in another case in which Justice Cardozo (Freund, et al., 1954, p. 244) wrote "To hold that motive or temptation is equivalent to coercion is to plunge the law in endless difficulties." We may agree with him, without implying that the proposition is therefore wrong. Sooner or later the law must be prepared to deal with all possible techniques of governmental control.

The uneasiness with which we view government (in the broadest possible sense) when it does not use punishment is shown by the reception of my utopian novel, *Walden Two* (Skinner, 1948b). This was essentially a proposal to apply a behavioral technology to the construction of a workable, effective, and productive pattern of government. It was greeted with wrathful violence. *Life* magazine called it "a travesty on the good life," and "a menace . . . a triumph of mortmain or the dead hand not envisaged since the days of Sparta . . . a slur upon a name, a corruption of an impulse." Joseph Wood Krutch devoted a substantial part of his book, *The Measure of Man* (1954), to attacking my views and those of the protagonist, Frazier, in the same vein, and Morris Viteles has recently criticized the book in a similar manner in *Science* (1955). Perhaps the reaction is best expressed in a quotation from *The Quest for Utopia* by Negley and Patrick (1952):

Halfway through this contemporary utopia, the reader may feel sure, as we did, that this is a beautifully ironic satire on what has been called 'behavioral engineering.' The longer one stays in this better world of the psychologist, however, the plainer it becomes that the inspiration is not satiric, but messianic. This is indeed the behaviorally engineered society, and while it was to be expected that sooner or later the principle of psychological conditioning would be made the basis of a serious construction of utopia—Brown anticipated it in Limanora—yet not even the effective satire of Huxley is adequate preparation for the shocking horror of the idea when positively presented. Of all the dictatorships espoused by utopists, this is the most profound, and incipient dictators might well find in this utopia a guidebook of political practice.

One would scarcely guess that the authors are talking about a world in which there is food, clothing, and shelter for all, where everyone chooses his own work and works on the average only 4 hours a day, where music and the arts flourish, where personal relationships develop under the most favorable circumstances, where education prepares every child for the social and intellectual life which lies before him, where—in short—people are truly happy, secure, productive, creative, and forward-looking. What is wrong with it? Only one thing: someone "planned it that way."

If these critics had come upon a society in some remote corner of the world which boasted similar advantages, they would undoubtedly have hailed it as providing a pattern we all might well follow—provided that it was clearly the result of a natural process of cultural evolution. Any evidence that intelligence had been used in arriving at this version of the good life would, in their eyes, be a serious flaw. No matter if the planner of *Walden Two* diverts none of the proceeds of the community to his own use, no matter if he has no current control or is, indeed, unknown to most of the other members of the community (he planned that, too), somewhere back of it all he occupies the position of prime mover. And this, to the child of the democratic tradition, spoils it all.

The dangers inherent in the control of human behavior are very real. The possibility of the misuse of scientific knowledge must always be faced. We cannot escape by denying the power of a science of behavior or arresting its development. It is no help to cling to familiar philosophies of human behavior simply because they are more reassuring. As I have pointed out elsewhere (Skinner, 1955), the new techniques emerging from a science of behavior must be subject to the explicit countercontrol which has already been applied to earlier and cruder forms. Brute force and deception, for example, are now fairly generally suppressed by ethical practices and by explicit governmental and religious agencies. A similar countercontrol of scientific knowledge in the interests of the group is a feasible and promising possibility. Although we cannot say how devious the course of its evolution may be, a cultural pattern of control and countercontrol will presumably emerge which will be most widely supported because it is most widely reinforcing.

If we cannot foresee all the details of this (as we obviously cannot), it is important to remember that this is true of the critics of science as well. The dire consequences of new techniques of control, the hidden menace in original cultural designs —these need some proof. It is only another example of my present point that the need for proof is so often overlooked. Man has got himself into some pretty fixes, and it is easy to believe that he will do so again. But there is a more optimistic possibility. The slow growth of the method of science, now for the first time being applied to human affairs, *may* mean a new and exciting phase of human life to which historical analogies will not apply and in which earlier political slogans will not be appropriate. If we are to use the knowledge that a science of behavior is now making available with any hope of success, we must look at human nature as it is brought into focus through the methods of science rather than as it has been presented to us in a series of historical accidents.

If the advent of a powerful science of behavior causes trouble, it will not be because science itself is inimical to human welfare but because older conceptions have not yielded easily or gracefully. We expect resistance to new techniques of control from those who have heavy investments in the old, but we have no reason to help them preserve a series of principles that are not ends in themselves but rather outmoded means to an end. What is needed is a new conception of human behavior which is compatible with the implications of a scientific analysis. All men control and are controlled. The question of government in the broadest possible sense is not how freedom is to be preserved but what kinds of control are to be used and to what ends. Control must be analyzed and considered in its proper proportions. No one, I am sure, wishes to develop new master-slave relationships or bend the will of the people to despotic rulers in new ways. These are patterns of control appropriate to a world without science. They may well be the first to go when the experimental analysis of behavior comes into its own in the design of cultural practices.

II—ROGERS

There are, I believe, a number of matters in connection with this important topic on which the authors of this article, and probably a large majority of psychologists, are in agreement. These matters then are not issues as far as we are concerned, and I should like to mention them briefly in order to put them to one side.

POINTS OF AGREEMENT

I am sure we agree that men—as individuals and as societies—have always endeavored to understand, predict, influence, and control human behavior—their own behavior and that of others.

I believe we agree that the behavioral sciences are making and will continue to make increasingly rapid progress in the understanding of behavior, and that as a consequence the capacity to predict and to control behavior is developing with equal rapidity.

I believe we agree that to deny these advances, or to claim that man's behavior cannot be a field of science, is unrealistic. Even though this is not an issue for us, we should recognize that many intelligent men still hold strongly to the view that the actions of men are free in some sense such that scientific knowledge of man's behavior is impossible. Thus Reinhold Niebuhr, the noted theologian, heaps scorn on the concept of psychology as a science of man's behavior and even says, "In any event, no scientific investigation of past behavior can become the basis of predictions of future behavior." (1955, p. 47). So, while this is not an issue for psychologists, we should at least notice in passing that it is an issue for many people.

I believe we are in agreement that the tremendous potential power of a science which permits the prediction and control of behavior may be misused, and that the possibility of such misuse constitutes a serious threat.

Consequently Skinner and I are in agreement that the whole question of the scientific control of human behavior is a matter with which psychologists and the general public should concern themselves. As Robert Oppenheimer told the American Psychological Association last year (1956a) the problems that psychologists will pose for society by their growing ability to control behavior will be much more grave than the problems posed by the ability of physicists to control the reactions of matter. I am not sure whether psychologists generally recognize this. My impression is that by and large they hold a laissez-faire attitude. Obviously Skinner and I do not hold this laissez-faire view, or we would not have written this article.

POINTS OF ISSUE

With these several points of basic and important agreement, are there then any issues that remain on which there are differences? I believe there are. They can be stated very briefly: Who will be controlled? Who will exercise control? What type of control will be exercised? Most important of all, toward what end or what purpose, or in the pursuit of what value, will control be exercised?

It is on questions of this sort that there exist ambiguities, misunderstandings, and probably deep differences. These differences exist among psychologists, among members of the general public in this country, and among various world cultures. Without any hope of achieving a final resolution of these questions, we can, I believe, put these issues in clearer form.

SOME MEANINGS

To avoid ambiguity and faulty communication, I would like to clarify the meanings of some of the terms we are using.

Behavioral science is a term that might be defined from several angles but in the context of this discussion it refers primarily to knowledge that the existence of certain describable conditions in the human being and/or in his environment is followed by certain describable consequences in his actions.

Prediction means the prior identification of behaviors which then occur. Because it is important in some things I wish to say later, I would point out that one may predict a highly specific behavior, such as an eye blink, or one may predict a class of behaviors. One might correctly predict "avoidant behavior," for example, without being able to specify whether the individual will run away or simply close his eyes.

The word *control* is a very slippery one, which can be used with any one of several meanings. I would like to specify three that seem most important for our present purposes. *Control* may mean: (i) The setting of conditions by B for A, A having no voice in the matter, such that certain predictable behaviors then occur in A. I refer to this as external control. (ii) The setting of conditions by B for A, A giving some degree of consent to these conditions, such that certain predictable behaviors then occur in A. I refer to this as the influence of B on A. (iii) The setting of conditions by A such that certain predictable behaviors then occur in himself. I refer to this as internal control. It will be noted that Skinner lumps together the first two meanings, external control and influence, under the concept of control. I find this confusing.

USUAL CONCEPT OF CONTROL OF HUMAN BEHAVIOR

With the underbrush thus cleared away (I hope), let us review very briefly the various elements that are involved in the usual concept of the control of human behavior as mediated by the behavioral sciences. I am drawing here on the previous writings of Skinner, on his present statements, on the writings of others who have considered in either friendly or antagonistic fashion the meanings that would be involved in such control. I have not excluded the science fiction writers, as reported recently by Vandenburg (1956), since they often show an awareness of the issues involved, even though the methods described are as yet fictional. These then are the elements that seem common to these different concepts of the application of science to human behavior.

1.   There must first be some sort of decision about goals. Usually desirable goals are assumed, but sometimes, as in George Orwell's book *1984*, the goal that is selected

is an aggrandizement of individual power with which most of us would disagree. In a recent paper Skinner suggests that one possible set of goals to be assigned to the behavioral technology is this: "Let men be happy, informed, skillful, well-behaved and productive." (1955–1956). In the first draft of his part of this article, which he was kind enough to show me, he did not mention such definite goals as these, but desired "improved" educational practices, "wiser" use of knowledge in government, and the like. In the final version of his article he avoids even these value-laden terms, and his implicit goal is the very general one that scientific control of behavior is desirable, because it would perhaps bring "a far better world for everyone."

Thus the first step in thinking about the control of human behavior is the choice of goals, whether specific or general. It is necessary to come to terms in some way with the issue, "For what purpose?"

2.   A second element is that, whether the end selected is highly specific or is a very general one such as wanting "a better world," we proceed by the methods of science to discover the means to these ends. We continue through further experimentation and investigation to discover more effective means. The method of science is self-correcting in thus arriving at increasingly effective ways of achieving the purpose we have in mind.

3.   The third aspect of such control is that as the conditions or methods are discovered by which to reach the goal, some person or some group establishes these conditions and uses these methods, having in one way or another obtained the power to do so.

4.   The fourth element is the exposure of individuals to the prescribed conditions, and this leads, with a high degree of probability, to behavior which is in line with the goals desired. Individuals are now happy, if that has been the goal, or well-behaved, or submissive, or whatever it has been decided to make them.

5.   The fifth element is that if the process I have described is put in motion then there is a continuing social organization which will continue to produce the types of behavior that have been valued.

SOME FLAWS

Are there any flaws in this way of viewing the control of human behavior? I believe there are. In fact the only element in this description with which I find myself in agreement is the second. It seems to me quite incontrovertibly true that the scientific method is an excellent way to discover the means by which to achieve our goals. Beyond that, I feel many sharp differences, which I will try to spell out.

I believe that in Skinner's presentation here and in his previous writings, there is a serious underestimation of the problem of power. To hope that the power which is being made available by the behavioral sciences will be exercised by the scientists, or by a benevolent group, seems to me a hope little supported by either recent or distant history. It seems far more likely that behavioral scientists, holding their present attitudes, will be in the position of the German rocket scientists specializing in guided missiles. First they worked devotedly for Hitler to destroy the U.S.S.R. and the United States. Now, depending on who captured them, they work devotedly for the U.S.S.R. in the interest of destroying the United States, or devotedly for the

United States in the interest of destroying the U.S.S.R. If behavioral scientists are concerned solely with advancing their science, it seems most probable that they will serve the purposes of whatever individual or group has the power.

But the major flaw I see in this review of what is involved in the scientific control of human behavior is the denial, misunderstanding, or gross underestimation of the place of ends, goals or values in their relationship to science. This error (as it seems to me) has so many implications that I would like to devote some space to it.

ENDS AND VALUES IN RELATION TO SCIENCE

In sharp contradiction to some views that have been advanced, I would like to propose a two-pronged thesis: (i) In any scientific endeavor—whether "pure" or applied science—there is a prior subjective choice of the purpose or value which that scientific work is perceived as serving. (ii) The subjective value choice which brings that scientific endeavor into being must always lie outside of that endeavor and can never become a part of the science involved in that endeavor.

Let me illustrate the first point from Skinner himself. It is clear that in his earlier writing (1955–1956) it is recognized that a prior value choice is necessary, and it is specified as the goal that men are to become happy, well-behaved, productive, and so on. I am pleased that Skinner has retreated from the goals he then chose, because to me they seem to be stultifying values. I can only feel that he was choosing these goals for others, not for himself. I would hate to see Skinner become "well-behaved," as that term would be defined for him by behavioral scientists. His recent article in the *American Psychologist* (1956) shows that he certainly does not want to be "productive" as that value is defined by most psychologists. And the most awful fate I can imagine for him would be to have him constantly "happy." It is the fact that he is very unhappy about many things which makes me prize him.

In the first draft of his part of this article, he also included such prior value choices, saying for example, "We must decide how we are to use the knowledge, which a science of human behavior is now making available." Now he has dropped all mention of such choices, and if I understand him correctly, he believes that science can proceed without them. He has suggested this view in another recent paper, stating that "We must continue to experiment in cultural design . . . testing the consequences as we go. Eventually the practices which make for the greatest biological and psychological strength of the group will presumably survive" (Skinner, 1955, p. 549).

I would point out, however, that to choose to experiment is a value choice. Even to move in the direction of perfectly random experimentation is a value choice. To test the consequences of an experiment is possible only if we have first made a subjective choice of a criterion value. And implicit in his statement is a valuing of biological and psychological strength. So even when trying to avoid such choice, it seems inescapable that a prior subjective value choice is necessary for any scientific endeavor, or for any application of scientific knowledge.

I wish to make it clear that I am not saying that values cannot be included as a subject of science. It is not true that science deals only with certain classes of "facts" and that these classes do not include values. It is a bit more complex than that, as a simple illustration or two may make clear.

If I value knowledge of the "three R's" as a goal of education, the methods of science can give me increasingly accurate information on how this goal may be achieved. If I value problem-solving ability as a goal of education, the scientific method can give me the same kind of help.

Now, if I wish to determine whether problem-solving ability is "better" than knowledge of the three R's, then scientific method can also study those two values but *only*—and this is very important—in terms of some other value which I have subjectively chosen. I may value college success. Then I can determine whether problem-solving ability or knowledge of the three R's is most closely associated with that value. I may value personal integration or vocational success or responsible citizenship. I can determine whether problem-solving ability or knowledge of the three R's is "better" for achieving any one of these values. But the value or purpose that gives meaning to a particular scientific endeavor must always lie outside of that endeavor.

Although our concern in this symposium is largely with applied science, what I have been saying seems equally true of so-called "pure" science. In pure science the usual prior subjective value choice is the discovery of truth. But this is a subjective choice, and science can never say whether it is the best choice, save in the light of some other value. Geneticists in the U.S.S.R., for example, had to make a subjective choice of whether it was better to pursue truth or to discover facts which upheld a governmental dogma. Which choice is "better"? We could make a scientific investigation of those alternatives but only in the light of some other subjectively chosen value. If, for example, we value the survival of a culture, then we could begin to investigate with the methods of science the question of whether pursuit of truth or support of governmental dogma is most closely associated with cultural survival.

My point then is that any endeavor in science, pure or applied, is carried on in the pursuit of a purpose or value that is subjectively chosen by persons. It is important that this choice be made explicit, since the particular value which is being sought can never be tested or evaluated, confirmed or denied, by the scientific endeavor to which it gives birth. The initial purpose or value always and necessarily lies outside the scope of the scientific effort which it sets in motion.

Among other things this means that if we choose some particular goal or series of goals for human beings and then set out on a large scale to control human behavior to the end of achieving those goals, we are locked in the rigidity of our initial choice, because such a scientific endeavor can never transcend itself to select new goals. Only subjective human persons can do that. Thus if we chose as our goal the state of happiness for human beings (a goal deservedly ridiculed by Aldous Huxley in *Brave New World*), and if we involved all of society in a successful scientific program by which people became happy, we would be locked in a colossal rigidity in which no one would be free to question this goal, because our scientific operations could not transcend themselves to question their guiding purposes. And without laboring this point, I would remark that colossal rigidity, whether in dinosaurs, or dictatorships, has a very poor record of evolutionary survival.

If, however, a part of our scheme is to set free some "planners" who do not have to be happy, who are not controlled, and who are therefore free to choose other values, this has several meanings. It means that the purpose we have chosen as our goal is not a sufficient and a satisfying one for human beings but must be supplemented. It also means that if it is necessary to set up an elite group which is free, then this shows all too clearly that the great majority are only the slaves—no matter by what high-sounding name we call them—of those who select the goals.

Perhaps, however, the thought is that a continuing scientific endeavor will evolve its own goals; that the initial findings will alter the directions, and subsequent findings will alter them still further, and that science somehow develops its own purpose. Although he does not clearly say so, this appears to be the pattern Skinner has in mind. It is surely a reasonable description, but it overlooks one element in this continuing development, which is that subjective personal choice enters in at every point at which the direction changes. The findings of a science, the results of an experiment, do not and never can tell us what next scientific purpose to pursue. Even in the purest of science, the scientist must decide what the findings mean and must subjectively choose what next step will be most profitable in the pursuit of his purpose. And if we are speaking of the application of scientific knowledge, then it is distressingly clear that the increasing scientific knowledge of the structure of the atom carries with it no necessary choice as to the purpose to which this knowledge will be put. This is a subjective personal choice which must be made by many individuals.

Thus I return to the proposition with which I began this section of my remarks —and which I now repeat in different words. Science has its meaning as the objective pursuit of a purpose which has been subjectively chosen by a person or persons. This purpose or value can never be investigated by the particular scientific experiment or investigation to which it has given birth and meaning. Consequently, any discussion of the control of human beings by the behavioral sciences must first and most deeply concern itself with the subjectively chosen purposes which such an application of science is intended to implement.

IS THE SITUATION HOPELESS?

The thoughtful reader may recognize that, although my remarks up to this point have introduced some modifications in the conception of the processes by which human behavior will be controlled, these remarks may have made such control seem, if anything, even more inevitable. We might sum it up this way: Behavioral science is clearly moving forward; the increasing power for control which it gives will be held by someone or some group; such an individual or group will surely choose the values or goals to be achieved; and most of us will then be increasingly controlled by means so subtle that we will not even be aware of them as controls. Thus, whether a council of wise psychologists (if this is not a contradiction in terms), or a Stalin, or a Big Brother has the power, and whether the goal is happiness, or productivity, or resolution of the Oedipus complex, or submission, or love of Big Brother, we will inevitably find ourselves moving toward the chosen goal and probably thinking that we ourselves desire it. Thus, if this line of reasoning is correct, it appears that some form of *Walden Two* or of *1984* (and at a deep philosophic level they seem indistinguishable) is coming. The fact that it would surely arrive piecemeal, rather than all at once, does not greatly change the fundamental issues. In any event, as Skinner has indicated in his writings, we would then look back upon the concepts of human freedom, the capacity for choice, the responsibility for choice, and the worth of the human individual as historical curiosities which once existed by cultural accident as values in a prescientific civilization.

I believe that any person observant of trends must regard something like the foregoing sequence as a real possibility. It is not simply a fantasy. Something of that sort may even be the most likely future. But is it an inevitable future? I want to devote the remainder of my remarks to an alternative possibility.

ALTERNATIVE SET OF VALUES

Suppose we start with a set of ends, values, purposes, quite different from the type of goals we have been considering. Suppose we do this quite openly, setting them forth as a possible value choice to be accepted or rejected. Suppose we select a set of values that focuses on fluid elements of process rather than static attributes. We might then value: man as a process of becoming, as a process of achieving worth and dignity through the development of his potentialities; the individual human being as a self-actualizing process, moving on to more challenging and enriching experiences; the process by which the individual creatively adapts to an ever-new and changing world; the process by which knowledge transcends itself, as, for example, the theory of relativity transcended Newtonian physics, itself to be transcended in some future day by a new perception.

If we select values such as these we turn to our science and technology of behavior with a very different set of questions. We will want to know such things as these: Can science aid in the discovery of new modes of richly rewarding living? more meaningful and satisfying modes of interpersonal relationships? Can science inform us on how the human race can become a more intelligent participant in its own evolution—its physical, psychological and social evolution? Can science inform us on ways of releasing the creative capacity of individuals, which seems so necessary if we are to survive in this fantastically expanding atomic age? Oppenheimer has pointed out (1956b) that knowledge, which used to double in millennia or centuries, now doubles in a generation or a decade. It appears that we must discover the utmost in release of creativity if we are to be able to adapt effectively. In short, can science discover the methods by which man can most readily become a continually developing and self-transcending process, in his behavior, his thinking, his knowledge? Can science predict and release an essentially "unpredictable" freedom?

It is one of the virtues of science as a method that it is as able to advance and implement goals and purposes of this sort as it is to serve static values, such as states of being well-informed, happy, obedient. Indeed we have some evidence of this.

SMALL EXAMPLE

I will perhaps be forgiven if I document some of the possibilities along this line by turning to psychotherapy, the field I know best.

Psychotherapy, as Meerloo (1955) and others have pointed out, can be one of the most subtle tools for the control of A by B. The therapist can subtly mold individuals in imitation of himself. He can cause an individual to become a submissive and conforming being. When certain therapeutic principles are used in extreme fashion, we call it brainwashing, an instance of the disintegration of the personality and a reformulation of the person along lines desired by the controlling individual. So the principles of therapy can be used as an effective means of external control of human personality and behavior. Can psychotherapy be anything else?

Here I find the developments going on in client-centered psychotherapy (Rogers, 1951) an exciting hint of what a behavioral science can do in achieving the kinds of values I have stated. Quite aside from being a somewhat new orientation in psychotherapy, this development has important implications regarding the relation of a behavioral science to the control of human behavior. Let me describe our experience as it relates to the issues of this discussion.

In client-centered therapy, we are deeply engaged in the prediction and influencing of behavior, or even the control of behavior. As therapists we institute certain attitudinal conditions, and the client has relatively little voice in the establishment of these conditions. We predict that if these conditions are instituted, certain behavioral consequences will ensue in the client. Up to this point this is largely external control, no different from what Skinner has described, and no different from what I have discussed in the preceding sections of this article. But here the similarity ceases.

The conditions we have chosen to establish predict such behavioral consequences as these: that the client will become self-directing, less rigid, more open to the evidence of his senses, better organized and integrated, more similar to the ideal which he has chosen for himself. In other words, we have established by external control conditions which we predict will be followed by internal control by the individual, in pursuit of internally chosen goals. We have set the conditions which predict various classes of behaviors—self-directing behaviors, sensitivity to realities within and without, flexible adaptiveness—which are by their very nature unpredictable in their specifics. Our recent research (Rogers and Dymond, 1954) indicates that our predictions are to a significant degree corroborated, and our commitment to the scientific method causes us to believe that more effective means of achieving these goals may be realized.

Research exists in other fields—industry, education, group dynamics—which seems to support our own findings. I believe it may be conservatively stated that scientific progress has been made in identifying those conditions in an interpersonal relationship which, if they exist in B, are followed in A by greater maturity in behavior, less dependence on others, an increase in expressiveness as a person, an increase in variability, flexibility and effectiveness of adaptation, an increase in self-responsibility and self-direction. And, quite in contrast to the concern expressed by some, we do not find that the creatively adaptive behavior which results from such self-directed variability of expression is a "happy accident" which occurs in "chaos." Rather, the individual who is open to his experience, and self-directing, is harmonious not chaotic, ingenious rather than random, as he orders his responses imaginatively toward the achievement of his own purposes. His creative actions are no more a "happy accident" than was Einstein's development of the theory of relativity.

Thus we find ourselves in fundamental agreement with John Dewey's statement: "Science has made its way by releasing, not by suppressing, the elements of variation, of invention and innovation, of novel creation in individuals." (Ratner, 1939, p. 359). Progress in personal life and in group living is, we believe, made in the same way.

POSSIBLE CONCEPT OF THE CONTROL OF HUMAN BEHAVIOR

It is quite clear that the point of view I am expressing is in sharp contrast to the usual conception of the relationship of the behavioral sciences to the control of human behavior. In order to make this contrast even more blunt, I will state this possibility in paragraphs parallel to those used before.

1. It is possible for us to choose to value man as a self-actualizing process of becoming; to value creativity, and the process by which knowledge becomes self-transcending.

2. We can proceed, by the methods of science, to discover the conditions which necessarily precede these processes and, through continuing experimentation, to discover better means of achieving these purposes.

3. It is possible for individuals or groups to set these conditions, with a minimum of power or control. According to present knowledge, the only authority necessary is the authority to establish certain qualities of interpersonal relationship.

4. Exposed to these conditions, present knowledge suggests that individuals become more self-responsible, make progress in self-actualization, become more flexible, and become more creatively adaptive.

5. Thus such an initial choice would inaugurate the beginnings of a social system or subsystem in which values, knowledge, adaptive skills, and even the concept of science would be continually changing and self-transcending. The emphasis would be upon man as a process of becoming.

I believe it is clear that such a view as I have been describing does not lead to any definable utopia. It would be impossible to predict its final outcome. It involves a step-by-step development, based on a continuing subjective choice of purposes, which are implemented by the behavioral sciences. It is the direction of the "open society," as that term has been defined by Popper (1945), where individuals carry responsibility for personal decisions. It is at the opposite pole from his concept of the closed society, of which *Walden Two* would be an example.

I trust it is also evident that the whole emphasis is on process, not on end-states of being. I am suggesting that it is by choosing to value certain qualitative elements of the process of becoming that we can find a pathway toward the open society.

THE CHOICE

It is my hope that we have helped to clarify the range of choice which will lie before us and our children in regard to the behavioral sciences. We can choose to use our growing knowledge to enslave people in ways never dreamed of before, depersonalizing them, controlling them by means so carefully selected that they will perhaps never be aware of their loss of personhood. We can choose to utilize our scientific knowledge to make men happy, well-behaved, and productive, as Skinner earlier suggested. Or we can insure that each person learns all the syllabus which we select and set before him, as Skinner now suggests. Or at the other end of the spectrum or choice we can choose to use the behavioral sciences in ways which will free, not control; which will bring about constructive variability, not conformity; which will develop creativity, not contentment; which will facilitate each person in his self-directed process of becoming; which will aid individuals, groups, and even the concept of science to become self-transcending in freshly adaptive ways of meeting life and its problems. The choice is up to us, and, the human race being what it is, we are likely to stumble about, making at times some nearly disastrous value choices and at other times highly constructive ones.

I am aware that to some, this setting forth of a choice is unrealistic, because a choice of values is regarded as not possible. Skinner has stated:

Man's vaunted creative powers . . . his capacity to choose and our right to hold him responsible for his choice—none of these is conspicuous in this new self-portrait (provided by science). Man, we once believed, was free to express himself in art, music, and literature, to inquire into nature, to seek salvation in his own way. He could initiate action and make spontaneous and capricious changes of course. . . . But science insists that action is initiated by forces impinging upon the individual, and that caprice is only another name for behavior for which we have not yet found a cause. (1955–1956, pp. 52–53).

I can understand this point of view, but I believe that it avoids looking at the great paradox of behavioral science. Behavior, when it is examined scientifically, is surely best understood as determined by prior causation. This is one great fact of science. But responsible personal choice, which is the most essential element in being a person, which is the core experience in psychotherapy, which exists prior to any scientific endeavor, is an equally prominent fact in our lives. To deny the experience of responsible choice is, to me, as restricted a view as to deny the possibility of a behavioral science. That these two important elements of our experience appear to be in contradiction has perhaps the same significance as the contradiction between the wave theory and the corpuscular theory of light, both of which can be shown to be true, even though incompatible. We cannot profitably deny our subjective life, any more than we can deny the objective description of that life.

In conclusion then, it is my contention that science cannot come into being without a personal choice of the values we wish to achieve. And these values we choose to implement will forever lie outside of the science which implements them; the goals we select, the purposes we wish to follow, must always be outside of the science which achieves them. To me this has the encouraging meaning that the human person, with his capacity of subjective choice, can and will always exist, separate from and prior to any of his scientific undertakings. Unless as individuals and groups we choose to relinquish our capacity of subjective choice, we will always remain persons, not simply pawns of a self-created science.

III—SKINNER

I cannot quite agree that the practice of science *requires* a prior decision about goals or a prior choice of values. The metallurgist can study the properties of steel and the engineer can design a bridge without raising the question of whether a bridge is to be built. But such questions are certainly frequently raised and tentatively answered. Rogers wants to call the answers "subjective choices of values." To me, such an expression suggests that we have had to abandon more rigorous scientific practices in order to talk about our own behavior. In the experimental analysis of other organisms I would use other terms, and I shall try to do so here. Any list of values is a list of reinforcers—conditioned or otherwise. We are so constituted that under certain circumstances food, water, sexual contact, and so on, will make any behavior which produces them more likely to occur again. Other things may acquire this power. We do not need to say that an organism chooses to eat rather than to starve. If you answer that it is a very different thing when a man chooses to starve, I am only too happy to agree. If it were not so, we should have cleared up the question of choice long ago. An organism can be reinforced by—can be made to "choose"—almost any given state of affairs.

Rogers is concerned with choices that involve multiple and usually conflicting consequences. I have dealt with some of these elsewhere (Skinner, 1953) in an analysis of self-control. Shall I eat these delicious strawberries today if I will then suffer an annoying rash tomorrow? The decision I am to make used to be assigned to the province of ethics. But we are now studying similar combinations of positive and negative consequences, as well as collateral conditions which affect the result in a laboratory. Even a pigeon can be taught some measure of self-control! And this work helps us to understand the operation of certain formulas—among them value judgments—which folk-wisdom, religion, and psychotherapy have advanced in the interests of self-discipline. The observable effect of any statement of value is to alter the relative effectiveness of reinforcers. We may no longer enjoy the strawberries for thinking about the rash. If rashes are made sufficiently shameful, illegal, sinful, maladjusted, or unwise, we may glow with satisfaction as we push the strawberries aside in a grandiose avoidance response which would bring a smile to the lips of Murray Sidman.

People behave in ways which, as we say, conform to ethical, governmental, or religious patterns because they are reinforced for doing so. The resulting behavior may have far-reaching consequences for the survival of the pattern to which it conforms. And whether we like it or not, survival is the ultimate criterion. This is where, it seems to me, science can help—not in choosing a goal, but in enabling us to predict the survival value of cultural practices. Man has too long tried to get the kind of world he wants by glorifying some brand of immediate reinforcement. As science points up more and more of the remoter consequences, he may begin to work to strengthen behavior, not in a slavish devotion to a chosen value, but with respect to the ultimate survival of mankind. Do not ask me why I want mankind to survive. I can tell you why only in the sense in which the physiologist can tell you why I want to breathe. Once the relation between a given step and the survival of my group has been pointed out, I will take that step. And it is the business of science to point out just such relations.

The values I have occasionally recommended (and Rogers has not led me to recant) are transitional. Other things being equal, I am betting on the group whose practices make for healthy, happy, secure, productive, and creative people. And I insist that the values recommended by Rogers are transitional, too, for I can ask him the same kind of question. Man as a process of becoming—*what?* Self-actualization —for what? Inner control is no more a goal than external.

What Rogers seems to me to be proposing both here and elsewhere (Rogers, 1956), is this: Let us use our increasing power of control to create individuals who will not need and perhaps will no longer respond to control. Let us solve the problem of our power by renouncing it. At first blush this seems as implausible as a benevolent despot. Yet power has occasionally been foresworn. A nation has burned its Reichstag, rich men have given away their wealth, beautiful women have become ugly hermits in the desert, and psychotherapists have become nondirective. When this happens, I look to other possible reinforcements for a plausible explanation. A people relinquish democratic power when a tyrant promises them the earth. Rich men give away wealth to escape the accusing finger of their fellowmen. A woman destroys her beauty in the hope of salvation. And a psychotherapist relinquishes control because he can thus help his client more effectively.

The solution that Rogers is suggesting is thus understandable. But is he correctly interpreting the result? What evidence is there that a client ever becomes truly *self-directing*? What evidence is there that he ever makes a truly *inner* choice of ideal or goal? Even though the therapist does not do the choosing, even though he encourages "self-actualization"—he is not out of control as long as he holds himself ready to step in when occasion demands—when, for example, the client chooses the goal of becoming a more accomplished liar or murdering his boss. But supposing the therapist does withdraw completely or is no longer necessary—what about all the other forces acting upon the client? Is the self-chosen goal independent of his early ethical and religious training? of the folk-wisdom of his group? of the opinions and attitudes of others who are important to him? Surely not. The therapeutic situation is only a small part of the world of the client. From the therapist's point of view it may appear to be possible to relinquish control. But the control passes not to a "self," but to forces in other parts of the client's world. The solution of the therapist's problem of power cannot be *our* solution, for we must consider *all* the forces acting upon the individual.

The child who must be prodded and nagged is something less than a fully developed human being. We want to see him hurrying to his appointment, not because each step is taken in response to verbal reminders from his mother, but because certain temporal contingencies, in which dawdling has been punished and hurrying reinforced, have worked a change in his behavior. Call this a state of better organization, a greater sensitivity to reality, or what you will. The plain fact is that the child passes from a temporary verbal control exercised by his parents to control by certain inexorable features of the environment. I should suppose that something of the same sort happens in successful psychotherapy. Rogers seems to me to be saying this: Let us put an end, as quickly as possible, to any pattern of master-and-slave, to any direct obedience to command, to the submissive following of suggestions. Let the individual be free to adjust himself to more rewarding features of the world about him. In the end, let his teachers and counselors "wither away," like the Marxist state. I not only agree with this as a useful ideal, I have constructed a fanciful world to demonstrate its advantages. It saddens me to hear Rogers say that "at a deep philosophic level" *Walden Two* and George Orwell's *1984* "seem indistinguishable." They could scarcely be more unlike—at any level. The book *1984* is a picture of immediate aversive control for vicious selfish purposes. The founder of *Walden Two*, on the other hand, has built a community in which neither he nor any other person exerts any *current* control. His achievement lay in his original *plan*, and when he boasts of this ("It is enough to satisfy the thirstiest tyrant") we do not fear him but only pity him for his weakness.

Another critic of *Walden Two*, Andrew Hacker (1955), has discussed this point in considering the bearing of mass conditioning upon the liberal notion of autonomous man. In drawing certain parallels between the Grand Inquisition passage in Dostoevsky's *Brothers Karamazov*, Huxley's *Brave New World*, and *Walden Two*, he attempts to set up a distinction to be drawn in any society between conditioners and conditioned. He assumes that "the conditioner can be said to be autonomous in the traditional liberal sense." But then he notes: "Of course the conditioner has been conditioned. But he has not been conditioned by the conscious manipulation of another *person*." But how does this affect the resulting behavior? Can we not soon forget the origins of the "artificial" diamond which is identical with the real thing? Whether it is an "accidental" cultural pattern, such as is said to have produced the founder of *Walden Two*, or the engineered environment which is about to produce his successors, we are dealing with sets of conditions generating human behavior which will ultimately be measured by their contribution to the strength of the group. We look to the future, not the past, for the test of "goodness" or acceptability.

If we are worthy of our democratic heritage we shall, of course, be ready to resist any tyrannical use of science for immediate or selfish purposes. But if we value the achievements and goals of democracy we must not refuse to apply science to the design and construction of cultural patterns, even though we may then find ourselves in some sense in the position of controllers. Fear of control, generalized beyond any warrant, has led to a misinterpretation of valid practices and the blind rejection of intelligent planning for a better way of life. In terms which I trust Rogers will approve, in conquering this fear we shall become more mature and better organized and shall, thus, more fully actualize ourselves as human beings.

UNIT TEN | DISCUSSION QUESTIONS

34 | RESOURCES FOR PERSONAL GROWTH AND CHANGE

In what ways do intensive group experiences differ from psychotherapy?

Compare sensitivity training with encounter groups.

35 | SOME ETHICAL ISSUES IN SENSITIVITY TRAINING

What are some of the ethical questions and issues related to the processes of training groups?

From your viewpoint, what are some of the ethical issues in group experiences?

36 | A BEHAVIORAL APPROACH TO COUNSELING AND GUIDANCE

Compare "respondent conditioning" with "operant conditioning." Give examples of everyday behavior to support your discussion.

Discuss and compare "aversive" stimulus with "punishment."

37 | SOME ISSUES CONCERNING THE CONTROL OF
HUMAN BEHAVIOR: A SYMPOSIUM

What is your overall opinion of this symposium? Do you favor any one issue? Explain.

One of the goals of any science is eventual "control." Discuss whether there is a need for the control of human behavior.

UNIT ELEVEN
SELF-UNDERSTANDING AND SOCIAL FEELING

Many viewpoints and interpretations concerning methods for understanding ourselves and others have been introduced covering the range from "pop psychiatry" to complex personality theories. The theories of Sigmund Freud, Carl Jung, Alfred Adler, Erich Fromm, Karen Horney, and Harry Stack Sullivan all present ways of viewing the human psyche. Such theories and methods involved with self-understanding and social feeling have not been the sole province of the behavioral scientist; religious leaders, public speakers, and salesmen have made important contributions.

Each decade has its own language and methodology. Dale Carnegie in 1936 wrote *How To Win Friends and Influence People.* Two of his most famous maxims are "Believe that you will succeed and you will" and "Learn to love, respect, and enjoy other people." Norman Vincent Peale believed that one of the main tasks of religion is to help people. Peale wrote several books on this theme, of which *The Power of Positive Thinking* in 1952 gained national popularity. During the 1950's, Bishop Fulton J. Sheen became famous as a television personality for his "Life Is Worth Living" series. The mid-1960's found over 500,000 buyers of psychiatrist Eric Berne's book, *Games People Play.* All of these approaches have in common the objective of helping an individual recognize those self-defeating attitudes and behavioral patterns he should change. Present methods are directed toward the same end, but are expressed in new terms such as: *T-grouping, confrontation groups, awareness experience, human capacity movement, encounter session, marathons, sensitivity,* etc.

No one of these past and present theories *is in itself* entirely adequate; each has its own place and its own significance as a part of the complete picture. The student who gets the most out of his study of himself and others looks understandingly at the *whole* . . . and, having looked, he is able to select and integrate the viewpoints or interpretations best suited to his own needs. This kind of understanding enables *you* to decide what will explain *your* living, *your* behavior, and *your* relationship with *others* most satisfactorily. In attempting to direct your life pattern, full recognition should be made with careful consideration of your particular abilities, interests, and energies.

In *The Will to Meaning,* Viktor E. Frankl is concerned with man's taking into account values that have significance for him beyond self-expression. He emphasizes that a totally conformist and collectivist world would make it impossible for an individual to have personal meaning in his life.

Carl R. Rogers describes some of the changes that occur in the orientation of values by the individual between infancy and adulthood. This article presents some hypotheses on the origins of values. *Toward a Modern Approach to Values: The Valuing Process in the Mature Person* is a timely discussion of one of the major problems facing modern society.

In Rollo May's *Courage to Be One's Self*, he stresses the importance of personal courage in the development of the complete individual. May's existential approach offers much worthy of thought for today's student. Finally, Sidney M. Jourard's *A Humanistic Revolution in Psychology* discusses a contemporary direction in psychology: "the third force." Jourard feels that conventional psychology has learned more about man at his worst than at his best and that humanism in psychology will provide an opportunity for exploring the better possibilities in man.

Emotion and Understanding. A grief-stricken American infantryman whose buddy has been killed in action is comforted by another soldier. (*U.S. Army Photograph*)

38 | THE WILL TO MEANING

Viktor E. Frankl

Central to my psychiatric approach known as logotherapy is the principle of the will to meaning. I counterpose it both to the pleasure principle, which is so pervasive in psychoanalytic motivational theories, and to the will to power, the concept which plays such a decisive role in Adlerian psychology. The will to pleasure is a self-defeating principle inasmuch as the more a person really sets out to strive for pleasure the less likely he is to gain it. For pleasure is a by-product or side effect of the fulfillment of our strivings, and it is contravened to the extent that it is made a goal. The more a person directly aims at pleasure, the more he misses it. In my opinion this mechanism underlies most cases of sexual neurosis. Accordi gly, a logotherapeutic technique based on this theory of the self-thwarting character of pleasure intention yields remarkable short-term results. Even the psychodynamically oriented therapists on my staff have come to acknowledge the value of logotherapy, and one such staff member has used this technique exclusively in treating sexually neurotic patients.

In the final analysis both the will to pleasure and the will to power are derivatives of the will to meaning. Pleasure is an effect of meaning fulfillment; power is a means to an end. A degree of power—economic power, for instance—is generally a prerequisite of meaning fulfillment. But while the will to pleasure mistakes the effect for the end, the will to power mistakes the means to an end for the end itself.

We are not really justified, however, in speaking of a *will* to pleasure or power in connection with psychodynamically oriented schools of thought, since they assume that man pursues behavior goals unwillingly and unwittingly and that his conscious motivations are not his actual motivations. Thus Erich Fromm in *Beyond the Chains of Illusion* speaks of "the motivating forces which make man act in certain ways, the drives which propel him to strive in certain directions." But to me it is inconceivable that man can really be driven to strivings; either he strives or he is driven. To ignore this difference, to sacrifice one phenomenon to another, is a procedure unworthy of a scientist; to do so is to allow one's adherence to hypotheses to blind one to facts.

Freud and his epigones have taught us always to see something behind or beneath human volitions: unconscious motivations, underlying dynamics. Freud never took a human phenomenon at face value; as Gordon W. Allport states in *Personality and Social Encounter*, "Freud was a specialist in precisely those motives that cannot be taken at their face value." But are there no motives at all which should be taken at face value? Such an assumption is comparable to the attitude of the man who, on being shown a stork, said, "I thought the stork didn't exist!" Does the fact that the stork has been misused to hide the facts of life from children in any way deny that bird's reality?

From *Are You Nobody?* Richmond, Va.: John Knox Press, 1966. Reprinted by permission.

According to Freud, the reality principle is an extension of the pleasure principle and merely serves its purposes. But one could just as well say that the pleasure principle itself is an extension of the homeostasis principle and serves *its* purposes. Ultimately the psychodynamic approach views man as a being basically concerned with maintaining or restoring his inner equilibrium and seeking to do so by gratifying his drives and satisfying his instincts. Even Jungian psychology essentially interprets human motivation thus; the archetypes of Jungian thought are also "mythical beings" (as Freud called the instincts). Both Freud and Jung view man as bent on getting rid of tensions, be they aroused by drives and instincts clamoring for gratification (Freud) or by archetypes urging their materialization (Jung). In either case, reality, the world of beings and meanings, is reduced to instrumentalities for getting rid of unpleasant stimuli. What has been eliminated in this view of man is the fundamental fact that man is a being who encounters other beings, who also reaches out for meanings to fulfill.

This is why I speak of a will to meaning rather than a need for or a drive toward meaning. If man were really driven to meaning he would embark on meaning fulfillment solely to rid himself of this drive in order that homeostasis might be restored; at the same time he would no longer be really concerned with meaning but rather with his own equilibrium and thus with himself.

Nor is the concept of self-actualization or self-realization a sufficient ground for a motivational theory. Self-actualization is another phenomenon which can be realized only as a side effect and which is thwarted precisely to the extent that it is made a matter of direct intention. Self-actualization is of course a desideratum. But man can actualize himself only insofar as he fulfills meaning, in which case self-actualization occurs by itself—automatically, as it were. Like pleasure, self-actualization is contravened when deliberately sought after or more an end in itself.

While lecturing at Melbourne University some years ago I was given a boomerang as a souvenir. In contemplating this gift I concluded that in a sense it symbolized human existence. One generally assumes that a boomerang returns to the thrower; actually it returns only when the thrower has missed his target. Similarly, man returns to himself, to being concerned with his self, only after he has missed his mission, only after he has failed to find meaning in life.

In his doctoral dissertation Ernest Keen, one of my assistants during a teaching period at Harvard's summer session, seeks to demonstrate that the shortcomings of Freudian psychoanalysis are compensated for by Heinz Hartmann's ego psychology, and the deficiencies of ego psychology in turn by Erikson's identity concept. Keen goes on to contend, however, that despite these correctives there is still a missing link in psychotherapy, and that this link is supplied by logotherapy. It is my conviction that man should not, indeed cannot, struggle for identity in a direct way; rather, he finds identity to the extent to which he commits himself to something beyond himself, to a cause greater than himself. No one has put it as cogently as has Karl Jaspers: What man is he ultimately becomes through the cause which he has made his own.

Rolf von Eckartsberg, also a Harvard assistant of mine, has shown the insufficiency of the role-playing concept by pointing out that it avoids the very problem prompting it—that of choice and value. For the question remains: Which role to adopt, which cause to advocate? The same criticism holds for those who insist that

man's primary intention and ultimate goal are to develop his potentialities. One recalls the example of Socrates, who confessed that he had within himself the potentiality to become a criminal but nevertheless decided to turn away from such a potentiality.

What is behind all these arguments that man should try to live out his inner potentialities or—as it is sometimes put—to "express himself"? The hidden motive behind such notions is, I believe, to lessen the tension aroused by the gap between what a man is and what he ought to become, between the actual state of affairs and that which he should help secure, between existence and essence, or being and meaning. To say that man need not worry about ideals and values since they are nothing but "self-expressions" and that he should therefore simply embark on the actualization of his own potentialities is to say that he need not reach out for meaning to fulfill or values to realize, that everything is all right as it is. Pindar's injunction, "Become what you are," is thus deprived of its imperative quality and transmuted into an indicative statement, namely, that man has all along been what he should become and hence need not reach for the stars to bring them down to earth, since the earth is itself a star!

The fact remains, however, that the tension between being and meaning is ineradicable in man, is inherent in his humanness. And that is why it is indispensable for mental well-being. Having started from man's meaning orientation, i.e., his will to meaning, we have now arrived at another problem—his meaning confrontation. The first issue refers to what man basically is: oriented toward meaning; the second refers to what he should be: confronted with meaning.

To confront man with values which are interpreted merely as self-expression will not do. Still less valid is the approach which would have him see in values "nothing but defense mechanisms, reaction formations or rationalizations of his instinctual drives"—to use the definition of two outstanding psychoanalytically oriented therapists. Personally I would not be willing to live for the sake of my defense mechanisms, much less to die for the sake of my reaction formations.

To treat a patient in terms of psychodynamic ideas may very well serve the purpose of what I call existential rationalization. If a person is taught that his concern about ultimate meaning is no more than, say, a way of coming to terms with his early childhood Oedipal situation, then his concern can be analyzed away, along with the existential tension aroused by it. The approach of logotherapy is altogether different. Logotherapy does not spare a patient confrontation with the specific meaning which he must act on—and which the therapist should help him find. In his book *Logotherapy and the Christian Faith* Donald F. Tweedie recounts an incident in which an American visitor to Vienna asked me to tell him in one sentence the difference between logotherapy and psychoanalysis—whereupon I invited him first to tell me what he regarded as the essence of psychoanalysis. He replied: "In psychoanalysis the patient must lie down on a couch and tell you things which sometimes are disagreeable to tell." And I quickly responded: "In logotherapy the patient is allowed to sit erect but must hear things which sometimes are disagreeable!"

Erwin Straus has rightly stressed that in existential thinking the otherness of the other should not be attenuated. The same holds true for meaning. The meaning which a person has to fulfill is something beyond himself, never just himself. Only if this meaning retains otherness can it exert upon a person that quality of imperativeness which yields itself to a phenomenological analysis of one's experience of existence. Only a meaning which is not just an expression of the person himself can be a true challenge to him. The Bible tells us that when Israel wandered through the desert God's glory went before in the form of a cloud; only in this way was it possible for Israel to be guided by God. Imagine what would have happened if God had dwelled in the midst of Israel in the form of a cloud: rather than leading the people safely, the cloud would have obscured everything and Israel would have gone astray.

Meaning must not coincide with being; meaning must be ahead of being: meaning sets the pace for being. Existence falters unless lived in terms of transcendence, in terms of something beyond itself. Here we might distinguish between pacemakers and peacemakers: the former confront us with meanings and values, thus supporting our meaning orientation; the latter alleviate the burden of meaning confrontation. In this sense Moses was a pacemaker; he did not soothe man's conscience but rather stirred it up. Moses with his Ten Commandments did not spare his people a confrontation with ideals and values.

There is also the appeaser type of peacemaker who tries to reconcile others with himself. Let's face facts, he says. Why worry about one's shortcomings? Only a few live up to their ideals. So let's attend to peace of mind or soul rather than those existential meanings which only arouse tensions. What this kind of peacemaker overlooks is the wisdom of Goethe's warning: If we take man as he is, we make him worse; if we take him as he ought to be, we help him become it.

When meaning orientation becomes meaning confrontation, that stage of maturation and development has been reached where freedom becomes responsibleness. An individual is responsible for the fulfillment of the specific meaning of his own life, but he is also responsible *to* something, be it society or humanity or mankind or his own conscience. A significant number of people interpret their own existence not just in terms of being responsible to some *thing* but rather to some*one*—namely, to God. As a secular theory and medical practice logotherapy must restrict itself to such a factual statement, leaving to the patient the decision whether to interpret his own responsibleness in terms of religion or agnosticism. Logotherapy must remain available to everyone; to this I am obliged to adhere, if for no other reason, by my Hippocratic oath. In any case, logotherapy sees in responsibleness the very essence of human existence, and for that reason the patient must himself decide for what and to what, or to whom, he is responsible.

A logotherapist is not entitled consciously to influence the patient's decision as to how to interpret his own responsibleness or as to what to embrace as his personal meaning. The fact that a person's conscience is subject to error does not release him from his obligation to obey it; existence involves the risk of error. He must risk committing himself to a cause not worthy of his commitment. Perhaps my commitment to the cause of logotherapy is erroneous. But I prefer to live in a world in which man has the right to make choices, even if they are wrong choices, rather than one in which no choice at all is left to him. A world in which both fiends and saints are possible is infinitely preferable to a totally conformist, collectivist world in which man is a mere functionary of the party or the state.

39 | TOWARD A MODERN APPROACH TO VALUE: THE VALUING PROCESS IN THE MATURE PERSON

Carl R. Rogers

A description is given of the change in the value orientation of the individual from infancy to average adulthood, and from this adult status to a greater degree of psychological maturity attained through psychotherapy or fortunate life circumstances. On the basis of these observations, the theory is advanced that there is an organismic basis for the valuing process within the human individual; that this valuing process is effective to the degree that the individual is open to his experience; that in persons relatively open to their experiencing there is an important commonality or universality of value directions; that these directions make for the constructive enhancement of the individual and his community, and for the survival and evolution of his species.

There is a great deal of concern today with the problem of values. Youth, in almost every country, is deeply uncertain of its value orientation; the values associated with various religions have lost much of their influence; sophisticated individuals in every culture seem unsure and troubled as to the goals they hold in esteem. The reasons are not far to seek. The world culture, in all its aspects, seems increasingly scientific and relativistic, and the rigid, absolute views on values which come to us from the past appear anachronistic. Even more important, perhaps, is the fact that the modern individual is assailed from every angle by divergent and contradictory value claims. It is no longer possible, as it was in the not too distant historical past, to settle comfortably into the value system of one's forebears or one's community and live out one's life without ever examining the nature and the assumptions of that system.

In this situation it is not surprising that value orientations from the past appear to be in a state of disintegration or collapse. Men question whether there are, or can be, any universal values. It is often felt that we may have lost, in our modern world, all possibility of any general or cross-cultural basis for values. One natural result of this uncertainty and confusion is that there is an increasing concern about, interest in, and a searching for, a sound or meaningful value approach which can hold its own in today's world.

Carl R. Rogers, "Toward a Modern Approach to Values: the Valuing Process in the Mature Person," *Journal of Abnormal and Social Psychology*, LXVIII, 1964, pp. 160–170. Copyright © by the American Psychological Association, and reproduced by their permission and that of the author.

I share this general concern. As with other issues the general problem faced by the culture is painfully and specifically evident in the cultural microcosm which is called the therapeutic relationship, which is my sphere of experience.

As a consequence of this experience I should like to attempt a modest theoretical approach to this whole problem. I have observed changes in the approach to values as the individual grows from infancy to adulthood. I observe further changes when, if he is fortunate, he continues to grow toward true psychological maturity. Many of these observations grow out of my experience as therapist, where I have had the mind stretching opportunity of seeing the ways in which individuals move toward a richer life. From these observations I believe I see some directional threads emerging which might offer a new concept of the valuing process, more tenable in the modern world. I have made a beginning by presenting some of these ideas partially in previous writings (Rogers, 1951, 1959); I would like now to voice them more clearly and more fully.

SOME DEFINITIONS

Charles Morris (1956, pp. 9–12) has made some useful distinctions in regard to values. There are "operative values," which are the behaviors of organisms in which they show preference for one object or objective rather than another. The lowly earthworm, selecting the smooth arm of a Y maze rather than the arm which is paved with sandpaper, is giving an indication of an operative value.

There are also "conceived values," the preference of an individual for a symbolized object. "Honesty is the best policy' 'is such a conceived value.

There is also the term "objective value," to refer to what is objectively preferable, whether or not it is sensed or conceived of as desirable. I will be concerned primarily with operative or conceptualized values.

INFANT'S WAY OF VALUING

Let me first speak about the infant. The living human being has, at the outset, a clear approach to values. We can infer from studying his behavior that he prefers those experiences which maintain, enhance, or actualize his organism, and rejects those which do not serve this end. Watch him for a bit:

Hunger is negatively valued. His expression of this often comes through loud and clear.

Food is positively valued. But when he is satisfied, food is negatively valued, and the same milk he responded to so eagerly is now spit out, or the breast which seemed so satisfying is now rejected as he turns his head away from the nipple with an amusing facial expression of disgust and revulsion.

He values security, and the holding and caressing which seem to communicate security.

He values new experience for its own sake, and we observe this in his obvious pleasure in discovering his toes, in his searching movements, in his endless curiosity.

He shows a clear negative valuing of pain, bitter tastes, sudden loud sounds.

All of this is commonplace, but let us look at these facts in terms of what they tell us about the infant's approach to values. It is first of all a flexible, changing, valuing *process*, not a fixed system. He likes food and dislikes the same food. He values security and rest and rejects it for new experience. What is going on seems best described as an organismic valuing process, in which each element, each moment of what he is experiencing is somehow weighed, and selected or rejected, depending on whether, at that moment, it tends to actualize the organism or not. This complicated weighing of experience is clearly an organismic, not a conscious or symbolic function. These are operative, not conceived values. But this process can, nonetheless, deal with complex value problems. I would remind you of the experiment in which young infants had spread in front of them a score or more of dishes of natural (that is, unflavored) foods. Over a period of time they clearly tended to value the foods which enhanced their own survival, growth, and development. If for a time a child gorged himself on starches, this would soon be balanced by a protein "binge." If at times he chose a diet deficient in some vitamin, he would later seek out foods rich in this very vitamin. The physiological wisdom of his body guided his behavioral movements, resulting in what we might think of as objectively sound value choices.

Another aspect of the infant's approach to values is that the source or locus of the evaluating process is clearly within himself. Unlike many of us, he *knows* what he likes and dislikes, and the origin of these value choices lies strictly within himself. He is the center of the valuing process, the evidence for his choices being supplied by his own senses. He is not at this point influenced by what his parents think he should prefer, or by what the church says, or by the opinion of the latest "expert" in the field, or by the persuasive talents of an advertising firm. It is from within his own experiencing that his organism is saying in nonverbal terms, "This is good for me." "That is bad for me." "I like this." "I strongly dislike that." He would laugh at our concern over values, if he could understand it.

CHANGE IN THE VALUING PROCESS

What happens to this efficient, soundly based valuing process? By what sequence of events do we exchange it for the more rigid, uncertain, inefficient approach to values which characterizes most of us as adults? Let me try to state briefly one of the major ways in which I think this happens.

The infant needs love, wants it, tends to behave in ways which will bring a repetition of this wanted experience. But this brings complications. He pulls baby sister's hair, and finds it satisfying to hear her wails and protests. He then hears that he is "a naughty, bad boy," and this may be reinforced by a slap on the hand. He is cut off from affection. As this experience is repeated, and many, many others like it, he gradually learns what "feels good" is often "bad" in the eyes of significant others. Then the next step occurs, in which he comes to take the same attitude toward himself which these others have taken. Now, as he pulls his sister's hair, he solemnly intones, "Bad, bad boy." He is introjecting the value judgment of another, taking it in as his own. To that degree he loses touch with his own organismic valuing process. He has deserted the wisdom of his organism, giving up the locus of evaluation, and is trying to behave in terms of values set by another, in order to hold love.

Or take another example at an older level. A boy senses, though perhaps not consciously, that he is more loved and prized by his parents when he thinks of being a doctor than when he thinks of being an artist. Gradually he introjects the values attached to being a doctor. He comes to want, above all, to be a doctor. Then in college he is baffled by the fact that he repeatedly fails in chemistry, which is absolutely necessary to becoming a physician, in spite of the fact that the guidance counselor assures him he has the ability to pass the course. Only in counseling interviews does he begin to realize how completely he has lost touch with his organismic reactions, how out of touch he is with his own valuing process.

Perhaps these illustrations will indicate that in an attempt to gain or hold love, approval, esteem, the individual relinquishes the locus of evaluation which he has in infancy, and places it in others. He learns to have a basic *dis*trust for his own experiencing as a guide to his behavior. He learns from others a large number of conceived values, and adopts them as his own, even though they may be widely discrepant from what he is experiencing.

SOME INTROJECTED PATTERNS

It is in this fashion, I believe, that most of us accumulate the introjected value patterns by which we live. In the fantastically complex culture of today, the patterns we introject as desirable or undesirable come from a variety of sources and are often highly contradictory. Let me list a few of the introjections which are commonly held.

Sexual desires and behaviors are mostly bad. The sources of this construct are many —parents, church, teachers.

Disobedience is bad. Here parents and teachers combine with the military to emphasize this concept. To obey is good. To obey without question is even better.

Making money is the highest good. The sources of this conceived value are too numerous to mention.

Learning an accumulation of scholarly facts is highly desirable. Education is the source.

Communism is utterly bad. Here the government is a major source.

To love thy neighbor is the highest good. This concept comes from the church, perhaps from the parents.

Cooperation and teamwork are preferable to acting alone. Here companions are an important source.

Cheating is clever and desirable. The peer group again is the origin.

Coca-Colas, chewing gum, electric refrigerators, and automobiles are all utterly desirable. From Jamaica to Japan, from Copenhagen to Kowloon, the "Coca-Cola culture" has come to be regarded as the acme of desirability.

This is a small and diversified sample of the myriads of conceived values which individuals often introject, and hold as their own, without ever having considered their inner organismic reactions to these patterns and objects.

COMMON CHARACTERISTICS OF ADULT VALUING

I believe it will be clear from the foregoing that the usual adult—I feel I am speaking for most of us—has an approach to values which has these characteristics:

The majority of his values are introjected from other individuals or groups significant to him, but are regarded by him as his own.

The source or locus of evaluation on most matters lies outside of himself.

The criterion by which his values are set is the degree to which they will cause him to be loved, accepted, or esteemed.

These conceived preferences are either not related at all, or not clearly related, to his own process of experiencing.

Often there is a wide and unrecognized discrepancy between the evidence supplied by his own experience, and these conceived values.

Because these conceptions are not open to testing in experience, he must hold them in a rigid and unchanging fashion. The alternative would be a collapse of his values. Hence his values are "right."

Because they are untestable, there is no ready way of solving contradictions. If he has taken in from the community the conception that money is the summum bonum *and from the church the conception that love of one's neighbor is the highest value, he has no way of discovering which has more value for him. Hence a common aspect of modern life is living with absolutely contradictory values. We calmly discuss the possibility of dropping a hydrogen bomb on Russia, but find tears in our eyes when we see headlines about the suffering of one small child.*

Because he has relinquished the locus of evaluation to others, and has lost touch with his own valuing process, he feels profoundly insecure and easily threatened in his values. If some of these conceptions were destroyed, what would take their place? This threatening possibility makes him hold his value conceptions more rigidly or more confusedly, or both.

FUNDAMENTAL DISCREPANCY

I believe that this picture of the individual, with values mostly introjected, held as fixed concepts, rarely examined or tested, is the picture of most of us. By taking over the conceptions of others as our own, we lose contact with the potential wisdom of our own functioning, and lose confidence in ourselves. Since these value constructs are often sharply at variance with what is going on in our own experiencing, we have in a very basic way divorced ourselves from ourselves, and this accounts for much of modern strain and insecurity. This fundamental discrepancy between the individual's concept and what he is actually experiencing, between the intellectual structure of his values and the valuing process going on unrecognized within—this is a part of the fundamental estrangement of modern man from himself.

RESTORING CONTACT WITH EXPERIENCE

Some individuals are fortunate in going beyond the picture I have just given, developing further in the direction of psychological maturity. We see this happen in psychotherapy where we endeavor to provide a climate favorable to the growth of the person. We also see it happen in life, whenever life provides a therapeutic climate for the individual. Let me concentrate on this further maturing of a value approach as I have seen it in therapy.

As the client senses and realizes that he is prized as a person* he can slowly begin to value the different aspects of himself. Most importantly, he can begin, with much difficulty at first, to sense and to feel what is going on within him, what he is feeling, what he is experiencing, how he is reacting. He uses his experiencing as a direct referent to which he can turn in forming accurate conceptualizations and as a guide to his behavior. Gendlin (1961, 1962) has elaborated the way in which this occurs. As his experiencing becomes more and more open to him, as he is able to live more freely in the process of his feelings, then significant changes begin to occur in his approach to values. It begins to assume many of the characteristics it had in infancy.

INTROJECTED VALUES IN RELATION TO EXPERIENCING

Perhaps I can indicate this by reviewing a few of the brief examples of introjected values which I have given, and suggesting what happens to them as the individual comes closer to what is going on within him.

The individual in therapy looks back and realizes, "But I enjoyed pulling my sister's hair—and that doesn't make me a bad person."

The student failing chemistry realizes, as he gets close to his own experiencing, "I don't like chemistry; I don't value being a doctor, even though my parents do; and I am not a failure for having these feelings."

The adult recognizes that sexual desires and behavior may be richly satisfying and permanently enriching in their consequences, or shallow and temporary and less than satisfying. He goes by his own experiencing, which does not always coincide with social norms.

He recognizes freely that this communist book or person expresses attitudes and goals which he shares as well as ideas and values which he does not share.

He realizes that at times he experiences cooperation as meaningful and valuable to him, and that at other times he wishes to be alone and act alone.

VALUING IN THE MATURE PERSON

The valuing process which seems to develop in this more mature person is in some ways very much like that in the infant, and in some ways quite different. It is fluid,

---

*   The therapeutic relationship is not devoid of values. When it is most effective it is, I believe, marked by one primary value, namely, that this person (the client) has *worth*.

flexible, based on this particular moment, and the degree to which this moment is experienced as enhancing and actualizing. Values are not held rigidly, but are continually changing. The painting which last year seemed meaningful now appears uninteresting, the way of working with individuals which was formerly experienced as good now seems inadequate, the belief which then seemed true is now experienced as only partly true, or perhaps false.

Another characteristic of the way this person values experience is that it is highly differentiated, or as the semanticists would say, extensional. The examples in the preceding section indicate that what were previously rather solid monolithic introjected values now become differentiated, tied to a particular time and experience.

Another characteristic of the mature individual's approach is that the locus of evaluation is again established firmly within the person. It is his own experience which provides the value information or feedback. This does not mean that he is not open to all evidence he can obtain from other sources. But it means that this is taken for what it is—outside evidence—and is not as significant as his own reactions. Thus he may be told by a friend that a new book is very disappointing. He reads two unfavorable reviews of the book. Thus his tentative hypothesis is that he will not value the book. Yet if he reads the book his valuing will be based upon the reactions it stirs in *him*, not on what he has been told by others.

There is also involved in this valuing process a letting oneself down into the immediacy of what one is experiencing, endeavoring to sense and to clarify all its complex meanings. I think of a client who, toward the close of therapy, when puzzled about an issue, would put his head in his hands and say, "Now what *is* it that I'm feeling? I want to get next to it. I want to learn what it is." Then he would wait, quietly and patiently, trying to listen to himself, until he could discern the exact flavor of the feelings he was experiencing. He, like others, was trying to get close to himself.

In getting close to what is going on within himself, the process is much more complex than it is in the infant. In the mature person it has much more scope and sweep. For there is involved in the present moment of experiencing the memory traces of all the relevant learnings from the past. This moment has not only its immediate sensory impact, but it has meaning growing out of similar experiences in the past (Gendlin, 1962). It has both the new and the old in it. So when I experience a painting or a person, my experiencing contains within it the learnings I have accumulated from past meetings with paintings or persons, as well as the new impact of this particular encounter. Likewise the moment of experiencing contains, for the mature adult, hypotheses about consequences. "It is not pleasant to express forthrightly my negative feelings to this person, but past experience indicates that in a continuing relationship it will be helpful in the long run." Past and future are both in this moment and enter into the valuing.

I find that in the person I am speaking of (and here again we see a similarity to the infant), the criterion of the valuing process is the degree to which the object of the experience actualizes the individual himself. Does it make him a richer, more complete, more fully developed person? This may sound as though it were a selfish or unsocial criterion, but it does not prove to be so, since deep and helpful relationships with others are experienced as actualizing.

Like the infant, too, the psychologically mature adult trusts and uses the wisdom of his organism, with the difference that he is able to do so knowingly. He realizes that if he can trust all of himself, his feelings and his intuitions may be wiser than his mind, that as a total person he can be more sensitive and accurate than his thoughts alone. Hence he is not afraid to say, "I feel that this experience [or this thing, or this direction] is good. Later I will probably know *why* I feel it is good." He trusts the totality of himself, having moved toward becoming what Lancelot Whyte (1950) regards as "the unitary man."

It should be evident from what I have been saying that this valuing process in the mature individual is not an easy or simple thing. The process is complex, the choices often very perplexing and difficult, and there is no guarantee that the choice which is made will in fact prove to be self-actualizing. But because whatever evidence exists is available to the individual, and because he is open to his experiencing, errors are correctable. If this chosen course of action is not self-enhancing, this will be sensed, and he can make an adjustment or revision. He thrives on a maximum feedback interchange, and thus, like the gyroscopic compass on a ship, can continually correct his course toward his true goal of self-fulfillment.

SOME PROPOSITIONS REGARDING THE VALUING PROCESS

Let me sharpen the meaning of what I have been saying by stating two propositions which contain the essential elements of this viewpoint. While it may not be possible to devise empirical tests of each proposition in its entirety, yet each is to some degree capable of being tested through the methods of psychological science. I would also state that though the following propositions are stated firmly in order to give them clarity, I am actually advancing them as decidedly tentative hypotheses.

Hypothesis I. There is an organismic base for an organized valuing process within the human individual.

It is hypothesized that this base is something the human being shares with the rest of the animate world. It is part of the functioning life process of any healthy organism. It is the capacity for receiving feedback information which enables the organism continually to adjust its behavior and reactions so as to achieve the maximum possible self-enhancement.

Hypothesis II. This valuing process in the human being is effective in achieving self-enhancement to the degree that the individual is open to the experiencing which is going on within himself.

I have tried to give two examples of individuals who are close to their own experiencing: the tiny infant who has not yet learned to deny in his awareness the processes going on within; and the psychologically mature person who has relearned the advantages of this open state.

There is a corollary to this second proposition which might be put in the following terms. One way of assisting the individual to move toward openness to experience is through a relationship in which he is prized as a separate person, in which the experiencing going on within him is empathically understood and valued, and in which he is given the freedom to experience his own feelings and those of others without being threatened in doing so.

This corollary obviously grows out of therapeutic experience. It is a brief statement of the essential qualities in the therapeutic relationship. There are already some empirical studies, of which the one by Barrett-Lennard (1962) is a good example, which give support to such a statement.

PROPOSITIONS REGARDING THE OUTCOMES OF THE VALUING PROCESS

I come now to the nub of any theory of values or valuing. What are its consequences? I should like to move into this new ground by stating bluntly two propositions as to the qualities of behavior which emerge from this valuing process. I shall then give some of the evidence from my experience as a therapist in support of these propositions.

Hypothesis III. In persons who are moving toward greater openness to their experiencing, there is an organismic commonality of value directions.

Hypothesis IV. These common value directions are of such kinds as to enhance the development of the individual himself, of others in his community, and to make for the survival and evolution of his species.

It has been a striking fact of my experience that in therapy, where individuals are valued, where there is greater freedom to feel and to be, certain value directions seem to emerge. These are not chaotic directions but instead exhibit a surprising commonality. This commonality is not dependent on the personality of the therapist, for I have seen these trends emerge in the clients of therapists sharply different in personality. This commonality does not seem to be due to the influences of any one culture, for I have found evidence of these directions in cultures as divergent as those of the United States, Holland, France, and Japan. I like to think that this commonality of value directions is due to the fact that we all belong to the same species—that just as a human infant tends, individually, to select a diet similar to that selected by other human infants, so a client in therapy tends, individually, to choose value directions similar to those chosen by other clients. As a species there may be certain elements of experience which tend to make for inner development and which would be chosen by all individuals if they were genuinely free to choose.

Let me indicate a few of these value directions as I see them in my clients as they move in the direction of personal growth and maturity.

They tend to move away from façades. Pretense, defensiveness, putting up a front, tend to be negatively valued.

They tend to move away from "oughts." The compelling feeling of "I ought to do or be thus and so" is negatively valued. The client moves away from being what he "ought to be," no matter who has set that imperative.

They tend to move away from meeting the expectations of others. Pleasing others, as a goal in itself, is negatively valued.

Being real is positively valued. The client tends to move toward being himself, being his real feelings, being what he is. This seems to be a very deep preference.

Self-direction is positively valued. The client discovers an increasing pride and confidence in making his own choices, guiding his own life.

One's self, one's own feelings come to be positively valued. From a point where he looks upon himself with contempt and despair, the client comes to value himself and his reactions as being of worth.

Being a process is positively valued. From desiring some fixed goal, clients come to prefer the excitement of being a process of potentialities being born.

Sensitivity to others and acceptance of others is positively valued. The client comes to appreciate others for what they are, just as he has come to appreciate himself for what he is.

Deep relationships are positively valued. To achieve a close, intimate, real, fully communicative relationship with another person seems to meet a deep need in every individual, and is very highly valued.

Perhaps more than all else, the client comes to value an openness to all of his inner and outer experience. To be open to and sensitive to his own inner reactions and feelings, the reactions and feelings of others, and the realities of the objective world —this is a direction which he clearly prefers. This openness becomes the client's most valued resource.

These then are some of the preferred directions which I have observed in individuals moving toward personal maturity. Though I am sure that the list I have given is inadequate and perhaps to some degree inaccurate, it holds for me exciting possibilities. Let me try to explain why.

I find it significant that when individuals are prized as persons, the values they select do not run the full gamut of possibilities. I do not find, in such a climate of freedom, that one person comes to value fraud and murder and thievery, while another values a life of self-sacrifice, and another values only money. Instead there seems to be a deep and underlying thread of commonality. I believe that when the human being is inwardly free to choose whatever he deeply values, he tends to value those objects, experiences, and goals which make for his own survival, growth, and development, and for the survival and development of others. I hypothesize that it is *characteristic* of the human organism to prefer such actualizing and socialized goals when he is exposed to a growth promoting climate.

A corollary of what I have been saying is that in *any* culture, given a climate of respect and freedom in which he is valued as a person, the mature individual would tend to choose and prefer these same value directions. This is a significant hypothesis which could be tested. It means that though the individual of whom I am speaking would not have a consistent or even a stable system of conceived values, the valuing process within him would lead to emerging value directions which would be constant across cultures and across time.

Another implication I see is that individuals who exhibit the fluid valuing process I have tried to describe, whose value directions are generally those I have listed, would be highly effective in the ongoing process of human evolution. If the human species is to survive at all on this globe, the human being must become more readily adaptive to new problems and situations, must be able to select that which is valuable for development and survival out of new and complex situations, must be accurate in his appreciation of reality if he is to make such selections. The psychologically mature person as I have described him has, I believe, the qualities which would cause him to value those experiences which would make for the survival and enhancement of the human race. He would be a worthy participant and guide in the process of human evolution.

Finally, it appears that we have returned to the issue of universality of values, but by a different route. Instead of universal values "out there," or a universal value system imposed by some group—philosophers, rulers, priests, or psychologists —we have the possibility of universal human value directions *emerging* from the experiencing of the human organism. Evidence from therapy indicates that both personal and social values emerge as natural, and experienced, when the individual is close to his own organismic valuing process. The suggestion is that though modern man no longer trusts religion or science or philosophy nor any system of beliefs to *give* him values, he may find an organismic valuing base within himself which, if he can learn again to be in touch with it, will prove to be an organized adaptive, and social approach to the perplexing value issues which face all of us.

REFERENCES

Barrett-Lennard, G. T. Dimensions of therapist response as causal factors in therapeutic change. *Psychol. Monogr.*, 1962, 76 (43, Whole No. 562).

Gendlin, E. T. Experiencing: A variable in the process of therapeutic change. *Amer. J. Psychother.*, 1961, 15, 233–245.

Gendlin, E. T. *Experiencing and the creation of meaning.* Glencoe, Ill.: Free Press, 1962.

Morris, C. W. *Varieties of human value.* Chicago: Univer. Chicago Press, 1956.

Rogers, C. R. *Client-centered therapy.* Boston: Houghton Mifflin, 1951.

Rogers, C. R. A theory of therapy, personality and interpersonal relationships. In S. Koch (Ed.), *Psychology: A study of a science.* Vol. 3. *Formulations of the person and the social context.* New York: McGraw-Hill, 1959. Pp. 185–256.

Whyte, L. L. *The next development in man.* New York: Mentor Books, 1950.

40 | COURAGE TO BE ONE'S SELF

Rollo May

Courage is the capacity to meet the anxiety which arises as one achieves freedom. It is the willingness to differentiate, to move from the protecting realms of parental dependence to new levels of freedom and integration. The need for courage arises not only at those stages when breaks with parental protection are most obvious—such as at the birth of self-awareness, at going off to school, at adolescence, in crises of love, marriage and the facing of ultimate death—but at every step in between as one moves from the familiar surroundings over frontiers into the unfamiliar. "Courage, in its final analysis," as the neurobiologist Dr. Kurt Goldstein well puts it, "is nothing but an affirmative answer to the shocks of existence, which must be borne for the actualization of one's own nature."

The opposite to courage is not cowardice: that, rather, is the lack of courage. To say a person is a coward has no more meaning than to say he is lazy: it simply tells us that some vital potentiality is unrealized or blocked. The opposite to courage, as one endeavors to understand the problem in our particular age, is automaton conformity.

The courage to be one's self is scarcely admired as the top virtue these days. One trouble is that many people still associate that kind of courage with the stuffy attitudes of the self-made men of the late nineteenth century, or with the somewhat ridiculous no matter how sincere "I-am-the-master-of-my-fate" theme in such a poem as "Invictus." With what qualified favor many people today view standing on one's own convictions is revealed in such phrases as "sticking one's neck out." The central suggestion in this defenseless posture is that any passer-by could swing at the exposed neck and cut off the head. Or people describe moving ahead in one's beliefs as "going out on a limb." Again what a picture! The only things one can do out on a limb are to crawl back again, saw the limb off and come down, dramatic as Icarus in a martyr-like and probably useless crash, or remain out on the limb, vegetating like a Hindu tree-sitter and exposed to the ridicule of a populace which does not think highly of tree-sitting, till the limb breaks off of its own dead weight.

Both of these expressions highlight the fact that what is most dreaded is getting out of the group, "protruding," not fitting in. People lack courage because of their fear of being isolated, alone, or being subjected to "social isolation," that is, being laughed at, ridiculed or rejected. If one sinks back into the crowd, he does not risk these dangers. And this being isolated is no minor threat. Dr. Walter Cannon has shown in his study of "voodoo death," that primitive people may be literally killed by being psychologically isolated from the community. There have been observed cases of natives who, when socially ostracized and treated by their tribes as though they did not exist, have actually withered away and died. William James, furthermore, has reminded us that the expression "to be cut *dead*" by social disapproval has much more truth than poetry in it. It is thus no figment of the neurotic imagination that people are deathly afraid of standing on their own convictions at the risk of being renounced by the group.

What we lack in our day is an understanding of the friendly, warm, personal, original, constructive courage of a Socrates or a Spinoza. We need to recover an understanding of the positive aspects of courage—courage as the inner side of growth, courage as a constructive way of that becoming of one's self which is prior to the power to give one's self. Thus, when . . . we emphasize standing on one's own belief, we do not at all imply living in a vacuum of separateness; actually, courage is the basis of any creative relationship. . . .

From the time of the ancient story of Prometheus onward, it has been recognized that to create requires courage. Balzac, who well knew this truth from his own experience, has so vividly described this kind of courage that we let his words speak for us:

The quality that above all deserves the greatest glory in art—and by that word we must include all creations of the mind—is courage; courage of a kind of which common minds have no conception, and which is perhaps described here for the first time. . . . To be sure. . . . But to produce, to bring to birth, to bring up the infant work with labor, to put it to bed full-fed with milk, to take it up again every morning with inexhaustible maternal love, to lick it clean, to dress it a hundred times in lovely garments that it tears up again and again; never to be discouraged by the convulsions of this mad life, and to make of it a living masterpiece that speaks to all eyes in sculpture, or to all minds in literature, to all memories in painting, to all hearts in music—that is the task of execution. The hand must be ready at every minute to obey the mind. And the creative moments of the mind do not come to order. . . . And work is a weary struggle at once dreaded and loved by those fine and powerful natures who are often broken under the strain of it. . . . If the artist does not throw himself into his work like a soldier into the breach, unreflectingly; and if, in that crater, he does not dig like a miner buried under a fall of rock . . . the work will never be completed; it will perish in the studio, where production becomes impossible, and the artist looks on at the suicide of his own talent. . . . And it is for that reason that the same reward, the same triumph, the same laurels, are accorded to great poets as to great generals.*

We now know through psychoanalytic studies, as Balzac did not, that one of the reasons creative activity takes so much courage is that to create stands for becoming free from the ties to the infantile past, breaking the old in order that the new can be born. For creating external works, in art, business or what not, and creating one's self—that is, developing one's capacities, becoming freer and more responsible—are two aspects of the same process. Every act of genuine creativity means achieving a higher level of self-awareness and personal freedom, and that, as we have seen in the Promethean and Adam myths, may involve considerable inner conflict.

A landscape painter, whose main problem was freeing himself from ties to a possessive mother, had for years wanted to paint portraits but had never dared.

Finally pulling his courage together, he "dove" in and painted several portraits in the course of three days. They turned out to be excellent. But, strangely enough, he felt not only considerable joy but strong *anxiety* as well. The night of the third day he had a dream in which his mother told him he must commit suicide, and he was

---

❊   Honoré de Balzac, *Cousine Bette*, New York, Pantheon Books, p. 236–8.

calling up his friends to say good-bye with a terrifying and overwhelming sense of loneliness. The dream was saying in effect, "If you create, you will leave the familiar, and you will be lonely and die; better to stay with the familiar and not create." It is highly significant, when we see the nature of this powerful unconscious threat, that he could paint no more portraits for a month—until, that is, he had overcome the counterattack of the anxiety which had appeared in the dream.

In Balzac's beautiful statement there is one point with which we would disagree, that is, "common minds have no conception" of this courage. This is the error which comes from identifying courage with obviously spectacular acts like the soldier's charge or Michelangelo's struggles in completing the paintings on the ceiling of the Sistine Chapel. With our present knowledge of the unconscious working of the mind, we know that struggles requiring courage equal to that of the soldier's charge take place in almost anyone's dreams and deeper conflicts in times of difficult decision. To reserve courage for "heroes" and artists only shows how little one knows of the profundity of almost any alive human being's inner development. Courage is necessary in every step in a person's movement from the mass—symbolically the womb—to becoming a person in his own right; it is at each step as though one suffers the pangs of his own birth. Courage, whether the soldier's courage in risking death or the child's in going off to school, means the power to *let go* of the familiar and the secure. Courage is required not only in a person's occasional crucial decision for his own freedom, but in the little hour-to-hour decisions which place the bricks in the structure of his building of himself into a person who acts with freedom and responsibility.

Thus we are not talking about heroes. Indeed, obvious heroism, such as rashness, is often the product of something quite different from courage: in the last war the "hot" pilots in the air force who appeared to be very brave in taking risks were often the ones who were unable to overcome their anxiety inwardly and had to compensate for it by courting danger in external rash deeds. Courage must be judged as an inner state; otherwise external actions can be very misleading. Galileo compromised externally with the Inquisition and agreed to recant his view that the earth moves round the sun. But what is significant is that he remained inwardly free, as is shown in his aside, according to legend, "It still does move round the sun." Galileo was able to go on working; and no one from the outside can say for another what decisions constitute a giving up or a preserving of freedom. We could imagine that the temptation to escape from freedom might have been present in a voice within Galileo, "Just refuse to agree—meet a martyr's death, and think of the relief from having to continue to make these new scientific discoveries!"

For it requires greater courage to preserve inner freedom, to move on in one's inward journey into new realms, than to stand defiantly for outer freedom. It is often easier to play the martyr, as it is to be rash in battle. Strange as it sounds, steady, patient growth in freedom is probably the most difficult task of all, requiring the greatest courage. Thus if the term "hero" is used in this discussion at all, it must refer not to the special acts of outstanding persons, but to the heroic element potentially in every man.

Is not all courage basically moral courage? What is generally called physical courage, meaning the capacity to risk physical pain, may be simply a difference in physical sensitivity. Whether children or adolescents have the courage to fight depends only minorly on the pain involved. It depends rather on whether the child dares risk parental disapproval, or whether he can bear the added isolation of having enemies, or whether the role he has unconsciously assumed for himself as a way of getting his security is standing up for himself or endeavoring to be liked by being compliant and "playing weak." Persons who have been able to fight wholeheartedly and without inner conflict report that generally the physical pain is overcome by the zest of the conflict. And is not the so-called physical courage of risking death really a moral courage—the courage to commit one's self to a value greater than one's existence, as such, and thus the courage to let go of one's life if need be?

In my clinical experience, the greatest block to a person's development of courage is his having to take on a way of life which is not rooted in his own powers. We can see this point in the case of a young man who came for therapy because of homosexual tendencies, great feelings of anxiety and isolation, and rebellious tendencies which regularly disrupted his work. As a child he had been regarded as a sissy and could never fight despite being attacked by schoolmates almost daily. He had been the youngest child of six, there being four older brothers and, directly above him, a sister. The sister died in early childhood, and the mother, who had passionately wanted a girl after the four sons, was inconsolable. She then became very close to this youngest boy and began to treat and dress him like a girl. For him to develop feminine interests, not to learn sports with other boys, not to fight even though he was offered financial rewards by his elder brothers if he would do so, were quite logical developments: *he must not risk his position with his mother.* For it was clear that acceptance and approval could be gained if he accepted the proffered role of a girl—but where would he be as a fifth son? His mother already unconsciously rejected him because he was not in fact a girl; if he acted like a boy, he would be hated by her as a symbol that she had no girl and as a reminder that the little girl died. These requirements, obviously contrary to his innate male tendencies, led to great resentment, hatred, and later rebellion—none of which he could dare express toward his mother. The basis for his development of courage as a male had been taken out from under him. As an adult he now showed great courage in socially rebellious acts; if a revolt against male authority was called for, he leapt into the fray. But he was terrified when any issue arose of his standing against any older woman, that is, any mother substitute—his actual mother having by this time died. What could not be risked was the final disapproval by and isolation from the mother image in his own mind.

Thus a person is unable to know *what* he believes, let alone stand up for it, or what his own powers are, if he has had all along to live up to some role of himself in his parents' eyes—an image he carries on and perpetuates within himself. His courage is a vacuum before he ever begins to act, since it has no real basis within himself.

Normally a child can take each step in differentiation from his parents, each step in becoming himself, without unbearable anxiety. Just as he learns to climb the steps despite the pain and frustration of falling back time and again, and eventually succeeds with a laugh of joy, so he normally feels out his own psychological independence step by step. Aware of his parents' love, and aware of a security present in proportion to his degree of immaturity, he can take the occasional crises with parents and such crises as going to school, and his growing courage is not overwhelmed. He is not required to stand alone to a greater degree than he is prepared to do. But if the parents need, like the mother above, to force the child into a role or dominate or overprotect the child out of their own anxiety, his task is made that much more difficult.

Parents who have inner, often unconscious, doubts about their own strength tend to demand that their children be especially courageous, independent and aggressive; they may buy the son boxing gloves, push him into competitive groups at an early age, and in other ways insist that the child be the "man" they inwardly feel they are not. Generally parents who push the child, like those who overprotect him, are showing in actions which speak louder than words their own lack of confidence in him. But just as no child will develop courage by being overprotected, so no child will develop it by being pushed. He may develop obstinacy or bullying tendencies. But his courage grows only as an outcome of his confidence, generally unverbalized, in his own powers and his indigenous qualities as a human being. This confidence gets its base from his parents' love for him and their belief in his potentialities. What he needs is neither overprotection nor pushing, but help to utilize and develop his own power, and most of all to feel that his parents see him as a person in his own right and love him for his own particular capacities and values.

Only rarely, of course, do parents require that the child assume the role of the opposite sex. Much more often their requirements are that the child fulfill the social amenities of the parents' social group, get good grades and be elected to societies in college, be "normal" in every respect so he never will be talked about, marry a suitable mate or go on in father's businss. And when the son or daughter conforms to these requirements, even though, let us say, they do not believe in them, they generally rationalize their actions by saying they need to keep parental support, financial and otherwise. But on a deeper level there is usually another motive which is even more relevant to the problem of courage. That is, living up to parental expectations is the way to gain admiration and praise from the parents, and to continue as the "apple of the parental eye." Thus vanity and narcissism are the enemies of courage.

We define vanity and narcissism as the compulsive need to be praised, to be liked: for this people give up their courage. The vain and narcissistic person seems on the surface to overprotect himself, not to take any risks and in other ways to act as a coward because he thinks too highly of himself. Actually, however, just the opposite is the case. He has to preserve himself as a commodity by which he can buy the praise and favor he needs, precisely because without mother's or father's praise he would feel himself to be worthless. Courage arises from one's sense of dignity and self-esteem; and one is uncourageous because he thinks too poorly of himself. The persons who require that others continually say, "He is so nice," or so intelligent or good, or "She is so beautiful," are persons who take care of themselves not for the reason that they love themselves, but because the beautiful face or the clever mind or the gentlemanly behavior is a means of purchasing the parental pat on the head. This leads to a contempt for one's self: and thus many gifted persons whose qualities have made them lauded in the public eye will confess in the confidence of therapy that they feel like fakers.

Vanity and narcissism—the compulsive needs to be admired and praised—undermine one's courage, for one then fights on someone else's conviction rather than one's own. In the Japanese movie *Rashomon*, the husband and robber fight with complete abandon when they themselves have chosen to fight. But in another scene, when the wife screams taunts at them, and they fight because of their compulsion to live up to her requirement of their masculine prowess, they fight with only half their strength: they strike the same blows, but it is as though an invisible rope held back their arms.

When one acts to gain someone else's praise, furthermore, the act itself is a living reminder of the feeling of weakness and worthlessness: otherwise there would be no need to prostitute one's attitudes. This often leads to the "cowardly" feeling which is the most bitter humiliation of all—the humiliation of having co-operated knowingly in one's own vanquishment. It is not so bad to be defeated because the enemy is stronger, or even to be defeated because one didn't fight; but to know one was a coward because one chose to sell out his strength to get along with the victor— this betrayal of one's self is the bitterest pill of all.

There are also specific reasons in our culture why acting to please others under-mines courage. For such acting, at least for men, often means playing the role of one who is unassertive, unaggressive, "gentlemanly," and how can one develop power, including sexual potency, when he is supposed to be unassertive? With women, too, these ways of gaining admiration militate against the development of their indigenous potentialities, for their potentialities are never exercised or even brought into the picture.

The hallmark of courage in our age of conformity is the capacity to stand on one's own convictions—not obstinately or defiantly (these are expressions of de-fensiveness not courage) nor as a gesture of retaliation, but simply because these are what one believes. It is as though one were saying through one's actions, "This is my self, my being." Courage is the *affirmative* choice, not a choice because "I can do no other"; for if one can do no other, what courage is involved? To be sure, at times one has simply to cling with dogged determination to a position he has won through courage. Such times are frequent in therapy when a person has achieved some new growth and must then withstand the counterattack of anxious reaction within him-self as well as the attacks of friends and family members who would be more com-fortable if he had remained the way he was. There will be plenty of defensive ac-tions at best; but if one has conquered something worth defending, then one defends it not negatively but with joy.

When in a person's development courage begins to emerge—that is, when the person begins to break out from the pattern of devoting his life to getting others to admire him—an intermediate step generally occurs. The persons in this stage take independent stands, to be sure, but they defend their actions at the court in which the laws are written by the very authorities they have been trying to please. It is as though they demanded the right to be free, but, like the American colonists before the Revolution, they have to argue their case on the basis of laws written by those from whom they demand their rights. People in therapy in this stage often dream literally of trying to persuade their parents of the justice of their cause, of their "right" to be themselves. It may well be that this stage is the farthest that many people reach in their development toward freedom and responsibility.

But in the final analysis this halfway station leaves the person in a hopeless dilemma: for in granting his parents or parental substitutes the right to draft the laws, and in arguing before their court, he has already tacitly admitted their sovereignty. This implies his lack of freedom, and his guilt if he asserts his freedom. We have already seen that this was the dilemma of the hero in Kafka's novel *The Trial*, who was always caught because he tried to argue his case on the assumption of the complete authority of his accusers. He was then in a hopelessly frustrating position, and was reduced, quite logically, to a position in which he could only beg from them. Imagine what would have occurred if Socrates at his trial had tried to argue against his Athenian accusers on the basis of their assumptions, their laws. All the difference in the world is made by his presupposition, "Men of Athens, I will obey God rather than you," which, as we have seen above, meant for him finding his guides for conduct in the innermost center of himself.

The hardest step of all, requiring the greatest courage, is to deny those under whose expectations one has lived the right to make the laws. And this is the most frightening step. It means accepting responsibility for one's own standards and judgments, even though one knows how limited and imperfect they are. This is what Paul Tillich means by the "courage to accept one's finiteness"—which, he holds, is the basic courage every man must have. It is the courage to be and trust one's self despite the fact that one is finite; it means acting, loving, thinking, creating, even though one knows he does not have the final answers, and he may well be wrong. But it is only from a courageous acceptance of "finitude," and a responsible acting thereon, that one develops the powers that one does possess—far from absolute though they be. To do this presupposes the many sides of the development of consciousness of self which we have discussed . . . including self-discipline, the power to do the valuing, the creative conscience, and the creative relation to the wisdom of the past. Obviously this step requires a considerable degree of integration, and the courage it requires is the courage of maturity.

41 | A HUMANISTIC REVOLUTION IN PSYCHOLOGY

Sidney Jourard

If I complain I have no will of my own, that people are influencing me in subtle and mysterious ways, you'll accuse me of being paranoid, and direct me to a psychotherapist.

If I put on a white laboratory coat, and assert that you have no will of your own, that your action and experience can be manipulated, predicted, and controlled, then I am recognized as a scientific psychologist, and honored.

This is most peculiar.

A revolution is going on in psychology. A different image of man is being tried as a guide to research, theory, and application. Over the years, theorists have conceptualized man as a machine; as an organism comparable to rats, pigeons, and monkeys; as a communication system; as an hydraulic system; as a servo-mechanism; as a computer—in short, he has been viewed by psychologists as an analogue of *everything but what he is:* a person. Man is, indeed, like all those things; but first of all he is a free, intentional subject. The closest analogue we psychologists can find as a model for man is *ourselves.* The other man is more like me than he is like any machine, rat, or pigeon. We have found that the earlier models of man produced unintended consequences at the hands of those who apply psychology. The consumers of psychological writing tended to take our models too seriously and actually started to treat people as if they *were* the models that theorists used only as tentative guides to inquiry.

The disciplines of existentialism, phenomenology, humanism, and personalism are gradually being absorbed by workers in the field; and psychology is in process of being reworked, rewritten, and reapplied. Psychologists are using their experience of themselves as persons as a guide to exploring and understanding the experience of others. This is not the death of "objective," scientific psychology. Rather, it may prove to be the birth of a scientifically informed psychology of human persons—a *humanistic* psychology.

Humanistic psychology is a goal, not a doctrine. It owes its renaissance to the growing conviction that current and past approaches to the study of man have reached their limits in elucidating man's behavior and his "essence." It is a growing corpus of knowledge relating to the questions, "What is a human being, and what might man become?" Thus, humanistic psychology can be regarded in analogy with industrial psychology or the psychology of mental health or of advertising. These specialties are systems of knowledge bearing on particular families of questions: e.g., what variables affect morale, or the output of workers, or the maintenance of wellness, or the purchasing behavior of potential customers. Humanistic psychology asks, "What are the possibilities of man? And from among these possibilities, what is *optimum man,* and what conditions most probably account for his attainment and maintenance of these optima?"

The aim of science is to know, to gain understanding of some phenomenon which is in question. Sciences addressed to nature, the "natural sciences," seek understanding of natural phenomena in order to tame them, to bring them under control of human beings, for human purposes. Understanding of the processes and phenomena in nature enables man to predict, alter, and control them.

Psychology, the science addressed to man's being, likewise seeks to know and understand. But a sharp distinction must be drawn here between the science of psychology and the natural sciences. While psychologists and physicists seek to understand the phenomena they study, it is appropriate only for the physicists to aim at increased control of these phenomena. If psychologists aim to predict and control human behavior and experience, as in their textbooks they claim, they are assigning man to the same ontological status as weather, stars, minerals, or lower forms of animal life. We do not question anyone's right to seek understanding in order the better to control his physical environment and adapt it to his purposes. We properly challenge any man's right to control the behavior and experience of his fellows. To the extent that psychologists illumine human existence to bring it under the deliberate control of someone other than the person himself, to that extent they are helping to undermine some person's freedom in order to enlarge the freedom of someone else. If psychologists reveal knowledge of "determiners" of human conduct to people other than the ones from whom they obtained this understanding, and if they conceal this knowledge from its source, the volunteer subjects (who have offered themselves up to the scientist's "Look"), they put the recipients of the knowledge in a privileged position. They grant them an opportunity to manipulate men without their knowledge or consent. Thus, advertisers, businessmen, military leaders, politicians, and salesmen all seek to learn more about the determiners of human conduct, in order to gain power and advantage. If they can sway human behavior by manipulating the conditions which mediate it, they can get large numbers of people to forfeit their own interests and serve the interests of the manipulator. Such secret manipulation of the masses or of an individual by some other person is possible only if the ones being manipulated are kept mystified as to what is going on, and if their experience of their own freedom is blunted.

Psychologists face a choice. We may elect to continue to treat our Ss as objects of study for the benefit of some elite; or we may choose to learn about determiners of the human condition in order to discover ways to overcome or subvert them, so as to enlarge the Ss'—that is, Everyman's—freedom. If we opt for the latter, our path is clear. Our ways of conducting psychological research will have to be altered. Our definition of the purpose of psychology will have to change. And our ways of reporting our findings, as well as the audiences to whom the reports are directed, will have to change. We shall have to state openly whether we are psychologists-for-institutions or psychologists-for-persons.

The trouble with scientific psychologists—among whom I number myself—is that we have, in a sense, been "bought." We have in our hands the incredible power to discover conditions for behavior or for ways of being in the world. We have catalogued many of the factors which have a determining effect on human behavior and on our condition. We know that, in every experiment that we analyze, there is always an error term, "residual variance"; and we seek to exhaust this residual variance to the best of our ability. We get better at it as we learn how to identify and measure more and more relevant variables. The trouble is, as I see it, that if we exhaust all the variance, the subject of our study will be not a man, a human person, but rather a robot.

Scientific psychology has actually sought means of artificially reducing variance—humanness—among men, so that they will be more manipulable. Our commendable efforts (from a technical viewpoint) in the fields of human engineering, teaching methods, motivation research (in advertising), and salesmanship have permitted practitioners in those realms to develop stereotyped methods that work at controlling outcomes—outcomes that are good for the businessman or politician, but not necessarily good for the victim. We have taught people how to shape man into a way of being that makes him useful. We have forgotten that an image of man as useful grows out of a more fundamental image of man as the being who can assume *many* modes of being, when it is of importance to him to do so.

I think that a scientific psychologist committed to the aims of humanistic psychology would utilize his talents for a different purpose. For example, if individuality and full flowering growth as a person were values, he would seek means of maximizing or increasing the odds for maximization of these ways of being. An example of the biased use of scientific know-how is brainwashing. The brainwasher, through scientific means, seeks to insure that the prisoner will behave and believe as his captors wish. The same psychologists who invented the means of brainwashing know how to prevent it from happening. The latter class of knowledge is more in keeping with the aims of humanistic psychology and should be more avidly sought and then applied in more realms than presently is the case, if humanistic psychology is to be furthered.

How odd it seems that psychology has learned more about man at his worst than at his best. How sad it seems that psychology has employed its powers of truth-finding to serve ignoble masters. I would like to propose that we don't wait until the scarcity of "full-functioning men" becomes a national emergency. Rather, I would propose that we psychologists reconcile our aims and commitment to truth and our adherence to the canons of scientific inquiry with our human concerns that man be free, that he grow. I propose that we commence an all-out program of investigation on many fronts to seek answers to the questions humanistic psychology is posing. For example, we need psychologists with the most informed imaginations and talent for ingenious experimentation to wrestle with such questions as, "What are the outer limits of human potential for *transcending* biological pressures, social pressures, and the impact on a person of his past conditioning?"; "What developmental and interpersonal and situational conditions conduce to courage, creativity, transcendent behavior, love, laughter, commitment to truth, beauty, justice, and virtue?" These questions themselves, and even my proposal that we address them, once struck me as less than manly, as tender-hearted and sentimental. I would never have dared pose them to most of my mentors during my under-graduate and gradu-ate-student days. We were supposed to be tough and disciplined, which meant that we were only to study questions about some very limited class of behavior, not questions about larger human concerns. "Leave those to the philosophers, ministers, and politicians," we were told. Questions about the image of man smacked too much of philosophy and were not our proper concern. Actually, our teachers in-tended only that we learn the tools of our trade, not that we stifle our humanistic concerns; but they produced that outcome anyway.

Wilse B. Webb has pointed out, in his paper "The Choice of the Problem," that there are many reasons entering into the selection of an area for scientific investiga-tion. I am proposing that the quest for a more adequate image of man, for specifica-tion of peculiarly human optima, and the quest for the conditions which maximize or actualize these optima are worthwhile and important areas for study. I guess that, from another point of view altogether, I am inviting more of us to become educated men as we become trained psychologists. I suspect that psychologists who are edu-cated men cannot help but be active humanistic psychologists. One measure of a man is the questions he raises, and another is the goals for which he uses his powers and talents. I am not making a plea for less rigorous inquiry. I am making a plea for the powers of rigorous inquiry to be devoted to questions, answers to which will inform a growing, more viable image of man as a human being with potentiality, not solely a biological or socially determined being.

When researchers are transparently pledged to further the freedom and self-actualizing of their subjects, rather than be unwitting servants of the leaders of institutions, then they will deserve to *be* and *to be seen* as recipients of the secrets of human being and possibility. I envision a time when psychologists will be the guardians of the most intimate secrets of human possibilities and experience and possessors of knowledge as to how man can create his destiny because man has shown him; and I hope that if we "sell" these secrets to advertisers, businessmen, politicians, mass educators, and the military, we shall not do so until *after* we have informed our subjects, after we have tried to "turn them on," to enlarge their awareness of being misled and manipulated. I hope, in short, that we turn out to be servants and guardians of individual freedom, growth, and fulfillment, and not spies for the institutions that pay our salaries and research costs in order to get a privileged peep at human grist. Indeed, we may have to function for a time as coun-terspies, or double spies—giving reports about our subjects to our colleagues and to institutions, and giving reports back to our subjects as to the ways in which insti-tutions seek to control and predict their behavior for their (the institutions') ends.

UNIT ELEVEN | DISCUSSION QUESTIONS

38 | WILL TO MEANING

Define and discuss the origin of "logotherapy."

Distinguish between "pacemakers" and "peacemakers." Which are you?

39 | TOWARD A MODERN APPROACH TO VALUES: THE VALUING PROCESS IN THE MATURE PERSON

Describe some of the changes that occur in valuing orientation of the individual between infancy and adulthood.

What are some specific value directions that you have adopted? Do these values increase your psychological maturity? Discuss.

40 | COURAGE TO BE ONE'S SELF

In what specific ways can "courage" increase the satisfaction of an individual's life-goals?

Discuss ways in which a parent can guide his children toward increased self-identity.

41 | A HUMANISTIC REVOLUTION IN PSYCHOLOGY

Compare the goals of humanistic psychology with those of any other view in psychology (i.e., behaviorism, etc.).

Is humanism in psychology contrary to the aims of psychology as a science? Defend your views.

UNIT TWELVE
SEX, COURTSHIP, AND MARRIAGE

Each stage of life requires fulfillment of particular kinds of roles. The "developmental task" theory of Robert Havighurst holds that the role for the 18–35 year-old group includes: (1) selecting a mate, (2) learning to live with a marriage partner, (3) starting a family, (4) rearing a family, and (5) managing a home. Most colleges and universities enjoy large enrollments in classes that are specifically designed to cover these topics; while discussions in courses in several other areas frequently find themselves centered around these subjects. Magazines, books, motion pictures, forums, and social gatherings address these issues. Television programs, such as "The Dating Game" and "The Newlywed Game," provide additional examples of the attention focused on young people during courtship and marriage. It is of no surprise that during the late 1960's, college students were clamoring for a chance to let computers choose agreeable dating companions for them. The vast majority of those who tried this method did not give the machines very high ratings. It seems that the successful dates occurred at about the same frequency rate as by chance. Nevertheless, the dating-by-computer companies continue to profit, and more and more companies appear on the dating scene. It has been estimated that a quarter-of-a-million Americans participate in lonely-hearts clubs founded on pursuit of interests or hobbies ranging from letter writing to so-called scientific endeavors.

Regardless of the methods used, the selection of a mate is by far the most significant decision confronting a person. The foundation of our society is centered around the successful home and family. No one clear method for marriage-partner selection exists; however, sociologists have recognized certain factors that are found in successful marriages; e.g., similarity of attitudes, interests, and values. The recognition of and adherence to these factors will undoubtedly increase the possibility of a happy union. The first reading in this unit is a reprint of a 1970 Gallup Poll survey regarding premarital sex and virginity. The findings of *Generation Gap Shown in Sex View* offer great opportunities for discussion of changing attitudes and views. That these changes in sexual behavior and attitudes are undoubtedly related to a number of factors is the subject taken up in the second reading in this unit. Erwin O. Smigel and Rita Seiden in *The Decline and Fall of the Double Standard* examine the social changes which have occurred since the late nineteenth century and have initiated changing sex attitudes. This article presents documentary evidence supporting the fact that female attitudes are undergoing rapid transition. Many observers consider the "pill" as the most significant single force behind increased sexual freedom. Ashley Montagu in *The Pill, the Sexual Revolution, and the Schools* discusses birth control and its role in the humanization of man; sexual emancipation of the sexes, social emancipation of women, and sexual responsibility. The final reading by the staff of *Changing Times* explores the question of marital happiness and disharmony. *The Unsolved Mystery of Marriage* questions why seemingly perfect matches fail and why the unlikely ones last for years.

42 | GENERATION GAP SHOWN IN SEX VIEW

George Gallup

Dramatic evidence of the generation gap is seen in a comparison of the views of college students on premarital sex and virginity with those of older persons.

A recent Gallup survey of 55 campuses showed three students in four saying it is not important that the person they marry be a virgin, with about equal proportions of college males and females holding this opinion.

By way of contrast, a survey conducted last fall showed 68% of adults, 21 and older, saying premarital sex is "wrong."

RELIGION A FACTOR

While three out of every four students at both private or state-supported schools place little importance on marrying a virgin, opinion is much more closely divided among students at denominational or church-affiliated colleges.

Students who say that religion is a "relevant part of their life" are far more inclined to stress the importance of virginity than are students who say religion is "not a relevant part of their life."

A correlation is found between a student's attitudes on the importance of virginity and his political and social philosophy.

Among students who classify themselves as liberals, 79% say it is not important to marry a virgin, whereas the percentage among conservatives is 58%.

The proportion of students who think marrying a virgin is important declines steadily class by class, with freshmen most inclined to say it is important and seniors and graduate students least inclined to say this.

The findings of this survey are based on personal interviews with 1,114 college students, who were selected so as to be representative of the total college student population of the country. Here is the question asked:

There's a lot of discussion about the way morals and sex are changing in this country. Here is a question that is often discussed in women's magazines. What is your view on this: Would it be important to you that the person you marry be a virgin, or not so important?

Following are the findings based on the total sample and by key groups within the sample:

	Important	Not important	No opinion
All students	23%	73%	4%
Men	24	71	5
Women	21	77	2
Private colleges	21	75	4
Public or state-supported	21	75	4
Denominational or church affiliated	42	56	2
Freshmen	29	68	3
Sophomores	23	76	1
Juniors	21	70	9
Seniors	16	80	4
Graduate students	15	83	2
"Liberals"	18	79	3
"Conservatives"	39	58	3
Religion is relevant part of life	39	58	3
Not relevant	12	85	3

43 | THE DECLINE AND FALL OF THE DOUBLE STANDARD

Erwin O. Smigel and Rita Seiden

To find meaningful correlations,[1] especially in a pluralistic society, between the multitude of social forces and sexual behavior is difficult; to determine these correlations accurately, when appropriate data on sexual behavior are not available, is impossible. Nonetheless, it is our assignment to examine these social forces in order to see what

Reprinted from The Annals, 376 (March 1968), pp. 7–17, by permission of the authors and The American Academy of Political and Social Science.

effect they have had on sexual behavior and attitudes—specifically on sexual behavior and attitudes of unmarried heterosexuals of college age and younger in the United States.

Most recent examinations of sexual behavior still cite Kinsey's data[2] (1938–1949) and/or Terman's[3] (1934–1935). No one has published a Kinsey-type study for the United States in the 1960's. However, a few limited studies[4] on premarital sexual behavior have been completed since Kinsey published *The Human Male* in 1948. The various studies of college students show percentages of premarital coitus for males and females which range from 54:35 in 1929;[5] 51:25 in 1938;[6] to 56:25 in 1951;[7] and, in 1953, 68:47, 41:9, or 63:14, depending on whose figures are accepted.[8] The most recent examination of sexual behavior puts the rate of college female premarital experience at 22 per cent.[9] This is consistent with Kinsey's findings that 20 per cent of all college women had had premarital intercourse.[10]

Most of the studies of sex completed after Kinsey's main works appeared have been limited to collecting statistics on attitudes. The most extensive of these studies, for which data was collected through 1963, was conducted by Ira Reiss, on sexual permissiveness.[11] Reiss's findings point to a coming together of sexual practices, and, for the young at least, of attitudes about sex. He found definite movement away from the orthodox double standard toward a standard of permissiveness with affection (shorthand for "premarital sex is acceptable when there is mutual affection between the partners").

The earlier statistics of Kinsey and Terman point up important differences in sexual behavior between the generation of women born before 1900 and the generation born in the following decade. Kinsey found that 73.4 per cent of women born before 1900 had had no premarital intercourse, but among those born between 1900 and 1909, only 48.7 per cent had been virgins at marriage. The figures for those born in the 1920–1929 generation are the same—48.8 per cent.[12] Terman's findings are essentially in agreement. The statistics for both the Kinsey and Terman studies referred to here are for women of all ages, and not just for college women.[13] Terman found that 74 per cent of the females born between 1890 and 1899 had had no premarital intercourse, whereas among those born between 1900 and 1909, the percentage of virgin brides had dropped to 51.2. His figures reveal that this trend also held for men: of those interviewees born between 1890 and 1899, 41.9 per cent had had no premarital coitus, whereas of the interviewees born in the next generation, 32.6 per cent had had no such premarital experience.[14] Clearly, the major change in sex practices occurred in the generation born in the decade 1900–1909, which came to sexual age during or immediately after World War I, a period characterized by marked social change and innovation.

It may well be true that changes in sexual behavior and attitudes are related to the social changes which began in the late nineteenth century and accelerated rapidly over the past 67 years. It is not as clear, except perhaps for the post-World War I years, exactly what the effects of these social changes have been on sexual behavior. Reiss argues that, despite popular belief to the contrary, "the sexual revolution [is] a myth and the only basic change [is] a trend toward more equality between the sexes. . . . There has been less change than [is] popularly believed between modern American males and their Victorian grandfathers."[15]

It is generally thought, however, that the late-nineteenth-century break with Victorian morality was a tangential result of the Industrial Revolution, urban migration, war, the feminist movement, and the scientific study of once-taboo topics. Wilbert Moore, a leading authority on social change, credited industrialization with certain effects on the social structure;[16] and it is our opinion that industrialization affected sex attitudes and behavior as well. He specified increased social and geographic mobility; growth of industrial centers with concomitant concentration of population in urban areas; emphasis on rationality as a necessary part of an industrialized society (for example, a lessening of the influence of religion); transition from extended (rurally located) families to nuclear (urban) families; emphasis on individualism resulting from the breakdown[17] of the extended kinship system; decreased family size accompanied by a decline in the economic significance of the family unit as the unit of survival; and, finally, increased education.

Each of these general effects of social change can be shown, at least theoretically, to have potential impact on sexual behavior and attitudes. As the population moves from small towns and intimate personal relationships to urban centers, old forms of social control break down. This disintegration and the accompanying anonymity is speeded by new and faster forms of transportation which further increase the possibilities of anonymity and independence. A rational society affects the individual's world view, and he tends to see his own life in terms of more rational standards. As the extended kinship system dissolves or loses its importance, mate-selection processes become a more personal responsibility, and increase the importance of peer group norms, which take precedence over family norms. In the evolving industrial society, women take a new and larger part in the working world, thereby securing greater independence for themselves and increased equality in male-female relationships. The general increase in education has made possible widespread dissemination of sex information to the public.

In sum, the family has declined in importance as the unit upon which or around which society is organized, and individualism, in relationship to the family, is in the ascendency. As individualism has grown, sexual behavior has become more a personal matter and is less exclusively influenced by family and procreational considerations.

The complex social changes discussed have been gradual, but the impact of war can be immediate and abrupt. This is clearly indicated in the data on sexual behavior during and immediately after World War I. In any war, the mores governing family life tend to decay. Removed from some of the responsibilities, restrictions, and supports of the family, removed from the all-seeing eye of the small town or the neighborhood, soldiers are suddenly subject only to the mostly approving observations of their fellow soldiers. In the face of death or the possibility of being severely wounded, hedonism becomes the prevailing attitude. This attitude appears to be contagious and spreads to the civilian population. In World War I, it particularly affected the young women who were working in factories, taking on roles and responsibilities that had once belonged exclusively to men, often for the first time living alone in relative anonymity, and in many instances emotionally involved with men who were scheduled to be sent overseas. (This same hedonistic philosophy may be held by contemporary young people who are faced with the dangers of limited wars and the always present possibility of extinction by nuclear explosion.)

Many soldiers had contact with prostitutes and contracted venereal diseases. The United States Interdepartmental Social Hygiene Board reports: "Between September, 1917, and February 14, 1919, there were over 222,000 cases of venereal disease in the army and there were over 60,000 in the navy."[18] Venereal disease and the prostitute taught the soldier more about sex in his relatively short career in the armed services than he might normally have learned. The incidence of venereal disease was so high that it became a matter of both private and official army talk. The consequence was that most soldiers left the service knowing not only the protective effects but also the birth control uses of prophylactic sheaths. This kind of sex education became a standard part of the army curriculum.

The soldier who went abroad had new sexual experiences and came in contact with women whose behavior derived from different and more permissive sex norms; the returned veteran brought back with him sexual attitudes shaped by these new norms. Although they were not consciously intended for his mother, sister, wife, or wife-to-be, they tended to affect them as well.

War also tends to spread industrialization and to extend the need for women in industry, and, in turn, to increase their economic independence. The war and wartime experiences intensified the gradual way in which industrialization was changing the social structure.

War, industrialization, and an increase in political democracy seem to have led to the struggle for equal rights for women. The nineteenth-century feminists, who fought for financial and social rights and by 1920 had been enfranchised, were now also demanding more sexual freedom. Margaret Sanger, an American housewife, was a leader in this war. She waged a courageous battle for the control of pregnancy, and she was brought to trial for making birth control information available to interested persons. It was the trial, the wide publicity she received, and her persistence which helped to acquaint the public with the possibilities of birth control. She and other fighters for female sexual freedom were supported by a backdrop of the new norms of the returning soldiers, the effects of economic gains for women, and an increase in the scientific study of sex.

Although Krafft-Ebing,[19] Havelock Ellis,[20] and others were writing about sex pathology and sexuality, Freud's writings about the unconscious and the effect of sex on personality had the most influence upon American behavior and attitudes. Although *Studies in Hysteria*, written by Freud and Breuer, which made these ideas available to the public, was published in 1895, "it was not until after the war that the Freudian gospel began to circulate to a marked extent among the American reading public."[21] No one can estimate what popularization of psychoanalytic theory has done to free individuals—particularly women—from the puritan anxieties about sex. The fact of its influence, however, cannot be doubted. These studies by the sexologists and those by the sociologists, anthropologists, and psychologists studying and writing in the late 1920's and early 1930's provided the setting for the public acceptance of Kinsey's impressive work—which may in turn have had great influence on a society already impatient with Victorian sex mores. In any event, studies of sex were being undertaken, and they provided information about taboo topics which helped to free the average individual from the restraint against serious discussion of sexual behavior. Each generation of sex researchers has extended the study and broadened the understanding of sex, from Kinsey's counting of sexual outlets in the 1940's to Masters and Johnson's detailed study of human sexual response[22] in the early 1960's.

In addition to those factors already described, which have affected so many aspects of the social structure, other elements, although less powerful forces for general change, have also contributed to the alteration of sexual mores in a more immediate sense. Cultural interchange resulting from wartime contact since World War I and from the great increase in travel has led to a broadened participation with other societies. Furthermore, the disappearance of the chaperon undoubtedly created opportunities for sexual freedom which are not subject to the social sanctions of one's own society. The availability of the automobile, the affluent society which permits young people to live apart from their parents, and the growth of community size made privacy much more accessible. There has been a virtual removal of "fear-evoking" deterrents with the development of effective contraceptive devices.

All of these factors seem to be related to the change in sexual practices and to the apparent liberalization of sexual standards reflected in Reiss's data.[23] Since these social forces are still operating in the same direction, we should also expect to see changes in the direction of permissive sexual attitudes and behavior to continue.

The data we have on sexual behavior are limited; but more data are available on attitudes.

The research statistics are analyzed in Tables 1, 2, 3, and 4.[24]

TABLE 1

Attitudes toward premarital intercourse, per cent

Approve of	Cornell, 1940[*]			Michigan State University, 1947[†]			11 Colleges, 1952–1955[†]			University of Florida, 1958[††]		
	M	F	Total	M	F	Total	M	F	Total	M	F	Total
Sex relations for both	15	6	9	16	2		20	5		42	7	25
Abstinence	49	76	65	59	76		52	65		20	86	52
Sex relations for men only	23	11	16	10	15		12	23		33	0	17
Sex relations for engaged/ in love	11	6	8	15	7		16	7		5	7	6
N	(73)	(100)	(173)			(2000)			(3000)	(45)	(42)	(87)

[*] Percentages are based on N of 173, but 3 per cent (1 per cent male, 2 per cent female) did not answer the question. The total per cent appearing in Reiss is 101; therefore, ours totals 98.
[†] Separate N's for the male and female samples were not given; therefore, it was not possible to compute total percentage advocating each standard.
[††] Total percentages were not shown by Reiss and were computed by the authors of this article.

Reiss's later data, collected in 1959 and 1963,[25] confirm the trends evidenced in the findings of the earlier studies (see Table 2).

We can probably safely conclude from these data:

1. Abstinence and permissiveness with affection are the favored standards for both males and females.

TABLE 2

Percentage accepting each standard, 1959*

Standard	Male	Female	Total
Permissiveness with affection	24	15	19
Permissiveness without affection	13	2	7
Abstinence	28	55	42
Orthodox double standard	9	13	11
Transitional double standard†	18	10	14
N	(386)	(435)	(821)

*   The sample was drawn from the student populations of five schools: two Virginia colleges (one Negro, one white); two Virginia high schools (one Negro, one white); and one New York college. Percentages of adherents to the reversed double standard have been omitted. Therefore totals do not equal 100 per cent.

†   Transitional double standard means that sex relations are considered all right for men under any condition, but are acceptable for women only if they are in love.

2.   There has been a rise in female approval of permissiveness with affection and a decline in approval of the abstinence standard.

3.   Permissiveness without affection, if we consider it comparable to a blanket endorsement of casual sex relations for both, is apparently on the decline—even more sharply for men than for women.

4.   The orthodox double standard is also on the decline if we compare the Table 1 data (sex relations for men only) with the Table 2 data (orthodox double standard).

5.   The percentage of men who favor permissiveness with affection has increased markedly while the female endorsement remains about the same. The redistribution of women's attitudes seems to be away from abstinence and the orthodox double standard toward greater endorsement of the transitional double standard—coitus is all right for men under any condition, but is acceptable for women only if they are in love. Therefore, while women still endorse abstinence more highly than other standards, they are coming to favor sexual relations in the context of affection. Reiss's 1963 data support the 1959 evidence which indicates an increasingly favorable attitude on the part of females[26] toward sex with affection. Eighteen per cent favor permissiveness with affection; one per cent endorse permissiveness without affection; 56 per cent support abstinence. The percentage endorsing the transitional double standard was not given.[27]

6.   Succinctly: The percentage of both men and women who accept increased permissiveness with affection as their standard has increased (see Table 3).

Since the 1947, 1952–1955, and 1959 studies used the largest number of subjects and employed somewhat more rigorous sampling techniques, they are probably more reliable indicators of the trend in these attitudes. They strongly support the assumption that there has been an important change in attitudes toward sex in the direction of permissiveness.

TABLE 3

*Percentage accepting the standard of sex relations
for engaged/in love**

1940		1947		1952-1955		1958		1959		1963†	
M	F	M	F	M	F	M	F	M	F	M	F
11	6	15	7	16	7	5	7	24	15		18

* We are considering Reiss's "permissiveness with affection" as equivalent to "sex relations for engaged/in love."
† Figure for men has been omitted as total number of male
interviews is a small proportion of the total sample.

In explaining the differences between statistics on sexual behavior and statistics
on attitudes (namely, that behavior seems to have changed little since the 1920's,
but attitudes have become more liberal), Reiss suggests that we are seeing a "consolidation process" taking place, that is, "a change in attitudes to match the change
in behavior" is occurring.[28] Nelson Foote cites a variety of evidence which, he claims,
indicates the decline of the double standard: decline in prostitution, increasingly
equal sexual opportunities and experiences for women, increase in orgasm in marital
sex relations, "the steady approach to equivalence of male and female premarital
petting and marital sex play techniques," the increase of extramarital coitus, decreasing insistence on virginity in females at marriage, and "some decline in frequency of
marital coitus implying more mutual consent and less unilateral demand."[29]

Finally, in line with both Reiss's and Foote's arguments that there is a trend
toward a new single standard of permissiveness with affection, Robert Bell suggests
that for young adults, sex becomes acceptable today when the couple feels they are in
love. Peer group members accept and approve of sex without marriage, but not of
sex without love.[30]

For the unmarried, there is an increasing tendency to reject marriage as the
arbitrary dividing line between "socially approved and socially disapproved sexual
intimacy."[31] And in the same way that male and female roles have become more
equal in other areas of life, greater equality has come to the area of sexual relations:
"fair play has been replacing chastity as the badge of honor in the interpersonal
relations of the sexes."[32]

The results of the various studies of attitudes show two particularly interesting
and possibly related findings:

First, there has been an increase in permissive attitudes toward sex since the
1940's. This may be due to the accumulating reforming influence of those social
factors which was operating in the twentieth century. Certainly, the changed attitude
shows itself sharply in the increase in sexual content of movies, the candid use of
sexual lures in advertising, an increasing social sanctioning (if not precisely approval)
of sexual material in popular literature, and a generally freer atmosphere which
permits open talk about sex. But the new standard for coital involvement insists on
permissiveness with affection.

Second, the parent generation (sampled in 1963 by Reiss) is far more conservative than the younger generation—and is apparently more conservative than it was when it was the younger generation. In Reiss's 1963 adult sample, only 17 per cent endorsed permissiveness with affection for males and only 5 per cent endorsed this standard for females.[33]

Apparently, the conservative parent generation refuse to endorse for their children standards of behavior in which members of their generation, and perhaps they themselves, engaged. What appears to be a "generation gap," however, is probably a manifestation of a change in role.[34] Reiss's data on his adult sample give a concise picture of the relationship between role position and attitudes (see Table 4).

Permissiveness evidently reaches its highest point on one curve (for the college student) while it reaches its lowest point on another curve (for the parents of the college student). What the data describe, then, are changes which occur as individuals come to occupy parental role positions, and they are not descriptive of differences between individuals of the post-World War II generation and their parent's generation.

In part, this information suggests that parents try to modify behavior in their children in which they themselves participated as young adults. This reaction may portend how the current young adult generation will feel when they are parents themselves. However, the qualification to be noted here is that the generation which came to maturity in the 1920's broke with previous generations in terms of behavior. The following generations continued in the same kind of practices but gradually came to express more liberal attitudes. The new liberalism of the younger generation may very well contribute to a shift in expressed adult values for the parent generations of the late 1960's and 1970's.

We know that sexual attitudes have changed and that sexual standards appear to be in a period of transition. "What was done by a female in 1925 acting as a rebel and a deviant can be done by a female in 1965 as a conformist."[35]

Data based on a large sample are available on sex behavior up to 1949 and on attitudes up to 1963. We do not know what has happened during the last five years or what is happening now. The general public impression is that there has been a very recent sexual revolution and that it is still going on. Most researchers do not believe that this is the case. The authors of this article, as social observers and recent reviewers of the literature on sexual behavior and attitudes toward sex, will attempt to "crystal ball" what has occurred during the last five years and what is occurring now. What follows, then, is not fact, but guess.

Past trends in social change, in behavior, and in attitudes toward sex are continuing. What seems to be taking place (except for pockets of our society) is a growing tendency toward more sexual permissiveness among the young unmarried. Sex with affection appears to be increasingly accepted. More and more this norm is based on personal choice, and it manifests itself for middle-class college youth in the form of trial marriage, for the girl, and for the boy at least as a stable, monogamous relationship, to the point of setting up housekeeping. Increasingly, this happens with parental knowledge though not necessarily with parental approval. If Kinsey repeated his study today, he would probably find premarital virginity slightly lower and figures for those who have had premarital intercourse only with their spouse, a circumstance which was already on the increase in 1947 (born before 1900, 10.4 per cent; born 1920–1929, 27.3 per cent),[36] somewhat higher.

Promiscuity, a word objected to by many young people, probably has lessened. Certainly the use of prostitutes has diminished. If we are correct in believing that more young people are living monogamously together, and if marriage for both men and women (the figures are: median age of first marriages in 1890 for brides was 22.0 and for grooms was 26.1;[37] for 1966, the median age for brides was 20.5 and for grooms 22.8[38]) is occurring at earlier ages, then the statistical probabilities of premarital promiscuity have lessened, except when it is a reflection of mental illness. Today, except for the "hippies," who, according to the press, indulge in group sex, promiscuity as a form of rebellion is significantly on the decline.

TABLE 4*

Marital and family status and permissiveness in the adult sample

Marital and family status	Per cent permissive	N
Single	44	(108)
Married		
No children	23	(124)
All preteen	22	(384)
Preteen and older	17	(218)
All teen and older	13	(376)

*   Source: Ira L. Reiss, *The Social Context of Premarital Sexual Permissiveness*, New York: Holt, Rinehart and Winston, 1967, p. 142, table 9.2 (some data omitted).

We are living in a much more permissive society, and we are much more vocal about sex. As Walter Lippman put it, even as early as 1929: "It was impossible to know whether increased openness about sex reflected more promiscuity or less hypocrisy."[39] While we do not have much new evidence concerning sexual behavior, we do have nonsystematic overt indications about attitudes. It is seen in advertisements which are much more suggestive than they used to be. At one time, an advertiser would indicate to a male reader that, if he used a certain product, a pretty girl would kiss him. Now the ads suggest that she will have intercourse with him: "When an Avis girl winks at you she means business," and as Chateau Martin asks, leering only slightly, "Had any lately?" Movies have become less suggestive and more obvious; nudity as well as intercourse have become not uncommon sights. The Scandinavian picture *I, A Woman* for example, consists of a number of seductions with a number of different men. Perhaps what is more significant is that censorship boards, the courts, and power groups in this country have sharply amended their definitions of obscenity. The theater has, for some time, been more open about sex and its various ramifications, and four-letter words are becoming a theatrical cliché.

Another indicator of this generation's expressed attitudes toward sex are the omnipresent buttons, which express not only political, but also sexual opinions. The buttons are designed for fun and shock, and for public declaration for sexual freedom. Sold in large cities all over this country, they range from simple position-statements such as "Make Love Not War," "I'm For Sexual Freedom," or "Equality for Homosexuals," to invitations which read "Roommate Wanted," "Join the Sexual Revolution—Come Home With Me Tonight," to such shock jokes as "Phallic Symbols Arise," "Stand Up For S-X," and "Come Together."

More sophisticated young people feel that the dirty-word movements or the shock words no longer have any impact. In the October 26, 1967, *Washington Square Journal,* a New York University publication, the student reviewer of an off-Broadway production, *The Beard,* which freely uses four-letter words and ends with an act of cunnilingus on stage, says: "Unfortunately the force of the play rests on the anticipated violation of social taboo, and violating social taboos just isn't what it used to be."

Except for the rediscovered poor, the United States is a society of unprecedented abundance. Upper- and middle-class white Americans pamper their children, give them cars and money, send them to college and abroad, and set them up in their own apartments while they are going to school. These young people have leisure and the wherewithal to use it in amusing themselves—only the war is real, which gives a special significance to college as a way of avoiding the war. This abundance means that college-age men and women can travel together, live together, and have a sex life encouraged by their peers, whose opinions they have now come to value more than those of their elders.

Abundance for the young unmarrieds in the city has made it possible to meet other young unmarrieds in new ways. Apartment houses are being built for them; clubs are formed for them, but perhaps the most significant of all the developments is the use of bars, now often called pubs, which serve as meeting places where singles can meet without prejudice. A girl who visits the pub is under no obligation to "go to bed" with the man whom she meets and with whom she may leave. These pubs (and they begin to specialize in different kinds of singles), in a sense, institutionalize a system of bringing together like-minded people; they speed the dating and the trial-and-error process, for they offer this particular group of affluent young people a wide variety of partners to choose from, and they can choose quickly, independently, and frequently.[40]

Many observers of the current scene consider the "pill" the most significant single force for increased sexual freedom. A count of the articles listed in the *Reader's Guide to Periodical Literature* reveals that more articles were published about birth control in the period March 1965 to February 1966 than were listed in a ten-year sampling starting with 1925 and ending with 1957. The sampling yielded 89 titles. But we doubt that the pill has added materially to the increase in the number of young adults or adolescents who have had premarital sex. Effective techniques of birth control existed, and were used, before the pill. True, the pill makes birth control easier to manage (except for the memory requirement), but romantic love is still important; it makes taking the pill, when no definite partner is available, undesirable. What the pill does is to give sexual freedom to those who are having steady sexual relationships, for then the use of the pill adds to romantic love by making elaborate preparations unnecessary.

According to our crystal ball, which, of course, may be clouded, we have not had a recent or current sexual revolution in terms of behavior. However, there probably has been some increase in the proportion of women who have had premarital intercourse. It is our guess that the increase has occurred largely among women who have had premarital sex only with their spouses-to-be. If there has been a sexual revolution (similar to the 1920's but ideologically different[41]), it is in terms of frankness about sex and the freedom to discuss it. Women have demanded and have achieved more education, more independence, and more social rights; one of these is the right to choose a partner for sex. Men are accepting many of these changes in the status of women and are tempering their insistence on what have generally been considered male prerogatives, for example, the right to demand that a bride be a virgin. Young men today are probably less promiscuous and more monogamous, and their relationships tend to be more stable. Both sexes are approaching a single standard based on sex with affection. We are still in a stage of transition. Despite the title of this article, the only indisputable conclusion which we can draw from the current scene is that we are witnessing the decline, but not yet the fall, of the double standard.

REFERENCES AND NOTES

1. It is understood that even if it were possible to determine these correlations accurately, we would not have an explanation of causation.
2. Alfred C. Kinsey, Wardell B. Pomeroy, Clyde E. Martin, Paul Gebhard, *et al.*, *Sexual Behavior in the Human Female*, Philadelphia: W. B. Saunders, 1953. The data on the female subjects were collected from 1938 through 1949. Alfred C. Kinsey, Wardell B. Pomeroy, and Clyde E. Martin, *Sexual Behavior in the Human Male*, Philadelphia: W. B. Saunders, 1948. Data on the male subjects were collected from 1938 to 1947.
3. Lewis M. Terman *et al.*, *Psychological Factors in Marital Happiness*, New York: McGraw-Hill Book Co., 1938.
4. Gilbert Youth Research, "How Wild Are College Students?," *Pageant*, vol. 7 (1951), pp. 10–21; Ernest W. Burgess and Paul Wallin, *Engagement and Marriage*, Chicago: J. P. Lippincott, 1953; Judson T. Landis and Mary Landis, *Building a Successful Marriage*, 3d ed., Englewood Cliffs, N.J.: Prentice-Hall, Inc., 1957; Winston Ehrmann, *Premarital Dating Behavior*, New York: Holt, Rinehart and Winston, 1959; Mervin B. Freedman, "The Sexual Behavior of American College Women: An Empirical Study and an Historical Study," *Merrill-Palmer Quarterly*, vol. 2 (1965), pp. 33–48; Ira L. Reiss, *The Social Context of Premarital Sexual Permissiveness*, New York: Holt, Rinehart and Winston, 1967, chap. VII. Reiss's primary purpose was not to examine behavior (at least not in this latest presentation); he was interested in attitudes. He asked 268 students (42 of them males) in an Iowa college about their behavior. What he did was to correlate expressed feelings of guilt with behavior, and found relationships with age and behavior and relationships between expressed standards and behavior. The Institute for Sex Research at Indiana University conducted a 1967 study of sex behavior among college students, but the final results have not yet been published.
5. Gilbert V. Hamilton, *A Research in Marriage*, 2d ed., New York: Lear, 1948, p. 348.
6. D. D. Bromley and F. H. Britten, *Youth and Sex*, New York: Harper & Brothers, 1938, p. 36.
7. Gilbert Youth Research *op. cit.*, p. 15.
8. Burgess and Wallin, *op cit.*, p. 330; Landis and Landis, *op cit.*, pp. 216 and 212; Ehrmann, *op. cit.*, pp. 33–34 and 46.
9. Freedman, *op. cit.*, p. 47.
10. Kinsey, *The Human Female*, p. 288.
11. Reiss, *op. cit.*

12. Ira L. Reiss, "Standards of Sexual Behavior," in Albert Ellis and Albert Abarbanel (eds.), *Encyclopedia of Sex*, New York: Hawthorne Books, 1961, p. 999. "These data were based on Kinsey (1953), but were especially prepared for [Reiss's] paper . . . [by] Drs. Gebhard and Martin of the Institute of Sex Research. These were based on 2,479 women who either were or had been married by the time of the interview."

13. Confirming this change are data reported by K. B. Davis, *Factors in the Sex Life of Twenty-two Hundred Women*, New York: Harper & Brothers, 1929, p. 232. Of those women who attended college in the early 1900's (that is, were born before 1900), only 7 per cent had premarital intercourse. According to Bromley and Britten, *loc. cit.*, 25 per cent of the college women of the 1930's had premarital intercourse. And according to Freedman (*op. cit.*, p. 45), "the rate of premarital nonvirginity tripled from 1900 to 1930."

14. Terman, *op. cit.*, p. 321; Kinsey, *The Human Male*, *op. cit.*, p. 395. Kinsey noted generational differences within his male sample; but the "generations" were formed by dividing his subjects into "younger" (under 33 years of age at the time of the interview) and "older" (over 33 years of age at the time interviewed) groups. He did not compare them by decade of birth as he did the women. The median age of the younger group was 21.2 years, that is, born approximately between 1917 and 1926. The median age of the older group was 43.1 years, that is, born approximately between 1895 and 1904 (Kinsey, *The Human Female*, *op. cit.*, chap. VII). Information is provided here that premarital petting had increased with each generation since 1920 even though incidence of premarital coitus had not. One of the possible explanations for the continued relatively high number of virgins is that heavy petting is now very common, so that there are a large number of "technical" virgins who engage in almost everything except coitus.

15. "Iowa Sociologist Calls Sex Revolution a Myth," *New York Times*, Oct 22, 1967, sec. I, p. 80.

16. Wilbert E. Moore, *Social Change*, Englewood Cliffs, N.J.: Prentice-Hall, Inc., 1963, pp. 100–103.

17. In a recent article, Thomas K. Burch casts doubt on whether there has indeed been a breakdown of the extended family or a decline in the size of the family because of urbanization. See Thomas K. Burch, "The Size and Structure of Families: A Comparative Analysis of Census Data," *American Sociological Review*, vol. 32 (1967), pp. 347–363. We feel, however, that there can be little doubt about the relation between urbanization and changes in function and meaning of the family.

18. T. A. Storey, *The Work of the United States Interdepartmental Social Hygiene Board*, New York: United States Interdepartmental Social Hygiene Board, 1920, p. 6.

19. *Psychopathia Sexualis*, the best known work of Krafft-Ebing, was originally published in German in 1886. The first English translation was published shortly thereafter.

20. *The Psychology of Sex*, which represents Ellis' main body of work, was published in English in six separate volumes from 1900 to 1910 by F. A. Davis, Philadelphia. Volumes I and II had appeared in French (1897) before they appeared in English.

21. Frederick Lewis Allen, *Only Yesterday: An Informal History of the Nineteen-twenties*, New York: Blue Ribbon Books, 1932, p. 98.

22. William H. Masters and Virginia E. Johnson, *Human Sexual Response*, Boston: Little, Brown, and Company, 1966.

23. Ira L. Reiss, *Premarital Sexual Standards in America*, New York: The Free Press, 1960, pp. 219–221.

24. These tables are rearranged in chronological order and condensed for our purposes from the ones appearing in Reiss, *The Social Context of Premarital Sexual Permissiveness*, *op. cit.*, pp. 16–18. The categories used by L. Rockwood and M. Ford in their

(1940) study of Cornell students, *Youth, Marriage, and Parenthood*, New York: John Wiley & Sons, Inc., 1945, p. 40, were used for classifying the data of the other studies. The 1947 and 1952–1955 studies were made by J. T. Landis and M. Landis and reported in *Building a Successful Marriage*, p. 215. Their categories were "Sexual Relations: For both, None for either, For men only, Between engaged only." The 1958 study by Ehrmann, *op, cit.,* p. 189, used the standards: "Double (comparable to Sex Relations for men only), Conservative single (Abstinence), General liberal single (Sex Relations for both), and Lover liberal single (Sex Relations for those engaged or in love)" as categories.

25. Reiss, *The Social Content of Premarital Sexual Permissiveness, op. cit.,* tables 2.5, 2.6, and 2.7, pp. 25–27. The reverse double standard category has been omitted, for Reiss says that this "response is almost certainly an error." For his discussion of this point, see *ibid.,* p. 24. Reverse double standard adherents are understood to believe that women should have greater sexual freedom than men. Percentage accepting this standard were: 1959—9 per cent male, 6 per cent female, 7 per cent total; 1963—0 per cent male, 5 per cent female, 4 per cent total.

26. *Ibid.,* p. 128. The data for males have not been utilized because the men represent only a small percentage of the total number of cases in the sample.

27. Reiss reported 20 per cent of the females endorsing the double standard, but did not break down the figure to show the percentage accepting the orthodox standard nor the percentage accepting the traditional standard.

28. Reiss, *Premarital Sexual Permissiveness in America, op. cit.,* p. 233.

29. Nelson N. Foote, "Sex as Play," *Social Problems,* vol. I (1964), p. 161.

30. Robert Bell, "Parent-Child Conflict in Sexual Values," *Journal of Social Issues,* vol. 22 (1966), pp. 38–39.

31. *Ibid.,* p. 43.

32. Foote, *op. cit.,* p. 161.

33. Reiss, *The Social Context of Premarital Sexual Permissiveness, op. cit.,* table 2.7, p. 142.

34. *Ibid.,* pp. 140–143; and Bell, *op. cit.,* pp. 38–39.

35. Ira L. Reiss, "The Sexual Renaissance: A Summary and Analysis," *Journal of Social Issues,* vol. 22 (1966), p. 126.

36. Reiss, "Standards of Sexual Behavior," *loc. cit.*

37. U.S. Department of Health, Education, and Welfare, *Vital Statistics: National Summaries,* vol. 50, no. 28 (November 1959). Source: U.S. Bureau of the Census, "Population Characteristics," *Current Population Reports,* Series P–20, 105–3.

38. U.S. Bureau of the Census, *Statistical Abstracts of the United States, 1967,* 88th ed., Washington, D.C.: U.S. Government Printing Office, 1967, table 75: "Median Age at First Marriage, by Sex: 1920–1966." Source: U.S. Bureau of the Census, *Current Population Reports.* Series P–20, No. 159.

39. Walter Lippman, *A Preface to Morals,* New York: The Macmillan Company, 1960, p. 228.

40. For an interesting comment on this phenomenon see "The Pleasures and Pain of the Single Life," *Time,* Sept. 15, 1967, pp. 26–27.

41. See Bennett M. Berger, "The New Morality," paper read at the Plenary Session of the Society for the Study of Social Problems, Aug. 27, 1967.

44 | THE PILL, THE SEXUAL REVOLUTION, AND THE SCHOOLS

Ashley Montagu

The Pill! The fact that it is referred to so magisterially represents something of the measure of importance that is generally attached to this genuinely revolutionary development. For it *is* a revolutionary development, probably to be ranked among the half-dozen or so major innovations in man's two or more million years of history. In its effects I believe that the pill ranks in importance with the discovery of fire, the development of the ability to make and employ tools, the evolution of hunting, the invention of agriculture, the development of urbanism, of scientific medicine, and the release and control of nuclear energy.

This is rather a large claim to make, but I do not think that it is in the least exaggerated, and I should like to underscore this statement in the best way possible: by setting out the facts and the consequences that are likely to flow from the changes they imply. Since the consequences of the pill are likely to be manifold and profoundly alterative of age-old beliefs, practices, and institutions, it will be helpful to deal with the most significant of these in a systematic manner.

BIRTH CONTROL AND ITS ROLE IN THE HUMANIZATION OF MAN

For the first time in the history of man, the pill provides a dependable means of controlling conception. For the first time, the pill makes it possible to make every individual of reproductive age completely responsible for both his sexual and his reproductive behavior. It is necessary to be unequivocally clear concerning the distinction between sexual and reproductive behavior. Sexual behavior may have no other purpose than pleasure, pure hedonism or impure hedonism, or without the slightest intention of reproducing, or it may be indulged for both pleasure and reproduction. Sexual behavior is much more rarely indulged in for the purposes of reproduction than it is for the purposes of pleasure. Hedonistic sex is to be regarded as purely sexual behavior. Sex that is indulged with a view to the generation of children constitutes reproductive behavior. In these senses the female tends to be the reproductive creature and man more often the sexual creature.

No society can long tolerate any form of anarchic behavior in its midst, and therefore sexual promiscuity especially has been prohibited in all human societies. In all societies, every individual is made responsible (1) for his sexual behavior, and (2) for his reproductive behavior. In nonliterate societies this has been regulated

Ashley Montagu, "The Pill, the Sexual Revolution, and the Schools," from *Phi Delta Kappan*, May 1968, pp. 480–484. Reprinted by permission.

in the following manner. Sex for the sheer pleasure of it has been allowed everyone, but reproductive behavior has been permitted only to those persons who are married to one another. Since in almost all such societies girls marry at or shortly after the attainment of the first menstruation (menarche), premarital sexual relations practically never result in children,[1] so there are no problems. In marriage the number of children, especially at the food-gathering hunting level of economic development, is planned. For example, in order to control the size of their families the Bushmen of the Kalahari desert simply abstain from sexual intercourse as the most effective means of birth control. The same is true of many other nonliterate peoples. The love and respect these peoples have for their children and for each other, and the vital necessity of controlling the size of their families and total population, are things that the so-called more developed peoples, who have gone so far in the opposite direction, must learn if they are again to be able to love their children and each other—indeed, if they are to survive at all.

With the gift of the pill we now have the power placed comfortably in our hands for accomplishing all these ends, and more. And unless we begin immediately, the debasement of humanity which has proceeded at such an alarming rate in the recent period will continue in its destructive effects at an accelerating pace, for we are not far now from the very edge of doom. With the pill, not to mention the improved versions which are already in process of development, we have it in our power to begin the rehumanization of man at the very foundations. The task of making human beings out of people literally becomes impossible when their numbers exceed the limits consonant with a successful issue to such an undertaking. That, then, is the first of the contributions made by the pill: It provides the basis for the humanization of man.

THE SEXUAL EMANCIPATION OF THE SEXES

In civilized societies the fear of conception has produced anxieties about sex in the female which have had a variety of effects upon the sexual relationship. Among these has been the strong resistance which females have traditionally offered to the male's sexual advances. Largely because of this resistance the male has been forced into a predatory exploitative attitude toward the female. With the freedom to enjoy sex for its own sake which the pill affords, women's attitudes towards sex will change, becoming less anxiety-ridden, more relaxed—and the attitudes of men towards women will undergo a complementary change. The double standard, which has had so damaging an effect upon both sexes and upon our society, will make way for a healthier view of sex and of the relations between the sexes.

It will become possible for the first time for the sexes genuinely to complement each other, and to live and love together on a basis of full equality. The shortsighted "viewers with alarm" will be relegated to their proper places when what they so wrongheadedly deplore, namely, the alleged feminization of men and the alleged masculization of women, are discovered to be advances in the right rather than in the wrong direction.

It is only in recent years that we have learned that what we have always taken for granted as biologically determined, namely, masculinity and femininity, are in fact genders which are virtually wholly culturally determined. We now know, beyond dispute, that whatever the sex of the child may be, its gender role is what it *learns*.

One learns to be either male or female according to the manner in which one is socialized, or to put it more accurately, *genderized*.[2] Hence, when one sex assumes some of the behaviors traditionally associated with the other, no violence is done to any supposed biological functions. Males have long stood in need of such feminine qualities as tenderness, sensitivity, compassion, gentleness, and the like. Women, for their part, will benefit from the adoption of traits hitherto considered purely masculine, such as courage, adventuresomeness, enterprise, intrepidity, and the like. Men need to be humanized; women to be energized. Men need to become more secure, compassionate, and less violent. Women, to achieve their full status as human beings, need men to go with them who have also acquired or are on the way to acquiring that status.

THE SOCIAL EMANCIPATION OF WOMEN

Possibly the greatest revolution resulting from the advent of the pill is the social emancipation of women that this will bring about. Menstruation, for example, for virtually all women has been to some extent socially handicapping. Because of it, in a male-dominated world, the female has everywhere been relegated to "the menstrual hut," discriminated against, and permanently demoted in the status hierarchy. Furthermore, many women during the menstrual cycle have been the captives of their hormones, often moody, characterized by premenstrual tensions, and not infrequently "ill." All these things have in the past combined to make menstruation a "curse" for women physiologically and psychologically. The pill by inhibiting the processes that lead to menstruation suppresses that function, and frees women for the first time from the discomforting and often disabling effects of menstruation and the possibility of unwanted pregnancy. With all these psychologically handicapping conditions which were formerly incident to her physiology removed, the last of the grounds for discrimination against women is gone, and women may at long last enter into that full social equality which, until the development of the pill, has been so long denied them.

The pill in its present form, effective as it is, is but the precursor of more sophisticated forms of hormone regulators, as they may be called. Pills are already in process of development which are designed to produce long-term inhibition of ovulation, conception, and menstruation. A single pill will produce immunity for years, its inhibitory effects being cancelable at will by taking another pill that restores the normal physiological functions.

Foresight is the last of the gifts granted by the gods to man. All the more reason, therefore, to reflect upon and prepare for the developments which these revolutionary changes, in the very beginnings of which we are now living, will bring about. This is nowhere more important than in its effects upon the young.

PREMARITAL SEX

The prohibition against sex in civilized societies, in which societies the age of marriage is delayed well into reproductive age, has a long and interesting history behind it. In the Western world the attitudes, customs, practices, and beliefs concerning the relations of the sexes to one another in all age-grades and statuses has largely been transmitted through the teachings of the Judaeo-Christian tradition. Since in such societies children born out of wedlock had no legal father, nor for that matter a legal mother, and since society was so structured as to offer no means of incorporating the child, and often the mother, into the society, and since sexual intercourse outside of wedlock was itself stigmatized as a sin, the negative sanctions against such immoral and illicit sex were severely enforced. Thus premarital sex came to be held as both morally and legally and socially abhorrent. Virtually all the reasons created to justify the prohibitions against premarital sex were little more than rationalizations. These concealed the real reasons why premarital sex could not be tolerated in such societies, namely, the havoc caused by such disallowed conduct to the social and religious organization of such societies. The ostracism and punishments that were often inflicted upon the offenders served as sufficient deterrents to keep premarital intercourse from growing to unmanageable proportions. But with the advent of two world wars and the breakdown in moral, religious, and social values that followed upon them there was a notable increase in all forms of forbidden sex.

The Kinsey Report, in part, constitutes a monumental record of the status of sexual mores in mid-twentieth century. Kinsey found that there was a great deal more covert sexual activity of every forbidden kind than was overtly admitted or even suspected. In the Sixties the pregnancy rate of girls of school age has risen spectacularly. These are facts which must be squarely faced.

It is not, for many reasons, desirable for girls of school age to bear children. In the first place, they are physiologically unprepared in most cases for such a function, with the result that a large proportion of children born to such immature mothers suffer from all sorts of deficiencies. This would be reason enough to discourage early pregnancy, but in fact this first is the last of the reasons why early pregnancy should be discouraged. The primary reason for such discouragement is that adolescent girls are themselves in process of development, of maturation as persons, and are in every way socially and psychologically unready for the responsibilities of motherhood. The optimum age for childbearing from every point of view, physiological, psychological, and social, is between 21 ± 2 years and 27 ± 2 years. Childbearing before the age of 21 ± 2 years should therefore be discouraged.[3]

With the pill, premarital sex without any fear of sex or the birth of children becomes for the first time possible, and hence the principal barrier against it is removed. But with the removal of this barrier the responsibilities involved in this particular relationship are maximized beyond anything that has hitherto been anticipated or required. For, once the barrier has been lowered, the danger of the debasement of this delicate, this tender, this most sensitive of all human relationships, is greatly increased. Hence no one should ever consider entering into such a relationship who is incapable of behaving responsibly in it. Responsibility to others is something one must learn. It is not something one is born with. It is here that the schools must assume *their* responsibility, for it is in the schools that the parents of future generations must be prepared in the meaning of sex and responsibility. What, then, is sexual responsibility, and how can it be taught in the schools?

SEXUAL RESPONSIBILITY

By "responsibility" I mean essentially involvement in the welfare of the other. It seems to me that involvement in the welfare of others should be the basis of all human relationships. If one cares about others, it is difficult, possessed of the requisite knowledge and responsibility, to behave in such a manner as to harm one's fellowman. It is necessary, however, to underscore the fact that involvement is not enough, because without the requisite knowledge and sensitivity, it is possible, with the best of intentions, to wreak havoc upon others. The evil that well-intentioned people have done adds up to a sizable quantity. It is not enough to be good, it is necessary also to be knowledgeable and understanding. All these qualities can be and should be taught in the schools.[4] They should, of course, also be taught in the home. But unless we can satisfactorily establish the criteria by which the good, the true, and the beautiful can be measured we shall not get very far in the discussion of sexual responsibility. I mention the "true" and the "beautiful" because these are fundamentally the same as "knowledge" and "understanding." Let us further define our terms. Goodness or love is behavior calculated to confer survival benefits in a creatively enlarging manner upon others. It is conduct which not only enables others to live, but to develop and live more fully realized than they would have done had you not communicated to them your involvement in their welfare.

By "knowledge" is to be understood verifiable information, and by "understanding" is to be understood the ability to appreciate what that knowledge is capable of doing—not merely what knowledge *is*, but what it is *for*.

Sexual responsibility, like every other kind of responsibility, implies moral involvement, the moral strength to be responsible to others for oneself and to them. This implies the goodness, the knowledge, and the understanding of what, in the special case of sexual behavior, are the indispensable qualifications before one may enter into any sexual relationship. Spelled out in practical terms, what this means is that our schools must become institutes for the teaching of human responsibility, with this as the primary purpose of education, and instruction in the three "R's" as purely secondary to this main purpose. To understand the nature of human nature is not beyond the capacity of a child. Nor is it beyond the child's capacities to understand the vulnerabilities of human beings, to respond with sensitivity to the needs of others with thoughtfulness and consideration, to learn to understand the facts about sex (including its philosophy, psychology, and ethics). These are matters that can be taught at every school age. Courses in these subjects, can, of course, be graduated to meet the requirements of the young at every age.

What will be required will be skillfully organized teaching materials and well-trained, congenially sophisticated teachers. Our teachers colleges are at the present time, for the most part, wholly unequipped to prepare such teachers. Hence a tremendous amount of work must be done, and most of it, it is to be feared, will be done by trial and error—which is better than not being done at all. However it will be done, it were well that it were done as soon as possible, for the hour is late and human beings much in need of that goodness, knowledge, and understanding for lack of which so many avoidable tragedies have blighted the lives of countless individuals and families. Never was there a period more favorable than the present in which to introduce into our schools the teaching of sexual responsibility. The sexual revolution should precipitate the educational revolution, which should in turn swiftly lead to the human revolution.

Let me explain. The teaching of sexual responsibility can be a fascinating experience for both teacher and pupil. It is not only an extremely interesting subject in itself, but since it gets down to the fundamentals of human relationships, it constitutes a uniquely sensitive introduction to the whole world of human relations. This is how, I believe, the course on sexual responsibility (or whatever other name it may be called by) should be taught, not as a course on sex but as a part of the course on human relations. Thus one would begin with the exciting evolutionary history of the manner in which human beings got to be the way they now are. What it means to be human from the evolutionary point of view, the nature of human nature, the facts about the physiology and psychology of reproduction, birth, the needs of the newborn and the means of its humanization.[5] By such a route we might for the first time genuinely realize the purposes of education: the making of fulfilled humane beings, the making of humane beings out of people.

It will take time. How long will depend on how widespread this kind of teaching becomes throughout the land. Toward the furtherance of that end it would be a great boon if we could drop the euphemistic phrase, "the facts of life." "The facts of life" are strictly for the birds, the bees, and the bats, especially the bats that are addicted to belfries. What growing young human beings need is the understanding of their own growth and development, how they came into being, and what their presence in fact means upon this earth for the great and continuing enterprise of human relations. And that is the point, I believe, that should be the main theme of education in sexual responsibility—what one owes to others and what one has a right to expect from others as humanely accomplished human beings. As I have already remarked, education in sexual responsibility becomes essentially education in human sensitivity, in knowledge, understanding, and lovingkindness. I *know* the teacher can do this. I know because I had such teachers.

Young unmarried individuals who are sufficiently responsible will be able, in the new dispensation, to enter into responsible sexual relationships in a perfectly healthy and morally acceptable and reciprocally beneficial manner, which will help the participants to become more fully developed human beings than they would otherwise have stood a chance of becoming. The dead hand of ugly traditional beliefs (such as the nastiness and sinfulness of sex, the wickedness of premarital sex), which has been responsible for untold human tragedies, will be replaced by a new flowering of human love. This is a critical point.

LOVE

Love, for far too many males in the Western world, has been identified with sex. Females for such men have amounted to little more than sexual objects. Such attitudes on the part of men have resulted in the debasement of the most important of all human relatednesses—the ability to love.

Love is by far the most consequential of all the needs which must be satisfied if the growing creature is to be humanized. It stands at the center of all the other needs, like the sun in our solar system around which the other planets move in their orbits. It is the one and only need which must be adequately satisfied if we are to become healthy human beings. By health I mean the ability to love and the ability to work. Spelled out, love means the communication of one's deep involvement in the welfare of the other, the communication of one's profound interest in the realization of the other's potentialities for being the kind of human being you are being to him, the communication of the feeling that you will always be standing by, that you will never commit the supreme treason that human beings so frequently commit against their fellowman, of letting him down when he most stands in need of you, but that you will be standing by giving him all the supports and sustenances and stimulations that he requires for becoming what it is in him to be, and knowing that to be human is to be in danger, to be terribly vulnerable to the damage that people are capable of inflicting upon one another, that you will be particularly careful in caring for the other not to commit such errors against him. If one can communicate these messages to the other, then I believe one can be said to love him. And this is the sort of thing that we should be teaching in our schools. As I have said, this should be the primary purpose of the schools. Within the matrix of such teaching a special course on sexual responsibility would hardly be necessary, except insofar as details were concerned.

As a corollary of this discussion on love, it should follow that those who are unable to love in this manner should refrain from entering into human relationships involving the deepest sensibilities of others. Such persons should be rehabilitated as human beings before they are permitted to enter into such relationships.

MARRIAGE

From the above discussion it should also follow that no one who is unprepared for it as a person aware of all that is required of one in the marital relationship should be permitted to marry. Certainly everyone should always remain free to choose who he desires to marry, but fitness for marriage should be determined by the state, until such time as human beings have attained the maturity and responsibility to make such decisions for themselves. At the present time most persons are certainly not able to do so, hence the enormous separation, divorce, and broken-home rates. The state requires us to go to school, to be vaccinated, and to prove our ability to drive a car before we can get a license to do so. Surely, evidence of ability to marry and bring up a child is not less important.

Furthermore, those who are able to pass the tests of marriageability are not thereby to be construed as giving evidence that they are necessarily prepared to deal responsibly with children. Hence I would not permit persons to bring children into the world who failed to give adequate evidence of their ability to minister responsibly to the needs of children. Nor, of course, should anyone be permitted to adopt children who is unfit for the task of responsible parenthood.

Those who do pass the tests for responsible parenthood will understand the importance of spacing the births of their children. They will plan the spacing and the number of children they propose to have, and in this connection there are unlikely to be the slightest problems. However, these are matters which will require careful teaching long before the principals involved reach the stage of seriously contemplating parenthood. Hence as part of the teaching of sexual responsibility I would make the teaching of birth control and the spacing of births an integral part of the course taught at progressively sophisticated levels as the levels of maturity of the students increase.

Since nothing can concern the individual or the state more than the quality of the citizenry, the state must assume the regulation of that quality. This is dangerous doctrine, for obviously in the hands of the wrong people great havoc could by this means be wrought. But I am not thinking in terms of the wrong people or of dictators. I am thinking of a democracy. Democracy is, however, a form of government which can only work as well as its citizens want it to. It demands a great deal of work on the part of its citizens. The citizens of a democracy must be taught to be worthy of it, otherwise they will get exactly the kind of government they deserve. Democracy is a privilege, and privileges entail obligations. Our job as teachers should be to make democracy work by teaching the young what obligations a citizen worthy of a democratic government should know and discharge. The first thing I would teach our developing citizen is that the most important quality of a human being is the ability to relate himself to others in a warm, loving manner, and as one who is capable of using his mind as the finely analytical instrument it is capable of becoming, joining knowledge, understanding, sensitivity, and responsibility to loving-kindness.

And where does one begin making the required changes? The answer is clear and unequivocal: in oneself. A teacher cannot mean any more to his pupils than he means to himself. A school is an institution, and an institution is an agreement among people to behave in certain ways. How teachers agree to behave about sex education or anything else is what their schools will be, and what their products will be.

NOTES

1.   For a discussion of the physiology of this see Ashley Montagu, *The Reproductive Development of the Female*. New York: Julian Press, 1957.

2.   See John Money (ed.), *Sex Research: New Developments*. New York: Holt, Rinehart & Winston, 1965.

3.   See Ashley Montagu, *The Reproductive Development of the Female*. New York: Julian Press, 1957.

4.   See my three books: *The Direction of Human Development*. New York: Harper, 1955; *On Being Human*, Second Edition. New York: Hawthorne Books, 1967; *Education and Human Relations*. New York: Grove Press, 1957.

5.   In these connections see Ashley Montagu, *The Human Revolution*. New York: Bantam Books, 1967; Ashley Montagu, *The Direction of Human Development*. New York: Harper, 1955; Ashley Montagu, *The Humanization of Man*. New York: Grove Press, 1963.

45 | THE UNSOLVED MYSTERY OF MARRIAGE

Staff, Changing Times, The Kiplinger Magazine

Francine has almost decided to leave Jack, after three years of marriage. The trouble seemed to begin when she told him she wanted to quit her job and have children. He was against it. Although he had a promising future, he was not yet earning enough to maintain their household as it was. They could wait a few more years before starting a family, he argued; they were still young enough.

For a while they quarreled on and off. Then an uneasy truce set in. Now they rarely speak to each other for any length of time. And they avoid topics that might touch off a fight.

Jack often brings work home from the office and volunteers for out-of-town sales assignments. Francine recently started feeling attracted to a man at her office and allowed him to take her out for a drink. He wants to take her out again. She feels guilty about her desire to see him and would like to "confess" to Jack. But she knows he won't understand.

Tonight Jack is away. While watching television alone, Francine suddenly begins sobbing. Their marriage seems so joyless . . . a trap. Wouldn't it be better to get out now?

THE ROAD TO SEPARATION

At work or at a social gathering, Francine and Jack seem to be a contented pair. Behind appearances are two anguished people who have lost faith in each other.

If they do break up, they will be one of more than 400,000 couples to be divorced or have their marriages annulled this year. For every four couples who vow to stay together until death, one couple decides not to wait that long.

All sorts of people get divorces. Most, though, are under 35, and about half of the childless couples have been married five years or less. The divorced share other characteristics, too. Sociologist William J. Goode says these conditions indicate a "greater proneness" to divorce.

Urban background.

Marriage at 15 to 19 (the teen-age divorce rate is about three times the general rate).

Short acquaintanceship before marriage.

Parents had unhappy marriages.

Nonattendance at church.

Mixed faith.

Disapproval of the marriage by relatives and friends.

Dissimilarity in social and economic status.

Differing ideas between husband and wife as to their marital obligations.

Naturally, not every couple whose marriage happens to include some—or even most—of these factors is doomed to divorce. If they were, there would be few marriages left. It's still normal for a couple to marry and stay married. Yet staying married is far from being a measure of married happiness.

For each marriage that ends in divorce, says Dr. Nathan W. Ackerman, a psychiatrist who specializes in treating families, there are many in which the partners stay together but are emotionally alienated from one another.

"They stay joined not out of reasons of love, but out of economic need, duty to children, personal dependency, fear of loneliness, or simply because there is no place else to go. The family unit remains together physically, but there is, in effect, an emotional divorce." Others have called those unions "empty shell" marriages.

The longer a couple stays married, the less likely they are to get divorced. However, one study of couples married from two to twenty-one years indicates that the longer a marriage endures, the less satisfaction the partners find in it, another suggestion that a marriage is not necessarily good just because it lasts. The real problem is not so much that a couple may separate as it is that they might not achieve happiness together.

WHERE HARMONY BEGINS

Why is nonhappiness so prevalent? What makes one couple happy, another unhappy? Where does the trouble begin?

Probably many more marriages start off "right" than "wrong." Young men and women don't pick mates at random. The process seems haphazard, but in practice their field of choice is usually confined to people much like themselves. They tend to marry someone from the same area, race, religion, ethnic background and social and economic class. Young men who have never been married tend to marry women who have never been married. Divorced people tend to marry other divorced people. Widows tend to marry men who have been married.

People from like groups have like attitudes toward many aspects of life, and this agreement is a bond.

But with hundreds of possible mates from their own or outside groups to choose from, how do people narrow the choice to one person?

Many experts believe love springs from a meshing of basic needs. Each person wants people to act in a certain way toward him; he also wants to be able to act in a certain way toward others. When a person finds someone who helps him function in accord with his underlying motivations, love develops. Thus a man who likes to dominate is inclined to seek out a submissive woman, a submissive woman will be attracted to a dominating man.

Selecting a mate with complementary needs is not a conscious, deliberate procedure, for a person may not be aware of his own needs, let alone those of a prospective spouse. Ask what he sees in her and he will cite some ill-defined attribute: "She's kind and gentle." She finds him irresistible because he's "so gay and happy." A probing psychiatrist may discover that the man really wants to be mothered and perceives a mothering disposition in the woman's solicitous attitude. She may in fact be a mothering type who sees in his high spirits a little boy who has to be taken care of.

Naturally, a man and woman can't interlock psychologically on every point. Nor do their needs always have to be opposite. Both may have needs that run in the same direction but are present in one to such a small degree that they do not cause conflict during courtship.

A study of college students who were engaged or seriously considering marriage suggests that similar background and attitudes and complementary needs may act like a series of filters, to sort out appropriate partners. In the early stages of courtship, likeness of social status and ideas brings couples together. Later on, complementary needs move toward a permanent union.

IT'S AN IMPERFECT SYSTEM

With all the forces at work to bring together men and women suited to one another, it seems strange that so many marriages turn out wrong.

One reason is that the like-to-like attraction is at best a rough way of matching people. And it doesn't operate effectively for everyone. Many couples never get a chance—or take the opportunity—to find out much about each other.

Moreover, the courtship itself is not an infallible method of matching young people for marriage. The boy is more interested in the girl's feminine charm than in, say, whether she is likely to comfort him or berate him if he should lose a job. The girl is often more concerned with his outward displays of masculinity than in whether he's mature enough to accept responsibility for a family. Each is inclined to idealize the other. The person that emerges after marriage can be shockingly different.

A man and woman from dissimilar backgrounds can enter marriage with sharply conflicting expectations and values. But that happens among people with similar backgrounds, too, for there is diversity within any group. The husband, for example, may have been brought up to expect women to do all the household chores, the wife brought up to expect the men to help out. He may end up washing dishes—and resenting it.

Some people carry neuroses into marriage that are bound to cause trouble. Take the acquiescent, deferential man married to an aggressive woman. In a sense, they fit together. She runs things, makes the important decisions. He defers to her because he sees himself as unworthy and helpless. Yet he resents his inferior position and may rebel occasionally by exploding with rage, perhaps on an irrelevant or inconsequential issue. Neuroses do not necessarily destroy a marriage, though. On the contrary, psychiatrists have found that some neurotics make good partners and good parents.

Even well-conceived marriages may falter under the impact of a crisis. The arrival of the first child, for example, can be a crucial turning point. Often an occasion of great personal fulfillment, this is also a time of stress for both husband and wife. A study of first-time parents showed that all had experienced some degree of shock, and 25% of the couples interviewed said they had gone through a "severe" crisis. Mothers feared they were neglecting their husbands, doubted their ability to be good mothers and had trouble adjusting to being tied down and having to give up outside interests. Fathers were disturbed by the disruption of the old household routines and the prospect of supporting a larger family.

WHAT THEY FIGHT ABOUT

One problem in identifying the causes of marital unhappiness lies in the fact that all couples do fight at times, and about much the same things.

University of Pennsylvania researchers interviewed 300 couples to determine why and how often they quarreled. Two hundred were chosen from families that had at one time sought family counseling help. The others were from a group of couples who considered their marriages sufficiently successful to compete in a nationwide contest for "representative families" from each state. The husbands and wives were given a list of possible points of disagreement and asked to indicate (independently of each other) what they fought about and how often. The 300 couples rated their problems in this order, going from the points of most conflict to those of least conflict:

finances	wife's mother
household management	other relatives
personality disagreements	wife's working
sexual adjustment	husband's father
sharing household tasks	religious matters
children	infidelity
recreation	health
husband's mother	wife's father
personal habits	social background
jealousy	education
husband's work	

When the answers of the two groups—the 200 and the 100—were tabulated separately, it was found that the couples who had had marital trouble ranked the problems in about the same order as those who considered themselves happily married. The difference was not in the nature of the issues but in the extent of disagreement. Ironically, the one thing husbands and wives in both groups tended to agree on was which issues they disagreed about.

The young man and woman who start marriage believing that they love each other too much ever to quarrel are sure to be disillusioned before long. In fact, their chances of achieving a stable marriage probably are better if they anticipate spats and learn how to cope with them. Sometimes an argument helps clear the air and starts a couple toward reconciliation. Part of the trouble between the couple described at the beginning of the article is that they have bottled up their anger and lost contact with each other.

Although happily married couples do fight occasionally, they manage to preserve an appreciation of their mates.

Dr. Eleanore B. Luckey of the University of Connecticut has discovered that in successful marriages each spouse tends to agree with the other's estimation of his or her own qualities. The husband, for example, will think of himself as considerate and helpful, and the wife rates him the same way—or as even stronger and more loving than he sees himself.

Among less satisfied couples, there was significantly less agreement. The wives thought of their husbands as colder than the men considered themselves. The husbands saw their wives as considerably more bossy than the wives were in their own view.

THE MOST PRECIOUS GIFTS

A good marriage, then, seems to be a fairly harmonious union in which a little conflict is tempered by a great deal of mutual respect. But what makes it that way?

Psychiatrist Joseph Barnett suggests that perhaps the most important quality a man and woman can contribute to a marriage is a sense of "esteem" for one's self and other people. The two usually go together. A person with an inner sense of his own worth does not have to make unreasonable demands on his partner. Nor does he have to win an argument or disparage someone else in order to protect his prestige.

In a happy marriage, the partners can act as friends as well as mates. And that kind of rapport appears to be more treasured than other values commonly associated with marital compatibility. When some 400 couples were asked to rank what they considered conducive to a satisfying marriage, their first choice was companionship. Being in love was second, followed by being needed, having children, calmness, financial security, sexual relationships, developing personal interests, an orderly home, and intellectual stimulation. Last on the list, incidentally, was good food.

UNIT TWELVE | DISCUSSION QUESTIONS

42 | GENERATION GAP SHOWN IN SEX VIEW

What are your views concerning the questions posed to the college students in this survey? Discuss.

How do you account for the 'generation gap' as shown in the Gallup Poll? Explain.

43 | THE DECLINE AND FALL OF THE DOUBLE STANDARD

What are some of the reasons the authors give for the late nineteenth-century break with Victorian morality?

The Woman's Liberation Movement supports the removal of the "double standard" in sexual behavior. In light of this reason, do you support the removal of the double standard in sexual behavior? Discuss.

44 | THE PILL, THE SEXUAL REVOLUTION, AND THE SCHOOLS

Montagu calls for sexual responsibility. In what ways do you suggest that this be introduced as a desirable goal in the public schools? If you do not agree that sexual responsibility should be taught, explain why.

The author suggests that some persons should not be permitted to bring children into the world. Do you agree? Discuss.

45 | THE UNSOLVED MYSTERY OF MARRIAGE

Why do some unlikely marriages manage to survive while some so-called "perfect marriages" fall apart?

What are some of the qualities of a happy marriage, as opposed to one that just endures?

UNIT THIRTEEN
APPLIED BEHAVIORAL SCIENCES

Application of behavioral science to the daily tasks of life is apparent; no field of endeavor dealing with life is unaffected by it. During our age in which man investigates the most distant galaxies and explores the depths of the ocean floor, a full understanding of behavior and its requirements is necessary. Whatever the structure of tomorrow's world, the contributions of behavioral scientists will play a vital role.

Sheldon Rosenberg and James H. Koplin discuss a number of major trends in psycholinguistic research and theory in their *Introduction to Psycholinguistics*. The authors reveal how language structure is acquired and describe the role of individual differences in verbal behavior. Charles E. Osgood's *The Psychologist in International Affairs* explores the function the psychologist can perform in international relations and the contributions the psychologist can and must make to the easing of world tensions. Marvin D. Dunnette and Wayne K. Kirchner summarize the various areas of decision which exist in industrial psychology and the corresponding psychological research activities implied by each of them. *Industry: A Place to Study Human Behavior* provides a convenient system in which to classify examples of contributions made by psychology to personnel decisions in industry.

Joachim F. Wohlwill, in *The Emerging Discipline of Environmental Psychology*, discusses the growing involvement of psychologists in this field. Wohlwill points to the paradox of psychology's relative neglect of the role of the physical environment in behavioral research and he calls for a deeper commitment.

46 | INTRODUCTION TO PSYCHOLINGUISTICS

Sheldon Rosenberg and James H. Koplin

Psycholinguistics, in spite of its youth, has become in recent years a major area of basic research and theoretical effort in psychology. Symptomatic of this growth, for example, was the publication in 1962 of the first broadly distributed psychological journal devoted entirely to work in verbal learning, verbal behavior, and psycholinguistics, *The Journal of Verbal Learning and Verbal Behavior*.[1] In addition, papers of the sort that in previous years were published in technical reports and nonpsychological publications are now appearing with greater frequency in the regular psychological journals.

THE FIELD OF PSYCHOLINGUISTICS

Although the field that we are concerned with is clearly not the sole province of the psychologist, the emphasis of the present volume is psychological. As Miller's (1951) review, *Language and Communication*, indicates, interest in the psychological study of language behavior is not new; the recent intensification of interest in what has come to be known as psycholinguistics can be traced at least in part to the psycholinguistics monograph (1954),[2] edited by Osgood and Sebeok. Nurtured by the work of learning theorists, communication engineers, and descriptive linguists, the monograph attempted to conceptualize the area in the context of the general study of human communication, an emphasis which Osgood (1963a) has reiterated in a recent review of the field. In his own words, ". . . *psycholinguistics is the science of encoding and decoding processes in individual communicators.*" Encoding processes are involved in language production and *decoding* processes in language reception.

Judging from the behavior of psychologists, this definition is usually interpreted to include, among other things, studies of (1) the influence of verbal and nonverbal antecedent conditions upon verbal behavior and verbal learning, (2) the influence of verbal stimuli upon nonverbal behavior and learning, (3) the role of verbal mediators in behavior, (4) interrelationships among various dimensions of verbal response, (5) relationships between verbal and nonverbal response dimensions, (6) language acquisition and language development, and (7) strictly normative studies of language behavior.

Since the publication of the monograph, in addition to the review by Osgood (1963a) already mentioned, such works have appeared as Brown's (1958) *Words and Things;* the two volumes of papers on verbal learning and verbal behavior edited by Cofer and Musgrave (1961, 1963); Gough and Jenkins' (1963) chapter on theory in verbal learning and psycholinguistics; Miller's (1962) paper on psychology and

From *Directions in Psycholinguistics,* Sheldon Rosenberg (ed), The Macmillan Company, New York, 1965.

grammar; Osgood's (1936b) recent attempt at rapprochement between Markov process and hierarchic sentence-to-word models of sentence encoding and decoding; the book on meaning by Osgood, Suci, and Tannenbaum (1957); a collection of readings edited by Saporta (1961); Skinner's (1957) *Verbal Behavior;* and a review of research literature by Rubenstein and Aborn (1960). Recently, there has been increased interest in the development of mathematical formulations relevant to psycholinguistics, especially with respect to the problem of grammar (see, for example, Jakobson, 1961; Luce, Bush, and Galanter, 1963).

That there are differences in opinion as to the kinds of research problems psycholinguists should concern themselves with is not surprising in a field as young as this one. For example, traditional research on verbal learning may not be seen by some as contributing directly to our understanding of natural language processes. That there are areas of overlapping interest for the fields of verbal learning and psycholinguistics, however, as well as areas of separation, has been pointed out by Gough and Jenkins (1963).

The position taken in the organization of the present Institute, although not necessarily shared by all of the contributors to this volume, was that the field of verbal learning has much to contribute to our understanding of natural language behavior. For example, if there is any "psychological reality" to the linguist's (e.g., Gleason, 1961) concept of "levels of linguistic structure" (sentence, phrase, morpheme, etc.), as we suspect there is (Miller, 1962; Rosenberg and Baker, 1964), it becomes important to identify and determine the influence of verbal habits that operate at levels that include isolated words, syllables, and letter combinations. Research of the sort that is included in *Meaningfulness and Verbal Learning.* (Underwood and Schulz, 1960) is representative of work at these levels. In addition, research on paired-associate learning can be viewed, in a sense, as an attempt to identify conditions that influence the establishment of sequential dependencies between verbal units or between classes of units. Studies of mediation in verbal paired-associate learning which have involved the establishment of stimulus and response equivalences have already contributed to the development of a mediational theory of grammatical phenomena (see the article by Jenkins in this volume).

Another area in which the traditional field of verbal learning may contribute to psycholinguistics is language development. Specifically, while the sentence may be at the top of the linguist's hierarchy, and while it may turn out that psychologically (at least in encoding) sentence structures determine relationships at the level of the isolated word (Miller, Galanter, and Pribram, 1960), the developmental picture is, of course, just the opposite. The sequence of relevant unit-stages suggested by the results of a number of studies (e.g., Chen and Irwin, 1946; Lewis, 1936; Shirley, 1933) is phoneme, syllable, word, phrase, sentence. This is an oversimplification, of course, and these stages overlap to a certain extent, but it is important to note that there are periods in the development of language facility during which what may be the units of verbal behavior resemble some of those that have been studied extensively in the area of verbal learning. Research relevant to unit formation, for example, in nonsense syllables (Underwood, 1964; Underwood and Schulz, 1960), may have implications for the ways in which units are formed during language acquisition.

As a final point, even if one prefers to limit his definition of psycholinguistics, it would be impossible to use rote verbal learning tasks to study, for example, the effect of variations in grammatical structure, without proper attention to the contribution of variables (e.g., word frequency, intralist similarity, method of presentation, method of testing) that have been found to be of importance by psychologists working in the area of verbal learning.

Additional discussions of the relationship between verbal learning and psycholinguistics can be found in the article by Johnson and in the article by Underwood in this volume.

Although the contribution of learning theory to the development of psycholinguistic thinking has been considerable (see, for example, Osgood, 1963a, 1963b; Skinner, 1957), another area that may not always be seen as being clearly relevant to the more general concerns of psycholinguistics is verbal conditioning. From a psychological standpoint, however, unless we can identify the variables that determine whether or not verbal behavior will be emitted and at what rate it will be emitted, knowledge of other aspects of language activity may be of limited practical significance. Spielberger, in this book, is particularly concerned with the contribution of cognitive and motivational determinants to verbal conditioning.

CURRENT ISSUES IN PSYCHOLINGUISTICS

While this volume does not pretend to cover the entire field of psycholinguistics, the articles included in it are representative of a number of the major trends in research and theory today. The discussion that follows is an attempt to conceptualize what appeared to be the most important questions of concern to the contributors.

WHAT IS THE ROLE OF LINGUISTIC SCIENCE IN THE PSYCHOLOGY OF LANGUAGE?

Jenkins points out forcefully that the work of the linguist "focuses our attention on a set of neglected problems with which the psychologist *must* cope." Jenkins asserts further that observations of language behavior "demand an account of behavior that can deal with structure, hierarchy, class, and combination."

The importance attributed to the "linguistics" in psycholinguistics takes the form of concern with (1) *the psychological implications of linguistic models of grammar*—i.e., descriptive and generative (Johnson), finite state, phrase structure and transformational (Jenkins, Johnson, Saporta, *et al.*)—and with (2) *the need to discover possible behavioral correlates of linguistic structures.* Jenkins views the search for behavioral correlates of linguistic structures as a major approach to the study of the structure of language behavior, and much of the research he discusses, as well as much of the material discussed by Johnson, Rosenberg, and Saporta *et al.*, is relevant to this approach. Throughout these articles one sees the contribution of linguistic science in the form of specification of manipulable dimensions of verbal materials and in the form of hypotheses about the functional units of language behavior.

HOW IS LANGUAGE STRUCTURE ACQUIRED?

The research and theory discussed by Jenkins are directed primarily to the question of how linguistic classes and their sequential arrangements—from the level of the phoneme to the level of the sentence—are learned. A possible solution to part of this problem is offered in terms of a mediation model for the establishment of stimulus and response equivalences.

Jones and Wepman, working from the vantage point of research on language pathology, propose a conceptual scheme to account for the general development of language based upon the work of a number of investigators.

How are Sentences Generated Psychologically?

Johnson's central concern is with this very basic question. He proposes a theory of language encoding based upon Chomsky's (1957) theory of grammar and the results of research which suggest strongly that language materials might be recoded into units (describable in terms of linguistic phrase structure rules) larger than the individual word or morpheme for processing. The hierarchic structure of language, as it is revealed both linguistically and psychologically, is made a basic ingredient of the theory.

What is the Role Played by Pre-Established Verbal Habits in the Acquisition and Retention of Verbal Materials?

This question is the central concern of Underwood and of Rosenberg. Underwood discusses research that has contributed to the identification of some of the verbal habits from a subject's "linguistic repertoire" that appear to influence performance in verbal learning situations. These include, for example, stimulus selection habits, item coding habits (transformations of verbal units), and second-order habits (i.e., habits that determine the class of a response, such as sequential grammatical habits and conceptual habits). Recent research on the possible role of the "linguistic repertoire" in forgetting is also evaluated.

Rosenberg discusses some of the implications of recent developments in linguistics for the area of verbal learning, and he stresses the need for research on the relationship between grammatical structure (sequential grammatical habits, grammatical form class, level of linguistic structure) and such traditional verbal learning variables as associative habit and word frequency. A series of studies is reported on in which an attempt was made to compare the effects of sequential grammatical habits with the effects of sequential associative habits upon performance in simple verbal learning situations.

Much of the work discussed by Jenkins, by Johnson, and by Nunnally, since it involves studies of the effects of pre-established (experimentally and by assessment through norms of verbal behavior) verbal habits upon subsequent verbal learning, is also relevant here.

What are the Conditions for the Modification of Verbal Behavior?

Experiments in verbal conditioning originated in the laboratories of psychologists who embrace stimulus-response theories. Later cognitive theorists began to attack this problem. Spielberger examines the research and theorizing that have been produced by these divergent approaches. A major point developed is that the rival theories are leading to vigorous research and sensitive experiments, but the sets of accumulating facts are *not* leading to a convergence of the points of view. This convergence is seen as one of the goals of any scientific enterprise.

He contends that basic epistemological assumptions associated with each of the theoretical positions influence the design and analysis of experiments to such a degree that comparable data will not be collected. The chief issue concerns the status of the concept "awareness" in each of the systems. Awareness is interpreted as a dependent variable by stimulus-response theorists, while cognitive investigators design their experiments using awareness as an independent variable.

Having established this position, Spielberger presents a critical review of the background of verbal conditioning research and the major techniques that have been applied. The last section of the article reports several experiments by the author and his students in which it is convincingly demonstrated that the amount of variance accounted for in verbal conditioning experiments is significantly increased if awareness is viewed as an independent variable in the design.

WHAT IS THE ROLE OF INDIVIDUAL DIFFERENCES IN VERBAL BEHAVIOR?

Everyone agrees that individual differences in verbal behavior must be important, but little successful effort has been directed toward a systematic account of this variable. Nunnally presents a general theory to embrace the effects of word usage in learning, perception, and personality.

The theoretical formulation begins with some statements about the acquisition of particular words by individuals. One of the most important parts of the theory pertains to the role that motivational states play in the words produced and the rate at which they are produced by subjects.

The essential notion is that subjects do not have a single response hierarchy to a given stimulus word. Rather they have many hierarchies related to different need states.

The next section of the article expands the application of the theory to the three problem areas mentioned above and discusses the work of the author and his associates in developing instruments to measure the individual differences in word usage of subjects. These measures are labeled "semantic habit scales."

Three experiments are cited which demonstrate the fruitfulness of the approach in studies of learning, perception, and personality variables. The article concludes with some methodological cautions that are of particular importance to investigators in this area.

WHAT CAN WE LEARN ABOUT THE GENERAL STRUCTURE OF LANGUAGE BEHAVIOR FROM A CONSIDERATION OF THE RESULTS OF RESEARCH ON LANGUAGE PATHOLOGY?

One of the major hypotheses put forth by Jones and Wepman is that the study of aphasia will lead to general principles of language organization. "By determining the communication processes that are differentially affected by brain damage, we become aware of language processes that must contribute to the language skills of a normally functioning person."

From data collected in a highly structured situation and from the grammatical analysis of free speech samples from aphasics and normal adults (along with the results of observations of language development in normal children), a conceptual model of the language processing units in normal persons is proposed.

Part of the research these authors discuss was facilitated by the development of a computer program for the analysis of the grammatical form class of words.

NOTES

1. Published by the Academic Press, Inc., New York.
2. During this year we also saw the publication of Mowrer's influential paper on language.

REFERENCES

Brown, R. *Words and things.* New York: The Free Press, 1958.

Chen, H. P., and O. C. Irwin. "Infant speech vowel and consonant types." *J. Speech Disorders,* 1946, **11**, 27–29.

Chomsky, N. *Syntactic structures.* The Hague: Mouton, 1957.

Cofer, C. N., and Barbara S. Musgrave (eds.). *Verbal learning and verbal behavior.* New York: McGraw-Hill, 1961.

———, and ——— (eds.). *Verbal behavior and learning.* New York: McGraw-Hill, 1963.

Gleason, H. A. *An introduction to descriptive linguistics,* rev. ed. New York: Holt, Rinehart and Winston, 1961.

Gough, P. B., and J. J. Jenkins. "Verbal learning and psycholinguistics." In M. H. Marx (ed.). *Theories in contemporary psychology.* New York: Macmillan, 1963.

Jakobson, R. (ed.). *Structure of language and its mathematical aspects.* Proceedings of symposia in applied mathematics. Vol. XII. Providence, R.I.: American Mathematical Society, 1961.

Lewis, M. M. *Infant speech: a study of the beginnings of language.* New York: Harcourt, Brace, 1936.

Luce, R. D., R. R. Bush, and E. Galanter (eds.). *Handbook of mathematical psychology,* Vol. II. New York: Wiley, 1963.

Miller, G. A. *Language and communication.* New York: McGraw-Hill, 1951.

———. "Some psychological studies of grammar." *Amer. Psychologist,* 1962, **17**, 748–762.

———, E. Galanter, and K. H. Pribram. *Plans and the structure of behavior.* New York: Henry Holt, 1960.

Mowrer, O. H. "The psychologist looks at language." *Amer. Psychologist,* 1954, **9**, 660–694.

Osgood, C. E. "Psycholinguistics." In S. Koch (ed.). *Psychology: a study of a science,* Vol. 6. New York: McGraw-Hill, 1963a.

———. "On understanding and creating sentences." *Amer. Psychologist.* 1963b, **18**, 735–751.

———, and T. A. Sebeok (eds.). "Psycholinguistics: a survey of theory and research." *J. Abnorm. Soc. Psychol.,* 1954, **49**, Suppl. to No. 4.

———, G. J. Suci, and P. H. Tannenbaum. *The measurement of meaning.* Urbana, Ill.: University of Illinois Press, 1957.

Rosenberg, S., and Norma J. Baker. "Grammatical form class as a variable in verbal learning at three levels of linguistic structure." Paper presented at meetings of Southeastern Psychological Association, Gatlinburg, Tenn., April, 1964.

Rubenstein, H., and M. Aborn. "Psycholinguistics." *Annual Rev. Psychol.,* 1960, **11**, 291–322.

Saporta, S. *Psycholinguistics: a book of readings*. New York: Holt, Rinehart and Winston, 1961.

Shirley, M. M. "The first two years: a study of twenty-five babies. II. Intellectual development." *Inst. Child Welf. Monogr. Ser.* Minneapolis: University of Minnesota Press, 1933.

Skinner, B. F. *Verbal behavior*. New York: Appleton-Century-Crofts, 1957.

Underwood, B. J. "The representativeness of rote verbal learning." In A. W. Melton (ed.). *Categories of human learning.* New York: Academic Press, 1964.

————, and R. W. Schulz. *Meaningfulness and verbal learning.* Philadelphia: J. B. Lippincott, 1960.

47 | THE PSYCHOLOGIST
IN INTERNATIONAL AFFAIRS

Charles E. Osgood

This essay is divided into two parts. The first might be subtitled "How I Became a Hard-nosed Peacenik"; it is a personal report which I hope will be informative and perhaps encouraging to my colleagues. The second part will deal more directly with the if's, how's, when's, and where's of what has come to be called "peace research."

The reader will not find the word "taboo" mentioned in the body of the chapter. This is not to say that there is nothing taboo about peace, for, certainly, peace has become a highly emotionally charged topic, and taboos are characterized by blind and violent emotions. Peace, hopefully, however, has not yet become completely taboo, although there are enough similarities to cause unease. The university professor who becomes involved with political questions, as peace has now become, must know that he subjects himself to question and even suspicion. Background, affiliations, ideology—all come under scrutiny. Character, beliefs, convictions become fair game to critical people in government.

But if we are ever to enjoy peace and pursue the investigations into more specifically taboo topics, such as sex and death, we must be alive to do it. The headlong rush of peace toward the undesirable status of a taboo needs to be arrested. Instead, peace needs to be advanced, investigated, and understood, tasks to which I now find myself deeply committed.

PERSONAL

What ingredients are required to make an ordinary, self-satisfied experimental psychologist—with more scientific jobs planned than his life can encompass anyway—into a peacenik who spends nearly half his time writing, lecturing, consulting, and doing research aimed at reducing international tensions? One ingredient is felt concern about the significance of the problem; a second is felt efficacy; a third is having something to work for, a new alternative, an idea; and the fourth ingredient, I think, is some ability to run uphill.

FELT CONCERN

If one has a modicum of intelligence coupled with a modicum of imagination, it is not difficult to get concerned about the present world situation. No one who looks at the evidence and thinks about it can deny that: (1) never before in history have so few been able to destroy so many and so much in so short a time (indeed, there is no physical reason for not building a weapon that would irradiate the entire surface of the earth, and some say that we must do this because the Russians might); (2) nuclear weapons are almost entirely offensive, not defensive, in nature, and therefore the continuing arms race produces less, not greater, security; and (3) the only "defense" against the use of such weapons lies in mutual fear of annihilation—a fragile defense, indeed, humans being human.

Yet, how many intellectuals have lifted their brilliantly plumed heads out of the sand and looked into the face of a nuclear holocaust? How many have asked themselves the traumatizing question: Of what value is present work if this larger problem is not solved? Why write this scholarly treatise on the hair styles of the ancient Egyptians if no one will be around to read it? Why run more rats through the maze if there will be no more human behavior or rat behavior to have a theory of? Some psychologists, being only human and subject to the laws of cognitive dissonance, will close this book firmly at this point. Yet, they cannot deny that almost instant elimination of everything they consider valuable is now possible in a way it never before in human history has been.

I claim my modicum of intelligence and my due share of imagination. Perhaps the fact that my father was a reader of science fiction had something to do with it. I began reading the old, large-size *Amazing Stories* in the attic at the age of eight. The end of the world and the details of its death throes—by a freezing flight away from the sun, by the evolution of strangling plants, as well as by self-annihilation with incredible weapons—became something conceivable for me. (I might add that about five years ago I stopped reading science fiction.) I believe that the capacity to hold in mind the probable nature and possible occurrence of nuclear war is one element necessary for active involvement in trying to do something about it.

But, in my case, at least, felt concern had another source as well. This was an intense devotion to rationality; I cannot think of any better way to say it. Annoyance with human irrationality has been a constant in my make-up (except, of course, when it is I who am irrational). For the first thirty years or so of my life, this was not directed in any way toward the political behavior of the human animal. I could not even bother to vote.

In 1945, while I was working on the training of B-29 gunners at the Smoky Hill Army Air Force Base in Kansas, came announcement of our first use of an atomic bomb against Hiroshima, then soon after announcement of our second use against Nagasaki. I considered these acts both immoral and stupid, and I still do. I suppose that I should have asked myself what I was doing training B-29 gunners, but I did not. Being still an avid science-fiction reader, I made dire predictions about the end of the world in a few years. My time scale was a bit off, as my wife has often reminded me, but such an eventuality is not becoming less probable. I even joined the Americans for Democratic Action to work on a special committee of the New Haven chapter for internationalizing control of nuclear energy and weapons. But when it became obvious that nothing along these lines was going to be accomplished quickly, I went back to being a struggling young psychologist.

And then McCarthyism struck home to me. When McCarthy began attacking academic freedom (which I had been taking more-or-less for granted), when he began destroying people with irrational smear techniques and was obviously getting away with it, I came charging out of my scholarly cave like a wounded bear. I began *reading* the newspaper, including columns and editorials, rather than just glancing at the headlines and enjoying my favorite comics. This just jangled my rationality factor all the more. Occasionally I would get angry enough to write a letter to the editor. I even made an outline and began collecting clippings, for a book aimed at McCarthyism and all it represented. I am certain that McCarthy had similar effects on many of us. But McCarthy finally picked the wrong target, got his "comeuppance," and went the way of all flesh. And I went back to psycholinguistics, still muttering and growling at what I saw in the newspapers and on television.

FELT EFFICACY

Concern at the irrationality of man and the extraordinary danger of such irrationality in a world of competing nation-states armed with nuclear weapons are not enough. One must also feel capable of doing something about them. This comes partly, I think, from self-confidence and security in one's own profession; it comes partly from the discovery that some people, at least, are willing to listen. Of course, some would say that it takes a fool who is willing to rush in where wise men fear to tread.

In 1958, I had a chance to spend a year at the Center for Advanced Study in the Behavioral Sciences. It was an opportunity to get disentangled from the usual routines of academic life and to get entangled with the ideas of fifty other Fellows. I went there to write a book on psycholinguistics; I never wrote a word of it. I hardly opened the twenty or so fat folders containing materials for its various chapters. I did a variety of minor scholarly jobs, but the main reason the book did not get written (it still is not) was that I found myself in an office next to Jerome Frank, a psychiatrist from Johns Hopkins. Jerry shared my concern, but he was doing something about it. He had already written an article for the *Atlantic* that had had great impact, and he was preparing to serve as a witness before the Humphrey Subcommittee on Disarmament.

This was the catalyst I needed, but had not been looking for. It threw me into the most severe conflict I have ever suffered. For years, I had been saying "What can I do?" as a means of convincing myself that I could not do anything, which is a wonderful rationalization for going on with the research that might make no difference and the book that no one might read. Yet here was a constant reminder that one could do something relevant and even get people to listen. The more I looked at my own areas of competence in psychology—human learning, the dynamics of human thinking, and human communication—the more relevance I began to see. More than this, I convinced myself that the psychological factors in international relations, though by no means the whole story, were particularly significant precisely because they were so largely unrecognized.

A NEW ALTERNATIVE

The kind of action into which one is thrust by the combination of concern and felt efficacy depends on who one is. It thrusts some into joining protest marches, signing petitions, and even howling at the moon in sheer outrage. It thrusts others into direct political action. It is most likely to thrust the scientist or scholar into *his* characteristic problem-solving activities—reading, talking, researching, and writing. So we set up a weekly seminar at the center on "Social Science Aspects of Policy in a Nuclear Age"; it included lawyers, economists, sociologists, anthropologists, a few political scientists, and almost every foreign scholar resident that year. We read the literature, talked informally, wrote papers and read them to each other, and since a broad spectrum of opinion was represented, occasionally became embroiled in heated debate.

I began as an ardent unilateral disarmer. It seemed perfectly logical to me that, if one side threw away its weapons, the other would soon follow suit. Just as we would not leap to destroy a disarmed Russia with nuclear weapons, neither would it leap to destroy us. I felt confident that we could win the real war for men's minds by nonmilitary means in a disarmed world. In fact, I believed that a nonthreatening, economically healthy, and openly communicating environment would gradually serve to strengthen democratic as against totalitarian ways of life, both at home and abroad. I still believe these things.

But now we come to the hardening of this peacenik. When I sat down to write out my ideas for presentation to the seminar—my first paper in this area, entitled "Suggestions for Winning the Real War with Communism"—and kept trying them out on my colleagues over coffee in the California sunshine, it became perfectly clear that, logical or not, ordinary unilateral disarmament simply was not feasible. My own arguments about the irrationality of human thinking under stress—such mechanisms as denial, semantic remoteness of concepts, projection, psychologic, and stereotypy in perceiving alternatives—which I used to characterize the Cold War mentality also offered apparently insurmountable obstacles to acceptance of any nonviolent resolution of international conflict. I became obsessed with the criterion of *feasibility*. The problem became to devise and justify a strategy that could move us toward a more peaceful world and reduce the likelihood of nuclear weapons being used, yet operate within reasonable limits of national security as perceived by people in decision-making positions.

The original paper introduced the basic ideas of "Graduated and Reciprocated Initiatives in Tension-Reduction" (which, in the way of such things, is now usually referred to as GRIT). It met solid criticism from participants in the seminar and from others to whom I sent it, but it also generated interest as a somewhat novel policy idea. So I went back to the typewriter to try to meet the criticisms. The next major version was published in *The Liberal Papers,* edited by James Roosevelt, and was entitled "Reciprocal Initiative." The book was seized upon by the Republican National Committee as campaign material; it called the book "the Democratic plan for surrender" and my particular contribution, "surrender on the installment plan." But, with an assist from 'The Ev and Charlie Show," they also helped make the book a best-selling paperback.

This book, coupled with my own distribution efforts, began to bring these ideas to the attention of hard-nosed but equally dedicated and concerned people both in and out of government. (It also brought my correspondence to a level where it could not be handled.) I discovered that once one gets his nose up into that atmosphere, it serves as a lightning rod, attracting all kinds of things—good and useful things, such as lecturing opportunities and consulting activities, but also bad and wasteful things, such as letters from crackpots and invitations to too many conferences. These experiences and contacts gave me an even clearer idea of the weaknesses and strengths of my own proposal, however.

The most recent version of the plan is a fairly hard-nosed job, I think. It is a paperback published by the University of Illinois Press entitled *An Alternative to War or Surrender.* The subtitle in my own mind was "Osgood's Last Gasp," but it probably will not be. It accepts the necessity of temporarily retaining our capacity for nuclear retaliation, but proposes using this capacity as a security base from which to take limited risks in the direction of tension-reduction, rather than using it merely as a deterrent. It accepts the necessity of temporarily retaining diversified conventional forces to firmly resist aggressive probes by an opponent (the "stick") while applying a pattern of deliberate initiatives designed to reduce and control tensions (the "carrot"). It elaborates in considerable detail the strategy and tactics of GRIT —how to create and maintain the right kind of credibility (firm but potentially cooperative), how to induce reciprocation by an opponent, how to design and execute programs of independent initiatives.

But there is still at least one aspect needing tightening. I am becoming convinced that the most complex and difficult problems we face in trying to ease out of the present, dangerous situation are internal rather than external. How can the irrational cries of "appeasement" and "surrender" be handled? How can the quite rational but short-sighted use of foreign affairs as political football be managed? How can the self-fulfilling but vicious cycles of the military, industrial, and scientific complexes, energized by billions of dollars a year, be slowed and reversed? To borrow an insightful tennis analogy from the Princeton sovietologist, Robert Tucker: we are engaged in doubles, not singles; on each side there is an irrational player who wants to beat the other side at any cost, including breaking up the game, and on each side there is a rational player who wants to keep the game going and win within the rules; paradoxically, the rational players have to play in such a way as to keep their opposite numbers in control of the game, which means sometimes giving them spectacular points.

ABILITY TO RUN UPHILL

I know that this sounds like patting oneself on the back, but I cannot claim to have got very far up. An ant at the bottom of a teacup has no place to go but up. The fact of the matter is that, when one has an unconventional idea in a political area of intense feeling and must get the idea moving through the complex and curious mass media, he has an uphill battle on his hands. He tries to reach the minds of key people in the decision-making process (decidedly uphill!) while at the same time, by writing and lecturing, tries to reach the general public. With one hand he does research or supports research that seems to have a critical bearing on the major issues, while with the other he acts like a lobbyist and applies what he thinks he already knows. He is simultaneously impelled by the urgency of the issue and restrained by the necessity (if he is to be effective) of maintaining his balance and dignity as a scientist and scholar.

I am often asked such questions as "Are you getting anywhere?" "Are your ideas having influence in Washington?" "Is anyone listening?" These are difficult questions to answer, for several reasons. For one thing, it is easy to overestimate one's own influence, to indulge in wishful thinking. When a pattern of events, such as the handling of the Cuban crisis and its aftermath, looks like what one has been suggesting, it is only too easy to assume that one's advice has been taken, when, in fact, the advisers are many and the possible reasons for actions multiple. For another thing, I suspect that, even if unconventional policy ideas are eventually to be successful, they will become so in a fashion analogous to "sleeper effects" in attitude-change studies; that is, they will have their first effects quietly in the minds of men, and, only when enough people are thinking differently and the time is ripe, will the unconventional approach achieve public acceptance. All of which, of course, assumes that the unconventional ideas in question have merit and *should* be accepted by the public and by leadership.

Is anyone listening? This much I can say: a great number of people, both in and out of government, have been exposed to GRIT by one means or another; how seriously it is taken and how much weight it has in competition with more conventional policy ideas, I cannot say. The entire notion of independent United States initiatives in arms control and tension control now appears to be respectable, although I cannot by any means claim sole responsibility for this. Several sizable research projects, some supported by government agencies and others by private funds, are now investigating the feasibility of unilateral initiatives. What does all this add up to? Not much, but it is something. I realize that this first section reads like the story of a one-man battle. It is not: there are constantly increasing numbers of people going the same general direction and working just as hard or harder.

PROFESSIONAL

It may be professional myopia, but I think that psychologists as a group have been more actively involved in "peace research" and over a longer period than any other behavioral or social science. For a long time, we have had the Society for the Psychological Study of Social Issues, whose members have done research and written about problems in such areas of public concern as race relations, civil rights, and peace and war. More recently, in 1960, beginning with a "working group" under Roger Russell, a continuing committee for the profession as a whole on Psychology in National and International Affairs was established. Members of this committee have been Raymond Bauer, Urie Bronfenbrenner, Morton Deutsch, Fred Fiedler, Harold Guetzkow, John Finan, Ed Hollander, Herbert Kelman, Joseph Weitz, and I, but this represents only a small sample of the professional psychologists actually involved. Most recently, through a grant from the Marshall Fund, we have been able to support a full-time person, Larry Solomon, in Washington to work on the committee's tasks.

Why should it be so, if indeed it is, that psychologists have got themselves involved in this earlier and more deeply? Perhaps it is because psychology had about the right "distance" from public issues—close enough to have developed a scientific concept of man and his behavior, but not so close as to have become intimidated. Perhaps the fact that psychology is more like the physical and biological sciences in method and in quantification created a feeling of security and efficacy. In the past few decades, psychologists have been quite self-conscious about scientific methods and have generally convinced themselves that, "even though they may not know the answers, they know how to find out." Or perhaps it is the outward-reaching tendencies of psychological theories of behavior, which have their moorings in the Skinner box, the tachistoscope, or the therapeutic interviews, but are generalized as much as possible.

The natural, legitimate tendency of a theory to generalize carries with it the real danger of overgeneralization. Put less kindly, psychologists face the danger of "overselling" wares which they may not have. This has been a constant concern of the Committee on National and International Affairs. There is nothing that would more effectively undercut the potential contribution of psychology to public affairs than repeated failure to follow through on explicit commitments to solve practical governmental problems. This is probably why professional psychologists have preferred to advertise themselves as equipped to do research, rather than to promise solutions or even advise from a body of established principle. And the danger here, of course, is that of leaning over so far backward to avoid "overselling" that we rule ourselves out for real contributions we might well be able to make. The committee has tried to steer between these two reefs.

The psychologist working on public issues may wear any of three hats, but he should be aware of which hat is appropriate for which occasion. On some occasions, he may legitimately don his "professional" hat—when he speaks as a psychological scientist on the basis of hard facts and generally accepted principles. On other occasions, he should wear his "specialist" hat—when he speaks as an individual psychologist who, by virtue of his special training and experience, may claim a higher probability of correct insights and opinions in certain areas than those not so trained. On yet other occasions, he must explicitly display his "citizen" hat—when he speaks his opinions, expresses his attitudes, and takes his stand on matters where neither his science nor his expertise give him any obvious advantage over other equally intelligent citizens.

An example of this arose in the meetings of the APA Council several years ago. There was strong pressure from some members for the association to take a public stand against the United States resuming nuclear testing, following the resumption of testing by the Soviet Union. The committee's policy recommendation, which was finally accepted, was as follows:

The Association should speak for the psychological profession on social and political issues only when psychologists have a professional expertise which is clearly relevant to the issues involved and when there is a substantial convergence of judgment among psychologists on the nature and implications of relevant scientific data. There are, of course, many urgent issues in which the need for psychological knowledge is apparent. When such knowledge is not available, the Association should encourage research to foster its development. At all times, the Association maintains its traditional interest in having its members participate as individual psychologists and citizens in the presentation and discussion of psychological facts and ideas as they bear on current national and international problems.

The three hats I mentioned above are clearly described in this statement. It is not always easy to maintain these distinctions, and some will argue that, with an issue as urgent as avoiding nuclear war, trying to maintain them involves a delicacy verging on the ludicrous. The answer, I think, is that to fail to make these distinctions is to destroy whatever contribution we can make as psychologists.

There are two other caveats I must make before saying something about action and research on international affairs. One concerns what we mean by "peace." Perhaps it is because of the grinding process which I have been through in the search for feasibility, but I often get the feeling that many of my colleagues have never thought very hard about what they mean by this term. It is the opposite of "war," which we are all against, and there surely is a good feel to it. But do we mean "peace" in the no-war sense? In the no-nuclear-war sense? In the complete-disarmament sense? In the permanent-tranquility sense? In the sense of establishing and observing the rule of international law? In the sense of peaceful (competitive) co-existence? In the *Pax Americana* sense? How one answers this question will determine what he includes under "peace research," how much effort he will put into short-term versus long-term action and research programs, and so forth. The controversy now going on between the "arms-management-and-control" proponents and the "general-and-complete-disarmament" proponents in part reflects differences in what kind of peaceful world people have in mind.

The other caveat concerns our own stereotypes and intolerance. Being merely human, psychologists are prone to the same cognitive dynamics they study in others. In our own striving for a simplified, comprehensible world, it is easy for us to set up bogeymen of our own—the Pentagon, Congress, the Mass Media, the Defense Industries, and so forth. Here are the Warmongers, here are the evil men who, for selfish and aggressive motives, are deliberately risking all our lives. There probably are a few such people, but I have yet to meet them. I have yet to find a person, in government, in industry, in the mass media, in the military, or elsewhere who does not profess to desire "peace" (on his own terms) as ardently as I do (on mine). We might differ absolutely on our assumptions and prescriptions, but not on our basic motives—to preserve both our lives and our way of life. But, most importantly (as we should realize as psychologists), to impugn these men's motives, to accuse them of being immoral and callous to the best interest of humanity as a whole, is promptly to establish an antagonism through which it is impossible to exert any positive influence. I do not want what I have just said to be misinterpreted. I am convinced that there are many people in the institutions we are discussing who are misguided, who have dangerous misconceptions about the nature of the world today and the nature of the people who inhabit it, and who are following policies that have a high probability of eventuating in the destruction of everything we hold valuable; but as a social scientist I cannot consider them evil, and I must consider them modifiable.

ACTION

By "action" for a more peaceful world, I refer to the whole spectrum of endeavors to change people's minds and thereby their behavior through utilizing what we know (or think we know) as psychologists and as intelligent citizens. It involves all the skills we have as individuals in personal relations, in persuasive communication, and in problem-solving. It means trying to inject psychological insights and skills wherever they are relevant; and often the first and most difficult step is to convince others of their relevance.

One type of action is, frankly, *lobbying*, in the best sense. By "best sense," I mean trying to influence decision-making in government for altruistic rather than selfish ends. I believe that there is a difference between lobbying for support of inter-American exchange among students and scholars and lobbying for higher status and pay for psychologists in government. Lobbying for increased support of research in the behavioral and social sciences would, I suppose, be equivocal. The Committee on National and International Affairs, particularly through the good offices of its full-time executive officer, Larry Solomon, has been trying to develop effective contacts with relevant government agencies and activities (Agency for International Development, Arms Control and Disarmament Agency, Peace Corps), as well as with members of Congress. One side of this activity is necessarily educational; it is surprising how many nonpsychologists, both in government and in the public at large, see us *only* as clinicians interested in and competent with personality problems. Another side of this activity is predictive—trying to anticipate public issues and prepare for them. Yet another side is a mediating role—bringing the public official with a problem and the psychologist with relevant skill and experience into fruitful contact.

Another type of action is trying to inject the psychologists' conception of the nature of man into the decision-making process. Again, being merely human, we tend to project our own conception onto others and are often shocked to discover how different other people's conceptions may be. Among the generally, if not completely, agreed-upon elements in the psychological conception of man are: man's behavior is determined by both innate and acquired factors and, as a kind of corollary, no individual is inherently evil; differences among individuals within nations, races, and the like are typically greater than differences between them; war is not inevitable, although many of its contributing elements (for example, aggression, fear, perceptual distortion under stress) may be; much of man's behavior, particularly as it relates to group solidarity and conflict, is learned and hence modifiable; and much of man's behavior is determined by irrational rather than rational factors. One means to inject our conception of man into the decision-making process is to bring psychologists into continuous contact with people in government; the APA committee has already made arrangements for several Congressional fellowships for psychologists, and we hope to have our own program under way soon.

Yet another type of action is the role of devil's advocate, questioning general assumptions. Examples of such assumptions are: that our opponent (whoever he may be) is motivated by aggression and hatred, whereas we are motivated by insecurity and fear: that we must maintain military superiority in order to be secure; that our nuclear deterrent is nothing more than that (it is also a security base from which to take limited risks); that credibility of our deterrent requires that we present the face of implacable hostility to an opponent: that prior commitment from both sides by means of negotiation is a prerequisite for tension-reducing action by either; and that we can have unlimited national sovereignty and unlimited international security at the same time. It is precisely because such assumptions are often implicit that they must be questioned and raised to the level of public debate. They create a rigid and narrow framework for policy, within which only a small number of possibilities seem to be available.

A sample of the activities undertaken by the Committee on National and International Affairs will serve to illustrate the variety of actions open to us. With support from the Brookings Institution, it was possible to hold four informal, two-day conferences among representatives of the mass media, government, and the universities on the general topic of communications and public policy, with different people participating in each conference. In connection with the Peace Research Institute, a working conference on the behavioral and social-science aspects of the Civilian Defense program was held, and a pamphlet called *The Shelter Centered Society* resulted. More widespread involvement of the profession as a whole is being pursued by developing a roster of psychologists competent and informed on various relevant topics, by arranging all-APA and divisional symposiums at regional and national meetings, and the like. Interprofessional cooperation in this area is being stimulated. Fruitful contacts with the United Nations Secretariat have been made, and a number of studies relevant to UN problems (particularly in the communications area) have been begun. An easy-access-and-retrieval coding and filing system for literature, personnel, and research proposals relevant to psychological factors in peace and war is being prepared. . . . It is hoped that such a facility will enable us to respond promptly to requests for digests and even position papers that come to us from people in government.

RESEARCH

Psychologists are as prone to fads as anyone else. There are fads in research. There was a period when learning theory was astride the white stallion; now it seems to be mathematical models. Young people quickly develop a sixth sense for what is "paying off" in job offers and promotions; a few regional and national meetings are sufficient to set a pattern, and such patterns are difficult to change over short periods. Although a great deal of research that has been going on steadily in social psychology, communications, cognitive processes, and many other areas is clearly relevant, "peace research," under that name, at least, is certainly not prestigious in our profession. However, the attractive power of a research area depends both on the stature of the senior people in it and on the availability of funds (which, incidentally, are not independent factors), and the situation seems to be becoming more favorable. Recent trips to university and other research centers throughout the country by my colleague, Shel Feldman, indicated a rather surprising density of relevant research, much of it quite explicitly (in the thinking of the investigators) on problems of war and peace, arms control, disarmament, international tensions, and related areas.

ACTION-ORIENTED RESEARCH

Some research is designed to produce dependable information that can be translated directly into action programs. This is particularly characteristic of research oriented to public issues. One illustration is the monograph, *Psychological Factors in Peace and War*, being prepared by Shel Feldman, Joseph de Rivera, and me with the support of the National Institute of Mental Health and Earl Osborn, president of the Institute of International Order. The general purposes are to make available to behavioral and social scientists in a readily digestible form the existing evidence on psychological propositions explicitly or implicitly made in the literature in this field, the hypotheses that need investigation, and the available personnel in terms of contributions and interests.

Another example is the production of what might be called "instant public opinion" on foreign-policy issues and assumptions. Under Dee Norton's general direction, the Iowa City Consensus on International Affairs has been polling its membership on a variety of issues of the moment (for example, Proposition #4: "We urge the United States Government to take immediate steps to re-establish diplomatic, cultural and trade relations with Cuba") and transmitting the results to various people in government. The point is that decisions are often made on the basis of assumptions about "public opinion" that may well be invalid. If such informed opinion could be collected in synchronized fashion from a broad sample of the population, it could have impressive impact.[1]

Yet another illustration is a panel study done by Feldman and Fishbein at our institute of the performance of a peace candidate in the last election; he lost, to be sure, but the action-oriented research was designed to find out why.

UNDERSTANDING-ORIENTED RESEARCH

What we usually refer to as "pure" or "basic," research is directed toward increasing our understanding of human behavior without any immediate concern for social action. What impresses one when he starts searching the literature for material relevant to the present topic is the fact that, if one forgets the particular substantive material, almost everything we are investigating has some relevance. A William McGuire does ingenious experiments on susceptibility to, and immunization against, persuasion: the persuasive materials may be counter-arguments to unquestioned assumptions about the value of brushing one's teeth, but they might just as well have been counter-arguments to the unquestioned assumptions about national security listed above. The point is that there is much that we are doing already, just because we want to find out more about human beings—how they think, how they make decisions, and how they behave—that could be made directly relevant to the crucial issues of our time by a minor shift in materials, subjects, or emphasis.

Some will argue that it is impossible to be truly objective when the topics under investigation are policy-relevant, are emotion-laden, or involve the investigator himself. I think that this is sheer nonsense. As soon as one has become involved in his own theory, his mentor's theory, or even his own previous findings, he is equally liable to bias. The whole purpose of our training in rigorous, objective, quantitative methods is to protect ourselves from such bias, and objective methodology will protect us if adhered to.

Merely by way of illustration, here are some areas of understanding-oriented research which I think particularly relevant: the simulation of complex human decision-making processes, whether by computers (e.g., Herbert Simon's work) or by people (e.g., Harold Guetzkow's internation simulations); studies of the dynamics of human perception or cognition as they affect choice behaviors of all types (e.g., extending and refining the theories of Heider, Festinger, and others); research on interpersonal, intergroup, and internation communication (e.g., the problem of multiple audiences receiving the same message and that of information restriction because of the structure and function of the mass media); crosscultural and crosslinguistic studies of psycholinguistic and other cognitive phenomena, both as a means of quantifying what might be called "subjective culture" and as a means of specifying cultural similarities and differences more rigorously.

The principles and tools developed in the course of such understanding-oriented research could be transferred rather directly to the "applied" research that is needed by society. Take, for example, internation simulation (which is not very different from the "war games" played by the military). If the validity of such simulations can be demonstrated and they can be shown to significantly reduce uncertainty in policy decisions, one can imagine a massive program of such research designed to simulate and thereby anticipate critical decision points in the constantly expanding "near future." Our present transportation and communication technologies make crosscultural tests of hypotheses and international surveys entirely feasible; we no longer need to be provincial in the behavioral and social sciences. Indeed, many of our hypotheses require testing against a crosscultural and crosslinguistic matrix in order to distinguish that which is culturally and linguistically unique from that which is common to the human species. Research on this scale would require a great deal of money, to be sure, but no more than is thrown away every time an experimental missile or space vehicle plops into the ocean as a failure.

NOTE

1.   I once had the fantasy that there was a huge map of the United States on a building near the White House. Above the map, a flashing sign announced "The Issue of the Day." With each county in each state represented by a small panel that would be turned to either black or white depending on the responses obtained there, the whole map would represent, by shades from white through gray to black, "instant public opinion" on the issue, as well as regional variations. Congressmen and men in various agencies could not help but steal a peek at what was happening as they went to and from their offices; the mass media would obviously have to carry these displays as regularly as they now carry the weather maps, and, when visiting the capital, every Mr. and Mrs. Jones from Podunk would want to see the display and point to *their* community. Sheer fantasy, but it could easily be done.

48 | INDUSTRY: A PLACE TO STUDY HUMAN BEHAVIOR

Marvin D. Dunnette and Wayne K. Kirchner

We shall define *industry* as comprising all organizations established to create goods and services. Such institutions as government agencies, hospitals and clinics, educational institutions, hotels, theaters, and research institutes as well as manufacturing organizations, advertising agencies, banks, and insurance companies all fall within this definition. Adopting this broad point of view makes apparent the vast theater of human behavior which is available for systematic observation and study in industry. Psychology, as one of the major sciences dealing with human behavior, is well equipped to make observations and to conduct studies on the problems and issues arising out of human behavior in industry. Opportunities for human behavior research in industry have not gone unheeded by psychologists. Over the last forty years the application of psychological methods, principles, and resulting personnel techniques has become widespread in the industrial setting. If present demands by industry for the methods and services of psychologists are indicative of the future, we may expect an impressive burgeoning of applications of psychology in industry in the years ahead.

With this in mind, let us take a brief look at the science of psychology.

PSYCHOLOGY: THE SCIENCE OF HUMAN BEHAVIOR

Psychology is usually defined as the science of human and animal behavior. For our purposes we may exclude animal behavior from the definition. Industry is not particularly concerned about animal behavior, and it would be an extremely uncommon event for any industrial psychologist to be asked to give attention to the behavior of animals. This is not to say that principles derived from the study of animals may not be useful in industry. In fact, they have been, and we note later some of the interesting instances of such applications in industrial settings.

Thus we are left with the disarmingly simple statement that psychology (in industry) is the *science of human behavior.* Simple as it seems, this definition contains elements deserving of careful thought. The important words are *science* and *behavior.* Since psychology is a science and since it deals with behavior, we gain immediate implications concerning its stance, its methods, and its subject matter. As a science psychology seeks to discover or to develop explanatory concepts. Explanation demands the identification, description, and observation of variables. The observation should be of a special sort. At the very least it needs to be planned and systematic; ideally, it should be experimental, that is, certain variables should be controlled (either actually or by statistical techniques) while others are systematically varied and their effects studied. Most important perhaps, the observations and experiments of science are specified or spelled out ahead of time. Observations of science are subject to confirmation or invalidation by any other scientist who wishes to repeat any particular observation. Opinions, whims, argumentation, pet notions, or theories do *not*, therefore, constitute an appropriate source for scientific conclusions. Facts, developed by specified observational and experimental procedures, *do* constitute the appropriate basis for scientific conclusions. The prime contribution that psychology can make in industry is to introduce the scientific method as *the* basis for deriving decisions involving and bearing on human behavior. In fact, Skinner (1953) has suggested that science (and therefore, psychology) consists of a set of attitudes which direct us to accept facts even though they may run counter to our expectations, hopes, or desires. Psychology does not work in the realm of wishful thinking about human behavior; instead, it works with facts and with *all* the facts. Some years ago, a psychologist, working in industry, developed a promising new diagnostic test for potential use in the selection of employees. Performing further research, he discovered, to his consternation, that responses on the test could not be depended upon to be consistent nor even honest self-appraisals of examinees. To his credit, he immediately published these facts against his test and refused to sell further copies of it. Such is the stance of intellectual integrity demanded of a person who would call himself a scientist or a psychologist.

HUMAN BEHAVIOR RANGES FAR AND WIDE

As suggested, the subject matter of psychology in industry is human behavior. Behavior refers, simply, to what a person or persons may be doing. Psychologists study behavior in all its forms—ranging from the very simple to the extremely complex, from the involuntary blinking of an eyelid to the intricate configuration of actions and reactions which may be demonstrated by a team of astronauts charged with controlling and directing a mooncraft. The range of human behaviors studied by psychologists in industry is fully as great as that studied by other psychologists. For example, human factors psychologists are intent on assuring that the design of equipment takes account of the special abilities or limitations of the human beings who may be assigned to operate it. A human factors specialist is, therefore, concerned with human sensory and motor behavior, and his research will often involve the study of seemingly simple forms of human behavior such as sensory discrimination and motor response characteristics. At the other end of the continuum, the industrial social psychologist or the organizational psychologist is intent on learning about human behavior as it is evidenced in group situations. Such specialists are concerned with the total behavior of groups and organizations and with the interactions between individuals as they affect the total group or organizational effort. Between these two extremes the differential psychologist is most concerned with the behavior of individuals in an effort to predict their behavior in different industrial circumstances. To be sure, these different levels of complexity never occur alone; the psychologist working in industry must be broadly trained and able to cope with the entire range of human behavior whether it be simple or complex. He must avoid tendencies toward provincialism in his enthusiasm for his specialty. The human factors specialist, intent as he is on designing equipment for *all* human beings, must be careful not to ignore differences among humans which may dictate significant design modifications in certain equipment. The differential psychologist, intent as he is on relating individual abilities to different forms of industrial behavior, must nevertheless remain constantly aware of the important potential influence of social factors—human interactions and group and organizational characteristics—on the nature and magnitude of the relationships he is studying.

STANDARDS OF SCIENCE MUST BE APPLIED
TO PSYCHOLOGY IN INDUSTRY

Our discussion of psychology as a science of human behavior makes apparent our orientation as we consider *applications* of psychology in industry. It is unfortunately true that current psychological practice in industry is far from uniform, and in a distressingly large number of instances, it has departed rather far from the standards set by scientific rules of evidence. Some observations have been poorly planned and inappropriately conducted; occasionally, experiments have lacked proper controls, thereby resulting in conclusions which may not flow necessarily from the data presented; studies have been conducted which do not meet the necessary standards of replicability, and occasionally, it has seemed that certain individuals have been more intent on proving a pet theory than on developing valid explanatory concepts. It can be argued that the lack of uniformity and the varying degrees of excellence merely reflect the growing pains that may be expected as a science moves from the laboratory into the real world. The standards of science must not, however, be forgotten or mislaid. In this small volume we have attempted to examine examples of psychology applied to industry from the scientist's point of view. We hope the reader will thereby gain an awareness not only of applications but also of misapplications of psychology in industry. Such awareness, if it becomes widespread, should insure in the years ahead that standards of scientific excellence will come to be more broadly and more uniformly applied to the practice of psychology in industry, with a resulting decline in the number of bad examples that may be cited.

PSYCHOLOGY APPLIED TO INDUSTRY
IS DIFFICULT BUT EXCITING

It is to be hoped that such standards of excellence may prevail, for industry does afford a magnificent opportunity for studying human behavior. Gainfully employed men and women spend nearly half their waking hours in the world of work; the non-employed members of our society have an obvious stake too in what goes on in industry. Thus, industry, as a setting in which to study behavior, is exciting because behavior there has such great relevance to the continued well-being of our society. A psychologist working on industrial behavior is concerned most broadly with creating optimum circumstances for the utilization of human resources in industry. He is concerned with enormously complex problems of human productivity and work performance, of human learning and the acquisition of skills, of human motivation and the effects of various incentives and environmental circumstances on the utilization of human capabilities, of physical safety and of mental health, and of the interaction between industry's needs or goals and individual employees' needs for the full development and actualization of their personalities. These are exciting problems; they also are eminently practical problems. The student who is pragmatic, who values opportunities to see the day-to-day results of his efforts, but who also seeks and enjoys studying complex problems involving human beings, will be deeply gratified by the study of psychology applied to industry.

AN OUTLINE FOR THE STUDY OF
HUMAN BEHAVIOR IN INDUSTRY

We have said that a major aim of psychology in industry is to introduce the scientific method as the basis for decisions involving human behavior or the utilization of human resources. Let us consider the various kinds of decisions which involve different aspects of human behavior. The following outline summarizes areas of decision and the corresponding psychological research activities implied by each of them:

I. Decisions based on institutional requirements.
Such decisions assume that certain aspects of industry or of the organization are constant. The problem becomes one of selecting people whose job behaviors conform to the requirements of the institution.

A. Personnel selection.
A careful study of job requirements will suggest the necessary human qualities for performing a job successfully. Scientific selection demands that these inferences be tested empirically by showing that the assessment methods developed for measuring the appropriate human qualities actually are related to successful job performance. The typical industrial firm has many jobs of various types to be filled and must assess the characteristics of applicants in an effort to assign them to the jobs so as to maximize the total organizational efficiency. Decisions bearing on such assignments are the ones involved in any program of personnel selection.

B. Personnel training and development.
A second method of assuring efficient performance on a job is to teach or to train employees in the skills or knowledges required by the job. The psychologist's role in training includes determining what things need to be learned, setting up procedures for teaching employees, and, most important, designing and carrying out experiments to determine whether or not the training programs have achieved their desired aims. The areas of personnel selection and personnel training are inextricably intertwined. Persons must be selected who are capable of being trained, and the design of training programs must take into account the individual qualities of the persons to be trained. In some instances the psychologist will need to develop several training procedures in order to take into account the varying levels of ability, experience, and present knowledge of the individuals who are to be trained.

C. Personnel counseling.
The counseling relationship affords the most individualized and most intimate learning situation in industry. Institutional requirements may occasionally come into conflict with an individual's capabilities and aspirations. In such instances personal guidance from a psychologist may be helpful. Such counseling may simply take the form of determining discrepancies between an individual's qualities and the demands of his job in which case placement on a more appropriate job or a learning program to help the individual develop new skills, attitudes, nor knowledges (to fit the de-

mands of his job) would be the usual outcome. Or, counseling may go deeper into situations or personal problems which affect the individual's total life experience. It is difficult to assess how far a firm should go in bearing responsibility for the personal and emotional well-being of its employees. The area of personnel counseling in industry is in sad need of careful research. Unfortunately, nearly none is being performed.

II. Decisions based on or modified by individual characteristics.

The assumption here is that institutional requirements or characteristics may need to be modified because of the so-called human element, that is, the special characteristics, capabilities, and limitations of human beings. One possible implication of such an assumption is that individual differences among humans may be relatively unimportant. Such an inference would seriously weaken the net effectiveness of psychological research in industry, and it should be strenuously avoided. Thus, research questions become far more complex than is the case if individual differences are ignored. Instead of asking how industry must be modified to take account of the abilities of *man*, we must ask in how many ways must industry be modified in order to take account of the varying capabilities (and modifiabilities) of *men*.

A. Engineering psychology.

World War II witnessed the emergence of teamwork between engineers and psychologists necessitated by several instances in which it was obvious that equipment had been designed and produced without giving sufficient attention to limitations of the human being who would be required to operate it. Many accidents and near accidents in aircraft were traced directly to inadequacies in equipment design characteristics (Fitts & Jones, 1947; Fitts & Jones, 1961). Broadly speaking, the engineering psychologist studies the characteristics of human operators in order to learn how equipment should be designed or how a complex production system consisting of men, materials, and machines should be put together so as to insure optimum efficiency of operation. The purpose, then, is to learn how the mechanical components of an industrial system need to be arranged or modified in order to utilize most efficiently the capabilities of the human elements of the system.

B. Human Motivation.

Among the most important of the decisions made in industry are those involving human motivation. Even when care has been used in the selection, training, and placement of employees, there is no assurance that they will show the intensity of effort in the industrial setting of which they may be capable and which they do demonstrate in other settings (e.g., in pursuing their hobbies and leisure time activities). There is no shortage of theories concerning human motivation in industry; there is an unfortunate shortage of experimental evidence bearing on it. The task for industrial psychologists is to discover the kinds of conditions within the industrial milieu which do result in high employee motivation. Again, individual differences must not be ignored; different persons probably are differentially motivated by different circumstances. It is up to the psychologist in industry to discover principles of human motivation which may form the basis for recommendations concerning modifications necessary for maximizing employee motivation.

C. Organizational psychology.

Only within the last decade has widespread attention been given to the possible effects on human efficiency of different organizational structures. In the early 1950's,

Sears Roebuck and Co. moved from a vertical organization with many levels of management to a flat or horizontal structure. This resulted in greater responsibility and autonomy for persons at lower levels in the firm; authority was decentralized and decision making became diffused among many persons throughout the organization. It was argued that this change was made because the new structure gave employees a greater sense of importance and more opportunities for self-fulfillment than the old structure. It is not certain that this contention can be sustained, but the Sears reorganization is an important illustration of the impact of organizational psychology. This is the broadest and most complex area of psychology applied to industry. The organizational psychologist is intent on developing a better understanding of total organizations and the human interactions which comprise them. His discipline represents a merging of differential, experimental, and social psychology and is, perhaps, the most concerted effort so far undertaken in the effort to understand human behavior in industry.

III. Decisions based on group perceptions and group influences.

Many industrial decisions grow out of the need to evaluate and act upon the opinions or perceptions of groups. Often this may require the resolution of group conflict. The desire to belong seems to be an elemental human characteristic; humans of like interests and needs form groups, and when they do, their goals become defined and intensified. Every employee in industry belongs to many groups ranging from his own work group to his union or professional society and to religious, political, or community groups outside the premises of his firm. Decisions in industry often require information about the attitudes and desires of such groups. The psychologist can help to gain such information.

A. Industrial communications and union-management relations.

Industrial activity—the creation of goods and services—cannot proceed without communication between people and between groups. One of the major barriers to accuracy in communication is engendered by the differing perceptions people have. A sincere request by a manager for help on a difficult assignment might be viewed by an insecure employee as a deliberate effort to show him up. A more secure and confident employee might more accurately view such a request as an opportunity to show his true merit. Accuracy in communications implies not only the faithful transmission of the mechanical components of a message but also the faithful transmission of the purposes and meanings intended by the sender. The wisdom of personnel decisions in industry depends, therefore, on the fidelity of processes for gathering information relevant to the decisions. In turn, the implementation of decisions demands accurate transmission to persons and groups in the organization. Psychological research on communications is directed at identifying and eliminating the important barriers to accurate communication in industry with the desirable result that the frequency of individual and group conflicts based on misunderstanding will be significantly decreased. One of the major sources of potential group conflict in industry comes from the differing perceptions and goals of labor and management. Both groups would probably agree that their broad goal is to insure the efficient and humane utilization of human resources, but they often differ on the definitions and relative emphases to be placed on such terms as "efficient," "humane," and "utilization." They most certainly encounter differences in defining the employment conditions which may lead to such a goal. Katzell identifies a number of psychological issues generated by the potential conflict between union and management, "including the degree to which their identification with the union may either facilitate or interfere with employees' loyalty to their employer, the circumstances contributing to union-management conflict or cooperation, the factors leading to employees' satisfaction or dissatisfaction with their union, and the characteristics of successful and unsuccessful negotiating sessions between labor and management representatives" (Katzell, 1961, p. 198). Psychologists have thus far performed only a limited amount of research in the area of union-management relations, but it does represent an extremely important and rich field for future psychological research in industry.

B. Consumer psychology and survey research.

The consuming public obviously constitutes an important group for industrial decision making. The opinions of the public concerning a firm's products or services can mean the difference between success and failure for the firm. Thus, more and more firms check consumer reactions to new products before they are released en masse on the market. Similarly, marketing decisions demand information about the most effective techniques for telling the public about the firm's product or service (advertising) and a careful evaluation of the public's reaction to the various products and services. Psychologist experts in the sampling and measurement of public opinion have become active in these important areas. By developing and perfecting methods of survey research, psychologists are able to provide information about various groups of consumers. In turn, this information aids in making marketing decisions and in developing marketing strategies, product modifications, and improved company services.

---

49 | THE EMERGING DISCIPLINE
OF ENVIRONMENTAL PSYCHOLOGY

Joachim F. Wohlwill

Everywhere about us, from Sunday-supplement features to the pages of *Science*, from town hall meetings to the halls of Congress, we are witnessing a concern for the quality of our physical environment, and the effects that the pressures of an

---

Joachim F. Wohlwill, "The Emerging Discipline of Environmental Psychology," *American Psychologist*, April (1970), No. 4, pp. 303–311. Copyright © by the American Psychological Association, and reproduced by permission.

expanding population and industrial civilization are exerting on it. This movement is making itself felt not only in those professions that deal directly with environmental problems—architecture, city and regional planning, civil and sanitary engineering—but likewise in a number of academic disciplines, notably biology, geography, and sociology. Indeed, there are few if any fields that do not at some points touch on the relationship between man and his environment; conversely any concerted attack on environmental problems, or program of study and research focused on them, inevitably takes on a strong interdisciplinary flavor—as witness the contributions to some of the major anthologies in this field: Thomas (1956), Duhl (1963), Ewald (1967), and Kates and Wohlwill (1966).

Involvement on the part of psychologists in this field is similarly growing, though more slowly and sporadically than one might have expected, if we consider the emphasis that psychologists have traditionally placed on the influence of the environment on behavior, and if we recognize further the direct relevance of many of the concepts, methods, and principles of general psychology to problems in this area. Thus one suspects that two of the most significant events of interest to psychologists, which might be said to mark the launching of the new discipline of environmental psychology, have thus far remained largely unnoticed on the part of psychologists at large. I am referring to the inauguration of a graduate training program in environmental psychology under the auspices of a Psychology Department, at the City University of New York, and the founding of a new journal devoted to this area, under the editorship of Gary Winkel of the same institution. The first issue of this journal, *Environment and Behavior,* has most recently appeared; it consists of a set of five papers reporting diverse research studies concerning the perception of and reaction to features and qualities of our physical environment. Yet it is interesting, and somewhat disconcerting, to note that only two of the six authors of these papers are psychologists by training or professional affiliation.

It is the intent of this article to outline the major dimensions of this still embryonic field, in order to show the intimate connection between some of the major questions that those concerned with environmental management and control are facing and particular problem areas from the study of motivation, cognition, attitude-formation, development, etc. The hope is that this outline will help to stimulate awareness of and interest in this field on the part of psychologists generally, and to point to some of its many researchable problems on which psychologists could profitably focus, much as Craik (1966, 1968) has most effectively done in two recent papers directed primarily at those in the design and planning professions.[*] We will note the benefit, not only for the formulation of environmental planning and policy, but for the testing of psychological hypotheses and the clarification of behavioral phenomena, of an increased involvement on the part of psychologists in this area. Finally, we will point to some of the institutional problems, within academia as well as concerning the relationships between those in academic life and those "in the field," that will need to be met to promote optimally effective training and research in these areas.

THREE FORMS OF THE INTERRELATIONSHIP BETWEEN BEHAVIOR AND ENVIRONMENT

This writer (Wohlwill, 1966) has pointed previously to the paradox of psychology's relative neglect of the role of the physical environment in behavior, in the face of the insistence on the environmentally determined basis of behavior. The fact is that when psychologists have talked of environmental influences, they have rarely been specific about the meaning for them of the concept of environment. It has been used to refer to the most diverse set of conditions of experience, ranging from attendance in nursery school to socialization practices of the parents; from the provision for practice or training on a task to the role of culture or society in a global sense. Yet, with the notable exception of some of the Hebbian animal research on the effects of early experience, and the work of ecological psychologists such as Barker, Wright, and their associates, the physical environment that serves as background and context for behavior has been of little interest to psychologists; the role of the "environment" has almost invariably referred to social or interpersonal influences, or else to effects presumed to be ascribable to the milieu in an altogether unspecified sense.

Yet, even without the current concern over environmental problems, it should be evident that behavior is in important and most diverse ways functionally related to characteristics and attributes of the physical environment. It is useful to distinguish among three forms of this relationship.

First of all, behavior necessarily occurs in some particular environmental context, which imposes major constraints on the range of behaviors permissible in it, and frequently serves to determine in a more positive sense particular aspects or patterns of an individual's behavior. The title of a best seller of some years back, *A Tree Grows in Brooklyn,* does more than remind us of the obvious fact that children growing up in a congested urban environment will have only limited experience in climbing trees; it may serve as a hint of the pervasive differences between their life space (in the literal sense) and that of a small-town child or one raised on a farm (cf. Wright, 1961). Furthermore, behavior, and particularly movement, occurs within a given type of space; the use made of environmental spaces, and the manner in which the spatial environment may itself be constructed or modified to accord with an individual's preferences, values, etc., becomes itself an important subject for study, of interest not only to psychologists, but to architects and planners as well (cf. Hall, 1966; Sommer, 1969).

Second, certain qualities of the environment, such as under- or overstimulation, crowding, severity of climate, etc., may exert generalized effects on broader systems of response within the individual. To cite just one example, consider the wonted brusqueness of the typical New York City bus driver on the job, or the proverbial "mad cabbie" of Manhattan. To the extent that these stereotypes have a basis in fact, it seems plausible to relate them to the conditions of stress and tension to which these individuals are subjected in their daily battle with urban traffic and congestion.

Third, behavior is in a variety of ways instigated by and directed at particular attributes and characteristics of the physical environment. Individuals give evidence of more or less strongly defined attitudes, values, beliefs, and affective responses relating to their environment—as witness the tumult and shouting evoked by current environmental problems. They develop diverse forms of adjustment and adaptation to environmental conditions. They exhibit temporary and permanent responses of approach to and avoidance or escape from given environmental situations, ranging all the way from recreation and tourism to migration to the suburbs, or to a different part of the country. (Consider, for example, the frequent specification of geographic areas in professional job-availability notices, such as "East or West Coast preferred.")

Of the three facets of behavior-environment relations named above, the first has received by far the most concentrated attention. To begin with, it is encompassed in the ecological approach to the study of behavior represented by Barker, Wright, and their associates and disciples (cf. Barker, 1963, 1965). The use of space in everyday behavior, that is, *proxemics,* forms the subject of two further recent volumes by Hall (1966) and Sommer (1969) dealing with such questions as the perception of space and spatial relations among objects and persons; habits, attitudes, and values concerning the use of space and interpersonal distance; behavioral consequences of architectural design, etc. The effects of crowding on behavior are the subject of the by now well-known animal research studies by Calhoun (1962, 1966), while an extensive literature has come into being on the images and "mental maps" formed by individuals of their geographic environment (Lynch, 1960; Stea, 1969). Not the least of the reasons for the comparatively large amount of attention that has been devoted to these problems has been the strong interest that has emanated from the field of architecture in their study and discussion.

The second facet, that of influences of environmental variables on general attributes of behavior and personality, is by contrast the least studied and least well-known, in spite of its obvious relevance to considerations of environmental quality, as well as to general psychological theory. Its investigation would take off from the controlled laboratory experimentation on the effects of early experience in animals and attempt to apply these to the relationship between variables of the physical environment and the development of the human individual, as well as its modification in adulthood and later life. There are obvious problems of control and isolation of determining variables involved in such an enterprise, though it is interesting to note that the effects of institutionalization in infancy have with some plausibility been related to the principles derived from the study of early experience in animals (e.g., Casler, 1961; Yarrow, 1961). We might also refer to the sensory-deprivation literature, which has been applied, for example, to the effects of prolonged exposure in the antarctic (Gunderson, 1963). And epidemiological work in the field of mental health has similarly pointed to environmental and ecological variables in the incidence of mental disease and emotional disorder, as well as more positive forms of adjustment. Thus we may look forward to future reports linking particular behavioral syndromes to prolonged exposure to noxious (or beneficial) environmental factors, in much the same way as the incidence of certain diseases (e.g., respiratory disorders) has been linked to particular environmental conditions such as pollution.

It is the third of the above mentioned forms of environment-behavior interrelationships, however, that not only ties in most directly with some of the most urgent and publicized of our environmental problems, but at the same time lends itself most easily to analysis in terms of principles or hypotheses derived from certain areas of basic psychological research. This point bears more extended exposition and illustration. To this end, let us distinguish among three more specific facets of this interrelationship: affective and attitudinal responses to present environmental attributes; approach and avoidance responses to environments potentially or actually available to the individual; and adaptation to environmental qualities as a function of prolonged exposure.

MOTIVATIONAL FORCE OF ENVIRONMENTAL STIMULATION
ENVIRONMENT AS A SOURCE OF AFFECT AND ATTITUDES

What accounts for the remarkable power of the physical environment to elicit affect, ranging from pleasure and excitement to aversion and boredom, and to try to become the object of pervasive attitudes varying from identification and loyalty to detachment or outright hostility? The bases for these reactions should prove to be subsumable under the principles of arousal and motivation, as related to such stimulus attributes as complexity, incongruity, novelty, variety, etc. These have become thoroughly researched and fairly well understood over the past decade, largely because of the pioneering work of Berlyne (1960) and of others that have followed (cf. Fiske & Maddi, 1961; Walker, 1964). Thus the present writer (Wohlwill, 1968a) has demonstrated that responses to photographic slides of the physical environment vary as a function of the judged complexity of these scenes in much the same fashion as do responses to artificially constructed stimuli varying in complexity. This correspondence extends to the recovery of two different functions, one representing interest or amount of voluntary exploratory activity, which increases monotonically with complexity, the other representing affective or evaluative responses, which reach an optimal value at a low or intermediate level of complexity. This differentiation is in good accord with the findings from the experimental literature (e.g., Day, 1967) and relates directly to Berlyne's (1960, p. 80) distinction between specific and diversive exploration, representing two modes of exploratory activity, one directed at information seeking, the other at affective arousal.

The author (Wohlwill, 1968b) has similarly analyzed the role of novelty, incongruity, and surprise—the other "collative" variables emphasized by Berlyne (1960)—in responses to features of the physical environment. Thus we see opening up a potentially fruitful link between laboratory experimentation and important applied research concerning attitudes and affective reactions to features of our physical surroundings, which promises to be of direct relevance to architects, city planners, natural resource personnel, etc. Indeed, it does not seem to be beyond the scope of our present knowledge to try to account in the terms of the stimulus-complexity and variation-seeking literature for such phenomena as the attractions of our large cities, with all their problems, their crowded conditions, and areas of dissolution and squalor, as a place to live as well as to visit, for so many people. An impressive attempt in this direction has been contributed by Rapoport and Kantor (1967). Addressing themselves to architects and urban planners, they have provided an interesting analysis of people's affective responses to the urban environment, which utilizes the research on stimulus exploration and stimulation seeking as a base, and places particular stress on the positive function of ambiguity and uncertainty in the layout of buildings and urban areas.

APPROACH AND AVOIDANCE RESPONSES DETERMINED BY ENVIRONMENTAL ATTRIBUTES

The intent of the distinction between this topic and the preceding one is to bring out the point that the physical environment does not only arouse strong affective reactions in the individual, but is frequently an object of approach and avoidance behavior, in a literal sense and on a large scale, which is of obvious importance for the study of questions of demography and ecology, as well as for environmental management. We may point in this connection to such phenomena as the move from the inner city to the suburbs (and the more recent movement in the opposite direction), to migration patterns from country to city, from East to West, from severe to temperate climates. While the influence of the physical environment per se in determining patterns of migration and residential choice is difficult to disentangle from the undeniable role played by economic and sociological factors, surely no one would question the important part played by the city qua city, as a determinant both of in-migration (e.g., from country to city) and out-migration (from inner city to suburb). Similarly, the attraction of certain geographic areas such as Florida and California, is clearly related to particular features of those environments, of which climate is probably only one. Some hints concerning the possible dimensions involved are provided in Gould's (1967) principal component analysis of preferences for the various states of the Union.

Relatively little research has been directed thus far at trying to isolate the physical environment variables that influence decisions involving residential choice and migration. Where sociologists have occupied themselves with the study of such questions (Gans, 1963; Gutman, 1966; Rossi, 1965), the predominant focus has, not surprisingly, been on such factors as intergroup relations, social mobility, economic opportunity and the like. Yet, in principle, it should be feasible to approach the study of human behavior of this type in terms of the affective and attitudinal components of our responses to the environmental attributes discussed in the previous section. Any attempt to apply such a framework to this realm of human behavior will, however, need to take into account the phenomena of adaptation to given environmental conditions, to which we will turn presently, as well as to the phenomena of selective perception and image formation, which may frequently bear little relationship to the experienced stimulus environment—compare Stea's (1967) concept of the "invisible landscape."

There is another category of approach-avoidance behavior that appears more readily amenable to analysis in terms of specific environmental variables, and to which the principles of stimulation seeking and variation seeking should prove directly applicable. I am referring to the grossly neglected area of *temporary* movement through the environment, taking the form of vacationing and tourism. The seeming triviality of these activities should not obscure the important role that such short-term environmental search and exploration movements may play in the individual's adaptation to and tolerance of his permanent environmental circumstances, nor the effects of such behavior on the social and economic life, and frequently on the ecology, of the areas of visitation. The problems faced by our National Park administrators, for example, at Yellowstone and Yosemite, provide one illustration of the nature and magnitude of these effects.

But, above all, behavior of this type is of interest to psychologists in much the same way as that cited previously, for example, in revealing the power of the environment as a source of affect, arousal, and exploratory activity. A variety of questions can be formulated with respect to this realm of behavior. Thus, what characteristics of a particular site, structure, or area account for its attractiveness as a vacation spot or as a goal for the tourist, and in terms of what stimulus dimensions may these be conceptualized (cf. Shafer, 1969)? Are there fundamental differences in the values attached to natural as opposed to man-made features, and if so what are their correlates? How do the frequently deleterious effects of overuse or overpopulation of a given locale or region modify the individual's response to it? What are the correlates of interindividual differences in preferences for vacation spots, as in the seemingly pervasive dichotomy between mountain and seashore?

These are highly concrete questions, to be sure. Their relevance to immediate practical concerns, such as the use and conservation of natural resources, the control of access to areas of heavy visitation to preserve ecological systems and natural values, etc., is inescapable. But they are mentioned here as much for their direct relevance to psychological principles and theory. To begin with: What is the primary psychological function of behavior of this type? Does it serve to raise the individual's level of stimulation, or to lower it, or does it perhaps provide rather for qualitative change (i.e., novelty)? What is the role of curiosity-related motivation, in the sense of the epistemic curiosity discussed by Berlyne (1960), in touristic activity?

There is surely a challenge here for psychology to identify and unravel the various motivations underlying this kind of behavior, and to determine their relative importance for different individuals (cf. Wohlwill, 1966, for a very cursory attempt in this direction). At the same time the behavioral scientist studying these phenomena will be forced to broaden his focus, so as to take into account the role of socially and culturally determined habits, attitudes, and values in this realm, as reflected, for instance, in the curious finding that 80% of all visitors to certain selected wilderness areas were found to have a college education; in addition, 27% had some postgraduate education (Gilligan, 1962).

ADAPTATION TO ENVIRONMENTAL QUALITIES AS A FUNCTION OF PROLONGED EXPOSURE

Any analysis of problems that relate to the individual's response to his environment, once it transcends the realm of momentary or short-term effects, inevitably comes up against the phenomenon of adaptation. For man is at once a seeker and a neutralizer of stimulation (Wohlwill, 1968b). He is not only able to adapt behaviorally and biologically to the most varied and extreme environmental conditions, from the zero gravity of space to the no less peculiar conditions of life below sea level, but his affective and attitudinal responses similarly change as a result of prolonged exposure to any given environment, generally in the direction of neutralizing its effects. This situation touches directly on findings and principles derived from adaptation level theory (Helson, 1964), and in particular on the role of deviation of stimuli from a preestablished adaptation level as a source of both positive and negative affect, as well as on the role of experience and extended exposure in setting and shifting adaptation levels (cf. Sonnenfeld, 1967; Wohlwill, 1966).

If we examine more closely the operation of adaptation processes in the mediation of effects of environmental attributes on us, several questions arise. First of all, what are the dimensions along which adaptation takes place? This question has been studied in the past mainly with reference to simple dimensions of sensory intensity (temperature, brightness, weight). How do they apply with reference to such stimulus attributes as complexity, incongruity, ambiguity, or to the multidimensional character of such workaday experiences as that to which a commuter on the New York subways or the Los Angeles freeways is subjected?

Second, what is the residue, in behavioral terms, of prolonged exposure to certain environmental conditions for which adaptation exerts a neutralizing effect at the level of conscious affect? And what is the cost of the adaptation process itself? These are questions that have been of considerable concern to physiologists (Dubos, 1965, esp. pp. 100–109, 254–279, 280–318; Selye, 1946), but we know very little as yet concerning the long-term *behavioral* effects of exposure to the visual and auditory stimulus world (and perhaps olfactory and thermal world as well) of our urban ghettos, of center-city or urban freeway traffic conditions at rush hour, of life in the immediate vicinity, for example, of a jetport or industrial plant. In this respect our knowledge of real life conditions parallels that obtained from laboratory studies, both from the sensory-deprivation literature and that on the effects of early stimulus experience in animals: we have a much better picture of the effects of under- than of overstimulation; similarly we are better informed of the psychological hazards of extended stays in the antarctic (Gunderson, 1963, 1968) than in megalopolis.

Finally, what are the limitations on the individual's tolerance of environmental conditions that may subject his adaptation powers to continual strain, in the face of conflicting forces impelling him to "escape from the field," that is, to exchange these conditions for less stressful ones? To be sure, exposure to such a conflict itself presupposes that the individual has a realistic choice of moving away from his present environment, which is certainly not the case for a majority of those individuals of our population experiencing such strains; yet, to judge from the wonted geographic mobility of large segments of our population, this type of conflict is probably a fairly common one. This question has been dealt with in an interesting, if perhaps overly formalized, form by Wolpert (1966), who has tried to provide a model for the study of what he has termed the "mover-stayer" problem. This model, and more generally the experience and resolution of this type of conflict situation, clearly warrants more extensive analysis by behavioral scientists.

Let us mention, in the same context, the distinction made by Sonnenfeld (1966) between adaptation and adjustment as alternative models of handling discomfort and stress emanating from the environment, calling our attention to the fact that we not only get used to environmental circumstances by adapting, but frequently arrive at more active modes of adjustment to them, which have the effect of reducing the strain placed on our adaptation processes themselves. These adjustments, whose role has been enormously enhanced through technological advances, at times function in lieu of adaptation mechanisms, where the latter are inadequate to deal with particular environmental conditions—as in the case of the pressurized cabin of the jetliner, or the space suit of the astronaut on the moon. More frequently, however, they act so as to supplant normally functioning adaptation processes. The installation of air-conditioning in buildings and cars, or of stabilizing fins on our ocean liners, is an example of this type. One intriguing question that suggests itself is whether reliance on such artificial adjustments in any way impairs the individual's capacity for adaptation; for example, does prolonged dependence on air-conditioning reduce one's tolerance for extreme degrees of heat?

CHALLENGE FOR PSYCHOLOGY

It does not take a very fertile imagination to raise questions such as the above. The point in reciting them was to indicate something of the range of important questions touching on central issues of environmental control and design and of our modes of dealing with environmental problems that should be of interest and concern to psychologists, relating as they do to basic concepts and principles from diverse areas of behavioral science.

For obvious reasons, the coverage of these problems given in this paper has been highly selective, and quite possibly rather idiosyncratic. For instance, no attention has been paid to the mediation and transformation of environmental effects through symbolic activity and interpersonal societal and cultural influences. Related to this point is the slighting of questions of individual differences in response to the environment, although some of these have been touched on in incidental fashion. The recent development of "sensation-seeking" scales and other similar instruments (McCarroll, Mitchell, Carpenter, & Anderson, 1967) and Craik's (1966) analysis of interpersonal differences in terms of "environmental dispositions" attest to both the interest in and importance of systematic attacks on these differential questions. Furthermore, the important area of attitude formation and change, and its application to environmental problems such as pollution, congestion, depletion of natural resources, etc., has been left out of account.

The range of problems considered is, thus, far from comprehensive, even in terms of its coverage of the field of environmental psychology, conceived of as a subdivision directly affiliated with the discipline of general psychology (much as is educational psychology). Still less is it representative of the broad range of problems referred to under the rubric of man-environment relationships, which would include the analysis of man-environment systems as it is increasingly entering into discussions of problems of environmental design, the interdisciplinary study of ecological systems, etc. Finally, it is important to recognize that there are many seemingly environmental problems, notably the critical ones of life in our cities, which cannot possibly be analyzed by an exclusive reference to the physical environment, overlayed as they are with factors of an economic, social, and political order. The subject of urban renewal, for instance, and of the responses of people to proposals involving the eradication of slums or the rehabilitation of a neighborhood, could not be encompassed adequately within the type of analysis provided in this article.

Yet, in spite of the bias inherent in our coverage, it should suffice to bring into focus the central point of this article, that psychology has a major stake in this area, and is indeed presented with a major challenge in making a contribution to the solution of environmental problems commensurate with their direct pertinence to diverse domains of psychological investigation. At the same time, attention to these problems on the part of psychologists can be expected to have a far from negligible feedback value for the advancement of basic psychological knowledge, by aiding us in conceptualizing the nature and psychological effects of the environment, of environmental stimulation, of ecological relationships, etc. In particular, we can distinguish among four primary forms that our involvement in this area can take. These are:

1. *Research, both basic and applied.* In contrast to certain fields currently enjoying popularity as subject matter for research, the area of the relationships between the

physical environment and behavior remains decidedly underresearched at present. Indeed, we have scarcely begun to scratch the surface of the vast array of questions awaiting our attention. Efforts are called for to stimulate and support research in this area.

2. *Training of and consultation with prospective and actual workers in professions dealing with environmental problems.* Schools of architecture and environmental design, as well as other environmental disciplines, are increasingly turning to psychologists to provide needed background in behavioral science concepts, techniques, and principles pertinent to their problems, and to consult with them in their attempts to cope with these problems. This demand will grow undoubtedly as the potential place of psychology among the environmental sciences becomes more firmly established.

3. *Graduate training for psychologists.* This would seem to be an auspicious time for certain departments of psychology to consider the institution of graduate programs in this area. The initiation of one such program, at the City University of New York, was noted in the introduction to this article; a more limited program, in architectural psychology, has been in existence at the University of Utah, while at Clark University the Departments of Psychology and Geography are collaborating in the development of a joint program emphasizing problems of environmental perception. Other behaviorally oriented training programs have been started in such institutions as colleges or schools of environmental design (e.g., Berkeley), as well as in divisions specifically set up to deal with man-environment problems (e.g., at Pennsylvania State University and Wisconsin, and in Canada at the University of Waterloo).

The question of the particular kinds of institutional settings that are most effective for the training of behavioral scientists in this area has, as yet, received little systematic attention. At this point experimentation with a wide variety of structures is undoubtedly advantageous. For reasons which will be argued at greater length presently, however, it is highly desirable that departments of psychology participate in this area of training.

4. *The undergraduate psychology curriculum.* A particular challenge confronts us in leading the beginning student to an appreciation of the relevance of the body of psychological knowledge for an understanding of environmental problems. An effective demonstration of the pertinence of basic psychological phenomena and principles in this area can only serve to make our field more meaningful to the student, and at the same time to increase his sensitivity to the modes of the individual's relation to his environment. Surely such questions as the motivational force of the environment or the behavioral implications of alternative forms of the design of new environments cannot fail to excite and involve the alert undergraduate; they are, in fact, ideally suited to bring out the value and power of intellectual analysis to a social problem of direct concern to him. Or, consider the fundamental question of our attitudes toward achieving control over our environment, and our changing view of the interdependence of the elements of ecological systems: it would be difficult to find more dramatic examples through which to approach the study of core problems in such diverse areas as perception, cognition, motivation, and attitude formation.

PREREQUISITES FOR ESTABLISHMENT OF ENVIRONMENTAL
PSYCHOLOGY AS VIABLE OFFSPRING OF OUR DISCIPLINE

While the time is clearly ripe for psychologists to become actively involved in this field, the soil is more fertile in certain departments and institutions than others. The vigorous growth of this new specialty area demands, in fact, that a number of conditions be satisfied, among which the following three are perhaps the most critical.

First, the development of the field is in large part dependent on the attention and support given to particular fields within psychology proper that can provide an adequate scientific foundation for it. We have already given extensive illustrations of some of the areas within psychology that are of direct relevance for the treatment of man-environment relations. Beyond the topics of stimulus exploration and related motivational phenomena and of adaptation processes, which were specifically considered, we can point to such areas as sensory deprivation, effects of sensory experience on development, psychological stress—its definition, determinants, and behavioral consequences (cf. Carson, 1968)—attitude formation, spatial perception and cognition, psychological ecology, etc. It may be suggested that environmental psychology will prosper in the environment of a particular institution only to the extent that some of the areas just mentioned are given adequate representation and support.

Second, it should be recognized that much of the work in this field is situated at the boundary between basic and applied research. The fact is that in the environmental sciences the lines between basic and applied problems are particularly blurred (e.g., the science of ecology). Psychologists are not unfamiliar with such a situation; it has characterized, for instance, the relationship between psychology and education, particularly in recent years. The growing interest on the part of many of our most prominent psychologists in the study of classroom learning, for theoretical as much as practical reasons, as represented in the work of such persons as Bruner, Skinner, and Eleanor Gibson, gives reason for optimism in this respect.

Finally, there must be a receptiveness to inter-disciplinary activity. The study of environmental problems touches on a particularly broad array of scientific and applied fields, and psychologists professing to specialize in this area will inevitably find themselves caught in a web of ties to diverse other disciplines, and of contacts with individuals in such diverse fields as physiology and sociology, architecture and resource management. This suggests not only the need for an environment and an institutional structure in which the boundaries between the individual disciplines can be easily crossed, for the purposes of the organization of research, of scientific communication, of the planning of curricula and programs of training; it further requires that the diversity of languages and concepts, of backgrounds, and of prevailing models of research and of modes of formulating problems in the various fields be recognized and adapted to, so as to permit effective communication and collaboration.

The rapidly growing activity in this field suggests that persons attracted to and suited for this type of scientific and professional activity will not be too difficult to find. A more uncertain question is whether the institutions in which they are located will prove sufficiently flexible to provide effective support for it. Herein lies a challenge, not only for psychology, but for our academic and scientific establishments, which will need to encourage experimentation with new structures and formats for interdisciplinary graduate programs and for the administration of collaborative research across disciplinary boundaries. Fortunately there are already in existence a variety of precedents and models that environmental psychology can follow in this regard, both from the realm of the environmental sciences and from other areas of interdisciplinary activity, such as that at the interface between psychology and biology.

The question may well be asked, why should we burden psychology, and academic departments of psychology in particular, fragmented and subdivided as they are, with yet another specialty area? Since architects, designers, and environmental scientists are apparently willing to bring behavioral scientists into their programs, why not concentrate on such settings as those cited already, for example, schools of design, divisions of environmental science, and special purpose institutes, to carry out the teaching and research functions in this area? There is no question that these settings will play a central role in dealing with the broad range of problems in the field of man-environment relationships. Yet it would be a mistake if psychology were thus to abrogate entirely its responsibility to become more directly involved in this area, and to ignore the stake it has in developing it.

The case of the field of educational psychology provides a valuable analogue in this respect. Until comparatively recent times and with very few exceptions (e.g., the work of Thorndike; the field of mental testing), the development of this field took place in large measure in independence of the mainstream of psychology. The result was for the most part a pragmatic and ultimately sterile approach to questions of classroom learning, curriculum development, etc. More recently, as noted above, general psychologists have become involved in the study of the learning process as it applies to the development of basic skills and concepts in the area of the "Three R's." leading to a much more effective interrelationship that has clearly benefited both education and psychology itself. Similarly, behavioral work inspired by the necessarily practical perspective of the designer, undertaken in an environmental science context, needs to be supplemented by work carried out in more direct relationship to the field of general psychology. This is essential if this emerging discipline is not to become divorced from the empirical, conceptual, and theoretical substrate of psychology that can provide a broader framework for the study of many environmental problems. At the same time, cognate areas of psychology will be presented with an important testing ground for the verification and elaboration of their basic principles.

CONCLUSION

We can confidently venture a prediction that the near future will see the construction of novel types of environments for living, ranging from individual dwellings to whole cities and regional communities here on earth—to say nothing of the possible colonization of the moon and conceivably other planets. The imaginative and exciting proposals for the city of the future (cf. Spilhaus, 1968) provide a taste of what we may look forward to in this regard. Such proposals are inevitably predicated on critical assumptions about behavior, about the use of space and environmental facilities, about preferences in regard to features of the environment, about tolerance for and adaptation to particular environmental conditions. It is hardly too soon for psychologists to become acquainted with and actively participate in these plans, so that we can be assured that these assumptions are based on an adequate foundation of psychological fact and tested theory. To a discipline that has for all too long paid lip service to the primary importance of environmental variables on behavior, this should represent an exciting challenge indeed.

REFERENCES

Barker, R. G. On the nature of the environment. *Journal of Social Issues,* 1963, **19,** 17–38.
Barker, R. G. Explorations in ecological psychology. *American Psychologist,* 1965, **20,** 1–14.
Berlyne, D. R. *Conflict, arousal and curiosity.* New York: McGraw-Hill, 1960.
Calhoun, J. B. Population density and social pathology. *Scientific American,* 1962, **206,** 139–146.
Calhoun, J. B. The role of space in animal sociology. *Journal of Social Issues,* 1966, **22,** 46–58.
Carson, D. Environmental stress and the urban dweller. *Michigan Mental Health Research Bulletin,* 1968, 2(4), 5–12.
Casler, L. Maternal deprivation: A critical review of the literature. *Monographs of the Society for Research in Child Development,* 1961, 26(2, Whole No. 80).
Craik, K. H. The prospects for an environmental psychology. *IPAR Research Bulletin.* Berkeley, Calif.: Institute of Personality Assessment and Research, University of California, 1966.
Craik, K. H. The comprehension of the everyday physical environment. *Journal of the American Institute of Planners,* 1968, **34,** 29–37.
Craik, K. H. Environmental psychology. In, *New directions in psychology.* Vol. 4. New York: Holt, Rinehart & Winston, in press.
Day, H. Evaluation of subjective complexity, pleasingness and interestingness for a series of random polygons varying in complexity. *Perception and Psychophysics,* 1967, **2,** 281–286.
Dubos, R. *Man adapting.* New Haven: Yale University Press, 1965.
Duhl, L. (Ed.) *The urban condition: People and policy in the metropolis.* New York: Basic Books, 1963.
Ewald, W. R., Jr. (Ed.) *Environment for man: The next fifty years.* Bloomington: Indiana University Press, 1967.
Fiske, W., & Maddi, S. R. (Eds.) *Functions of varied experience.* Homewood, Ill.: Dorsey Press, 1961.
Gans, H. J. Effects of the move from city to suburb. In L. Duhl (Ed.), *The urban condition: People and policy in the metropolis.* New York: Basic Books, 1963.
Gilligan, J. P. (Ed.) *Wilderness and recreation.* (Study Report No. 3) Washington, D.C.: Outdoor Recreation Resources Review Commission, 1962.
Gould, P. R. Structuring information on spatio-temporal preferences. *Journal of Regional Science,* 1967, **7,** 259–274.
Gunderson, E. K. E. Emotional symptoms in extremely isolated groups. *Archives of General Psychiatry,* 1963, **9,** 362–368.
Gunderson, E. K. E. Mental health problems in antarctica. *Archives of Environmental Health,* 1968, **17,** 558–564.
Gutman, R. Site planning and social behavior. *Journal of Social Issues,* 1966, **22,** 103–115.
Hall, E. T. *The hidden dimension.* Garden City, N.Y.: Doubleday, 1966.
Helson, H. *Adaptation-level theory.* New York: Harper & Row, 1964.
Kates, R. W., & Wohlwill, J. F. (Eds.) Man's response to the physical environment. *Journal of Social Issues,* 1966, 22(4), 1–140.
Lynch, K. *The image of the city.* Cambridge, Mass.: Harvard University Press and M.I.T. Press, 1960.

McCarroll, J. E., Mitchell, K. M., Carpenter, R. J., & Anderson, J. P. Analysis of three stimulation-seeking scales. *Psychological Reports*, 1967, **21**, 853–856.

Rapoport, A., & Kantor, R. E. Complexity and ambiguity in environmental design. *Journal of the American Institute of Planners*, 1967, **33**, 210–221.

Rossi, P. H. *Why families move: A study in the social psychology of urban residential mobility.* Glencoe, Ill.: Free Press, 1965.

Selye, H. The general adaptation syndrome and the diseases of adaptation. *Journal of Clinical Endocrinology*, 1946, **6**, 117–230.

Shafer, E. L., Jr. Perception of natural environments. *Environment and Behavior*, 1969, 1, 71–82.

Sommer, R. Personal space. Englewood Cliffs, N.J.: Prentice-Hall, 1969.

Sonnenfeld, J. Variable values in space landscape: An inquiry into the nature of environmental necessity. *Journal of Social Issues*, 1966, **22**, 71–82.

Sonnenfeld, J. Environmental perception and adaptation level in the arctic. In D. Lowenthal (Ed.), *Environmental perception and behavior.* (Department of Geography Research Paper No. 109) Chicago: University of Chicago Press, 1967.

Spilhaus, A. The experimental city. *Science*, 1968, **159**, 710–715.

Stea, D. Reasons for our moving. *Landscape*, 1967, **17**, 27–28.

Stea, D. Environmental perception and cognition: Towards a model for "mental maps." In G. J. Coates & K. M. Moffett (Eds.), *Response to environment.* (*Student Publications,* Vol. 18) Raleigh: School of Design, North Carolina State University, 1969.

Thomas, W. L., Jr. (Ed.) *Man's role in changing the face of the earth.* Chicago: University of Chicago Press, 1956.

Walker, E. L. Psychological complexity as a basis for a theory of motivation and choice. *Nebraska Symposium on Motivation*, 1964, **12**, 47–95.

Wohlwill, J. F. The physical environment: A problem for a psychology of stimulation. *Journal of Social Issues*, 1966, **22**, 29–38.

Wohlwill, J. F. Amount of stimulus exploration and preference as differential functions of stimulus complexity. *Perception and Psychophysics*, 1968, **4**, 307–312. (a)

Wohlwill, J. F. Man as a seeker and neutralizer of stimulation. Presented at the Sanitarian's Institute of Environmental Quality Management, University of Connecticut, December 1968. (b)

Wolpert, J. Migration as an adjustment to environmental stress. *Journal of Social Issues*, 1966, **22**, 92–102.

Wright, H. F. The city-town project: Interim research report. Unpublished manuscript, University of Kansas, 1961.

Yarrow, L. J. Maternal deprivation: Toward an empirical and conceptual reevaluation. *Psychological Bulletin*, 1961, **58**, 459–490.

UNIT THIRTEEN | DISCUSSION QUESTIONS

46 | INTRODUCTION TO PSYCHOLINGUISTICS

What is the role of linguistic science in the psychology of language? Discuss.

Discuss the kinds of research problems psycholinguists encounter.

47 | THE PSYCHOLOGIST IN INTERNATIONAL AFFAIRS

Discuss some of the basic ideas of Osgood's "Graduated and Reciprocated Initiatives in Tension-Reduction (GRIT)."

Osgood suggests several "actions" for a more peaceful world. In what ways do you agree or disagree with his suggestions?

48 | INDUSTRY: A PLACE TO STUDY HUMAN BEHAVIOR

Discuss the kinds of human behavior decisions studied by industrial psychologists.

In what ways does engineering psychology differ from organizational psychology?

49 | THE EMERGING DISCIPLINE OF ENVIRONMENTAL PSYCHOLOGY

Discuss the interrelationship between behavior and environment.

What do you consider to be the challenge for psychology in the study of the environment? Support your selection.

UNIT FOURTEEN
ADDITIONAL CONTEMPORARY ISSUES
IN PSYCHOLOGY

Psychology has emerged as an outgrowth of philosophical tenets. Controversies of the 1920's centered about such topics as the presence or absence of instincts in man, the dichotomy of mind and matter, and the value of introspection as a scientific tool. The confrontation of issues such as these was necessary to the development of later psychological theories. Sciences thrive on controversy. The 1970's find behavioral scientists involved in a wide array of problems facing this nation. At the present time, there are more than 30,000 American psychologists involved in a myriad of activities. The fact that the American Psychological Association (APA) is subdivided into twenty-nine divisions* testifies to the diversity that exists within the field.

This unit is a potpourri of issues not covered elsewhere in this volume. It covers the areas of homosexuality, psychological effects of racism, IQ controversy, and predictions about the future of behavioral science.

Irving Bieber's *Speaking Frankly On A Once Taboo Subject* dispels some of the common beliefs regarding homosexuality. Bieber feels that in order to prevent the development of childhood homosexual symptoms, it is necessary to consider the behavior of parents.

Kenneth B. Clark's *The Psychology of the Ghetto,* outlines various defense mechanisms of the black American. He further discusses the black matriarchy and the distorted black masculine image.

During 1969, Dr. Arthur R. Jensen's view of heredity as a determinant of intelligence initiated anew one of the oldest disputes in psychology—nature versus nurture. *Science News* in "Genetics versus Headstart" gives some background information about the IQ dispute and presents opposing views.

Finally, Gardner Murphy explores 10 topics that he feels will have significance for *Psychology In The Year 2000*. Murphy feels that the twenty-first century can offer less terror and more joy only if psychologists learn both "how to look inside and how to look outside" in their study of human behavior.

---

*   See the Introduction to Unit One for a listing of these divisions.

50 | SPEAKING FRANKLY ON A ONCE TABOO SUBJECT

Irving Bieber

Until recently, homosexuality was a taboo subject in most households. In many families, it still is—just as cancer was only a short time ago. As a practicing psychiatrist, I am glad that the discussion of homosexuality is moving more and more from the old hush-hush atmosphere into the open. This increasing candor benefits everybody. For, uncomfortable as many people feel when the problem is talked about, nothing less than our self-interest as parents and enlightened citizens demands it. Our children can be helped by such discussion, and I believe we owe it to them to use our constantly developing insight into the problem so that in the future they may fulfill their roles as healthy men and women.

The discussion has been hampered by something even more basic than our discomfort. There still is much that science doesn't know about homosexuality; that is, continuing erotic activity between members of the same sex. Even the number of homosexuals in the United States is unknown. At a guess, there are about two million. What is far more important is that many—perhaps most—are desperately unhappy about it. Fortunately, new research indicates that homosexuality can, in many instances, be headed off during childhood and adolescence. And it is parents who are usually in the best possible position to prevent homosexual tendencies from developing in their youngsters in the first place.

Few parents know how to go about this, yet science today can give them guidelines to help relieve much human misery.

Like most researchers interested in homosexuality, I have long been impressed by the gnawing frustrations, which chronically cast a shadow over the lives of these patients. Homosexual relationships are generally turbulent and shortlived. Few last more than a matter of months or a year or two. Moreover, we know that most homosexuals live in constant fear of exposure which can result in loss of employment as well as social ostracism or even imprisonment. Every child, then, who can be guided away from prehomosexual influences is being spared untold pain as an adult.

In the present state of our knowledge, this is a delicate task indeed. Many uncertainties remain. Some responsible researchers still believe, for example, that a predisposition to homosexuality can be inborn, perhaps because of hereditary factors or such physical characteristics as frailness in boys or unusual sturdiness in girls. Nor do we know all that we should about the consequences of exposing children to young homosexual classmates or to the sizable homosexual communities in our large cities.

However, there is increasing evidence that all adult homosexuals were normal infants and that their sexual maladjustment is caused by unhealthy relationships with their parents.

Personally, I came to this conclusion after completing a study in which 77 psychoanalysts supplied detailed information on 206 men. This was a nine-year investigation conducted under my chairmanship by a research committee of eight members of the Society of Medical Psychoanalysts, plus a clinical psychologist and a social psychologist. One particularly vital fact emerged from our research: it is highly improbable that a family will produce a homosexual if at least one parent has a reasonably sound relationship with the child.

While we can now pinpoint some specific danger signals for parents to watch for, both within themselves and their children, it is easy to become over-zealous in the search for symptoms and arouse concern and suspicions where none are warranted. This is not an area for angry parental accusations or anxious questioning.

Before outlining the signs of impending danger in the development of children, then, let me dispel some widespread misconceptions.

First, the male homosexual is popularly thought to be effeminate and sissyish; the female homosexual is almost invariably pictured as a tough (if man-hating) masculine type. The confusing and uncomfortable truth is that only a minority of homosexuals conform to these stereotypes. Most male homosexuals are by no means effeminate and most Lesbians don't look like Amazons. Sexually normal people (heterosexuals) by and large have no way of identifying most homosexuals. Homosexuals, on the other hand, recognize each other through characteristic language and subtle behavior cues and patterns; they usually adopt these without even being consciously aware of it.

Second, again contrary to common belief, homosexuality is not a trait that develops because of individual choice. Essentially, it comes about because homosexuals have been conditioned, from early life, to be afraid of long-term romantic relationships with the opposite sex. They avoid normal sexual activity because they have developed overwhelming fears of their sexual capability and enjoyment with members of the opposite sex. Having been thus cut off from the normal channels for romantic and sexual gratification, homosexuals seek it with members of their own sex. Nevertheless, although basic sexual urges may thus be fulfilled to varying degrees, a feeling of complete attainment of romantic longings probably never occurs. This is one important reason why nearly all homosexual relationships turn out to be frustrating.

To prevent childhood homosexual symptoms from developing—or possibly even to "immunize" youngsters against them—it is necessary to consider the behavior of parents.

We know, for instance, that mothers of male homosexuals usually behave in characteristic and abnormal ways. They are overly intimate with their sons. They are also excessively possessive, over-protective and inclined to discourage the son's masculine ways. In families with more than one child, the mother generally favors the prehomosexual son. One mother of a patient who showed clear signs of homosexuality by the age of 6, had begun quite deliberately, as far back as his birth, to make a "sissy" out of him simply because she already had one son and had badly wanted her second child to be a girl.

Such a mother spends an inordinate amount of time with the favored son and demands that he be unusually attentive to her. She may encourage an alliance with him against his father and often openly prefers the son to her husband.

There is more to this unhealthy pattern. Mothers of homosexuals frequently make their sons their principal confidants sometimes even in sexual matters. They interfere with the boy's heterosexual interests in childhood and adolescence, often by discouraging their sons from dating. If the sons show interest in girls, the mothers quickly find fault with them and usually succeed in disrupting the relationships ("You can't trust women; all they want is a meal ticket"). Typically, these mothers baby their sons by being excessively concerned about illness and injuries and tend to discourage participation in sports and other boyhood activities, presumably out of concern for their sons' welfare.

A boy with prehomosexual tendencies responds to this kind of mothering by becoming submissive. Typically, he is likely to worry excessively about displeasing his mother or hurting her feelings. That this is a very big worry indeed to such a boy is not at all surprising. After all, his whole life has led him to believe that his mother is the center of his world, and usually he loves and admires her out of all proportion. He turns to his mother—and only rarely to his father—for protection against his many fears.

Mothers of homosexuals, incidentally, are usually inadequate wives. They tend to dominate and minimize their husbands and frequently hold them more or less openly in contempt. The plain fact is that, unconsciously, these mothers are engaged in romances with their sons. Sometimes this shows itself in seductive behavior toward prehomosexual boys.

We have come to learn that fathers of most homosexuals also tend to behave in typical ways. They are usually unaffectionate and spend little time with their boys. You don't find many homosexuals whose fathers took them on camping trips or to baseball games. The prehomosexual son reacts to his father's indifference or hostility with fear, lack of respect and sometimes even hatred. Perhaps most damaging of all, he does not see in his father a masculine image with whom he can identify. In fact, he tries to be as much unlike his father as possible. It stands to reason, therefore, that homosexual sons (or heterosexual sons with severe homosexual problems) are most likely to develop in families where mothers are close-binding, intimate and seductive toward their sons and at the same time dominate their husbands who are detached or hostile as fathers.

Here is a fairly characteristic case from our study "Homosexuality," (Basic Books, Inc.). The patient was a 35-year-old college professor who was severely depressed, drank heavily and threatened to commit suicide. He was an only son. As a child, he lived in a small New England city. His mother was beautiful and pridefully traced her ancestry to early American colonists. Her father had always hoped she would marry a man of social distinction. Instead, she married the patient's father, who owned a little haberdashery.

The mother never set foot in the store; it was clearly beneath her. Neither did the son, who was being brought up by the mother to fancy himself a young gentleman and scholar. The patient was ashamed of his father's occupation. He took pains to conceal it from his college friends. While the boy was small, the father occasionally tried (if not too hard) to have the boy accompany him on hunting and fishing trips.

But the mother always found excuses to prevent such masculine activities. Moreover, the boy was very badly beaten by his mother when she found him, at the age of 6, playing mildly sexual games with a little girl. Thereafter, the youngster stopped playing with girls.

By the age of 12, he was an active homosexual. It was only after more than 20 years of self-torture and four years of intensive psychiatric treatment that he became —and now is—a normally married man.

Our knowledge of prehomosexual girls is more limited. Detailed studies of sufficiently large samples of female homosexuals have not yet been reported, but present evidence indicates that this condition, too, is caused by destructive psychological conditions within the family. Again, certain telltale patterns exist. Mothers of female homosexuals are usually hostile and extremely competitive with these daughters. These girls are rarely taught feminine behavior by learning how to cook, sew or perform other homemaking functions. They may not even be permitted in the kitchen while Mama presides over the stove and exercises her role as Queen Bee. Of course, tailored suits without frills and ribbons are not necessarily unfeminine. And homosexual girls do not necessarily wear severe clothes. Many, however, are not *becomingly* dressed by their mothers.

The mother of the prehomosexual girl is unconsciously envious and openly critical of her daughter. She is likely to ignore evidence of the girl's grace, but she will be eager to criticize any show of clumsiness. With such mothers, beautiful girls learn to underestimate their own attractiveness; and plain girls come to consider themselves ugly ducklings.

Fathers may behave in an openly possessive or seductive manner toward their daughters or may reject them completely. These fathers commonly side with their wives against their daughters in family disputes. They usually fail to be protective whenever the mothers are treating their daughters unfairly or destructively.

Thus, one parent (and usually both) interferes with the child's natural sex identification and in a romantic interest in the opposite sex.

How should parents behave to discourage prehomosexual tendencies? First, it is essential for a child's normal development that a mother be able to demonstrate affection toward her son and show respect for his masculine needs and behavior. She should be able to kiss, hug and pet her son and not be afraid of physical contact with him; then her maternal respect for her son's masculinity permits her to recognize that he will respond sexually as a male. Therefore she won't habitually undress before him, bathe him once he can do this for himself or intrude on his privacy in the bathroom or bedroom. She won't permit inappropriate sleeping arrangements, such as sleeping in the same bed with him or sharing the parental bedroom with him or assigning him to the same bedroom as his sisters. She will encourage his participation in activities typical of boys his age. Correspondingly, fathers should be able to demonstrate affection toward their children and behave so they will show recognition, respect and approval of a daughter's femininity and of a son's masculinity.

All children pass through a phase in which boys compete with fathers and girls with their mothers. A girl may accuse her mother of being homely, useless and suggest that mommy may as well leave; *she* will take care of daddy. She may demand new clothes each time her mother buys something new for herself. The boy may minimize his father, "playfully" hit him with full force or try to out-do his father whenever an opportunity presents itself, perhaps when playing cards or football. Children may also become cross and resentful when they witness a parental embrace and try to break it up.

This kind of behavior is entirely normal. Understanding parents react to this phase good-humoredly, lovingly and wisely. Without permitting the child to become disrespectful, they help him work through these problems. On the other hand, parents who make the mistake of entering into competition with their children— fathers with sons, mothers with daughters—intimidate the youngsters and distort their personality development, both sexual and social. Among homosexuals, the cross-sex parent is almost always competitive with this child.

What about children for whom a homosexual pattern has been set? With the development of modern techniques of psychotherapy, homosexuality is now a treatable condition. The younger the homosexual, the more favorable the outlook for cure. For best results, treatment is best begun before active homosexual behavior has started and before a deviant sexual pattern becomes firmly established. Parents who have reason to suspect homosexual tendencies in a child should consult their family physician who may refer them to a psychiatrist or to any agency specializing in family problems. Teachers are likewise in a favorable position to observe behavior typical of prehomosexual children and should bring such problems to the attention of parents and school personnel who can assist in referring the child for help—always keeping in mind that their suspicions may be unfounded and that the diagnosis can only be established through qualified professional channels.

Much can be done to prevent the chronic suffering of homosexuality, but science can do nothing unless parents look searchingly and honestly within themselves and into their relationship with their youngsters.

51 | THE PSYCHOLOGY OF THE GHETTO

Kenneth B. Clark

It is now generally understood that chronic and remediable social injustices corrode and damage the human personality, thereby robbing it of its effectiveness, of its creativity, if not its actual humanity. No matter how desperately one seeks to deny it, this simple fact persists and intrudes itself. It is the fuel of protests and revolts. Racial segregation, like all other forms of cruelty and tyranny, debases all human beings—those who are its victims, those who victimize, and in quite subtle ways those who are merely accessories.

This human debasement can only be comprehended as a consequence of the society which spawns it. The victims of segregation do not initially desire to be segregated, they do not "prefer to be with their own people," in spite of the fact that this belief is commonly stated by those who are not themselves segregated. A most cruel and psychologically oppressive aspect and consequence of enforced segregation is that its victims can be made to accommodate to their victimized status and under certain circumstances to state that it *is* their desire to set apart, or to agree that subjugation is not really detrimental but beneficial. The fact remains that exclusion, rejection, and a stigmatized status are not desired and are not voluntary states. Segregation is neither sought nor imposed by healthy or potentially healthy human beings.

Human beings who are forced to live under ghetto conditions and whose daily experience tells them that almost nowhere in society are they respected and granted the ordinary dignity and courtesy accorded to others will, as a matter of course, begin to doubt their own worth. Since every human being depends upon his cumulative experiences with others for clues as to how he should view and value himself, children who are consistently rejected understandably begin to question and doubt whether they, their family, and their group really deserve no more respect from the larger society than they receive. These doubts become the seeds of a pernicious self- and group-hatred, the Negro's complex and debilitating prejudice against himself.

The preoccupation of many Negroes with hair straighteners, skin bleachers, and the like illustrates this tragic aspect of American racial prejudice—Negroes have come to believe in their own inferiority. In recent years Negro men and women have rebelled against the constant struggle to become white and have given special emphasis to their "Negroid" features and hair textures in a self-conscious acceptance of "negritude"—a wholehearted embracing of the African heritage. But whether a Negro woman uses hair straightener or whether she highlights her natural hair texture by flaunting *au naturel* styles, whether a Negro man hides behind a neat Ivy League suit or wears blue jeans defiantly in the manner of the Student Nonviolent Coordinating Committee (SNCC), each is still reacting primarily to the pervasive factor of race and still not free to take himself for granted or to judge himself by the usual standards of personal success and character. It is still the white man's society that governs the Negro's image of himself.

FANTASY PROTECTIONS

Many Negroes live sporadically in a world of fantasy, and fantasy takes different forms at different ages. In childhood the delusion is a simple one—the child may pretend that he is really white. When Negro children as young as three years old are shown white- and Negro-appearing dolls or asked to color pictures of children to look like themselves, many of them tend to reject the dark-skinned dolls as "dirty" and "bad" or to color the picture of themselves a light color or a bizarre shade like purple. But the fantasy is not complete, for when asked to identify which doll is like themselves, some Negro children, particularly in the North, will refuse, burst into tears, and run away. By the age of seven most Negro children have accepted the reality that they are, after all, dark skinned. But the stigma remains; they have been forced to recognize themselves as inferior. Few if any Negroes ever fully lose that sense of shame and self-hatred.

To the Negro child the most serious injury seems to be in the concept of self-worth related directly to skin color itself. Because school is a central activity at this age, his sense of inferiority is revealed most acutely in his lack of confidence in himself as a student, lack of motivation to learn, and in problems of behavior—a gradual withdrawal or a growing rebellion. The effects of this early damage are difficult to overcome, for the child who never learns to read cannot become a success at a job or in a society where education and culture are necessary. In addition, there is the possibility that poor teaching, generally characteristic of the ghetto schools, tends to reinforce this sense of inferiority and to give it substance in the experience of inferior achievement. The cycle that leads to menial jobs and to broken homes has then begun; only the most drastic efforts at rehabilitation can break that cycle.

The obsession with whiteness continues past childhood and into adulthood. It stays with the Negro all his life. Haryou recorded a conversation between teen-age boys about their hair styles that reflected this obsession.

You know, if he go in there with his hair slick up like white, they might go for him better, you know.

They might use him for a broom or a mop.

Well, why do you wear "brushes?"

Why do I wear "brushes?" It's a blind, a front. Are you saying that I'm ignorant?

He's a playboy. He like to do his hair like that. He's ashamed of his own hair, you know. He feels bad that he's black and now he wants to be half and half. He wants to be a half-breed.

When your great granmammy was taken advantage of in the fields, what was happening then? Have you ever seen a light-skinned African? Have you ever seen an African your color?

No.

All right then; two bird dogs don't make nothing but a bird dog.
You don't have to go all the way, getting your hair slicked.
I don't have to go all the way black either, do I?
What are you going to do? You can't go all the way white.

Teen-age Negroes often cope with the ghetto's frustrations by retreating into fantasies related chiefly to their role in society. There is, for example, a fantasy employed by many marginal and antisocial teen-agers, to pretend to knowledge about illicit activities and to a sexual urbanity that they do not, really, have. They use as their models the petty criminals of the ghetto, whose colorful, swaggering style of cool bravado poses a peculiar fascination. Some pretend falsely to be pimps, some to have contacts with numbers runners. Their apparent admiration of these models is not total but reflects a curious combination of respect, of contempt, and, fundamentally, of despair. Social scientists who rely on questionnaires and superficial interviews must find a way to unravel this tangled web of pretense if their conclusions are to be relevant.

Among the young men observed at Haryou, fantasy played a major role. Many of these marginal, upward-striving teen-agers allowed others to believe that they were college students. One young man told his friends that he was a major in psychology. He had enrolled in the classes of a Negro professor with whom he identified, and he described those lectures in detail to his friends. The fact is that he was a dropout from high school. Others dressed like college students and went to college campuses where they walked among the students, attempting to feel a part of a life they longed for and could not attain. Some carried attaché cases wherever they went—often literally empty. One carried ordinary books camouflaged by college

bookcovers and pretended to "study" in the presence of friends. Most of these young men were academically at the fifth- or sixth-grade reading level; none was in college. Another youngster who said he was in college planned to become a nuclear physicist. He spoke most convincingly about his physics and math courses and discussed the importance of Negroes' going into the field. Within a year, however, he had been dropped for nonattendance from the evening session of the municipal college at which he was enrolled. He had not taken even a first course in physics and had not been able to pass the elementary course in mathematics. He explained this failure in a complicated story and reported that he now intended to get a job. Later he described his new job in the executive training program of a high-status department store downtown. He was saving for college where he would continue with nuclear physics. He carried an attaché case to work each day. But the truth was that he was not in an executive training program at all; he had a job as a stock clerk. Yet the fantasy was one of performance; there was truth in his dreams, for if he had been caught in time he might have become a scientist. He did have the intellectual potential. But as a Negro, he had been damaged so early in the educational process that not even the surge of motivation and his basic intelligence could now make his dreams effective. His motivation was sporadic and largely verbal; his plans were in the realm of delusion. To some, this form of social schizophrenia might seem comic, but a more appropriate response is tears, not laughter.

SEX AND STATUS

In Negro adults the sense of inadequate self-worth shows up in lack of motivation to rise in their jobs or fear of competition with whites; in a sense of impotence in civic affairs demonstrated in lethargy toward voting, or community participation, or responsibility for others; in family instability and the irresponsibility rooted in hopelessness.

But, because, in American life, sex is, like business advancement, a prime criterion of success and hence of personal worth, it is in sexual behavior that the damage to Negro adults shows up in especially poignant and tragic clarity. The inconsistency between the white society's view of the Negro as inferior and its sexual exploitation of Negroes has seemed to its victims a degrading hypocrisy. Negroes observe that ever since slavery white men have regarded Negroes as inferior and have condemned interracial marriage while considering illicit sexual relationships with Negro women appropriate to their own higher status. The white man in America has, historically, arranged to have both white and Negro women available to him; he has claimed sexual priority with both and, in the process, he has sought to emasculate Negro men. Negro males could not hold their women, nor could they defend them. The white male tried to justify this restriction of meaningful competition with the paradoxical claim that Negro males were animal-like and brutish in their appetites and hence to be feared and shunned by white women. The ironic fact has been that, given the inferiority of their racial status, Negro males have had to struggle simply to believe themselves men. It has long been an "inside" bit of bitter humor among Negroes to say that Negro men should bribe their wives to silence.

Certain Negro women of status who have married white men report that their choice was related to their discovery that the Negro men they knew were inferior in status, interests, and sophistication and hence unsuitable as partners. Many problems of race and sex seem to follow this principle of the self-fulfilling prophecy. The Negro woman of status may see the Negro male as undesirable as a sexual partner precisely because of his low status in the eyes of whites. Unlike a white female who may reassure herself that the lower the status of the male, the more satisfying he is as a sexual partner, the upper-class Negro female tends to tie sexual desirability to status and exclude many Negro males as undesirable just because their status is inferior. It is a real question whether this "discovery" is based on fact or whether these women are not accepting the white society's assumption of the low status of Negro men and therefore expecting them to be weak. On the other hand, frustrated, thrill-seeking white males or females who have been told all their lives that Negroes are primitive and uninhibited may seek and find sexual fulfillment among the same Negroes who are cool, distant, or hostile in their relationship to other Negroes. In sexual matters it appears that those who expect weakness or gratification often find what they expect.

As Negro male self-esteem rises in the wake of the civil rights movement, one interesting incidental fact is that any Negro woman who is known to be the mistress of a white public official—and particularly any mistress of a segregationist—has been put under a growing pressure to break that relationship. In the past, Negroes tended to suppress their bitterness about such illicit relationships, accepting the white male's evaluation of himself and of them, and in a sense forgiving the Negro woman for submitting to the temptation of protection and economic gain. In the last decade, however, Negro mistresses of white officials are more openly rejected and are regarded as one of the "enemy."

White men were accustomed to possessing Negro women without marriage, but today the fact that a number of white men are married to Negro women of status, particularly those who are well known in the theatrical world, indicates that Negro women are placing higher value upon their own dignity than many other Negro women were permitted to in the past—and so are the white men who marry them. But, though a Negro woman may gain status by marrying into the white community, Negro men, even in the North, remain vulnerable if they seek to cross racial lines and to break this most fearsome of social taboos. When they have done so they have paid a tremendous price—lynching, murder, or a prison sentence in the South, social condemnation in the North—but, above all, the price of their own self-doubt and anxiety. The full complexity of social disapproval and personal doubt is difficult to resist psychologically even when the law allows and protects such nonconformist behavior.

The emerging, more affirmative sexual pride among Negro males may have as one of its consequences an increasing trend toward more open competition between white and Negro males for both white and Negro females. One of the further consequences would probably be an intensification of hostility of white males toward interracial couples and toward the white female participants, reflecting the desire on the part of the white male to preserve his own competitive advantage. One would expect him then to employ his economic and political power—without suspecting the fundamental basis of his antagonism—to maintain the inferior status of the Negro male for as long as possible. An important level of racial progress will have been reached when Negro and white men and women may marry anyone they choose, without punishment, ostracism, ridicule, or guilt.

THE NEGRO MATRIARCHY AND THE DISTORTED MASCULINE IMAGE

Sexual hierarchy has played a crucial role in the structure and pathology of the Negro family. Because of the system of slavery in which the Negro male was systematically used as a stud and the Negro female used primarily for purposes of breeding or for the gratification of the white male, the only source of family continuity was through the female, the dependence of the child on his mother. This pattern, together with the continued post-slavery relegation of the Negro male to menial and subservient status, has made the female the dominant person in the Negro family, Psychologically, the Negro male could not support his normal desire for dominance. For the most part he was not allowed to be a consistent wage earner; he could not present himself to his wife and children as a person who had the opportunity or the ability to compete successfully in politics, business, and industry. His doubts concerning his personal adequacy were therefore reinforced. He was compelled to base his self-esteem instead on a kind of behavior that tended to support a stereotyped picture of the Negro male—sexual impulsiveness, irresponsibility, verbal bombast, posturing, and compensatory achievement in entertainment and athletics, particularly in sports like boxing in which athletic prowess could be exploited for the gain of others. The Negro male was, therefore, driven to seek status in ways which seemed either antisocial, escapist, socially irresponsible. The pressure to find relief from his intolerable psychological position seems directly related to the continued high incidence of desertions and broken homes in Negro ghettos.

The Negro woman has, in turn, been required to hold the family together; to set the goals, to stimulate, encourage, and to protect both boys and girls. Her compensatory strength tended to perpetuate the weaker role of the Negro male. Negro boys had the additional problem of finding no strong male father figure upon which to model their own behavior, perhaps one of the reasons for the prevalent idea among marginal Negroes that it is not masculine to sustain a stable father or husband relationship with a woman. Many young men establish temporary liaisons with a number of different women with no responsibility toward any. Among Negro teen-agers the cult of going steady has never had the vogue it seems to have among white teen-agers; security for Negroes is found not in a relationship modeled after a stable family—for they have seen little of this in their own lives—but upon the relationship they observed in their own home: unstable and temporary liaisons. The marginal young Negro male tends to identify his masculinity with the number of girls he can attract. The high incidence of illegitimacy among Negro young people reflects this pervasive fact. In this compensatory distortion of the male image, masculinity is, therefore, equated with alleged sexual prowess.

The middle-class white and Negro male often separates women into two categories, good women with whom he will go steady and marry, and others with whom he has and will continue to have sexual relations alone. The lower-class Negro is, in a way, more sophisticated than either in his refusal to make undemocratic distinctions between "good girls" and "others." The consistently higher illegitimacy rate among Negroes is not a reflection of less virtue or greater promiscuity, but rather of the fact that the middle-class teen-agers are taught the use of contraceptives and learn how to protect themselves from the hazards of premarital and illicit sexual contacts. The middle-class girl is able to resort to abortions, or she gives birth secretly, surrendering the child for adoption. In the case of marginal young people, or the upwardly mobile Negro, what contraceptive ideas he has are unreliable; and rarely does the girl participate in protection, in part because it is taken as a sign of masculinity for the male to supervise such matters. Illegitimacy among these groups, therefore, is a consequence, in large part, of poverty and ignorance.

Among Negro middle-class families the attitude toward sex is vastly different from that among marginal and lower-class Negro groups. The middle-class Negro fears he will be identified with the Negro masses from whom he has escaped or tried to escape, and sex is a focal point of anxiety. The middle-class girl is often so rigidly protected that normal sexual behavior is inhibited, or she learns to be sophisticated about the use of contraceptives. For her, as for white middle-class girls, sex is tied to status and aspirations. She wants to make a good marriage—marriage to a white man might even be available—and the motivation to avoid illegitimate pregnancy is great.

The marginal young people in the ghetto, through their tentative and sporadic relationships, are seeking love, affection, and acceptance perhaps more desperately than young people elsewhere. Person-to-person relationships are, for many, a compensation for society's rejection. They are, in a sense, forced to be quite elemental in their demands, and sex becomes more important for them than even they realize. They act in a cavalier fashion about their affairs, trying to seem casual and cool, but it is clear nonetheless that they are dominated by the complexity of their needs.

The girl, like the boy, has no illusions. Unlike the middle-class girl who believes —or demands—that each relationship should be forever, and who tries to hold on to the boy, the marginal Negro lower-class girl is realistic about the facts of the situation. Nor does she expect to hold the boy. Sex is important to her, but it is not, as in middle-class society, a symbol of status, to be used to rise into a better family or a higher income bracket. The marginal Negro female uses her sex, instead, to gain personal affirmation. She is desired, and that is almost enough. The relationship, whatever its social and psychological limitations, is pure in the same sense as innocence—that is, it is not contaminated by other goals. For her and for the boy, sex is time-contained, with its own intrinsic worth and value, not animal in its expression, but related to the urgent human need for acceptance; it is sophisticated, not primitive.

This innocent sophistication includes the total acceptance of the child if a child comes. In the ghetto, the meaning of the illegitimate child is not ultimate disgrace. There is not the demand for abortion or for surrender of the child that one finds in more privileged communities. In the middle class, the disgrace of illegitimacy is tied to personal and family aspirations. In lower-class families, on the other hand, the girl loses only some of her already limited options by having an illegitimate child; she is not going to make a "better marriage" or improve her economic and social status either way. On the contrary, a child is a symbol of the fact that she is a woman, and she may gain from having something of her own. Nor is the boy who fathers an illegitimate child to lose, for where is he going? The path to any higher status seems closed to him in any case.

Illegitimacy in the ghetto cannot be understood or dealt with in terms of punitive hostility, as in the suggestion that unwed mothers be denied welfare if illegitimacy is repeated. Such approaches obscure, with empty and at times hypocritical moralizing, the desperate yearning of the young for acceptance and identity, the need to be meaningful to some one else even for a moment without implication of a pledge of undying fealty and foreverness. If, when the girl becomes pregnant, the boy deserts or refuses to marry her, it is often because neither can sustain an intimate relationship; both seem incapable of the tenderness that continues beyond immediate gratification. Both may have a realistic, if unconscious, acceptance of the fact that nothing else is possible; to expect—to ask—for more would be to open oneself to the inevitable rejections, hurts, and frustrations. The persistent experience of rejection spills over into the anticipation and acceptance of rejection in a love relationship. This lack of illusion stems from the fact that there can be no illusion in any other area of life. To expose oneself further to the chances of failure in a sustained and faithful relationship is too large a risk. The intrinsic value of the relationship is the only value because there can be no other.

Among most lower-class Negroes, competition in sex is predominantly heterosexual and free. In the Negro middle class sexual freedom and expression are often identified with lower-class status, and many men and women are therefore governed chiefly by their inhibitions and cannot act freely in matters of sex. The men may be impotent, the women frigid, and both afflicted with guilt. Some compensate for the restraints on sexual adequacy and fulfillment through fantasies and boasting about a false prowess. Other middle-class Negro men retreat into noncommittal peripheral relationships with women, avoiding all alternatives—homosexuality, heterosexuality, or verbal bombasts—as risks requiring more ego strength than their resources permit. Instead, a blank and apathetic sexlessness dominates their lives. They withdraw from all commitment to another person seeking refuge from the dangers of personal vulnerability.

Considering the depth and the complexity of the need, aggressive sexual behavior may, for many of the racially damaged, make the difference between personal stability and instability. Until the lower-class Negro is free to compete for and to win the socially acceptable rewards of middle-class society, the ghetto's pattern of venereal disease, illegitimacy, and family instability will remain unbroken. But when that time comes, no one can expect destructive sexual activity to cease abruptly. What is more likely is a shift to another, some would say "higher," level of behavior; then the Negro's sexual "misbehavior" will be indistinguishable in all respects from that of the respectables—with full participation in divorce, abortions, adultery, and the various forms of jaded and fashionable middle- and upper-class sexual explorations. There might even be the possibility of sexual fulfillment and health.

WHITE RATIONALIZATIONS

It is now rare even for the most ardent apologist for the *status quo* seriously to assert that the American pattern of segregation has beneficial consequences. Some do, however, continue to argue that the Negro's inferiority and inherent character defects demand that he be segregated. Others suggest that the chances of his developing those traits and characteristics which would make him more acceptable to the white community would be greater if he would function within his own community until he demonstrates that he is worthy of associating with others. Among the questions which remain unanswered by this type of argument are: Under what circumstances is the Negro ever adjudged worthy or deserving of association with others, and how can he be expected to develop these traits of "worthiness" under conditions which tend to perpetuate characteristics of unworthiness as described by the proponents of this position themselves? In the belief no doubt that this was a statement of compassion, one white opponent of New York's school integration plan said: "If I were God, what would I do to improve the lot of the Negro? If I were God, I'd make everybody white."* To sensitive Negroes, this betrays the ultimate condescension—the belief that to *be* Negro means irrevocable rejection.

Even this point of view is not logically consistent, since the same individuals who reject Negroes as offensive have no difficulty, as we have noted above, in accepting Negroes in close and at times intimate association and relationship, for example, as servants or menials or mistresses, as long as the inferior position of the Negro and the dominant position of the white is clearly perceived and accepted by both.

The answers to these questions cannot be found in any single devil—but must be sought in the compliant or accessory role of many in society. However, more privileged individuals understandably may need to shield themselves from the inevitable conflict and pain which would result from their acceptance of the fact that they *are* accessories to profound injustice. The tendency to discuss disturbing social issues such as racial discrimination, segregation, and economic exploitation in detached, legal, political, socio-economic, or psychological terms as if these persistent problems did not involve the suffering of actual human beings is so contrary to empirical evidence that it must be interpreted as a protective device. After World War II, the bulk of the German people *could not know* what was going on in the death camps. The people of Mississippi *had to believe* in 1964 that the disappearance and death of the three civil rights workers in that state was a diversionary strategy plotted by civil rights groups. Negroes generally expected that a grand jury in New York City *would have found* that it was justifiable homicide performed in the line of duty for a white policeman to kill a fifteen-year-old Negro boy who was "attacking him with a penknife." Insensitivity is a protective device. Among its more primitive examples are: The prevalent beliefs that the predicament of the masses of Negros reflects their inherent racial inferiority; that the poor are to blame for the squalor and despair of the slums; that the victims of social injustice are somehow subhuman persons who cause and perpetuate their own difficulties; that the more responsible and superior people of the society not only have no obligation for the "irresponsibles" but must be vigilant to see that all of the power of government is used to protect them and their children from them; and that any contrary or compassionate interpretation of the plight of the poor or the rejected is merely the sentinel and naive expression of impractical do-gooders or "bleeding hearts."

More subtle and obscure forms of protection against facing the consequences of social injustice are to be found among those social scientists who cultivate that degree of academic detachment which blocks meaningful or insightful study of human affairs. The preoccupation with trivia—as if this were the ultimate scientific virtue and goal—leads to the irrelevance of much social science research. It is interesting to speculate on the significance of the fact that during the ten years after the U.S. Supreme Court school desegregation decision, an increasing number of social scientists have raised questions concerning the "scientific validity" of the psychological and sociological data cited by the Court as evidence of the damage

---

*   *New York Times Magazine,* September 20, 1964, p. 122.

which segregation inflicts upon personality. Not one of these critics had questioned these data and their interpretations prior to the Court's decision, although the studies on which they were based had been published and available for critical reactions for many years prior to their use in the historic decision.

Certain students of jurisprudence have also criticized the Court's decision on the grounds that the Brown decision, which ruled that state laws requiring or permitting racial segregation in public schools violated the equal protection clause of the Fourteenth Amendment, was based upon flimsy sociological and psychological data rather than upon more stable and heretofore determining legal grounds. This, too, is a purist approach rooted in the belief that detachment or enforced distance from the human consequences of persistent injustice is objectively desirable. It may rather be of service primarily as a subconscious protection against personal pain and direct involvement in moral controversies.

The language and the emphasis of the Court's decision made any such evasion of the human costs of racial segregation quite difficult. The Court insisted upon a simple and direct statement of the reality: *

To separate them from others of similar age and qualifications solely because of their race generates a feeling of inferiority as to their status in the community that may affect their hearts and minds in a way unlikely ever to be undone. The effect of this separation on their educational opportunities was well stated by a finding in the Kansas case by a court which nevertheless felt compelled to rule against the Negro plaintiffs:

Segregation of white and colored children in public schools has a detrimental effect upon the colored children. The impact is greater when it has the sanction of the law: for the policy of separating the races is usually interpreted as denoting the inferiority of the Negro group. A sense of inferiority affects the motivation of a child to learn. Segregation with the sanction of the law, therefore, has a tendency to retard the educational and mental development of Negro children and to deprive them of some of the benefits they would receive in a racially integrated school system.

The obscuring function of legal technicalities and the equivocations of social science jargon were rejected and in their place was offered an understandable statement of the inevitable anguish of rejected and stigmatized human beings.

The pervasive need to turn one's back on any clear evidence of man's inhumanity to man exemplified in the cool objective approach is probably most clearly seen, though in a more subtle form, in the detached "professionalism" of many social workers and in the selective isolation of many psychiatrists and clinical psychologists. Some members of these "helping fields," too, have often defended as objectivity what, to the client, feels more like insensitivity. Furthermore, in their preoccupation with the problem of the individual and their insistence upon reducing him to a manageable system of assumptions, the disturbing and dehumanizing social realities behind his personal agony may be avoided. With the professional perspective which constricts social vision to the impulses, strengths, and weaknesses of the individual "client" as if these can be isolated from the injustices and pathologies of his life, these professionals need not confront the difficult problems of the nature and

---

* *Brown v. Board of Education,* 347 U.S. 483 (1954).

origin of the social injustices nor run the risks of conflict with the many vested interests which tend to perpetuate the problems of the poor and the rejected. This posture is built into the nature of their training and reinforced by their complex role as agents of the more privileged classes and the admitted and irrevocable fact of their identification with the middle classes. The professionals themselves would point out, also, that the routinizing pressure of bureaucratic procedures, and a heavy case load of human suffering dull the edge of concern and that the most sensitive among them feel, within the structure, uncertain and helpless as to how to address themselves to the problem of social change. It is not surprising, altogether, that compassion is usually sooner or later subordinated to accommodation; yet it is hard for many to understand why they are irrelevant to the root problems of the poor.

Some theorists and practitioners maintain that it is not within their power or training to attempt to help workingclass and low-status people because the problems of these people are psychosocial and, since they cannot be "reached," are not amenable to the psychotherapeutic and casework techniques thought to be helpful in working with middle-class individuals. Some professionals tend to limit their role to that of models or interpreters of the middle-class norms of speech, behavior, dress, values, and ways of handling problems and feelings. In view of their status and psychological distance, the social worker's concern to "relate to" the "client" seems pathetic in its failure of elemental empathy. The stated or unstated goal of this type of "therapeutic" relationship must then become that of helping the client "adjust" to his life realities, i.e., to keep him from "acting out" his rebellion in antisocial or self-destructive ways and thereby to function more effectively *within* the continuing pathology of his society. These goals are consistent with the *status quo* convenience of the middle class. They are consistent with the benign artificiality of response from these professionals which repels the members of the working class, for whom the immediate and pressing realities of their daily lives alone seem relevant. That middle-class individuals are not equally repelled may be an indication of the extent to which pretenses and protective detachment have become norms of middle-class adjustment —particularly in a society of accepted injustice. This is not to say that individual therapy is not needed and cannot be effective. It is to say that such procedures are not effective where social pathology is at the root of the individual's maladjustment. It is a real question whether adjustment or indifference to the reality of injustice is not the real neurosis, and rebellion the evidence of health.

MORAL OBJECTIVITY

Objectivity, without question essential to the scientific perspective when it warns of the dangers of bias and prejudgment in interfering with the search for truth and in contaminating the understanding of truth, too often becomes a kind of a fetish which serves to block the view of truth itself, particularly when painful and difficult moral insights are involved. The question of the nature of objectivity in law, in science, in human relationships, is complex and cannot be resolved by attempts to make it synonymous with the exclusion of feeling and value. Objectivity that implies detachment or escape from psychological reality decreases understanding and can be used merely to avoid the problem. In the social sciences, the cult of objectivity seems often to be associated with "not taking sides." When carried to its extreme, this type of objectivity could be equated with ignorance. When the social psychology department of an outstanding Eastern university received a substantial grant to endow a chair in the field of race relations, the responsible officials of that department decided that, in order to obtain the most objective person, they should consider no one who had worked extensively in the field of race relations. Indeed, they decided to appoint someone who had had no experience in this field at all, and chose a man whose major contribution to psychology was rather in the field of the experimental psychology of visual discrimination. Perhaps the guiding assumption was that the problem of American race relations was to be understood in the most fundamental terms of the capacity of the rods and cones of the human retina to differentiate color! Imagine, however, if, a chair in nuclear science were to be filled in any university, how transparently absurd it would seem to choose a man with no experience in the field, on the grounds that he thereby would be more objective! The fact that this did not seem absurd to scholars in the case of race relations is a revealing commentary. It may be that where essential human psychological and moral issues are at stake, noninvolvement and noncommitment and the exclusion of feeling are neither sophisticated nor objective, but naive and violative of the scientific spirit at its best. Where human feelings are part of the evidence, they cannot be ignored. Where anger is the appropriate response, to exclude the recognition and acceptance of anger, and even to avoid the feeling itself as if it were an inevitable contamination, is to set boundaries upon truth itself. If a scholar who studied Nazi concentration camps did not feel revolted by the evidence no one would say he was unobjective, but rather fear for his sanity and moral sensitivity. Feeling may twist judgment, but the lack of feeling may twist it even more. And to insist on quantitative measurement and analysis of certain phenomena, of, for example, love or friendship, is to distort the nature of the phenomenon itself. It is not to enlarge truth, but to constrict it.

Even to pose an hypothesis is to move away from literal objectivity, *if* objectivity is to be defined as total openmindedness. Objectivity should play a role not in the refusal to make hypotheses, but in the rigorous assessment of the evidence accumulated for that hypothesis, so as to guard, as far as possible, against any distortion of these facts. When one cares deeply what the answer to a question is, one must exercise even greater care to examine the evidence than if the answer is of no personal consequence. To refuse science the right to deal with such phenomena is to set intolerable limits, for moral decisions, like all others, should be based on fact. Responsible objectivity includes the totality of reality, not a part alone.

52 | GENETICS VS. HEADSTART

Staff of Science News

The embers of the oldest dispute in psychology—nature versus nurture—have been fanned to white heat once again, this time by a Berkeley professor. And the flames are beginning to lick through the academic woods, creating heat and even a little light.

The pyrotechnic scholar is Dr. Arthur R. Jensen, a psychologist at the University of California's School of Education.

His view of the overwhelming primacy of nature—or heredity—as a determinant of intelligence is set forth in a 123-page article in the Winter 1969 issue of the prestigious *Harvard Educational Review*.

After arguing that environmental factors are not nearly as important in determining the Intelligence Quotient as genetic factors, Dr. Jensen analyzes the environmental influences which may be most critical in determining I.Q. He concludes that prenatal influences may contribute the largest environmental factor, but genetics dominate nevertheless.

A basic finding of Dr. Jensen's research is that environment acts as what he calls a threshold variable. Extreme environmental deprivation can keep a child from performing up to his genetic potential, but an enriched educational program cannot lift him above this potential.

Dr. Jensen emphasizes the point that new educational methods must be developed which take advantage of the mental abilities of children from deprived backgrounds.

But there is more to the Jensen study than just another vote for heredity in its ancient struggle with environment for the allegiance of behavioral scientists. Dr. Jensen also contends that the Federal Government's widely publicized effort at compensatory education for the children of deprived minority groups is a failure.

He attacks what he sees as the central notion upon which these programs are based: the idea that I.Q. variations are almost completely a result of environmental differences and the cultural bias of the tests themselves (SN: 3/8, p. 243). He also argues that it would be better to teach specific skills to the children born into poverty than to try to raise their I.Q. scores through emphasis on abstract learning.

As though all this were not enough to bring the intellectual pot to a boil, Dr. Jensen speculates that social class and racial variations in intelligence cannot be accounted for by differences in environment.

"The idea that the lower average intelligence and scholastic performance of Negroes could involve not only environmental, but also genetic factors has indeed been strongly denounced," Dr. Jensen says, "but it has been neither contradicted nor discredited by evidence." And, he adds, "the fact that a reasonable hypothesis has not been rigorously proved does not mean that it should be summarily dismissed."

Asked whether he was concerned that racists might seize upon portions of his research and, by quoting them out of context, belabor those who seek to improve race relations, Dr. Jensen says: "I don't want to give these people the power of censorship over my research. I know many fine scholars who didn't submit research because of the fear that it might be misinterpreted. I think it is important that people read my article before making interpretations of it."

He observes that the part of his study that dealt with racial differentials on I.Q. scores constituted less than five per cent of the total research, although this was the part that has received the most attention. Dr. Jensen was also careful to note in his paper that "since, as far as we know, the full range of human talents is represented in all the major races of man and in all socioeconomic levels, it is unjust to allow the mere fact of an individual's racial or social background to affect the treatment of him."

Dr. Jensen's genetic explanation for intelligence variation does not satisfy Harvard's Dr. Jerome Kagan, who is among those invited by the *Review* to counter Jensen's points in the upcoming spring edition. Dr. Kagan illustrates his objections with an analogy to physical stature:

"There is no doubt that stature is inherited," he says. "Height is controlled by genetic factors. The more closely related two people are, the more similar their height. It is also true that Indian children living in the rural areas of most Central or South American countries are significantly shorter than the Indian children living in the urban areas of those countries."

According to Dr. Kagan, the flaw in Dr. Jensen's logic is that it suggests that the shorter stature of the rural children is due to a different genetic constitution.

Dr. Kagan finds the essential error in the genetic argument to be the conclusion that if a trait is under genetic control, differences between two populations on that trait must be due to genetic factors.

Prof. J. McVicker Hunt of the University of Illinois notes that the stature of human beings "appears to have increased by nearly a foot without benefit of selective breeding or natural selection."

Dr. Hunt also disagrees strongly with Dr. Jensen's assertions on genetic differences in intelligence among the races, as does Prof. Lee J. Cronbach of Stanford. "The genetic populations we call races no doubt have different distributions of whatever genes influence psychological processes," Cronbach says. "We are in no position to guess, however, which pools are inferior."

In Dr. Kagan's child psychology laboratory variations in test scores among white children of different backgrounds are observed as early as one or two years of age.

"Lower class mothers spend less time in face-to-face mutual vocalization and smiling with their infants; they do not reward the child's maturational progress, and they do not enter into long periods of play with the child," Dr. Kagan reports.

"Our theory of mental development suggests that specific absence of these experiences will retard mental growth and will lead to lower intelligence test scores."

Applying this argument to racial differences on such tests, Dr. Kagan notes that "the most likely determinants of the black child's lower I.Q. score are his experiences during the first five years of life."

Mental tests administered by Dr. Francis Palmer of the City University of New York to middle- and lower-class black children in Harlem resulted in few differences in scores after the examiners had established emotional rapport with the children. Dr. Kagan observes that such results lend support to the idea that it is important that a child understand the nature of the test he is taking, and that he feel comfortable in the presence of those who are giving him the examination.

Another objection to genetic explanations of I.Q. scores is raised by William F. Brazziel, director of general education at Virginia State College in Norfolk, who points out that "if 90 per cent of the black people in America have ancestors that include white people, how can we tell when black genes or white genes make for a wrong mark on a test score sheet?"

Dr. Jensen's criticism of Federal compensatory education programs draws a spirited dissent from Dr. Hunt. "Compensatory education has not failed," he says. "Programs which made an effort to inculcate cognitive skills, language skills and number skills show fair success. If the parents are drawn into the process, the little evidence available suggests that the effect on the children, and on the parents as well, increases in both degree and duration."

In reply to critics who charged him with failure to give compensatory education enough time to prove its case, Dr. Jensen says: "These programs have already been evaluated by the Government itself, so I think it was appropriate for me to comment on them."

53 | PSYCHOLOGY IN THE YEAR 2000

Gardner Murphy

Our profound ambivalence about human futures, and our hopes and fears regarding the possibility of intelligent planning for the future, appears in a charming phrase of Sir George Thomson. Regarding the role of science in planning for new potentialities within the human germ cell, he says that the likelihood of genetic improvements is about like the probability of improving a statue by spraying it with machine gun bullets. Instantly, however, he catches himself up in the remark that with the electron microscope, the localization of individual genes is already very close. One dares not be overbold for fear the critics will laugh, while actually the science fiction, and the casual predictions of scientists for the last hundred years or so, have been much too modest—in fact, much too myopic—as to what actually can be achieved. The best guide here is a systematic and reasonable extrapolation from identifiable trends and, at the same time, a cautious but systematic utilization of the principle of emergence in which new realities constantly come into being, not through the extrapolation of separate curves, but through specific interaction processes. Many of these new emergents are known in metallurgy, in embryology, and in the field of psychology. Some of them have to do with new perceptual and conceptual wholes as shown in countless studies of music and of painting; some of them have to do with dyadic or group patterns that come into existence when new relationships are achieved, for the first time, as shown in the dynamic leadership patterns of Lewin, White, and Lippitt. In a symposium like the present one, an ultracautious note may indeed *sound* like science, but only like the plodding science of Sir Francis Bacon's *Novum Organum,* not the creative science that indeed has remade the world, and is remaking the world through the extravagant inventiveness of a Planck and an Einstein. In this spirit, I shall attempt some predictions that, I believe, are just as likely to prove shallow and banal as to prove ultimately extravagant and exotic.

The ten topics which I shall attempt to survey are extrapolations based upon (*a*) the current extraordinary development of *psychophysiology;* (*b*) together with such psychophysiology, the new possibilities of *internal scanning,* in the discovery of the inner human world; the renewed capacity to *observe, with full objectivity, a great deal that has long been regarded as hopelessly subjective;* (*c*) herewith, the direct *confrontation of the unconscious world* that merges into, and is isomorphic with, the world of physiology; (*d*) following these discoveries, the development of *voluntary*

Gardner Murphy, "Psychology in the Year 2000," *American Psychologist* **24,** May 1969, No. 5, pp. 523–530. Copyright © 1969 by the American Psychological Association, and reproduced by permission.

Presented to the Wayne State University Centennial Symposium, Detroit, Michigan, May 10, 1968.

control over the inner world, such as scientists previously never dared to dream; (*e*) a new definition of a wide variety of nameless states, *psychological states for which there are no good names,* including feeling states, cognitive states, and volitional states, upon which human destiny almost literally may depend, with resulting understanding of those profound alterations in states of consciousness, well known to the East, regarding which Western man usually has expressed doubt or scorn; (*f*) together with these, the objective exploration of the vast sphere of *parapsychology,* at the edges of which science is nibbling, but so far has failed massively to invade; (*g*) a fresh *reconsideration of the relations of psychology to the biological sciences,* especially genetics; (*h*) a renewed *consideration of psychology in relation to the social sciences,* notably in the new science of social ecology, entailing cross-cultural collaboration of cross-cultural realities; (*i*) a note on the way in which changes in research *methods* alter all these basic concepts; (*j*) finally, a consideration, in all these terms, of the nature of the *human predicament* to which expanding science, which I am describing, may make a serious and indeed a crucial contribution.

PSYCHOPHYSIOLOGY

First, then, as to psychophysiology. Partly as a result of new concepts of the wholeness, the integrity, of the living system, as voiced for example by Sir Charles Sherrington in the *Integrative Action of the Nervous System,* and partly as a result of the sheer power of the research tools that have been developed, psychophysiology has become a dramatically new science in recent decades. Problems of specialization and subspecialization of tissues, as within the mammalian cerebral cortex, have assumed astonishing forms with Penfield's discovery of specific memory localization, with various techniques for studying the electronic functional realities inside the individual nerve cell, with X-ray studies of lattices, and with fine localization of sensory and motor function through implanted electrodes. Both the cruder spot localizations, earlier used in the study of aphasias, and also the extreme equipotentiality concepts, based largely on extirpation studies, have yielded to a dialectical reconsideration of both local and general aspects of functioning, and with an extraordinary directness of application to the world of immediate experience. Donald Hebb's brilliant breakthrough in the study of sensory deprivation has helped scientists to think of the amazing possibilities of sensory enrichment. One can no longer speak of sensory deprivation or sensory enrichment without thinking, in the manner of David Krech, about the biochemistry and physiology of the mammalian cortex, as profoundly affected by very early postnatal experience. One begins to see, quite literally, the likelihood, in the next few decades, of a thoroughgoing isomorphism of physiological process right across the board. Biochemical and neurophysiological progress has been so astonishing in the last few years that psychologists may look quite confidently for a rapidly advancing series of discoveries related specifically to the different kinds of human experience, essentially the sensory, the imaginal, the conceptual, the affective, and indeed certain types of experience that have never been analyzed finely enough to name. Psychopharmacology, long considered to be limited to the specific effects of toxins, is rapidly taking on the form of a powerful organist having at his command banks upon banks of keys, and hundreds of stops, calling into existence an incredible gamut of new experiences.

INTERNAL SCANNING

Following from, or upon, this concurrent study of psychophysiology and biochemistry on the one hand, and the phenomenal world of immediate experience and function on the other hand, psychologists will be drawn, as in a vortex, into the rich field of the study of internal scanning. By this I mean, first, the process by which delicate messages from the striped musculature can be identified more accurately as our subjects carry out reflex or skilled movements. Like a tea taster or a wine sampler, the subject, in several laboratories today, recognizes quickly the kinesthetic messages in different magnitude from different muscles. Specific muscular activities are experienced kinesthetically at the same time he sees on the panel the electronic evidence of what is occurring in specific muscle groups, so that he learns to identify and name them. He is learning, in the same way, to recognize on the panel many other messages that come from organs that are under autonomic control. One may think of the studies by the U.S.S.R. scientists, Bykov and Lisina, relating to proprioceptive and interoceptive conditioning.

But the work will soon move further along. Giving the subject feedback on a panel that shows him what specific internal activities are going on, he can be taught to make more and more refined differentiation within the inner world. His searching, his sweeping, his scanning, and his identifying of the different components from the proprioceptive world, as identical or isomorphic with the same messages from the exteroceptive world on the panel or convey to him through tones, give him more and more information as to the rich system of internal messages that have previously been nearly a blur, so precise that he can begin to play the instrument himself. The ancient prejudice that exteroceptive information has a kind of place in the reality world, which is lacking for the other sensory functions, has begun to collapse. A rich variety of internal messages has exactly the same possibility of cross-checking, consensual validation, as has held for sight, hearing, and touch. It is hard to set any limits. Something is known about discriminability when working with teas and wines, or even two-point thresholds on the finger tip, but these studies have never been pushed to their true physiological limits. Nor is it known how they are affected by a variety of parameters, anatomical distribution of receptors and afferent fibers, which in the past have never been sufficiently important to investigate; but today they are being seen in terms of individuality—an individuality based upon heredity, growth, and the learning process. A whole internal world is awaiting discovery.

CONFRONTATION OF THE UNCONSCIOUS WORLD

Third, this internal world, as Gregory Razran has pointed out, would include the entire world of the "observable unconscious," the world of psychologically meaningful, but hitherto not directly observable, processes discovered by Freud and his followers. More and more it appears to be the same world as that which anthropologists, playwrights, poets, and prophets have often enjoined without knowing, in any scientific sense, what they were doing.

But it is one thing to observe the separate components, of course, and another thing to study creatively how they can be put together into new and emergent wholes. Both Arnheim, in *Art and Visual Perception,* and Freud, in *The Interpretation of Dreams,* have applied some of the first informative steps regarding the synthesis, the creative organization, of a world that offers vast possibilities. Literally there are hundreds of experiences waiting patiently to be discovered through experimentation. It will not be just the clinicians and the "encounter" groups that will discover them; such discoveries will soon yield rich new harvests to general experimental psychology. I might remind you that while Chaucer, 600 years ago, had only a few words for colors, there are today some thousands of color terms, mostly representing *new* colors that have evolved in the last century as a result of industrial chemistry—colors that do not appear in any rainbow, natural sunset, or natural color schema. There are not only the stock experiences that human beings have by virtue of their anatomical equipment and their physiological capacity as human beings, but thousands of newly created colors. There also are many new kinds of inner experiences, ranging from the effects of new foods, drugs, smogs, exercise, fatigue, strain, anxiety, and ecstasy— scores upon scores of new kinds and shades of inner experience. Of course, many of the new methods may involve risks, and many of them will come under some sort of social control. Whether it will be control by a wise and humane Federal agency, or by public opinion, no present reliable clues are extant.

Inner responses include those called affective and impulsive states, and the vast range of expressions of mood and temperament used in the aesthetic world and in the personal world generally. There are new worlds just waiting; and they will not have to wait very long. Experimental methods for the study of differentiation are developing; for example, experiments in the Soviet Union proved that two-point thresholds within the body, say from the gastric mucosa, can be measured. It is believable that as such differentiations are carried out by classical psychophysical methods, experimenters may first identify a very large range of internal messages and, second, may learn how to integrate them in thousands of new ways.

VOLUNTARY CONTROL

Fourth, insofar as these new messages can be differentiated, tagged, and named, they apparently can be brought under voluntary control. A wide array of new possibilities exists, for example, in Hefferline's study of rapid acquisition of operant control over slight movements that are effective in cutting out a disagreeable hum spoiling music at the time. That is, individuals who could differentiate at all, could also learn, even though unwittingly, to bring in or shut out particular messages. Other laboratories are now continuing what Hefferline started. It appears to be a very refined, delicate, and far-below-threshold type of activity that can bring in an astonishing range of experimentally prepared visual and auditory material. Soviet work on voluntary control of cardiovascular processes appears to concur with what Robert Malmo has reported in Montreal. There are studies of bladder and of capillary control, using panel feedback techniques, strongly suggesting that the autonomically controlled organs are capable of being brought rapidly into the same sphere of voluntary control as that which obtains for the striped muscle responses. Within the next decade or two certainly a very significant control of cardiovascular and gastrointestinal responses may be anticipated, not only with immediate clinical values in bringing in or shutting out various classes of bodily informaton, but with the deeper scientific value of giving a much wider view of what the human potentialities for such inner experience and such inner control may be. Wenger and Bagchi studied adepts in yoga in various ashrams in India, while Anand and his collaborators pushed their studies further. The keen interest of Indian investigators in putting to experimental tests the classical yoga sutras of Patanjali means not only cross-national research collaboration but, what is more important, the serious awakening of Western psychologists to the fact that experiences treasured and cultivated on the other side of the globe may be as worthy of investigation as those encountered in Detroit, Cambridge, or Topeka.

Last, but by no means least, the process of directly observing one's own electroencephalogram, notably one's own alpha, was developed by Joe Kamiya at Langley Porter and independently by Barbara Brown at the Sepulveda Veterans Admininstration Hospital. With Kamiya, a 400-cycle tone is activated by the individual's own alpha rhythm, so the subject given the task of increasing the amount of alpha he is exhibiting can rapidly learn, through the feedback that this tone gives him, to bring this under his control. Soon he is turning on or turning off his own alpha. Apparently alpha is not the only rhythm that he can control. There are staggering possibilities both for the understanding of the nature of central nervous system control by the organized central nervous system itself in the form that is called voluntary, but likewise a vast area of further implications for the understanding of the isomorphic relation between a variety of subjective states that accompany the alpha and the exteroceptive patterns that are seen when observing the visual tracing or hearing an appropriate tone. While the clinical applications are important, it is this larger vision of learning to control the brain rhythms themselves that is likely to mean most to the scientist oriented to the year 2000.

NAMELESS STATES

Fifth, while neither Kamiya, nor anyone else, so far as I know, has published the implications that these new methods have for the study of whole new areas of experience only dimly describable today, it is highly probable that before the year 2000 there will be both identification of many kinds of phenomenological states that are anchored upon particular types of EEGs, and the invention of appropriate *names*, appropriate language to describe the newly identified and newly integrated components. I am thinking particularly of cognitive states, conceptualizing states, creative states that may, while retaining all their charm and all their majesty, become far more describable, controllable and achievable.

PARAPSYCHOLOGY

Sixth, it is characteristic of science at any given period to cultivate the belief that it has a rather well-integrated system into which new observations can fit. While it is at many points open-ended, with really fuzzy edges, there would be chaos indeed if scientists relinquished their passion for a unified field of science. Suppose science was an archipelago of little, spotty, factual details, with no possibility of an implied closed system, an ocean bed unifying all the little islands that appear at the surface level. There is very good psychological reason why science, as it grows, takes on the conservative, the resistive character that is apparent. Under these conditions it is hardly surprising that there is some restlessness, or even resistance, when talking about the discovery of kinds of experience about which nothing has been known. Of course, there are many good reasons, in polite society, why people do not know too much about their insides. These have to do with delicate and complex systems of human expression, some related very broadly to love, some related very broadly to destructiveness, but a great many others that almost every human individual encounters, but does not really want at this time to communicate on a massive basis. I do not anticipate very much actual interference with science on this count, but I do think one must be honest in admitting that this quest of the inside will entail not only triumphs but occasional acrimonious encounters.

While saying this I must add that the resistance toward types of human communication, which presently are not understood, has shown the same attributes. One can understand very clearly the natural fear of scientists that their whole tough labor would be disturbed if they should admit perceptual, memoric, affective, or volitional processes that now are not explainable in terms of the basic biochemistry and biophysical realities of human conduct. Even the thought elements that the Würzburg School brought into Wundt's psychological system led to much hostility. Today more serious difficulties are being dealt with as the study of *parapsychology* moves into more systematic experimental form. Most of the data, when closely observed, are like the perceptual and affective data already known, but appear to occur under conditions in which the time and space parameters are unfamiliar. For exmple, in several recent studies, the telepathic phenomena occur when sender and receiver are separated by very long distances; and while the data can be described psychologically without any mystery, a physical difficulty is encountered because how to conceptualize energies that could carry over these long distances is not known. In other words, the difficulty is at the level of physics, not at the level of psychology. Psychologists may be a little bewildered when they encounter modern physicists who take these phenomena in stride; in fact, take them very much more seriously than psychologists do, saying, as physicists, that they are no longer bound by the types of Newtonian energy distribution, inverse square laws, etc., with which scientists used to regard themselves as tightly bound. In the same way, new physical conceptions regarding the nature of time seem to remove a large part of the trouble that appears in precognition experiments, in which a randomly determined target order of stimulus materials can be foreseen by certain subjects. I think that with the computer methods that are now coming into use, and with the progressive rigidity in experimental controls, psychologists probably will witness a period of slow, but definite, erosion of the blandly exclusive attitude that has offered itself as the only appropriate scientific attitude in this field. The data from parapsychology will be almost certainly in harmony with general psychological principles, and will be assimilated rather easily within the systematic framework of psychology as a science when once the imagined appropriateness of Newtonian physics is put aside, and modern physics replaces it.

PSYCHOLOGY AND BIOLOGY

As I turn to genetics, I would venture to predict a period of massive reorientation of psychology to the biological roots of which it used to boast. The very substance of growth, of motivation, of the learning process, and indeed of most of the basic realities with which the modern evolutionary psychology will have to cope, are provided by the DNA-RNA system; the elements of field physics as they are known in the embryology of Spemann and Weiss; the intricacies of polygenic determination of structure and function; and the broad recognition that individuality in tissue systems, as described by Roger Williams, rewrites the psychology of individual differences in astonishing terms. These genetic terms, of course, will be held by some to be fatalistic, as indicating the genetically given limitations upon all human endeavor. But in two respects these discoveries will be most encouraging: (a) It will be realized that individuality always applies to the growth *potential*, which can be utterly different when a new environmental situation is supplied. An example is the discovery of the Mendelian basis of the phenylpyruvic type of mental defect that has nevertheless yielded, to a large degree, to a carefully prepared diet. In other words, that which was genetically determined was controllable. Through respect for the genetics of human individuality, how to become better environmentalists will be understood. (b) As Sir George Thomson's statement, quoted earlier, implied, scientific insight is moving rapidly to a point such that the electron microscope can greatly aid in studies of the internal organization of individual cells. This, together with some control of mutations and a great deal of control of selective breeding and the application of the principles of population genetics, makes it likely that, within a few generations, to a considerable degree, some of the most abhorrent threats to human development may be eliminated. In anticipating the year 2100 or 2500, biologists could talk quite rationally about not only the prevention of deterioration, but plans for the actual long-range improvement of genetic potentials.

PSYCHOLOGY AND SOCIAL SCIENCE

But the biological sciences do not have the whole exigent message. There is equal need for big gains in the social sciences, especially in the development of a social ecology. Ecology has been the most neglected aspect, I think, of the entire behavior field. The experimental psychologist may control, say, a $10 \times 10 \times 10$ foot area, and, with enormous and devoted attention to detail, think of everything that is in that space at a given time. Organisms, however, have life histories in segments of space time about which a fair amount is known if they are hatched or born in the laboratory. But if not, the higher they are in the phylogenetic tree, the more likely they are to bring more from their past into the laboratory. Mark May used to say that the American sophomore, from whom are derived findings from humanity at large, was expected to "park his culture outside." Only the regions of time and space that are involved in the experiment are observed, ignoring the whole vast area from which the individual organism comes.

The needed studies of ecological organization are vastly more complex than anybody has imagined so far. The maps that Roger Barker has drawn of a Kansas town, and the lists of situational pressures that Saul Sells has devised as a preparation for space travel, will be only a tiny sampling of that vast conception of past and present environmental totalities that Egon Brunswik asked scientists to imagine. It will be a genetics that is oriented to a systematic and scientific science of ecology that will really give new field clues to human behavior. By field clues I hope to suggest the modalities of interaction between the edge of the organism and the edge of the environment, such that a complete and real fusion is created. I mean the kind of thing that is involved in interaction between the visual centers in the brain, the retina, the external light source, the laboratory conditions, personalities of the experimenters, the laboratory tradition, and laboratory culture, all of which must be considered when a person sees an inkblot or a social scene enacted before him. There must be whole organisms and whole environments to be studied for the sake of the modalities of reciprocity that develop between them. Psychologists began to learn from Lewin, as earlier they began to learn from Clerk-Maxwell, how to think in field terms; but they really have not done much of the sort on a scale demanded by present knowledge. The subspecialization has driven them more and more from organs to tissues, from tissues to cells, from cells to molecules, from molecules to atoms, from atoms to microparticles. All this specialization is, of course, absolutely necessary. The job of seeing psychological function, however, in combined biological and cultural terms is mostly a promissory note with as yet very little backing.

Because of its rarity, I shall mention the example of audiogenic seizures in mice, which Benson Ginzburg showed to have a not too complex Mendelian basis. But some of the mice that were expected to have convulsions and die had no convulsions, or had convulsions but did not die. He then attacked the problem from the pharmacological viewpoint and, in terms of biochemistry, found a way to buffer the lethal effects of the genes. Allow me a free analogy in the field of human ecology: What will happen when one finds a human environment of space-time-sensory enrichment, maternal warmth, generous and skillful experimental reinforcement that will allow a poorly endowed, frightened, aggressive ghetto child to develop into full humanness? This is exactly the type of experiment now being launched at several outposts of research on disadvantaged children. Before long thought in terms of biology versus the social sciences will cease; an ecological science will be developed so rich and so concrete that it will articulate closely with the new biology of individual growth.

And if psychologists mean quite seriously that man, as man, is richly intertwined with his ecology, it follows that the psychology of the next two decades will depend enormously upon the discovery of new forms of cross-cultural, cross-national communication. Indeed, it follows that unless there is very broad cross-national communication and action, there will be no human race to investigate. It will not do for American psychology, now having about 92% of the world's psychological personnel and about 92% of its published communications, to undertake a bland and supposedly disinterested study of the rest of the world in order that the wise and productive science, which they represent, can convey appropriate knowledge to those struggling along in less enlightened paths of endeavor. The study of the human predicament can come from a human race familiar with the method of science, but a human race speaking many tongues, regarding many values, and holding different convictions about the meaning of life sooner or later will have to consult all that is human. There are a few living today who will still be alive in the year 2000, if there is a year 2000; and I hope they will still be battling the problem of developing a sufficiently coherent, human enough point of view to speak for all kinds of human beings. This will mean that the genetic and ecological progress that I am describing will have actually helped toward a psychology that is common human, that entails not only a study of all human beings, but a study by trained and devoted individuals within all human groups. Following the American habit of delivering "State of the Union" messages, the Secretary-General of the United Nations has been asked to report on the "state of the human race." I personally do not understand why governments, and indeed professional psychologists, as well, are almost wholly ignoring the challenge to study directly the possibilities of achieving an international and intercultural plan for world order. Aiming at this goal, it is conceivable that there will be worldwide human modalities of investigation like those already existing in astronomy and in medicine, but oriented to the behavioral sciences. And it is even possible that they will be oriented not only to the behaviors as such, but toward the deep inner humanness that I have tried to describe as an object of study. This, in relation to the dyadic and group problems of the behavior sciences, may give both insight and control over the more destructive tendencies, and may utilize the common human aspiration to live not only more safely and a little more comfortably, but also a little more creatively and a great deal more humanly.

THE ROLE OF METHOD

You have noted that new discoveries in the field of psychology, and, I believe, in all scientific fields, are largely the children of new *methods*. Consider what the compound microscope did to histology, what X-rays did for diagnostic procedure, and what the puzzle box, the maze, the Skinner box have done in the development and documentation of seminal scientific theories. I am raising these issues not simply to welcome the computer to our side, as a new brother, but to ask one final question. Psychologists can, as A. H. Maslow has pointed out, strip down the study of man to those methods common to the other sciences that do not deal with man; they can assume that the human sciences can best do their job by leaving humanness out. There is, however, another possibility. They might conceivably find that science can become big enough to develop fully human methods oriented to the complete panoply of human problems, that empathy, "tlc," rich dyadic methods of communication between subjects and experimenters, through patience, discipline, and imagination, might give them in the year 2000 a science more competent to deal with all the discoverable aspects of human nature.

But a still more basic problem of method relates to the way in which they try to hook together the data from laboratory, from clinic, from field observation, from home, from neighborhood, and from observation of human gatherings in schools, churches, juries, parliamentary bodies. On the one hand, they have neglected the use of laboratories, and today they are beginning to discover a more suitable laboratory approach to a wide variety of spontaneous human situations. They are discovering that inventive experimentalists can do even better work in free human situations than they can in the classical, highly planned, settings. But now I am referring mainly to the manner in which the experimental method does its work. Long ago, psychologists established for themselves the impossible task of creating a psychology through intensive observation of those phenomena that occur under controlled laboratory conditions, and then systematizing a psychology based solely on such findings. They tried to set up physics and chemistry, sometimes the biological sciences of genetics, embryology, and physiology, as models. Belatedly they have discovered that beautiful scientific structures, such as that of modern geology, with only slight use of experimental method, can be developed through the integration of many types of observations, short-term and long-term, outdoors and indoors, pinpointed or extravagantly blown up to cosmic proportions. The geologists uses experimental methods, but he uses them in the total context of his work. It is mother earth, not her fingernails, that interests him. Psychology, which attempted to pinpoint its existence in the nineteenth-century terms of Weber and Fechner, is now beginning a great awakening, a sort of Rip Van Winkle awakening; for we are discovering, and will discover more fully in the next few decades, the vast dimensions in which a mature psychology can be conceived. It will make even more use of experimental method than it does at present. But the experiments will be suggested, and the techniques controlled, rather largely by the broad perception of the nature of the human animal in his whole ecological setting. The observational systems that will develop cannot be categorized by any one word that is now known. The word *experimental* is a fine word, but it will have to be replaced by something much more systematic. Even the developmental approach will mean something quite new when conceived in the kind of general systems terms, the kind of life science terms, that I am trying to suggest. Mathematical models certainly will both benefit and be benefited by the transitions that I am suggesting; and, of course, the engineering skills, already so important in psychophysiology, will become even more important.

I think psychologists will have to admit that many of this era will be unable to see the promised land that begins to be sketched out. Psychologists who will be extant in the year 2000 will have to be smarter than the psychologists today, as well as enormously better trained—I might add, enormously more *broadly* trained—than the subspecialized people turned out today. The blade of the modern mind is sharpened until it breaks, and we damn the blade instead of asking the metallurgist to develop tools from which sharp weapons can be prepared that, while still unscathed, can cut through the hard inscrutable rock of man's basic resistance to discovering his own nature.

THE HUMAN PREDICAMENT

The year 2000 can come, and the twenty-first century can offer less terror and more joy, but only if psychologists have learned both *how to look inside* and *how to look outside;* how to recognize the reciprocities of inner and outer, through methods that are as far ranging and as deeply human as is the human stuff that is being studied.

UNIT FOURTEEN | DISCUSSION QUESTIONS

50 | SPEAKING FRANKLY ON A ONCE TABOO SUBJECT

According to Bieber, the mothers of male homosexuals behave in characteristic and abnormal ways. Explain.

In what ways would you suggest society should deal with homosexuality? Discuss.

51 | PSYCHOLOGY IN THE GHETTO

The female-dominated black family has been called pathological. Some authorities say it may be a healthy adaptation to ghetto conditions. Which viewpoint do you accept? Support your views.

List the defense mechanisms commonly employed by blacks from the ghetto. In what ways are these mechanisms different from those used by the majority?

52 | GENETICS VERSUS HEADSTART

Dr. Arthur Jensen's research supports genetics as the dominant factor in determining the IQ. Support or criticize this view from your observations.

In what ways would you design an educational program for disadvantaged youngsters to improve their condition? Discuss.

53 | PSYCHOLOGY IN THE YEAR 2000

Discuss the views of Murphy toward parapsychology.

In what ways do you agree or disagree with the author's ideas concerning the future of psychology? Discuss.

COLOR ILLUSTRATIONS ON BACK COVER

Progress of a disease. A famous series of paintings by Louis Wain, a London illustrator who became schizophrenic in middle age, reflects the artist's mental deterioration.

Because the subject of the paintings is constant—always a cat—the artist's representation of that subject vividly reflects his own changing perception of his environment. Presumably, Wain saw not only the environment but also himself in his cats. Most of his life he remained relatively isolated from the society of other people, living instead with seventeen cats and three spinster sisters.

At the age of fifty-seven, Wain began to show indications of psychosis. Under the influence of a delusion of persecution, he insisted that enemies were influencing his mind with electrical impulses. From this time on, his paintings also began to change radically, seeming so clearly to reflect the progress of his illness.

Top left: An early painting, showing a contented, appealing, and friendly cat.

Top right: A much more highly stylized painting. The rainbow-like halo effect is typical of psychotic art.

Bottom left: Increasingly intricate geometric patterns fill the painting.

Bottom right: In the last painting of the series, all resemblance to a catlike form is gone; the intricate patterning has become a design in itself.

CDE7987654321